Reading for Results

Reading for Results

Thirteenth Edition

Laraine E. Flemming

Jordan Fabish, Long Beach City College
Contributing Consultant

"It is not true that we have only one
life to live; if we can read, we can
live as many more lives and as many
kinds of lives as we wish"

—S.I. HAYAKAWA

WADSWORTH
CENGAGE Learning·

Australia • Brazil • Mexico • Singapore • United Kingdom • United States

Reading for Results, Thirteenth Edition
Laraine E. Flemming

Product Director: Nicole Lloyd

Product Manager: Andrew Rawson

Senior Content Developer:
    Elizabeth Neustaetter

Freelance Development Editor:
    Maggie Barbieri

Associate Content Developer:
    Jacob Schott

Senior Marketing Manager:
    Necco McKinley

Senior Content Project Manager:
    Aimee Bear

Senior Designer: Diana Graham

Manufacturing Planner: Betsy Donaghey

IP Analyst: Ann Hoffman

IP Project Manager: Kathryn Kucharek

Production Service:
    S4Carlisle Publishing Services

Compositor:
    S4Carlisle Publishing Services

Text Designer: Janis Owens,
    Books By Design, Inc.

Cover Designer: Wing-Ip Ngan,
    Ink Design, Inc.

Cover Image Credit:
    Brothers Good/Shutterstock.com

For product information and technology assistance, contact us at
Cengage Learning Customer & Sales Support, 1-800-354-9706.

For permission to use material from this text or product, submit all requests online at **www.cengage.com/permissions**. Further permissions questions can be emailed to **permissionrequest@cengage.com.**

Library of Congress Control Number: 2015936369
Student Edition:
ISBN: 978-1-305-50052-5

Cengage Learning
20 Channel Center Street
Boston, MA 02210
USA

Cengage Learning is a leading provider of customized learning solutions with employees residing in nearly 40 different countries and sales in more than 125 countries around the world. Find your local representative at **www.cengage.com**.

Cengage Learning products are represented in Canada by Nelson Education, Ltd.

To learn more about Cengage Learning Solutions, visit **www.cengage.com.**

Purchase any of our products at your local college store or at our preferred online store **www.cengagebrain.com.**

Printed in the United States of America
Print Number: 01 Print Year: 2015

Contents

7 Focusing on Supporting Details in Longer Readings   347

8 Focusing on Inferences in Paragraphs   397

9   Understanding the Role of Inferences in Longer Readings   469

10   Learning from Organizational Patterns in Paragraphs   529

11   Combining Patterns in Paragraphs and Longer Readings   609

12   Responding to Persuasive Writing   659

Compelling readings. Innovative writing assignments. Research-based explanations and exercises. *Reading for Results,* now available in its thirteenth edition, includes these and other trademark features you've come to expect from this leader in developmental reading instruction.

Reading for Results

Thirteenth Edition

Laraine E. Flemming

Jordan Fabish, Long Beach City College
Contributing Consultant

"It is not true that we have only one life to live; if we can read, we can live as many more lives and as many kinds of lives as we wish"

—S.I. HAYAKAWA

WADSWORTH
CENGAGE Learning

Australia • Brazil • Mexico • Singapore • United Kingdom • United States

"I really appreciate the informal, friendly, nonthreatening tone of the explanations and examples in the book. I find the explanations to be clear, effective, and of an appropriate length."

—DINA LEVITRE, Community College of Rhode Island

"The explanations and clarity of explanations/format of models for key concepts are my favorite parts of this book. My students tell me that they are very clear and like the summary boxes that give them tips, summaries of key points, or those that ask them to recall main points ("check your understanding" boxes)."

—AILEEN GUM, San Diego City College

"I really like the "Reader to Writer" assignments and WebQuests."

—JENNI WESSEL-FIELDS, Black Hawk College

"*Reading for Results* makes learning to read at a higher level an accessible, achievable challenge."

—JOHN KLYCZEK, Lake Land College

"Many students comment how they have learned so much from the readings in the exercises. They say they often share their information and get comments like, 'How do you know that?' and they answer, 'I learned it in my college reading book!'"

—MARY ROUSE, Bluegrass Community and Technical College

"Some of the content assumes a certain maturity level, and I appreciate that. The examples describe diverse populations and are a way to broaden the horizons of my students."

—STACEY FOSTER, Pine Technical College

● Brand New Pointers on Screen Reading

Research comparing reading from print books versus reading from screens frequently shows a drop in comprehension when students read on screens. However, since the digital age is not about to end any time soon, more recent research[†] has focused on how using specific strategies can combat this effect. This edition of *Reading for Results* makes use of those studies by suggesting concrete strategies for screen reading that will help students switch from paper to screen without missing a beat.

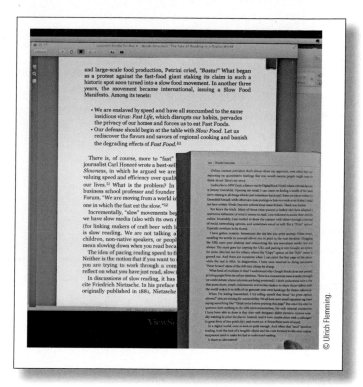

© Ulrich Flemming.

● New Discussions of Visual Aids

Research shows that inexperienced readers tend to skip visual aids, not realizing what they add to comprehension. This edition of *Reading for Results* explains why ignoring visual aids is a huge mistake. It also shows students, step by step, how to interpret the graphs, charts, and photos they encounter in their reading.

Bar graphs display data so that readers can make comparisons. They are perfect for showing differences in frequency or amounts. Bar graphs are great for illustrating differences between any number of things from salary ranges to health care in different countries. Bar graphs often accompany texts that focus on how two or more groups differ from one another in relation to spending, growth, decline, or behavior. Here's a typical bar graph:

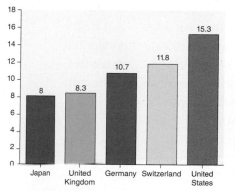

Source of figures: www.pbs.org/frontline/
sickaroundthe world.

[†]See Sources page in the manual for all references to research mentioned in the preface.

● Increased Focus on Evaluating Web Information

While your students might be great at using Instagram, the research suggests they haven't completely mastered how to search for and evaluate information found on the Web. Chapter 1 now includes revised explanations and a new exercise focusing on website evaluation. Special attention is also paid to the way photographs can reveal bias.

1. Imagine that the chapter section you are surveying is titled "1962: Integration Comes to Southern Campuses." It is accompanied by the photograph below, which has the caption "James Meredith arrives on the campus of Ole Miss." Thus, you think it's a good idea to learn a little bit about James Meredith before you read the chapter.

Library of Congress Prints and Photographs Division [LC-DIG-ppmsca-04292]

What search term will you use to find the information that will help you understand the chapter section?

● A Host of New *From Reader to Writer* Assignments

Reading is always a collaborative enterprise, with writers leaving clues that enable readers to recreate the writer's message. What better way to illustrate this essential point than by having readers switch places and become the writers, who leave clues for others to follow? Each chapter in this edition contains numerous new writing assignments asking readers to take on the role of writer and make use of the very cues and clues they just learned about as readers.

From Reader to Writer The reading you just finished described different ways to make sure that new information gets into long-term memory. Some memories, however, require no effort. Called "flashbulb" memories, they pack such an emotional wallop, they require no rehearsal or elaboration to find their place in memory's storehouse.

Some flashbulb memories are collectively shared. For instance, anyone who was alive at the time never forgot the bombing of Pearl Harbor or the assassinations of John F. Kennedy, Robert Kennedy, Malcolm X, or Martin Luther King. Others are more personal. Memories of our first love, the death of a parent, and moments of triumph or humiliation are likely to stay with us forever.

Describe a flashbulb memory that you think will always be with you. Start with a sentence that introduces the term and its definition. Then introduce the experience that you think qualifies as a flashbulb memory, for instance, "Flashbulb memories are based on experiences so vivid and so emotionally powerful, we couldn't forget them if we wanted to. The definition certainly fits how I felt when I. . . ."

● Introducing Argument Diagrams for Revision Analysis

Having learned in Chapter 12, *Responding to Persuasive Writing*, about the ways readers identify the underlying structure of an argument in order to evaluate it, students are encouraged to write their own argument essays, choosing from a list of compelling issues, such as children's beauty pageants, pet owners serving jail time when their dogs attack, how women's colleges are dealing with transgender students, and monitoring employee movements in the workplace. To help students master argument structure as

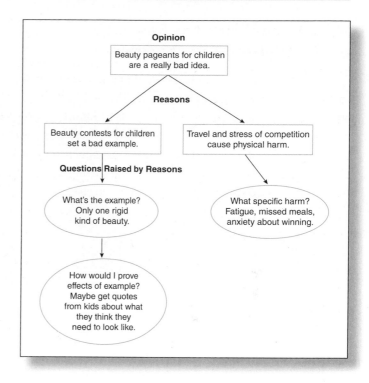

writers, Chapter 12 introduces diagrams that encourage students to visualize their evidence, consider its relevance, and imagine the questions readers might pose in response.

● Completely Revised Chapter on the Key Reading Terms *General* and *Specific*

As the new title suggests, Chapter 3, "Looking for Specific Topics and General Main Ideas," now forges a stronger link between understanding the terms *general* and *specific* and then using that understanding to identify the key elements of a paragraph or reading: the topic, main idea, and supporting details. Chapter 3 also makes greater use of diagrams that visually echo what's been explained in the text.

● Influenced by New Research on the Workings of the Brain

The decades-old idea that learning increases when readers activate several senses at the same time—reading, writing, and reciting aloud—has gained additional credence from current studies of the brain. The research shows different areas of the brain responding, depending on how content is presented, in spoken, written, or pictorial form. Guided by these findings, *Reading for Results* 13 includes numerous, new visual aids that enhance the text's explanations. It also places more emphasis on learning through a multi-sensory approach: read it, write it, hear it, and, if possible, teach it to someone else.

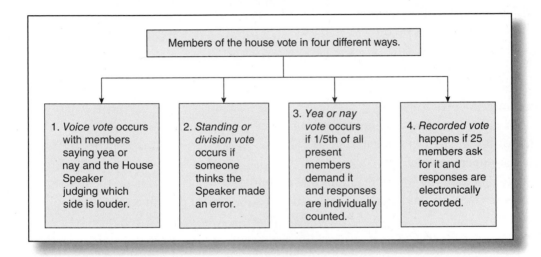

● An Enlarged Section on Finding the Topic

While experienced readers might think determining the topic of a paragraph is an easy task, it's actually not all that simple for those who aren't long-time readers. In recognition of that difficulty, this edition of *Reading for Results* links locating the topic more tightly to an understanding of general and specific words, showing students how specific topics can be made to branch out into larger, more general main ideas.

● A Host of New Topical Readings

From its first appearance on the market, *Reading for Results* has been lauded for reading selections that keep even the most reluctant readers glued to the page. This edition is no exception, and the range of topics is lively and diverse. Among the numerous new topics covered are the origin of Emoji, the scary results of Stanley Milgram's notorious obedience experiments, the enforced enrollment of Native Americans in reservation schools, and the complicated struggle to maintain one's personal privacy while going public on the Web.

As in Previous Editions, the Following Highly Acclaimed Features Remain:

● Overviews and Review Tests for every chapter

● Numerous follow-up exercises for practice and review

● Clear and comprehensive research-based explanations

● Concise reading tips sprinkled throughout chapters

● Multi-paragraph readings conclude each chapter

● Web Quest assignments encourage research on the Web

● *Summing Up the Key Points* and *Check Your Understanding* help students review what they've learned as well as monitor comprehension

Additional Resources
● For Students

Aplia™, an online reading and learning solution, helps students become better readers, motivating them with compelling subject matter, interactive assignments, and clear, detailed explanations for both skills and concepts. All Aplia assignments and explanations correspond to those appearing in *Reading for Results*, providing students with additional practice when they need it. Aplia's *Grade It Now* technology gives students multiple chances to complete specific exercises designed to reinforce learning. Through diagnostic tests and Aplia's user-friendly grading and performance interface, instructors are able to quickly and easily assess and track both individual and class-wide student performance. Aplia also allows instructors to generate and download detailed reports. In addition, instructors have the option of using an Individual Study Path course format that generates a unique list of assignments for each, student, with all assignments based on diagnostic data.

MindTap is a customizable, easy-to-use learning platform that supports both skills assessment and personalized learning. Based on *Reading for Results*, MindTap includes an interactive ebook, Aplia follow-up assignments for practice and review, additional readings, related writing assignments, pre-made digital flashcards, and multimedia activities that connect directly to what students are learning. Instructors who use MindTap will find it easy to create a carefully sequenced and individualized learning path that adapts to students' needs while tracking both engagement and progress.

● For Instructors

The Instructor's Resource Manual and Test Bank offers suggestions for teaching each chapter and supplementary exercises for skills introduced in *Reading for Results*. These suggestions and exercises are great for the new instructor looking for support or the more experienced teacher looking for ideas. The Instructor's Resource Manual also provides a list of all the vocabulary words introduced in the book, along with follow up exercises and tests. The manual also includes a sample midterm and final. Also helpful for both the new and the experienced teacher is the author's companion website at laflemm.com, which provides a host of follow up exercises along with explanations of key terms used in the text.

Cengage Learning Testing Powered by Cognero® is a flexible online system that allows instructors to author, edit, and manage test-bank content from multiple Cengage Learning solutions, including the quizzes and exams included in the Instructor's Resource Manual and Test Bank for *Reading for Results*.

The Instructor Companion Website offers chapter-specific PowerPoint presentations and vocabulary exercises for words introduced in the text, along with the Instructor's Manual and Test Bank. Instructors can request an access code from their sales representative. If they wish, they can also access the companion website via login.cengage.com. Additional exercises and explanations of key terms can also be found at the author's personal website www.laflemm.com

Acknowledgements

Many thanks to the terrific reviewers, all of whom offered concrete suggestions for improvements that have made this new edition one of the best ever. I couldn't have done it without you:

Judy Bennett, Lake Land College
Stacey Foster, Pine Technical College
Lesley Fredericks, Camden County College
Aileen Gum, San Diego City College
Michelle Hollitz, Lane Community College
John Klyczek, Lake Land College
Dina Levitre, Community College of Rhode Island
Pamela Prokop, Anoka Technical College
Mary Rouse, Bluegrass Community and Technical College

Matthew Sorrento, Camden County College
Jenni Wessel-Fields, Black Hawk College

I am grateful, too, to my Cengage editors Andrew Rawson and Elizabeth Neustaetter for their patience, advice, and support. With them on my team, this revision went more smoothly than I could ever have imagined.

Innumerable thank yous to Chris Feldman, the copyeditor for this book. I have been writing textbooks for more decades than I care to think about, and Chris is, without question, the finest copyeditor I have ever had the pleasure of working with.

Many thanks to Roxanne Klaas from S4Carlisle who guided this book through production from first page to last, always with great efficiency and close attention to detail. It's our first time working together, and I devoutly hope it's not our last. The same goes for Diana Graham, whose revised design for the 13th edition of *Reading for Results* is the perfect complement to the book's focus on achieving success.

As in the past, a huge thanks to the talented Maggie Barbieri, whose gifts as an editor are surpassed only by her talents as a writer. Her own books are a must read for anyone who loves a good mystery.

Another big thank you to Jordan Fabish at Long Beach City College, who patiently lets me talk interminably about my latest theory of teaching reading and writing. And last, but certainly not least, to Ulrich Flemming who, from the beginning of my career, first as a teacher and then as an author, always said, without a moment's hesitation, "Yes, you can!"

1 Strategies for Learning from Textbooks

IN THIS CHAPTER, YOU WILL LEARN

- how to use *SQ3R*, a reading method specifically created for learning from textbooks.

- why paraphrasing is an essential reading skill.

- which methods of reading and review might work best for you.

- how to match your reading rate to the material.

- how to use the Web to expand your background knowledge.

- how to adapt your reading to a computer screen.

"Skeptics say college is overrated, but those with degrees make more even when their jobs don't require higher education."

—"EVEN FOR CASHIERS, COLLEGE PAYS OFF,"
NEW YORK TIMES, JUNE 26, 2011

"It turns out that . . . mindsets predict how well students end up doing. Students with growth mindsets tend to stick with it, tend to persevere in the face of difficulty, and tend to be successful in challenging classes."

— PSYCHOLOGIST CAROL DWECK

Created more than half a century ago, *SQ3R*, the study system for learning from textbooks described in this chapter, has sometimes been called obsolete, or out of date. Yet, in fact, it's anything but.

Francis P. Robinson, the educational psychologist who created *SQ3R* in the 1940s, spent years teaching both college students and military personnel how to learn from textbooks. Due to his extensive teaching experience and his training in psychology, Robinson had an in-depth understanding of how people learn. For that reason, his system,[†] used consistently and with some modifications, still offers big benefits.

[†]*SQ3R* has spawned numerous similar study systems like *PQRST*—i.e., *Preview, Question, Read, Summary, Test*. If you have used another system that gets the results you want, feel free to stick with it.

Chapter 1 also emphasizes the importance of writing while reading as a way of improving both comprehension and remembering. It pays particular attention to **paraphrasing**, or translating someone else's words into your own. Because paraphrasing is a critical academic skill, you'll hear about it in several chapters. Chapter 1, however, gives you the basics.

Finally, Chapter 1 tells you how to use the Web to expand your background knowledge and improve your comprehension of textbook assignments.

Introducing *SQ3R*: Survey, Question, Read, Recall, Review

If you are reading a bestseller by a writer like Dean Koontz[†] or Charlaine Harris,[†] you probably let your mind drift along with the story, almost like you were dreaming it. However, this dreamy, unfocused approach, perfect for leisure reading, isn't particularly effective with textbooks.

With textbooks, you need a systematic but flexible system that can take into account the difficulty of the material, the author's writing style, and the goals of your assignment. *SQ3R* is flexible enough to include all three elements. What follows are the steps in the system, all of which can and should be adapted to your needs.

S: Survey to Get a General Overview and Make Predictions

When you start a textbook assignment, don't just open your textbook and begin reading. Instead, **survey** or preview the material using the general sequence of steps described in the following box. The purpose of the survey is for you to develop expectations about the content. That way, when you start reading, you will have a **purpose**. You'll be reading to confirm or revise your expectations. Having a purpose improves both comprehension and remembering.

Although the steps in a survey may increase or decrease according to text difficulty and your knowledge of the material, these seven steps are almost always essential.

[†]Dean Koontz is the author of numerous thrillers like *Odd Thomas* and *Frankenstein: The Dead Town*. If you like crime novels, you will love his.
[†]Charlaine Harris is the author of *The Southern Vampire Mysteries* series of novels, on which the hit HBO series *True Blood* is based, and the books are as good as the HBO series.

Seven Basic Steps in a Survey

1. Read the title. Consider what it suggests about the chapter's contents.

2. Read all introductory material. That includes opening anecdotes, or stories, chapter outlines, lists of questions, goals, and objectives. These are all ways in which textbook authors identify a chapter's key concepts, or ideas.

3. Use the title and introduction to form a general question or two about what's covered in the chapter. Check your memory to see if you have any prior knowledge, or previous experience, with the topic discussed.[†]

4. Read the headings and opening sentence of chapter sections. **If the material is especially difficult or unfamiliar, expand this step**: Read the last sentence of every chapter section or even the first and last sentence of every paragraph. Use this material as the basis for focus questions that will guide your reading and help you maintain concentration.

5. Read the title and look closely at all visual aids. Visual aids include pictures, photos, maps, charts, boxes, icons, or visual symbols, and graphs. If captions, or explanations, accompany the visual aids, read them, too. Ask yourself what each visual aid suggests about the chapter's content. If specific icons, or symbols, are used consistently in the chapter, see if you can detect a pattern in the kinds of information they identify.

6. Pay attention to words printed in boldface or in the margin of the page. With particularly important or difficult courses, expand this step to include jotting boldface or italicized terms in the margins. As you read, add brief definitions to the terms noted in the margins.

7. Read end-of-chapter summaries and questions. If there is no end-of-chapter summary or list of questions, read the last page of the chapter.

[†]More on developing prior knowledge using the Web is found on pages 47–59.

The Four Goals of a Survey

Whatever the length and depth of the survey, it should always give you the following: (1) a general overview of the content covered; (2) a feeling for the writer's style; (3) an idea or sense for what's important; and

(4) a sense of the chapter's (or article's) natural breaks or divisions, which you can then use to decide the number and length of your study sessions. While most articles assigned for outside reading can be read and at least generally understood in a single study session, chapter assignments should be divided up so that you read in chunks, completing only ten or so pages in each study session.

Ten Questions to Consider During Your Survey
●

1. What does the title suggest about the author's emphasis or focus?

2. According to the heading and highlighted terms, what issues or topics will the author address?

3. Are any visual aids included? What do they suggest about the chapter's content and emphasis?

4. Do any chapter sections look especially difficult?

5. Does any of the material look familiar?

6. What method does the author consistently use for emphasis? Does the author favor **boldface** and marginal annotations? Or does she make heavy use of opening questions and boxed information? Textbook authors are likely to favor a particular method of presenting important information. Try to determine the author's preference.

7. How many pages should I plan to complete during each study session?

8. Do I have any background knowledge about the topics or issues addressed in this chapter?

9. Do the headings include any questions I can use to focus my attention while reading?

10. Is there a summary I can use to figure out what's central to the chapter?

The Importance of Reading Flexibility

"A how-to-study program must be individualized to each student's needs."
—Francis P. Robinson

Reading flexibility refers to a reader's willingness to change strategies depending on what he or she is reading and why. For example, if flexible readers are studying a textbook chapter on marriage and the family in preparation for a class discussion and don't feel that the material is especially difficult, they might abbreviate their survey, reading just the introduction and headings while ignoring the pictures and other visual aids. They would probably also increase their reading rate from the average rate of 250 words per minute to a rate more appropriate to familiar material, around 350 words per minute.

But if those same readers were studying a difficult biology chapter and assuming they might have a quiz on it in the next class, they would make their survey longer and more detailed. They would look at every clue to meaning in the chapter. They might even read the first and last sentence of every paragraph.

Flexible readers feel the same way about taking notes or reviewing. Difficult texts get a separate sheet of detailed notes and numerous reviews. Less difficult texts might get just marginal notes and underlining, followed by one or two reviews.

READING TIP Be a flexible reader who consciously adapts reading strategies to the text. If, for instance, reading your history and health texts at the same rate of speed leaves you feeling confused, adapt to the more difficult material by slowing down your reading rate.

Don't Skip Those Visual Aids

"I tend to skip over the graphs or charts that I come across, hoping that I can get the information I need from the text."
—Kathleen Gilmartin and Karen Rex, *Working with Charts, Graphs, and Tables*

The student who provided the previous quote is not alone. Whether they are surveying or reading every page, many readers tend to skip over the visual aids that authors provide. Usually, they do so because they aren't as familiar with visual representations of **data**, or information, as they are with printed versions. Yet the more practice readers have with information presented in visual form, the more likely they are to look at it and understand what it adds to the discussion. The less practice they have, the more inclined they are to skip the diagrams, charts, tables, and graphs that accompany a text.

Beginning right now, this book offers you repeated practice with a variety of visual aids in the hope that, from now on, you won't skip them when you see them, **especially when you are doing a survey**. Often, the visual aids an author uses can reveal the main idea, or central point, of an entire chapter section. Include them in your survey, and you'll be in a better position to determine what's important in the chapter section and what's not. Instead of skipping over visual aids when you see them, learn the typical characteristics of each type, along with the kind of information each one is most likely to display.

Matching the Text with the Visual

When you spot a number reference to a specific figure in the text while you are reading, look at the visual aid identified by that number. Make sure you know if the specific chart, table, or graph illustrates what's just been said or adds to it. The title and caption will usually help you figure out the point of the visual display.

Unfortunately, there will be times when the chart, table, or graph accompanying a chapter section is on the following page rather than on the same page as the text. When this happens, remember to be a flexible reader. If you are struggling to understand the author's message, then take the time to look at the figure on the next page before continuing to read. However, if you think you understand what's being said, wait until you finish the chapter section to check out the visual aid accompanying it.

Beginning with Bar Graphs

We'll start here with bar graphs. The chapters that follow will tell you more about other kinds of visual support likely to turn up in academic writing.

Bar graphs display data so that readers can make comparisons. They are perfect for showing differences in frequency or amounts. Bar graphs are great for illustrating differences between any number of things from salary ranges to health care in different countries. Bar graphs often accompany texts that focus on how two or more groups differ from one another in relation to spending, growth, decline, or behavior. Here's a typical bar graph:

Figure 1-1 Percentage of Gross Domestic Product (GDP) 5 Countries Spend on Health Care

Source of data: www.pbs.org/frontline/sickaroundthe world.

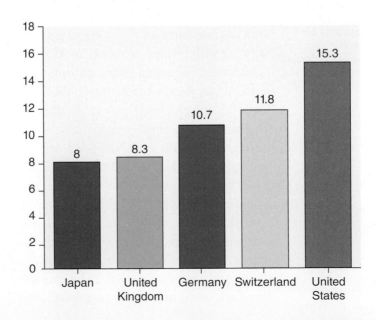

Bar Graphs Are Visual Aids That

●

- use the height or length of two or more bars to illustrate the differences in quantity or frequency among separate groups of data (e.g., the amount of corn grown in Ukraine versus Iowa, developmental milestones achieved in the first three years for males and females, tax rates in countries around the world).

- are often used as proof of generalizations (e.g., "When it comes to salaries, women are still not equal to men in the corporate world").

- are usually identified and referenced in the text with the word *Figure*, a number, and a title.

- are composed of two axes, or lines: one horizontal axis going across the bottom—called the **X axis**—and another vertical axis that extends up the side and is called the **Y axis**. The X axis usually identifies the type of information being compared. The Y axis identifies amounts or frequency.

- usually include a **legend**, which indicates what the different colors or patterns of the bars in the graph represent.

- are most appropriate for showing large differences in quantities or groups.

SUMMING UP THE KEY POINTS

1. Surveying a chapter before you read it should fulfill four objectives: Your survey should (1) give you a general overview of the chapter, (2) give you a feel for the writer's style and method of organization, (3) help you figure out what's important in the chapter, and (4) identify chapter breaks that will help you decide how many pages you want to read in each study session.

2. Flexibility is crucial to surveying and every other aspect of reading. Each new reading assignment calls for a different set of reading strategies that reflect the kind of material you are reading, the author's style, and your own reading purpose.

3. Visual aids are important to your understanding of the author's message. Never skip them during a survey. Frequently they'll reveal the author's main point even before you actually read the written text.

▶ EXERCISE 1   Surveying Visual Aids

DIRECTIONS   Read just the heading and opening question of the full text shown on page 37. Then look at the bar chart that follows and see if you can predict the answer to the question *before* reading the passage.

Maternal and Paternal Influences

Do mothers and fathers parent differently?

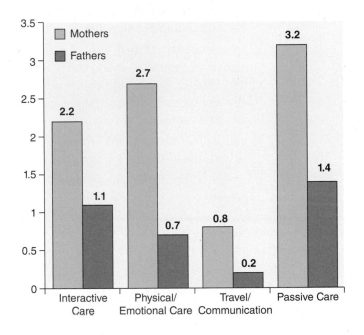

Figure 1-2   Type of Child Care

Coon and Mitterer. *Introduction to Psychology*, 12th ed., p. 92, © Cengage Learning.

Write a complete sentence that answers the previous question.

_____

Now look at the reading on pages 37–38 [Exercise 7]. Were you able to get the right answer just from looking at the bar graph? What about the bar graph influenced your answer?

_____

_____

_____

▶ **EXERCISE 2**   **Surveying for Advance Knowledge**

DIRECTIONS   Survey the reading "Long-Term Memory: Preserving the Past" on pages 64–66, using the steps listed below. Then, based on the information drawn from your survey, answer the questions that follow by circling the correct answer.

1. Read the title and all the topic headings.

2. Read the definitions following all **boldface** terms and anything written in italics.

3. Pose questions based on the title, headings, boldface terms, and visual aids.

4. Read the first and last paragraphs.

5. Because this is a fairly complex textbook excerpt, read the first and last sentence of every paragraph.

Questions Based on Your Survey of Pages

1. *True* or *False.* Long-term memory allows us to retain new information for just a few seconds longer than short-term memory can manage.

2. *True* or *False.* During consolidation, the brain eliminates information that it considers unimportant.

3. *True* or *False.* Maintenance rehearsal of new information relies heavily on sound repetition.

4. *True* or *False.* The reading is likely to explain how information needs to be organized in long-term memory for us to recall it.

5. *True* or *False.* The red-breasted sparrow will, in some way, be connected to an explanation of the **semantic network model**.

✔ **CHECK YOUR UNDERSTANDING**

1. What are the four goals of a survey?

   _____

   _____

   _____

   _____

2. What does the term *reading flexibility* mean?

   _____

   _____

   _____

   _____

3. During a survey, what can visual aids frequently tell you about a chapter section?

   _____

4. Bar graphs are useful for what purpose?

   _____

Q: Ask and Answer Questions While Reading

Many students struggle to maintain concentration while reading. This isn't unusual. We all struggle when we try to absorb new and difficult material for an extended length of time.

Still, the problem of failing concentration can be considerably reduced. One way to reduce it is to ask questions while reading. Raising and answering questions during a study session will help you remain mentally active throughout. Using questions to maintain your concentration can also alert you to key points addressed in the chapter. What follows are several methods you can use to develop questions that guide your attention and keep you focused.

Use Opening Lists

Many textbook chapters open with a list of ready-made questions that the author or authors expect to answer in the chapter. Use these lists to focus your reading. Questions based on introductory lists of questions will keep you alert to especially important passages. Here, for instance, are three questions that could open a chapter of a psychology text:

- What Are the Basic Brain Structures and Their Functions?

- How Does the Nervous System Operate?

- How Does the Brain Change?

With questions like these to guide your reading, you are bound to be alert to passages that provide an answer. You are also more likely to stay alert because you won't be reading aimlessly and wondering what you should be looking for.

Some textbook chapters open with a list of specific objectives that tell you what you should know after reading the chapter. When that's the case, use words like *what*, *why*, and *how* to turn the objectives into focus questions. For an illustration, look at the list of objectives from a health textbook titled *An Invitation to Health* and compare the objectives on the list to the questions they evoke:

Objectives	Questions
Define health and wellness	What does it mean to be healthy? What does it mean to be well?
Name three ways in which gender impacts health	How does gender affect health?
Describe the *Healthy People 2010–2020* initiative	What is the *Healthy People 2010–2020* initiative?
List three to five attributes of credible medical information websites	What are three to five ways medical information websites indicate that they are trustworthy?

However you develop your questions, it pays to jot down an abbreviated version of the questions or objectives on a piece of paper *before* you begin reading. The list will make you more alert to places in the text where questions get answered or objectives are met.

Each time you find a passage that answers a question or meets an objective, put a check mark next to the passage. Then cross the question or objective off your list. That way you will have a record of what's really significant in the chapter.

Taking the time to check off the questions and objectives gives your brain extra time to mull over what you have read. That extra time will help anchor the information in your long-term memory.

Turn Headings into Questions

Most textbook chapters are divided by major and minor headings. **Major headings** introduce the topics or issues addressed within the chapter. **Minor headings** further subdivide topics and issues introduced by the major headings. Here's an example of each:

The major heading introduces the topic under discussion.

It should also make readers pose the question, "What are the causes of violence?"

The minor heading suggests questions such as "Are the two causes always in combination?" "Can someone become violent due to psychological causes without there being a biological one?"

The Causes of Violence

What sets off a violent person? Criminologists have a variety of views on this subject. Some believe that violence is a function of human traits and makeup. Others point to improper socialization and upbringing.

Psychological/Biological Abnormality

On March 13, 1996, an ex-Boy Scout leader named Thomas Hamilton took four high-powered rifles into the primary school of the peaceful Scottish town of Dunblane and slaughtered 16 kindergarten children and their teacher. This horrific crime shocked the British Isles into implementing strict controls on all guns. Bizarre outbursts such as Hamilton's support a link between violence and some sort of mental and biological abnormality. (Siegel, *Criminology*, 10th ed., p. 302, © Cengage Learning.)

Most textbook writers make use of major and minor headings to divide up chapters. You should make use of them too. Use them to help you make predictions about what will follow. Use them as well to create questions that will focus your attention on the text even when the material is new and complex.

Form Questions Based on Key Terms

Authors make it a point to highlight vocabulary words essential to their subject matter. They highlight the words using **boldface**, *italics*, colored ink, and marginal notes. Often they use a combination of visual devices to get your attention.

When you spot those highlighted terms during a survey, use them as the basis for questions. For example, the following words, *mnemonic* and *acronym*, appear as marginal notes in a chapter on memory. Together they provide the basis for the two questions listed below.

Mnemonic[†]	a device for improving memory
Acronym[†]	a word composed of the first letter of a series of words
Questions:	1. What are some examples of mnemonics that I already know? Are they useful for all kinds of remembering?
	2. What are some examples of acronyms, and how can they aid memory?

Use Whatever's Available as the Basis for Questions

Some textbook chapters won't use headings, icons, marginal annotations, and so on, to highlight key points. This is particularly true of history books. When your textbook doesn't offer many visual clues to significance, be a flexible reader. Use whatever is available as the basis for your questions.

You could, for instance, read the first sentence and last sentence in each paragraph of a chapter section to see if they provide a basis for questions. Note the questions that can be derived from the opening and closing sentences of each paragraph in this excerpt from a history text.

[†]An example of a mnemonic would be the expression "Spring forward and fall back" to remember how to wind your clocks with the change of season.
[†]Some examples of acronyms are ASAP for As Soon As Possible and SCUBA for Self-Contained Underwater Breathing Apparatus.

Mexican-American Activism

How did
migrant
workers start a
movement for
social justice?

How did
Chávez and
the union
draw attention
to these
conditions?

Do all of these
still exist?

The national Mexican-American movement for social justice began with migrant farm workers. From 1965 to 1970, labor organizers César Chávez and Dolores Huerta led migrant workers in a strike (*huelga*) against large grape growers in California's San Joaquin Valley.

Chávez and the AFL-CIO affiliated United Farm Workers (UFW) drew national attention to the working conditions of migrant laborers, who received as little as 10 cents an hour (the minimum wage in 1965 was $1.25) and were often lodged by employers in squalid housing without running water or indoor toilets. A national consumer boycott of table grapes brought the growers to the bargaining table, and in 1970 the UFW won better wages and working conditions. The union resembled nineteenth-century *mutualistas*, or cooperative associations. Its members founded cooperative groceries, a Spanish-language newspaper, and a theater group. (Adapted from Norton et al., *A People and a Nation*, 8th ed., pp. 892–93, © Cengage Learning.)

SUMMING UP THE KEY POINTS

1. Readers who pose questions are less likely to lose their concentration while reading. They are also more likely to spot the most important passages in a chapter.

2. Questions used to guide your reading can be based on (1) introductory lists of questions and objectives, (2) major and minor headings, (3) key words highlighted in the text, (4) first and last sentences in paragraphs, and (5) whatever is available.

▶ **EXERCISE 3**   **Using Questions to Focus Your Attention**

DIRECTIONS   Survey the following selection. Pose a question or questions in the margins for each heading or underlined sentence. The first two questions are examples of the kinds of questions you might ask.

What is a "sense" of maleness or femaleness?

Does that mean that before the age of three, children don't know if they are male or female?

_____
_____
_____
_____

Gender Identity: Our Sense of Maleness or Femaleness

<u>By the age of three, most children have acquired a firm sense of their gender identity, of being either male or female</u>. But what determines gender identity? The answer is not yet clear. Some research points to biological influences. Investigators suspect that prenatal hormones sculpt the developing brain in ways that influence the later development of gender identity (Reiner & Gearhart, 2004). But research suggests that gender identity may not be fully stamped in at birth. In this research, children who were born with ambiguous[†] genitalia because of inherited birth defects developed a gender identity that was consistent with the gender to which they were assigned and raised accordingly, even when the assigned gender conflicted with their chromosomal (XY or XX) sex (Slijper et al., 1998). <u>All in all, most scientists believe that gender identity arises</u> from a complex interaction of nature (biology) and nurture (rearing influences) (Diamond, 1996).

Whatever the sources of gender identity may be, it is almost always consistent with one's biological sex. But for a few individuals, their gender identity and their biological sex are mismatched. These individuals have the gender identity of one gender but the sexual organs of the other.

_____

[†]ambiguous: unclear because a choice has not been made.

Transsexualism: A Mismatch of Identity and Biology

<u>People with transsexualism feel trapped in the body of the opposite gender by a mistake of nature.</u> A transsexual man is anatomically a man but has the gender identity of a woman. A transsexual woman is anatomically a woman but possesses a male gender identity. <u>Myths around transsexualism abound.</u>

<u>Transsexual men and women may be repulsed by the sight of their own genitals.</u> Many undergo gender reassignment surgery to surgically alter their genitals to correct what they see as nature's mistake. Gender reassignment surgery transforms the genitalia to a workable likeness of those of the opposite gender. But since it cannot transplant the internal reproductive organs that produce the germ cells—the testes in the man and the ovaries in the woman—reproduction is impossible. Thus, surgery does not change a man into a woman or a woman into a man, if what it means to be a man or a woman depends on having the internal reproductive organs of their respective sex. <u>Nonetheless, gender reassignment surgery generally permits the individual to perform sexual intercourse.</u> Hormonal replacement therapy is used to foster growth of the beard and body hair in female-to-male cases and of the breasts in male-to-female cases. (Adapted from Nevid, *Psychology: Concepts and Applications*, 3rd ed., pp. 406–7, © Cengage Learning.)

Chastity, now known as Chaz, Bono is someone for whom changing genders was worth the physical pain and mental readjustment a sex change requires.

Ron Galella/WireImage/Getty Images.

Barry King/FilmImage/Getty Images.

✔ CHECK YOUR UNDERSTANDING

1. Why is posing questions while reading important?

   _____

   _____

2. What are some of the sources readers can use as the basis for questions?

   _____

   _____

   _____

R1: Read in Sections or Chunks

Once you finish your survey and have a sense of what you need to look for, you are ready to start reading. But that doesn't mean you should sit down and read an entire chapter. Instead, assign yourself a specific number of pages or sections to cover during the time you have set aside for study.

Each time you return to the text to read the next part of your assignment, try to recall what was said in the previous one. These spaced reviews of the previous material *before* you process what's new will help you remember what you read.

How much you read per session should be determined by (1) how difficult the material is and (2) how much you already know about it. If you don't know anything about the subject under discussion, if the content is complex and the style difficult, consider reading only eight to ten pages per session. Just make sure you plan on at least three or four study sessions to get through the chapter.

Think about reading a whole chapter in one sitting *only* if the material is familiar and the style easy to read.

For Really Difficult Textbook Assignments, Consider the 10/5 Approach

When a textbook assignment is filled with new terms, concepts, and facts, reading can seem like torture. What can help is a variation on the technique productivity gurus like Alan Lakein call *The Swiss Cheese Method.*

The principle behind the Swiss Cheese Method is to accomplish a large task by completing small pieces of it step by step. The name comes from the idea of poking holes into a cheese until the cheese disappears.

To apply this principle to reading, set a stop watch on your computer or your phone—if you don't have either, use a kitchen timer—for ten minutes. Read during every minute of the ten. No interruptions allowed, so turn off your cell phone.

But when the timer goes off, stop and take five minutes for a quick stroll from say your desk to the kitchen. While you stroll think about what you've read, mentally summing it up. You don't necessarily have to be right. All you have to do is to **paraphrase**, or put into your own words, what you think the author said. The more you read of the chapter, the more the pieces will fall into place, and you may well revise your first thoughts about the author's message. When the five minutes are up—time them too—go back to reading for another ten.

Follow this routine for at least an hour. If you can, push it to an hour and fifteen minutes. Do this every day until you finish the chapter. When you are done, you will be surprised at how much you know, and the process will be much less painful than laboring over a hard-to-read chapter for thirty-minute or hour-long stretches.

Vary Your Assignments to Stay Sharp

If you've set aside an hour and a half to study, vary your assignments so that you aren't spending all your study time on one subject. Changing from assignment to assignment helps concentration and remembering. Each time you switch to new material, your brain will feel refreshed and more alert simply because it's working on something different.

For best results, alternate between related subjects so that one reinforces the other. If you are reading a psychology chapter on the parts and functions of the brain, follow it with a health chapter on injuries and diseases of the brain. If you have set aside an hour to study, spend thirty minutes on each subject. If you set aside two hours, give each subject an hour.

READING TIP A willingness to re-read is critical to understanding a difficult textbook. But just as important is a willingness to re-read *in a different way*. If a first reading left you confused, do the second reading at a slower rate. You might also try reading aloud. If the text describes a physical event or process, try visualizing. Again be flexible and adapt to the material.

Write While You Read

"I write all over the pages of every book I read. It helps me have a conversation with the author and allows me to keep track of my thinking while I am reading."
—Teacher and blogger, John Howell

If I could personally give every student who reads this book one piece of advice, it would be this: Keep a pen or pencil in hand while you read, and use it—*a lot*. For somewhat familiar material written in an easy-to-absorb style, underline key words and jot brief notes in the margins of pages. With more complicated texts, especially those essential to your college career, do both—take brief marginal notes and make a more detailed set of notes in a separate notebook.

If you are reading a print text, keep a highlighter close by. Use the highlighter for sentences that seem especially significant—for example, ideas that might turn up on exams or prove useful for term papers. Because writing while reading is critical to academic success, you'll hear more on this subject later on in the chapter.

E-Books Are No Exception

If you are using an e-book, it probably allows you to highlight, attach sticky notes, jot your own notes in pop-up boxes, and so on. Use every single one of the features available to you. Whether print or digital, writing in a book is a way of personalizing the information and making it your own. The more you personalize new information, the better you will understand and remember it.

Writing and the Brain

In addition, more recent research on the brain shows how truly specialized it is. Different parts of the brain respond to different language activities. When you read new material and write about it at the same time, your brain is absorbing the information via two separate pathways, one devoted to reading, the other to writing. The dual processing involved in reading and writing about the same passage makes the material in that passage more memorable.

Personal Experience Counts

The more you know about a subject, the more informed your marginal notes are going to be. Take a government and an economics course, and you might be able to jot a note that compares Supply Side and Keynesian solutions[†] to an economic crisis. But initially, college textbooks introduce

---

[†]The Supply Side school claims tax cuts stimulate the economy, whereas Keynesians would ask that the government create jobs.

largely unfamiliar subjects about which you know very little. That doesn't mean, however, that you can't comment on the author's statements in order to deepen your understanding of them. Often, you can compare what the author says to something you know about in your own life, for instance:

This is just like fraternities and sororities where people get mistreated and forever after treasure their membership.

In 1959, researchers Elliot Aronson and Judson Mills published a groundbreaking article titled "Severity of Initiation and Liking for a Group." In it, the two researchers argued "that persons who go through a great deal of trouble or pain to attain something tend to value it more highly than persons who attain the same thing with a minimum of effort." To prove their point, Aronson and Mills described the behavior of 63 college women, who had to take an "embarrassment test" in order to join a discussion group about sexual behavior that had been touted as highly informative. The tests had been designed by the researchers to range from mildly to very embarrassing. Some women, for example, had to listen to descriptions of moderately sexual situations. Others had to listen to four-letter words and stories of an explicitly sexual nature. Whatever the nature of the material, they were told not to show embarrassment. If they did, they wouldn't be allowed to attend the discussion group. Those who passed the test, which many later described as humiliating, were then allowed into the discussion group. What they didn't know was that the discussion group had been designed to be as boring as possible. Yet the women who had suffered the severest humiliation during "testing" were the ones who most strongly insisted the discussions were really interesting.

They can't face thinking they went through it for nothing.

As the poet and textbook author John Frederick Nims said so correctly, "When a new piece of information is fed into the brain, it is whirled around the circuits until it finds its place with similar things."[†] When you make marginal comments that compare new information to your own personal experiences, you are ensuring that your brain holds on to the new by connecting it to what you already know or have experienced.

Match Your Reading Rate to the Material

Unless you are reading a very difficult text, where the complexity of the material forces you to maintain a low, phrase-by-phrase reading rate (see

---

[†]John Frederick Nims and David Mason, *Western Wind: An Introduction to Poetry*, 4th ed. (Boston: McGraw-Hill, 1999), p. 18.

"Readers make choices in the kinds of attention they give to texts—from scanning, skimming, and speed reading to deep reading and re-reading."
—Catherine L. Ross, professor, University of Western Ontario

the following chart), the speed with which you read should vary. While re-reading the introduction you already surveyed, for instance, you can speed up to 500 or 600 words a minute. You need to slow down, though, when you start a chapter section, reducing your rate to around 250 or 300 words a minute.

With material that is familiar and not too difficult—introductions in textbooks, for instance, are often lists of single sentences rather than paragraphs—your reading rate can be on the boundary between skimming—that is, very fast reading to understand just a few main points—and study reading. If you are reading a chapter on childhood nutrition, for example, and already know much of the information from another course, then keep your reading rate fairly high, between 350 and 400 words a minute. If the text becomes difficult, don't be afraid to slow down and do an analytical, or close, reading, probably at 100 or 150 words a minute.

Reading Rates
●

Good readers are flexible about reading rate. They vary it to suit the material and their reading purpose.

Reading Strategy	Purpose	Type of Assignment	Rate
Scanning	To locate a specific piece of information	You are searching for a specific fact, statistic, or study.	700 to 1,000 words a minute
Skimming	To get a very general overview of an article or a chapter	You are preparing to read a chapter and previewing it to determine how much time and how many study sessions you will need to master the material.	400 to 800 words a minute
Study Reading	To understand an author's message or follow the plot of a novel or short story	You are reading a detailed but clearly written chapter in preparation for class.	250 to 400 words a minute
Close or Analytical Reading	To understand a very difficult passage or unfamiliar and complex material	You are trying to understand a chapter filled with new material and written in a hard-to-read style.	100 to 250 words a minute

▶ **EXERCISE 4**   **Reviewing What You've Learned**

DIRECTIONS   Fill in the blanks by explaining what each piece of advice introduced in the previous chapter section means. The first one is done for you.

1. Read in sections or chunks.	Don't try to read the whole chapter. Divide it into sections and read a section at a time.
2. When material is difficult, consider the 10/5 approach.	
3. Vary your assignments to stay sharp.	
4. Write while you read.	
5. Match your reading rate to the material.	

> **SUMMING UP THE KEY POINTS**
>
> 1. Unless the material is really easy to learn, don't think you have to read entire chapters in one sitting. Break the chapter up into sections with a limited number of pages that you can read in about an hour.
> 2. Varying your assignments during a study session is a good way to maintain concentration.
> 3. Whether your textbook is print or digital, write while you read. Writing while reading gives your brain a chance to process the new material, making it easier to remember.
> 4. Vary your reading rate according to the difficulty of the material and your knowledge of the subject. Slow down when a text is difficult and unfamiliar. Speed up when you are dealing with material that is familiar or uncomplicated.

R2: Recall† Right After Reading

When an author's words are right in front of us, we usually think we understand them. Yet if we look away from the page and try to recall what we've read, we often discover that our understanding is muddled or incomplete. That's what makes the recall step of *SQ3R* so important. It's a way of monitoring your understanding before going on to the next section of a chapter or an article.

Slowing Down Forgetting

There's another reason why recalling immediately after reading is critical: Most people are inclined to forget new information right after reading it. But with the passage of time, the rate of forgetting slows down, and we forget less as time goes by. That means anything we do to fix newly absorbed information into long-term memory *right after reading*—when the rate of forgetting is highest—improves our chances of remembering it, weeks or even months later.

---

†Francis Robinson used the word *recite*, but he included under that term "mentally reviewing the answer or writing it out," which is another way of saying "recall."

As always with *SQ3R*, there are different ways to complete this step. The one you choose depends on the kind of material you are reading and the depth of understanding you want to achieve. Here again, flexibility is key. Here are just some of the ways you can fulfill this key step in *SQ3R*.

1. Recite the Answers to Your Questions

With material that's not too difficult or too unfamiliar, try mentally reciting answers to the following questions: What topic, or subject, was discussed? What point did the author make about the topic? How did the author illustrate or argue the point? The last question of the three is usually the toughest to answer. If you can think of one illustration or reason after a first reading, you are doing just fine.

You might also consider reciting the answers aloud. That would give your brain an external and internal repetition of key material. The more pathways your brain uses to receive information, the greater your chances of remembering it.

2. Write Out the Answers to Your Questions

Robinson believed that readers were inclined to fool themselves if they only recited answers to their questions. In his opinion, it was too easy to accept a vague and confused answer. Posing questions about the material and writing out the answers was, from Robinson's perspective, a better comprehension check.

3. Make an Informal Outline

Some students panic when they hear the word *outline*. They panic because they think they have to create formal outlines in which every *a* is followed by a *b*, and strict rules dictate how the outline has to be completed. But the outlines you use for the recall step of *SQ3R* don't have to be formal ones. They just have to provide a quick review of the content covered and show the relationship between ideas.

Start your outline by looking only at the heading of the chapter section and asking yourself, "What was the main idea or central message of this section?" Write the heading and your answer down at the top of the page. Then indented underneath the main idea, in your own words, list any reasons, illustrations, studies, facts, or figures that the author used to explain or prove that overall point.

Here to illustrate is a brief textbook excerpt about "Convenience Products" followed by an outline. Read the text first. Then look over the outline to see how it matches up.

> **Convenience products** are goods and services consumers want to purchase frequently, often immediately, and with minimal effort. Milk, bread, and toothpaste are convenience products. Convenience services include 24-hour quick-stop stores, walk-in hair or nail salons, copy shops, and dry cleaners.
>
> Marketers further subdivide the convenience category into impulse items, staples, or emergency services. **Impulse goods and services** are purchased on the spur of the moment—for example, visit a car wash or buy a pack of gum while at the super market register. . . . **Staples** are convenience goods and services consumers constantly replenish to maintain a ready supply: gasoline, shampoo, and dry cleaning are good examples. **Emergency goods and services** are bought in response to unexpected and urgent needs. A snow blower purchased during a snowstorm and a visit to a hospital emergency room to treat a broken ankle are examples. (Adapted from Boone and Kurtz, *Contemporary Marketing*, 15th ed., pp. 348–49, © Cengage Learning.)

> Convenience Products: Marketers divide into three categories.
>
> 1. impulse buys like grabbing a candy bar when you reach the cash register
> 2. staples like gas
> 3. emergency purchases like batteries during a tornado

Informal outlines are a great way to figure out just how much you have understood of what you've read. They will also serve you well when you want to review for exams. Just make sure to leave plenty of space between the items in your outline so you can add to it during early reviews.

4. Draw Rough Diagrams and Pictures

If you think you are a **visual learner**, that is, you remember what you see even better than what you hear, consider translating words into pictures or diagrams during the recall step of your reading. Then check your drawing against the actual text to see what you've missed.

Just be aware that not every text will easily translate into a picture. If you are reading about the developmental stages of frogs in biology, then a picture might well be worth a thousand words. But if you are trying to remember the meaning of "probable cause"[†] in criminology, making a drawing will be tough because the definition is more **abstract** (i.e., an idea that can't take visual form) than **concrete** (i.e., something that can be physically seen and touched).

What follows is a passage about the layers of the Earth. It's perfect for the reader-made diagram that follows it.

Four different layers make up the Earth: the inner core, outer core, mantle, and crust. The rocky and brittle crust is the outermost and thinnest layer. In contrast, the thickest part of the Earth's mass is in the mantle, which is composed of iron (Fe), magnesium (Mg), aluminum (Al), silicon (Si), and oxygen (O) silicate compounds. Below the mantle lies the core, composed mostly of iron so hot that it's molten, or so hot that it has turned to liquid. The inner portion of the core, however, is under such intense pressure, it remains solid.

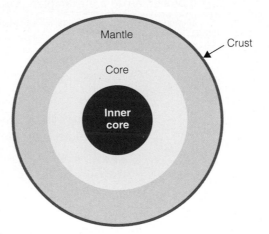

5. Work with a Friend

If you can work with someone who is serious about studying, consider completing assignments in pairs. Read each chapter section at the same time. Then take turns doing the recall. While one person does the recall, the other should look at the chapter section. When the person doing

---

[†]probable cause: refers to the circumstances under which law enforcement can obtain a search warrant.

the recall finishes up, the person doing the reading should add anything missed that seemed important.

SUMMING UP THE KEY POINTS

1. Recalling right after reading is important for two reasons. First, it's a way of monitoring your understanding. It tells you how well you have or have not understood what you've read. Completing the recall step in *SQ3R* also slows down the rate of forgetting and increases your chances of remembering what the text actually said.

2. Flexibility is important in choosing the method of recall. In addition to mentally reciting after reading, you should also consider the following: (1) reciting the key points aloud, (2) writing out answers to the questions you came up with during your survey, (3) creating an informal outline, (4) making rough diagrams or drawing pictures, and (5) working with a friend. The method you choose depends on the kind of material you are reading and your understanding of how you learn most easily.

▶ **EXERCISE 5**　　**Recalling After Reading**

DIRECTIONS　　Read the following excerpt. Then, from memory, fill in the boxes.

Steps in Delegation

The process of **delegation** essentially involves three steps. First, the manager **assigns responsibility**. That is, the manager defines the employee's duty to perform a task. For example, when a manager tells someone reporting to him to prepare a sales report, order additional raw materials, or hire a new assistant, he is assigning responsibility.

Second, the manager must also **grant the authority** necessary to carry out the task. Preparing a sales report may require analyzing previous sales reports, ordering raw material may require negotiations on price and delivery dates, and hiring a new assistant may mean submitting a hiring notice to the human resource department. If these activities are not a formal part of the group member's job, the manager must give her the authority to do them anyway.

Finally, the manager needs to **create accountability**. This suggests that the group member incurs, or takes on, an obligation to carry out the job. If the sales report is never prepared, if the raw materials are not ordered, or if the assistant is never hired, the group member is accountable to her boss for failing to perform the task. Indeed, if the manager is not careful, it is possible for some personnel to lose sight of their major task because they become focused on the wrong objectives. (Adapted from Van Fleet and Peterson, *Contemporary Management*, 2nd ed., Boston: Houghton Mifflin, pp. 252–53.)

Delegation Process

```
┌──────────────┐     ┌──────────────┐     ┌──────────────┐
│              │     │              │     │              │
│              │ ──▶ │              │ ──▶ │              │
│              │     │              │     │              │
└──────────────┘     └──────────────┘     └──────────────┘
```

✔ CHECK YOUR UNDERSTANDING

1. What are two reasons why recalling right after reading is useful?

   _____

   _____

   _____

2. What are some of the methods readers can use to recall what they've read after finishing a chapter section?

   _____

   _____

   _____

R3: Review Right After Completing the Assignment

Robinson's suggestion to review right after reading is a good one. But it needs some modification and clarification. Perhaps because he assumed students were also outlining chapters while they read, Robinson allotted only five minutes for review. Actually, you need at least fifteen to make this step productive.

Robinson also didn't always make it clear that the third *R* in his system represented only *the first* of several reviews. Trained as an educational psychologist, Robinson knew full well that *mastery of new material occurs with repeated reviews that extend over time.* He never assumed that the first review would be the reader's last.

The Goal of the First Review: See the Big Picture

The first goal of a review is to understand how the individual parts of the chapter fit together. For example, in a chapter titled "The Professional Sports Business," you would need to determine the author's overall intention or objective. Is the author trying to give you a historical overview of how sports have become more about making money than a celebration of athletic prowess? Or perhaps the chapter focuses on the various elements that make up the business of sports, such as scouts, agents, contracts, owners, trainers, and endorsements. Once you have the larger chapter objective in mind, it becomes easier to see what each chapter section contributes to that objective.

Pick a Review Method That Suits You and Your Assignment

For some assignments and some readers, outlining is an ideal learning strategy. But there are other ways to complete a first review. The following are some suggestions.

Draw Diagrams and Charts. If you remember pictures or images more readily than words, you might consider reviewing with diagrams. One popular diagram used for study purposes is called a **concept map**.

With a concept map, you put the overall point of the chapter or article in the middle of the page or top of the page and enclose it in a circle or box. Then using arrows and indentation, you can show how ideas relate to one another. Here, for instance, is a concept map that gives visual form to the ideas and relationships introduced in a chapter about the internment of Japanese Americans during World War II:

Despite having their families suffer the fate of internment during World War II, Japanese-American soldiers served their country with distinction.

The Nisei[†] 100th Infantry Battalion and 442nd Regimental Combat Team saw heavy action.

21 members of battalion received Medal of Honor

6,000 Japanese Americans served in Military Intelligence Service

October 5, 2010: Congressional Gold Medal awarded to 100th Infantry Battalion, the 442nd Regimental Combat Team, and all 6,000 Japanese Americans in the MIS

[†]Nisei: refers to children born of Japanese parents who immigrated to other countries and raised their children in those countries, rather than in Japan.

Don't think, however, that you are restricted to concept maps. If another format suits the text and your purpose, use it. Here, for instance, is part of a chart created for a chapter on disorders of the digestive system. Note how the reader has tried to fill in some of the details about the headings and left question marks under headings about which she recalled little or nothing.

Common Disorders of the Digestive System

stomatitis	hiatal hernia	pyloric stenosis	gastritis	enteritis	peptic ulcers	IBD[†]
inflammation of soft tissue in mouth	stomach protrudes above dia-phragm into esophagus opening	?	chronic inflammation of stomach lining	?	lesion in stomach lining, most bacterial caused	Crohn's disease and ?

[†]IBD: inflammatory bowel disease.

Look at All the Major Headings. Go through the chapter page by page or screen by screen. Look at each major heading and then look away to see how much you remember about what's included under that heading. Give yourself just a few seconds to respond. If nothing comes to mind at the end of ten or fifteen seconds, mark the chapter or article section for another reading.

While being able to recall the main point introduced under each heading is wonderful, recognizing that you can't recall much of anything is also useful. Your lack of recall tells you that the chapter section needs a second reading.

Work with a Classmate. Here again, think about working with someone in your class. Ask him or her to say the major headings aloud. Then respond by reciting what you remember about each one. Any time you draw a blank or remember very little, your partner should mark the passage for another reading.

Whittle Recall Cues Down to Size

Reviews done right after reading and the follow-up reviews you do for exam preparation have slightly different goals. Your first review should tell you what the chapter covers and how the different parts fit together. Are they ordered, for instance, according to sequence in time? Or do they tell you how different parts of the United States reacted to the same key event? It should also help you determine what you do and don't know about the material you've just finished reading.

However, the reviews you do in preparation for exams should focus on creating **recall cues**, words or phrases that call up the information you have learned. Although you may well start out reviewing with notes or diagrams based on complete sentences—"Gender identity refers to our sense of being male or female" or "Delegation involves three basic steps"—you should end up with notes that include only a few key words and phrases, for example, "gender identity," or "steps in delegation." You can tell you are prepared for exams when just glancing at those key words and phrases triggers the explanations they represent.

SUMMING UP THE KEY POINTS

1. The third *R* in *SQ3R* refers to the review that takes place after a chapter is completed. However, Robinson knew that several reviews over an extended period of time were essential to mastery of new material. He never assumed that one review right after finishing a chapter would be enough.

2. The first goal of a review is to get a sense of how the parts of a chapter connect. Are they all effects of one cause, for instance, or do they describe a progression of events? Like the first step of *SQ3R*, the survey, use the review step to establish a sense of the chapter's general, or overall, goal.

3. Robinson suggested readers should review by looking over their informal outlines, but other methods can be used as well. You can look at all the major headings and then look away to see how much information you recall about each heading. You can make a concept map, which shows the chapter's central point in the center along with the sub-topics or issues used to explain it. Or you can go over the chapter with a classmate who asks you what each major heading contributes to the overall point of the chapter.

Writing and Reading

"Your memory is not a product of what you want to remember or what you try to remember; it's a product of what you think about."
—Daniel T. Willingham, *Why Don't Students Like School*

Whether you are reading a print or digital book, writing while reading will help you understand and remember what you read. When you underline or jot notes, you analyze the text, trying to decide what's important and what's not. It's the thought involved that deepens your understanding and anchors new facts and ideas in long-term memory.

What follows are suggestions about how you can write and read at the same time. Over the course of several study sessions, try them all to see which ones work best, and which ones are appropriate to specific kinds of texts. Underlining key words, for instance, probably works well with any kind of material from history to science. Diagramming, in contrast, is usually more effective with descriptions of physical events or processes.

Suggestions for Writing While Reading
●

1. As you do a first reading, underline in pencil or highlight key words in selected sentences that you think are essential to the author's explanation.

2. When you do a second reading (or even a third one) for exam reviews, make final decisions about what's essential and what's not. This time around, consider if you need to erase or eliminate any words you underlined or highlighted.

3. Use boxes, circles, or stars to highlight key names, dates, and events.

4. If you have any personal knowledge about the subject matter, make personal comments in the margins or note boxes.

Examples:

Uncle Bob went to Wild West show this summer.

Between 1872 and 1878, William "Buffalo Bill" Cody alternated between his career as a scout for the U.S. Cavalry and his starring roles in a series of melodramas popular in the East. By 1882, he had founded the enterprise that brought him even greater fame and shaped the country's view of itself, "Buffalo Bill's Wild West."

5. Use numbers to itemize individual parts of a definition, process, or procedure.

6. Paraphrase, or restate, the author's ideas in your own words.

Examples:

4 parts of emotions:
1. how you feel
2. how body responds
3. thoughts
4. purpose of

Emotions have several components: feelings ❶, physiological ❷ responses ❸, cognitions ❹, and goals.

7. Use the margins or note boxes to identify points of view that agree or disagree with the author's.

8. Use the top margin to summarize the contents of the page.

Examples:

Marshall Plan Provides Massive Aid

Comp. Howard Zinn on role of Marshall Plan.

The Marshall Plan was a four-year program proposed by U.S. Secretary of State George C. Marshall on June 5, 1947. Its goal was to provide foreign assistance to seventeen western and southern European nations as part of post–World War II reconstruction. Between 1948 and 1951, over $13 billion was dispensed through the Marshall Plan.

9. Whenever you find yourself struggling to understand an author's meaning for more than two or three sentences, mark the passage for a second and slower reading (e.g., *RR, x2, ??*).

10. Use arrows, labels, and abbreviations to make relationships between sentences clear.

11. Double underline, star, or otherwise highlight definitions.

Examples:

If you boil water on a stove, you can see a steamy mist above the kettle, and then higher still the mist seems to disappear into the air. Of course, the water molecules have not been lost. Step ❶ → In the pan, water is in the liquid phase, and in the mist above the kettle, water exists as tiny droplets. These Step ❸ → droplets then evaporate, and the water Step ❹ vapor mixes with air and becomes invisible. Air generally contains some water vapor. **Humidity** is a measure of the amount of water vapor in air. (Turk and Turk, *Physical Science,* p. 410.)

12. Put quotation marks or rectangles around statements you think are particularly significant.

13. Mark a statement or passage you think might be a test question (e.g., *T.Q.*).

14. Highlight any statements you think could be the jumping-off point for a paper. In your notes, comment on the statement in a way that suggests how the paper might be developed.

Examples:
Effect of 1918 Influenza

How <u>lethal</u> was the 1918 influenza? It was <u>twenty-five times more deadly than ordinary influenzas</u>. This flu <u>killed 2.5 percent</u> of its <u>victims</u>. Normally just one-tenth of <u>1 percent of people</u> who get the flu <u>die</u>. And since <u>a fifth of the world's population got</u> the <u>flu</u> that year, including <u>28 percent of Americans</u>, the number of deaths was stunning. So many died, in fact, that the average lifespan in the United States fell by twelve years in 1918. If such a plague came today, killing a similar fraction of the U.S. population, 1.5 million Americans would die. (Adapted from Kolata, *Flu*, p. 216.)

T.Q.
Paper: There are signs bird flu could be worse than 1918.

Effect on mortality: average lifespan decreased.

▶ EXERCISE 6   Marking a Text

DIRECTIONS   Read each marked excerpt. Circle the letter of the one that better illustrates the advice given on pages 32–35. Then, in the blanks at the end, explain why you chose one over the other.

a. How Short-Term Memory Works

1   <u>Most psychologists refer to short-term memory as *working memory*, since information held in short-term memory is actively "worked on," or processed, by the brain</u> (Baddeley, 2001; Braver et al., 2001). <u>Working memory is a kind of mental workspace or blackboard for holding information long enough to process it and act on it</u> (Stoltzfus, Hasher, & Zacks, 1996). For example, <u>we engage working memory when we form an image of a person's face and hold it in memory for the second or two it takes the brain to determine whether it is the face of someone we know</u>. We also employ working memory whenever we

perform arithmetical operations in our heads or engage in conversation. In a conversation, our working memory allows us to retain memory of sounds long enough to convert, or change, them into recognizable words.

2   In the 1950s, psychologist George Miller performed a series of groundbreaking studies in which he sought to determine the storage capacity of short-term memory. Just how much information can most people retain in short-term memory? The answer, Professor Miller determined, was about seven items, plus or minus two (Kareev, 2000). Miller referred to the limit of seven as the "magical number seven."

3   The magic number seven appears in many forms in human experience, including the "seven ages of man" in Shakespeare's *As You Like It*, the Seven Wonders of the World, the Seven Deadly Sins, and even the seven dwarfs of Disney fame (Logie, 1996). Investigators find that people can normally repeat a maximum of six or seven single-syllable words they have just heard (Hulme et al., 1999). Think about the "magical number seven" in the context of your daily experiences. Telephone numbers are seven-digit numbers, which means you can probably retain a telephone number in short-term memory just long enough to dial it. (Adapted from Nevid, *Psychology: Concepts and Applications*, 3rd ed., p. 221, © Cengage Learning.)

b. How Short-Term Memory Works

1   Most psychologists refer to short-term memory as *working memory*, since information held in short-term memory is actively "worked on," or processed, by the brain (Baddeley, 2001; Braver et al., 2001). Working memory is a kind of mental workspace or blackboard for holding information long enough to process it and act on it (Stoltzfus, Hasher, & Zacks, 1996). For example, we engage working memory when we form an image of a person's face and hold it in memory for the second or two it takes the brain to determine whether it is the face of someone we know. We also employ working memory whenever we perform arithmetical operations in our heads or engage in conversation. In a conversation, our working memory allows us to retain memory of sounds long enough to convert, or change, them into recognizable words.

2   In the 1950s, psychologist George Miller performed a series of groundbreaking studies in which he sought to determine the storage capacity of short-term memory. Just how much information can most people retain in short-term memory? The answer, Professor Miller

Form images, holding in memory to see if familiar

EX

T.Q.

<u>determined</u>, was <u>about seven items</u>, plus or minus two (Kareev, 2000). Miller referred to the limit of seven as the "magical number seven."

Miller says we hold about 7 items in s.t. memory.

3   The magic number seven appears in many forms in human experience, including the "seven ages of man" in Shakespeare's *As You Like It*, the Seven Wonders of the World, the Seven Deadly Sins, and even the seven dwarfs of Disney fame (Logie, 1996). Investigators find that people can normally repeat a maximum of six or seven single-syllable words they have just heard (Hulme et al., 1999). Think about the "magical number seven" in the context of your daily experiences. Telephone numbers are seven-digit numbers, which means you can probably

Keep phone number in mind.

retain a telephone number in short-term memory just long enough to dial it. (Adapted from Nevid, *Psychology: Concepts and Applications*, 3rd ed., p. 221, © Cengage Learning.)

_____

_____

▶ EXERCISE 7   Writing While Reading

DIRECTIONS   Here is the rest of the text introduced on page 8. Using underlining and marginal notes, mark up this text in a way that you think would help you remember the key points. When you finish, compare what you've done to the sample provided by your instructor.

Maternal and Paternal Influences

Do mothers and fathers parent differently? Although maternal influences—all the effects a mother has on her child—have a great impact, fathers do make a unique contribution to parenting (Bjorklund & Hernández Blasi, 2012). This is true despite the fact that mothers still do most of the nurturing and caretaking, especially of young children.

Studies of paternal influences (the sum of all effects a father has on his child) reveal that fathers are likely to play with their children and tell them stories. In contrast, mothers are typically responsible for the physical and emotional care of their children.

It might seem that the father's role as a playmate makes him less important. Not so. Playtime is very important for children. From birth onward, fathers pay more visual attention to children than mothers do. Fathers are much more tactile (lifting, tickling, and handling the baby), more physically stimulating (engaging in rough and tumble play), and more likely to engage in unusual play (imitating the baby, for example). In comparison, mothers speak to infants more, play more traditional games (such as peekaboo), and, as noted, spend much more time in caregiving. Some studies have shown that young children who spend a lot of time playing with their fathers have a high level of competence in certain areas.

Overall, fathers can be as affectionate, sensitive, and responsive as mothers are. Nevertheless, infants and children tend to get very different views of males and females. Females, who offer comfort, nurturance, and verbal stimulation, tend to be close at hand. Males come and go, and when they are present, action, exploration, and risk taking prevail. It's no wonder, then, that the parental styles of mothers and fathers have a major impact on children's gender role development. (Dennis Coon and John O. Mitterer. *Psychology: A Journey*, 5th ed., p. 108, © Cengage Learning.)

READING TIP Using a variety of page-marking techniques will keep you focused on what's important. You might also try using different colors to highlight various kinds of information. Underline in red for the main idea, or key point. Use a yellow highlighter for sentences that provide essential support for the main idea. Write potential test questions in blue ink or in bold.

Putting the Spotlight on Paraphrasing

While you may think of paraphrasing as something you do only when you write papers, paraphrasing, or putting someone else's ideas into your own words, is actually an essential part of reading and note-taking. When we really want to understand something, we paraphrase, using our words to express the author's ideas.

Think about it. Even if you are just reading instructions for how to put a simple bookcase together, you're going to paraphrase. The directions say "Place board 1 at a right angle to board 2," and you say to yourself, "This board goes on the corner of this one." What you've done is automatically paraphrase, or re-word, the directions to make sure you have understood them.

Paraphrase to Check Comprehension

But paraphrasing while reading isn't just essential to concrete tasks like building a bookshelf. It's critical for reading textbooks as well. Paraphrasing while reading acts as a **comprehension check**. It tells you how well you have understood what you've just read. If you can paraphrase it, you can rest easy. You and the author have made contact. But if you can't, a re-reading is in order.

When the author's words are right in front of your eyes, it's easy to think you've understood their message. But if you can't recap the meaning in your own words, you probably haven't really understood the author's point.

Clearly, you don't want to make that discovery the day before a test. On the contrary, you need to identify passages you don't understand *while* you are reading. That way you can (1) adjust your reading rate and re-read the passage more slowly, (2) mark it for a later re-reading, or (3) ask someone for help understanding the passage.

Paraphrase to Remember

Equally important, paraphrasing gives your brain a chance to store what you have learned from your reading in long-term memory. As you search your mind for word substitutes that allow you to paraphrase, your brain is re-processing what you have just read. The double processing is a memory booster.

▶ **EXERCISE 8**   **Practice with Paraphrasing**

DIRECTIONS   Read the following quotations from famous people. Put each one into your own words. *Note*: Your paraphrase may be longer than the original. All the people quoted are famous writers and that was part of their gift—to say a lot in few words.

EXAMPLE   "Many of the things you can count, don't count. Many of the things you can't count, really count." —Albert Einstein

Concrete things like possessions and money are not what's important. What's

important are more abstract things like happiness, love, and a sense of well-being.

EXPLANATION   The original text has two parts. The first half tells you about the kind of things that don't truly count in life. The second half tells you about the things that do. The goal of the paraphrase, then, is to find the words that would describe each category. "Possessions and money" are good substitutes for things we can count. What about things we can't count? In the paraphrase shown above, the words "happiness, love, and a sense of well-being" were used. But actually, for both sides of the sentence, there were other choices as well. And that's typical for paraphrasing. Each person's paraphrase is likely to be different.

1. "Genius is born, not paid." —Oscar Wilde, writer

_____

_____

2. "The cure for boredom is curiosity." —Dorothy Parker, writer

_____

_____

3. "Life isn't about finding yourself. It's about creating yourself." —George Bernard Shaw, playwright

_____

_____

4. "When the going gets tough, the tough get going"—origin not known

_____

_____

Pointers on Paraphrasing for Reading

The more you practice paraphrasing, the better you will get at doing it, even when you have more than one sentence to translate into your own words. But your ability to paraphrase will also improve if you know some basic pointers about how to go about it. Some general suggestions are presented here. Later chapters will add more specifics to these instructions. However, these pointers will get you off to a good start.

Be Selective ← what is it?

The goal of paraphrasing for reading is to see how well you have understood the author's overall message. Thus, the most you want to paraphrase would be the sentence (or sentences) that express the main idea, or point, and a supporting detail or two. If you can do that, you know that you have not only understood the author's message but can explain it to someone else.

Use Language That Is Equally General or Equally Specific

↑
How?

As you search for words that can replace the author's, try to match the level of generality or specificity in the original language. Don't, for instance, replace the specific word *train* with the more general phrase *mode of transportation*. By the same token, *dog* is a good replacement for *canine*. *Animal* is not.

Accept the Fact That Some Words Don't Translate

Some words have no substitutes. You won't find replacements for names and scientific terminology, so don't waste time looking for them. In a sentence like this one, you can probably find replacements for every word except Freud's name and the name of his book: "Based on new studies of the brain, Sigmund Freud's famous book *The Interpretation of Dreams* is no longer considered relevant to an understanding of what happens when we dream." It follows, then, that a paraphrase would retain those words without any change: "Given what we currently know about the brain, Sigmund Freud's once-important text *The Interpretation of Dreams* is now considered hopelessly out of date."

Feel Free to Change the Order of Ideas

A paraphrase shouldn't alter the original meaning. Sometimes, though, it helps to change the order of ideas, putting, say, the beginning of the original sentence at the end of your paraphrase.

Changing the order of ideas is especially useful if words for the end of a sentence come to mind more readily than those for the beginning. Once you complete the part of the sentence that's easier for you to paraphrase, you may find that the puzzling piece has become clear too. Notice here how the original order has been reversed in the paraphrase:

Original: There are two major changes that occur in the central nervous system.

Paraphrase: Within the central nervous system, two key changes take place.

Look Away from the Text When You Paraphrase

What is the author trying to say?

answer

When the original words are right in front of you, it's tempting to use them. But that leads to copying the author's words without really understanding them. When you find a sentence or passage you want to paraphrase, read it carefully. Maybe even read it twice. Underline key words. Then, without looking at the sentence or passage, jot the paraphrase in the margins of your textbook or in your notebook.

Don't Confuse Paraphrasing for Reading Notes with Paraphrasing for Term Papers

Reading paraphrases don't require you to be as complete and grammatically correct in the same way paraphrasing for term papers does. For reading paraphrases all you have to do is re-create, in your own words, a bare bones version of the main idea or key point. For an illustration, here are some original statements followed by reading and writing paraphrases.

Original	In the nineteenth century, baseball emerged as the most popular new urban sport.
Reading Paraphrase	19th century baseball big in cities.
Writing Paraphrase	Baseball became a favorite urban sport in the nineteenth century.
Original	The Antarctic seals, however, after almost becoming extinct, have made an astonishing comeback, and the population is now rapidly increasing.
Reading Paraphrase	After almost dying out, Antarctic seals make big comeback.
Writing Paraphrase	Once almost extinct, Antarctic seals are rebounding and their numbers are increasing.

Original	Although much of the behavior of lower animals appears to be regulated by instincts, this is not true of human behavior.
Reading Paraphrase	Instinct doesn't control our behavior like in animals.
Writing Paraphrase	Instinct regulates almost all behavior among lower animals, but it does not have the same control over human actions.
Original	For a period of about seventy-five years (1765–1840), the Gothic novel, an early relative of the modern horror story, was popular throughout Europe.
Reading Paraphrase	1765–1840, Gothic horror novels big sellers.
Writing Paraphrase	Between 1765 and 1840, the ancestor of the modern-day horror story, the Gothic novel, was widely read throughout Europe.

SUMMING UP THE KEY POINTS

1. Paraphrase to check your understanding. But paraphrase selectively. Pick out a few sentences to paraphrase rather than huge chunks of text.

2. If a paraphrase for an entire sentence doesn't come to you immediately, try paraphrasing in pieces. Paraphrase one half of the sentence and then the other. Or else, paraphrase the parts of the sentence enclosed in commas.

3. Look away from the text while you paraphrase so that you are not tempted to copy the original.

4. Feel free to change the order of ideas and words as long as you don't change the meaning.

5. In choosing words to replace the original ones, come up with words that are equally specific rather than being more general.

6. Remember, names, titles, and many terms have no replacements. Thus, they can be used in your paraphrase.

> **EXERCISE 9**   **Picking the Better Paraphrase**

DIRECTIONS   Circle the letter of the better paraphrase. Then explain what's wrong with the one you didn't choose.

Original **EXAMPLE**   When we are in our twenties, we are confronted with the question of how to take hold in the adult world. (Adapted from Gail Sheehy, *Passages*, p. 25.)

Paraphrase a. As we age, we have to learn how to function as adults.
(b.) Once we reach our twenties, we have to learn how to function as adults.

EXPLANATION   The opening words in the original text were quite specific about the time frame. "When we are in our twenties. . . ." Thus, paraphrase *a* is incorrect. It makes the time frame, "As we age," too general. Sentence *b* is the better paraphrase because it keeps the opening phrase specific.

Original 1. The greatest threats to any species are the loss or degradation* of habitat, harmful invasive species, human population growth, pollution, climate change, and overexploitation. However, according to many researchers, the greatest threat to wild species is habitat loss. (Adapted from G. Tyler Miller and Scott E. Spoolman, *Sustaining the Earth*, 9th ed., p. 100, © Cengage Learning.)

[handwritten annotation: Same — pointing to "degradation"]

Paraphrase a Habitat destruction and loss due to the invasion of humans is forcing many species into extinction, as humans drive out existing species in order to build housing developments and recreational parks.
(b.) Although species extinction has a number of causes from loss of habitat and pollution to the arrival of new and invasive species, habitat loss is the most serious threat.

Explanation *Because B is the same as the original.*

degradation: the spoiling or wearing down of something that once functioned effectively.

America's grizzly bears are endangered by the deterioration and loss of habitat due to housing and recreational development.

© Ulrich Flemming.

Original **2.** The processes to which a dead body may be subjected are, to some extent, restricted by law.

Paraphrase a. The law places some restrictions on the handling of dead bodies.

b. The law restricts all handling of dead bodies that are being processed for burial.

Explanation *Because the first one repeat same meaning as the original.*

Original **3.** When Ulysses S. Grant and Robert E. Lee met in the parlor of a modest house at Appomattox Court House, Virginia, on April 9, 1865, to work out the terms for the surrender of Lee's Army of Northern Virginia, a great chapter in American life came to a close, and a great new chapter began. (Bruce Catton, *Grant and Lee: A Study in Contrasts. The American Story*, p. 56.)

Paraphrase   a. An important chapter in life closed when Ulysses S. Grant and Robert E. Lee met in Virginia in 1865, while a brand new and more promising chapter got started.

               b. One chapter opened and another one closed when Ulysses S. Grant and Robert E. Lee met at Appomattox Court House in Virginia to determine the conditions under which Lee's Army of North Virginia would admit defeat.

Explanation   *Because B is the same as the original.*

Original   **4.** Psychologists try to diagnose chronic boredom with question- naires: the Boredom Proneness Scale, for instance, was developed in 1986 and asks subjects twenty-eight separate questions about boredom.

Paraphrase   a. Psychology researchers use questions to measure chronic bore- dom. The Boredom Proneness Scale, for example, tests how consistently bored people are by asking twenty-eight different questions.

               b. The Boredom Proneness Scale is the major test psychologists use to determine the number of years people have been experiencing intense and constant boredom.

Explanation   *Because B is talking about constant boredom.*

CHECK YOUR UNDERSTANDING

1. Why should you paraphrase while reading?

Because paraphrase could that you understand the story or not.

2. Should you try to paraphrase everything you read? Please explain.

No —that is not necessary. Only for the one might help you to understand the article better.

3. What should you do if the paraphrase for a key sentence doesn't occur to you immediately?

4. When you paraphrase, can you change the order of ideas? Please explain.

5. When you paraphrase, is it acceptable to make the words you use more general than the original ones? Please explain.

Mining the Web for Background Knowledge

Around 1970, reading researchers began focusing on the relationship between background knowledge and comprehension. Almost unanimously they came to one conclusion: The more readers know about a subject *before* they begin reading, the more their comprehension improves.

In the 1970s, though, student readers couldn't really put this insight into practice. It would have required too much time searching for sources. Fortunately the arrival of the Internet and the World Wide Web has changed all that.

The Web Makes a Difference

Today, if you survey a textbook chapter and think, "Oh no, this reads as if it were written in a foreign language, that's how little I know about the subject," you can turn to the Web, a huge network of computerized documents linked together in cyberspace. The Web has information on just about any topic you can think of. With the Web to assist you, it is possible to develop some basic background knowledge about whatever subject you are studying, and you can do it in minutes.

Build Background Knowledge Before Reading

You can add a Web step to your survey by quickly jotting down some headings that describe unfamiliar people or events. Say, for instance, in a chapter titled **Moving Westward**, you spotted the name Quanah Parker and thought to yourself, Who's that?

You can find out in less than a minute by typing the name into a search engine box. Within seconds the screen will show you a list of websites, any one of which will tell you that Quanah Parker was a Comanche Chief who never lost a battle against white soldiers or settlers and whose mother was a white captive, who refused to return home when she had the chance.[†]

Your Timing Matters

It's fine to look up names and events while you read as well. If that works for you, wonderful. But be careful. It's easy to get distracted and start aimlessly browsing the Web *while* you are supposed to be reading your assignment. If you find that you are easily distracted when you do a Web search, then make it a point to look up unfamiliar names, events, and terms *before* you actually settle down to start reading.

Be a Savvy Searcher

Web searches are a great way to quickly build background knowledge. But they can also waste time as you sift through lists of irrelevant, or unrelated, websites. To avoid that pitfall, keep the following pointers in mind.

[†]Many people believe that the 1956 movie *The Searchers* was based on the abduction and return of Quanah's mother, Cynthia Parker.

Pointers on Choosing a Website
●

1. **Give your search term a sharp focus**. Make your search term state, as precisely as possible, what you are looking for. If, for instance, you are trying to find out more about the Battle of Saratoga in the Revolutionary War and the heading of your chapter section reads, "Saratoga—A Watershed," don't use the heading. The word *watershed* is going to make the search too **general**, or broad in meaning. You will end up sifting through websites about water drainage.

   Instead, make your search term more restricted in meaning. Use, for instance, the search term "Battle of Saratoga." That will get you a much more relevant list of websites. It will also eliminate all references to bodies of water. Overall, making your search term a phrase rather than a single word is likely to improve your search results.

2. **Be selective**. Whatever you do, don't just start at the top of the list that comes up on the screen and work your way down. Instead, give the list a quick once-over to get a sense of which sites might be most appropriate to your purposes. *Don't make the mistake of thinking that the order of the sites represents their quality*. For the most part it doesn't. The first website on the list that comes up on the screen is not necessarily the best. So evaluate the websites before hitting any Web links.

3. **Check for relevance**. Look for references to words used in your search term. Keep an eye open, too, for references to people and events related to your chapter assignment. Search engines introduce each link with a title, description, and Web address. The most relevant links will usually include at least one or two words from your original search term. The least relevant won't contain any words from your search term or your chapter assignment.

4. **Review the language**. If the website description is hard to read, skip it altogether. The website probably won't be easier to understand.

5. **Stay focused on your topic**. Avoid websites that mention your search term as a sub-topic of some larger, more general discussion. If you are researching the role José Martí played in winning Cuba's independence from Spain, don't get sidetracked by a site that mentions his name as one of several Latin American poets. Martí was a poet. But his poetry is not your focus. You want to learn about his role as a revolutionary.

6. **Skip sites referring to documents, conference proceedings, addresses, interviews, and journal articles**. These will probably be too limited in scope to enlarge your general background knowledge adequately. Hold off clicking on websites identified as outlines or timelines. These kinds of sites work better for later reviews. Because outlines and timelines reduce information to the bare minimum, they are usually too abbreviated to be valuable as pre-reading preparation.

7. **Ignore sponsored sites or sites selling products**. Sponsored sites weren't just found by the Web crawler searching the Web. Someone paid a fee to make them come up in response to a particular set of search terms. They are likely to be **biased**, or inclined to show favoritism. With Google, sponsored sites generally appear on the right-hand side of the screen and at the very top. But they can also make their way into the list of sites compiled randomly, or without plan, by the Web crawler. If a site seems to be selling products of any kind, don't use it for background knowledge.

8. **Use any shortcuts that let you view the website before hitting the link**. If there's a magnifying glass to the right of the website description, hit that icon. You'll get a brief snapshot of the opening Web page. If the snapshot shows a long piece of text with few paragraph breaks or pictures, pick another site to preview. Your goal is to get as much information as quickly as you possibly can. Stay away from sites that are still putting Word files on the Web without making them appropriate for Web reading.

READING TIP

If the chapter you are ready to read has an unfamiliar name or date in the heading, do a quick Web search for background knowledge before you start to read.

▶ **EXERCISE 10**   **Using the Web for Background Knowledge**

DIRECTIONS   Read the description of each search goal. Then answer the questions that follow. *Note*: Some of the questions require that you have access to the Web.

1. Imagine that the chapter section you are surveying is titled "1962: Integration Comes to Southern Campuses." It is accompanied by the photograph below, which has the caption "James Meredith arrives on the campus of Ole Miss." Thus, you think it's a good idea to learn a little bit about James Meredith before you read the chapter.

Library of Congress Prints and Photographs Division [LC-DIG-ppmsca-04292]

What search term will you use to find the information that will help you understand the chapter section?

_____

What happened when James Meredith arrived on the campus of Ole Miss?

_____

_____

_____

2. You are about to read a chapter section titled "Birds in Decline." Your survey suggests that the text focuses on *why* birds are disappearing in rapid numbers. You think it's a good idea to find out more about the *causes* before you begin reading. Here are two of the many website descriptions that come up when you type "birds in decline" into a search box. Which one would you choose to read first and why?

    a. **Top 20 Common Birds in Decline | National Audubon ...**
    birds.audubon.org/**species**-by-program/cbid ▾ National Audubon Society ▾
    Since 1967 the average population of the common **birds** in steepest **decline** has fallen by 68 percent; some individual **species** nose-dived as much as 80 ...

b. **North American Birds Declining as Threats Mount**
new.nationalgeographic.com/.../130621-thr... ▾ National Geographic Society ▾
Jun 21, 2013 - Increasingly, though, both casual **bird**-watchers and ornithologists note a
steady **decline** in numbers—not just of endangered **species**, but also ...

Please explain your choice. _____

_____

_____

3. You think a paper on the way psychics fraudulently manipulate their clients to suggest that they have special powers would be fun to write. When you search the Web, these are two of the websites that come up. Which one do you think will be most helpful for your paper and why?

a. **They didn't see that coming: Psychics fail scientific test ...**
www.independent.co.uk › News › Science ▾ The Independent ▾
by Richard Hall - Nov 1, 2012 - **Scientists** from Goldmiths, University of London,
challenged Kim Whitton and Patricia Putt – **psychics** with more than two decades of ...

b. **Psychic Science - explore psychic abilities, psychical ...**
www.psychicscience.org/ ▾ Psychic Science ▾
Psychic Science - free educational-entertainment resources for psychical research and
parapsychology, including ESP tests and psychic games and ...

Please explain your choice. _____

_____

_____

4. You are writing a paper on the effects of vitamins on the body's health. To find information for your paper, you type the word "vitamins" into the search box of your browser. What problem do you encounter?

_____

_____

_____

What do you do in response? _____

_____

Evaluating Websites

Once you zero in on the websites to look at, you'll still need to evaluate each site individually. The following suggestions will help you decide if you have made the right choice or need to keep looking.

"On the Internet, nobody knows you're a dog."

Know Who's Supplying the Information

If you find a site that seems to have good information, but it isn't managed by an educational institution (look for ".edu" at the end of the Web address) or linked to a traditional news source (for instance, the Public Broadcasting Service or the *New York Times*), look for a link that says *About Us*, *About the Author*, *Biography*, or *Home*. If you can't find any indication of who's responsible for keeping the material on the website accurate and up-to-date, go back to your original list. You need to know the source of the information you are getting in order to decide if it's credible, or trustworthy.

Look for Sources

Some information—like the dates of the American Civil War or the fate of the *Titanic*—is so widely known that **documentation**, or the citing of sources used, isn't necessary. However, as soon as a writer, on the Web or anywhere else, starts judging or evaluating people and events—"The Civil

War was more about economic interests than it was about the abolition of slavery"; "Had the *Titanic* been built with better materials, it never would have sunk"—then you need to see some sources. The only time this isn't absolutely necessary is if the person is such a well-known expert on the topic, it's highly unlikely he or she would be making unsupported claims.

If, for instance, the economist Paul Krugman mentions in his blog that Congress raised the debt limit seven times under George W. Bush and doesn't cite a source, you can probably still trust that Krugman isn't passing on inaccurate information.[†] He is, after all, one of the most well-known and respected economists in the United States.

However, if a Web writer who is not a well-known expert expresses an opinion and cites facts to support that opinion but doesn't cite sources *or* credentials, then you probably need to use a different website for gathering background knowledge.

Don't Absorb the Opinions with the Facts

Using words that have strong, positive or negative **connotations**, or associations, writers can weave opinions into statements that might seem like **facts** but aren't. In other words, the statements haven't been and cannot be **verified**, or proven true, by reference to outside sources, which is the hallmark of factual information. Statements that cannot be verified are a matter of **opinion**, or personal preference, and can vary from person to person.

Here, for instance, is one writer's negative take on Hugo Chávez, the former president of Venezuela: "Hugo Chávez masqueraded as a democratic leader but behaved like a dictator." Compare that statement to this one, which **implies**, or suggests, a positive judgment: "Relieved that he had survived cancer surgery, the people of Venezuela celebrated the return of Hugo Chávez to power." Both statements are more opinion than fact, and you need to be aware of that, rather than taking in the opinions with the information.

If the website you choose to use for background knowledge turns out to be heavy with connotative language like the previous examples, you have two choices. You can simply hit another link on the list. Or—and this is my preference—you can read what the author says and then look at another site on the same topic to see if the language or opinions differ. That approach will probably give you a deeper understanding of the topic, even though it's going to take a bit more time.

[†]In fact, Krugman did make this claim, and it was correct.

Be Aware That Photos Can Convey a Bias

Sometimes **bias**, or prejudice for or against someone or something, is conveyed through photos even more than words. For instance, a website that recounts the controversial trial of Julius and Ethel Rosenberg, a couple executed for spying in the fifties, may reveal a hidden bias in the photographs used. Pictures of the couple's courtship, wedding, and two small sons may have been selected to favorably influence your impression of the pair, who some people believe, to this day, were railroaded into the electric chair.

If that's the only site you use to get background knowledge about this controversial case, you might end up sharing the bias expressed in the pictures, and you don't want to do that until you can be sure you have formed your own opinion, rather than unthinkingly absorbing someone else's.

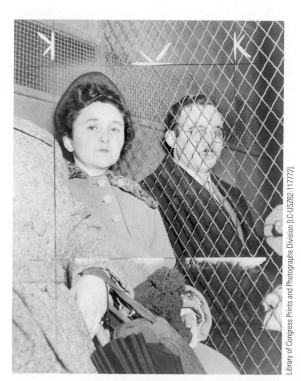

Unlike a photo of the Rosenbergs at their wedding, this is not a photo likely to arouse sympathy.

Library of Congress Prints and Photographs Division [LC-USZ62-117772].

Don't Ignore YouTube

YouTube has a reputation it doesn't deserve. Many people think of it as the site to visit for videos about a goose scaring off a Doberman or a cat romancing a pig. But YouTube offers much more than crazy pet antics.

Do you need to understand the meanings of the two numbers you get when the doctor takes your blood pressure? Do you want to hear the Gettysburg Address? Or maybe you want to see a dramatization of the Poe short story you are reading for American Literature class. You can find all this and more on YouTube, so do not rule it out, *especially* when you are in need of background knowledge. It's a fabulous resource!

SUMMING UP THE KEY POINTS

1. The more background knowledge you have about a textbook topic before you begin reading, the easier it will be for you to understand and remember the material.

2. The Web is an excellent source of background knowledge. Just make sure you use a search term specific enough to generate a list of websites related to your topic. Usually that means a phrase rather than a single word.

3. Once you get a list of websites on the screen, be selective about which ones you actually look at. Check the website descriptions to be sure the site is relevant to your search purpose.

4. Don't assume that the top spot on a list of websites provided by a search engine is an indication of the site's quality. It is not.

5. If the website you choose uses emotionally charged language, switch to a different site. Even better, compare two (or three) different sites on the same topic.

6. When your goal is building up background knowledge, YouTube is a better resource than you might think.

▶ **EXERCISE 11**   **Using the Web for Background Knowledge**

DIRECTIONS   Answer the questions by filling in the blanks or circling the correct response.

1. What's the point of using the Web before or during reading?

_____

_____

2. The letters *edu* indicate that a website is affiliated with, or connected to,

_____.

3. If you are using a personal website for background knowledge, what do you need to look for?

_____

4. If you are searching the Web *while* you read, what should you be cautious about?

_____

5. During World War II, there was a resistance organization in Germany made up of teenagers who fought the Nazis until the entire group of young people was rounded up and executed. The group was called the "White Rose." Imagine that you are looking for more information about this organization. Would the search term "White Rose" be a good one? After circling your answer, please explain it.

Yes or *No*. Please explain.

_____

_____

6. If this were the heading in a chapter you were assigned—"The Chesapeake Bay—an Estuary[†] in Trouble" (from *Living in the Environment*)—you should search the Web using as your search term

a. Chesapeake Bay estuary in trouble.

b. the phrase "Chesapeake Bay."

c. the phrase "estuaries in trouble."

Please explain your answer.

_____

_____

[†]Estuary: a partially enclosed body of water along a coastline.

7. When a list of websites comes up in response to your search term, read the description to see if it contains _____

_____.

8. Imagine that you were looking for background information on President Franklin Delano Roosevelt and you landed on a website where you found the following description. Would this be a good site to use for background knowledge? Please circle your answer. Then explain your reasoning.

> Franklin Delano Roosevelt held office during a time of financial crisis and economic instability: the Great Depression of the 1930s. Roosevelt, however, rose to the occasion. Gathering around him some of the finest minds in the country, known as "Roosevelt's brain trust," the president introduced a radical economic program called the "New Deal." At the heart of the New Deal was Roosevelt's willingness to intervene in the free market through government funding of programs that would create jobs and, at the same time, improve the goods and services available to U.S. citizens. The Works Progress Administration (WPA) was the largest federal agency in the government's program of economic relief. It provided close to 8 million jobs. The WPA affected almost every section of the country and was responsible for the building of much-needed bridges and roads still in use today. More than any president before or since, Roosevelt successfully used the government to enact essential social and political reforms.

Yes or *No*. Please explain.

_____

_____

9. What about this site's description? Do you think it could be useful for background knowledge about another president, Andrew Jackson (1829–1837), and his role in what's come to be called "The Trail of Tears"?

> President Andrew Jackson has been justly criticized for forcing Native Americans to walk the "Trail of Tears," which pushed Indian

tribes off of their lands and relocated them to lands that white settlers did not want. Many Indians died on the almost thousand-mile walk, and the "Trail of Tears" represents a truly shameful chapter in America's history. But it's also true that Jackson's reasons for being a proponent of what was called "Indian Removal" are often inaccurately described.

Jackson was not an Indian-hater. He had fought in wars against the Indians and had a military man's respect for their skills as warriors. The fact that he adopted an Indian child and cared for him also provides evidence for a more complex view of his character. If it had been up to Jackson, he would have sent the child to West Point, but West Point would not accept someone of Native-American heritage.

Jackson was, however, a man of his time. He lived in an era when white superiority was simply assumed. If white settlers needed more land, then Jackson, like many other Americans, believed that the Indians had to leave theirs and make room for white "civilization." No one with any sense of justice could defend Jackson's actions. Still, his motives and attitudes toward the Indians are often inaccurately represented as his personal failing rather than a reflection of the times in which he lived. (Source of this interpretation of Jackson's behavior: http://histclo.com/pres/Ind19/jackson.html.)

Yes or *No*. Please explain.

_____

_____

_____

10. *True* or *False*. When you are searching for background knowledge, it doesn't pay to waste time looking at the photos on websites. Please explain.

_____

_____

Screen Reading

"The idea of pacing reading speed to fit your purpose is hardly new. Neither is the notion that if you want to savor an author's language, if you are trying to work through a complex passage, if you want to reflect on what you have just read, slow is the way to go."
—Naomi Baron, *Words Onscreen: The Fate of Reading in a Digital World*

Numerous studies show that students speed up when they read from a screen. Unfortunately, that increase in reading rate is not a conscious decision. It's a habit. Student readers speed up because that's how they are used to reading online. Accustomed to checking Facebook posts, looking at Instagram photos, or shopping online, they just naturally kick their reading rate into higher gear, even when they are reading more complex and more difficult material. But guess what? That's one of the reasons studies also show lower rates of comprehension with screen reading. Students are speeding up their reading when they should be slowing down.

If you are trying to find background knowledge about your topic and are zooming from heading to heading while you are searching online, that's fine. You can skim at high rates of speed while you are searching. But when you find what you are looking for, consciously slow down and read carefully. In other words, regulate your reading based on the purpose and material, advice that applies to digital devices as much as it does to print.

Here are a few pointers that can help you take control of your reading from a screen:

1. Set your purpose in reading and use it to guide your attention. If, for example, you are reading about how the human heart functions for your biology class, consciously consider what you need to know from the reading. That would probably include both the heart's structure and process. Pay special attention to sections of the text that describe the heart's parts and mentally itemize the steps that make up its functioning.

2. If you have finished reading the text following one heading, see if you can sum up the main point or points of what you just read. If you can't, read the section again.

3. Recognize the difference between writing for the Web and writing for print. Text written for the Web tends to include the key points at the beginning of the reading. Web writers know that Web readers are impatient and expect to get information fast. Thus, they pack the opening paragraphs with the most important facts and ideas. Read the opening paragraphs carefully. If they seem to tell you everything

you need to know, they probably do because the writer has followed the basic rule of Web writing, "Don't keep readers waiting. If you do, they'll click on another website!"

A lot of what we read on the Web, however, wasn't written just for that digital medium. The article, essay, or chapter may well have first appeared in a print book or a journal. Therefore, you can't assume that the key point will *always* open a piece of Web text. Keep reading until you can answer the question, "What's the author's message in this segment or section?" There may come a time when everything you find on the Web was written explicitly for that medium. But that time is not now, so don't assume that the information you need is always in the opening paragraphs. If the origin of the content was print, the opening paragraphs may well be introductory.

4. If you are using a digital device that provides you with note-taking functions, use as many of them as you can. But if the material you are reading is essential to your major, don't just take digital notes.[†] Cut and paste key passages into a file and take notes on those passages as well.

5. Leave plenty of space between the passages you've cut and pasted. When you review what you've cut and pasted, briefly paraphrase each major point. Cutting and pasting passages doesn't engage the brain the way paraphrasing does. Yes, in selecting the passages to cut and paste, you have thought about the content. But you haven't thought deeply enough to really master it. Paraphrasing will lead to mastery.

6. For really important subjects, take your notes in longhand *after* you have printed out the page of cut and paste notes. The movement of your hand is going to record the information you read using an additional pathway of the brain. As you already know, the more pathways you use to learn, the more likely you are to understand and remember what you've read.

7. If the material you are reading provides hypertext links, don't randomly click on them. Read the section following each topic heading

---

[†]PDF files that allow you to write in the margins would be an exception to this rule of thumb. Because you can flip through the files and see your actual notes on the page, you don't need to cut and paste and then paraphrase.

first to see if there are definitions you really need to know in order to understand the passage. Then click on the hypertext links you think will provide that information.

8. If you need to clarify a concept that seemed unclear in the passage you just finished, seek clarity from the Web before continuing with your reading. Did you read about how the brain consolidates memories while we sleep but didn't really understand the term *consolidate*? Type the search term "consolidation and sleep" into your search engine. Make sure to put quotes around the phrase to indicate that the two terms have to appear together as shown.

9. In addition to checking out the website captions for a site that might provide the appropriate information, make sure to hit videos when the list of websites comes up. Read the video captions to see if there is one that seems related to your area of interest. If there is, watch the video first, then check out a more text-heavy website. By the time you are through reading the text and watching the video, you'll be armed, in this case, with a verbal and a visual understanding of how the brain consolidates information while we sleep.[†]

CHECK YOUR UNDERSTANDING

1. What role can the Web play in helping you complete your reading assignments?

_____

_____

2. When using a search term, why is it better to use a phrase instead of a single word?

_____

_____

[†]The pointers shown here are suggested by research like the following: Roger Azevedo and Jennifer G. Cronley, "Does Self-Regulated Learning Facilitate Students' Learning with Hypermedia," *Journal of Educational Psychology*, 96, No. 3, 523–35. Additional sources appear in the manual.

3. Why wouldn't a personal blog be the best place to look when you are trying to gain background knowledge about topics in a textbook assignment?

_____

_____

_____

_____

4. When a list of websites comes up in response to your search term, should you start at the top and look at each website until you find one that is useful? Please explain.

_____

_____

5. What common mistake do many students make when they switch from reading print on paper to reading words on a screen?

_____

_____

6. When reading from a screen, why should you paraphrase the notes you have already cut and pasted into a file?

_____

_____

DIGGING DEEPER   Long-Term Memory: Preserving the Past   *Jeffrey Nevid*

Looking Ahead   Textbook author Jeffrey Nevid describes how the brain manages to translate just-formed, short-term memories into long-term ones that stay with us, perhaps forever. Unlike many people who think a good memory is a gift, Nevid argues that if we take the time, we can make sure short-term memories stick around.

Getting Focused   Based on the title and the description in *Looking Ahead*, focus on spotting the specific suggestions the author makes for ensuring that new memories don't vanish like smoke.

1   **Long-term memory (LTM)** is a storage system that allows you to retain information for periods of time beyond the capacity of short-term memory. Though some information may remain in long-term memory for only days or weeks, other information may remain for a lifetime. The storage capacity of short-term memory is limited, but long-term memory is virtually limitless in what it can hold. In all likelihood, we can always squeeze more facts and more experiences into long-term memory *if we know how to go about it.*

2   **Consolidation** is the process by which the brain converts unstable, fresh memories into stable-long-term memories. The first 24 hours after information is acquired are critical for consolidation to occur. Sleep appears to play an important role in the process by which the brain consolidates or solidifies newly formed memories of daily experiences into more lasting remembrances. This means that if you are studying for a test you have the next day and want to increase the chances of retaining information you've just learned, make sure to get a good night's sleep. Sleep even helps consolidate memory of new learning in other animals, such as birds (Brown, Nusbaum, & Margoliash, 2010).

3   Whereas short-term memory relies largely on acoustic (by sound) coding, long-term memory depends more on semantic coding, or encoding into long-term memory by meaning. Thus, one way of transferring information from short-term memory to long-term memory is through **maintenance rehearsal**, which is the repeated rehearsal of words or sounds.

    But a better way is through **elaborative rehearsal,** a method of rehearsal in which you focus on the meaning of the material. A friend of mine has a telephone number that ends with the digits 1991, a year I

Elaborative rehearsal: The process of transferring information from short-term to long-term memory by consciously focusing on the meaning of the information and relating it to other things you know.

remember well because it was the year my son Michael was born. I have no trouble remembering my friend's number because I associate it with something meaningful, the year of my son's birth. However, I need to look up other friends' numbers that end in digits that have no personal significance for me.

4   How do we manage to organize the information in our long-term memory, so we can retrieve what we want to know when we want to know it? Well, imagine being in a museum where bones, artifacts,* and other holdings were strewn about without any organization. It would be difficult, perhaps impossible, to find the exhibit you were looking for. Now imagine how difficult it would be to retrieve specific memories if they were all scattered about in your long-term memory without rhyme or reason. Fortunately, long-term memory is organized in ways that provide fairly quick access to specific memories.

5   The leading model of how long-term memory is organized is called the **semantic network model**. Within this model or framework, it's assumed that information is contained within networks of related or interlinking concepts. Thus, we understand new information by relating it to previously stored words and meanings. For example, when we learn, say, about the red-breasted sparrow, we link it to previous concepts about *birds* and understand it via our stored ideas about birds.

6   We know immediately, for instance, that the red-breasted sparrow can fly and gives birth to its young via eggs. However, within the category of *bird,* there are also sub-categories of information logged into long-term memory. Thus, we know that the red-breasted sparrow has a red chest—something like a robin's, but nothing like a blue jay's. Since we also are likely to know something about sparrows, we understand immediately that the red-breasted sparrow is probably not a very big bird. The *ripple effect* that the learning of new information causes is called **spreading activation**. According to this model, new information triggers memories of related concepts, which then help contribute to your understanding and remembering of the new idea.

7   Although no one knows exactly why it's so, it's also true that elaborative rehearsal (connecting ideas by relating them to what's previously known or experienced e.g., the red-breasted sparrow looks like a small robin) encourages the storing of information in long-term memory more effectively than **maintenance rehearsal**, or rehearsal by

---

*artifacts: remains of an earlier time.

repetition (Thomas Jefferson was our third president; Thomas Jefferson was our third president . . .). Researchers think that making connections via meaning encourages the brain to think more deeply about whatever it's trying to learn while maintenance rehearsal focuses not on meaning but on sound and doesn't encourage the brain to do any analysis.

(Adapted from Jeffrey S. Nevid, *Psychology*, 4th ed., © Cengage Learning.)

Sharpening Your Skills

DIRECTIONS   Answer the following questions by filling in the blanks or circling the letter of the correct response.

Paraphrasing   1. Using your own words, explain what consolidation means when the context, or subject, is remembering.

_____

_____

2. Explain the difference between **elaborative rehearsal** and **maintenance rehearsal**.

_____

_____

Applying What You Read   3. Imagine that you need to understand and remember the meaning of *cognitive dissonance,* a term that refers to the mental discomfort caused when humans believe that something is true yet act in a way that contradicts their beliefs. People who smoke, for instance, but at the same time fear that they might get lung cancer definitely experience cognitive dissonance. How would you apply elaborative rehearsal to remember the meaning of the term?

_____

_____

_____

Important

4. When the authors describe "spreading activation" as the "ripple effect," they are suggesting that the entry of new information into long-term memory

   a. causes previous memories to be re-evaluated and then eliminated from long-term memory in order to make room for new short-term memories.

   b. causes a chain reaction in which new information activates already stored memories that help explain and retain what's recently been learned.

   c. causes other already stored memories to be either altered or forgotten, so that they need to be re-learned at another time and in a different way.

From Reader to Writer The reading you just finished described different ways to make sure that new information gets into long-term memory. Some memories, however, require no effort. Called "flashbulb" memories, they pack such an emotional wallop, they require no rehearsal or elaboration to find their place in memory's storehouse.

Some flashbulb memories are collectively shared. For instance, anyone who was alive at the time never forgot the bombing of Pearl Harbor or the assassinations of John F. Kennedy, Robert Kennedy, Malcolm X, or Martin Luther King. Others are more personal. Memories of our first love, the death of a parent, and moments of triumph or humiliation are likely to stay with us forever.

Describe a flashbulb memory that you think will always be with you. Start with a sentence that introduces the term and its definition. Then introduce the experience that you think qualifies as a flashbulb memory, for instance, "Flashbulb memories are based on experiences so vivid and so emotionally powerful, we couldn't forget them if we wanted to. The definition certainly fits how I felt when I. . . ."

▶ **TEST 1**   **Reviewing Key Concepts**

DIRECTIONS   Answer the following questions by filling in the blanks or circling the letter of the correct answer.

1. What are the four goals of a survey?

    1. _____

    2. _____

    3. _____

    4. _____

2. How does a flexible reader respond to a text?

    _____

    _____

3. Why should visual aids be included in a survey?

    _____

4. Why pose questions before reading?

    _____

5. Why should your reading rate vary?

    _____

    _____

6. What are the two reasons why it is important to recall right after reading?

    1. _____

    _____

    2. _____

7. What kind of text lends itself to taking notes using diagrams or drawings?

   _____

8. What are recall cues?

   _____

9. Why is paraphrasing crucial to reading?

   _____

10. When reading textbook material on a screen, what common mistake are readers inclined to make and why?

    _____

    _____

▶ **TEST 2**   **Understanding Bar Graphs**

DIRECTIONS   Answer the following questions by filling in the blanks.

1. Bar graphs are best used _____

   _____

2. The line along the bottom of a bar graph is called the _____

   _____ . Usually it identifies _____

   _____

3. The bar along the left side is called the vertical _____ . It almost

   always identifies _____

4. According to the bar graph below, how many people were polled

   to create the graph? _____ What category shows the highest

   percentage of responses? _____

   Based on the graph, would it be accurate to say that the major-

   ity of people surveyed reject store or generic brands? _____

   _____

   _____

Brand Names versus Generic Products

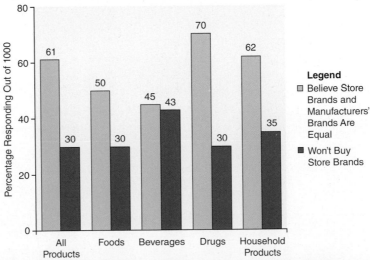

Source of Data: Pride and Ferrell, *Marketing*, 10e, p. 303, © Cengage Learning.

▶ **TEST 3**   **Paraphrasing**

DIRECTIONS   Choose the paraphrase that more effectively sums up the original text. Then explain why you chose your answer. Explain as well what was wrong with the paraphrase you did not select. *Note*: The paraphrases in this test are writing paraphrases rather than the ones you might use for notes on your reading.

1. *Synergy* [the interaction or cooperation of two or more people, organizations, or substances to create an effect greater than the sum of their separate effects] is one of the key words used by business professionals to indicate that they have no clue as to what business they are actually in.

    —Dave Barry, "Idiot's Guide To English," *Mr. Language Person*

    a. When professional business people feel the need to impress, they are likely to talk about the word *synergy*, which refers to the interaction of two or more persons, groups, or substances combined into some larger whole.

    b. Whenever business people don't really know what they are talking about, you are likely to hear the word *synergy* pop up. It refers to the way people, groups, or substances can combine to produce something greater than any of its parts.

    Please Explain Your Choice

    _____

    _____

    _____

    _____

2. We hear a lot about how the online spaces that teens frequent are sinister worlds populated by sexual predators* or bullies. But we rarely if ever hear that many teenagers are scarred by the same experiences offline.

    —Danah Boyd, *It's Complicated*, p. 21

    a. Although we seldom hear about teenagers being bullied or lured into dangerous sexual situations in real life, we are always hearing about these kinds of things happening online.

---

*predators: people or animals that do others harm.

b. Parents who worry about their kids being online because cyber-space is filled with bullies and people looking to do their kids sexual harm have cause for their concerns since these kinds of things happen all too often in real life.

Please Explain Your Choice

_____

_____

_____

_____

3. Thanks to the process we loosely call "globalization,"* women are on the move as never before in history. In images familiar to the West from television commercials for credit cards, cell phones, and airlines, female executives jet about the world phoning home from luxury hotels and reuniting with eager children in airports. But we hear much less about a far larger flow of female labor and energy: the increasing migration of millions of women from poor countries to rich ones, where they serve as nannies, maids, and sometimes sex workers.

—Adapted from Barbara Ehrenreich, *Global Woman: Nannies, Maids, and Sex Workers in The New Economy*, p. 2

a. Globalization has benefitted many women. As a result, we are used to seeing images of women executives flying around the world and then re-uniting with their enthusiastic children. But we don't hear much about the effect of globalization on poor women, whose opportunity consists of going around the world in order to get low-paid jobs as housekeepers, baby sitters, and sex workers.

b. Globalization has offered women a host of new opportunities. As a result, we are bombarded with images of successful women flying around the globe and phoning home to their families, who are eagerly waiting to welcome them back. We are, at the same time, increasingly faced with stories about women doing poorly paid work as caretakers, maids, and sex workers.

---

*globalization: the growing economic and financial connections among nations that do business with one another.

Please Explain Your Choice

_____

_____

_____

_____

_____

4. Greta Ehrlich is a woman who knows about being in the wrong place at the wrong time. In 1992, out with her dogs for a walk, she was struck by lightning and came close to dying. Saved by her devoted dogs and attentive friends who heard her cries for help, she never really recovered because her heart had been badly damaged by the bolt of electricity that surged through her body. Nevertheless, her book, *A Match to the Heart*, about her fight to come back to at least partial life, has inspired many people to keep fighting even when life seems to have counted them out.

   a. Out for a walk in 1992, Greta Ehrlich was struck by lightning and almost died. In her book about her experience, *A Match to the Heart*, she dedicates her life to helping others recover from traumatic experiences that have left them with damaged hearts.

   b. In 1992, Greta Ehrlich, out for a walk with her dogs, was struck by lightning and almost died. But her dogs and her friends helped pull her through, even though she never completely recovered from the damage the lightning had done. Her book, *A Match to the Heart*, describing her struggles to get back as much of her life as possible, has inspired others to do the same.

Please Explain Your Choice

_____

_____

_____

_____

2

Building Word Power

> "Words and eggs must be handled with care."
>
> —POET ANNE SEXTON
>
> "The beginning of wisdom is the definition of terms."
>
> —PHILOSOPHER SOCRATES

Enlarge your vocabulary while sharpening your comprehension skills and you'll be amazed at your increased ability to understand and remember what you read. As Wilfred Funk, one of the great dictionary makers of all time, aptly expressed it, "The more words you know, the more clearly and powerfully you will think . . . the more ideas you will invite into your mind."

 ## Making the Meanings "Automatic"

The pages that follow are going to give you numerous strategies for improving your reading vocabulary.[†] However, as you learn those techniques, keep in mind the ultimate, or final, goal of vocabulary work:

[†]Reading vocabulary includes all the words you know on sight when you read, but you may or may not use those same words when you write. The word *cognition*, for instance, refers to the mental processes you engage in to understand something. To read psychology textbooks, you have to know the word, but you may never use it in your writing.

to develop **automatic word recognition**. That means seeing the word and knowing its meaning, automatically, without having to consciously think about it.

Learning researchers call this *automaticity*. That's a fancy way of saying your grasp of word and meaning is so firmly embedded in your memory that you don't have to mentally search for a definition. It's just there.

Understanding words at this automatic level is like driving a car for a long time. You have practiced your driving skills to such a degree that, after a certain point, they feel like a natural instinct rather than a learned activity.

But like driving, having word meanings automatically at your disposal doesn't come without practice. You'll need to do several reviews to develop that level of word recognition.

Active Reviews and Memory Pegs

As soon as you get ten new words together, write them in a notebook or on flash cards.[†] On a regular basis, actively review both words and meanings. That means look at the word first and then try to come up with the meaning. If you can't recall the meaning from memory, make up a memory peg that will help you in later reviews.

Memory pegs are connections you make between what you already know and what you are trying to learn. When it comes to words, memory pegs can take many different forms. Here are just a few to get you started:

© Ulrich Flemming.

This aerial photo shows the striking topography of southern Utah.

Topography refers to the physical appearance of an area or region, particularly the elevations or heights.

Memory Peg: A *top*ography map shows you what's on *top* of the land like trees, bushes, rocks, and mountains.

[†]I'd vote for online flash cards, where you won't be tempted to turn the card over and look at the definition. You won't get the definition until you get to another screen.

Depiction refers to a representation of something, for instance, in a drawing, painting, or sculpture.

Memory Peg: A de*pic*tion is a *pic*ture of something.

Alleviate means to improve, reduce, or eliminate some difficulty or pain.

Memory Peg: *Alleve* is a commonly used medication for *alleviat*ing pain.

▶ **EXERCISE 1**   **Using Memory Pegs**

DIRECTIONS   Here are three words that commonly turn up in textbooks, particularly history texts. Make up a memory peg for each one.

Impromptu means unrehearsed or done spontaneously without being planned beforehand. "The candidate gave an impromptu speech and as usual said the wrong thing."

Memory Peg:

Ramifications refers to the results or consequences of an action. "The discovery of the explorer's long-buried journal was going to have widespread ramifications for historians."

Memory Peg:

Enigma describes someone or something who is always mysterious and can never be completely understood. "Because no one could ever predict his actions, Thomas Jefferson, America's third president, was called 'The Great Enigma.'"

Memory Peg:

Using Context Clues

What do you do when you come across an unfamiliar word? Do you just skip over it? Or do you pick up your dictionary and look for the definition? You probably already know that the first method is not recommended. Yet actually, the second one—turning to the dictionary every time—also has drawbacks. Looking up too many words can hurt your concentration. Look up too many words and you can lose track of where you were on the page. A better strategy is to see if you can figure out an approximate definition and continue reading.

Developing Approximate Definitions

Frequently, the sentence or passage in which the word appears can help you determine an **approximate definition** that allows you to keep reading without interruption. An approximate definition may not perfectly match a dictionary's definition. Still, it is close enough so that you can continue reading without interruption, and that's what's essential.

> When Russia was under the control of Josef Stalin, *dissidents* were routinely shot or imprisoned in hospitals for the mentally ill. Stalin did not allow anyone to express disagreement or discontent with his policies.

If you didn't know what the word *dissidents* in the first sentence meant, you could probably **infer**, or figure out, a definition from the sentence that follows. That sentence offers an example of what dissidents do: They disagree with their government.

Although there are several different kinds of context clues, most fall into one of four categories: *example*, *contrast*, *restatement*, and *general knowledge*.

Example Clues

As you already know from the previous illustration, the context of an unfamiliar word sometimes provides you with an example of the behavior or thinking associated with the word. Here's another sentence in which an example can lead you to a definition of the word *personification*:

> The eighteenth-century poet William Blake had a gift for using *personification* in his work as these two tired sunflowers delightfully illustrate:

> Ah, William, we're weary of weather,
> said the sunflowers, shining with dew.
> Our traveling habits have tired us.
> Can you give us a room with a view?[†]

As the example suggests, the word *personification* means that a writer describes something non-human as if it were capable of human feelings,

---

[†]I wish I had found this example of personification on my own, but I did not. More great examples can be found here: http://literarydevices.net/personification/

thoughts, and actions. And poets are not the only ones who use it. Just about all writers do, but poets more than most.

Contrast Clues

Context clues can also tell you what a word does not mean. Fortunately, knowing what a word doesn't mean can often lead you to a good approximate definition. Here's an example of a passage that provides a contrast clue:

> As a child, she liked to be alone and was fearful of people; but as an adult, she was remarkably *gregarious*.

This sentence suggests that someone who is *gregarious* does not exactly flee the company of others. In fact, the sentence implies just the opposite: People who are gregarious like to be in the company of others. Thus, "liking the company of others" would be a good approximate definition.

Words That Signal Contrast Clues

In addition to knowing what a contrast clue is, you should also know that words such as *but*, *yet*, *nevertheless*, and *however* frequently introduce contrast clues. These words are all **transitions**—verbal bridges that help readers connect ideas. The transitions mentioned here tell readers to be on the lookout for a shift, reversal, or change in thought. Look at the word *however* in the following example. Do you see how it changes the author's train of thought and paves the way for a contrast clue that helps define the word *frivolous*?

> After having had a really bad day, she wanted to read something *frivolous*. Normally, *however*, she preferred serious novels.

So what does the word *frivolous* mean? "Silly," "light," or "not serious" are all good approximate definitions.

Restatement Clues

To avoid tedious word repetition, authors often use a word and then follow it with a **synonym**, a word or phrase similar in meaning:

> The journalist had the *audacity* to criticize the president to his face. Oddly enough, her boldness seemed to amuse rather than irritate him.

In this case, the author doesn't want to overuse the word *audacity*, so she follows it with a synonym, *boldness*. For readers not sure what *audacity* means, the synonym *boldness* restates the word in language they can understand and provides them with a definition.

Restatement Clues in Textbooks

Intent on supplying readers with the **specialized vocabulary** essential to mastering an academic subject, textbook authors often introduce a word and then carefully define it. For example, the authors of the following passage want to be sure that their readers have exact definitions for the terms *brand recognition* and *ad recognition*. To make sure their readers have no doubt what these two terms mean, the authors define them in parentheses:

> Two important types of recognition in marketing are *brand recognition* (we remember having seen the *brand* before) and *ad recognition* (we remember having seen the *ad* before). (Hoyer and MacInnis, *Consumer Behavior*, 5th ed., p. 17.)

In addition to parentheses, authors use other devices to tell readers, "Here is the definition for the word I just introduced." Colons and dashes, for instance, are also common.

> Most people have experienced brain freeze: This is the painful sensation in the temples that follows the consumption of food or drink that is very cold.

> Union density—the percentage of workers who belong to unions—grew in the 1930s and peaked in the 1940s and 1950s, when 35 percent of U.S. workers were unionized. (Linda Mooney et al., *Understanding Social Problems*, 8th ed., © Cengage Learning.)

In addition to colons, dashes, and parentheses, textbook authors often signal a restatement clue by first introducing the word being defined, in either boldface or italics. Then they follow the word with a comma and a definition. Here's an example:

> A major buzzword in leadership and management is *vision*, the ability to imagine different and better conditions and the ways to achieve them. (Dubrin, *Leadership*, 5th ed., p. 6.)

Here, the author is well aware that readers might think they know the meaning of the word *vision*—the ability to see. Yet within this particular context, the author has a specialized definition in mind. To avoid any confusion, he provides that definition right after he introduces the word.

Textbook authors go to great lengths to make sure you have the right definitions for the words essential to their academic field. In turn, your job as a reader is twofold: (1) pay attention to the devices that signal the presence of restatement or definition clues; and (2) when those definitions appear, read them carefully.

Consider as well jotting both words and definitions in a notebook or on flash cards, whether online or in print, for later review. The chances are good that the definitions will not reappear in later chapters, though the words themselves will. That's why it's a good idea to record the definitions when you first see them.

Mobilize Your Vocabulary Reviews

Think, too, about making a file of words you need to know for different courses. Put the file in a Cloud-based storage site like Dropbox and open it from your cell phone any time you have a few minutes to spare while waiting in line in the grocery store or at the bank or ATM.

General Knowledge Clues

Example, contrast, and restatement context clues are important. However, some context clues are not so obvious. Often your knowledge of the situation or events described will be your only real clue to word meaning. The following passage illustrates this point:

> For months he had dreamed of being able to *redeem* his medals. He had been unable to think of anything else. Now, with the vision of the medals shimmering before him, he hurried to the pawnshop.

None of the context clues previously discussed appears in the passage. However, your general knowledge should tell you that the word *redeem*, in this context at least, means "reclaim" or "recover." Most people go to a pawnshop to buy or to sell, and the man described as hurrying to the pawnshop probably wouldn't be in such a rush to sell something he had dreamed of for months. He is going to buy back what he has already sold.

1. Example Clue	"The discussion was becoming increasingly *belligerent*; no matter what was said, someone in the group would challenge it in an angry voice."
2. Contrast Clue	"At first the smell was almost flower-like, but in a matter of minutes it became harsh and *acrid*."
3. Restatement Clue	"*Cognition*—thinking or knowing—has been the subject of numerous studies."
4. General Knowledge Clue	"Football and basketball coaches are frequently known for their *volatile* tempers."

SUMMING UP THE KEY POINTS

1. The goal of learning new vocabulary is to make your understanding of the word automatic.

2. Memory pegs are links between what you already know and what you want to learn.

3. Often, the sentence or passage in which an unfamiliar word appears can tell you what the word means. The words or sentences that supply the meaning are called *context clues*.

4. Context clues don't necessarily give you an exact dictionary definition, but they can supply an "approximate definition" that allows you to keep reading without interruption.

5. Of the many different kinds of context clues, four are particularly common: example, contrast, restatement, and general knowledge.

6. An example clue describes the behavior, attitude, event, or experience associated with a word.

7. A contrast clue provides the reader with a word that is opposite in meaning.

8. A restatement clue follows the unfamiliar word with a synonym substitute. In textbooks, authors explicitly define the word, often within dashes or parentheses.

9. General knowledge clues are descriptions of events or experiences that are likely to be familiar to readers because they are familiar with both the events and the experiences.

▶ EXERCISE 2 Using Context Clues

DIRECTIONS Use context clues to develop an approximate meaning for each italicized word.

EXAMPLE To the old dog lying under the table, the smell of frying bacon was almost unbearably *tantalizing*, and he stared at the pan with obvious doggy longing.

Tantalizing means appealing, exciting; desirable but out of reach .

EXPLANATION In this case, the sentence offers a general knowledge clue. Even readers who don't have pets would undoubtedly know that to a dog, the smell of frying bacon is extremely appealing or exciting.

1. According to the myth, the hero Achilles was *vulnerable* in just one area of his body. He could be killed only if he was wounded in the heel.

   Vulnerable means _____.

2. The candidate had expected to win, but instead she was *trounced* by her opponent, who won by a landslide.

   Trounced means _____.

3. Forced to sell their lands and homes at whatever prices they could obtain, Japanese Americans were herded into detention camps in the most desolate areas of the West. Sadly, few Americans protested the *incarceration* of their Japanese-American countrymen. (Boyer et al., *The Enduring Vision*, 7th ed., p. 778, © Cengage Learning.)

   Incarceration means _____.

Despite no evidence indicating that Japanese-Americans were spies, they were imprisoned in isolated camps like this one for the duration of World War II.

4. Before allowing someone to deliver a personal opinion on the air, most television news programs issue a *disclaimer* denying all responsibility for the views expressed.

   Disclaimer means _____.

5. Killed by an obsessed fan in 1995, the Latina entertainer Selena was deeply mourned because she was so much more than an entertainer: Selena was the *embodiment* of Mexican-American culture—representing devotion to the family, hard work, and a sense of community. (Adapted from Hoyer and MacInnis, *Consumer Behavior*, 5th ed., p. 295, © Cengage Learning.)

   Embodiment means _____.

6. Unjustly accused of spying, Captain Alfred Dreyfus[†] (1859–1935) was convicted and sentenced to life in prison on the ill-famed Devil's Island; pardoned in 1899, Dreyfus was fully *exonerated* of all charges in 1906.

   Exonerated means _____.

7. The novelist Alice Hoffman is an amazingly *inventive* writer: her plots range from teenage coming-of-age novels to historical fiction.

   Inventive means _____.

[†]What came to be known as the "Dreyfus Affair" polarized the French people. Many rightly suspected that Dreyfus was being persecuted because he was Jewish. That fact appalled some and pleased others.

8. Confusion and *delusions* (false and distorted beliefs) are typical signs of sleep deprivation. (Coon, *Essentials of Psychology*, p. 34.)

   Delusions means _____ .

9. Queen Marie Antoinette's *hedonistic* lifestyle was one of the things that made her hated by the people of France; close to starvation themselves, they could not love a queen who seemed to care about nothing but pleasure.

   Hedonistic means _____ .

10. If she wants to get her finances under control, she will have to *consolidate* her debt; she can't continue paying all of her debts and interest individually.

    Consolidate means _____ .

▶ **EXERCISE 3**   **Using Context Clues**

DIRECTIONS   Use context clues to write an approximate meaning for each italicized word.

1. The reporters were sent out to cover the fighting that had broken out in the streets, but under no condition were they to get involved in the *upheaval.*

   Upheaval means _____ .

2. The millionaire did not expect the judge to hand down such a *punitive* sentence, and his face went white with shock when he heard the verdict.

   Punitive means _____ .

3. All over the country, people were starving and desperately *scavenging* for food.

   Scavenging means _____ .

4. Looking filthy and *disreputable* after an all-night bender, the reporter tried to spruce up in the men's room before going into work.

   Disreputable means _____ .

5. Her boss didn't need to make an effort to be nasty; he was *inherently* so and thought nothing of publicly humiliating his employees.

   Inherently means _____.

6. Because I can't spell very well, I was happy to learn there is no apparent *correlation* between the ability to spell and a high IQ.

   Correlation means _____.

7. Impossible as it seems, for close to thirty years, between the 1920s through the 1950s, a woman named Gertrude Pitkanen delivered and sold babies of unwed mothers to whoever had the money to pay for them, and she did it without ever facing the legal *repercussions* of her actions.

   Repercussions means _____.

8. Inventors don't necessarily care if their inventions are *lucrative*; often they just have an idea they are desperate to make a reality, and money doesn't matter.

   Lucrative means _____.

9. Research on people who have lived to be more than eighty years old has consistently revealed a connection between low body weight and *longevity*.

   Longevity means _____.

10. How is it that so many doctors who *advocate* diet and exercise are overweight couch potatoes?

    Advocate means _____.

▸ EXERCISE 4   Using Context Clues

DIRECTIONS   Use context clues to write an approximate definition for each italicized word.[†]

_____

[†]The italicized words in Exercises 4 and 5 are all from the Academic Word List developed by the School of Linguistics and Applied Language Studies at Victoria University of Wellington in New Zealand.

EXAMPLE People driven by *intrinsic* motivation don't need external rewards such as praise from others; instead, they find satisfaction in simply completing a task.

Intrinsic means <u>internal, inside or within oneself</u>.

EXPLANATION In this case, the sentence offers a contrast clue. If people do not need external rewards, they must be motivated by rewards that are internal, or inside themselves.

1. African-American novelist James Baldwin was an outspoken advocate of civil rights, who did not believe that racism would disappear on its own. Friends enjoyed relaying *anecdotes* about Baldwin's fiery and often funny responses to anyone claiming it would.

   Anecdotes means _____.

2. In the sixth century, Emperor Justinian turned Rome's disorganized laws into a *coherent* legal system.

   Coherent means _____.

3. Although scientists disagree about whether frogs are in danger of becoming extinct from the fungus that has killed them in huge numbers, some scientists argue that frogs' long-standing ability to adapt to changes in their environment may save them from *extinction*.

   Extinction means _____.

The poison dart frog is one of the species of frog that may be in line for extinction.

4. By embracing drug use, rock music, "free love," and non-Western religions, the rebellious hippies of the 1960s and 1970s rejected *conventional* rules.

   Conventional means _____ .

5. If *preliminary* testing of a new drug indicates potential benefits, the drug is then tested again for a longer period of time and on a larger sample population.

   Preliminary means _____ .

6. Electricity is *generated* from a variety of energy sources, including coal, oil, wood, nuclear reactors, wind, sunlight, and water.

   Generated means _____ .

7. *Proponents* of the bill were disheartened when the vote was put off until spring; the bill's critics, however, were thrilled.

   Proponents means _____ .

8. Milton Hershey certainly didn't invent chocolate, but his *innovations* to the recipe and manufacture of it turned a luxury for the wealthy into an affordable treat for all.

   Innovations means _____ .

9. The lawyer's *cogent* argument convinced the court, and she was allowed to submit the fibers as evidence.

   Cogent means _____ .

10. After the Twenty-Second Amendment to the U.S. Constitution took effect in 1951, all *ensuing* presidents were limited to two terms each.

    Ensuing means _____ .

▶ **EXERCISE 5**   **Using Context Clues**

DIRECTIONS   Use context clues to write an approximate definition for each italicized word.

1. Although global warming has been *attributed* to the burning of fossil fuels, a few scientists argue that it's actually caused by natural climate cycles.

   Attributed means _____ .

After the bombing of Hiroshima and Nagasaki in 1945, a huge mushroom cloud bloomed in the sky.

2. U.S. military officials believed that dropping atomic bombs on Japan was the only way to save millions of American lives and end World War II; however, others have argued that there was no *justification* for killing more than 140,000 Japanese citizens and injuring another 100,000.

   Justification means _____ .

3. Based on research and observation, scientists propose theories, or explanations, of events; then they conduct experiments that either prove a theory's *validity* or reveal its inaccuracy.

   Validity means _____ .

4. In the U.S. Army, a general is the highest rank of officer, whereas the most *subordinate* officer rank is second lieutenant.

   Subordinate means _____ .

5. The final event of the American Civil War occurred on April 9, 1865; Confederate General Robert E. Lee officially *terminated* the conflict by surrendering to Union commander Ulysses S. Grant at the Appomattox, Virginia, courthouse.

   Terminated means _____ .

6. Medical research rules require that human subjects know they are participating in an experiment; therefore, scientists must obtain each subject's *consent*, or permission, before giving him or her any treatment.

   Consent means _____ .

7. When scientists attempt to create a clone, they *extract* the DNA from the cell of one organism and then insert it into the egg cell of another organism of the same species.

   Extract means _____ .

8. The kilometer is a unit of length used in Europe, Canada, and other countries; it is *equivalent,* or equal, to 0.62 miles.

   Equivalent means _____.

9. Because they can explode when mixed together, *incompatible* chemicals spelled with the same first letter, like cadmium chlorate and cupric sulfide, must be kept apart; they should never be stored alphabetically in a laboratory.

   Incompatible means _____.

10. The *Oxford English Dictionary* aims to present all words from the earliest records to the present day. Its over 600,000 entries make it our language's most *comprehensive* dictionary.

    Comprehensive means _____.

 ## Context and Meaning

Generally speaking, there are few situations in life where context isn't important. Words are no exception. Change a word's context and you very likely change its meaning. For instance, if you are buying a new air conditioner, you might ask the salesperson how big a room the unit can *cool.* Here the word means "lower the temperature." But if someone asks your opinion of Prince Royce's new song, you might say, "It's cool," and you wouldn't be talking about the temperature.

From Reader to Writer What follows are five uncommon words. Look them up in a print dictionary or online. Then create sentences for each one in which the context makes the meanings clear. The first one is done for you.

| gossamer | mellifluous | nostrum | palaver | redolent |

She wore a white shawl made of some gossamer material that was so sheer he could see her pale freckles beneath it.

What elements of the sentence suggest that *gossamer* is a material that is easy to see through?

✔ CHECK YOUR UNDERSTANDING

1. When readers get definitions from context, should the definition be almost the same as the one that appears in a dictionary? Please explain your answer.

   _____

   _____

2. What are the most common kinds of context clues?

   _____

3. The following sentence gives what kind of context clue for the italicized word?
   "*Stressors*, the external events that disrupt our daily functioning, are unavoidable but still manageable."

   Type of context clue: _____

4. The following sentence gives what kind of context clue for the italicized word?
   "The administration offered the older teachers *incentives* for taking early retirement: They could have one full year of health benefits and a three-hundred-dollar bonus."

   Type of context clue: _____

5. The following sentence gives what kind of context clue for the italicized word?
   "In the 1960s, members of opposing political parties in Congress worked together, but today members of Congress are much more *polarized*."

   Type of context clue: _____

6. The following sentence gives what kind of context clue for the italicized word?
   "After all the cars leaving the game streamed onto the highway, there was complete *gridlock* going north and away from the stadium."

   Type of context clue: _____

7. What are memory pegs?

   _____

   _____

Defining Words from Their Parts

In addition to using context clues to determine approximate meanings for unfamiliar words, check to see if you know any of the word's parts. For example, imagine you read this sentence and were initially puzzled by the word *dermatitis*: "The deadly disease began with a seemingly minor symptom—a light *dermatitis* on the arms and legs." Even if you had never heard or used the word *dermatitis*, you could come up with a definition simply by knowing that *derma* means skin and *itis* means inflammation, or outbreak. Given the context and your knowledge of the word's parts, you would be correct to say that *dermatitis* means "inflammation of the skin," or "rash."

Learning Roots, Prefixes, and Suffixes

To determine meaning from word parts, you need to know some of the most commonly used roots and prefixes, along with a few suffixes. The exercises in this chapter will introduce you to a good many. It's worth your while to learn a few new word parts every day, averaging about twenty a week. If you review them regularly, you will be amazed at how quickly your vocabulary expands.

1. **Roots** give words their fixed meaning. Prefixes and suffixes can then be attached to the roots to form new words. For example, the following words are all based on the root *spec*, which means "look" or "see": re*spec*t, in*spec*tion, *spec*tacles, *spec*ulation.

2. **Prefixes** are word parts that appear at the *beginning* of words and modify the root meaning, as in *in*clude and *ex*clude or *in*voke and *re*voke.

3. **Suffixes** are word parts that appear at the *end* of many words. Although suffixes do occasionally affect word meaning, they are more likely to reveal what part of speech a word is, as in quick*ness* and quick*ly*. Words ending in *ness* are usually nouns. Those ending in *ly* are usually adverbs.

STUDY TIP

When you make a list of word parts, put the definitions on the far right. Each time you review, cover one side of the list and *recall from memory* either the word part or the definition. This kind of active recall will give your brain time to anchor the new word and definition in your long-term memory.

▶ **EXERCISE 6**   **Learning Word Parts**

DIRECTIONS   Read each sentence and note what meaning the missing or partial word should convey. Then fill in the blanks with one—or, in some cases, two—of the word parts listed below.

Prefixes	Roots
bi = two	*chron* = time
im = not	*gam* = marriage
per = through	*lat* = side
poly = many	*mob* = move
	pel = force
	popul = people
	rect = straight, straighten

EXAMPLE   When we talk about events being ordered according to time, we are talking about events that are described in chron ological order.

EXPLANATION   The partially completed word needs to say something about "time." Thus, we need a word part that brings that meaning to the blank. The obvious choice would be the root *chron*, meaning "time."

1. When a situation can't be fixed or straightened out, we say that it cannot be _____ ified.

2. If a city is filled with people, it can be described as _____ ous.

3. When a disease goes away and repeatedly comes back over time, it is called _____ ic.

4. Human skin is called _____meable because substances, both good and bad, can pass through it.

5. An interesting book that almost forces you to keep reading is often described as com _____ ling.

6. An agreement that has to be signed by two sides is called ____ ____ eral.

7. Being married to two people at the same time is called ____ _____ y.

8. Being married to several people at the same time is called _____ _____ y.

9. If someone or something can move, we say that he, she, or it is _____ ile.

10. In contrast, someone or something that cannot move would be described as ____ _____ ile.

STUDY TIP

Because the word parts introduced in Exercise 6 appear in many different words, you should start learning them right now. Repeated reviews done over an extended period of time are the key to mastery. See a list of common word parts at the end of this chapter.

Combine Forces: Use Context Clues *and* Word Parts

Recognizing word parts and using context clues are, by themselves, effective methods of determining meaning. However, they are even more powerful when combined. Take, for example, the following sentences:

> I can't imagine a more *credulous* person. He actually believed I saw a flying saucer on the way home.

To a degree, knowing that the root *cred* means "belief" and the suffix *ous* means "full of" are helpful clues to meaning. We can start off, then, by saying that to be *credulous* is to be "full of belief." Yet what exactly does that mean? You can imagine a bottle full of juice or wine. But how can a person be "full of belief"?

This is where context comes in. Look at the example clue the author offers: "He actually believed I saw a flying saucer on the way home." Apparently, a credulous person is likely to believe a story that most people might laugh at or question. After a closer look at the context, we can come up with a more precise definition of *credulous*: "gullible" or "easily fooled."

A knowledge of word parts can also help you sharpen or improve an approximate definition derived from context. Suppose you are not sure how to define the word *ambiguous* in a sentence like this one: "The finest poems are usually the most *ambiguous*, suggesting that life's big questions defy easy answers."

Relying solely on context, you might decide that *ambiguous* means *puzzling* or *difficult*. Those definitions are certainly acceptable. But once you know that the prefix *ambi* means "both," you could make your definition more precise by defining *ambiguous* as "open to more than one interpretation."

SUMMING UP THE KEY POINTS

1. Recognizing the meaning of prefixes or roots within a word can unlock a word's meaning, especially if you can combine that knowledge with context clues.

2. Roots give words their central, or core, meaning. Attaching new beginnings (prefixes) or endings (suffixes) to the word will change the meaning of the whole word, but the essential meaning of the root won't change. Just think, for instance, of how the meaning of *invent* stays the same in the following sequence, *re*invent, inven*tor*, inven*tion*, even though the words as a whole assume different (but related) meanings.

3. Prefixes modify root meanings, and they can do so rather dramatically. Consider, for example, the difference between the words "do" and "*un*do."

4. Suffixes can tell you something about word meaning. Suffixes like *er* and *or* at the end of a word indicate that the word refers to a person who can perform or do something mentioned in the root—for example, farm*er*, creat*or*, invent*or*. On the whole, though, suffixes

reveal more about a word's grammatical function—noun, verb, adjective, and so on—than they do about the definition.

5. By combining context clues and word parts you double your chances of getting the exact definition for unfamiliar words. Thus, it pays to learn as many common word parts as you possibly can, giving special attention to those drawn from Greek and Latin. The words appearing in academic texts rely heavily on these two languages.

▶ **EXERCISE 7**   **Using Word Parts and Context Clues**

DIRECTIONS   Use context clues and word parts to come up with an approximate definition for each italicized word. *Note*: Some of the words in the following sentences use prefixes or roots from the previous exercise.

Prefixes	Roots	Suffixes
mono = one	*for* = to bore into	*ism* = state, condition, or quality
pseudo = false	*the* = god	
mal = bad	*vit* = life	*ize* = to cause to be, to treat or affect
re = again, back	*pel, puls* = throw, push	
syn, sym = together		*onym* = name, word

1. The Egyptian pharaoh Akhenaten rejected *polytheism*, advocating *monotheism* instead, but his decision to worship one god over many led to his downfall.

   Monotheism means _____ .

   Polytheism means _____ .

2. The International Olympic Committee debated for years before acknowledging how difficult it is for *synchronized* swimmers to execute the same movement at the same time while being submersed in water.

   Synchronized means _____ .

3. The kidnapper's actions were so *repellent* that it was hard to have any sympathy for her. Most agreed with the prosecution and hoped to see her incarcerated for a very long time.

   Repellent means _____.

4. During the operation, the surgeon's knife almost *perforated* the patient's lung.

   Perforated means _____.

5. The injection had completely *immobilized* the bear, allowing the ranger to approach it without fear.

   Immobilized means _____.

6. Amazingly, the drug had *revitalized* him after everyone thought he would not last the night.

   Revitalized means _____.

7. In the nineteenth century, many women writers used *pseudonyms* because they were afraid of being labeled "unladylike" and didn't want their real names to be known.

   Pseudonyms means _____.

8. It can be brief, but management wants to see your *vita*, even if there is not much on it, before any contract gets signed.

   Vita means _____.

9. In an effort to win elections, politicians spend too much time *maligning* one another.

   Maligning means _____.

10. Even at an advanced age, the legendary salsa singer Celia Cruz had the *vitality* of a much younger performer.

    Vitality means _____.

CHECK YOUR UNDERSTANDING

1. Why should you learn as many Greek and Latin prefixes and roots as you possibly can?

_____

_____

_____

2. How is a prefix different from a root?

_____

_____

_____

3. What do suffixes reveal about a word?

_____

4. Why is it a good idea to use both kinds of clues to meaning, context and word parts?

_____

 # Learn Word History to Expand Your Vocabulary

When you look up words, either online or in print, some definitions will include the word's **etymology**, or a history of its origin and entry into English. Sometimes, in fact, there will be a colorful story behind the word you look up. When there is, make sure you learn it. Knowing the story behind the word will function like a memory peg and anchor both word and meaning into your long-term memory. Here are five words with a story in their past.

Ostracize	When the ancient Greeks wanted to vote on whether someone should be banished from their community, they would write their vote on a piece of pottery, called an *ostracon*. From that practice came the word *ostracize*, which means to banish or exclude.
Chauvinist	Nicolas Chauvin was the name of a soldier in a nineteenth-century French play. The character was presented as being completely devoted to France's ruler Napoleon Bonaparte. From the name of that character comes the word *chauvinist*, meaning someone unthinkingly prejudiced in favor of one's country or group.
Martinet	Jean Martinet was a seventeenth-century French general, who passionately believed in strict discipline for his soldiers. Disagreement with his rules was neither encouraged nor allowed. From the general, then, comes the word *martinet*, meaning someone who follows rules to the letter and expects others to do the same.
Titan	According to Greek mythology, the Titans were members of a gigantic family of gods who inhabited the Earth before people did. The Titans were huge and powerful. Today when we describe something as "titanic," we mean that it is huge or enormous. When we say that someone is a "titan," we mean that he or she has a great deal of power or is outstanding in some field.
Herculean	Hercules was a Greek hero who possessed extraordinary strength. It was said that he could perform fantastic feats. Today when we use the word *herculean*, we are talking about something that demands a great deal of effort or someone in possession of enormous strength.

Now see if you can correctly match those words to the blanks in the following sentences.

1. The creators of Google are ready to take on the _____ task of putting whole libraries online.

2. The new recruits were disappointed to discover that their drill sergeant was a _____.

3. In the rock world of the 1970s and 1980s, Freddie Mercury, lead singer of the group Queen, was a _____, but fame did not save him from AIDS, and he died in 1991.

4. As a tourist, he was inclined to be a _____; anything different from what he was accustomed to in his own country just had to be bad.

5. After a pair of male penguins stole eggs from some of the other birds, replacing them with stones, the two birds were _____ by the rest of the flock.

READING TIPS

To learn new words, make it a point to connect them to sample sentences or to people (e.g., "The word *anecdote* reminds me of how my dad gives advice. He always starts with an anecdote").

Connecting new words to images will also help you remember their meaning. The word *succulent*, for instance, means "juicy and tasty." Linking it to an image like the one shown here will help you remember that meaning long term.

In other, warmer parts of the world, open air markets displaying piles of *succulent* fruit are common all year round.

© Ulrich Flemming.

WEB QUEST
What links these three men together: Samuel Johnson, Noah Webster, and James Murray?

_____

Connotations and Denotations of Words

The more words you add to your reading vocabulary, the more inclined you will be to try them out in your own writing. However, to use words effectively, you need to know more than their **denotation**, or dictionary definitions. You also need to know whether a word carries with it any connotations. **Connotations** are the associations or implications some words develop over time with repeated use. Consider, for instance, the different connotations of the words *house* versus *home*. *House* has neutral connotations. It calls up few associations or feelings. *Home* is different. It's associated with positive feelings about family and safety.

The sense of a word's connotations will become clearer the more you see it in different contexts. That's one of the reasons why you usually need a good deal of experience with new words before you use them in your writing.

Matching Up Connotation with Context

For example, the words *house* and *domicile* both refer to a place where people live. Thus, a non-native speaker who looked the two words up might think they were interchangeable. But a native speaker who had seen and heard the words repeatedly would know they require different contexts. Yes, a "domicile" is a house or a building where people live. However, it's likely to turn up in a formal context, like tax, travel, or insurance forms, e.g., "Indicate your legal domicile on the second page of the passport form."

It would be very unusual, though, to see the word *domicile* in a sentence like the following: "The dog hated to sleep in his new dog domicile; he much preferred the living room couch." In this context, only *house* is appropriate because its connotations are more informal than those attached to the word *domicile*.[†]

Changing the Connotation with the Context

Words don't necessarily have positive *or* negative connotations. Some words have strong connotations in one context and negative or no connotations in another.

Take, for example, the words *cans* and *bags* in the following sentence: "He threw the empty cans and bags into the trash." In that sentence, the

---

[†]The *house* versus *domicile* example is thanks to my friend and colleague Joan Hellman formerly of Catonsville Community College.

two words have no emotional impact. They evoke, or call up, only their dictionary definitions.

But that changes dramatically when the two words appear in the context of this poem called "Hard Evidence," written by poet and textbook author Carol Kanar.

Hard Evidence
for Wolf

I'm stumbling on signs of life
throughout the empty house,
bones buried under rugs,
a leash snared by a table leg.

These and other of your effects—
cans and bags of uneaten food,
assorted toys and grooming aids—
a legacy now for homeless dogs.

Habits die, but need remains:
the walk I will not take today.
Silence whimpers at my door.
I still can smell you in the rain.[†]

See how the connotations of those ordinary words change with the context? Now the words *cans* and *bags* are hard evidence of a beloved dog's death. They carry with them associations of sadness and loss. Changing the context of a word often changes not just its meaning but its emotional impact as well.

SUMMING UP THE KEY POINTS

1. The term *etymology* refers to the history or story behind a word. The etymologies of words can often serve as memory pegs. Learn the history of the word and the history will anchor the meaning in your memory.

2. The more you want to use the words you learn, the more attentive you need to be to their context. The dictionary will give you

[†]Poem used by permission of Carol Kanar.

a word's *denotation*, or formal meaning. But the *connotations*, or associations, the word carries only become clear after you have seen it used in multiple contexts.

3. Context can dramatically shift a word's meaning along with its connotations. Teachers telling "stories" to children are just doing their job. But an employee who tells "stories" about co-workers probably doesn't have many friends. Context makes the difference.

4. When you learn a new word, it's a good idea to get some experience with how it is used in context (or contexts) before using it in your own writing. A sense of the correct context only comes with practice.

▶ **EXERCISE 8**   **Understanding Connotation**

DIRECTIONS   Underline the word with more positive connotations.

1. (Crude, Direct) in the way he expressed himself, he often offended people even when he meant no harm.

2. She (giggled, guffawed) her amusement at her husband's quick-witted response.

3. Today's fashion models are almost always tall and (slender, skinny).

4. He didn't expect to pay such a high price for a (preowned, used) vehicle.

5. Clothes for (overweight, husky) boys are located on the second floor.

▶ **EXERCISE 9**   **Understanding Connotation**

DIRECTIONS   Underline the word with more negative connotations.

1. The student (called, blurted) out the answer before the teacher had finished reading the question.

2. The couple spent days (debating, disputing) how to spend their tax refund.

3. She was (stubborn, determined) and refused to change her mind.

4. His (carelessness, recklessness) caused the accident.

5. He (tossed, hurled) her suitcase out the window.

✔ CHECK YOUR UNDERSTANDING

1. What does the word *etymology* refer to?

_____

2. What's the difference between a word's *connotation* and its *denotation*?

_____

_____

3. Once you learn a new word, can you assume that it means the same thing in every context? Please explain your answer.

_____

4. Why is it a good idea to see a new word used repeatedly before you use it in your own writing?

_____

 ## Looking Up Words While You Read

The specialized vocabulary words necessary to understand a particular subject are often defined in **annotations**, or notes in the margins of textbooks. Or they can be found in the **glossary**, or list of key terms located in the back of your textbook. Context clues can also provide you with approximate definitions for both specialized and non-specialized vocabulary.

Yet even with the help of context clues, there will be times when you have to look up a word's meaning. And despite my belief that print books are not going away any time soon, I would suggest that you look those occasional words up online. Much of the time, the search box of your browser (Firefox, Safari, Opera, or Chrome) will provide the meaning you need to keep on reading without interruption.

Looking Up Words Online

Web dictionaries have become so crowded with ads, it's sometimes hard to find the words being defined, so consider using online dictionaries only when your browser doesn't supply a definition that makes sense for the text you are reading. To use your browser, type *define* followed by a colon plus the word you are looking for into your browser's search box.

For example, if you were trying to define the word *reiterate*, your search term would look like this: **define: reiterate**. And that search term would call up the definition shown below, which includes not just the meaning but some synonyms as well. The synonyms are a bonus of online definitions. They will help you better understand the word's meaning. Another bonus of online definitions is the presence of an audio file ◀⏴. Click on the icon and you can hear the word pronounced. For non-English speakers, that feature is a godsend.

re·it·er·ate
/rēˈitəˌrāt/ ◀⏴
verb

say something again or a number of times, typically for emphasis or clarity.
"she reiterated that the administration would remain steadfast in its support"
synonyms: **repeat**, say again, **restate**, **retell**, **recapitulate**, go over (and over), **rehearse**
More

If you are more comfortable using an online dictionary, then sort through the various ones available to find one that's easy to read, has the fewest number of ads, and supplies you with sample sentences using the word in different contexts. My current favorite is the Merriam-Webster Online Dictionary. But whichever one you like, bookmark it or add it to your browser's toolbar for easy access while you read.

Use a Print Dictionary for Writing

For reading, you have a choice about how you look words up that other people have written. But if you are the one doing the writing, you should probably stick with a print dictionary, preferably hardback rather than paperback. Print dictionaries are more likely to provide information about where and when a word or phrase is appropriate. "Spot on," for example, meaning perfect or exactly right, would not be appropriate in a formal piece of writing but would be fine in conversation with friends. Print dictionaries are also likely to provide usage tips explaining the difference between words such as *all ready* (meaning completely prepared) and *already* (meaning happening before the time expected). As a writer, this is the kind of thing you need to be aware of and that you are less likely to find by looking up words online.

A Note on Dictionaries and Writing

"Never use a long word where a short one will do."
—Writer George Orwell

Where writing is concerned, you should probably avoid using words you have to look up before using. So much of word meaning is related to the associations that come with its context, and words with the same meaning don't necessarily share the same context. Like *home*, the word *residence* refers to a place where someone lives. But if you are writing a narrative about where you grew up and write, "When my dad couldn't pay the mortgage on our residence, my mom went to work so we wouldn't have to move and my brother and I could stay in the school we loved," the reader is going to think it's odd that you used the word *residence*, which normally appears in formal applications for passports and insurance. That's the kind of thing that can happen when writers use words they aren't really familiar with but think sound important. When you write, definitely use the dictionary to double check meanings and learn about proper usage or find out how to break a word into syllables. Avoid using it as a source of words that you aren't especially familiar with but think your audience might consider impressive.

Getting Down the Basics: Syllable Count, Pronunciation Guide, and Parts of Speech

Whether you are looking up words online or in a print dictionary, you can expect the **entry word**, or word being defined, to appear in boldface. The entry word will be divided into syllables. It might be divided by dots (jus·ti·fi·ca·tion) or hyphens (jus-ti-fi-ca-tion). Dots or hyphens fulfill the same function. They indicate where the syllable breaks appear. That way you know how many syllables there are in a word.

Digital and print dictionary entries both provide a sequence of letters with symbols in parentheses (ĭn-strŭkt'). The letters and symbols tell you what sounds to give the vowels[†] and consonants that make up the word. Consonants almost never present any pronunciation difficulty.

But long and short vowel sounds occasionally do. That's why dictionaries provide pronunciation keys, even online, where you can usually hear the word pronounced.

An accent mark (dī-dăk'-tĭk') or **boldface** (dahy-**dak**-tic)† tells you what syllable gets the stronger emphasis. Following the guide to pronunciation enclosed in brackets or parentheses comes the part of speech either spelled out (*noun, adjective*) or abbreviated (*n, adj, adv*). Often at the very end of an entry, enclosed in brackets, you'll also find a brief etymology of the word.

▌ **EXERCISE 10**   **Understanding More Than the Definition**

DIRECTIONS   Use a dictionary to answer the following questions. It can be an online or a print dictionary.

1. The word *heinous*, meaning "horribly wicked," is often *mispronounced*. Should the first syllable rhyme with *hey* or *hi*? _____hi_____

2. What part of speech is the word *heinous*? _____

3. How many syllables are there in the word *prevaricate*, meaning to mislead or lie? _____

4. *Hyssop* is a woody plant with small blue flowers. How many syllables does the word have, and which one gets the strongest accent? _____ Is the *y* in *hyssop* pronounced like the *i* in "hi" or the *i* in "him"? _____

5. During World War II, a *kamikaze* was a pilot trained to make a suicidal attack, usually on ships. How many syllables does the word have? _____ Which one gets the strongest accent? _____ Is the *e* at the end of the word silent or spoken? _____ Are the *a*'s in the word pronounced like the *a* in *father* or the *a* in *pat*? _____ The word is a noun, but it can also play what other part of speech? _____

---

†Long vowel sounds: wāy, wē, bīte, nō, cūte. Short vowel sounds: săt, lĕt, lĭt, lŏt, bŭt.
†The word is spelled *didactic* and means "intended to instruct."

Sorting Through Multiple Meanings

As you already know, a word can have multiple meanings. Those different meanings, however, can seem confusing when they appear together in a dictionary entry.

To avoid feeling overwhelmed when faced with multiple meanings, keep in mind that your goal is to determine what an unfamiliar word means *within a specific context*. That specific context will help you sort through any number of definitions and find the right one.

Say, for instance, that the word *scald* in the following sentence sent you to the dictionary. "Clinicians need to carefully scald their dental instruments before reusing them." Here are some of the meanings you would find:

1. to burn with hot liquid or steam

2. to cook slightly

3. to criticize harshly

4. to sterilize, or clean thoroughly, by washing in boiling water

5. *Botany*: a disease that affects some grasses

Faced with so many different definitions, you may feel unsure about which meaning to pick. Yet, usually, you can find the meaning through the simple process of elimination. For example, you can eliminate the definition following the word "Botany," which is a **special context label**. Special context labels tell you that the meaning provided is only appropriate within discussions of a particular subject, for instance, law, medicine, or architecture.

The special context label shown above tells you that the word *scald* means "a disease that affects some grasses" *only* when used in discussions of botany, the study of plants. Because our sample sentence has nothing to do with plants, we can eliminate this definition.

Once you eliminate this meaning, you have four left. However, notice that meaning 3 applies to something done to people whereas the sample sentence talks about "dental instruments" being scalded. That means that definition 3 won't work with the sample sentence. Nor will definition 2, since you cook in order to eat and you are not going to eat dental instruments.

Of the five meanings, the fourth one makes the most sense. No self-respecting dentist is going to use dirty dental instruments. He or she is going to sterilize them so they don't spread germs and disease. Thus, meaning 4 perfectly fits the sentence in which *scald* appears and that's what you are aiming for.

> **EXERCISE 11**   **Choosing the Correct Meaning**

DIRECTIONS   Read each sentence and look carefully at the italicized word. Then look at the various meanings and pick the one that best fits the context.

1. *Sentence:* The young reporter volunteered to act as a *conduit* between the rebels and the government.

    Meanings: **con•duit** *n.* **1.** a pipe that carries liquids, such as water **2.** a tube or duct that covers or encases electric wires or cable **3.** a means by which something is communicated or transmitted: *Throughout the war, she had been a conduit for the enemy's messages* **4.** *Archaic*† a fountain

    What is the best meaning for the word *conduit* in the above sentence? _____

2. *Sentence:* The prime minister generally had a *sanguine* temper but there were times when the weight of his duties plunged him into depression.

    Meanings: **san•guine** *adj.* **1.** having the color red **2.** having a healthy reddish skin tone **3.** inclined to be cheerful **4.** bloody

    What is the best meaning for the word *sanguine* in the above sentence? _____

3. *Sentence:* The so-called financial analyst was a *patent* liar, but he had powerful friends and those who knew him were afraid to challenge him.

    Meanings: **pat•ent 1.** *n.* a grant by a government acknowledging exclusive ownership of an invention **2.** *v.* to obtain an exclusive right to ownership **3.** *adj.* open, obvious, unconcealed **4.** *Biology. adj.* open, unblocked

    What is the best meaning for the word *patent* in the above sentence?

    _____

---

†archaic: used to describe an early meaning no longer in use.

4. *Sentence*: After his *vital* organs shut down, only machines were keeping him alive.

   Meanings: **vi•tal 1.** *adj*. pertaining or related to life **2.** necessary to the continuation of life **3.** being full of life **4.** destructive to life

   What is the best meaning for the word *vital* in the above sentence?

   _____

READING TIP Next time you turn to a dictionary to look up an unfamiliar word and find several definitions, quickly eliminate any meanings that have no bearing on the word's context. Then look for the meaning that makes the most sense within the context of the sentence or passage.

Figurative and Literal Word Meanings

Because most of the definitions for *scald* on page 108 involved heat in some form, you may have been surprised by the meaning "to criticize harshly." That definition seems to have nothing to do with the other definitions listed. There's a reason for that. The meaning "to criticize harshly" doesn't completely fit the others because it's figurative rather than literal.

Words used in a **figurative sense** don't describe an experience in realistic terms. Instead, they suggest a resemblance. It's through the resemblance or comparison that a meaning is conveyed. If we say we were *scalded* by harsh criticism, we are talking about a person saying something so hurtful it feels *as if* the words could burn.

For another example of words used figuratively, we can go to the other end of the temperature scale. Take, for instance, the word *frozen*. We can certainly use it to describe ice cream. That would be using the word **literally**, or realistically, to describe the actual state or consistency of ice cream.

But we can also say that someone's opinions have "frozen with time." That phrase uses the word *frozen* figuratively. It suggests that a person's opinions haven't changed in any way with the passage of time, much like frozen ice cream hasn't changed from its original state to a more liquid one. With figurative language, there is always an implicit comparison tucked somewhere in the words.

SUMMING UP THE KEY POINTS

1. In addition to providing definitions, dictionary entries tell you how a word is pronounced, broken into syllables, and used in a sentence.

2. Special context labels tell you that certain meanings apply only within a particular setting such as botany, architecture, or law.

3. Many dictionaries include a word's etymology at the end of the entry, usually enclosed in brackets.

4. If you are looking up an unfamiliar word from your reading, don't panic if the entry contains several definitions. Just sort through them using the original context of the word as a guide to your selection. Different definitions are often somewhat related in meaning, so even if you don't pick the exactly right one, you may still be able to get an approximate definition. That approximate definition will allow you to continue your reading.

5. Words used in a figurative sense convey their meaning by implying, or suggesting, a resemblance. Thus, in the following sentence, the man's face is not made of wood. But it resembles wood due to the lack of movement: "The stroke had turned his face into a wooden mask."

▶ **EXERCISE 12**   **Going from Literal to Figurative Language**

DIRECTIONS   Fill in the blanks with the word that matches the literal and figurative description of each word.

1. Used literally the word describes something you take when you are ill, but you could also use it figuratively to say that someone is really annoying. The word is _____ .

2. Used literally the word describes something you put in tea or on fish, but you could also use it figuratively to describe something that doesn't work well. The word is _____ .

3. Used literally the word describes male cattle, but you could also use it to describe a story you think has been made up. The word is

_____ .

4. Used literally the word describes a legless creature that slithers through grass and can contain poison, but you could also use it to describe someone who can't, under any conditions, be trusted. The word is _____ .

✔ CHECK YOUR UNDERSTANDING

1. Online definitions and dictionary entries always give you three basic elements. What are the three elements?

_____

2. If an entry contains several different definitions, what should guide your choice of meaning?

_____

3. What does etymology refer to?

_____

4. Look over the pairs of sentences that follow and circle the letters of the sentences that use the italicized words figuratively.
   a. The coach had to call a "time out" when two parents of the players got into a *heated* argument.
   b. The little boy *heated* the soup on the stove and then carried the pot to the table.
   a. The cookies were on a very *high* shelf where the dog could not reach them.
   b. The Tejano singer was *high* on nothing more than the enthusiasm of the crowd.

5. Look over the pairs of sentences that follow and circle the letters of the sentences that use the italicized words literally.
   a. The young girl had learned how to *weave* from her Cherokee grandmother.
   b. Unlike writers in the nineteenth century, modern writers are not inclined to *weave* morals, or lessons, into their short stories.
   a. The surgeon *cut* a hole on the top of the man's head in order to relieve the pressure on his brain.
   b. The police captain told his lieutenant to *cut* the chatter and get to the point.

Evaluating Websites About Words

However you choose to use the Web to define words, make sure the site you're drawing definitions from fulfills these criteria:

1. The web page should be easy to read. If you have to study the page to separate the entry from the ads and promotional sidebars, keep looking. Busy web pages can prove a distraction. You may end up browsing weight loss ads and forget what word you were looking up.

2. The various elements in the entry—for example, pronunciation guide, audio link, and word history—should be clearly laid out. If you have to look at the page for a long time to determine where, say, the meanings leave off and the history begins, this is not the site you want to be using.

3. The definitions of words should be clearly written. If you have to puzzle over how a definition is worded because it doesn't quite make sense, it's probably the definition and not you.

4. The definitions should come from several different sources so that you can compare the meanings from various sources. If an online dictionary uses only one source for its definitions, the meanings listed in the entry should be fairly similar to the meanings listed in other dictionary entries for the same word. (Yes, this means you have to do some cross-referencing.) If you find a definition for a word that doesn't appear anywhere else, you should probably not use this site again.

5. The best sites for looking up words will give you actual examples of the word used in sentences. The sentences will illustrate the range of meanings.

READING TIP

Web-based definitions fall under the same rule as those in print: Turn to the Web only when you can't continue reading without determining the meaning of an unfamiliar word.

DIGGING DEEPER

Scrabble for the Internet Age   *Terence Cullen*

Looking Ahead   It once took close to a decade for newly minted words to earn their way into the ***Official Scrabble Player's Dictionary***. But as the following reading shows, that has changed. New words are being incorporated, or added, at a much faster pace.

Getting Focused   The point, or main idea, of this article is that new words are being incorporated into the *Official Scrabble Player's Dictionary* at a much faster pace. As you read, be on the lookout for an explanation of why this is happening.

1   Scrabble is about to have a *bromance* with the *selfie*. And, no, it's not a *buzzkill*. These words are three of the 5,000 new terms that have been added to Merriam-Webster's *Official Scrabble Player's Dictionary*—the 76-year-old game's ultimate argument-settler and also a mirror of modern language. It's Scrabble for the Internet age. "These are words that have become part of the culture, part of the language and part of the dictionary," says Peter Sokolowski, editor at large for Merriam-Webster.

2   Among the other new pop culture words added are *chillax* and *frenemy*, now recognized as common parts of our speech. Foreign words such as *qigong*—a Chinese exercise routine—and *qajaq*, which is the Inuit spelling for *kayak*, were also added to the updated version of the book, available August 11.

3   Many of the thousands of words have essentially become "naturalized citizens" and are getting incorporated quickly into our vernacular (15 points!), says Sokolowski. "They can be foreign words that can become English words that are included in the English language," he says. So now the Yiddish term *schmutz*—a glob of something—can net you 23 points.

4   A word could normally take decades to make it into a collegiate dictionary, which is the rubric (ooh, 10 points!) for the Scrabble guide, says Sokolowski. But the pace of the Internet puts words in the news more often—changing how we talk every day. Hence, we have words like *texter* and *funplex*—slang for an entertainment center. "The public can be expected to encounter this word, and that means it has to be in the dictionary," he says. "In the case of these terms, they've come very

quickly and have been added to the dictionary." Established players aren't concerned about slang's incorporation (another 17 points!) into the game as long as it's sure to stick around. "(It's) a bit of a balancing act for us," says John Chew, co-president of the North American Scrabble Player's Association. "We don't have any issue with slang, we just want to make sure the words are going to be around in the long run."

5   In 2005, when Merriam-Webster put out its last "new" edition, it added high-scoring words like *qi* (Chinese for personal energy) and *za* (short for pizza), which one Scrabble expert said "completely changed the game. Each subsequent edition of the book, it makes the game richer," says Stefan Fatsis, author of *Word Freak: Heartbreak, Triumph, Genius, and Obsession in the World of Scrabble Players.* "Ultimately, it forces players to learn a bunch more words if they want."

6   Some of Scrabble's best will soon aim for the top right corner, where, if playing their tiles right, they can score 401 points with the Inuit word *quinzhee*—a combination of an igloo and a hole in the ground.

"'Selfie,' 'frenemy' now playable in Scrabble as game adds new words." By Terence Cullen from *New York Daily News,* August 4, 2014. © Daily News, L.P. (New York). Used with permission.

Sharpening Your Skills

DIRECTIONS   Answer the questions by circling the letter of the correct response or writing the answer on the blank lines.

Using Context Clues

1. The editor of the Scrabble dictionary says, "Many of the thousands of words have essentially become 'naturalized citizens' and are getting incorporated quickly into our vernacular."
   Based on the context, how would you define *incorporated*?

   _____

2. Which definition for *vernacular* makes the most sense?

   a. code of ethics

   b. method of spelling

   c. way of speaking

   d. ability to listen

3. Based on how it's used in the following sentence, what do you think a *rubric* is?

   "A word could normally take decades to make it into a collegiate dictionary, which is the rubric (ooh, 10 points!) for the Scrabble guide."

   a. a standard or method of judgment

   b. a color code

   c. a chain of command

   d. a pronunciation key

Paraphrasing 4. According to the article, and in your own words, what's the key criterion for deciding if a new word should be added to the Scrabble dictionary?

_____

_____

Literal and Figurative Language 5. In paragraph 3, the author speaks of words as "naturalized citizens." Chapter 2 introduced you to the word that describes language that speaks of non-human things as if they were flesh and blood human beings. What is that word?

_____

From Reader to Writer Use the Web to find sites that list words from other languages that the English language does not have. When the lists come up—and plenty will come up; count on it—look over several of them and pick two or three words you think would be a good addition to the language. Then write a paragraph or two explaining why you think these words would be useful additions to the English language.

Should we start a campaign, for instance, to get the Yiddish word *Shlimazl*, meaning someone whose luck is always bad, added to the language? Or is there already an English equivalent? Or how about the German word *jugendsünde*, meaning the mistakes made in your youth that you absolutely don't want brought up now that you are an adult? Do we need a specific word for those early mistakes or not?

▶ **TEST 1** **Reviewing Key Concepts**

DIRECTIONS Complete the following sentences by filling in the blanks.

1. If you don't know what a word means, before looking it up on-line or in a dictionary, see if _____ will provide an _____ .

2. There are many different kinds of context clues, but these four are particularly common: _____
_____ .

3. The _____ of a word will give you its core meaning. But a _____ can still dramatically change that meaning.

4. A _____ doesn't tell you much about word meaning, but it says a lot about _____ the word is.

5. Whenever possible, try to use _____ and _____ to determine the meaning of an unfamiliar word.

6. Words like *nitwit*, *gorgeous*, and *snarl* have strong _____ .

7. Words that have strong associations in one _____ may not have the same associations in another.

8. If a dictionary entry gives you several meanings for the same word, make sure the meaning you pick fits the _____ of the unfamiliar word.

9. The history of a word is its _____ .

10. In this sentence—"The rock hit the window and shattered it"—is the word *rock* used literally or figuratively? _____
What about in this sentence? Is the word *rock* used literally or figuratively? "She took her husband's death hard; he had been her *rock* for almost thirty years." _____

▶ **TEST 2**   **Using Context Clues**

DIRECTIONS   Use context clues to select an approximate meaning for each italicized word.

1. In the face of real danger, he didn't even try to display his usual *bravado*: When the bull charged, he ran like a scared rabbit.

   a. extreme shyness

   b. love of animals

   c. false bravery

   d. quick wit

2. With age, the financial wizard and penny pincher Hazel Green grew increasingly eccentric: She wore *bizarrely* unfashionable clothes, trusted no one, went on strange diets, and generally seemed to be out of step with the world.

   a. stingily

   b. weirdly

   c. colorful

   d. cleverly

3. In *The Country of the Pointed Firs*, the nineteenth-century writer Sarah Orne Jewett created the remarkable and compelling Mrs. Todd, a country woman who uses her vast store of herbal *lore* to cure the ailing and aging.

   a. knowledge

   b. mystery

   c. myths

   d. poisons

4. After her face was *disfigured* by an automobile accident, the super-model realized that there really were people in the world who could love her for who she was rather than what she looked like.

   a. enriched

   b. abandoned

   c. rebuilt

   d. ruined

5. In order to justify his claim to visitation rights, Adam was willing to undergo a *paternity* test that would prove David was indeed his son.

   a. relative

   b. brotherhood

   c. fatherhood

   d. chemical

6. In the nineteenth century, girls and boys were rigidly *socialized*: Girls were encouraged to be subordinate to boys, and boys were told they could conquer the world.

   a. restricted by class

   b. punished for misbehavior

   c. taught to obey

   d. taught appropriate social roles

7. Although the curse of Tutankhamen's tomb has never been scientifically proven, the *irrational* belief persists that those who discovered the tomb met an early death.

   a. dishonest

   b. sensational

   c. fast-spreading

   d. illogical

8. In the fairy tale, the wolf tried to disguise his *predatory* nature by dressing up as Little Red Riding Hood's elderly grandmother.

   a. insensitive

   b. youthful

   c. dangerous

   d. wild

9. He wanted to work on their relationship by regularly seeing a therapist; she opted for a more *radical* solution and filed for divorce.

   a. insignificant

   b. drastic

   c. quiet

   d. expensive

10. The lawyer *systematically* worked his way through the document and eliminated all references to the coauthor.

a. casually

b. slowly

c. quickly

d. carefully

▶ TEST 3   Using Context Clues

DIRECTIONS   Use context clues to develop an approximate meaning for each italicized word.

1. The artist, who is clearly a Democrat, uses his *satirical* cartoons to expose the follies of Republican politicians.

   Satirical means _____.

2. They decided against buying the house because of its *proximity* to the airport.

   Proximity means _____.

3. Having a child outside of marriage no longer carries the punitive *stigma* it did a half century ago.

   Stigma means _____.

4. On the highway running through the city, a vehicle accident can cause *gridlock* that stretches for miles.

   Gridlock means _____.

5. To provide her children with intellectual *stimulation*, the young mother often took them to museums, bookstores, and concerts.

   Stimulation means _____.

6. When Martha asked her husband if she was getting fat, he said "yes" without thinking and quickly regretted his *candor*.

   Candor means _____.

7. George Washington was the first and last U.S. president to govern from Philadelphia; all *subsequent* presidents have resided in the White House in Washington, D.C.

   Subsequent means _____.

8. When the *Apollo 11* astronauts landed on the moon, they found a rocky, *barren* landscape.

   Barren means _____.

9. The diplomat had a *supercilious* expression on his face and seemed to be looking down his nose at the other guests.

   Supercilious means _____.

10. The Rev. Martin Luther King Jr.'s *charismatic* leadership inspired millions of people to demand civil rights for black Americans.

    Charismatic means _____.

▶ **TEST 4**   **Using Context Clues**

DIRECTIONS   Use context clues to develop an approximate meaning for each italicized word.

1. The 1938 Fair Labor Standards Act signed by Franklin D. Roosevelt prevents the *exploitation* of children; it prohibits anyone under the age of thirteen from working in most jobs.

   Exploitation means _____.

2. The Louisiana Purchase, President Thomas Jefferson's *acquisition* of 530 million acres of French territory in 1803, doubled the size of the United States.

   Acquisition means _____.

3. Wilbur and Orville Wright succeeded in building the first "flying machine" because they systematically *modified* their design, making changes and improvements following each test flight.

   Modified means _____.

4. By the end of the twentieth century, America's economy had begun to shift from one based *predominantly* on manufacturing to one based mostly on employees' knowledge and skills.

   Predominantly means _____.

5. The American Civil War *commenced* on April 12, 1861, when the South fired the first shots at Union troops in Charleston, South Carolina, and ended on April 9, 1865.

   Commenced means _____.

6. In the years *preceding* the American Civil War, the country went through a period of rapid expansion: Between 1845 and 1853, for example, the country's boundaries were expanded to include territory that now covers 11 different states.

   Preceding means _____.

7. According to one *hypothesis*, the impact of an asteroid 65 million years ago led to the extinction of the dinosaurs, but this explanation is not a proven fact.

   Hypothesis means _____.

8. The legal document known as a "living will" provides *explicit* instructions about what caregivers should and should not do in the event that a person goes into a coma and requires long-term life support.

   Explicit means _____.

9. According to many scientists, global warming could have dangerous *implications* for the future, including a destructive rise in sea levels, damage to ecosystems and agriculture, and an increase in extreme weather events like hurricanes.

   Implications means _____.

10. In economics, *fluctuations* in the prices of goods are caused by similar increases and decreases in the availability of and demand for those goods.

    Fluctuations means _____.

> **TEST 5**   **Using Word Analysis and Context Clues**

> **DIRECTIONS**   Use context clues and word parts to develop an approximate meaning for each italicized word.

> **Prefixes**
> *anti* = against
> *extra* = over, outside, beyond
> *dis* = apart from, not, without
> *ad* = to, toward
>
> **Roots**
> *cred* = belief
> *dict* = say or speak
> *sect* = cut, divide
> *here* = stick

1. The doctors were fearful the boy would die because they had no *antidote* for the snakebite.

   Antidote means _____.

2. The girl refused to *dissect* the frog because she couldn't bear the thought of wasting a frog's life just so some student could cut up the body.

   Dissect means _____.

3. Because the Shaker religion forbade sex even in marriage, it had a hard time keeping *adherents*.

   Adherents means _____.

4. The report included too much *extraneous* information: The committee wanted only the essential facts of the situation, not silly gossip about dress and personal behavior.

   Extraneous means _____.

5. If she wants to run in the next campaign, she needs to *disassociate* herself from well-known gamblers and gangsters.

   Disassociate means _____.

6. Dr. Sorenson thinks of himself as an expert on ocean environment, but he lacks the proper *credentials*: He's a dentist, not a marine biologist.

   Credentials means _____.

7. My mother always told me to follow the *dictum* "neither a borrower nor a lender be," but I am always borrowing money from my friends.

   Dictum means _____.

8. The bank official desperately tried to *extricate* himself from the financial crisis he had helped to create, but all his influence couldn't get him out of trouble this time.

   Extricate means _____.

9. Once the suspect gave a *credible* account of his actions the night before, the police decided to let him go.

   Credible means _____.

10. Even with the glue in place, the pictures simply would not *adhere* to the shiny wallpaper.

    Adhere means _____.

▶ **TEST 6**   **Using Word Analysis and Context Clues**

DIRECTIONS   Use context clues and word parts to develop an approximate meaning for each italicized word.

Prefixes

in, im = in, into, not

multi = many

omni = all

circum = around

Roots

clin = lean

plac = calm, please

ven = come

sci = know

vor = eat

---

1. As my uncle got older, he became less *implacable*; more mellow with age, he was much easier to please.

   Implacable means _____ .

2. The entertainer Lena Horne was determined to *circumvent* the racism that once ruled Las Vegas. When hotel owners told her they didn't allow African Americans to rent rooms, Horne told them no room, no performance. As usual, Horne got her way.

   Circumvent means _____ .

3. President Lyndon B. Johnson's first *inclination* in a difficult situation was to sweet talk whomever he needed on his side; if that didn't work, he could quickly turn into a bully.

   Inclination means _____ .

4. In George Orwell's famous novel *1984*, "Big Brother" is an *omniscient* political leader, so all-knowing that privacy simply doesn't exist in the world he controls.

   Omniscient means _____ .

5. The United States had a *multiplicity* of reasons for not entering World War II, but after Japan bombed Pearl Harbor, every one of those reasons disappeared like smoke.

   Multiplicity means _____.

6. When millions died during the civil war in Rwanda, both Europe and the United States were harshly criticized for not *intervening* early on, when lives might have been saved.

   Intervening means _____.

7. Roaches have survived for centuries because they are *omnivorous*; they eat anything and everything—from paste to nail filings.

   Omnivorous means _____.

8. While the angry *multitudes* shouted outside the gates of the palace, the frightened king and queen tried to leave in secret, knowing full well that there was no way to calm their starving subjects.

   Multitudes means _____.

9. The mother *placated* the child with a chocolate chip cookie; in a matter of seconds, he went from tears to giggles.

   Placated means _____.

10. Not anxious to return to work, the boy took the most *circuitous* route he could think of and managed to make a fifteen-minute trip take three-quarters of an hour.

    Circuitous means _____.

▶ **TEST 7**   **Using Word Analysis and Context Clues**

DIRECTIONS   Use context clues and word parts to develop an approximate meaning for each italicized word.

Prefixes	Roots
pre = before or preceding, prior to	*locut, loqu* = speech
super = over, beyond, above	*voc* = voice, call
sub = under, from below, put under	*fic, fact, fect* = to make, to do
	gen = to give birth to, to produce, to cause

1. She has an amazing mind; in a single class session, she can *generate* one original idea after another, and most of them are quite good.

   Generate means _____.

2. After having their reports censored by military officials, the reporters were *vocal* in their complaints; they told anyone who would listen that their right to free speech had been ignored by the high command.

   Vocal means _____.

3. As a *prelude* to his speech, the scientist told a silly joke; as he had hoped, the comic introduction warmed up the audience and made them more attentive.

   Prelude means _____.

4. Patricia Henley's novel *Hummingbird House* wonderfully *evokes* the lush and beautiful landscape of Guatemala; she is particularly good at describing the country's colorful birds and gorgeous flowers.

   Evokes means _____.

5. What exactly is the *genesis* of the word "bedlam"? I've heard two different stories about its origin, and I am not sure which one is accurate.

   Genesis means _____.

6. Although the two men work together very well, they couldn't be more different: Bob is relaxed and *loquacious*, whereas Will is tense and silent most of the time.

   Loquacious means _____ .

7. To avoid being followed by reporters, the famous couple used *fictitious* names when they checked into the hotel, but they used their real names after they had crossed over the border into Mexico.

   Fictitious means _____ .

8. In an effort to trim her speech down to no more than fifteen minutes, the union organizer carefully crossed out any *superfluous* details that weren't directly related to her message.

   Superfluous means _____ .

9. The previous group leader encouraged independent thought; unfortunately, the current leader tries to *subdue* all signs of it.

   Subdue means _____ .

10. Many people believe that psychics are *clairvoyant*, and they, therefore, pay large sums of money to get their future told, but if psychics can see into the future, why don't they just game the stock market and retire?

    Clairvoyant means _____

    _____ .

Prefixes, Roots, and Suffixes You Should Know

●

Prefixes

a, ad = to, toward

anti = against

bene = well, good

bi = two

circum = around

dis = apart from, not, without

extra = over, outside, beyond

im = not

in, im = in, into, not

mal = bad

mono = one

multi = many

omni = all

per = through

phil = love

poly = many

pre = before, preceding, prior to

pseudo = false

re = again, back

sub = under, from below, put under

super = over, beyond, above

syn, sym = together

Roots

bellum = war

chron = time

clin = lean

cred = belief

derma = skin

dict = say or speak

fic, fact, fect = to make or to do

for = to bore into

gam = marriage

gen = to give birth to, to produce, to cause

here = stick

lat = side

locut, loqu = speech

mob = move

pe, pull = push, force

plac = calm, please

popul = people

rec, rect = straight, straighten

sci = know

sect = cut, divide

the = god

ven = come

vi, vit, viv = life

voc = voice, call

vor = eat

Suffixes

ism = state, condition, or quality

ist = person who does what's described in the root

itis = inflammation

ize = to cause to be, to treat or affect

onym = name, word

ous = full of

3

Looking for Specific Topics and General Main Ideas

IN THIS CHAPTER, YOU WILL LEARN

- about the difference between general and specific words.

- how readers need more specific words to identify the **topic**, or focus, of a paragraph.

- how specific statements of the topic lead readers more quickly to the author's **main idea**, or general message.

- why general sentences need specific **supporting details** to fully communicate the author's meaning.

- how to recognize three common patterns of general and specific sentences that appear in your textbooks.

"I went to a general store. They wouldn't let me buy anything specifically."

—COMEDIAN STEVEN WRIGHT

"I always wanted to be somebody, but now I realize I should have been more specific."

—COMEDIAN LILY TOMLIN

Throughout this book you'll see repeated references to the terms *general* and *specific*. You'll be asked, for instance, to come up with a *specific* word or phrase that identifies the *topic*, or subject, of a paragraph. You'll also be asked to explain the author's ***general* main idea** or point and then identify the ***specific supporting* details** that support or clarify it. Because the terms *general* and *specific* are both unavoidable and essential when talking about reading and writing, this chapter explains in detail what the terms mean when they are applied to both words and sentences.

Starting with General and Specific Words

Words, like the sentences that follow on pages 150–51, can be labeled *general* or *specific*. However, those labels don't mean much in isolation. To talk about a word being *general* or *specific*, you need to see it in relation to another word or words. In the following list, all of the words on the left are more general than the words on the right. Look over the two lists and compare each pair of words. See if you can explain what makes one word more general or more specific than another.

Military	Soldier
Technology	Software
Asia	China
Royalty	Queen
Government	Democracy
Language	Spanish
Music	Hymn
Weather	Blizzard

What you probably picked up on is the way in which the more general words could refer to or include the more specific ones. In other words, a soldier is a member of the military. Software is part of technology, and China is in Asia.

That ability of one word to subsume, or include, the other goes a long way toward explaining the difference between general and specific words: The more general a word is, the more it expands the range of possible meanings it can refer to. As words grow more general, they represent ever larger categories or groups that can be used to refer to a number of quite different people, events, ideas, experiences, or objects.

More specific words, in contrast, tend to narrow the range of meanings and refer to individuals rather than groups. They are the writer's way of saying, "I mean this, but I am excluding that." The more specific words are, the less they are used to refer to large numbers of quite different people, events, ideas, and places. General words serve that purpose, while more specific words nail down and make precise the meanings of words that are more general.

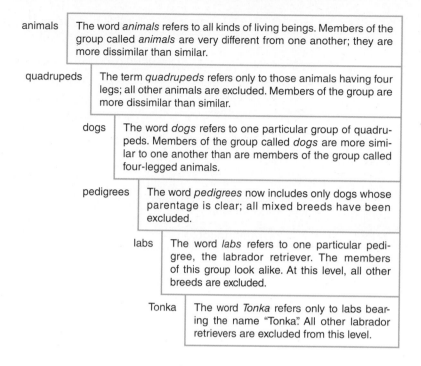

animals — The word *animals* refers to all kinds of living beings. Members of the group called *animals* are very different from one another; they are more dissimilar than similar.

quadrupeds — The term *quadrupeds* refers only to those animals having four legs; all other animals are excluded. Members of the group are more dissimilar than similar.

dogs — The word *dogs* refers to one particular group of quadrupeds. Members of the group called *dogs* are more similar to one another than are members of the group called four-legged animals.

pedigrees — The word *pedigrees* now includes only dogs whose parentage is clear; all mixed breeds have been excluded.

labs — The word *labs* refers to one particular pedigree, the labrador retriever. The members of this group look alike. At this level, all other breeds are excluded.

Tonka — The word *Tonka* refers only to labs bearing the name "Tonka". All other labrador retrievers are excluded from this level.

Figure 3-1 When read from top to bottom, this ladder shows how increasing specificity in language decreases the number of differences suggested by the words.

▶ **EXERCISE 1**   Telling the General from the Specific

DIRECTIONS   Add one more general or more specific word to each pair. The words on the left should be more general. The words on the right should be more specific.

EXAMPLE

Emotion   Rage

EXPLANATION   The word *rage* refers to a particular kind of emotion, one associated with anger. If you use the word *emotion*, then rage is a possibility but not specified as the meaning. A writer who wanted to make it clear to readers that he was talking about rage would have to use that word specifically. *Note: Feelings* is another more general word that could be written in the blank.

1. _____, measles

2. _____, robbery

3. document, _____

4. _____, Mars

5. _____, Dracula

6. singer/entertainer, _____

7. continent, _____

8. symbol, _____

9. gesture, _____

10. _____, scarves

Identifying the Author's Specific Topic

Understanding the difference between general and specific words comes in handy when you are reading a difficult paragraph. The quicker you can zero in on the paragraph's specific **topic**, or focus of discussion, the more easily you can determine the author's general **main idea** or message.

Take, for instance, the following paragraph. As you read it, ask yourself: What specific word identifies the subject that is the focus of the paragraph? The answer will help you come up with the paragraph's topic.

[1]One of the most dramatic sleep problems is narcolepsy (nar-koe-lep-see), or sudden irresistible sleep attacks. [2]Narcoleptic attacks last anywhere from a few minutes to a half hour. [3]Victims may fall asleep while standing, talking, or even driving. [4]Emotional excitement, especially laughter, commonly triggers narcolepsy. [5]Tell an especially good joke and a narcoleptic may fall asleep. [6]More than half of all narcolepsy victims also suffer from something called cataplexy (cat-uh-plec-see), a sudden temporary paralysis of the muscles, leading to complete body collapse. (Adapted from Coon and Mitterer, *Introduction to Psychology*, 11th ed., p. 102, © Cengage Learning.)

If you answered the previous question with the word *narcolepsy*, you are absolutely correct. The author addresses that topic in every single sentence.

However, if you decided that the word *problems* or even the phrase *sleep problems* were the topic, you would have been thinking too generally. Those topics are too general because they include ideas the author is not interested in discussing. The authors are not concerned with all of the many different problems related to sleeping, from insomnia to sleep apnea.* Instead, they focus on one specific type of sleep problem—narcolepsy.

Note, too, that the word *problems* isn't repeated or referred to throughout the paragraph. The word *narcolepsy*, however, gets repeated or referred to in every sentence. That's why the word *narcolepsy* best expresses the author's specific topic or focus.

Phrasing the Topic

Because you've looked at an example of a paragraph in which a single word summed up the topic, you might be thinking that a single word can always express the specific topic of a paragraph. But that would be a mistake. More often than not, you'll need more than one word to identify the specific topic of a paragraph. Here's an example:

> [1]In the mid-nineteenth century, the majority of immigrants to America's shores arrived at New York City's Castle Garden immigration center. [2]But as immigration began to increase in the latter part of the nineteenth century, the government built a bigger immigration center on New York's Ellis Island. [3]The Ellis Island immigration center officially opened in 1892, and until 1954, it provided millions of new immigrants with their first glimpse and taste of American life. [4]Although initially immigrants were barely given enough to eat upon arrival—dried bread and prunes—the U.S. government quickly improved the offerings and new arrivals were treated to hearty stews and soups, although many mistook white bread for cake and were puzzled by the presence of bananas on the table. [5]More strictly controlled than previous immigrations centers, the Ellis Island center carried out health inspections, and those suffering from minor ailments were allowed to rest up before leaving. [6]Only 2 percent of arriving immigrants were turned away from the country's shores, usually due to having a contagious illness or being considered incapable of living independently. [7]When the Ellis Island immigration center opened on January 1, 1892, the first passenger to register her arrival was a fourteen-year-old Irish girl named Annie Moore. [8]A statue of Annie still stands in what is now the Ellis Island museum.

*apnea: a condition in which breathing is interrupted during sleep.

Between 1892 and 1954, the Statue of Liberty welcomed immigrants to Ellis Island.

© Ulrich Flemming.

Consider *immigrants* or *immigration* the topic of the paragraph, and it might take you a while to arrive at the author's main idea or message: "Between 1892 and 1954 the Ellis Island immigration center provided new arrivals with an introduction to America." Words such as *immigrant* and *immigration* are too general to sum up the focus or emphasis of the paragraph. A better bet would be to use an entire phrase like "the Ellis Island immigration center," especially since that phrase appears or is referred to throughout the paragraph, as you can see from the highlighted words below.

In the mid-nineteenth century, the majority of immigrants to America's shores arrived at New York City's Castle Garden immigration center. But as immigration began to increase in the latter part of the nineteenth century, the government built a bigger immigration center on New York's Ellis Island. The Ellis Island immigration center officially opened in 1892, and until 1954, it provided millions of new immigrants with their first glimpse and taste of American life. Although initially immigrants were barely given enough to eat upon arrival—dried bread and prunes—the U.S. government quickly improved the offerings and new arrivals were treated to hearty stews and soups, although many mistook white bread for cake and were puzzled by the presence of bananas on the table. [[Here the phrase is not restated but it is implied]] More strictly controlled than previous immigrations centers, the Ellis Island center carried out health inspections, and those suffering from minor ailments were allowed to rest up before leaving. Only 2 percent of arriving immigrants were turned away from the country's shores, usually due to having a contagious illness or being considered incapable of living independently. When the Ellis Island immigration center opened on January 1, 1892, the first passenger to register her arrival was a fourteen-year-old Irish girl named Annie Moore. A statue of Annie still stands in what is now the Ellis Island museum. [[Here again there is an implied reference to the Ellis Island immigration center.]]

The repetition of and reference to the phrase "Ellis Island immigration center" does what more specific language is supposed to do for readers: It narrows down the range of meanings they can bring to the text.

The repeated references to that phrase make it clear that what's under discussion is not *immigration* or *immigrants* in general but rather immigration as it occurred in a particular location or context. That's not to say you couldn't come up with the main idea using more general terms for the topic. But it would take you longer. And that extra time provides no extra benefit in terms of your understanding. So why not take the shortest route?

Note, too, how the author introduces the topic in stages, starting with *immigration* but ending with the *Ellis Island immigration center*. That's a common pattern in academic writing. The opening sentence will introduce a general version of the topic and then make it more specific in succeeding sentences.

Following the Topic References

When you read to identify the topic—or for that matter, to discover the main idea—keep in mind that the author won't just repeat the same word or phrase. To avoid boring repetition, writers use pronouns and word substitutes to keep the topic in front of readers. In the following paragraph, for instance, the specific topic is "pedigreed dogs at Westminster." Note how the author threads that specific topic through the paragraph using a combination of word repetition and explicit and implicit references:

Mutual sniffing and tail-wagging plus the phrase "of the dog show" keep the topic in the forefront of the reader's mind.

The words *pedigreed* and *pooches* both keep the reader's attention on the dogs and the dog show.

By the last sentence the word *dogs* makes it clear that dogs at the Westminster Dog Show have to play a role in the main idea.

[1]For pedigreed dog owners, the Westminster Dog Show is a major event that arouses much rivalry in pet owners, each of whom thinks his or her dog deserves the blue ribbon. [2]But given the mutual sniffing and tail-wagging that takes place among the participants of the dog show, it's pretty clear they aren't especially concerned about who walks away with the Westminster blue ribbon. [3]Pedigreed or not, the pooches at dog shows are, for the most part, just happy to meet and greet a host of new four-footed friends. [4]The owners might consider who wins the Westminster Dog Show to be a big deal, but the dogs themselves could care less.

To Identify the Specific Topic of a Paragraph, You Should ●

a. ask yourself what word or phrase the author is talking about.

b. look for words or phrases that are repeated, referred to, or implied throughout the paragraph.

c. pay especially close attention to any words that are consistently mentioned or implied *toward the end of the reading*.

d. focus on references to words or phrases that turn up in almost all of the sentences of the paragraph rather than just two or three.

e. consider if pronouns, associated words, or specific examples might stand in for or suggest the author's topic.

▶ **EXERCISE 2**

DIRECTIONS   Read each passage. Then circle the letter of the word or phrase that best sums up the specific topic of the reading.

EXAMPLE

Sentences 1 and 2 strongly suggest "physical disabilities" as the topic.

Sentence 3 introduces the word *attitude* and mentions a change in attitude.

[1]There was a time when physical disabilities were routinely hidden. [2]People with disabilities were ashamed that they looked different from those whose bodies were considered normal. [3]But that attitude toward disability is changing fast, as more and more people are putting their disabilities on display and refusing to be apologetic about them. [4]In 2014, it was the talk of the Web when a gorgeous young woman posed in a bikini with her colostomy bag front and center on her six-pack abs. [5]After a contestant in a beauty contest walked on stage wearing her insulin pump because she

While the word *attitude* is not mentioned again, these are all examples of a change in attitude.

suffered from diabetes, she not only won the contest but got others with diabetes, both men and women, to post their photos on Facebook. ⁶The photos showed people happily smiling into the camera with their insulin pumps pointedly on display. ⁷*Pro Infirmis*, a Swiss charity devoted to giving the disabled a voice in the world, recently made a short film in honor of The International Day of Persons with Disabilities, which is celebrated on December 3rd. ⁸The film shows a series of storefront windows featuring models with a missing or deformed body part. ⁹There is a fashionably dressed man in a wheelchair, a pretty young girl with a curved spine, and a handsome man with one leg. ¹⁰This new, "don't hide it, flaunt it" attitude toward disabilities can be summed up in the bumper sticker that is appearing more and more frequently. ¹¹The bumper sticker shows a clenched fist and the words "Disabled and Proud."

Notice how sentence 10 reintroduces the word *attitude* in order to sum up what came before.

Topic   a.   disabilities

b.   beauty contestant displaying her insulin pump

c.   changing attitude toward disabilities

EXPLANATION   Answer *a* is a little too general. The paragraph deals specifically with physical disabilities. But the word *disabilities* can refer to mental or psychological disabilities as well. Answer *b* is too specific. The "beauty contestant displaying her insulin pump" is addressed in only two sentences. If that's the topic, how could we include the woman in a bikini who had her colostomy bag on display?

Answer *c* is just specific enough. It manages to include the content of all the sentences in the paragraph, all of which focus on the way attitudes toward having a disability are changing. *Note*: Sometimes you need to add a word or two to come up with the specific topic. The words *attitudes*, *changing*, and *disabilities* all appear in the paragraph. But it's the reader's job to add a word like *toward* or *about*.

1.   ¹Psychologists interested in the effect of positive mental states have begun to study the state of mindfulness, which involves feeling fully present, aware, and undistracted. ²In a mindful state, people are conscious of what's going on around them. ³But they do not judge the situation by labeling it good or bad. ⁴They simply experience it. ⁵It's that open, receptive mindful attitude that seems to have benefits. ⁶It appears, for example, that cancer patients who have learned to meditate in order to induce a state of mindfulness experience less distress and a greater sense of well-being than those patients who have no such

training. [7]One study (Brewer et al., 2011) suggests that being mindful also makes it easier to quit smoking. [8]Other studies suggest that mindfulness is associated with self-knowledge and a sense of well-being (Friese, Messner, & Schaffner, 2012; Siegel, 2010). [9]Anyone who has a tendency to sleepwalk through life—and that's probably most of us—would do well to be mindful of the value of mindfulness.

(Adapted from Coon and Mitterer, *Psychology: A Journey*, 5th ed., p. 208, © Cengage Learning.)

Topic

a. mental states

b. meditation

c. mindfulness

2. [1]Drought has been menacing the West and Southwest of the United States for at least a decade. [2]But in 2014, it reached crisis proportions with at least seven states suffering the crop loss, water shortages, usage restrictions, and fire hazards that come with a fast diminishing water supply. [3]Texas, Oklahoma, California, Kansas, Arizona, New Mexico, and Nevada were so severely hit by the drought that reservoir levels dropped way below normal and crop pasture burnt up in the extreme heat. [4]Texas, with its quarter of a million farms, struggled to keep both crops and farm animals alive. [5]A similar situation prevails in Oklahoma, where the Oklahoma Emergency Drought Relief Commission had to award more than $1 million to keep farming communities going. [6]In Arizona, drought and extreme heat, combined with a lighter-than-average snowfall, severely reduced soil moisture, thereby increasing the risk of fire hazards across the state. [7]Of all seven states, only California experienced *severe* drought throughout the entire state, with 76.7% of the states undergoing *extreme* drought.

(Source of statistics: "7 States Running Out of Water," *Huffington Post*, Last accessed 5/24/2014.)

Topic

a. California

b. reservoir levels

c. drought

3. [1]Among the millions of neurons, or cells, in the human brain, what role do specific neurons play in controlling movement or thought, or causing disorders like depression and autism?[†] [2]Figuring out the functions of various neurons and circuits in mice or other lab animals can offer

---

[†]autism: a psychological condition, present from childhood, in which the child has trouble making contact with the world outside of his or her own psyche.

answers to this question. [3]That's why scientists are interested in a technique called optogenetics, which gives scientists the power to turn neurons on or off. [4]Once a particular group of neurons have been turned off, scientists can then explore whether or not they are responsible for a particular behavior or disorder. [5]Using optogenetics, researchers have been able to manipulate neurons in worms, flies, mice, and even monkeys. [6]The technology has been used to study neural processes underlying epilepsy, addiction, depression, and more. (Adapted from Stephen S. Hall, "Neuroscience's New Toolbox." *MIT Technology Review*, July/August 2014, 22.)

a. scientific discoveries

b. optogenetics

c. neurons

4. [1]*Wesley the Owl* is a lovely book written by biologist Stacie O'Brien, who adopted an injured baby barn owl that lived with her for nineteen years until his death. [2]A gifted writer as well as a scientist, O'Brien tells a heartwarming and moving story, one that might make readers want to run out and adopt an owl. [3]Hedwig the owl, a key character in the Harry Potter series, has certainly had that effect, and numerous fans adopted (and then abandoned) owls after reading the books or seeing

© Ulrich Flemming.

With a few exceptions, it's illegal to own a barn owl in the United States.

the movies. [4]The Harry Potter fans got rid of their owls so quickly because owls, lovely and smart as they are, make terrible pets. [5]First off, rodents are a staple of the owl diet. [6]Wesley's human companion purchased by her own account 28,000 rats and mice over the course of their time together. [7]Owl owners who don't want to purchase rats and mice have to keep a large supply of frogs, lizards, and small birds on hand because that's what owls eat. [8]Owls also regurgitate the animal body parts they cannot digest, leaving a smelly trail of undigested food in their wake. [9]Perhaps most importantly, owls have very sharp talons, or claws. [10]Thus, they can be a danger to children and pets, who don't know that owls are not fond of being touched.

a. owls

b. owls as pets

c. Wesley the Owl

5. [1]With the outbreaks of childhood diseases such as whooping cough and measles that occurred in 2014 and 2015, many parents are angry at anti-vaxxers, parents who refuse to have their children vaccinated for standard childhood diseases. [2]While some parents don't vaccinate because they don't realize they can get help paying for vaccinations from the Vaccinations for Children program, the majority do not reject vaccinations for financial reasons. [3]Some parents get personal exemptions from vaccination requirements because they believe, incorrectly, that the vaccinations cause autism. [4]Others prefer to lead what they consider a "natural lifestyle." [5]They believe the body doesn't need the help of modern medicine but can fight off disease through the strength of its immune system. [6]Still others do not approve of vaccinations for religious reasons. [7]For a variety of reasons then, the anti-vaccination movement has grown over the last two decades. [8]It's so large, in fact, that between 2009 and 2012 thirty-one bills designed to make vaccine exemptions easier to come by were put in front of state legislatures. [9]Most of these bills have failed, and in hindsight* that seems like a good thing. [10]It's good because some states are reaching a point where the number of unvaccinated children challenges what's called "herd immunity." [11]In the simplest terms, herd immunity exists when enough people, close to 95 percent, are vaccinated against a disease that could otherwise spread quickly from person to person. [12]Herd immunity

---

*hindsight: being able to look back in time.

stops the disease from spreading as it normally would. [13]However, in some states, as many as 7 percent of children attending school have not been vaccinated, meaning that the chain of immunity is breaking down, which is why we are seeing a return of childhood diseases that we thought had disappeared and why members of the anti-vaccination movement are beginning to be the focus of community anger.

a. autism

b. childhood diseases

c. parents against vaccinations

From Reader to Writer Like the people described on page 140, military veterans are also making a point of not hiding their disabilities. Instead they are taking pride in showing them. Write a paragraph or two describing what you think of this new attitude toward having a disability. Focus on why you feel as you do. When you finish, circle every reference to the topic.

 ## Constructing the Topic with the Author

Inexperienced readers are inclined to think that writers supply every single word necessary to convey their message. Experienced readers know better. They know that readers frequently have to add to what the author says in order to come up with a specific topic that is partially suggested but not completely stated. Here's an example:

[1]Prior to the nineteenth century, America was a largely agricultural country and daily life required so much effort that there was little time for leisure. [2]But as industry grew, so did city life and leisure time. [3]With that dramatic change came an interest in sports. [4]However, in the cities, one sport in particular dominated. [5]By the nineteenth century, baseball had emerged as the most popular new urban sport. [6]The game first appeared in its modern form in the 1840s when a group of wealthy New Yorkers organized the Knickerbocker Club. [7]Then in 1862, in Brooklyn, William H. Cammeyer built the first enclosed baseball field in the country. [8]However, it was not until 1869 that *teams* began to charge admission and pay players. [9]In 1876, eight teams—New York, Philadelphia, Hartford, Boston, Chicago, Louisville, Cincinnati, and

St. Louis—came together to form the National League of Professional Baseball Clubs. [10]By the late 1880s, annual attendance at National League games had reached eight million, and both men and boys in vacant lots and empty streets were imitating the professional players they admired. (Adapted from Gillon and Matson, *The American Experiment*, 2nd ed., p. 747, © Cengage Learning.)

A reader who has finished the first three sentences of the paragraph would probably be ready to assume that the word *sports* might express the topic. But that same reader would be forced to revise that prediction based on the fourth sentence, which explicitly tells the reader, "No, I'm not talking about sports in general, but one sport in particular." Sentence 5 then identifies the specific sport under discussion—baseball.

Yet if you read to the end of the paragraph, it's clear that the author is not talking about all the possible sub-topics included under the word *baseball*, such as the positions, rules, and players. This is a paragraph about the "history of baseball." That's the best statement of the topic because all of the sentences following 5 discuss its historical development. Thus, "the history of baseball" is the topic that will lead you directly to the author's main idea, "The history of baseball begins in the nineteenth century when it became the country's most popular urban sport."

READING TIP

Experienced readers know that they frequently have to co-author the text with the writer. They are the ones who supply the words, phrases, and ideas that the author suggests but does not state.

▶ EXERCISE 3   Constructing the Topic

DIRECTIONS   Read each paragraph. Then in the blank that follows, write what you consider to be the topic. *Note*: In some cases, the topic will be stated for you. In others, you will have to construct or piece it together, adding some words to those already present.

EXAMPLE

[1]The eye is made up of many different parts, each one playing a significant role in an individual's ability to see. [2]The eyeball is surrounded by three layers of protective tissue. [3]The outer layer, called the *sclera*, is made from firm, tough, connective tissue and is white in color. [4]The middle layer, called the *choroid coat*, is a delicate network of connective tissue that

contains many blood vessels. [5]The inner layer, which is called the *retina*, contains the nerve receptors for vision and approximately ten different layers of nerve cells. [6]Two kinds of nerve cells are contained within the retina: *cones*, which are used mainly for light vision, and *rods*, which are used when it is dark or dim. (Clover, *Sports Medicine Essentials*, p. 385 © Cengage Learning.)

Topic   Parts of the Eye
_____

EXPLANATION   The sentences in the paragraph all focus on different parts of the eye, so "parts of the eye" is the only phrase general, or broad, enough to sum them all up. *Note*: Here again, the reader has to create the topic from words in different sentences.

1. [1]How often have you heard that laughter is the best medicine? [2]Cliché* or not, this saying really does have some truth to it. [3]Research has shown that stress weakens the immune system. [4]That's why people who suffer from long-term stress tend to get more colds than do people whose lives are relatively stress free. [5]People with strong positive attitudes toward life are likely to overcome illness more quickly than do those who consistently harbor negative feelings. [6]The reason for this lies in how the body functions. [7]During times of stress, the body secretes the hormone cortisol. [8]One of cortisol's effects is to lower or decrease the activities of the immune system. [9]It follows, then, that people who are constantly feeling stressed cannot easily fight off or quickly recover from illness. (Adapted from Donald C. Rizzo, *Introduction to Anatomy and Physiology*, p. 358, © Cengage Learning.)

Topic
_____

2. [1]More than two decades ago, school choice backers were persuasive enough to convince several American cities, such as Milwaukee, Cleveland, and New York City, to test voucher programs, state-funded programs that give students money awards to pay for private schools. [2]As a result, some 20 years after the initial school choice debate began, we can assess whether the claims about voucher programs have come true. [3]Unfortunately, the results of voucher programs have been mixed at best. [4]For example, in

_____

*cliché: An expression that has been said so often it suggests the author is not bothering to think about the language he or she is using.

Milwaukee, where low-income students received vouchers to private schools of their choice, researchers found that five years after school entry, students using vouchers were not doing markedly better than those attending public schools. [5]Overall, researchers found that the test scores of students who used vouchers didn't differ from the scores of students who were not part of a voucher program.

(Adapted from Dalton Conley, *You May Ask Yourself*, 2nd ed., p. 507.)

Topic _____

3. [1]When Americans think of the Wild West, they don't usually imagine a landscape inhabited by African Americans. [2]Yet this image of the West—one without the presence of black people—is inaccurate. [3]In truth, thousands of African Americans helped settle the West, a fact that Hollywood has generally ignored, further enhancing the image of an all-white Wild West that never existed. [4]The 1951 movie *Tomahawk*, for instance, features white actor Jack Oakie playing a character named James "Sol" Beckworth. [5]Beckworth, however, was black, not white, and he made his name as a Buffalo Soldier, who helped the army move Native Americans off of their rightfully owned land. [6]Mary Fields, a far more heroic figure than Beckworth, was a fierce, six-foot-tall black woman who drove a stagecoach and protected her passengers with a pair of six-guns that she wasn't afraid to use. [7]Exciting as her life was, Mary has never made it into a film about the West. [8]Similarly, Oklahoma, the location for many westerns, was the site of several African-American communities, although not one of those communities has ever appeared in a western.

Topic _____

4. [1]Schools, employers, and the government are increasingly using technology to monitor individuals' performance and behavior. [2]A 2005 study reports that 36 percent of companies use "keystroke monitoring so they can read what people type as well as track how much time they spend at the computer" and "55 percent retain and review e-mail messages." [3]In 2010, identity theft was the number-one complaint filed with the Federal Trade Commission for the eleventh year in a row. [4]Concerns over online privacy are so great that in 2011, officials from the Federal Trade Commission

testified before a House Subcommittee on issues related to online privacy. (Adapted from Mooney, Knox, and Schacht, *Social Problems*, 8th ed., p. 462, © Cengage Learning.)

Topic   _____

5. [1]For at least three decades, it was assumed that medical experts could clearly establish whether or not a child was the victim of *shaken baby syndrome*, a hard and repeated physical shaking that caused trauma to the brain, leading to serious injury or death. [2]However, in the last decade, both doctors and researchers have challenged the notion that shaken baby syndrome can be easily identified, even by medical experts. [3]More specifically, they question the idea that three specific symptoms—bleeding in the retina of the eyes, bleeding in the tissues surrounding the brain, and swelling in the brain—automatically indicate that these injuries were the result of an adult's brutally shaking the child. [4]In a 2001 study of the three symptoms, British neuropathologist Jennian Geddes set the stage for the current controversy concerning shaken baby syndrome. [5]Geddes found that most babies with the three critical symptoms were suffering not from trauma to the brain but from oxygen deprivation to the brain's cells, the symptoms of which do not occur immediately but can emerge slowly over time. [6]Rupture to the brain due to shaking, however, has an immediate effect with the child lapsing into unconsciousness. [7]That immediate cause-and-effect relationship was the main reason juries and judges were willing, in the absence of any witnesses or other evidence, to convict caretakers present right before a child lapsed into unconsciousness. [8]A number of those convictions were based almost solely on medical testimony, claiming that if the three symptoms were present upon examination, then whoever had been with the child prior to the child's becoming unconscious was responsible for harming the child. [9]The effects of oxygen deprivation, however, happen more slowly and can begin with a child being fussy or refusing to eat but not immediately losing consciousness. [10]That knowledge has had an influence on trials involving shaken baby syndrome.

Topic   _____

Moving on to General and Specific Sentences

The terms *general* and *specific* become even more critical to reading comprehension when readers want to expand a writer's topic into the **main idea** or point of the passage. After all, readers can't be satisfied with knowing what specific topic the author has chosen to discuss. They also need to know what the author wants to say *about* that topic. They need, that is, to get a handle on the author's general message.

Because the **purpose**, or goal, of textbook writing is to inform, textbook authors are inclined to use general sentences that sum up their main ideas. These sentences are called **topic sentences** or **main idea statements** in paragraphs (**thesis statements** in longer readings). Experienced readers of academic material are practiced in spotting these sentences, because their ability to tell the difference between general and specific sentences has become almost **automatic**. In other words, they do it without consciously thinking about it. Having worked for a while with general and specific words, can you say which of these three sentences is the most general?

a. Some people show anger by growing sulky and silent.
b. Others scream and shout to show their fury.
c. People show anger in different ways.

Sentence *c* is the correct answer. That's because sentence *c* suggests more possible meanings than sentences *a* and *b* do. Like more general words, general sentences can be understood in a number of different ways. That's the main reason why they require more specific sentences for clarification. If writers stay on a very general level, they risk being misunderstood because the reader is free to fill in too much information that the writer may never have intended. Left with only more general sentences, readers can happily come up with a meaning the writer never wanted to convey. Take, for instance, a passage like this one:

> People show anger in different ways. Not everyone expresses anger in exactly the same way. Although everyone feels anger at some point in life, the way that each person expresses it can differ.

Given only these sentences, you can assume that the author believes anger can be expressed in silence, shouting, smashing things, striking others, yelling insults, and the list can go on. But the writer may well have a more restricted range of responses in mind, and that's where more specific sentences, called **supporting details**, become essential. They are a writer's way of saying to readers, "This is what I meant, and what I meant doesn't include a number of other responses you might be ready to assume."

> [1]People show anger in different ways. [2]Some, when angered, grow pouty and silent. [3]Others scream and shout in fury. [4]Then there are those who like to mix the two. [5]After an initial outburst, they resort to a deep and prolonged sulk. [6]In general, though, physical aggression is not within the normal range of responses to feeling anger.

Notice how the more specific supporting details place limits on the general opening statement. That's important. This pattern of a broad, general topic sentence followed by more specific supporting details that nail it down more firmly, is common in academic writing. All the more reason for you to be able to spot, almost without thinking about it, where general sentences leave off and more specific ones begin.

▶ **EXERCISE 4**   **Recognizing General and Specific Sentences**

DIRECTIONS   Read each pair of sentences. Then label the general sentence *G* and the specific one *S*.

EXAMPLE

a. Political scandals are not a modern invention, and the nineteenth century certainly had its fair share of spectacular financial meltdowns, which left federal and state governments with big bills and nothing to show for them. ___G___

b. One of the most spectacular nineteenth-century scandals involved the building of a New York City courthouse that involved so much construction graft*, it cost $13 million. ___S___

EXPLANATION   Sentence *a* is more general because it can refer to any number of political scandals occurring in the nineteenth century. Sentence *b* is more specific because it focuses the reader's attention on one particular scandal that took place in a particular location, New York City.

1. a. Early newspapers made no pretense of being without political bias. _____

    b. In the eighteenth century, American politicians funded and controlled newspapers. _____

*graft: profiting by illegal means, especially through the use of political influence.

2. a. In Japan, revealing one's emotions to others is not encouraged, but in America the opposite is true. _____

   b. Culture affects behavior in a number of ways, particularly within the context of personal relations. _____

3. a. Like many of his victims, Jesse James was shot in the back. _____

   b. The outlaw Jesse James met what some have called a fitting end. _____

4. a. By 2050, the U.S. Census Bureau predicts that the number of Hispanic individuals living in the United States will increase from 50.5 million to 132.8 million. _____

   b. People of Hispanic origin make up about 17 percent of the total population in the United States, but the U.S. Census Bureau expects a dramatic increase in that number over the course of time. _____

5. a. The cow known as Molly B is a true survivor who refused to accept her miserable fate. _____

   b. Destined for the slaughterhouse, Molly B made her escape by leaping over the slaughterhouse gate and swimming across the Missouri River. _____

From Reader to Writer Write two or three more specific sentences that explain why this is good advice not just for hockey, but for life: "You miss 100% of the shots you don't take."

—Wayne Gretzky, A Legendary Hockey Player also known as "The Great One."

READING TIPS

1. Be alert to general sentences that are further clarified by specific sentences. These general sentences, called *topic sentences* or *main idea statements*, sum up the main idea or message of a paragraph. These are the sentences to paraphrase and record in marginal notes.

2. Above all, make sure you understand what words or phrases in the general sentence are further explained by the more specific *supporting details*.

3. Writers of business textbooks are particularly fond of making the first sentence of a paragraph the topic sentence. When reading a business text, check to see if the first sentence is more general than the two that follow. If it is, you have found the sentence that states the main idea.

From Reader to Writer Pick three well-known sayings and translate them into more general language. Read them aloud and see if your classmates can recognize the more specific point hidden in the general language. What specific advice, for instance, do you think is hidden in this general statement: Don't enumerate your winged creatures before they come to light?

▶ EXERCISE 5   Connecting General and Specific Sentences

DIRECTIONS   For each general sentence, circle the letter of the sentence that makes it more specific and clarifies its meaning.

EXAMPLE

General Sentence Pit bulls are not, by nature, vicious dogs that attack for no reason, and their current reputation is undeserved.

Specific Sentences a. Before pit bulls were trained as fight dogs by being subjected to repeated abuse and starvation, they were called "nanny" dogs because they were gentle and good caretakers for children.

b. People who are convicted of breeding and training pit bulls to fight one another should be sent to jail for a minimum of five years.

c. The poet and philosopher Vicki Hearne spent her life defending the rights of animals, using her poetry and prose to express her belief that animals are capable of both compassion* and loyalty.

EXPLANATION   Only sentence *a* offers a more specific explanation of why pit bulls don't deserve their current reputation as vicious dogs. If they were once considered the perfect pet for families with children, then they cannot be vicious by nature.

———————————
*compassion: a feeling for the suffering and pain of others.

General Sentence   1. Despite strong security efforts, pirates have become bolder in their attacks on vessels sailing off the African coast.

Specific Sentences   a. Pirates attack private boats in the hope of taking prisoners who can be held for ransom.

b. Pirates have increased attacks off the coast of East Africa in recent years despite an international flotilla* of warships dedicated to protecting vessels and stopping the pirate assaults.

c. The government of Somalia is barely functioning, which is one of the reasons the waters off the coast of Somalia are a hot spot for pirate attacks.

General Sentence   2. Betty Ford, the wife of President Gerald Ford, died in 2011 and was mourned by many who admired her courage and her commitment to helping others.

Specific Sentences   a. Unlike many first ladies, Betty Ford supported herself before getting married, and she knew the meaning of hard work: She was a women's clothing buyer for a large department store and an assembly-line worker in a frozen-food factory.

b. When Betty Ford had breast cancer and a mastectomy, she broke with tradition and publicly disclosed the details of her surgery because she believed knowing about her experiences would help other women feel less alone in their struggle.

c. In his inaugural address, Gerald R. Ford was the first president to ever credit his wife for his extraordinary political success.

General Sentence   3. Medical research has saved billions of lives through the development of vaccines and medicines that protected against or cured once deadly diseases, but at times medical research has done tragic, even deadly, harm.

Specific Sentences   a. Researchers are reporting that the sexually transmitted disease gonorrhea has become resistant to even the strongest antibiotics, a fact that is causing great concern in the medical community.

b. Professor of surgery at the Jefferson Medical College from 1856 to 1882, Professor Samuel Gross was one of the most famous surgeons of the nineteenth century, and his textbook, *A System of Surgery* (1859), provided the basis for surgeries performed during the Civil War.

---

*flotilla: fleet of small ships.

c. During World War II, researchers looking for treatments infected prisoners in American correctional facilities* with typhoid, dysentery, malaria, and a number of other dangerous diseases.†

SUMMING UP THE KEY POINTS

1. Broad in meaning, general sentences can be understood in different ways. While general sentences are essential to summing up events and experiences in order to make the writer's point, they often require specific sentences for clarification.

2. Specific sentences don't sum up as many events or experiences as general ones do. Their focus is narrower, and the more specific they are, the more they focus on individual people, places, events, ideas, and experiences. As a result, they are less open to different interpretations.

3. General and specific sentences work together to ensure that communication between writer and reader takes place. Without specific sentences to place restrictions on key words and phrases, general sentences can be easily misunderstood because they are open to different interpretations.

4. The general sentence summing up the main idea is called the topic sentence or the main idea statement. The more specific sentences that explain it are called supporting details.

▶ EXERCISE 6   **Connecting General and Specific Sentences**

DIRECTIONS   Read the three specific sentences. Then look at the more general sentences that follow. Put a check in the blank next to the one that could sum up the specific sentences.

EXAMPLE

Specific Sentences   a. Before 1980, most doctors were self-employed, but today more than half are salaried employees who work in medical groups.

b. The number of general practitioners has been steadily declining as more and more medical students choose to become specialists.

---

*facilities: spaces and/or equipment for performing some specific activity.
†From the blog of Leonard Glantz, professor of bioethics at Boston University (http://primr.blogspot.com/2011/01/another-look-at-guatemala-research.html).

    c. Increasingly, doctors are the subject of lawsuits for medical malpractice, and the damages awarded in many of those lawsuits have increased sharply over the last decade.

General Sentences		
_____	1.	The number of women and minorities applying to medical school has increased greatly.
✓	2.	The professional life of physicians has changed dramatically over the past few decades.
_____	3.	Most people who enter medical school do so because they have been influenced by family doctors.

EXPLANATION　　General sentences 1 and 3 are not good choices because the specific sentences do not mention medical schools or why people apply to them. Only sentence 2 is broad enough in meaning to include all three specific sentences.

Specific Sentences　**1.** a. The tradition of using candles at funerals began with the Romans, who used them to frighten away evil spirits.

    b. Tombstones originated as a way of keeping the dead in the underworld.

    c. The original purpose of coffins was to keep the dead safely underground.

General Sentences		
_____	1.	Anthropologists have found evidence that funeral traditions existed during the Neanderthal age (100,000–40,000 BCE).
_____	2.	Different cultures have different ways of mourning their dead.
_____	3.	Many of the modern customs associated with mourning came from a fear of what the dead might do to the living.

Specific Sentences　**2.** a. The citizens of Sparta, a city-state of ancient Greece, were not allowed to become farmers; they were made to train as warriors instead.

    b. Family life in Sparta was severely limited because both boys and girls spent long hours in physical training.

    c. From age seven to age thirty, the boys received instruction in the art of waging war.

General Sentences	_____ 1. The Spartans were obedient to the laws of their land.
	_____ 2. Spartan life was hard and devoted to war.
	_____ 3. Spartan men and women were known for their heroism in war.

Specific Sentences 3. a. During World War II, German invaders destroyed Russia's richest agricultural regions.

b. According to official reports, more than seven million Russians were killed while defending their country against German attacks.

c. Although precise figures are hard to come by, Russia seemed to be the country that had the greatest number of casualties during World War II.

General Sentences	_____ 1. The Russians suffered heavy losses in World War II.
	_____ 2. Russia suffered more than any other country during World War II, largely because it began the war on the side of Adolf Hitler before switching sides in 1941.
	_____ 3. Russia has never recovered from the tragedy of World War II.

Specific Sentences 4. a. During World War II, the U.S. War Department finally approved the training of African-American pilots.

b. In 1941 Benjamin O. Davis Jr. became the first African American to lead a squadron of pilots.

c. President Franklin D. Roosevelt's Executive Order 8802 required employers in defense industries to make jobs available "without discrimination* because of race, creed* or color."

General Sentences	_____ 1. For many African Americans, World War II offered a chance to break down racial barriers.
	_____ 2. During World War II, racial violence broke out on several military bases.
	_____ 3. When they returned home, many African-American veterans of World War II were shocked to discover that they were still being treated as second-class citizens.

---

*discrimination: the act of showing prejudice in favor of or against a particular group.
*creed: set of beliefs, religious beliefs.

✔ **CHECK YOUR UNDERSTANDING**

1. What's the function of general sentences, and why is it a good idea to follow them with more specific sentences?

_____

_____

_____

2. General sentences summing up the main idea are called _____

_____ . The more specific sentences that support them are called _____

_____ .

Recognizing Different Levels of General and Specific Sentences

As you can probably guess, writers don't alternate, or go back and forth, between general and specific sentences in any rigid pattern. Sometimes they introduce an idea with a series of general sentences before switching to a more specific illustration or explanation. At other times, they might start an explanation with one general sentence and make each succeeding sentence slightly more specific.

Look, for example, at the following diagram. It shows you how a writer moves an explanation forward from the very general to the very specific, with a series of increasingly specific sentences about temperament in artists.

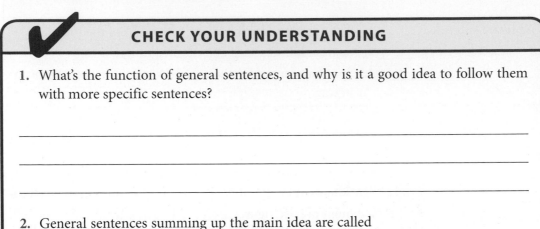

Based on sentence 1, the reader can assume that the writer is making a point about all artists, from sculptors to musicians.

By sentence 2, the reader can eliminate people who work in the fine arts, painting, architecture, etc.

Sentence 3 reduces possible interpretations even further. The author has one particular popular entertainer in mind.

1. Many artists are as famous for their temperament as they are for their talent.

2. Popular entertainers are no exception to this rule.

3. Super-talented rapper and singer-songwriter Nicki Minaj has made headlines more than once for letting her temper get the best of her.

Sentence 4 is even more specific than sentence 3. It focuses on defining what the author means by "letting her temper get the best of her."

Sentences 4 and 5 are equally specific. Both help explain how the rapper has let temper "get the best of her."

4. In 2011, in the space of a few months, Minaj's maid and her facialist accused her of having screaming temper tantrums.

5. When the singer felt the sting of criticism on Twitter, she retaliated by closing her account.

In this case, the writer becomes increasingly specific in order to explain the point of the opening general sentence. However, it's also possible to do the reverse. Writers sometimes build up to a larger, more general point by listing a series of more specific sentences:

Specific Sentences

1. In Brazil's celebration of Carnival, there are samba contests, with all the dancers wearing brightly colored costumes dripping in sequins and feathers.

2. In Italy, Carnival is the big winter festival, celebrated with colorful parades, but also with private parties and balls.

3. In the Netherlands, Carnival is the last chance to eat and drink before Easter, and much of the celebrating is done indoors in pubs, or bars.

4. In Croatia, the celebration of Carnival did not get started until 1982, but it is now an established tradition, with face masks being an essential part of the celebration.

5. The festival of Carnival is celebrated all across the Caribbean with steel-band music playing a huge role in the outdoor festivities.

General Statement

6. Carnival, once mainly a Christian tradition, has lost many of its religious associations, but it is still celebrated around the world, with each country adding its own individual flavor.

General and specific sentences can be combined in different ways. How they combine depends on the author's topic, purpose, and audience. What's important is that you, the reader, keep track of how and why the writer shifts back and forth between different levels of generality.

Why Recognizing Shifts in Level Is Important

As you read, you certainly don't have to make written diagrams of the sentences to indicate when the author is shifting from general to specific. But you do have to notice where sentences become more general or more specific. When a writer opens with a general statement and immediately becomes increasingly specific, then the main idea is probably expressed in the first or second sentence of the paragraph, meaning it has a form that looks something like this:

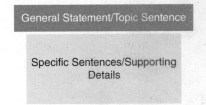

If the writer starts out with several specific sentences that offer background about the topic, then switches to a more general one—which is, in turn, followed by more specific sentences—it's likely that the main idea is somewhere in the middle of a paragraph. When diagrammed, it would have a shape that looks like this:

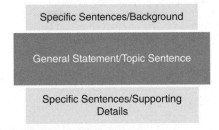

By the same token, a series of sentences that are equally specific often means that the author is building up to a larger point, which, in diagram form, would look something like this:

Specific Sentences/Supporting Details

General Statement/Topic Sentence

Overall, recognizing the relationships between general and specific sentences in writing is one of the main ways readers can follow the writer's train of thought. It's also one of the ways readers decide whether information is essential or not. But we'll talk more about that in later chapters.

SUMMING UP THE KEY POINTS

1. Writers combine general and specific sentences in different ways, depending on the subject matter, the kind of information they want to convey, and their purpose or reason for writing.

2. Readers need to be alert to shifts in general and specific language. Noticing when the language shifts can help readers follow the writer's train of thought.

3. Different disciplines are likely to combine general and specific sentences in different ways. Business texts start out general and become more specific. History texts, in contrast, are just as likely to start out specific and become more general.

▶ **EXERCISE 7** **Recognizing Shifts in General and Specific Language**

DIRECTIONS Fill in the accompanying diagrams with the appropriate letters. The letter of the most general sentence goes on the top level. The letter of the most specific sentence goes on the bottom level.

EXAMPLE

a. Among the Kapauku, ownership of many pigs is a sign of wealth and prestige.

b. Among the Kapauku of New Guinea, the wife is the one who cares for and raises the family's pigs, meaning that more wives allows for the raising of more pigs.

c. In our society, a man with more than one wife is likely to get into serious legal trouble, but in other societies, having several wives is considered both legal and desirable.

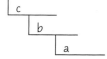

EXPLANATION   Sentence *c* is the most general. It introduces the notion that some societies encourage men to marry more than one woman. Sentence *b* restricts the number of societies being discussed and focuses on the role of wives in caring for pigs. Sentence *a* explains why pigs are important and, by implication, why wives are as well.

1. a. The biggest change in the American workforce involves gender.

    b. The American workforce is changing.

    c. Since 1960, the number of women in the American workforce has more than doubled.

2. a. In mathematics, for example, some words have meanings that are different from their usual ones.

    b. In mathematics, a *curve* is the path between two points, and a curve can be straight rather than rounded.

    c. Changing the context of a word can change its meaning.

3. a. There are many ways to fight insomnia and fall asleep more easily.

    b. The more carbohydrates—sugars, starches, and grains—you eat at night, the more easily you will fall asleep.

    c. Diet can help you fight insomnia.

4. a. In *The Net Delusion*, Morozov shows how the Internet can actually make it easier for repressive* governments to spy on activists who promote democracy.

    b. Not everyone is convinced that the Internet can be used to promote democracy around the world.

---

*repressive: inhibiting or restraining freedom.

c. Journalist Evgeny Morozov has insisted that those in the West need to liberate* themselves from the belief that the Internet can only be used to support democratic freedom.

5. a. While our own culture considers mutilation* of the body to be a sign of a psychiatric disorder, other cultures do not necessarily share this view.

   b. The culture we are born into has a strong influence on how we view or interpret behavior.

   c. In some African cultures, boys entering manhood have six cuts made into their forehead as a mark of their new status.

Three Common General and Specific Patterns in Paragraphs

While essay or novel writers might temporarily leave readers in the dark as they try out new styles of writing or build up suspense, textbook authors take a much more direct approach. Less concerned with originality of style and more concerned with familiarity of form, they want their readers to quickly recognize standard patterns of explanation, making use of them to determine the author's intended meaning.

What follows are three of the most common explanatory patterns in textbooks. Becoming familiar with them will enhance, or improve, your ability to understand textbook material.

Explanatory Pattern 1: Starting Off with the Topic Sentence

Topic Sentence

Specific Details

Textbook authors, particularly those writing business texts, frequently start off paragraphs with the topic sentence or main idea statement. These general sentences can be long, short, or somewhere in between. But they always perform the same function: They introduce the main idea that writers want readers to grasp or share. If someone were to ask

*liberate: free, break away from.
*mutilation: cutting or injuring the body.

you what the paragraph was meant to communicate to readers, you could answer by paraphrasing the opening sentence.

Here's an example of a paragraph, where the opening topic sentence has been underlined. Note how the topic sentence lays out the paragraph's general point. Then the remaining, more specific supporting details take over to answer any questions readers might have about the main idea expressed in the topic sentence.

The word *theory* doesn't get mentioned again. However, the remaining sentences all refer to it by describing it, so we can call "Hilgard's theory of hypnosis" the topic.

The topic sentence tells us that Hilgard's theory emphasized something called "split awareness."

The more specific sentences illustrate "split awareness."

The best-known theory of hypnosis was proposed by Ernest Hilgard (1904–2001), who argued that hypnosis causes a dissociative state, or "split in awareness." To illustrate, he asked hypnotized subjects to plunge one hand into a painfully cold bath of ice water. Subjects told to feel no pain said they felt none. The subjects were then asked if there was any part of their mind that did feel pain. With their free hand, many wrote. "It hurts," or "Stop it, you're hurting me," while they continued to act pain-free. In this split awareness state, one part of the hypnotized person says there is no pain and acts as if there is none. Another part, which Hilgard calls the hidden observer, is aware of the pain but remains in the background. The **hidden observer** is the detached* part of the hypnotized person's awareness that silently observes events. (Coon and Mitterer, *Introduction to Psychology*, 11th ed., p. 194, © Cengage Learning.)

In this case, the topic sentence tells readers that Ernest Hilgard believed hypnosis caused a state of split awareness. The supporting details then answer a key question readers might pose about the topic sentence: What exactly is "split awareness"?

▶ **EXERCISE 8** **Supplying the Topic Sentence**

DIRECTIONS Each item in this exercise gives you the topic and the supporting details. Your job is to come up with a general sentence that opens the paragraph and ties them all together.

EXAMPLE

Topic Myths about Abraham Lincoln

Topic Sentence A great many myths surround the figure of Abraham Lincoln.

*detached: separate and disconnected.

Supporting Details   One long-standing myth has persisted for years: the belief that Lincoln was a poor country lawyer. He wasn't. In the 1850s he successfully and profitably represented two huge companies, the Illinois Central Railroad and the Rock Island Bridge Company. A few gay rights activists have also insisted that Lincoln was homosexual. This claim seems to be flatly contradicted by fact. Lincoln had four children, and, prior to his marriage, occasionally visited prostitutes. Yet another story that doesn't hold up is the belief that Lincoln suffered for years from devastating depression. Given that serious and untreated depression make normal functioning all but impossible, it's hard to believe that Lincoln was deeply depressed. He was, after all, a remarkably effective president, who carried out all the tasks of his office.

EXPLANATION   The topic sentence shown above introduces the topic and tells readers, in general terms, what they need to know *about* the topic. As a topic sentence should, it can also effectively sum up the more specific supporting details that follow it.

Topic   **1.** Snake Handlers

Topic Sentence   _____

_____

Supporting Details   The Bible passage that snake handlers read quite literally comes from the gospel of Mark 16:17–18, where it says, "In my name, shall they cast out devils; they shall speak with new tongues. They shall take up serpents, and if they drink any deadly thing, it shall not hurt them. . . ." Following what they believe to be God's word, snake handlers reach into a box filled with poisonous snakes and pull out a pair of snakes, handling them as a sign of their faith in the Lord. Most states have laws against snake handling, but the practice persists, especially in the region known as Appalachia,† since those who believe in it see themselves as answerable to God's rather than human law. But in truth, snake handlers are following the law of God only as it is expressed in the King James version of the Bible. Many Biblical scholars do not consider the

†Appalachia: The region from southern New York to northern Mississippi that stretches across the Appalachian Mountains.

Snake handlers believe that God will protect them from the snakes' poison; they also keep the snakes starved and dehydrated so the venom is less potent.

© AP Images.

text about taking up serpents to be authentic, and it does not appear in all translations. Skeptics of the practice say there is a reason why snake handlers don't regularly get bitten. The snakes are kept in overcrowded conditions without food or water, so that they are perpetually stressed and weak. Every once in a while, however, a snake handler does die as a result of handling a poisonous snake. In February of 2014, Jamie Coots, a snake handler featured on National Geographic Television, died after a rattlesnake bit him on the hand. Coots refused medical treatment, trusting in the Lord to save him.

Topic   **2.** Hetty Green's financial savvy

Topic Sentence   _____

_____

Supporting Details   Hetty Green was born Hetty Robinson in 1834, during an era when it was believed that women needed men to handle their business affairs because females were, by nature, too soft-headed and -hearted to handle money. Hetty's mother, embarrassed not to have produced a male heir, got rid of Hetty early on, sending the girl off to live with her grandfather, who, like her father, had made his money in whaling. Because Hetty's grandfather couldn't see very well, the young girl read aloud the financial pages of the newspaper, so the old man could keep up with his investments. Meanwhile, little Hetty was learning about the stock market. When her parents died and the bulk of her inheritance went into trusts she had no control over, Hetty started making bets on Wall Street, buying low-priced stocks in companies she thought would do better in time. Almost always, Hetty was right, and her policy of buy low and sell high made her a millionaire many times over. She also had the policy never to borrow, and when major financial panic swept through the country at least four times in her adult life, Hetty was untouched by the financial collapse all around her. For Hetty, financial panic was an opportunity to buy up stocks she would have considered too expensive in better times. When she died in 1916, Hetty was worth $100 million (the equivalent of about $2.5 billion today). By that time, Wall Street, uncomfortable with the idea that a woman could have Hetty's extraordinary financial savvy, had nicknamed her "the witch of Wall Street."

Explanatory Pattern 2: Starting with an Introductory Sentence and a Reversal Transition

Introductory Sentence

Reversal Transition

Topic Sentence

Specific Details

It's certainly true that paragraphs starting with a topic sentence are popular in textbooks. However, that doesn't mean every textbook paragraph opens with a statement of the main idea. In and out of textbooks, paragraphs often open with an introductory sentence.

Introductory sentences are general sentences that provide background or context for the main idea, often mentioning the topic that is the focus of the reading. Following the introductory sentence (or sentences) comes the topic sentence expressing the main idea. Frequently that topic sentence opens with or includes a **reversal transition**. Reversal transitions signal to the reader that the writer's train of thought is about to move away from the point made in the introduction. Here's an example:

The introductory sentence suggests the writer is going to discuss

[1]One need spend only an hour or so in a supermarket of a shopping mall to observe instances of children being physically or verbally abused. [2]*Unfortunately*, such public behavior is but the tip of the iceberg; the

abusive behavior toward children in public places.

Note how the word *unfortunately* has reversed the writer's train of thought, moving it away from "public behavior" and into the "private" sphere.

private reality is much worse. [3]A 2005 PNS survey found that 64 percent of American adults agree that "a good hard spanking" is sometimes necessary in disciplining a child. [4]This is despite evidence that children who get spanked regularly are more likely to cheat or lie or be disobedient at school, to bully others, and have less remorse for what they did wrong. [5]Sadly, child abuse, in private, goes far beyond unnecessary spanking. [6]Abuse may involve burning, scalding, beating, and smothering. [7]In 2006 alone, there were 905,000 reported cases of child maltreatment. (Adapted from Hughes and Kroehler, *Sociology. The Core.* 10th ed., © McGraw Hill, 2010, p. 335.)

While not quite as common as paragraphs that open with a topic sentence, paragraphs like the sample above turn up frequently in textbooks and other kinds of writing. The introductory sentence usually alerts readers to the topic by providing some context or background about the main idea. The introductory sentence, however, gets no further development. Instead, a reversal transition introduces the topic sentence that puts the main idea into words. The supporting details take over from there.

Common Reversal Transitions   But   However   Nevertheless   Unfortunately   Surprisingly

▶ **EXERCISE 9**   **Spotting Explanatory Patterns**

DIRECTIONS   Circle the correct letter to indicate if the topic sentence is the first or second sentence in the paragraph.

1.   [1]A bad economy, reduced funds for animal control, and the despicable* popularity of dog fighting have created a hidden epidemic in many of America's biggest cities, where stray and wild dogs have banded together to survive. [2]Generally, the dogs congregate in areas where buildings have been

———

*despicable: disgusting, unworthy of respect.

abandoned, and they can go unnoticed. [3]Aware that they are often targets of human aggression, the dogs are smart enough to emerge only at night or during bad weather to hunt for food. [4]According to Randy Grim, who runs *Stray Rescue* in St. Louis, Missouri, the problem is huge and growing all the time. [5]Of specific concern is the fact that some of the unneutered strays are giving birth to pups, which then grow up without human contact. [6]Pups born into roaming dog packs are wild animals rather than former pets, which have been let loose or gotten lost. [7]Thus, they are a greater threat to humans and to other dogs. [8]Not surprisingly, the group People for the Ethical Treatment of Animals (PETA) has issued a warning about the growing urban epidemic. [9]PETA has even suggested that euthanizing, or putting the dogs down, is a better fate than their life on the streets. (Source of Information: Will Doig, "The Secret Life of Feral Dogs," *Salon*, retrieved January 14, 2012.)

a. Sentence 1

b. Sentence 2

2. [1]For centuries, earthquakes were considered warnings from the gods. [2]However, it's only in the twentieth century that a fully developed theory, called *plate tectonics*, seemed to adequately explain the cause of earthquakes. [3]According to this theory, the Earth's surface consists of about a dozen giant rock plates, each seventy miles thick. [4]Propelled by unknown forces, the plates are continuously in motion. [5]Sometimes they collide and temporarily lock together. [6]The locking of the plates builds up stress at the plates' edges, causing the rock to fracture. [7]The fracture causes the plates to resume their motion, but the sudden release of energy can also produce an earthquake. [8]The brainchild of Alfred Wegener, the concept of plate tectonics[†] was initially ridiculed when Wegener first proposed it in 1905. [9]Tragically, Wegener died in 1930 without ever knowing that his theory would one day gain the respect of the scientific world.

a. Sentence 1

b. Sentence 2

3. [1]Over the years, the food pyramid—with its six different food groups—has often been criticized for confusing consumers interested in understanding the basics of good nutrition. [2]The people at

---

[†]Wegener laid the groundwork for the theory of plate tectonics by introducing the idea of continental drift, which explained how one big supercontinent turned into seven individual ones.

Food Guide pyramid.

MyPlate graphic.

the U.S. Department of Agriculture, however, seem to have heard the complaints because the food pyramid has disappeared; in its place sits a brand new four-color image of sound nutrition, called MyPlate. [3]MyPlate is divided into four sections: fruits, vegetables, grains, and proteins. [4]Next to the brightly colored plate sits a little circle of dairy. [5]Fats, in contrast to the disgraced and dismissed food pyramid, are nowhere to be seen on the current nutritional symbol. [6]In contrast to the food pyramid, MyPlate's message is clear on sight. [7]Fruits and vegetables should be major players in our daily diet and on an equal footing with proteins and grains. [8]No one who sees My-Plate can ever again think that a quarter-pound cheeseburger is a nutritionally sound meal because it also happens to have a slice of lettuce and tomato sitting on top of the melted cheese.

a. Sentence 1

b. Sentence 2

WEB QUEST
How and where did Alfred Wegener die? Why is the exact day of his death unknown?

_____

_____

_____

Explanatory Pattern 3: Ending with the Topic Sentence

Specific Details

Topic Sentence

Especially at the beginning of individual chapter sections, textbook writers often reverse the typical relationship between general and specific sentences. Instead of starting out with a general sentence, they end with one, after listing the specific supporting details that back it up. Here's an example:

[1]Think of something funny. [2]What is the expression on your face? Now think of something in your past that made you sad. [3]Did your face change? Chances are it did. [4]Undoubtedly, you are aware that certain facial expressions coincide with specific emotions. [5]Now consider this. [6]Could you be equally successful in determining someone's emotional state based on facial expression if that person is from a different culture— say Romania, Sumatra, or Mongolia? [7]In other words, do you believe facial expressions of emotion are universal? [8]Think of the multitude of cultural differences in styles of dress, gestures, personal space, rules of etiquette, religious beliefs, attitudes, and so on. With all of these differences influencing behavior, it would be rather amazing if any human characteristics, including emotional expressions, were identical across cultures. (Adapted from Hughes and Kroehler, *Sociology: The Core*, 10th ed., McGraw-Hill, p. 44.)

This paragraph opens a chapter section discussing a famous study on facial expressions and emotions. Although the specific supporting details at the beginning lay the groundwork for the final topic sentence, it's the remaining paragraphs in the chapter section that would provide the real support.

While you are less likely to see this particular explanatory pattern in the middle of a chapter section, it's very likely to turn up at the beginning, particularly in history, sociology, and psychology texts.

The next time you start reading a chapter section and the first paragraph seems to consist largely of equally specific sentences, pay close attention to the last sentence. It might well be the topic sentence of the paragraph. However, by the time you are through reading the chapter section, it might also turn out to be the main idea of the entire section. But we'll talk more about that in the chapters that follow.

From Reader to Writer Pick a person, an animal, or a location that you know well. Write down all the specific details about that person, animal or place that make it meaningful to you. Then make the last sentence the general statement that expresses the meaning of the details, for instance, "Max was a dog whose loyalty knew no limits" or "The playroom was a space no child could resist."

SUMMING UP THE KEY POINTS

1. Because authors of textbooks know they have to supply readers with a lot of unfamiliar information, they are inclined to take a direct route. They frequently present the main idea, or key point, in a general sentence that either opens the paragraph or arrives right on the heels of the first sentence. Then they follow that sentence with more specific supporting details.

2. A common variation on this pattern is to use specific sentences that build up to the main idea. This pattern of piling up specifics to make a general point is typically found at the beginning of chapter sections and appears in the paragraph that immediately follows the heading.

3. The **main idea** is the key point or message of a paragraph or reading. The **topic** is the subject under discussion; the **topic sentence** or **main idea statement** conveys the paragraph's central point that the author wants readers to understand.

4. **Introductory sentences** pave the way for the main idea by providing background or context. Often, they identify or refer to the topic in the process. Introductory sentences are frequently followed by **reversal transitions** that modify or contradict the opening statement.

5. **Supporting details** further explain the main idea, often answering questions readers might have about the topic sentence.

6. Because their purpose is to inform, textbook writers usually get right to the point. They don't spend time building suspense or creating mood as they might when writing an essay or short story.

READING TIPS

1. If the second sentence in a paragraph explains the first, the opening sentence is probably the topic sentence expressing the main idea.

2. If the second sentence in the paragraph does not follow up on the idea introduced in the first sentence, check to see if the remaining sentences explain the second sentence. If they do, the second sentence is the topic sentence.

3. If the specific sentences in a paragraph seem to be piling up, look closely at the last sentence. It might well be the topic sentence.

▶ **EXERCISE 10**   **Recognizing Common Explanatory Patterns**

DIRECTIONS   Read each paragraph. Then circle the appropriate letter to indicate which sentence is the topic sentence.

EXAMPLE

¹Families have become as diverse as the American population and reflect different traditions, beliefs, and values. ²Within African-American families, for instance, traditional gender roles are often reversed, with women serving as head of the household. ³Kinship bonds often unite several households, as does a strong religious commitment. ⁴In Chinese-American families, both spouses may work and see themselves as breadwinners, but the wife may not have an equal role in decision making. ⁵In Hispanic families, wives and mothers are acknowledged and respected as healers and dispensers of wisdom. ⁶At the same time, they are expected to defer to their husbands, who see themselves as the strong, protective, dominant head of the family. (Adapted from Hales, *An Invitation to Health*, 7th ed., p. 219, © Cengage Learning.)

Topic Sentence   (a.) The first sentence is the topic sentence.
       b.   The second sentence is the topic sentence.
       c.   The last sentence is the topic sentence.

EXPLANATION   The general sentence opening the paragraph introduces the topic, "diversity among American families." This is the subject repeatedly referred to throughout the passage. The first sentence also expresses the author's general point about the topic: Families are as diverse as America itself. The remaining supporting details then provide specific examples of that diversity.

1. ¹Most adults want their love relationships to result in marriage. ²However, U.S. residents are in no hurry to achieve this goal, and the median age at first marriage has been rising for several decades. ³Between 1970 and 2006, the median age for first marriage rose nearly four years for both men and women, from roughly 23 to 27.5 for men and from roughly 21 to 25.5 for women. ⁴This trend is not bad. ⁵Women under age 20 at the time they are first married are three times more likely to end up divorced than women who first marry in their 20s and six times more likely to end up divorced

than first-time wives in their thirties. (Kail and Cavanaugh, *Human Development*, 5th ed., p. 410, © Cengage Learning.)

Topic Sentence

    a. The first sentence is the topic sentence.

    b. The second sentence is the topic sentence.

    c. The last sentence is the topic sentence.

2. [1]Prior to the 1960s, the definitive works on the sexual behavior of humans were the large-scale surveys of Americans' sexual activities published by Alfred Kinsey in the late 1940s and early 1950s. [2]The famous Kinsey Reports, *Sexual Behavior in the Human Male* (1948) and *Sexual Behavior in the Human Female* (1953), asked thousands of men and women about their sexual behavior and attitudes. [3]The topics of the questions ranged from frequency of intercourse to masturbation habits to homosexual experiences. [4]With the publication of the Kinsey Reports, humans suddenly had a measure against which to compare their own sexual lifestyles. [5]The Kinsey Reports are still cited today as a source of statistical information about sexual behavior. (Adapted from Hock, *Forty Studies that Changed Psychology*, 6th ed., Pearson, p. 159.)

Topic Sentence

    a. The first sentence is the topic sentence.

    b. The second sentence is the topic sentence.

    c. The last sentence is the topic sentence.

3. [1]In some Arab countries, where women do not have equal rights, men routinely cut in front of women waiting in line. [2]They see no reason why a man should wait in back of a woman. [3]In Britain and the United States, where men and women are at least officially considered equal, few men would dare cut ahead of a woman who was standing ahead of them in line. [4]In countries like Italy and Spain, where individuality is highly prized above social conformity, lines are little more than an annoyance to be ignored at will. [5]Men and women routinely jostle for the best position in line, and the poor soul who stands and waits his or her turn is thought to be lacking in spirit. [6]Culture clearly has an effect on the behavior of people waiting, or refusing to wait, in a line.

Topic Sentence

    a. The first sentence is the topic sentence.

    b. The second sentence is the topic sentence.

    c. The last sentence is the topic sentence.

4. ¹Among traditional Chinese families, marriage is less a matter of a man getting a wife than of bringing a child-bearer into the household. ²Because marriage has less to do with relations between husband and wife than with those between the husband's family and a daughter-in-law, marriages in traditional Chinese families are almost always arranged, often at an early age, and there is little if any courtship. ³When a boy is six or seven years old, his parents might hire a matchmaker to find a girl who will eventually be an appropriate bride. ⁴Because they believe that the time of a person's birth influences his or her personality and fate, the parents might also enlist the services of a fortune teller to make the appropriate match. . . . ⁵If the fortune teller deems* the girl appropriate, the matchmaker tries to convince the girl's parents to accept the match. ⁶If she is successful, the *bride wealth*, the marriage gifts of the husband's family to the wife's parents, is then negotiated. (Shaffer, *Social and Personality Development*, 6th ed., p. 122, © Cengage Learning.)

Topic Sentence

    a. The first sentence is the topic sentence.

    b. The second sentence is the topic sentence.

    c. The last sentence is the topic sentence.

✔ CHECK YOUR UNDERSTANDING

1. Name and describe the three common ways general and specific sentences are combined in textbook paragraphs.

_____

_____

_____

_____

_____

*deems: considers, judges, evaluates.

_____

_____

2. What's the difference between the introductory sentence and the topic sentence?

_____

_____

3. What role do supporting details play in a paragraph?

_____

_____

4. What is the purpose of textbook writing? _____ How does that
   purpose affect the author's method of writing?

_____

_____

DIGGING DEEPER When Wheelchairs Are Cool *Ben Mattlin*

Looking Ahead The passage on page 140 talked about the ways in which people with disabilities are no longer willing to feel ashamed because their bodies don't fit the norm. Does this writer share or object to that point of view?

Getting Focused The title is obviously meant to get your attention. When you finish, see if you can paraphrase the author's explanation of how wheelchairs can be cool.

1   LAST week, the celebrity gossip site TMZ posted pictures of Justin Bieber in a wheelchair. He was not at a hospital. He was at Disneyland. As everyone knows, Disney patrons in wheelchairs get to cut to the front of the lines. But as a dispute flared over whether this was Mr. Bieber's intent, becoming a trending topic on Twitter, one fact remained unassailable: I was there first.

2   One of the great perks of being in a wheelchair—as I have been since age four—is being able to cut lines. Sometimes people let you go ahead of them at the grocery store. Sometimes theater and sports arena box offices give you discount tickets. When I was a kid, I often got backstage passes. In short, you get to take advantage of others' pity—or at least their desire to keep things simple and not cause a scene. You get treated like a V.I.P. You get treated like Justin Bieber, except without the screaming fans.

3   The teen heartthrob's publicists said that he was just resting an injured knee, not trying to pretend he was, well, like me. But I prefer to think otherwise. After all, they also acknowledged that even without the wheelchair, he would still get to circumvent the endless queues, to avert a riot. The point is that he was not afraid to be seen in a wheelchair, which, to me, is a point for my team.

4   I've never pretended to be in a wheelchair to curry favor, of course, but I've often felt that I can play the disability card for all it's worth. I have, I confess, used it to hustle my kids through Disney lines, even though I knew full well that I wasn't actually going to get on the ride myself. Besides, sometimes you can't help it. People offer you stuff. Strangers smile at you, give you a thumbs-up, pat you on the shoulder and say, "Good for you for being outside today!" (I can never quite decide whether that's complimentary or condescending—or both.)

5   The mantra of disability rights is "no pity." Yet the truth is, taking advantage of one's disability—or rather, of other people's solicitousness—is one of the true joys of life on wheels. When I was a kid, before equal-access laws attempted to level the playing field, I often got into movies free. I never asked for it, but I never refused it either. "I'll just stay in my wheelchair," I sometimes said, as if it were a consolation for not taking an actual seat from a paying customer. (Still, I had my limits. When sweet old ladies offered to buy me candy or a cookie, it was decidedly creepy. I never once said yes.)

6   This kind of cloying generosity was a great source of laughter when I was growing up with spinal muscular atrophy. My older, nondisabled brother and I used to joke that if we were ever orphaned, or simply needed some extra spending money, we could clean up by begging on street corners. He would accost passers-by while I would act, well, as handicapped as possible, moaning and drooling and contorting my face. Sure, this gallows humor was a sort of defense mechanism. But the constant clash between what others thought they knew about me just from glancing at my skinny, floppy, wheelchair-riding limbs and what we actually knew about me—that I was a smart, alert, regular guy who happened to require a lot of assistance—occasioned much familial hilarity.

7   Now I know better, of course. It wasn't really funny. And if I want fairness and equality, I have to pay the price—even if it's full price.

8   But many well-meaning able-bodied folks remain frustratingly ignorant about people with disabilities. We even have a term for it now—"ableism"—though I'm not sure how much it helps. People may know that it's wrong to exclude or underestimate the disabled, but I fear they're rarely clear on exactly what that entails or how to behave. There is still something hopelessly "other" about folks with disabilities. Wheelie Justin may be a hopeful sign for the future, when the very image of disability no longer stigmatizes.

9   I've long believed in disability pride, a.k.a. Crip Cool (there's even the #cripswag hashtag on Twitter). To me, that has never meant being an awe-inspiring overachiever, someone who succeeds despite a disability. Rather, it's the opposite—someone who embraces his or her disability and isn't afraid to show it. Wheelchairs can be fun. Voice-recognition technology is a blast. Vans with automatic ramps are awesome. And don't forget our coveted parking spaces. All of which help mitigate the bad stuff.

10   So go ahead and play disabled. As long as it's done with joy and respect—not to tease or poke fun—I won't be offended. Just don't do it for the freebies, which are harder and harder to find these days anyway. Do it as you do anything else, because you think it's cool.

11   And if Mr. Bieber wants to give me a call, I'd be happy to show him how to pop wheelies. (Ben Mattlin, "When Wheelchairs Are Cool," *The New York Times*, July 31, © 2014, *The New York Times*. All rights reserved. Used by permission and protected by the Copyright Laws of the United States. The printing, copying, redistribution, or retransmission of this Content without express written permission is prohibited.)

Sharpening Your Skills

DIRECTIONS   Answer the questions by circling the letter of the correct response or writing the answer on the blank lines.

Using Context Clues and Word Analysis

1. The word *queues* in paragraph 3 is another way of saying "lines." What does the author mean when he says Justin Bieber wanted to *circumvent* the queues? What parts of the word offer readers a clue to its meaning?

   _____

2. In paragraph 5, the author says "the mantra of disability rights is 'no pity.'" Based on how the word *mantra* is used, which definition makes the most sense?

   a. triumph

   b. advantage

   c. mistake

   d. slogan

3. In the sentence about the mantra of disability rights, the author also talks about taking advantage of people's *solicitousness*. Based on how the word *solicitousness* is used, which definition makes the most sense?

   a. concern

   b. contempt

   c. embarrassment

   d. enthusiasm

4. Based on how the word *cloying* is used at the opening of paragraph 6, which definition makes more sense and why?

   a. affectionate

   b. sickening

   _____

   _____

Recognizing Explanatory Patterns

5. What explanatory pattern do you see at work in paragraph 1?

   a. Pattern 1

   b. Pattern 2

   c. Pattern 3

6. What explanatory pattern do you see at work in paragraph 4?

   a. Pattern 1

   b. Pattern 2

   c. Pattern 3

7. What explanatory pattern do you see at work in paragraph 5?

   a. Pattern 1

   b. Pattern 2

   c. Pattern 3

Following the Author's Train of Thought

8. In paragraph 8, what does the pronoun *it* refer to in this sentence: "We even have a term for it now—"ableism"—though I'm not sure how much it helps"?

   _____

   _____

9. Why does the author mention Justin Bieber? What's the point of referring to the pop idol?

_____

_____

Paraphrasing 10. In your own words, what does it mean to be "Crip Cool"?

_____

_____

From Reader to Writer Begin by defining _ableism_ in your own words. Then explain why the author is annoyed by people afflicted with ableism. (Feel free to refer to paragraph 8 if you need to.)

▶ TEST 1   Reviewing Key Concepts

DIRECTIONS   Answer the following questions by circling the letter of the correct response.

1. General sentences

   a. narrow the range of meanings a reader can apply to a word or phrase.

   b. sum up or comment on a number of different events, people, or ideas.

   c. are always at the very beginning of readings because they express the author's main idea.

2. Specific sentences

   a. are essential to general sentences because they help restrict the range of meanings a reader can apply to the author's words.

   b. are essential to writing because they provide the kind of colorful details that keep the reader interested in what the author has to say.

   c. always follow general sentences because they contain information that is less important.

3. The topic of a paragraph is

   a. the general point the writer wants to communicate to the reader.

   b. the subject most repeatedly referred to in the paragraph.

   c. the key thought introduced in the first sentence of the paragraph.

4. The main idea is

   a. the sentence that sums up the point of the paragraph.

   b. the central thought that the author wants to communicate to readers.

   c. the subject most often referred to in the paragraph.

5. The topic sentence

   a. mentions or refers to the topic without introducing the main idea.

   b. mentions or refers to the topic and makes a point about the topic.

   c. is always the first sentence of a textbook paragraph.

6. Supporting details

   a. restate the main idea in more specific language.

   b. provide examples and illustrations of the main idea.

   c. anticipate and answer questions readers might raise about the main idea.

7. Readers need to notice when the writer shifts between general and specific levels of language because

   a. they will forget the author's original point if they don't notice the specific examples accompanying it.

   b. it's impossible to understand general language without specific details.

   c. it will help them stay in touch with the author's train of thought.

8. Textbook authors usually come straight to the point because

   a. their purpose is to inform.

   b. they want their readers to take them seriously.

   c. they don't want their readers to be distracted by colorful details.

9. The most common location for paragraphs that introduce the topic sentence at the very end is

   a. at the beginning of a chapter section.

   b. in the middle of a chapter section.

   c. at the end of a chapter section.

10. The topic sentence is most likely to be the first sentence in which kind of textbook?

   a. sociology

   b. history

   c. business

▶ **TEST 2**   **Recognizing the Most General Sentence**

DIRECTIONS   In each group of sentences, one is more general than the others. Circle the letter of the most general statement.

1. a. In the African country of Dahomey, music historians were carefully trained to preserve important records.

   b. There was a time when the music of Africa was also the history of the African people.

   c. In the African country of Burundi, singers followed soldiers to war and recorded great actions in song.

   d. Many African countries trained men and women to be living books who could record important events in song.

   e. If the songs contained important information, some African musicians had to learn them in secret.

   f. In the Sudan, singers recited the history of the nation at public gatherings and sang the deeds of great heroes.

2. a. Tornadoes are clouds shaped like funnels: They reach all the way to the ground, doing enormous damage.

   b. Although all storms have fearful aspects, tornadoes are the most frightening.

   c. Winds within the funnel of the tornado can reach speeds of more than several hundred miles per hour.

   d. Tornadoes strike without warning: They seem to come out of nowhere.

   e. Sometimes buildings actually blow up as the tornado passes over them.

   f. The heavy rain and hail that accompany a tornado also do much damage.

3. a. Because of the way he looked, Joseph Merrick (1862–1890) could not go into the street without being mobbed by curious strangers who stared at and ridiculed him.

   b. Before he came under a doctor's care, Joseph Merrick was exhibited in the circus, like an animal.

    c. The victim of a terrible and deforming disease, Joseph Merrick could not sleep like other people; he had to sit up with his heavy head resting on his knees.

    d. The head of the Elephant Man was enormous and misshapen.

    e. Joseph Merrick, also known as the Elephant Man, had a brief and tortured life.

    f. Joseph Merrick never forgot the brutal beatings and terrible humiliation of his life in the circus.

4. a. It took a while for L. Frank Baum, author of *The Wonderful Wizard of Oz*, to find just the right title for his masterpiece.

    b. While the book was in production, Baum changed the title to *From Kansas to Fairyland*.

    c. An author sometimes has great difficulty choosing the title of a book.

    d. When Baum first submitted his manuscript in 1899, it was called *The Emerald City*.

    e. Just before the book appeared in print, Baum changed the title again, this time to *The City of the Great Oz*.

    f. In the end, the book was published in 1900 as *The Wonderful Wizard of Oz*.

5. a. During the American Revolution, British and American spies used a mixture of water and ferrous sulfate to create ink that was invisible until baking soda was brushed over the paper.

    b. There are references to the use of invisible ink in the writing of Pliny the Elder, a Roman general, who, as a military man, had a reason to keep secrets.

    c. Public interest groups have tried to get access to the formula for invisible ink developed in World War I, but the information remains classified.

    d. Many people think that invisible ink is the stuff of fiction, but it's real and has been around for centuries.

    e. In 2008, Habib Ahmed was given a ten-year sentence in Britain for bringing books written in invisible ink into the country.

▶ **TEST 3**   **Clarifying General Sentences**

DIRECTIONS   Read each general sentence. Then circle the letters of the three more specific sentences that support it.

General Sentence   **1.** The German psychologist Hermann Ebbinghaus was the first person to systematically study the process of forgetting.

Supporting Details
  a. One theory of forgetting suggests that we forget when new information interferes with what's previously been learned.

  b. Ebbinghaus spent thousands of hours memorizing nonsense syllables.

  c. After learning the nonsense syllables, Ebbinghaus measured the time it took to forget them.

  d. Another theory of forgetting stresses that we forget whenever we don't intend to remember.

  e. As a result of his research, Ebbinghaus discovered that the greatest memory loss occurs right after learning.

  f. Another memory researcher, A. P. Bumstead, discovered that several learning sessions stretched out over time actually decreased forgetting.

General Sentence   **2.** It's easy to understand why the threat of rabies inspires great fear.

Supporting Details
  a. In its final stages, rabies produces hallucinations.

  b. Few people recover from rabies once symptoms appear.

  c. Rabies has been around a long time; there are references to it as early as 700 BCE.

  d. Once the disease takes hold, the victim can neither stand nor lie down comfortably.

  e. Recently, scientists have improved the treatment for rabies; the new treatment is much less painful than the old.

  f. In the early stages of rabies, a dog is likely to appear tired and nervous; it will try to hide, even from its master.

General Sentence   3. Many people believe that mystery stories are a product of modern times, but the mystery story actually has a long history.

Supporting Details

    a. Historians of the detective story claim to have found elements of the mystery story in the pages of the Bible.

    b. Dorothy Sayers was for many years an enormously popular mystery writer.

    c. Poe's "The Murders in the Rue Morgue," published in 1841, introduced the classic mystery plot of a dead body found in a sealed room.

    d. Mystery historians like to argue about which books may or may not be classified as true mystery stories.

    e. Nineteenth-century authors Charles Dickens and Edgar Allan Poe are often cited as the fathers of the modern mystery.

    f. Raymond Chandler wrote mystery stories so good that literary critics called his crime novels art.

General Sentence   4. Facebook users should be careful about what they post on the social media website.

Supporting Details

    a. Facebook is all too ready to decide for its users what news is important and what news is not.

    b. When Dawnmarie Souza posted her thoughts on her employers at American Medical Response in Connecticut, she was fired.

    c. Facebook has made Mark Zuckerberg one of the richest men in the United States.

    d. When a high school supervisor in Cohasset, Massachusetts, complained about both her students and their parents, she lost her job.

    e. Many employers regularly check out job applicants on Facebook; if the applicant has posted pictures suggesting he or she leads a wild social life, potential employers tend to think twice about hiring that person.

    f. Facebook is more about earning advertising revenue than it is about keeping in touch with friends.

▶ **TEST 4**   **Locating Topic Sentences**

DIRECTIONS   Circle the appropriate letter to identify the location of the topic sentence that sums up the main idea.

1. [1]Textbooks have long taught that the seventeenth-century English settlement at Jamestown, Virginia, struggled and almost perished because the colonists didn't like hard work. [2]However, when scientists analyzed the rings of Jamestown cypress trees during a 1998 climate study, they found that the trees' growth was significantly stunted between 1606 and 1612. [3]Based on this information, the study's authors argued that when Jamestown was founded in 1607, a lack of rain caused fresh water supplies to dry up and parched corn to turn brown on the stalk. [4]The subsequent food shortage would have aggravated relations between the colonists and the Powhatan Indians, who were also forced to compete for scarce resources. [5]In 1608, Captain John Smith noted in his journal that the Indians would not trade corn for colonists' goods because that year's crop had been poor, and the Indians did not have enough for themselves. [6]Based on current research, it now seems possible that a drought, rather than laziness or greed, was to blame for Jamestown's disappearance. (Source of information: Jeffery L. Sheler, "Rethinking Jamestown," *Smithsonian*, January 2005, pp. 48–56.)

Topic Sentence   a. first sentence

b. second sentence

c. last sentence

2. [1]Fraternities have been around practically since the first university was founded. [2]Fraternity hazing, however, has never before been so brutal or so deadly; with good reason, schools are cracking down on the practice. [3]After a nineteen-year-old student died during a hazing episode that included mock kidnapping, public humiliation, and forced drinking, Cornell University banned all fraternity pledging. [4]New York State's Binghamton University halted all pledging in the spring of 2012 because of an "alarmingly high number of serious hazing complaints." [5]In 2011, the parents of Michael Starks, a nineteen-year-old student who died during a hazing ceremony, sued Utah State University and won. [6]But the parents' goal was not money. [7]Their goal was to get the university to publicize the dangers of hazing and the binge drinking that accompanies it. [8]The

university has agreed to do so. [9]After a drum major at Florida's A&M University was found dead from a brutal beating endured during a hazing ritual, the school introduced stricter controls over fraternity hazing.

Topic Sentence

a. first sentence

b. second sentence

c. last sentence

3. [1]To persons living in the industrialized countries, measles is a minor childhood disease. [2]Yet among children in developing countries, measles is a major cause of death. [3]Measles accounts for 6.3 percent of deaths among children under age five in the developing nations. [4]Deaths due to measles occur when children, already weakened by malnutrition and poor living conditions, become further weakened by measles. [5]Their bodies' ability to fight disease diminishes, leaving them susceptible to other potentially deadly diseases. [6]However, rates of measles have declined almost by half since 1990, following a worldwide World Health Organization (WHO) measles vaccination campaign. [7]Vaccination campaigns, though, have had far less effect in Africa due to the continent's ongoing and severe economic problems. (Adapted from Weitz, *The Sociology of Health, Illness and Health Care*, 5th ed., p. 329, © Cengage Learning.)

Topic Sentence

a. first sentence

b. second sentence

c. last sentence

4. [1]Men who are quick to express anger are more likely to develop heart disease than men who are calmer and more relaxed. [2]Hostility also appears to double the risk of recurrent heart attacks in men (but not in women). [3]Research has linked hostility to increased cardiac risk factors and to decreased survival in men with coronary artery disease if they are below the age of sixty-one. [4]Hostility has also been linked to an increased risk of heart attack and abnormal heart rhythms. [5]In a study that tracked more than 1,000 physicians for thirty-six years and took into account other physical and psychological risk factors, the angriest men were likely to suffer heart attacks by fifty-five and three times more likely to develop cardiovascular

disease. [6]At least where men are concerned, anger and hostility have both short- and long-term consequences for the heart. (Adapted from Hales, *An Invitation to Health*, p. 279, © Cengage Learning.)

Topic Sentence
a. first sentence
b. second sentence
c. last sentence

5. [1]Only in modern times have most people married for love. [2]In the "good old days," most married for money and labor—marriage was an economic arrangement between families and love was not an issue. [3]The key questions were how much land or wealth did the man have? [4]How large a dowry would the bride bring to the spouse? [5]Emotional attachments were of no importance to parents in arranging marriages and neither the bride nor the groom expected emotional fulfillment from marriage. [6]The most common emotions couples expressed seem to have been resentment and anger. [7]Not only was wife beating commonplace but so was husband beating. [8]And when wives beat their husbands, it was the husband, not the wife, who was likely to be punished by the community because he had shamed the village by not controlling his wife properly. (Adapted from Stark, *Sociology*, 10th ed., pp. 370–71, © Cengage Learning.)

Topic Sentence
a. first sentence
b. second sentence
c. last sentence

4 Getting to the Point of Paragraphs

"Understanding depends on mutual empathy, on reader and writer appreciating each other's task."

—LARRY WRIGHT, PROFESSOR, PHILOSOPHER, AND AUTHOR OF *CRITICAL THINKING: AN INTRODUCTION TO ANALYTICAL READING AND REASONING*

Chapter 4 reviews and enlarges what you learned about paragraphs in Chapter 3 (pp. 163–173). It further describes and illustrates the kinds of explanatory patterns textbook writers use when combining general and specific sentences in paragraphs. The chapter also gives you an additional strategy for dealing with paragraphs where you can't quite get a handle on the author's meaning, despite your understanding of how general and specific sentences relate to one another.

Additional Ways Authors Introduce Topic Sentences

As you know from Chapter 3, authors sometimes use an introductory sentence to get readers ready for the arrival of the main idea. What you might not realize is that these introductions often consist of more than one sentence. In the following paragraph, notice how

two sentences prepare readers for the main idea that is the true focus
of the paragraph:

[1]For the past twenty years, it's been claimed that low self-esteem
causes numerous social and psychological ills. [2]Think well of yourself
and you will behave better was the reigning theory. [3]**Yet, as it turns
out, exaggerated self-esteem seems to be more prevalent* and more
problematic than low self-esteem.** [4]In a wide range of studies focused
on self-esteem, participants consistently gave themselves higher ratings than they gave others. [5]They also overestimated their personal
contribution to team efforts; exaggerated their ability to control life's
events; and made unrealistic predictions about their future success.
[6]Participants in the studies also tended to get angry when things did
not turn out as expected. [7]Similar research on self-image also shows
that many people overestimate their intellectual and social skills. [8]What
was particularly interesting about this tendency was that those who
had the poorest intellectual and social skills were the most likely to
overrate their performance in both areas. [9]For instance, researchers
Justin Kruger and David Dunning found that college students with the
lowest scores on tests of logic and grammar generally assumed that
their scores would be among the highest. [10]Interestingly enough, when
these same students received training in grammar and logic, their self-
assessments became less confident and more realistic. (Adapted from
Brehm, Kassin, and Fein, *Social Psychology*, 5th ed., p. 138, © Cengage Learning.)

"That Was Then, This Is Now" Introduction

The above sample paragraph illustrates a typical textbook pattern authors
use to prepare readers for the main idea. The introductory sentences tell
readers what has been thought in the past *before* introducing them to
more current thinking on the topic. The description of the current thinking then becomes the true point of the paragraph.

You can confirm that the discussion of the current thinking is the
true point of the paragraph by a quick glance at the supporting details.
As you can see above, the details provide evidence for the current claim
that exaggerated self-esteem causes more trouble than low self-esteem.
If the more traditional concept, or idea, about self-esteem was the point
of the paragraph, the supporting details would tell readers more about
low self-esteem and its supposed effect on behavior and performance.

---

*prevalent: widespread.

When an opening sentence tells you what's been thought in the past *or* what most people are inclined or ready to believe, it's a strong signal that the opening sentence is *not* the topic sentence. Writers usually use these kinds of statements purely as introductions. They then follow up with more up-to-date or more evidence-based thinking that is the real point of the paragraph.

From Reader to Writer Write a paragraph that starts off something like this: "There was a time when I thought that _____ ." (You can substitute any number of words for *thought*, e.g., *believed, argued, insisted*, etc.) Fill in the blank by describing your previous thinking about any topic you choose, i.e., friendship, pets, politics, astrology, religion.

Then use a reversal transition to introduce a sentence explaining how your thinking on the subject has changed. Follow that sentence with a specific description of the event or experience that changed your mind. Here's a sample opening: "I used to think that spending time on Facebook was a total waste of time with no effect on real life. But now I know that Facebook can have a huge impact on the real world."

Line Graphs Illustrating "Then and Now"

Readings that describe how changes have taken place over time often include line graphs to support that point. Take, for instance, the following paragraph about the development of a vaccine for measles. It describes the effect the vaccine had on public health, and that point is echoed by the graph that follows.

[1]Although it was described at least two centuries prior, measles made its first appearance in print during the 9th century when a Persian physician wrote an account of the disease. [2]It was centuries, however, before anyone knew what caused it. [3]Measles, as the Scottish physician Francis Home demonstrated, was the product of an infectious agent. [4]It then took a few more centuries before the virus causing measles was isolated in 1954. [5]Less than ten years later, in 1963, a vaccine was made available to the public. [6]Then in 1968 a new and improved vaccine was distributed, and by 1980, measles was no longer a general threat to public health. [7]It had been a long time coming, but the measles vaccine had all but wiped out what had once been a plague.

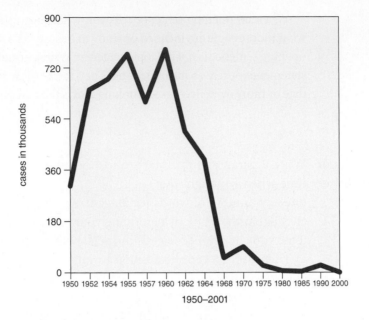

Figure 4-1 Measles United States 1950–2000
The first vaccine was available in 1963 and an improved vaccine appeared in 1968.
Measles seemed to be wiped out once the vaccine was widely distributed.

(Source of data: http://www.historyofvaccines.org/content/graph-us-measles-cases*)

*Figures for the individual years and disease rates are approximate.

When Lines on a Graph Double Up

Sometimes a paragraph describing how a change has taken place over time will track two groups, either to show that both have experienced a similar trend; or else, to indicate how much the two groups differ. When two groups are involved in the discussion, the accompanying graph will show two lines, each with its own set of peaks and valleys.* When a graph contains more than one line, it will have a **legend**, or key, to the various data plotted on the graph. See, for example, the graph on page 195. Note how the legend in the graph on page 195 identifies what group each color represents.

[1]There was a time when majoring in education was considered a smart move. [2]It was a guarantee of a safe and solid career that offered professional satisfaction and financial security. [3]As a result, many undergraduates made education their major. [4]Equally valuable was a Master's degree in Education. [5]It guaranteed not just an increase in knowledge but an increase in pay. [6]Yet as almost anyone working in education

Notice how sentence 6 gives the reader a clear transitional signal, telling readers a big change is coming up.

*Obviously, line graphs can track more than two groups as well.

today will tell you, that time has passed. [7]The current crop of students, both undergraduate and graduate, is much less inclined to think about becoming a teacher (see Figure 4-2). [8]According to Richard M. Ingersoll, a professor of education and sociology at the University of Pennsylvania, "teacher-bashing" is one powerful reason why graduate and undergraduate enrollment in education has suffered a severe decline. [9]Teaching is, in Professor Ingersoll's opinion, a "beleaguered occupation." [10]However, in addition to teacher bashing, budget cuts, struggles over tenure, and the increasing use of standardized testing to measure learning and teacher effectiveness have all made becoming a teacher a much less inviting prospect than it once was. (Source of Quotations: Rebecca Koenig, "Education-Degree Programs, Once Popular, Take a Nosedive," *The Chronicle of Higher Education*. Last accessed October 11, 2014.)

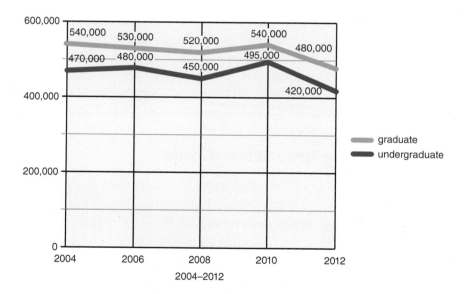

Figure 4-2   Enrollments in Educational Degree Programs Slide

(Source of data: Rebecca Koenig, "Education-Degree Programs, Once Popular, Take a Nosedive," *The Chronicle of Higher Education*. Last accessed October 11, 2014.)

How to Read Line Graphs ●	1. Make sure you know what's being measured. This information usually appears in the text when the figure is referred to e.g., "Conflict between Native-Americans and the U.S. Military decreased during the years of the Civil War and began to steadily increase as soon as it was over. See Figure 2-1." In addition, the title and caption usually indicate what information the graph is meant to illustrate.

2. Check the horizontal or X axis going from left to right in order to determine the amount of time covered.

3. Check the Y axis going from top to bottom to understand the increases or decreases over time.

4. Pay particularly close attention to the peaks and valleys created by the line or lines on the graph. The spikes and dips show you, in the most direct way, the effect of time on whatever is being measured. In our first sample graph (Figure 4-1), it's clear that hundreds of thousands of people were struck down by measles prior to the licensing of a vaccine. However, the steep decline in the line of the graph indicates a dramatic change once the vaccine had been distributed. Line graphs are particularly good at displaying such huge changes over time.

5. If the graph uses more than one line to help readers visualize the information the graph describes, read the *legend* carefully to make sure you know what each line represents. In our second example, the legend is a simple one indicating which color charts the enrollment of graduate versus undergraduate students.

Moving Toward the Middle

Specific details

Topic sentence

Specific details

As you might expect, introductions in paragraphs aren't limited to two sentences either. In fact, introductions can get so long they push the topic sentence closer and closer to the middle of the paragraph. This is especially true when the author wants to give you some history or background related to the topic or main idea prior to introducing the main idea.

Note, too, that when main ideas start moving way beyond the first sentence, writers frequently use the kind of reversal transitions already introduced in Chapter 3. (A more complete list of reversal transitions follows.) Such reversal transitions are the writer's way of saying to readers, "I'm shifting gears now. Here comes the real point of the paragraph."

In the following paragraph, for instance, the reversal transition *however* appears in the fourth sentence to tell readers that the writer is getting to the real point of the paragraph. From this point on, the emphasis is not just on Frankenstein's monster but also on Mary Shelley, whose creation of the monster is the paragraph's topic.

[1]Most people know the gruesome story of Baron Victor Frankenstein, the arrogant doctor who created a living creature from the bodies of

Dr. Frankenstein's monster.

corpses, only to see his creation turn murderous. [2]The story has been told and retold. [3]It has also been the subject of numerous films, and most people are familiar with the tale, so much so that we use allusions, or references, to Frankenstein's monster to describe a good idea gone very wrong. [4]**What many people don't know, however, is that the chilling story of Dr. Frankenstein and his creature was written by a nineteen-year-old newlywed named Mary Shelley.** [5]As a young bride, Shelley liked to take part in storytelling competitions with her husband, the poet Percy Bysshe Shelley, and his friend and fellow poet George Gordon Byron. [6]On one particularly long evening in 1816, Byron suggested that everyone compose a ghost story. [7]In response to Byron's suggestion, Mary Shelley spent the night writing and was ready the next day with the story of Dr. Frankenstein, the man who constructed a creature from body parts and galvanized* it into action. [8]When she read it aloud, everyone agreed Shelley's story was the best by far, and by 1818 she had published it as a novel.

Topic sentences in the middle or close to the middle of a paragraph are not as common as topic sentences at the beginning. But they do exist. Thus, you should be prepared for this variation on the more standard explanatory pattern of a one- or two-sentence introduction followed by a statement of the main idea.

You already know some reversal transitions from Chapters 2 and 3. What follows is a more complete and extensive list:

Reversal and Contrast Transitions ●		
	Be that as it may	On the other hand
	But	Regardless
	Conversely	Still
	Despite that fact	That fact notwithstanding
	Even so	Tragically
	However	Unfortunately
	In contrast	When in fact
	In spite of	While that might be true, it's also true that
	Nevertheless	
	Nonetheless	Yet
	On the contrary	Yet as it turns out

*galvanized: forced into action with electricity; caused to act, produced a strong reaction.

Because transitions can sometimes be full sentences, be on the lookout for transitional sentences like the following:

Sample Transitional Sentences ●	Things did not turn out as planned. But it was not to be. But that didn't happen. Then something strange occurred. The challenge wasn't long in coming. However, one thing is clear. Things did not stay that way, however.

READING TIP

If a paragraph opens with a series of general sentences, but only one general sentence gets the support of more specific details, the sentence getting the support is the topic sentence.

WEB QUEST

Mary Shelley called her novel *Frankenstein; or, The Modern Prometheus.* According to Greek mythology, who is Prometheus, and why did Shelley link her novel to this figure from Greek mythology? What's the connection?

_____

_____

_____

_____

Doubling Up on Topic Sentences

To make doubly sure that their readers get the main idea, writers sometimes use two topic sentences, making their point in the first *and* the last sentence of the paragraph. Here's an example:

The career of George Smith Patton Jr., the much-decorated four-star army general, stalled because he didn't know how to control his

Topic sentence

Specific details

Topic sentence

temper. During World War II, in August of 1943, Patton visited ailing and wounded soldiers in two separate army hospitals. On each visit he publicly slapped a soldier who complained about losing the nerve to fight. Patton viewed the men with contempt and insisted that "real" soldiers should not have to look at gutless cowards afraid of the battle field. Although Patton thought his behavior perfectly appropriate, his commanding officer, Dwight D. Eisenhower, did not. Eisenhower made Patton publicly apologize to the hospital staff and to the men themselves. Eisenhower also made sure that Patton never rose any higher on the ladder of military command. **Thanks to his uncontrollable temper, George S. Patton's brilliant military career stalled and never got re-started.**

If a paragraph says much the same thing in the first sentence and the last, you can be sure that the idea expressed in those two sentences is the main idea.

READING TIP

Any time you think you've found the topic sentence, you can confirm your guess by checking out how the remaining sentences relate to your presumed topic sentence. Do they explain it more precisely? Do they give reasons why it's true or provide examples to make it clearer? If the answer to questions like these is yes, then you've found the topic sentence. If the answer is consistently no, it's time to re-think your topic sentence.

▶ EXERCISE 1   Recognizing Topic Sentences and Reversal Transitions

DIRECTIONS   Some of the following paragraphs open with the topic sentence. Some don't. Identify the topic sentence by writing the number of the sentence in the blank. If you see a reversal transition, circle it.

1. ¹Most Americans are accustomed to thinking that lie detectors, because they are machines, can, without error, separate the guilty from the innocent. ²But, in fact, lie detectors can and do make mistakes. ³For one thing, those who administer the tests are not necessarily qualified

experts. [4]Many states don't employ licensed examiners trained to read and interpret lie detector printouts. [5]In addition, many subjects react to taking a lie detector test by becoming anxious. [6]As a result, their bodies behave as if the subjects were lying even when they are telling the truth. [7]Unfortunately, some people are smart enough to use relaxation techniques or tranquilizers to remain calm when they are actually telling a pack of lies.

Topic Sentence _____

2. [1]Charles Loring Brace was a young man with good intentions. [2]Arriving in New York City to complete his training as a minister, Brace was confronted by the sight of children roaming the streets in packs. [3]Some had homes. [4]Some didn't. [5]What they all had in common was poverty. [6]Even if they had parents who worked, there just wasn't enough money to keep the children fed, never mind in school and off the streets. [7]Brace's solution was to, in his words, get the children "utterly out of their surroundings and . . . send them away to kind Christian homes in the country." [8]The method Brace chose to accomplish his goal was the now infamous *orphan trains,* which, between 1854 and 1929, picked around 100,000 children up from the streets—even those who actually had living parents—and packed them off to rural areas, where they were supposed to get the fresh air and attentive, loving care they did not get at home. [9]While some of the children who rode the orphan trains did fare better as a result[†] of the move, many did not see much improvement in their lives. [10]After stepping off the trains and arriving at their new "home," the children would be looked over by those thinking to adopt them and taken to a new home if they were strong or pretty enough. [11]But no one involved in the process made sure that the people taking the children really meant them well. [12]Often, those adopting were looking for youthful farm hands or housekeepers, who could be worked hard and couldn't complain because, once the orphan trains departed, the children had nowhere else to go. (Source of quotation: http://www.pbs.org/wgbh/amex/orphan/. Last accessed September 9, 2014.)

Topic Sentence _____

[†]Two boys from the orphan trains, Andrew Burke and John Brady, ended up becoming governors of North Dakota and Alaska, respectively.

3. [1]When Anne Sullivan first arrived to teach her young pupil, six-year-old Helen Keller, she found a little girl who could not see, hear, or speak. [2]Cut off from the world because she was deaf, mute, and blind, Keller reacted like a frightened animal. [3]She would try to bite, scratch, and kick those who came too close. [4]But Anne Sullivan changed all that. [5]Playing the roles of teacher and friend, Sullivan transformed Keller's life, revealing to the little girl the true scope of her talents. [6]It wasn't long before Keller, with Sullivan as her guide, could name the things and people she saw around her. [7]She could even use those names to communicate with others. [8]Over time, and with Sullivan's help, Keller learned to read Braille, the system of writing for the visually impaired. [9]She read Braille in English, then in Latin, Greek, French, and German. [10]With Sullivan's assistance, Keller also learned sign language. [11]In the end, she proved the truth of the first words she spoke with Anne Sullivan's help, "I'm not dumb."[1]

Topic Sentence   _____

4. [1]The history of horror films is almost as long as the history of movie-going. [2]The first movie theater opened in 1905. [3]But it didn't take long, only five years, for J. Searle Dawley, along with producer Thomas Edison, to shoot the 1910 movie *Frankenstein* about Mary Shelley's man-made monster. [4]Ten years later, German directors Carl Boese and Paul Wegener returned to the subject of man-made monsters in *The Golem*, a classic horror film highly regarded to this day. [5]*The Golem* tells the story of a rabbi who created and brought to life a giant creature made of clay. [6]The 1919 film *The Cabinet of Dr. Caligari*, sometimes referred to as "the granddaddy of all horror films," portrayed a sadistic* doctor and played in what was to become a classic horror setting, an asylum.* [7]By 1922, famed director F. W. Murnau filmed the horror masterpiece, *Nosferatu*, a brilliant interpretation of the Bram Stoker novel *Dracula*. [8]But if the Germans owned the horror film in the twenties, it was the

---

[1]You can see videos of Keller and Sullivan on YouTube.
*sadistic: enjoying the inflicting of pain.
*asylum: in this context, an institution for the mentally ill; also used in the context of "seeking asylum," or safety from harm.

Americans who took over the genre* in the thirties. ⁹The thirties saw the arrival of films like *Dracula, The Mummy, Frankenstein, The Phantom,* and *Dr. Jekyll and Mr. Hyde,* all of them box office blockbusters, suggesting that movie-goers and horror films were made for one another. ¹⁰Judging by the popularity of modern horror films like *Paranormal Activity, Saw, Shutter Island,* and *The Babadook,* they still are.

Topic Sentence _____

5. ¹Artists from Mark Twain to Norman Rockwell have used the image of kids swimming in a river to suggest the ease and joy of childhood. ²That image certainly makes sense because kids, more than adults, do take to the river during summertime. ³Particularly in areas where the income level is not high, swimming in the river is the only alternative to the sweltering heat. ⁴Unfortunately, in some cases, the decision to jump into the river on a hot day can prove deadly. ⁵Although health officials report only a few cases per year, children sometimes die after a river swim, because they have come into contact with *Naegleria fowleri,* a deadly amoeba that destroys the brain. ⁶The amoeba enters the swimmer's body through the nose and finds its way to the brain, where it starts eating brain cells. ⁷By the time it's through, the victim cannot function normally, showing symptoms like confusion, loss of balance, and hallucinations. ⁸Most victims die within seven days after the symptoms start. ⁹The primary treatment for an attack is an antifungal medication that is injected into the veins and the brain. ¹⁰But so far, only one victim has survived the onset of symptoms thanks to the use of medication. ¹¹Although coming in contact with *Naegleria fowleri* is a rare occurrence, the results are so deadly, the Centers for Disease Control says that anyone swimming in freshwater ponds and rivers throughout the summer months should use nose clips.

Topic Sentence _____

_____

*genre: a particular category of film or literature with specific characteristics that identify it.

READING TIPS

1. To check that you have truly identified the topic sentence of a paragraph, turn the topic sentence into a question, e.g., What mistakes do lie detectors make? If the supporting details provide an answer, you have correctly identified the topic sentence.

2. If a reversal transition opens the second or third sentence of a paragraph, there's a very good chance the sentence starting with the reversal transition is the topic sentence.

From Reader to Writer

Charles Loring Brace, introduced in paragraph 2, had this to say about his decision to "help" the children of the poor: "The human soul is difficult to interfere with. You hesitate how far you should go." Start by quoting Brace, then write a paragraph or two explaining how far Brace went in his attempts to aid homeless children. Look over the following website (or others like it) so that you include specific details in your description of the orphan trains: http://www.kancoll .org/articles/orphans/or_hist.htm.

When you finish your description, explain why you think Brace went too far or not far enough in his attempts to save "the human soul."

SUMMING UP THE KEY POINTS

1. Writers don't necessarily limit themselves to one introductory sentence per paragraph. Often they want to provide their readers with more background and context, so they enlarge the introduction and push the topic sentence deeper into the paragraph.

2. Writers who do this are likely to introduce the topic sentence with a reversal transition like *however*, *but*, *yet*, or *unfortunately*.

3. Frequently, writers start paragraphs with introductions that identify past thinking about the topic. Or they identify what's traditionally assumed about the topic. Such introductions pave the way for the author to introduce a main idea that differs significantly from earlier thinking or traditional beliefs.

4. Writers sometimes need to provide so much background that the main idea doesn't get expressed until the middle of the paragraph.

5. Writers who discuss how an idea, attitude, or behavior has changed over time often use line graphs to support their main idea.

Introductory Questions Can Replace Introductory Sentences

Particularly in textbooks, writers are inclined to use introductory questions as much as introductory sentences. Like introductory sentences, **introductory questions** introduce the topic and pave the way for the main idea. In textbooks, introductory questions can appear in the heading of a chapter section. However, they are even more likely to open the paragraph. This is especially true for psychology texts, for instance:

Topic Sentence

[1]What determines our long-term satisfaction, and why are some of us happier than others? [2]**Seeking the roots of happiness, Ed Diener and his colleagues (1999) reviewed years of research and found that there are three key predictors of happiness.** [3]The first is social relationships: People with an active social life, close friends, and a happy marriage are more satisfied than those who lack these intimate connections. [4]The second is employment status. [5]Regardless of income, employed people are happier than those who are out of work. [6]Finally, people who are physically healthy are happier than those who are not. (Adapted from Brehm, Kassin, and Fein, *Social Psychology*, 5th ed., p. 536, © Cengage Learning.)

This paragraph illustrates a common way writers use questions to point the way to the topic sentence. Notice how the question paves the way for the topic by pointing readers in the direction of "happiness," preparing them for the actual paragraph topic, the roots or predictors of happiness. Then the topic sentence arrives to provide a general answer to the two-part opening question. After that, the supporting sentences provide the specific details that fully answer the opening questions.

The Answers Don't Always Arrive Right After the Question

When a question opens a paragraph, it's very common for the answer to come right after the question and for that answer to be the topic sentence. But textbook authors, who are especially fond of making a question either the heading or the first sentence, sometimes delay the answer to their question. Here's an example:

Opening Question

The second sentence does not provide the answer.

[1]What is the difference between civil and criminal law? [2]The distinction between civil and criminal actions is important to understanding the legal

The third sentence, however, does answer the opening question.

process. [3]**Civil actions** involve a conflict between private persons and/or organizations whereas **criminal law** applies to offenses against the public order and entails a specified range of punishments. [4]Typical of cases involving civil law are those involving disputes over contracts, claims for damages, and divorce cases. [5]In a civil case, the person bringing the suit is called the *plaintiff*, and the person being sued is the *defendant*. [6]Acts that are in violation of criminal law are specifically detailed in government statutes. [7]The party demanding legal action is called the *prosecution*, and the person being prosecuted is called the *defendant*. [8]Most of these cases arise in state courts, although there is a growing body of federal criminal law dealing with such issues as kidnapping, tax evasion, and the sale of narcotics. (Adapted from Gitelson, Dudley, and Dubnick, *American Government*, 10th ed., p. 352, © Cengage Learning.)

If the sentence immediately following an opening question does not provide the answer to that question, keep looking. The answer might well be delayed by a sentence or two. If by the end of the paragraph, you still haven't identified the answer, then you might have to infer, or come up with, your own. But we will talk more about that in Chapter 8.

READING TIP   If the writer opens a paragraph with a question, chances are good that the answer is also the main idea. There are times, too, when the question combines with the answer to make up the main idea.

▶ **EXERCISE 2**   **Recognizing Topic Sentences**

DIRECTIONS   Write the number of the topic sentence in the blank following each paragraph.

1. [1]Why do we dream? [2]The truth is no one really knows for sure why we dream; all we currently have are different theories. [3]Some evidence suggests that dreaming may help us consolidate* old memories with the new learning that occurred during the day. [4]Yet research for these claims is inconsistent. [5]Dreams may have other functions as well. [6]Ernest Hartmann, a leading dream investigator,

---

*consolidate: to combine separate elements into a unified whole.

believes dreams help us sort through possible solutions to every-day problems and concerns. [7]Yet another prominent theory holds that dreams are attempts by the brain to make sense of the random* discharges of electrical activity that occur during REM (Rapid Eye Movement) sleep. [8]The electrical activity arises from the brain stem, the part of the brain responsible for such basic functions as breathing and heart rate. [9]According to this hypothesis, the brain creates a story line to explain those random signals. (Adapted from Nevid, *Psychology: Concepts and Applications*, 3rd ed., p. 148, © Cengage Learning.)

Topic Sentence _____

2. [1]According to the National Safety Council, over 100,000 accidents per year involve texting while driving. [2]It is, the research shows, more dangerous even than drinking while driving. [3]With texting, there is an eight times greater chance of an accident occurring. [4]With drivers who have a blood-alcohol level of 0.08, there is a four-time greater chance that an accident will occur. [5]Yet when asked, nearly one half of all drivers polled in an AT&T survey admitted that they text while driving and don't plan to stop. [6]Reggie Shaw, however, is not one of those who refuse to stop texting no matter what the statistics show. [7]On the contrary, Shaw has become a spokesperson for the stop-texting-while-driving movement. [8]He is passionate about changing the mindset of drivers who think texting while driving isn't a habit they have to break, because he knows all too well what the consequences can be. [9]In 2006, nineteen-year-old Shaw was texting his girlfriend when his car crossed over into the opposing lane and killed two men, James A. Furfaro and Keith P. O'Dell, instantly. [10]Although Shaw initially denied that he had been texting when the accident occurred, his cell phone records told another story, and Shaw eventually admitted to the public what he had not been able to admit to himself: his text, the contents of which he can't even remember, had cost two men their lives. [11]Once he acknowledged his responsibility, Shaw became committed to convincing others that texting while driving is unsafe at any speed.

Topic Sentence _____

3. [1]Bats in the Northeast are dying in huge numbers. [2]But why should we care? [3]New figures released in 2014 by the U.S. Fish and Wildlife

_____
*random: not based on a consistent pattern, happening by chance.

Service estimate bat deaths in the millions, leaving the bat population at only a fraction of what it once was. [4]The bats are dying due to a disease called "white nose syndrome," a fungus that strikes bats during hibernation, leaving them with a white ring around the nose. [5]The fungus also attacks the bats' wings and appears to eat away at internal tissue. [6] In addition, the fungus irritates the bats' skin. [7]That irritation causes the bats to wake up repeatedly during hibernation in order to clean themselves off. [8]Once awake, they are likely to set off in search of food and water and end up dying from the unnatural exertion, or effort. [9]Many bat caves have lost as much as 90% of their population. [10]The death of millions of bats is of great concern because of their role in insect management. [11]On a nightly basis, bats eat up to half their body weight in bugs. [12]With bats dying from white nose syndrome in huge numbers, humans can expect to see large, and in some cases harmful, increases in the insect population.

Topic Sentence _____

Nancy Heaslip, New York Department of Environmental Conservation.

4. [1]What's the difference between a science and a pseudoscience? [2]Astronomers have low opinions of beliefs such as astrology because they are a form of pseudoscience, from the Greek *pseudo* meaning false. [3]A pseudoscience is a set of beliefs that appear to be based on scientific ideas but that fail to obey the most basic rule of real science: All scientific claims must be repeatedly tested and verified, or proved true, especially in the face of contradictory evidence. [4]For example, in the 1970s a claim was made that pyramid shapes focus cosmic forces and might even have healing properties. [5]Proponents of the pyramid theory claimed, for instance, that placing a pyramid made out of paper or plastic over a piece of fruit could preserve it from

rotting. [6]What real science showed, though, was that any material shape, not just a pyramid, protects fruit from airborne spores and allows it to dry without rotting. [7]When experiments contradicted the claims about the power of pyramids, those making the claims did not respond with carefully controlled experiments of their own. [8]Instead, they just ignored the contradictory evidence, yet another indication that their belief was based on pseudoscience. (Adapted from Seeds and Backman, *Foundations of Astronomy*, 11th ed., p. 25, © Cengage Learning.)

Topic Sentence   _____

5. [1]Cognitive theorists believe that the way in which people interpret events contributes to emotional disorders such as depression. [2]One of the most influential cognitive theorists is the psychiatrist Aaron Beck, the developer of cognitive therapy. [3]Beck and his colleagues believe that people who adopt a negatively slanted way of thinking are prone to depression when they encounter disappointing or unfortunate life events. . . . [4]A minor disappointment is blown out of proportion—experienced more as a crushing blow than as a mild setback. [5]Along with his colleagues, Beck has identified a number of faulty thinking patterns, called *cognitive distortions*. [6]These cognitive distortions are believed to increase vulnerability to the onset of depression following negative life events. [7]The more distorted thinking patterns dominate a person's thoughts, the greater the vulnerability to depression. (Adapted from Nevid, *Psychology: Concepts and Applications*, 3rd ed., p. 538, © Cengage Learning.)

Topic Sentence   _____

▶ **EXERCISE 3**   **Recognizing the Most Accurate Paraphrase**

DIRECTIONS   Read each paragraph. Write the number (or numbers) of the topic sentence in the blank. Then circle the letter of the best paraphrase. If the topic sentence is introduced with a reversal transition, please circle the transition. *Paraphrasing Note*: A paraphrase that makes specific words more general does not qualify as a good paraphrase. The same is true for paraphrases that add information or points of view not present in the original.

1. [1]Cocaine became an outlawed substance in 1914. [2]But, for centuries before that, cocaine was considered a beneficial drug that

served a variety of useful purposes. [3]Before the Spanish conquest of Peru, the coca plant was reserved for Incan[†] royalty, who used it in rituals and celebrations. [4]By the sixteenth century, when Spanish explorers first began arriving in South America, the native inhabitants had a 5,000-year history of chewing coca leaves to fight fatigue and hunger and increase endurance. [5]The Spanish explorers then introduced coca leaves to Europe, where the leaves were smoked or consumed only occasionally. [6]In 1860, however, Germany's Albert Niemann isolated the plant's active ingredient and processed it into powder and liquid forms. [7]Thanks to Niemann, doctors were able to dispense cocaine for a variety of ailments, from toothaches to hay fever. [8]They also used it as an anesthetic during surgery. [9]It didn't take long before cocaine was available over the counter and as an ingredient in cigarettes, chocolate, and wine. [10]In 1886, Atlanta surgeon and chemist John Pemberton introduced Coca-Cola, a drink that contained coca leaf extract and was advertised as a cure for nervous ailments, "offering the virtues of coca without the vices of alcohol." [11]Not until the early 1900s did the medical community begin to understand the drug's addictive nature, which led to its being banned. [12]Prior to being banned though, cocaine was legal and widely used. (Source of information: "In Search of the Big Bang," www.cocaine.org.)

Topic Sentence _____

Paraphrase

a. Cocaine is destructive and highly addictive; it should remain illegal.

b. Cocaine offers medical benefits, but the dangers outweigh any positive effects.

c. Cocaine should never have been made illegal.

d. Prior to the early twentieth century, cocaine was freely used in any number of ways.

2. [1]Many of the young heroes and heroines in children's literature—including popular characters like J. K. Rowling's Harry Potter, Roald Dahl's James Henry Trotter of *James and the Giant Peach*,

---

[†]Incan: related to the Peruvian people who established an empire from Ecuador to central Chile.

and Lucy Maud Montgomery's Anne of *Anne of Green Gables*—are orphans. [2]Although the presence of so many orphans in young adult fiction may seem to suggest a very sad outlook on life, literature experts say that orphaned characters actually serve a positive purpose. [3]According to English professor and children's literature specialist Philip Nel, an orphaned literary character expresses the powerlessness many young readers feel. [4]Still, says Nel, "many literary orphans are resilient characters who, despite their lack of power, find the emotional resources to beat the odds and make their way in the world." [5]Thus, orphaned characters make young readers believe it's possible to have some control over a world dominated by adults. [6]Nel also believes that literary orphans encourage children to think about growing up. [7]He says that a hero or heroine who has been prematurely separated from his or her parents encourages young readers to explore the idea of leaving and seeking independence. [8]By imagining a world free of their parents, young readers prepare for the transition from child to adult. (Source of quotation: Deirdre Donahue, "Orphans in Literature Empower Children," *USA Today*, July 3, 2003, p. 7D.)

Topic Sentence _____

Paraphrase

a. The large number of orphans in children's fiction suggests kids don't want adults in their lives.

b. Some experts think orphaned literary characters help young readers feel more in control of their world.

c. The pessimism in children's literature is cause for concern.

d. Youthful readers need to express resentment toward parents; that may be why there are so many orphans in children's literature.

3. [1]*Munchausen syndrome* is a psychiatric disorder in which people fake illness in order to get attention and treatment. [2]People affected with Munchausen syndrome will, for instance, scratch and cut themselves or add blood to their urine specimens. [3]They may also inject a variety of substances into their blood or veins in order to cause illness. [4]Those afflicted with Munchausen syndrome usually have enough medical knowledge to appear convincingly sick. [5]They will present themselves at emergency rooms, reporting a variety of symptoms, and willingly undergo any number of tests. [6]If the test results do not match their symptoms, these individuals will

turn around and report an entirely different set of symptoms. [7]If confronted, victims of Munchausen syndrome are inclined to get hostile and demand treatment at another facility. [8]Those afflicted with Munchausen syndrome will do just about anything to get the attention and treatment they crave. (Adapted from Neighbors and Tannehill-Jones, *Human Diseases*, 2nd ed., p. 420, © Cengage Learning.)

Topic Sentence _____

Paraphrase

a. Munchausen syndrome is a serious mental illness that afflicts millions of people who don't even know they have it.

b. People with Munchausen syndrome take sadistic pleasure in hurting themselves because, on some level, they feel guilty.

c. People with Munchausen syndrome worry constantly about their health and will get numerous medical tests in the hopes of finding they have an illness.

d. Victims of Munchausen syndrome are so desperate for attention, they will fake an illness so they can get noticed and treated.

4. [1]What makes a friendship? [2]Although a number of factors influence friendship, one of the most important is *proximity*, or nearness. [3]If you live in a college dormitory, your friends are more likely to live down the hall than across campus. [4]Your earliest friends were probably children who lived next door or down the block from you. [5]It's simple. [6]Proximity increases the chances of interacting with others and getting to know them better, thus providing a basis for developing feelings of affection for them. [7]Another explanation for the positive effects of proximity on friendship is the tendency for people to have more in common with people who live nearby or attend the same classes. (Adapted from Nevid, *Psychology: Applications and Concepts*, 3rd ed., p. 604, © Cengage Learning.)

Topic Sentence _____

Paraphrase

a. Although friendships are formed for many different reasons, proximity, or nearness, is the most important.

b. We are more likely to become friendly with people who live close by.

    c. Friendships form for different reasons, but proximity is an especially powerful factor.

    d. A shared childhood is probably the most important factor in the development of a lifelong friendship.

5. [1]Jury duty is an essential part of living in a democratic society. [2]But you'd never know it from the way some American citizens behave. [3]For many, jury duty is an inconvenience they try to avoid any way they can. [4]Some people simply throw away the summons to jury duty. [5]They know that if the state authorities come after them, it's easy enough to claim the notice never arrived. [6]Should the authorities pursue the issue—and they often don't—it's up to the state to prove that the notice actually got into the potential juror's hands, and that's not easy to do. [7]For those who lack the nerve to just chuck the notice into the wastebasket, there's a second choice. [8]During the interview stage of jury selection, jury dodgers can display their acting skills. [9]An agitated tone, much eyeball rolling, and excessive hand-wringing signal that the potential juror is overly biased or mentally unbalanced. [10]Both states of mind are reason for dismissal.

Topic Sentence   ————

Paraphrase

    a. Jury dodgers think nothing of lying in order to get out of jury duty.

    b. Many people pay no attention to jury duty notices because they are convinced the authorities will not pursue them if they don't show up.

    c. Many people treat jury duty as an annoyance and try to get out of it through any number of excuses.

    d. Pretending to be mentally disturbed is a very effective way of avoiding jury duty, but most people don't have the acting skill to pull it off.

From Reader to Writer Explain why you think people who try to get out of jury duty should be penalized for failing to do their duty as American citizens. Or else, explain why you perfectly understand that some people don't want to do jury duty and why you think they should not be penalized if they throw the notice away and don't show up.

Working with the Writer to Construct the Topic and Main Idea

"A writer only begins a book. A reader finishes it."
—Writer and poet Samuel Johnson

When a paragraph opens with a general sentence followed by two or three specific illustrations, skilled readers correctly conclude that the first sentence is the topic sentence. However, as you already know, writers don't always introduce the main idea in the first sentence. Nor do they always use a reversal transition to announce the delayed topic sentence is about to arrive.

For paragraphs that vary from the standard, or familiar, patterns of explanation, you need to use the same strategy you used for finding topics. You need, that is, to focus on the words or phrases most frequently repeated, referred to, or suggested in a reading. They are the author's way of saying to readers, "These are the words essential to creating the idea I am trying to communicate."

Tracking Repetition and Reference to Identify the Topic

For an illustration of how you can use repetition and reference as clues to the topic, read the following paragraph. As you do, pay close attention to the italicized words and phrases printed in red. They will lead you to the topic.

[1]Prior to the nineteenth century, America was a largely agricultural country and daily life required so much effort that there was little time for leisure. [2]But as industry grew so did city life and leisure time. [3]With that dramatic change came an interest in *sports*, and in the cities, *one sport in particular dominated*. [4]By the nineteenth century, *baseball* had emerged as the most popular *new urban sport*. [5]*The game* first appeared in *its* modern form in the 1840s when a group of wealthy New Yorkers organized the Knickerbocker Club. [6]Then in 1862, in Brooklyn, William H. Cammeyer built the first enclosed *baseball field* in the country. [7]However, it was not until 1869 that *teams* began to *charge admission* and pay *players*. [8]In 1876, *eight teams*—New York, Philadelphia, Hartford, Boston, Chicago, Louisville, Cincinnati, and St. Louis—came together to form the National *League of Professional Baseball Clubs*. [9]By the late 1880s, annual attendance at *National League games* had reached eight million, and both men and boys in vacant lots and empty streets were emulating the *professional players they admired*. (Adapted from Gillon and Matson, *The American Experiment*, 2nd ed., p. 747, © Cengage Learning.)

Although the author sets the stage for the topic with the more general word *sports*, it's already clear by the middle of the paragraph that the topic of this passage is the more specific word *baseball*. No other person, object, event, or place in the paragraph gets quite the same amount of repetition and reference. As you can see, the more general word *sports* disappears as the authors take up their true subject—baseball.

Topics Are Implicit as Well as Explicit

This sample paragraph, with all of its italicized references to baseball, illustrates what you already know from Chapter 3: Writers don't rely solely on repetition to keep key words front and center in the reader's mind. Instead, they refer to or suggest key words **implicitly**, or indirectly, through a variety of methods. (See the chart on pages 217–18 for a more detailed list.)

Look, for instance, at sentence 5 of the sample paragraph. Because context eliminates any questions about which "game" the writers have in mind, the word *game* acts as a substitute, or stand-in, for "baseball." It reminds readers that the writers are still discussing the beginnings of baseball *before* adding a new piece of information about the topic.

In this case, the new information concerns when the Knickerbocker Club, the first organized association for baseball fans, was formed. Similarly, sentence 9 doesn't even mention the word *baseball*. But the phrases *National League games* and *professional players* signal to readers that baseball is still the topic under discussion. The question now, of course, is what does the author want to say *about* that topic? What's the main idea?

READING TIPS

1. Texts are made up of words. But some words are more important than others. Looking for the words and phrases that the author consistently repeats and refers to is the way to determine the building blocks of both the topic and the main idea.

2. Sometimes topics are suggested even more than stated, so think on two levels while reading: What do the words mean and what do they suggest?

From Topic to Main Idea via Repetition and Reference

At this point, you may already know the main idea of the baseball paragraph. But for the sake of illustration, let's assume you don't and see how tracking repetition and reference can lead you to it.

Take another look at the sample paragraph. This time different words are italicized and printed in blue. These words and phrases aren't repeated or referred to as often as the word *baseball*. Still, they clearly get a lot of attention, which means they play a role in the author's main idea. Combine them with the topic and you will know what that main idea is.

As you re-read the paragraph and check out the italicized words, ask yourself (1) What words and phrases are consistently repeated, referred to, or suggested? and (2) How could they combine with the topic of baseball to convey a general message or point?

[1]*Prior to the nineteenth century*, America was a largely agricultural country and daily life required so much effort that there was little time for *leisure*. [2]But *as industry grew* so did *city life* and *leisure time*. [3]With that *dramatic change* came an interest in *sports*, and *in the cities*, one *sport in particular dominated*. [4]*By the nineteenth century, baseball had emerged* as the most popular *new urban sport*. [5]*The game first appeared* in *its modern form in the 1840s* when a group of wealthy New Yorkers *organized the Knickerbocker Club*. [6]*Then in 1862*, in Brooklyn, William H. Cammeyer built the *first* enclosed baseball field in the country. [7]However, it was not until *1869* that teams *began to charge* admission and pay players. [8]*In 1876, eight teams*—New York, Philadelphia, Hartford, Boston, Chicago, Louisville, Cincinnati, and St. Louis—*came together* to form the National League of Professional Baseball Clubs. [9]*By the late 1880s*, annual attendance at National League games *had reached eight million*, and both men and boys in *vacant lots* and *empty streets* were emulating the professional players they admired. (Adapted from Gillon and Matson, *The American Experiment*, 2nd ed., p. 747, © Cengage Learning.)

What the italicized words and phrases in the sample paragraph show is the authors' emphasis on three threads of thought. Note first of all the repetition of **time order transitions** such as "Prior to the nineteenth century," "In 1876," and "By the late 1880s." The time order transitions in the sample paragraph help readers follow the course of events as they occurred in real time. By their frequency, they also tell readers that change over time is critical to the main idea.

The arrival of something new and growing rapidly is another thread, suggested by the phrases *dramatic change, began to charge admission and pay players, first enclosed baseball field,* and *had reached eight million.* Important too is the chain of repetition and reference related to cities: *city life, in the cities, new urban sport, New Yorkers, vacant lots,* and *empty streets.*

Once you have identified the words that are repeated or referred to throughout a paragraph, you need to think about how you can combine what those words represent into a sentence that sums up the author's point. In the case of the sample paragraph, you might well come up with something that reads like this: "During the nineteenth century, baseball got its start as a popular sport in the cities," or like this: "In the nineteenth century, baseball first became the game to play in the cities."

Either of these statements is fine because they both rely on the clues threaded throughout the paragraph via repetition and reference. Both can also generally sum up the more specific details in the paragraph, which any self-respecting main idea needs to do.

The question now is this: Is there a topic sentence in the paragraph that matches either of these sentences? Certainly sentence 4 comes very close. The match between the author's topic sentence and our versions of the main idea is a solid indication that we are following the same train of thought as the author, which is essential to being a skillful reader.

Different Texts Require Different Approaches

Sometimes the topic sentence of a paragraph practically leaps off the page. You'll see a general sentence followed by specific illustrations and know immediately that you are dealing with a basic explanatory pattern—general topic sentence followed by specific illustrations. But for paragraphs that are a little more difficult, not quite so straightforward, you should try the approach just described. Use repetition and reference clues to come up with a main idea. Then look for a topic sentence that confirms you are correct.

And even if the paragraph you are reading doesn't have a topic sentence (more on those in Chapter 8), you can still test your main idea for accuracy by seeing how well it summarizes the more specific sentences in the paragraph. Do the more specific sentences flesh out some of the words used to construct your main idea? Do they answer questions that a reader might have about the main idea you have come up with? If they do, then you and the author are following the same mental path, which, at this stage of reading, is precisely what you want to be doing.

Tracking Repetition and Reference
●

The Writer's Clue: Word Repetition
The second sentence opens with a word that comes at the end of the previous sentence.

[1]Warren G. Harding could not be nominated today when, at the first mention of his name, a hundred reporters would be digging for <u>dirt</u> in his past. [2]<u>The dirt</u> was there. (Conlin, *The American Past*, p. 642, © Cengage Learning.)

The Writer's Clue: Transition Words
The sentence that comes after a sentence opens with a transition, which explicitly identifies its relationship to the previous sentence.

[1]Already as a young child, the writer knew that becoming fluent in English was separating him from his Spanish-speaking grandmother. [2]<u>Thus,</u> he tried to hide how well he had mastered the language of his new country and made a point of not speaking it at home, even when his parents, proud of his achievement, encouraged him to.

The Writer's Clue: An Implied Example or Clarification
The following sentence supplies a specific illustration of some idea, attitude, theory, or opinion that has just been mentioned.

[1]Warren G. Harding could not be nominated today when, at the first mention of his name, a hundred reporters would be digging for dirt in his past. [2]The dirt was there. [3]<u>For fifteen years in Marion, Ohio, he carried on a sexual affair with a neighbor.</u>

The Writer's Clue: Pronouns like *This* or *That*   The next sentence opens with a pronoun that refers to a general idea or action described in the previous sentence.

[1]In 2000, <u>Dow Chemical fired 24 employees and disciplined 235 others</u> after an email investigation turned up hard-core pornography and violent subject matter. [2]<u>This</u> is the type of response companies need to make if we are to have a harassment-free workplace. (Adapted from Kreitner, *Management*, p. 333, © Cengage Learning.)

The Writer's Clue: A General Category Word Used as a Stand-In for a More Specific Word

[1]The <u>first electrocution of a criminal</u> was carried out in New York's Auburn Prison on August 6, 1890. [2]<u>The event</u> drew a group of curious doctors who positioned themselves in a circle around the chair as

The second sentence opens with a more general word that includes or covers a more specific event in the previous sentence.

William Kemmler of Buffalo was strapped into the device.

The Writer's Clue: An Associated Word or Phrase Is Used as a Substitute The next sentence opens with a phrase commonly associated with what's just been mentioned.

[1]For pedigreed <u>dog</u> owners, the Westminster <u>Dog</u> Show is a major event that arouses much rivalry in pet owners, each of whom thinks his or her <u>dog</u> deserves the blue ribbon. [2]But given the <u>mutual sniffing and tail-wagging</u> that takes place among the participants, it's pretty clear they aren't especially concerned about who walks away with first prize.

The Writer's Clue: Variation on a Word Already Mentioned The sentence that follows includes the same word or words but the endings are different.

[1]Freud's idea of <u>therapy</u> consisted of long sessions of free <u>association</u> with the sessions sometimes going on for years. [2]The <u>therapists</u> who have followed in his footsteps, however, are far less interested in having their patients <u>free associate</u> their way through their childhood memories.

The Writer's Clue: An Implied Word or Phrase Echoes the Previous Sentence The second sentence suggests a word or phrase from the previous sentence but doesn't explicitly state it because the writer assumes the reader will supply it.[†]

[1]When <u>the killer flu of 1918</u> finally came to an end, the public breathed a sigh of relief, convinced that something so deadly was a one-time occurrence. [2]But those in the scientific community were not convinced. *Note*: The suggested but unstated phrase at the end of sentence 2 is something like "that the flu was a one-time occurrence."

[†]The formal term for an implied but unstated word or phrase that the writer expects readers to supply is *ellipsis*.

SUMMING UP THE KEY POINTS

1. Readers can determine the topic and the main idea of a paragraph by tracking the author's use of repetition and reference throughout the paragraph.

2. Notice how an author uses pronouns, examples, substitutes, associated words, and ellipsis to tell readers which words are especially important. (See the chart above for an example of ellipsis.)

3. Tracking repetition and reference is an additional reading strategy that should be used to identify the topic and main idea in combination with recognizing general and specific sentences.

▶ **EXERCISE 4**   **Recognizing Repetition and Reference**

DIRECTIONS   Read each passage. Then answer the questions about how the sentences connect through repetition and reference.

EXAMPLE   ¹If two people with sharply different spending styles commit to a relationship, problems usually arise. ²This is particularly true in a marriage. ³For example, the conflict of "his" and "her" money may come into play, and whoever earns the larger salary may want to tell the other how to spend. ⁴In disagreements over money, the larger earner may think or say, "I earned it and I'll spend it." (Adapted from Garman and Forgue, *Personal Finance*, 10th ed., p. 119, © Cengage Learning.)

a. Sentence 2 uses what word to refer to the point made in sentence 1?
   This

b. Sentences 2 and 3 both refer to and illustrate what key phrase in sentence 1?
   different spending styles; problems

c. Sentences 3 and 4 do not say so explicitly, but they assume readers know that the example they describe takes place in the context of what personal relationship?
   marriage

d. Which of the following main ideas fits the key words in the paragraph?

1. Marriages in which one person makes more money than the other are bound to have problems.

2. If two people marry and think of their money as his and hers, problems will arise.

3.) When people with different spending styles marry, the chance of conflict increases.

EXPLANATION   References to these two topics—different spending styles and problems between married couples—reappear in the sample paragraph, making answer 3 correct. The other answers are self-explanatory.

1. ¹Most well-designed studies show that although children almost always find divorce stressful, the bulk of them survive divorces without much, if any, long-term psychological damage. ²By and large, these investigations show that 75 percent to 85 percent of children studied coped quite well in the wake of their parents' divorces. ³Moreover, the studies indicate that when parents experience severe conflict prior to the divorce, the apparent adverse* effects of divorce appear to be minimal. ⁴That's probably because children find the divorce to be a welcome escape from their parents' bitter arguing. (Adapted from Lilienfield et al., *50 Great Myths of Popular Psychology*, Wiley Blackwell, 2009, p. 170.)

a. What word in sentence 2 is used as a stand-in for the word *studies* in sentence 1? _____

b. What general phrase from sentence 1 does sentence 2 make more specific? _____

c. What word in sentence 3 echoes the idea that children "survive divorces without much . . . long-term damage"? _____

d. The word *that's* in sentence 4 refers to what idea in sentence 3?

_____

_____

_____

*adverse: unpleasant, negative.

    e. Which of the following main ideas fits the key words in the paragraph?

      1. No matter how much parents may try to avoid it, children are bound to suffer during a divorce.

      2. Studies generally show that divorce usually makes children anxious but does not cause long-term harm.

      3. Studies show that children suffer no harm from their parents' divorcing.

2. ¹Brazil has the sixth largest economy in the world and is one of the richest countries on earth. ²But it is a rich country full of poor people. ³Brazil has the dubious distinction of having one of the most unequal distributions of wealth in the world. ⁴In 2002, the richest 20 percent of the population earned twenty-nine times as much as the poorest. ⁵Compare this to Mexico, where the richest 20 percent of the population earned sixteen times as much as the poorest, or the United States where the richest 20 percent of the population earned nine times as much as the poorest. (Adapted from Hirschberg and Hirschberg, *One World, Many Cultures*, p. 212.)

    a. What point from sentence 1 is repeated in sentence 2? What new information does sentence 2 add?

    _____

    _____

    b. What phrase in sentence 3 makes a connection to the word *poor* in sentence 2?

    _____

    c. Sentence 4 is a specific illustration of what general phrase in sentence 3?

    _____

    d. Which of the following main ideas generally fits the key words in the paragraph?

      1. Brazil is an extremely wealthy country.

      2. Despite the country's extreme wealth, much of Brazil's population is poor.

      3. Brazilian society has no class mobility, and there is no chance for a poor person to even become rich.

3. ¹An ancient Chinese form of medicine, acupuncture is based on the philosophy that energy circulating through the body controls health. ²Thus, pain and disease are the result of a disturbance in the energy flow, which can be corrected by inserting long, thin needles at specific points, or meridians, in the body. ³Each point controls a different corresponding part of the body. ⁴Once inserted the needles are rotated gently back and forth or charged with a small electric current for a short time. ⁵Research studies have found that acupuncture helps alleviate nausea in cancer patients undergoing chemotherapy. ⁶It also helps in treating chronic lower back pain and may or may not be of value for irritable bowel syndrome. (Adapted from Hales, *An Invitation to Health*, 7th ed., p. 438.)

Acupuncture is believed to bring about healing through the insertion and manipulation of needles.

Andrey_Popov/Shutterstock.com.

a. Where in sentence 2 is the first indication that the author is continuing the discussion of acupuncture philosophy begun in sentence 1? _____

b. The word *which* in sentence 2 refers to what phrase in the first part of the sentence? _____

c. In sentence 4, the author expects the reader to supply what phrase after the word *inserted*? _____

d. Sentence 6 offers another example of what phrase introduced in sentence 5? _____

e. Which of the following main ideas generally fits the key words in the paragraph?

   1. Originating in ancient China, acupuncture is based on the idea that good health depends on how energy moves through the body.

2. Research in the effectiveness of acupuncture, an ancient form of Chinese medicine, has shown mixed results.

3. Acupuncturists heal the body by inserting needles in meridians that correspond to and control different body parts.

4. [1]Between the nineteenth and twentieth centuries, the huge area in America known as the Great Plains underwent startling changes. [2]At the beginning of the nineteenth century, there were few settlements, and one could walk for miles without seeing a house. [3]But by the end of the century, settlements were springing up all over, and growing numbers of men and women were seeking their fortunes in the region that had once been known as "The Great American Desert." [4]In 1800 the plains had been covered by herds of buffalo. [5]These huge, dumb animals were the natural cattle of the plains, and the Indian tribes living in the area hunted them for food and for the animals' hides, which could be turned into clothing and blankets. [6]Many of the pioneers who came west followed suit. [7]Still the herds managed to survive. [8]But as trains entered the region, shooting buffalo for sport became a popular practice, and passengers would open up a window and take aim. [9]By the turn of the century, the buffalo's numbers had sharply dwindled. [10]Not surprisingly, the Apache, Sioux, and Navajo who had hunted the buffalo also disappeared from the plains. [11]By 1900 they were enclosed on reservations and no longer roaming the Great Plains.

a. Sentences 2 and 3 pick up on what word mentioned in sentence 1?

_____

b. In sentence 5, what word tells readers the writer is still talking about the buffalo introduced in sentence 4? _____

c. In sentence 6 the phrase "followed suit" refers to what activity described in sentence 5? _____

d. Sentence 9 describes the effect of what cause identified in sentence 8? _____

e. Which of the following main ideas generally fits the key words in the paragraph?

1. Although herds of buffalo have returned to the region once known as the Great Plains, the herds are markedly smaller than they were at the turn of the century.

    2. The years between 1890 and 1910 were the most devastating decades for the Indian tribes that had once ridden freely over the region of America known as the "Great Plains."

    3. Over the course of one century, between 1800 and 1900, the Great Plains underwent a huge transformation.

▶ EXERCISE 5   Using Repetition and Reference to Identify Main Ideas

DIRECTIONS   On the first line following the paragraph, write the words or phrases you think are consistently repeated, referred to, or suggested in the paragraph. On the next two lines write what you think is the main idea. Then write the number of the author's topic sentence in the blank. *Note*: This is the time to check if you and the author are following the same train of thought. The topic sentence and your version of the main idea should be similar.

EXAMPLE   [1]In the nineteenth century, American and British fishermen nearly wiped out the seals of Antarctica. [2]The Antarctic seals, however, after almost becoming extinct, have made an astonishing comeback. [3]The population is now rapidly increasing. [4]Although scientists admit that other factors may be responsible for the seals' rebound, they are convinced that the severe decrease in the baleen whale population is a major cause. [5]The baleen whale and the Antarctic seal once competed for the same food source—a tiny shellfish called krill. [6]With the baleen whale practically extinct now, the seals have inherited an almost unlimited food supply. [7]That increase in the seals' food supply is considered a major reason for the seals' comeback.

Against all odds, the Antarctic seal is still in existence.

© Ulrich Flemming.

a. What words and phrases are consistently repeated, referred to, or suggested throughout the paragraph?

Antarctic seals, comeback, increase, decrease, baleen whale

b. In your own words, what's the main idea?

Now that the baleen whale is no longer competing with them for food, the

Antarctic seals are starting to multiply.

c. Where's the topic sentence that matches your main idea? ___2___

EXPLANATION   Every sentence in the paragraph mentions or refers to the seals of Antarctica, so that's a dead giveaway to the topic. But almost every sentence also mentions their comeback. Consequently, the comeback of the Antarctic seals has to be part of the main idea.

The other oft-referred-to idea is how the "severe decrease" in the baleen whale population affected the Antarctic seal. Put all three elements together and you have the main idea. Look for the sentence closest to the main idea we inferred and you will find it expressed in sentence 2, which is the topic sentence of the paragraph.

1. ¹Throughout history, societies from all parts of the world have performed a ritual known as *couvade*, a ceremony in which the husband pretends he is suffering from labor pains while his wife actually gives birth. ²Although no one knows the exact origins of the couvade, there are several theories. ³According to one, the ritual of couvade began as a way of warding off evil spirits. ⁴Supporters of this interpretation suggest that the husband enacts a pregnancy in order to attract the evil spirits to himself and away from his wife. ⁵Yet another theory speculates* that the couvade is a way of publicly identifying the father so that his paternity is not in doubt. ⁶Among those anthropologists who study the habits and practices of other cultures, this particular theory about the couvade's origins has the most support.

a. What words and phrases are consistently repeated, referred to, or suggested throughout the paragraph?

_____

_____

*speculates: puts forth an as yet unproven theory, theorizes.

    b. In your own words, what's the main idea?

    _____

    _____

    c. Where's the topic sentence that matches your main idea? _____

2. [1]Sudden infant death syndrome (SIDS) is a mysterious and tragic disease in which a sleeping baby stops breathing and dies. [2]In the United States, SIDS strikes about two of every thousand infants, usually when they are two to four months old. [3]SIDS is less common in cultures where infants and parents sleep in the same bed, suggesting that sleeping position may be important. [4]Indeed, about half of apparent SIDS cases may be accidental suffocations caused when infants lie face down on soft surfaces. [5]Other SIDS cases may stem from problems with brain systems regulating breathing or from exposure to cigarette smoke. (Bernstein et al., *Psychology*, 8th ed., p. 173, © Cengage Learning.)

    a. What words and phrases are consistently repeated, referred to, or suggested throughout the paragraph?

    _____

    _____

    b. In your own words, what's the main idea?

    _____

    _____

    c. Where's the topic sentence that matches your main idea? _____

3. [1]Emergency medical technicians (EMTs) and paramedics are trained to respond quickly to medical emergencies. [2]Once the technicians and paramedics arrive at a scene, they determine the nature and extent of the patient's condition. [3]They also try to determine if the patient has any existing medical problem. [4]Following strict procedures, they give appropriate emergency care and then transport the patient to a medical facility. [5]Guidance for handling complicated problems is given by radio or phone from a physician. [6]EMTs and paramedics work both indoors and outdoors in all kinds of weather. [7]They are required to do considerable kneeling, bending, and heavy lifting. [8]Formal certification and training are needed in all states to

become an EMT or paramedic. [9]Job outlook is good, as demand is expected to grow faster than average. (Adapted from Scott and Fong, *Body Structures and Functions*, 11th ed., p. 274, © Cengage Learning.)

a. What words and phrases are consistently repeated, referred to, or suggested throughout the entire paragraph?

_____

_____

b. In your own words, what's the main idea?

_____

_____

c. Where's the topic sentence that matches your main idea? _____

4. [1]On her blog, Lenore Skenazy bills herself as the World's Worst Mom and proud of it. [2]Skenazy is the outspoken guru of the Free-Range Childhood movement, which, as her blog says, "fights the belief that our children are in constant danger" and encourages parents to give their children as much freedom as the kids can handle. [3]Critical of "helicopter parents," who hover constantly over their kids for fear something bad will happen to them, Skenazy insists that children need time to explore the world on their own without being under their parents watchful eyes. [4]They should, for instance, be allowed to walk or ride short distances to an afterschool activity or to visit a friend without being accompanied by an adult. [5] Skenazy first got the public's attention in 2008 when she wrote about letting her son find his way home on the New York subway. [6] Since then, she has developed quite a following among like-minded parents across the nation. [7]Among her supporters are Danielle and Alexander Meitiv, from Monterey County, Maryland, who also believe that kids need to take manageable risks to become self-reliant and independent adults. [8]Unfortunately, when the Meitivs put Skenazy's ideas for a free-range childhood into practice, their kids were rounded up by the police, because someone observing the two children playing unsupervised in a park had called 911. [9]The parents got their children back along with a visit from social services. [10]The Meitivs, however, intend to continue giving their kids a free-range childhood. [11]Like Skenazy, they argue that fears about threats to children are exaggerated by the media, and children are in no more danger now than they were fifty

years ago, when it was normal for kids to play outside by themselves. [12]While Skenazy has her critics—lots of them—many parents think she has the right approach. [13]Some also point out that they have no choice. [14]With the economy forcing them to work long hours, they don't have the time to hover over their kids twenty-four hours a day and don't want to be considered bad parents because of it.

a. What words and phrases are consistently repeated, referred to, or suggested throughout the entire paragraph?

_____

_____

b. In your own words, what's the main idea?

_____

_____

_____

c. Where's the topic sentence that matches your main idea? _____

5. [1]In 1927, when Charles Lindbergh decided to fly nonstop over the Atlantic, everyone said it was impossible. [2]But Lindbergh didn't listen. [3]He flew anyway, becoming an international hero, as the first person to make the trip. [4]In 1933, when the public demanded that he return a medal given to him by the Nazis, Lindbergh refused. [5]No matter how unpopular his decision, he was not about to bend to the opinion of others. [6]True to character, Lindbergh also planned his own funeral. [7]Typically, he refused to leave such an important event in anyone else's hands. [8]In the end, Charles Lindbergh's independent character shaped every event of his extraordinary life.

a. What words and phrases are consistently repeated, referred to, or suggested throughout the entire paragraph?

_____

_____

b. In your own words, what's the main idea?

_____

_____

c. Where's the topic sentence that matches your main idea? _____

READING TIPS

1. If a passage is particularly hard to understand, re-read it to make sure you can match every pronoun to its antecedent.

2. Especially important in this context are pronouns such as *what*, *this*, and *that*. They often refer to entire ideas rather than single words. That's why misunderstanding, or misinterpreting, them can interfere with your comprehension. It pays to give them special attention.

✔ CHECK YOUR UNDERSTANDING

1. What methods do authors use to make key ideas in a paragraph stand out for readers?

   _____

   _____

2. How should readers respond to an author's use of repetition and reference?

   _____

3. How can readers confirm that they have determined the main idea the author had in mind?

   _____

   _____

▶ **EXERCISE 6**   **Matching Your Main Idea to the Topic Sentence**

DIRECTIONS   Read each paragraph and note which words are repeated or referred to. Then write your version of the main idea in the blanks. Underline the author's topic sentence. *Note*: If you can't find a topic sentence that matches your main idea, you need to re-think your main idea.

1. [1]Inhalant abuse, an addictive habit with dangerous and sometimes deadly consequences, is the intentional breathing of common

household products in order to get high. [2]This intentional breathing is commonly called "huffing," "snuffing," or "bagging." [3]Bagging is the most dangerous as it entails placing a plastic bag over the head to get a longer effect. [4]Using inhalants over a period of time may result in permanent brain, heart, kidney, and liver damage. [5]Some products like paint and gasoline contain lead and may cause death from lead poisoning. [6]Inhalant abuse is the third most common kind of substance abuse by individuals aged twelve to fourteen years, surpassed only by alcohol and tobacco. [7]Symptoms of inhalant abuse include spots or sores around the mouth, a glassy-eyed look, fumes on the breath or clothing, anxiety, and loss of appetite. (Adapted from Neighbors and Tannehill-Jones, *Human Diseases*, 2nd ed., p. 414, © Cengage Learning.)

What's the main idea?

_____

_____

2. [1]The terms *introvert* and *extrovert* first came to public notice through the work of the psychotherapist Carl Jung (1875–1961). [2]Jung used the words *introvert* and *extrovert* to describe two different ways of relating to other people. [3]Introverts need a degree of solitude, or alone time, to be comfortable in the world because long stretches in a group exhaust them. [4]Extroverts, in contrast, are energized by the presence of others and seek to be around people as much as possible. [5]Although the terms *introvert* and *extrovert* have survived to the present day, long after Jungian psychology has been all but forgotten, Jung did not use the terms in the way most people do nowadays. [6]For Jung, there was "no such thing as a pure introvert or extrovert." [7]In his eyes, any person who was completely one or the other "would be in a lunatic asylum." [8]Instead, he saw personality as a mix of both traits, with one tendency usually outweighing the other.

What's the main idea?

_____

_____

_____

3. [1]In 2014, when reports about cases of the deadly Ebola virus in African countries began to soar into the thousands, medical researchers warned that the public, already terrified, didn't even know the whole story. [2]At the time, the public didn't know that tracking down cases of those infected with or dying from the Ebola virus was a difficult, dangerous, and often hopeless task. [3]Finding and confirming cases of Ebola began with potential cases of the disease being called in through telephone hot-lines. [4]The calls came from families and neighbors of the victims but also from nurses and doctors treating those infected. [5]These reports were then passed on to investigating teams sent out to find the suspected victims. [6]Tracking down those suffering from the disease meant investigative teams had to work their way through hard-to-travel areas with unreliable methods of communication. [7]Because the virus carries a social stigma*, investigators were often met by angry crowds and blockaded roads. [8]Sometimes they were physically attacked by villagers who didn't want anyone claiming the disease was in their midst. [9]On a few occasions, investigators were killed. [10]If the team did manage to locate the victim, the man or woman suffering from the disease wasn't always in any condition to provide information about how he or she might have been infected. [11]Often investigative teams arrived after the person reported as ill had already died, in which case the body would be tested for the virus and might or might not become part of the disease's growing body count gathered by the World Health Organization (WHO). [12]Locating victims of Ebola proved so difficult that the Centers for Disease Control and Prevention suggested in October of 2014 that, for every one case formally reported, there might actually be an additional 2.5 cases in existence.

What's the main idea?

_____

_____

———————————

*stigma: mark or sign of disgrace or shame.

4. [1]Which dream theory is most widely accepted? [2]Each theory has its strengths and weaknesses. [3]However, studies of dream content do support the neurocognitive[†] focus on the continuity between dreams and waking thought: Rather than being exotic or bizarre, most dreams reflect everyday events. [4]For example, athletes tend to dream about the previous day's athletic activities. [5]And in general, the favorite dream setting is a familiar room in a house. [6]Dream action usually takes place between the dreamer and two or three other emotionally important people—friends, enemies, loved ones, or employers. [7]Dream actions are also mostly familiar activities such as running, jumping, riding, sitting, talking, and watching a sports event. (Adapted from Coon and Mitterer, *Introduction to Psychology*, 11th ed., p. 193, © Cengage Learning.)

What's the main idea?

_____

_____

READING TIPS

1. Remember what you learned in Chapter 1. Good readers are flexible readers. When one strategy doesn't work, they try another.

2. Check your comprehension regularly when you read, right after you finish a difficult paragraph and at the end of chapter sections. If you can't paraphrase, you need to mark the passage for a second reading.

[†]neurocognitive: focusing on how specific parts of the brain react during different kinds of thinking.

DIGGING DEEPER Combatting Infectious Diseases *G. Tyler Miller and*
Scott E. Spoolman

Looking Ahead Unlike the passage on page 231, which focuses on the Ebola virus, this reading focuses on infectious diseases in general. It looks at diseases caused by both viruses and bacteria.

As the accompanying bar graph shows, the United States is not exactly a hotbed of infectious diseases. However, that fact is pretty irrelevant in a world where another continent is only a plane ride away.

Getting Focused The title announces the topic and goes a long way toward identifying the main idea of the entire reading. Read to identify and evaluate the efforts that have been made to combat infectious diseases.

1   Infectious diseases are caused by pathogens. A **pathogen** is a living organism that can cause disease in another organism. Some examples of pathogens are bacteria, virus, parasites, and fungi.

Transmissible Diseases

2   An **infectious disease** occurs when a pathogen such as a bacterium, virus, or parasite invades the body and multiplies in its cells and tissues. Examples are flu, HIV, malaria, tuberculosis, and measles. A **transmissible disease*** (also called a contagious or communicable disease) is an infectious disease that can be transmitted from one person to another.

3   In 1900, infectious disease was the leading cause of death in both the world and the United States. Since then the incidences of infectious diseases leading to death have been greatly reduced, especially in the United States, as Figure 4-3 on page 234 indicates. This reduction in the death rate from infectious disease has been achieved mostly by a combination of better health care, the use of antibiotics to treat infectious diseases caused by bacteria, and the development of vaccines to prevent the spread of some infectious viral diseases. As a result, average life expectancy has increased in most countries. In addition, the leading cause of death in the United States has shifted to non-transmissible cardiovascular disease. The percentage of people dying from cancers is increasing in both developed and developing countries.

---

*Some infectious diseases are not transmissible, although they can be spread to people by an animal or insect. Lyme disease, spread by ticks, would be an example of an infectious disease that is not transmissible.

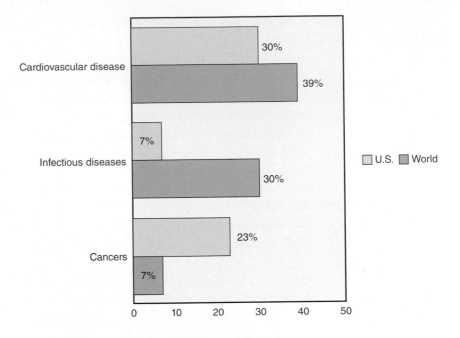

Figure 4-3 Major Causes of Death in World and United States, 2005

(Source of data: World Health Organization and U.S. Centers for Disease Control and Prevention.)

Infectious Diseases Are Still Major Health Threats

4   Despite the shift in higher risk levels from transmissible to non-transmissible diseases, infectious diseases remain a serious health threat, especially in developing countries, where conditions are often crowded. Infectious diseases can be spread through air, water, food, and body fluids. They can also be spread through droplets sprayed by sneezing and coughing.

5   Even with advances in identification and treatment, infectious diseases remain a threat. In some cases, disease-carrying bacteria have become immune to widely used antibiotics that once held the promise of eliminating the diseases they were used to treat. Some strains of tuberculosis, for instance, have become resistant to antibiotics. One form of incurable tuberculosis, known as multidrug-resistant TB, is on the rise in parts of Africa, China, India, and Russia. Because the disease cannot be treated with antibiotics, people who are infected with it have to stay in permanent quarantine.

6   Similarly, many disease-transmitting insects, such as mosquitoes, have developed immunity to widely used pesticides. In 2012, the World

Health Organization released a plan for alternating pesticides in order to combat malaria-carrying mosquitoes, which no longer seemed susceptible to the insecticides that had been in use for years. Complicating the picture is the ease of international travel, which is much more common now than it was half a century ago when it was assumed that science would one day conquer infectious diseases. Travel has encouraged the spread of contagious diseases, with distance no longer acting as a barrier to the infection. (Adapted from Miller and Spoolman, *Living in the Environment* 16e, © Cengage Learning, pp. 440–41.)

Sharpening Your Skills

DIRECTIONS   Answer the following questions by circling the letter of the correct response or writing the answer on the blank lines.

Making Predictions

1. A quick survey of the reading suggests the importance of what three key terms?

   _____

   _____

Using Context Clues

2. Based on the context, what do you think might be a good synonym for the word *incidences* in paragraph 3 ?

   _____

Recognizing the Main Idea

3. Which of the following statements do you think best sums up the main idea of the entire reading?

   a. Pathogens are organisms that cause disease.

   b. Although progress combatting infectious diseases has been made, some still remain a threat.

   c. The overuse of antibiotics has caused the return of infectious diseases that were once no longer a threat.

   d. Infectious diseases still plague other countries, but they are no longer a threat in the United States.

Main Ideas and Supporting Details

4. How would you label the following statement from paragraph 5, as major or minor, "In some cases, disease-carrying bacteria have become immune to widely used antibiotics that once held the promise of eliminating the diseases they were used to treat"? _____

5. In your own words, what is the main idea of paragraph 5? _____

_____

_____

Recognizing Explanatory Patterns

6. In paragraph 3, the author opens with

   a. an introductory sentence.
   b. the topic sentence.
   c. a supporting detail.

Following the Author's Train of Thought

7. In paragraph 4, the pronoun *they* in the last sentence refers to what?

_____

8. In paragraph 6, what does the first *which* in the paragraph refer to? _____ What does the second *which* refer to? _____

Paraphrasing

9. In your own words, explain why infectious diseases pose a threat even if they occur in countries distant from our own.

_____

_____

Understanding Visual Aids

10. The bar graph that accompanies this reading makes what point?

_____

_____

From Reader to Writer Pertussis, more commonly known as whooping cough, is a highly contagious respiratory disease that once seemed to have been eliminated as a threat. But as the following line graph shows, it is once again on the rise. (See Figure 4-4.) There seem to be two reasons for the disease's return. Use the Web to find out what those two reasons are. Then write a paragraph (or two if you need to) that describes the two main causes of the disease's sudden surge. To pave the way for the main idea, try using some form of a "that was then, this is now" introduction.

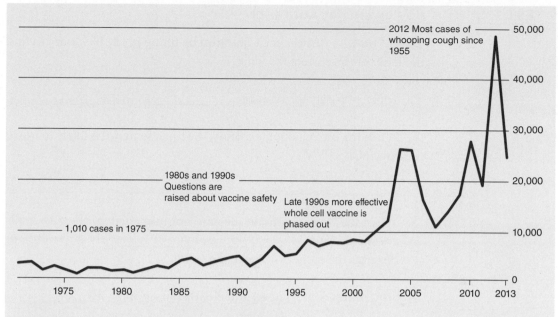

Figure 4-4 Whooping Cough Makes a Comeback

(Source of data: Science News https://www.sciencenews.org/article/whooping-cough-bounces-back. Last downloaded October 14, 2014.)

▶ **TEST 1**   **Reviewing Key Concepts**

DIRECTIONS   Answer each question by filling in the blank or circling the letter of the correct response.

1. Topics of paragraphs can be _____ as well as _____.

2. When the introduction expands, the topic sentence is likely to move toward

   _____

3. When the topic and main idea are not immediately obvious, readers should use _____ and _____ of key words to discover the author's subject and point.

4. Sometimes writers open and close a paragraph with _____ _____.

5. Writers who use the "that was then, this is now" pattern start by telling readers _____. Then they switch gears and _____.

6. Which one of the following is not a reversal transition?

   a. Yet unfortunately
   b. Still
   c. However
   d. Next

7. When the author opens a paragraph with a question, the answer is often the _____.

8. What word or phrase in sentence 2 is a reference to "the boy" introduced in sentence 1?

   ¹The search party had been looking for the boy since the night before. ²One moment he had been holding his mother's hand and the next he was seen entering the woods.

   _____

9. What word or phrase in sentence 2 is a reference to the pit bulls introduced in sentence 1?

   [1]Pit bulls have too often been misused by their owners. [2]The breed does not deserve its fearsome reputation.

   _____

10. What word or phrase in sentence 2 is a reference to the dance introduced in sentence 1?

    [1]The dance had attracted a huge number of people, none of whom wanted to go home. [2]It was three o'clock in the morning before the band stopped playing.

    _____

▶ **TEST 2**   **Identifying Topics and Main Ideas**

DIRECTIONS   Circle the letter of the topic and write the number of the topic sentence in the blank.

1. [1]For a period of about seventy-five years (1765–1840), the Gothic novel, an early relative of the modern horror story, was wildly popular throughout Europe. [2]Many of the most popular Gothic novels—those written by Horace Walpole, Ann Radcliffe, and Matthew Lewis—sold in the thousands. [3]They were quickly translated, and just as quickly plagiarized. [4]Gothic novels were popular largely because they described a mysterious world where ghostly figures flitted through the dark passageways of ruined buildings, usually in the dead of night. [5]Because Gothic novels were read and enjoyed by men and women of all classes, publishers, ever alert to a ready market, made sure that the books were available at bargain prices. [6]Even the poorest members of the working class could afford to pay a penny to enter the Gothic world of terror, and they paid their pennies in astonishing numbers.

Topic
   a. Horace Walpole
   b. horror stories of the eighteenth century
   c. Gothic novels
   d. modern horror novels versus Gothic novels

Topic Sentence   _____

2. [1]When we read or hear about the suffering of wild animals illegally caught, shipped, and sold, we are likely to sigh deeply for about fifteen seconds, then forget both the animals and their suffering. [2]However, we should be concerned about the wild animal trade, particularly right now, with the threat of bird flu still hovering in the air. [3]Imported animals don't come into the country alone. [4]They carry with them germs and diseases. [5]In 2005, for instance, British inspectors identified a parrot carrying the bird flu virus. [6]Because the parrot was being imported legally, it was kept in isolation for several weeks. [7]But many parrots sold in Britain come into the country illegally and are never checked for disease. [8]One of those birds could also be infected with bird flu and spread the virus to its human owner. [9]It wouldn't be long until the owner infected someone else, and cases of the disease would multiply.

Topic   a. exotic animals

    b. illegal wild animal trade

    c. the suffering of animals

    d. the dangers of importing parrots

Topic Sentence   _____

3. [1]During the Chinese festival called Qingming, relatives honor their ancestors by burning paper images of important personal and household items. [2]In the past, paper money, clothes, cars, cigarettes, beer, and pork buns were among the paper images consigned to the flames. [3]According to custom, fire transforms the paper objects, making them usable in the world of the dead. [4]But like so much else in the twenty-first century, technology has had a profound effect on this ancient tradition, adding new objects to the fires lighted during the yearly festival. [5]Paper cell phones, for instance, are now set aflame so that former users can have, even in the world of the dead, the latest models. [6]Particularly popular are paper iPhones. [7]So too are paper iPads complete with paper traveling cases and pretend fingerprints. [8]When a store announces the presence of iPhone and iPad paper images, they quickly sell out as relatives rush to make sure that their loved ones stay connected even in the afterlife.

Topic   a. the ancient tradition of Qingming

    b. technology's effect on Qingming

    c. paper images of personal products

    d. Chinese traditions involving fire

Topic Sentence   _____

4. [1]Researchers use interviews, rating scales, and questionnaires to identify observable psychological traits. [2]However, when seeking to uncover hidden or unconscious wishes, psychologists are likely to turn to *projective tests*. [3]In some projective tests, the subject is asked to tell a story about a picture or an image. [4]With others, subjects are told to respond to a word by calling up other words they associate with it. [5]Perhaps the most famous projective test is the Rorschach Technique. [6]Developed by Swiss psychologist Hermann Rorschach, the test consists of ten inkblots. [7]Subjects look at the inkblots and then describe what they see in them. [8]Yet another famous example of a projective test is the Thematic Apperception Test (TAT). [9]During the TAT, subjects are shown pictures and asked to make up stories about the people depicted. [10]Although projective tests like the Rorschach and the TAT have been popular for decades, many psychologists now question their reliability as diagnostic tools.

Topic

a. psychological testing

b. unconscious wishes

c. projective tests

d. the Thematic Apperception Test

Topic Sentence   _____

5. [1]As everyone knows, identity theft is on the rise. [2]What's the latest scheme to get people to reveal personal information that identity thieves can use? [3]Clever con artists are using jury duty to trick people into giving out personal information. [4]The scheme works like this. [5]The con artist calls his or her victim and tells the person that he or she has not appeared for jury duty despite a notice having been sent. [6]As a result, a warrant has been issued for the alleged jury dodger's arrest. [7]When the victim protests that he or she never got the notice, the identity thief asks for a birth date and Social Security number. [8]This information will supposedly allow the phony official to check the records and verify that a mistake has been made. [9]But, the con artist warns, the checking has to be done immediately in order to cancel the arrest warrant. [10]Otherwise the police may arrive at the victim's door within twenty-four hours. [11]It's this threat that often makes people so terrified they give out the requested information, and at that point their fate is sealed. [12]So far the jury duty scam has been reported in eleven different states.

Topic

a. jury duty scam

b. clever con artists

c. identity theft

d. the fear of police

Topic Sentence   _____

▶ TEST 3   **Constructing Main Ideas and Recognizing Topic Sentences**

DIRECTIONS   After identifying the words and phrases you think are repeated and referred to throughout the paragraph, write your version of the main idea in the blank lines. Then fill in the blank at the end with the number of the author's topic sentence.

1. ¹In the third century BCE, the Chinese were the first to sight Halley's comet. ²In the fourteenth, the Florentine painter Giotto put the whirling ball of light into one of his paintings; in the sixteenth, William Shakespeare mentioned it in two of his plays. ³But it took the eighteenth-century astronomer Edmund Halley (1656–1742) to recognize that the comet seen by the Chinese, the Italians, and the British was the same comet returning on a fixed schedule. ⁴While studying what seemed to be the appearance of many different comets, Halley realized that there might be only one comet that regularly appeared every seventy-six years. ⁵As a result of his studies, he predicted that the comet would return in 1758. ⁶His prediction was proven correct when the comet showed up on schedule. ⁷From that moment on, the comet bore his name. ⁸Unfortunately, Halley died without knowing that his prediction had come true.

    1. What words or phrases are repeated, referred to, or suggested throughout the paragraph?

      _____

      _____

    2. In your own words, what's the main idea of the paragraph?

      _____

      _____

    3. What's the topic sentence that matches your main idea? _____

2. ¹Corporate welfare refers to laws and policies that benefit corporations and allow them to avoid paying billions in federal taxes. ²For example, in 2010, General Electric (GE) earned $14.2 billion in profits. ³But thanks to tax laws benefitting corporations, GE did not pay any federal income tax. ⁴The company also received a

$3.2 billion tax credit. [5]Although the U.S. corporate tax rate is quite high, 35 percent, many large, profitable corporations take advantage of tax shelters* to avoid paying taxes. [6]From 2008 to 2010, Chevron Corporation paid less than 5 percent of profits in taxes. [7]The drug company Merck also paid only a 5 percent tax rate. [8]Hewlett Packard paid 3 percent while Exxon and IBM paid 2 percent. [9]In the same three-year period, Verizon, Boeing, Dow, and DuPont made profits but all paid zero taxes. [9]Citigroup and Bank of America, with a combined $8 billion in pretax earnings in 2009 and 2010, paid zero taxes two years in a row. [10]Indeed, 100 of the largest U.S. companies paid less than 10 percent of pretax profits in federal income tax in 2010. [11]If these 100 companies had paid the 35 percent official corporate tax rate, an additional $150 billion would have been collected in federal taxes in one year—an amount approximately equal to the total budget deficits for all 50 states. (Adapted from Linda Mooney et al., *Social Problems*, 8th ed., p. 174, © Cengage Learning.)

1. What words or phrases are repeated, referred to, or suggested throughout the paragraph?

   _____

   _____

2. In your own words, what's the main idea of the paragraph?

   _____

   _____

3. What's the topic sentence that matches your main idea? _____

3. [1]Some people express their personal philosophies by tattooing themselves with phrases like "Live Hard" or "Love Thy Neighbor." [2]Others consider tattoos a way of displaying their taste in art. [3]They might tattoo a William Blake[†] drawing or a Georgia O'Keeffe[†] flower on some part of their bodies. [4]But in different cultures and eras, tattoos have also served religious purposes. [5]Mexico's Mayan

---

*Tax shelters: Methods of legally avoiding the payment of taxes
[†]William Blake was a famous eighteenth-century poet, whose drawings were as famous as his poems; Georgia O' Keeffe was an American painter famous for her paintings of boldly colored flowers.

people expressed their religious beliefs by tattooing themselves with images of jaguars, snakes, turtles, and toads. ⁶From the 1700s until the present, many Muslims tattooed themselves to show their devotion to Allah. ⁷Some Native-American tribes used tattooing for medicinal purposes, believing that tattoos would ward off illness. ⁸The Cree, for instance, would tattoo a cross on each cheek to protect against toothaches, and members of the Ojibwa tribe tattooed small circles on their temples to prevent headaches. ⁹Tattooing has also been widely used as a means of identification. ¹⁰Before 787 CE, early Christians used tattoos to identify members of their faith. ¹¹Similarly, members of the military or fraternities may have themselves tattooed to publicly show their commitment. ¹²Some cultures have tattooed prisoners, the most sinister example being the Nazis, who tattooed numbers on the arms of concentration camp victims during World War II. ¹³Throughout history, tattoos have served many different purposes.

1. What words or phrases are repeated, referred to, or suggested throughout the paragraph?

   _____

   _____

2. In your own words, what's the main idea of the paragraph?

   _____

   _____

3. What's the topic sentence that matches your main idea? _____

4. ¹For hunters, fall is prime time. ²It's deer season, the time to stock the freezer with venison. ³Yet despite being enthusiastically hunted every fall, deer are not on the endangered list. ⁴Actually, for a number of reasons, the wild deer population in the United States is skyrocketing. ⁵Hunting regulations, including hunting bans and strict limits on the number of deer killed, have allowed the animals to thrive. ⁶The rate of deer reproduction, too, has contributed to the growing population. ⁷One doe usually gives birth to twins every year. ⁸Furthermore, reduced numbers of natural predators such as

wolves, along with a series of mild winters, have resulted in a lower mortality, or death, rate. [9]Deer have also successfully adapted to the destruction of their habitats[†] by humans. [10]Even when forests are cut down, deer manage to find enough food and shelter in the remaining vegetation. [11]They also boldly venture into suburbs to snack on tasty garden vegetables and flowers.

1. What words or phrases are repeated throughout the paragraph?

   _____

   _____

2. In your own words, what's the main idea of the paragraph?

   _____

   _____

3. What's the topic sentence that matches your main idea? _____

5. [1]The causes of depression in adolescents are complex. [2]The exact causes, in fact, are not completely understood by psychologists. [3]Researchers, though, have noticed a common link among depressed children. [4]While studies of family relationships suggest that depression can be inherited, they also suggest that certain family climates are typical among depressed children. [5]Children who witness or are victims of domestic violence seem to be particularly at risk for depression. [6]It may be that abusive parents, whose poor parenting skills may be caused by their own depressed state, weaken their children's ability to regulate their emotional highs and lows. [7]It might also be true that abusive parents encourage their children to develop negative ideas about social relationships and a depressed outlook on life. (Adapted from Bukatko and Daehler, *Child Development*, 5th ed., p. 396, © Cengage Learning.)

   1. What words or phrases are repeated, referred to, or suggested throughout the paragraph?

      _____

      _____

   _____

   [†]habitats: living areas.

2. In your own words, what's the main idea of the paragraph?

    _____

    _____

3. What's the topic sentence that matches your main idea? _____

5 Getting to the Point of Longer Readings

> "Learning thrives on structure, and one way to increase reading comprehension is to teach students about text structures that they are certain to encounter when reading."
>
> —WRITER JAMES WITHERS

Leaf through the pages of most college textbooks, and you'll see that the chapters break down into sections of various lengths. Some of those chapter sections are only a paragraph long. Occasionally as long as twelve to fifteen sentences, these single paragraphs still focus on one main idea.

However, as you can tell from even a brief survey, many textbook chapters are broken up into sections that extend beyond a single paragraph. Thus, in this chapter, we'll talk about how to apply what you know about explanatory patterns in single paragraphs to longer multi-paragraph readings.

Later on, we'll look more closely at longer reading selections. But for now we'll discuss how to think your way through readings that consist of no more than six paragraphs.

Pattern 1: Opening with the Main Idea

When background or context about the topic or main idea isn't a necessity, textbook authors are inclined to introduce the overall main idea of a chapter section in the very first paragraph. Actually, they are likely to introduce it in the very first sentence. Take, for example, the following reading. Note how, after the first sentence, the remaining paragraphs keep coming back to the idea it expresses: Heavy drinking in the old West was the norm.

Whiskey in the Old West

The title introduces the topic, while a general sentence expresses the overall main idea.

1   The men and women of the frontier days were heavy drinkers. They launched their days with an "eye opener" or "flem-cutter": raw, homemade whiskey. A jug sat on shop counters like a dish of mints today; general stores doubled as saloons. Westerners swigged whiskey like wine with their meals and like water when they worked. Preachers refreshed themselves with "the creature during their sermons. . . ."

This major heading signals the author is going to discuss one cause of heavy drinking in the Old West.

2   **Whiskey Lightened the Misery**. Illness explains some of the drinking. Frontier settlers suffered chronically from the alternating chills and fevers of malaria. (They called it the "ague.") The medicine for which they reached was alcohol. Isolation also contributed. Travelers in the Ohio Valley invariably described conversations with men, and especially women, who commented mournfully on the lack of company. Whiskey was their companion.

The second heading suggests another reason for heavy drinking.

3   **The Price Was Right**. Finally, whiskey was cheap. The corn and rye from which it was made were easy to grow. The technology was simple: Ferment[†] a mash of grain and water; boil it in an enclosed kettle; condense the steam that escaped and, presto, white lightning. Many family farmers kept a small still[†] percolating day and night. And on the frontier, whiskey was a cash crop.

(Adapted from Conlin, *The American Past*, 9th ed., p. 191, © Cengage Learning.)

This reading illustrates an explanatory pattern you already know from paragraphs. The first sentence in the reading introduces a general idea that is explained in more specific detail by the two supporting paragraphs, making it the overall main idea of the reading. The only real difference is in the label for the opening sentence. It's called a "thesis statement" instead of a topic sentence. Different, too, is the length of the supporting details. Supporting details are now paragraphs rather than sentences.

Thesis statements do for longer readings what topic sentences do for paragraphs: They generally sum up the main idea. With thesis statements, however, the main idea governs or controls several paragraphs rather than one. And unlike topic sentences, thesis statements aren't restricted to single sentences. They can consist of one, two, or even three sentences, depending on the complexity of the idea addressed.

[†]ferment: in this context, to cause a chemical change that turns sugar into alcohol; also to excite or stir up.
[†]still: apparatus for making whiskey.

Supporting Details: Connecting the Familiar to the New

Notice, too, how the author weaves references to the words *whiskey*, *frontier* (a synonym for *Old West*), and *drinking* throughout the supporting paragraphs. These words are repeated and referred to throughout in order to keep readers in touch with the building blocks central to the main idea introduced in the opening paragraph, "The men and women of the frontier days were heavy drinkers," while at the same time adding some new information to that main idea. People drank a lot because (1) they didn't feel particularly good most of the time and (2) whiskey was a cheap pick-me-up.

Subheadings for Supporting Details Are a Bonus

Multi-paragraph textbook readings often introduce the supporting details with subheadings like the ones shown on page 250. In this case, the subheadings spell out the main ideas of the supporting paragraphs. Sometimes, though, they simply identify the topic. If that were the case with the previous reading, then the headings would be only a word or phrase, for instance, "Loneliness" and "Low Cost of Whiskey."

READING TIPS

1. Whether they introduce the topic or the main idea, titles and subheadings in chapter sections are important clues. They help readers make the right connections between the overall main idea of the reading and the supporting details that serve to explain it.

2. If a heading is a complete sentence, then it very likely expresses the main idea of the chapter section or paragraph as well.

3. The title often provides a clue to the main idea. As you read, look for any references to words used in the title. References to the title are likely to be central to developing the overall main idea.

The Function of Supporting Details in Longer Readings ●

As they do in paragraphs, supporting details in longer readings

1. **show** how the main idea expressed by the thesis statement applies in different contexts or settings.

2. **provide** examples of people, events, or theories that illustrate the main idea.

3. **identify** key terms that are necessary to understanding the main idea.

4. **describe** the consequences of some situation or event related to the main idea.

5. **offer** reasons, studies, or statistics meant to prove the main idea correct.

6. **divide** some larger group down into smaller subcategories, describing each one in more specific detail.

7. **trace** a sequence of events that led up to or followed the event or events mentioned in the main idea.

▶ EXERCISE 1   Identifying the Thesis Statement

DIRECTIONS   Each reading is complete except for the first sentence or two. The missing sentence or sentences comprise, or make up, the thesis statement. After reading the chapter section, circle the letter of the thesis statement that would fit the entire reading.

1. The Ethics of Product Placement

1   _____. The goal of product placement is to capture viewers' attention while they're caught up in the fun or drama of a movie, television program, or video game. While viewers note the brand names on everything from cell phones to coffee makers, marketers don't have to announce that the presence of their products is not an accident. In other words, money exchanged hands in order for it to happen.

2   Proponents of this practice say that consumers are sophisticated enough not to be misled. They argue that consumers recognize marketers usually pay to have their brands featured. Critics, however, say that paid product placement should be identified as such. One way to avoid any misunderstanding is to run a notice at the bottom of the screen when the product appears. Another idea is to insert a brief announcement at the beginning or end of the entertainment, the way television shows are required to disclose product plugs.

3   Product placement is even more controversial when news programs are involved. Not long ago, for instance, McDonald's paid to put iced coffee drinks on anchors' desks during television newscasts in Las Vegas. Although the European Union doesn't allow product placement within news shows, the United States has no such ban. There are critics, though, who think a similar ban is needed here. (Adapted from Pride, Hughes, and Kapoor, *Business*, 10th ed., p. 434, © Cengage Learning.)

a. Product placement on news programs is inappropriate, and the United States should follow the Europeans in forbidding the practice of allowing advertising during a news program.

b. Companies routinely use product placement—the paid-for placement of branded products in videos, television, and movies—to lure consumers into buying their goods. While product placement is a profitable marketing strategy, not everyone approves of it.

c. Product placement—the paid-for appearance of brand names in videos, television, and movies—is not unethical as long as the viewer is aware that money has changed hands in order for the product to appear.

2. Encoding Strategies

1 _____. Failure to encode is one of the main reasons why new information does not make its way into long-term memory.

2 **Rehearsal** The more you *rehearse* (mentally review) information as you read, the better you will remember it. But maintenance rehearsal alone is not very effective. *Elaborative encoding*, in which you look for connections to existing knowledge, is far more useful.

3 **Selection** The Dutch scholar Erasmus said that a good memory should be like a fish net: It should keep all the big fish and let the little ones escape. If you boil down paragraphs in most textbooks to one or two important terms or ideas, your memory chores will be more manageable. Mark your texts selectively and use marginal notes to further summarize ideas.

4 **Create Chunks** Assume that you must memorize the following list of words: north, man, red, spring, woman, east, autumn, yellow, summer, boy, blue, west, winter, girl, green, south. This rather difficult list could be reorganized into chunks as follows: (directions) north-south-east-west, (seasons) spring-summer-autumn-winter, (colors) red-yellow-green-blue, (genders) man-woman-boy-girl.

5 **Construct Cues and Make Connections** The best memory cues (stimuli or triggers that call up the memory) are closely related to the information you want to remember and linked to something you already know. For instance, if you want to remember what the word *nebulous* means (cloudy or vague), you might link it to the phrase "cumulus cloud," which you know from science class. For extra insurance, match that cue to a visual image of a cumulus cloud. (Paragraphs 1–4 adapted from Coon and Mitterer, *Introduction to Psychology*, 11th ed., p. 277, © Cengage Learning.)

To remember *nebulous*, think *cumulus*.

© Laraine Flemming.

a. One way to improve your memory is to use techniques that make sure you fully *encode* information, organizing it into a usable or memorable form.

b. Creating chunks of information is an effective way of making sure that new information gets stored in long-term memory.

c. If you want to remember new information, make connections between the new information you want to remember and the already familiar information stored in your long-term memory.

 ## Pattern 2: Ending with the Main Idea

When a chapter section consists of one long paragraph, it's not that common for the main idea to appear at the end of the paragraph. The same, however, is not true for multi-paragraph chapter sections.

With a multi-paragraph chapter section, the opening sentences of the first paragraph often provide background about the topic or the overall main idea. Then the last sentence introduces the thesis statement. That thesis statement focuses and unifies the entire reading while the remaining paragraphs provide the specifics.

Here's an illustration. The heading introduces the topic, "negative campaigning." But notice that the main idea developed throughout the reading doesn't appear until the end of the opening paragraph.

The title suggests the topic.	**Negative Campaigning**
	1 The level of negativism in political campaigns, especially in advertising, has increased, even as the public registers its disapproval of mudslinging. The strident* tone projected in campaigns seems to have fueled mistrust of government and politics. It may also have the effect of reducing voter turnout. <u>Tired of the unrelenting nastiness, states are exploring different ways of controlling negative campaigning.</u>

Negative Campaigning

1 The level of negativism in political campaigns, especially in advertising, has increased, even as the public registers its disapproval of mudslinging. The strident* tone projected in campaigns seems to have fueled mistrust of government and politics. It may also have the effect of reducing voter turnout. <u>Tired of the unrelenting nastiness, states are exploring different ways of controlling negative campaigning.</u>

2 Negative campaign advertising comes in three flavors: *fair*, *false*, and *deceptive*. A fair ad might emphasize some embarassing aspect of an opponent's voting record or some long-forgotten personal mistake. A false ad, as the label implies, contains untrue statements. More problematic are deceptive advertisements, which distort the truth about an opponent. The task for states is to regulate negative campaign advertising without violating the free-speech guarantees of the U.S. Constitution. False advertising that is done with actual malice can be prohibited by a state. However, deceptive ads, complete with accusations and innuendo,* are more difficult to regulate.

3 States have enacted laws prohibiting false campaign statements; candidates who use false ads against their opponents can be fined. One of the problems with these laws is that the damage is done long before the remedy can be applied. Fining a candidate after the election is akin to latching the barn door after the horse has fled. Several states have adopted a fair campaign practices code. These codes typically contain broad guidelines such as "Do not misrepresent the facts" or "Do not make appeals to prejudice based on race or sex." The limitation of the codes is that following them is voluntary rather than mandatory. (Adapted from Bowman and Kearney, *State and Local Government*, 4th ed., p. 107, © Cengage Learning.)

Marginal notes:

The last sentence picks up the title phrase, which is a signal that this sentence is the thesis statement.

Here is where the author connects the paragraph to the overall main idea about the states taking action.

Note how the author opens with a reference to the states enacting laws. This is a way of telling readers, I'm continuing with the same point already under discussion. "States are looking for ways to eliminate or control negative campaigning."

The fact that paragraphs 2 and 3 explain, in more specific terms, the last sentence in the first paragraph is significant. It means that the last sentence is more than the topic sentence of paragraph 1. It is also the thesis statement of the entire reading.

Overall, single paragraphs with the topic sentence in the last position are far less common than paragraphs with the topic sentence in the first position. However, when it comes to the first paragraph of chapter sections, writers frequently make the topic sentence appear at the end. That's because the topic sentence will, as the reading unfolds, turn into the thesis statement that governs the entire section.

---

*strident: loud, angry.
*innuendo: a hint, usually about something unpleasant or damaging to someone else.

READING TIP

Sometimes textbook authors open a chapter section with an anecdote, or story, that illustrates the main idea. Then the last sentence of the paragraph sums up the point of the anecdote. The sentence expressing the point of the story is usually both the topic sentence and thesis statement.

▶ **EXERCISE 2**   **Recognizing Thesis Statements**

DIRECTIONS   Read each chapter section and underline the thesis statement to indicate if it opens or closes the first paragraph.

1. **The Many Faces of Buddhism**

1   Buddhism is the world's fourth largest religion, with around 360 million followers living all around the world, from China to the United States. One reason why Buddhism is so widespread is its spiritual flexibility. As a religion grounded not in the worship of a supreme being but in following the ancient teachings of Gautama Buddha, Buddhism has been able to accommodate many different practices and beliefs as long as they led to the same goal—the attainment of *nirvana*, or spiritual enlightenment, which freed one from the mental and emotional limitations of the human self. In one very early Buddhist sect, or group, for example, it was believed that enlightenment could be achieved by chanting the Buddha's sacred name, Amitābha.

2   Japanese Buddhists, however, believe that meditation focusing on mindful breathing is the central way to purify consciousness in preparation for achieving nirvana. Introduced in the sixth century but becoming truly influential in the thirteenth, Zen Buddhism remains the dominant form of Buddhist worship in Japan. The Zen form of Buddhism spread widely, in part at least because it was the favored form of religious belief for the samurai, the private soldiers of the wealthy. With its emphasis on self-reliance, rigorous discipline, and internal examination of the self, Zen practice perfectly fit the samurai's military code. Because the samurai were often seen as heroic figures, others were encouraged to imitate their religious beliefs.

3   Chinese Buddhists, in contrast, have taken a more communal approach to Buddhism with an emphasis on spiritual connectedness and caring for the larger community. Ironically, given that the Chinese invaded and occupied Tibet, Tibetan Buddhism, with its focus on the Dalai Lama as the spiritual leader, has taken hold in China, although

Chinese followers are not always willing to admit it. The Chinese government has denounced the Dalai Lama as a "wolf in monk's robes," and insists that the Tibetan leader's goal is to separate Tibet from China. Thus, those who practice Tibetan forms of Buddhist worship generally remain quiet about their beliefs. (Sources of information on Chinese Buddhism: http://www.pri.org/stories/2011-12-01/finding-balance-buddhism-and-modern-life-china, last accessed October 28, 2014; http://cla.calpoly.edu/~bmori/syll/Hum310japan/JBUDDHISM.html, last accessed October 29, 2014.)

Like the religion, statues of Buddha take many different forms.

© Ulrich Flemming.

2. Hate Crimes

1   In the fall of 1998, Matthew Shepard, a gay college student, was kidnapped and severely beaten. He died five days after he was found unconscious on a Wyoming ranch, where he had been left tied to a fence for eighteen hours in near-freezing temperatures. His two killers, Aaron J. McKinney and Russell A. Henderson, both twenty-two, were sentenced to life in prison after the Shepard family granted them mercy. *Hate* or *bias crimes*, like the one committed against Matthew Shepard, are violent acts directed toward a particular person or members of a group merely because the targets share a discernible* racial, ethnic, religious, or gender characteristic.

---

*discernible: capable of being seen, noticeable.

2   Hate crimes can include the desecration* of a house of worship or cemetery, harassment of a minority group family that has moved into a previously all-white neighborhood, or a racially motivated murder. For example, on August 23, 1989, Yusef Hawkins, a black youth, was killed in the Bensonhurst section of Brooklyn, New York, because he had wandered into an all-white neighborhood.

3   Hate crimes usually involve convenient, vulnerable targets, who are incapable of fighting back. For example, there have been numerous reported incidents of teenagers attacking the homeless in an effort to rid their town or neighborhood of people they consider undesirable. Another group targeted for hate crimes is gay men and women: gay bashing has become common in some U.S. cities.

4   Racial and ethnic minorities have also been the targets of attack. In California, Mexican laborers have been attacked and killed. In New Jersey, Indian immigrants have been the targets of racial hatred. Although hate crimes are often mindless attacks directed toward "traditional" minority victims, political and economic trends may cause this form of violence to be redirected. For example, Asians have been attacked by groups who resent the growing economic power of Japan and Korea as well as the commercial success of Asian Americans.

(Adapted from Siegel, *Criminology*, 10th ed., p. 322, © Cengage Learning.)

Pattern 3: Using Reversal Transitions to Introduce Thesis Statements

Textbook authors can set the stage for the thesis statement in any number of ways, from offering some history about the topic to recounting a news event related to the main idea. But whatever approach they take to the introduction, writers, particularly of textbooks, are likely to use reversal transitions to tell readers, "I've finished the introduction. Here comes the thesis statement."

In the following reading, for instance, the author introduces the thesis statement by first describing a common image of Thomas Jefferson. But that's not the overall main idea of the reading. In fact, the author's point is quite the opposite. Note how he prepares the reader for the shift from introduction to main idea by using the words *personally* and *however*.

---

*desecration: act of destroying or showing disrespect for objects or places considered sacred by some group.

Shop 'Til You Drop

The first two sentences offer the public image of Jefferson.

1   Jefferson[†] is the patron saint* of economical government, an honor he deserves. He insisted that his secretary of the treasury count by the penny when he drafted federal budgets. Personally, *however,* Jefferson was a spendthrift. He spent as much as $2,800 a year on wine, and up to $50 a day on groceries at a time when a turkey cost 50 cents. Twice when he had a new architectural idea, he had large parts of Monticello, his home, torn down and rebuilt.

Note how the word *personally* shifts the context from public to private while the word *however* paves the way for the thesis statement.

2   In Paris, during the 1780s, he lived as extravagantly as the French nobles with whom he hobnobbed. When he visited John and Abigail Adams in London, the frenzy* of his shopping spree appalled the thrifty New Englanders.

Paragraph 3 makes it seem that the author is turning away from Jefferson's money problems until the word *but* brings the subject of his money problems back into focus.

3   Already rich in land and slaves, Jefferson inherited more wealth from his wife when she died in 1782—but he also inherited a huge debt her father had bequeathed her. Jefferson was never again out of debt and he never made what can be called a serious attempt at belt-tightening to reduce it. He sold slaves, land, and even his beloved library when his creditors threatened to take legal action. When he died in 1826, he saddled his daughter with so much debt that she had to sell Jefferson's much renovated Monticello. (Adapted from Conlin, *The American Past*, 8th ed., p. 199, © Cengage Learning.)

The author of the reading on Jefferson uses the two opening sentences to tell the reader what's usually said about Jefferson. This introduction is a variation on the "that was then, this is now" introduction from Chapter 4. In this case, the author recounts Jefferson's public image only to point out how different the private one was.

Keep in mind as well that *introductions don't have a fixed length.* Even textbook authors, who are prone to getting quickly to the point, might use an entire paragraph, maybe even two paragraphs, to set the stage for the main idea. Thus, the thesis statement wouldn't appear until the second or even the third paragraph. Here's a good example:

Global Adoptions

While the thesis statement might be in the first paragraph, it's unlikely because these factual statements don't require much additional explanation.

1   Over the last decade, U.S. families have adopted on average 20,000 children from foreign nations each year. These families pay an average of $30,000 for an international adoption, including at least one visit to the country of their adopted child's birth.

[†]Thomas Jefferson: Jefferson was the country's third president and the author of the Declaration of Independence, which was a declaration of rebellion against British rule.
*patron saint: protecting and guiding spirit.
*frenzy: period of wild excitement and/or behavior.

Note how the opening transitional sentence guides the reader to the main idea expressed in the second sentence, which is also the thesis statement.

The last sentence in the second paragraph identifies a major concern. Here in the third paragraph, the author tells readers how UNICEF addresses that concern.

2   But while international adoptions can be filled with great joy, they sometimes have a more menacing side. Human rights abuses, including the abduction of children, within the context of international adoptions are frequently reported and are a significant issue of concern. Unfortunately, there are many examples of children being taken from their home countries under dubious circumstances.

3   While the United Nations International Children's Emergency Fund (UNICEF) does not strictly oppose international adoption, it has stated that it believes international adoption should be considered only when the child cannot be suitably cared for in his or her home country. UNICEF'S position has been that if a child has been abandoned, biological parents or extended family should be located. If that is not possible, placement for the child with a foster or in-country adoptive family should be looked into. Only when all other options have been exhausted should inter-country adoption be considered.

4   UNICEF has said that its policy seeks to ensure that international adoptions are conducted within a legal framework that protects the best interests of the child. The organization notes that many international adoptions are completed in good faith. However, UNICEF has also warned that a lack of legal oversight has resulted in child trafficking and kidnappings.

5   On April 1st, 2008, a new international treaty called the Hague Convention on Protection of Children and Co-operation in Respect of Inter-country Adoption entered into force in the United States. The Convention establishes important standards and safeguards to protect children in the process of inter-country adoptions. Adoptions are unable to proceed if such standards and safeguards are not met. As of early 2009, for example, the U.S. Department of State issued adoption alerts on Vietnam and Guatemala, noting that United States citizens are not able to register new adoptions in those countries due to lack of sufficient safeguards at this time. (Adapted from Theresa M. Hornstein and Jeri Lynn Schwerin, *Biology of Women*, 5th ed., p. 361, © Cengage Learning.)

In this reading, the author uses the opening paragraph to provide some background about international adoptions. Then a transitional sentence paves the way for the real point of the reading, introduced in the second, rather than the first, paragraph: International adoptions also have a dark side.

READING TIP   When it comes to following the author's train of thought, the opening sentence of each supporting paragraph is especially important. Much of the time, the first sentence of the supporting paragraph is where you will find out how the new paragraph links up to what came before.

WEB QUEST
What kind of government is suggested by the phrase "Jeffersonian Democracy"?

_____

_____

_____

▶ **EXERCISE 3**   Identifying the Main Idea in Multi-Paragraph Readings

DIRECTIONS   When you finish the reading, write your version of the main idea in the blanks that follow. Then underline the thesis statement.

EXAMPLE

Rebound Marriages

1   A rebound marriage results when people marry someone immediately after another person has ended a relationship with them. It is a frantic and usually unfortunate attempt on their part to reestablish their desirability in their own eyes and in the eyes of the partner who dropped them. One man said, "After she told me she wouldn't marry me, I became desperate. I called up an old girlfriend to see if I could get the relationship going again. We were married within a month. I know it was foolish, but I was very hurt and couldn't stop myself."

Note how the openings of paragraphs 2 and 3 keep on bringing the reader back to the topic of rebound marriages and the negative consequences they produce.

2   To marry on the rebound is questionable because the marriage is made in reference to the previous partner and not to the partner being married. In reality, people who engage in rebound marriage are using the person they intend to marry to establish themselves as a "winner" in a previous relationship.

3   To avoid the negative consequences of marrying on the rebound, wait until the negative memories of a past relationship have been replaced by positive aspects of a current relationship. In other words, marry when the satisfaction of being with the current partner outweighs any feelings of revenge. This normally takes between twelve and eighteen months. In addition, be careful about getting involved in a relationship with someone who is recently divorced or just emerged from the painful ending of a previous relationship.

(Knox and Schacht, *Choices in Relationships*, 10th ed., p. 199, © Cengage Learning.)

In your own words, what's the main idea of the reading?

People who marry someone else immediately after getting dumped and enter into a

rebound marriage may well live to regret it.

EXPLANATION   Recognizing the topic of this reading is not especially difficult. Every paragraph returns to the subject of rebound marriages. What might be less clear is why the first two sentences are underlined as the thesis statement. Maybe you are thinking that the first sentence, which defines rebound marriage, expresses the overall main idea. But that's not really true.

The "negative consequences" of marrying on the rebound are repeated and referred to. So if someone were to ask you what the reading was about, you couldn't just define the term *rebound marriage*. You would also have to mention that the reading outlines the drawbacks of rebound marriages. That's why you need to underline two sentences rather than one for the thesis statement.

1. Forced Sterilization of Women

1   A woman's reproductive rights are critical aspects of her broader independence. Yet many times, these rights are at risk. At particular risk are the reproductive rights of women from ethnic minority groups. Worldwide, the ugly practice of forced sterilization has been used to oppress women of various racial and ethnic groups. Forced sterilization is the process of permanently ending someone's ability to reproduce without her free consent.

2   There are several examples of situations where particular groups of women have been targeted with forced sterilization. In the United States, according to General Accounting Office reports, some 3,406 Native American women between the ages of 15 and 44 were sterilized between 1973 and 1976 by Indian Health Service medical personnel. The true numbers, however, may be much higher. The exact numbers remain unknown because the initial investigation was limited to four Indian Health Service hospitals. Thus, the total number of women sterilized remains unknown. The GAO's report listed many violations of the rights of Native American women undergoing sterilization procedures, such as inadequate consent forms, medical personnel ignoring a wide range of professional requirements, and the sterilization of girls.

3   Peru provides another example. In the mid-to-late 1990s in Peru, some 200,000 to 300,000 women were forcibly sterilized. In 2002, Peru's Minister of Health issued a national apology for the forced sterilization of these women. According to Peruvian rights advocate

Maria Esther Mogollon, sterilizations focused on poor and indigenous* women. The majority of these women never signed informed consent statements for their sterilization. In some cases, when women went into the hospital to give birth, doctors sterilized them without their consent. Many would not find out until several years later that they had, in fact, been sterilized.

4   In more recent years, Romani women in the Czech Republic, Slovakia, and Hungary have also faced forced sterilization. In 2005, the Czech Public Defender of Rights issued a report, which found more than 80 cases of forced sterilizations where doctors failed to ensure informed consent. As in Peru, sterilizations were performed on Romani women during their deliveries without their prior informed consent. Other Romani women gave their written consent to sterilization, but were coerced into doing so at the time when their delivery was in progress and they were in the midst of regular contractions. (Adapted from Theresa M. Hornstein and Jeri Lynn Scherin, *Biology for Women*, 5th ed., p. 337, © Cengage Learning.)

In your own words, what's the main idea of this reading?

_____

_____

2. Protecting Children from Toxic Chemicals

1   In 2005, the Environmental Working Group analyzed umbilical cord blood from ten randomly* selected newborns in U.S. hospitals. Of the 287 chemicals detected, 180 cause cancers in humans or animals, 217 damage the brain and nervous system in test animals, and 208 cause birth defects or abnormal development in test animals. Scientists do not know what harm, if any, the very low concentrations of these chemicals found in the infants' blood might cause, but they are deeply concerned.

2   Infants and young children are more susceptible to the effects of toxic substances than are adults for three major reasons. First, children breathe more air, drink more water, and eat more food per unit of body weight than do adults. Second, they are exposed to toxins in dust or soil when they put their fingers, toys, or other objects in their mouths. Third, children usually have less well-developed immune systems and body detoxification processes than adults have.

_____

*indigenous: native to the country, already there when it was settled by outsiders.
*randomly: with no particular pattern.

3   In 2003, the U.S. Environmental Protection Agency (EPA) proposed that in determining risk, regulators should assume children have ten times the exposure risk of adults to cancer-causing chemicals. Some health scientists contend that these guidelines are too weak. They suggest that, to be on the safe side, we should assume that the risk of harm from toxins for children is 100 times that of adults. Others support doing this on ethical grounds. They say it is wrong not to give children much greater protection from harmful chemicals in the environment.

(Adapted from Miller, *Living in the Environment*, 15th ed., p. 432, © Cengage Learning.)

In your own words, what's the main idea of the reading?

_____

_____

Pattern 4: Answering a Question with the Thesis Statement

As they do with single paragraphs, writers—textbook writers in particular—like to use questions to focus readers' attention on the main idea. Similar to single paragraphs, the answer to the opening question of a chapter section is likely to be the thesis statement expressing the main idea. This explanatory pattern appears in all disciplines, or subjects. But once again, it is particularly popular in psychology texts, for example:

The Function of REM Sleep

The opening question focuses readers' attention on the point of the reading—to tell readers about the purpose of REM sleep.

The thesis statement provides an immediate answer.

1   *What is the purpose of REM sleep?* REM[†] sleep appears to sharpen our memories of the previous day's most significant experiences. This is why daytime stress tends to increase REM sleep, which may rise dramatically when there is a death in the family, trouble at work, a marital* conflict, or other emotionally charged events. The value of more REM sleep is that it helps us sort and retain memories, especially memories about strategies for solving problems. This is why, after studying for a long period, you may remember more if you go to sleep, rather than pulling an all-nighter. (REMember to get some REM!)

_____

[†]REM is an acronym. That means it's made up of the first letter of each word in a term or phrase (in this case, Rapid Eye Movement) and used as a pronounceable word in its own right.
*marital: related to marriage.

Note how the opening phrase of paragraph 2 helps the reader shift the focus to infants.

2   Early in life, REM sleep may stimulate the developing brain. Newborn babies have lots of new experiences to process so they spend a hearty eight or nine hours a day in REM sleep. That's about 50 percent of their total sleep time. But infants may need that much REM sleep in order to take in all of the new experiences they encounter on a daily basis. (Adapted from Coon and Mitterer, *Introduction to Psychology*, 11th ed., p. 187, © Cengage Learning.)

As it so often does, a question like the one opening this two-paragraph selection, points the way to what the author wants you to learn from the reading. Once you finish it, you should be able to answer the question: What is the purpose of REM sleep?

The answer to that question comes in the second sentence of paragraph 1. That sentence is not just the topic sentence of the opening paragraph. It is also the thesis statement of the selection: REM sleep intensifies our awareness of the day's significant events. The remainder of the paragraph tells us more about the type of memories REM sleep heightens.

Typically, when a chapter section opens with a question—particularly if the question is a separate heading—the answer to the question is also the thesis statement of the entire reading. It's rare for writers to start off a chapter section with a question and then not make the answer the overall main idea. However, it's not always true that the answer immediately follows the question. Sometimes the question will appear in one paragraph, the answer in another.

READING TIP

Writers don't *always* answer their opening questions immediately. Sometimes they give a traditional or commonsense answer only to reverse it before introducing the answer they really intend to address. Writers who take this approach will usually introduce the real answer to the question (i.e., the thesis statement) with a reversal transition, so it will be easy to spot.

▶ **EXERCISE 4**   **Paraphrasing Thesis Statements in Multi-Paragraph Readings**

DIRECTIONS   Underline the author's thesis statement. Then paraphrase it in the blanks that follow.

1. Are Cross-Pressures a Problem for Adolescents?

1 In years gone by, adolescence was often characterized as a stormy period when all youths experience *cross-pressures*—strong conflicts

that stem from differences in the values or practices advocated by their parents and those favored by peers. How accurate is this life portrait of the teenage years? It may have some merit* for adolescents, particularly those "rejected" youths who form deviant peer cliques that endorse and promote antisocial conduct. But there are reasons why the so-called cross-pressures "problem" is simply not a problem for most adolescents.

2   One reason that parent/peer conflicts are kept to a minimum is that parents and peers tend to exert their influence in different domains.* Hans Sebald, for example, asked adolescents whether they would seek the advice of their parents or the advice of their peers on a number of different issues. Peers were likely to be more influential than parents on such issues as what styles to wear and which clubs, social events, hobbies, and other recreational activities to choose. By contrast, adolescents claimed that they would depend more on their parents when the issue involved school or work-related goals. Teenagers are unlikely to be torn between parent and peer pressure as long as parents and peers have different primary areas of influence.

3   A second, more important reason why parent/peer warfare is typically kept to a minimum is parents, by virtue of their parenting styles, have a good deal of influence on the company their adolescents keep. Authoritative parents who are warm, neither too controlling nor too lax, and who are consistent in their discipline generally find that their adolescents are closely attached to them and have internalized their values. These adolescents have little need to rebel or to desperately seek acceptance from peers when they are so warmly received at home. (Adapted from Shaffer, *Social and Personality Development*, 6th ed., p. 487, © Cengage Learning.)

In your own words, what's the overall main idea of this reading?

_____

_____

2. Are Men More Aggressive than Women?

1   Despite differences across cultures, one thing is universal: Men are more violent than women. This has been found in virtually all studies of

---

*to have merit: to show accuracy or truth; to be convincing.
*domains: areas or spheres of influence.

cultures around the world. According to U.S. Department of Justice data for 2011, 90 percent of the murders in the United States were committed by males. Men commit the majority of homicides and make up the majority of murder victims. Males are also physically more aggressive than females. This is true across all cultures that have been sampled.

2 So does this mean that the stereotype about males being more aggressive than females is correct? Not necessarily. Deciding who is more aggressive, males or females, depends on how one defines aggression, because there are many ways to harm someone other than by physical means. That difference was expressed by a remark a child made to researchers Britt Galen and Marion Underwood, "Boys may use their fists to fight, but at least it's over with quickly; girls use their tongues, and it goes on forever."

3 Research on aggression reveals that although boys tend to be more *overtly* aggressive than girls, boys do not tend to be more aggressive than girls when it comes to indirect or *relational aggression*. Indeed, for these types of aggression, girls sometimes are more aggressive than boys. Indirect forms of aggression include acts such as telling lies to get someone in trouble or shutting a person out of desired activities. Relational aggression is one kind of indirect aggression that targets personal connections and social status with threats to end a relationship or engaging in hurtful gossip.

4 Why are girls at least as aggressive as boys on relationship (but not physical) forms of aggression? Researchers believe that females typically care more about relationships and intimacy than males do, and that's why they employ relationship aggression. Injuring someone socially may seem a particularly effective form of punishment. Another reason may be that strong norms encourage boys to be physically aggressive, but these same norms discourage girls from doing so.

5 Numerous studies conducted in a variety of countries around the world have found that females tend to engage in indirect aggression more often than males. However, many others have found only minor or no significant gender differences. The results of meta-analyses* (Archer 2004; Card et al., 2008) that have reviewed the very large research literature on the topic have found very small but statistically significant gender differences, with girls exhibiting somewhat more indirect aggression than boys. (Adapted from Saul Kassin et al., *Social Psychology*, 8th ed., p. 443, © Cengage Learning.)

---

*meta-analyses: a study that looks at numerous studies on the same subject in order to identify general patterns of agreement or disagreement.

In your own words, what's the overall main idea of this reading?

_____

_____

3. The Truth About ADHD

1   Many myths surround Attention Deficit/Hyperactivity Disorder (ADHD). One myth concerns causes. At one time or another, TV, food allergies, sugar, and poor home life have all been proposed as causes of ADHD. But heredity is actually a much more important factor.

2   Twin studies show that identical twins are often diagnosed with ADHD, but this is uncommon for fraternal twins.[†] Similarly, adoption studies show that children are more prone to ADHD when a biological parent has been diagnosed with ADHD than when an adoptive parent has. In addition, prenatal exposure to alcohol and other drugs can place children at risk for ADHD.

3   Another myth is that children "grow out of" ADHD in adolescence or young adulthood. More than half of the children diagnosed with ADHD will have problems related to overactivity, inattention, and impulsivity in adolescence and adulthood. Few of these young adults complete college, and some will have work- and family-related problems.

4   One final myth is that many healthy children are wrongly diagnosed with ADHD. The number of children diagnosed with ADHD increased substantially during the 1990s, but this was not because children were being routinely misdiagnosed. The increased numbers reflected growing awareness of ADHD and more frequent diagnoses of ADHD in girls and adolescents.

(Adapted from Kail and Cavanaugh, _Human Development_, 5th ed., p. 230, © Cengage Learning.)

In your own words, what's the overall main idea of this reading?

_____

_____

4. Increasing Requirements for a Marriage License

1   Should marriage licenses be obtained so easily? Should couples be required, or at least encouraged, to participate in premarital education before saying "I do"? Given the high rate of divorce today, policy makers are considering this issue. Although evidence of long-term

---

[†]fraternal twins: siblings born at the same time but who are not identical.

effectiveness of premarital education remains elusive,* some believe that "mandatory* counseling will promote marital stability." . . .

2   Several states, for instance, have proposed legislation requiring premarital education. For example, an Oklahoma statute provides that parties who complete a premarital education program pay a reduced fee for their marriage license. Also in Lenawee County, Michigan, local civil servants and clergy have made a pact: They will not marry a couple unless that couple has attended marriage education classes. Other states that are considering policies to require or encourage premarital education include Arizona, Illinois, Maryland, Minnesota, Mississippi, Missouri, Oregon, and Washington.

3   Proposed policies include not only mandating premarital education and lowering marriage license fees for those who attend courses but also imposing delays on issuing marriage licenses for those who refuse premarital education. However, "no state mandates premarital counseling as a prerequisite to obtaining a license." (Adapted from Knox and Schacht, *Choices in Relationships*, 10th ed., p. 196, © Cengage Learning.)

In your own words, what's the overall main idea of this reading?

_____

_____

SUMMING UP THE KEY POINTS

1. In multi-paragraph readings, the stated main idea is called the *thesis statement*.
2. Like paragraphs, multi-paragraph readings in textbooks rely heavily on some basic explanatory patterns.
   - The thesis statement starts the reading and the remaining paragraphs function as the supporting details.
   - The reading opens with an introduction followed by a reversal transition that announces the arrival of the thesis statement.

---

*elusive: hard to prove or catch, or understand.
*mandatory: required or commanded by authority.

- The first paragraph introduces the main idea at the end and that main idea is further developed by the supporting paragraphs, making the topic sentence of one paragraph the thesis statement for the entire reading.
- The reading opens with a question and the thesis statement provides the answer.

3. Just as with single paragraphs, repetition and reference are clues to the meaning of longer, multi-paragraph readings. As you move from paragraph to paragraph, note the words and phrases that come up repeatedly. Try to determine how they combine into a main idea that governs the entire reading.

From Reader to Writer What's your opinion on the idea of linking a marriage license to mandatory marital counseling? Explain why you are for or against that idea, and, equally important, what your reasons are for holding the opinion that you do.

✓ CHECK YOUR UNDERSTANDING

1. Describe four common ways that textbook authors introduce the main ideas of chapter sections.

_____

_____

_____

_____

2. How does a thesis statement differ from a topic sentence?

_____

3. When you read, why is it important to keep an eye out for words that are repeated or referred to throughout the passage or reading?

_____

DIGGING DEEPER Can Physical Aggression Be Learned? *Saul Kassin, Steven Fein, and Hazel Rose Markus*

Looking Ahead On pages 266–67, you learned about gender differences in aggression. This reading looks at aggression from a slightly different perspective. It attempts to answer the question, Are aggressive people born that way or do they learn to be aggressive from their environment?

Getting Focused As with paragraphs, questions in the title or in the opening lines of a reading are significant. Anytime you see a question in the title, you should be able to answer that question by the time you finish the reading.

1   Regardless of the precise contribution of genetic and biological factors, it is clear that aggressive behavior is strongly affected by learning (Bandura, 1973). For example, rewards obtained by aggression today tend to increase its use tomorrow. Such rewards come in two flavors: *positive reinforcement,* when aggression produces desired outcomes, and *negative reinforcement*, when aggression prevents or stops undesirable outcomes. The child who gets a toy by hitting the toy's owner is likely to hit again. So, too, the child who can stop other children from teasing by shoving them away has learned a fateful lesson: aggression pays. Children who see aggression producing more good outcomes and fewer bad outcomes are more aggressive than other children (Boldizar et al., 1989).

2   Rewards are only one part of how people learn to be physically aggressive. What about punishment? Often promoted as a way to reduce aggressive behavior, punishment can also play a role in encouraging it. Some politicians and police officials in New York City believe that the dramatic reduction in crime in the city in recent years is due in large part to swift, more effective punishment of all crimes, even relatively minor crimes such as vandalism. They believe that speedy punishment sends the message that crime does not pay. Is it true, then, that punishment discourages physical aggression?

3   Research suggests that punishment is most likely to decrease aggression when it (1) immediately follows the aggressive behavior, (2) is strong enough to deter the aggressor, and (3) is consistently applied and perceived as fair and legitimate to the aggressor. However, such strict conditions are seldom met, and when they are not, punishment can backfire and encourage physical aggression. When courts are over-burdened and prisons are over-crowded, which is often the case, the relationship

between crime and punishment can seem more like a lottery than a rational system in which the punishment fits the crime. In short, the certainty of the punishment is more important than its *severity*.

4   There are other problems with using punishment to limit aggression. Punishment perceived as unfair or arbitrary* can provoke retaliation, thereby creating a cycle of aggression. Perhaps most troubling is that punishment, especially when delivered in an angry or hostile manner, offers an aggressive model to imitate in the future.

5   Researcher Murray Strauss and his colleagues have been outspoken critics of the use of corporal punishment, or physical force in the form of spanking, hitting, and pinching, intended to cause a child pain and used as a way of controlling behavior. Although the large majority of children in the United States experience spanking and other forms of corporal punishment, numerous studies suggest a connection between spanking and later aggressive behavior. In other words, more corporal punishment now is associated with aggressive behavior later on. (Adapted from Saul Kassin et al., *Social Psychology*, 8th ed., pp. 448–9, © Cengage Learning.)

Sharpening Your Skills

DIRECTIONS   Answer the questions by filling in the blanks or circling the letter of the correct response.

Using Context Clues   **1.** What kind of context clue do the authors provide for the word *corporal* in paragraph 5?

    a. example

    b. contrast

    c. restatement

    d. general knowledge

Main Ideas and Explanatory Patterns   **2.** What explanatory pattern do the authors use for this reading as a whole?

    a. The first paragraph opens with the thesis statement that governs the rest of the reading.

    b. The first paragraph ends with the thesis statement that governs the rest of the reading.

---

*arbitrary: lacking in reason or system, based on personal whim.

c. The first paragraph provides an introduction and uses a reversal transition to introduce the thesis statement that governs the rest of the reading.

d. The first paragraph provides an introduction while the second paragraph uses a question and answer format to introduce the thesis statement that governs the rest of the reading.

3. Where do the authors answer the question they pose at the end of paragraph 2: "Is it true, then, that punishment discourages physical aggression"?

a. They answer the question immediately after asking it.

b. They delay the answer until the second sentence of the third paragraph.

c They answer the question in paragraph 4.

4. What explanatory pattern do the authors use in paragraph 3?

a. They open with the topic sentence.

b. They put the topic sentence at the end.

c. After the introduction, they use a reversal transition to pave the way for the topic sentence.

Following the Author's Train of Thought

5. In paragraph 4, the authors say there are other "problems" associated with using punishment to control behavior. How many and what problems are then identified?

_____

_____

Understanding the Function of Supporting Details

6. In paragraph 1, what do these supporting details illustrate: "The child who gets a toy by hitting the toy's owner is likely to hit again. So, too, the child who can stop other children from teasing by shoving them away has learned a fateful lesson: aggression pays"?

_____

7. Why is Murray Strauss quoted in this reading?

_____

_____

Paraphrasing　8. How would you paraphrase this statement from paragraph 1: "For example, rewards obtained by aggression today tend to increase its use tomorrow"?

_____

_____

9. In your own words, how do the authors answer the question posed in paragraph 2: "But rewards are only one part of how people learn to be physically aggressive. What about punishment"?

_____

_____

10. In your own words, explain the difference between positive and negative reinforcement.

_____

_____

_____

From Reader to Writer Write a few paragraphs explaining why, if you have—or plan to have—children, you will or will not use spanking to correct their behavior. Use the reading you just completed as part of your introduction by pointing out what the authors suggest about spanking and aggression. Once you summarize the reading in a sentence or two, introduce your thesis statement, which should indicate that you are or are not influenced by the author's conclusions.

▶ TEST 1   Reviewing Key Concepts

DIRECTIONS   Answer the following questions by filling in the blanks.

1. What is the function of a thesis statement?

   _____

   How does it differ from a topic sentence?

   _____

   _____

2. When a textbook author gets right to the point, how does he or she start a chapter section?

   _____

3. With a multi-paragraph chapter section, the opening sentences of the first paragraph often provide background about the topic and the overall main idea. Then the last sentence introduces _____ of the paragraph, which also functions as the _____ .

4. If the author opens a chapter section with a question, what will be the function of the thesis statement?

   _____

5. When an author opens a chapter section by telling you what was traditionally thought or said about a topic or main idea, you should be on the lookout for a _____ that signals _____ .

▶ **TEST 2**   **Recognizing Thesis Statements**

DIRECTIONS   Underline the thesis statement in each reading.

1. Is Joint Custody Becoming the Norm?

1   As men have become more involved in the nurturing of children, the courts no longer assume that "parent" means "mother." Instead, a new family relations model is emerging. It suggests that even nonbiological parents may be awarded joint custody or visitation rights as long as they have been economically and emotionally involved in the life of the child.

2   Given that fathers are no longer routinely excluded from custody considerations, over half of the states have enacted legislation authorizing joint custody. About 16 percent of separated and divorced couples actually have a joint custody arrangement. In a typical joint physical custody arrangement, the parents continue to live near one another. The children may spend part of each week with each parent or may spend alternating weeks with each parent. New terminology is even being introduced in the lives of divorcing spouses and in the courts. The term "joint custody," which implies ownership, is being replaced with "shared parenting," which implies cooperation in taking care of children.

3   There are several advantages to joint custody or shared parenting. Ex-spouses may fight less if they have joint custody because there is no inequality in terms of involvement in their children's lives. Children will benefit from the resulting decrease in hostility between parents who have both "won" them.

4   Unlike sole-parent custody, in which one parent wins (usually the mother) and the other parent loses, joint custody allows children to continue to benefit from the love and attention of both parents. Children in homes where joint custody has been awarded might also have greater financial resources available to them than children in sole-custody homes.

5   Joint physical custody may also be advantageous in that the stress of parenting does not fall on one parent but rather is shared. One mother who has a joint custody arrangement with her ex-husband said, "When my kids are with their dad, I get a break from the parenting role, and I have a chance to do things for myself. I love my kids but I also love having time away from them." Another joint-parenting father

said, "When you live with your kids every day, you can get very frustrated and are not always happy to be with them. But after you haven't seen them for three days, it feels good to see them again." (Adapted from Knox and Schacht, *Choices in Relationships*, 10th ed., p. 510, © Cengage Learning.)

2. Lost in the Fog of War

1 Decimated by war, first with France in the 1950s, then with the United States, the southeast Asian country of Vietnam appears to be booming again, with many of the country's citizens enjoying a sense of peace and well-being. That's true at least for those citizens who don't have freckles, white skin, or blue eyes. In Vietnam, freckles are a source of shame. They announce American parentage and make their owners despised because they are Vietnamese Amerasians, the children of mothers who slept with American soldiers during the country's war with the United States. Considered offspring of a once-hated enemy, Vietnam's Amerasians are despised by the people they live with and rejected by the country to which they believe they rightly belong: the United States.

2 Initially, though, the United States did make attempts to reach a hand out to the children U.S. soldiers had left behind after the Vietnam War ended in 1975. The 1987 Congressional "Homecoming Act" even funded a city center for Vietnamese Amerasians. At the same time, the government also offered visas to the offspring of American soldiers. At that point, the only thing needed to qualify for a visa was an obviously mixed-race appearance. That alone could guarantee resettlement in the United States. But these good intentions on the part of the Americans were undermined when con artists began picking kids up off the streets and attaching them to fake relatives, who also wanted a new life in the United States.

3 The easy visas, dried up as officials began demanding hard evidence—documents, letters, and pictures—as proof of an American father. The problem was that any such evidence had been quickly destroyed after the war with the United States ended and the Viet Cong took over Vietnam. No woman who had been involved with the enemy wanted visible proof of the relationship. In addition, a country in wartime doesn't usually excel at filing documents.

4 Thus, Vietnam's Amerasians, most of whom desperately want to leave a country that despises them because of their parents, are left to search for their fathers on the Internet, using what little they know

about their past to search out a father who may not even care to know they exist. For a number of years, they have had an ally in a Danish furniture painter named Brian Hjort, who created a website called FatherFounded.org. Backpacking through Vietnam in the 1990s, Hjort became friendly with some Amerasian war orphans, and was impressed by their generosity and warmth. He became determined to aid their cause, even though he knew most of the fathers he was searching for would probably never be found.

5   Hjort's website has brought about a few successful reunions. But he depends on donations for continuing his work, and it's not clear how long he can carry on. Still, for now at least, the site remains in existence, and Hjort does his best to reunite American fathers with the children they fathered during war time, because as he says on his website, "Amerasians are paying the price for past events in Vietnam." In his mind, at least, someone needs to take responsibility for their plight.

(Source of information: Patrick Winn, "Vietnam War Babies: Grown Up and Low on Luck," September 2, 2011, Salon.com.)

▶ **TEST 3**   **Recognizing and Paraphrasing Thesis Statements**

DIRECTIONS   Underline the thesis statement. Then paraphrase it in the blanks that follow.

1. Dreams and Creativity

1   History is full of cases where dreams have been a pathway to creativity and discovery. A striking example is provided by Dr. Otto Loewi, a pharmacologist and winner of a Nobel Prize. Loewi had spent years studying the chemical transmission of nerve impulses. A tremendous breakthrough in his research came when he dreamed of an experiment three nights in a row. The first two nights he woke up and scribbled the experiment on a pad. But the next morning, he couldn't tell what the notes meant. On the third night, he got up after having the dream. This time, instead of making notes he went straight to his laboratory and performed the crucial experiment. Loewi said later that if the experiment had occurred to him while awake, he would have rejected it.

2   Loewi's experience gives some insight into using dreams to produce creative solutions. Inhibitions are reduced during dreaming, which may be especially useful in solving problems that require a fresh point of view. Even unimaginative people may create amazing worlds each night in their dreams. For many of us, this rich ability to create is lost in the daily rush of everyday life when we are pulled in so many different directions.

3   The ability to take advantage of dreams for problem solving is improved if you "set" yourself before retiring. Before you go to bed, try to visualize or think intently about a problem you wish to solve. Steep yourself in the problem by stating it clearly and reviewing all relevant information.

4   Although this method is not guaranteed to produce a novel solution or a new insight, it is certain to be an adventure. In one study, at least half of the subjects, all of them college students, recalled a dream that helped them solve a personal problem. (Adapted from Coon and Mitterer, *Introduction to Psychology*, 11th ed., p. 214.)

Paraphrase   _____

_____

2. The Content Cleaners

1   Stories about the luxuries provided to those employed by big tech companies abound. Among the many perks tech employees are given are gyms, game rooms, yoga classes, juice bars, and made-to-order stir fry stands. Work for one of the big guns in the tech business, say Google, Facebook, or even Dropbox, and you are guaranteed to be living the American dream, unless, of course, you are a *content moderator*. Content moderators are the people social media companies employ to make sure that those using their services are not confronted by pornographic pictures, racist slurs, sexist rants, or murder threats. Tech employees who moderate content are definitely not living the dream.

2   There are well over 100,000 content moderators employed by social media companies. Many of them work overseas, a large number of them in the Philippines. But they also work out of Morocco, China, and Africa. Generally, those working overseas do "basic" moderation. Their job is to monitor the raw feeds of social networking sites and delete any obvious images or messages that would nauseate, insult, wound, or terrorize a social media user. They are cautioned to be on the lookout for threats of forced sex, gory or sexualized images of body parts—both human and animal—and anything considered racist, pornographic, or homicidal. For policing the lunatics of the world, overseas content moderators make around one dollar an hour, usually earning between four or five hundred dollars a month.

3   Content moderators who work in the United States are generally tasked with evaluating posts that require a better understanding of the cultural context, for instance, when is a statement a racial slur rather than a lyric from a rap song? These moderators are better paid than their overseas colleagues. But they, too, like the moderators overseas, often spend their days sifting and sorting their way through posts that do not place humanity in its best light. According to one former moderator who worked for YouTube, U.S.-based moderators generally can take the job for somewhere between three and five months before they start worrying about the effect of the content on their psyche. For moderator Jake Swearingen, the last straw was yelling to a co-worker that he had just seen a video of a beheading and having his colleague turn around and casually ask, "Which one?" At that moment—the moment witnessing a beheading seemed no big deal to a co-worker—Swearingen knew he had to move on and find another form of employment before he developed the same casual attitude

toward violent and brutal acts. (Source of information: www.wired.com/2014/10/
content-moderation/, last accessed October 28, 2014.)

Paraphrase _____

_____

▶ **TEST 4**   **Recognizing and Paraphrasing Thesis Statements**

DIRECTIONS   Underline the thesis statement. Then paraphrase it in the blanks that follow.

1. Debt and the Federal Government

1   Like most Americans, you probably think about the way the government spends its money the same way you think about how you ought to spend yours. If you spend more than you earn, you will have to borrow money and pay it back to the bank. If you want to buy a car or a house, you will have to get a loan and make monthly payments on it. If you run up so many charges on your credit card that it is maxed out, you won't be able to charge anything more on it. Surely the government ought to work the same way: spend no more than it earns and pay back its loans.

2   But it doesn't. And there are two basic reasons why the government can, on a regular basis, spend more than it earns. One reason is that a debt is important or worrisome only insofar as the government cannot make the payments on its bonds in a currency that people regard as stable and valuable. As long as people believe that the American dollar is stable and valuable, they line up to buy Treasury bonds. As a result, the government in Washington, like the owners of Walmart, can pay for whatever they want.

3   The government can also run up debt because it can afford to pay the interest. The total federal debt is a very large number (in 2015 it was already over eighteen trillion dollars). But the number, while huge, does not mean much when taken alone. Currently interest rates have remained low and the economy can afford the interest payments. Federal interest payments take up about 1.7 percent of the total value of all of the goods and services the nation produces, called the *Gross Domestic Product* or *GDP*. If interest rates stay low, the government may be able to continue to do what consumers can't do, which is spend more than it earns. But if interest rates start climbing, the government might have to look more closely at spending versus debt.

(Adapted from Wilson and Dilulio, *American Government*, 10th ed., p. 486.)

Paraphrase   _____

               _____

2. On the Trail of Typhoid Mary

1 November 11, 1938, a woman called Mary Mallon died of a stroke. She was seventy years old at the time, and at her death, at least three deaths and fifty-three cases of typhoid had been attributed to her. Due to her deadly history, the press had dubbed Mary Mallon "Typhoid Mary," a nickname she richly deserved because everywhere she went, the disease called "typhoid" was not far behind, until, that is, one man decided to stop her.

2 In 1906, while working as a cook for New York City banker Charles Henry Warren, Mallon prepared a delicious dinner—cold cucumber soup, lobster, wild rice, and strawberry ice cream with peaches. Warren and his guests ate heartily. But less than ten days later, several guests ended up in the hospital. All of them were eventually diagnosed with typhoid fever.

3 Careful research and some clever detective work by Dr. George Soper, a sanitary engineer employed by the New York Department of Health, traced the disease to Mary Mallon. Unfortunately, by the time Soper had identified Mallon as the source of infection, she was gone, on to yet another job as a cook or housekeeper. Hot on Mallon's trail, Dr. Soper discovered that the woman changed jobs frequently; wherever she worked, someone developed typhoid fever.

4 When Soper finally caught up with Mallon in 1907, she was hardly apologetic. On the contrary, she chased him away with a carving knife. Mallon only submitted to testing when Soper returned with three police officers. Tests done over her objections showed Mallon carried the bacteria that caused typhoid. But, for some reason, she herself showed no symptoms of the disease. Told to have her gallbladder removed— the gallbladder was believed to be the site of the infection—Mallon refused and began a lengthy court battle to gain her freedom from hospital isolation.

5 In 1910, Mary Mallon was released. However, she had to promise never to work as a cook again. She also had to report to the New York Department of Health every ninety days, allowing officials to keep her under a watchful eye. But by now, the newspapers all knew who Mallon was. Hounded by reporters, Mallon disappeared again only to resurface in 1915 when an outbreak of typhoid was reported at the Sloane Hospital for Women. As George Soper had suspected, Mary Mallon had been working in the hospital kitchen shortly before the

outbreak. This time, when police caught up with Mallon, they arrested her. By court mandate, she was confined to Riverside Hospital in New York, where she spent the rest of her life.

Paraphrase _____

_____

▶ **TEST 5** **Recognizing and Paraphrasing Thesis Statements**

DIRECTIONS Underline the thesis statement. Then paraphrase it in the blanks that follow.

1. **Learning the Lesson of Gabriel's Rebellion**

1 After the American and French Revolution, Haiti's slave population took the slogans of the rebellions altogether seriously and rebelled against the country's overlords. By 1793, they had triumphed under the leadership of the great military genius Toussaint L'Ouverture, and by 1804, they had gotten rid of their French rulers and established the Republic of Haiti. Thousands of former slave owners fled the island, taking with them their slaves, in order to seek asylum in the United States. But while the slaveholders may have been welcomed with open arms, their slaves were not, particularly in the South.

2 The arrival of so many people of color, both free and enslaved, haunted southern plantation owners, who feared that the new arrivals might be too familiar with notions of freedom and equality and, thus, might follow in the footsteps of Gabriel Prosser,[†] the former slave who had attempted a rebellion in 1800. Drawing on both Haitian and American revolutionary experiences, Prosser, a blacksmith by trade, had recruited other skilled African American workers, who, like himself, lived under minimal supervision. Prosser believed that both slaves and poor white people would be animated by the spirit of revolution that had changed the course of history in France, Haiti, and the United States. Appropriately the banner he designed echoed the defiant words of the American revolutionary Patrick Henry, "Give me liberty or give me death." Only in Prosser's version, the slogan became "Death or Liberty."

3 Prosser's attack was planned for August 30, 1800. It was intended to target the most prominent residents in the city of Richmond, Virginia. Prosser and his followers would set fire to the city, seize the capitol building, and capture the governor, James Monroe. During the rebellion's planning stage, Prosser thought other slaves and poor whites would rally to his cause and join the movement to bring equality to all people living on American soil, not just to those who were white. Tragically for Prosser and his supporters, heavy rainfall on the

---

[†]Prosser was actually the slave name that was bestowed upon the blacksmith, which is the main reason why the revolt is called Gabriel's Rebellion.

day of the rebellion forced a postponement of the revolt, giving a traitor the chance to inform the authorities.

4   While no white residents were killed in the revolt that never really got started, the authorities were furious that a black man had taken the notion of liberty so seriously. Although Prosser escaped initially, he was hunted down and hanged along with twenty-six of his fellow rebels. Outraged at the idea of slaves rebelling, southern legislatures responded to the plot by passing severe laws regulating the movement and behavior of slaves. What came to be known as "Gabriel's Rebellion" ended up not in more freedom for people of color, but in greater restriction of freedom. Formerly loose rules and laws were tightened and more fiercely observed than they had been prior to the revolt. (Very loosely adapted from Mary Beth Norton et al., *A People and a Nation*, Brief 10th ed., p. 193, © Cengage Learning.)

Paraphrase   _____

_____

2. Why Should We Be Concerned About a Warmer Earth?

1   So what is the big deal? Why should we worry about a possible rise of only a few degrees in Earth's average surface temperature? We often have that much change between May and July, or even between yesterday and today. So why should we care about a few degrees change in temperature?

2   Climate scientists warn that the concern is not only how much the temperature changes but how rapidly it occurs. Most past changes in the temperature took place over thousands to a hundred thousand years. The problem we face now is a significant increase in temperature *during this century*. Such rapid climate change could have dramatic and drastic effects on Earth's environment.

3   A 2003 U.S. National Academy of Sciences report laid out a nightmarish worst-case-scenario in which human activities or a combination of human activities and natural climate changes succeed in triggering a new and abrupt climate change. At this point, the global climate system reaches a tipping point, when it will be too late to reverse catastrophic change for tens of thousands of years.

4   The report describes whole environments in complete collapse, low-lying cities being flooded, forests consumed in vast fires, while grasslands dry out and turn into dustbowls. It also calls up the threat of wildlife disappearing, more frequent and intensified coastal storms,

and hurricanes with tropical waterborne and insect-transmitted infectious disease spreading rapidly beyond their current ranges.

5   The possibilities outlined in the National Academy report were supported by a 2004 analysis carried out by Peter Schwartz and Doug Randall for the U.S. Department of Defense. The authors concluded that global warming "must be viewed as a serious threat to global stability and should be elevated beyond a scientific debate to a U.S. national security concern." In 2004, the United Kingdom's chief science adviser David A. King wrote, "In my view, climate change is the most severe problem we are facing today—more serious than the threat of terrorism." (Adapted from Miller, *Living in the Environment*, 15th ed., p. 471, © Cengage Learning.)

Paraphrase   _____

_____

6 Focusing on Supporting Details in Paragraphs

IN THIS CHAPTER, YOU WILL LEARN

- more about the relationship between topic sentences and supporting details.
- how to distinguish between major and minor supporting details.
- how to evaluate minor details.

> "God is in the details."
>
> —ARCHITECT LUDWIG MIES VAN DER ROHE
>
> "The devil is in the details."
>
> —ANONYMOUS

Chapter 6 returns to the paragraph to look more closely at supporting details and how they combine with topic sentences to explain the author's main idea. You'll learn how major supporting details directly support the main idea while minor details reinforce major ones, sometimes in very important ways that should not be ignored despite the label "minor."

You'll also learn how concluding sentences in paragraphs can get slightly off the track of the main idea yet still need to be accounted for in your notes. As before, your work with this chapter will lay the groundwork for the next chapter, where you will look at supporting details in longer readings drawn primarily from textbooks.

The Function of Supporting Details

Paul: I thought June's behavior at that meeting was extraordinary.

Marisa: I thought the same thing. I couldn't believe how rude she was. She's too outspoken for my taste.

Paul: That's not what I meant at all. I thought she was great. When she believes in something, she's not afraid to speak her mind.

When the conversation between Paul and Marisa stays on a general level, both speakers are inclined to agree. It's only when Marisa moves to a more specific level that the speakers realize they actually disagree. This is a good example of how important supporting details are to the exchange of ideas. They make general statements more specific and place restrictions on how the listener or speaker can interpret, or understand, what's been said. Supporting details help both speakers and writers avoid a communication breakdown.

Supporting Details and Main Ideas

Supporting details in paragraphs are the specific sentences that clarify, prove, or suggest the author's main idea. Supporting details can provide reasons, examples, studies, definitions, and so on, that are essential to getting a clear understanding of the author's central point. The form they take depends on the main idea expressed in the topic sentence or implied by the author's selection of details (more about implied main ideas in Chapter 8).

But whatever their form, the function of supporting details remains the same: They are there to make sure readers understand the main idea. To see how topic sentences and supporting details work together in a paragraph, read the following statement:

> Prolonged unemployment can create serious psychological problems that, in the long run, actually contribute to continued joblessness.

By itself, the sentence tells us that long-term unemployment can do psychological damage. But what does the author mean by that general phrase "prolonged unemployment"? Is she talking about six months or six years? Exactly what kind of psychological problems does she have in mind? After all, that phrase is fairly general and covers a lot of ground. Also, how do psychological problems contribute to or help cause continued joblessness?

Left on its own, the sentence raises several questions. Those questions get answered when the sentence is followed by specific supporting details:

> [1]Prolonged unemployment can create serious psychological problems that, in the long run, actually contribute to continued joblessness. [2]In

a society that stresses the relationship between productive work and personal value, it is easy enough to equate long-term unemployment with personal worthlessness. [3]That is, in fact, precisely what many unemployed men and women begin to do. [4]Out of a job for a year or more, they start to see themselves as personally worthless and without value to society. [5]In what amounts to a vicious cycle, this sense of personal worthlessness further diminishes their chances of gaining employment. [6]Sometimes the unemployed stop looking for work altogether, sure in their despair that no one will hire them. [7]Or else they go to interviews but present themselves in such a defeated and hopeless fashion that the interviewer is unimpressed and rejects their application.

Do you see how the specific supporting details in the paragraph help readers understand the topic sentence? Sentences 2 and 3 limit the interpretations of the phrase "serious psychological problems." Sentence 4 defines "prolonged unemployment."

Sentence 5 explains the second half of the topic sentence by telling us how a sense of personal worthlessness can "contribute to continued joblessness." Sentences 6 and 7 provide two specific illustrations of how this happens.

Topic Sentences Can't Do It All

When reading a paragraph, you should certainly be on the lookout for a sentence expressing the main idea. However, by itself, that topic sentence or main idea statement is bound to raise some questions. It's the job of the supporting details to provide the answers.

In fact, if you don't understand how the supporting details relate to the main idea, you haven't truly understood the paragraph. Imagine, for example, that you were asked this question on an exam: "Explain how prolonged unemployment can contribute to continued joblessness." Without a thorough understanding of the previous paragraph's supporting details, you wouldn't be able to answer the question.

You can usually determine what supporting details contribute to your understanding of the main idea expressed in the topic sentence by asking two questions: (1) What type of supporting details—examples, reasons, studies, definitions, statistics—does the author supply? (2) What questions about the main idea do the supporting details answer?

READING TIP Once you think you have identified the topic sentence that sums up the main idea, ask yourself which of the remaining sentences provide clarification or evidence for that sentence. If the remaining sentences don't clarify or prove the sentence you have selected, you need to rethink your choice of topic sentence.

▶ **EXERCISE 1** **Recognizing Supporting Details**

DIRECTIONS The first sentence in each group of sentences is the topic sentence. That topic sentence is followed by five supporting details. Circle the letters of the three sentences that make the topic sentence clear and convincing.

EXAMPLE

Topic Sentence In April 1986, a tragic accident occurred at a nuclear power plant known as Chernobyl.

Supporting Details (a.) An explosion ripped through one of Chernobyl's four reactors, and a dangerous amount of radiation entered the atmosphere.

(b.) The plant burned for two weeks because technicians were unable to plug the leak caused by the explosion.

c. America had had its own nuclear scare when a meltdown occurred at Pennsylvania's Three Mile Island.

(d.) Immediately following the explosion at Chernobyl, thirty one people died; thousands of others suffered and eventually died of radiation sickness.

e. Western Europe relies on nuclear power for much of its electricity.

EXPLANATION The three circled supporting details tell us more about the tragic accident mentioned in the topic sentence. These three sentences help make the topic sentence clear and convincing. The other two do not help explain the topic sentence.

Topic Sentence **1.** The life of the Maasai, a group of people who make their home in East Africa, is tightly linked to the raising of cattle.

Supporting Details a. In Maasai culture, wealth is measured by the number of cattle a person owns.

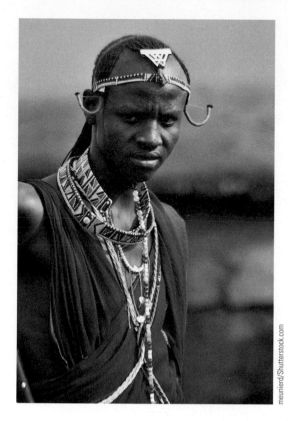

The Maasai are easily recognizable by their clothing, jewelry, and body art.

meunierd/Shutterstock.com

 b. Because they consider cattle sacred, the Maasai do not slaughter them.

 c. Through a series of treaties, the British evicted the Maasai from most of their homeland.

 d. The Maasai follow their cattle from grazing site to grazing site.

 e. The Maasai's way of life has remained basically the same for hundreds of years.

Topic Sentence   2. All over the world, landmines still lie waiting for unsuspecting victims.

Supporting Details   a. Landmines were first used on a large scale in World War I.

 b. Probably the most effective critic of using landmines in wartime was Britain's Princess Diana, who supported an international ban on their use.

 c. In African Angola landmines still litter the country despite strong efforts to remove them.

d. In Afghanistan, children are still suffering and dying because the landmines left behind by the Russians look like toys.

e. Although some areas have been cleared, large areas of Cambodia in Southeast Asia remain threaded with landmines.

Topic Sentence 3. In order to label and describe the techniques cult leaders use to control their members, psychologist Margaret Singer studied former cult members and found some recurring patterns of behavior and thought.

Supporting Details
a. In 1978, on the command of their leader, Jim Jones, more than nine hundred members of the Peoples Temple drank purple Kool-Aid laced with the deadly poison cyanide.

b. Singer found that adolescents are more likely to be recruited into a cult because they are more insecure about who they are and what they want to accomplish in life.

c. Interviews with former cult members revealed that isolation from family and loved ones outside the cult is central to keeping members obedient.

d. Heaven's Gate was a doomsday cult in California that ended with the death of twenty-one women and eighteen men, all of whom voluntarily committed suicide.

e. When asked, most former cult members told Singer that cult leaders made them feel guilty if they even mentioned wanting a life outside of the cult.

Topic Sentence 4. Before the introduction of a vaccine in 1954, polio was a terrifying and feared disease around the world, with the United States no exception.

Supporting Details
a. In 1916, a polio epidemic hit New York City; there were twenty-seven thousand cases and six thousand deaths.

b. The virus that causes polio was identified in 1908.

c. In the early 1900s, physicians believed that polio was associated with the teething of infants, despite the fact that plenty of infants cut new teeth with no signs of fever or paralysis.

d. In 1946, twenty-five thousand cases of polio were reported in the United States; most of them were children who were left paralyzed from the waist down.

e. The year 1952 saw the largest polio outbreak, with 57,879 cases reported nationwide; 3,145 people died of the disease and 21,269 suffered paralysis.

> **EXERCISE 2**   **Identifying Irrelevant or Unrelated Supporting Details**

DIRECTIONS   Read each paragraph. Write the number of the topic sentence in the first blank. If the paragraph contains an irrelevant detail, write the number of that sentence in the second blank.

EXAMPLE   [1]Orthorexia nervosa is an eating disorder that occurs when health-conscious individuals become obsessed with the quality of the food they eat. [2]People who suffer from this disorder base their self-esteem on their ability to maintain a diet of only healthy foods. [3]They decide, for example, that beans and rice are healthy and restrict themselves to eating only those two foods. [4]Should they go off their restricted diet, they feel intensely guilty and depressed. [5]Bulimics overeat and then feel guilty about the amount of food they have consumed. [6]Victims of orthorexia nervosa don't seem to realize that excessive reliance on a few select foods can deprive their bodies of critical nutrients.*

Topic Sentence   _____

Irrelevant Detail   _____

EXPLANATION   With the exception of sentence 5, the supporting details in the sample paragraph all describe the eating disorder orthorexia nervosa. Sentence 5, however, talks about the eating disorder bulimia and never relates it to orthorexia, making the detail in sentence 5 irrelevant to the rest of the paragraph.

1. [1]Child abuse can take several forms. [2]Sometimes the child is injured physically and may suffer from an odd or a disturbing combination of cuts, burns, bruises, or broken bones. [3]Usually the parents or guardians claim that the child "had an accident," even though no normal accident could cause such injuries. [4]Abused children have a greater chance of becoming abusive parents. [5]But child abuse may also take the form of emotional neglect; the parents will simply ignore the child and refuse to respond to bids for attention. [6]Children suffering from this kind of abuse often show symptoms of the *failure to thrive* syndrome*, in which physical growth is delayed. [7]In still other cases of maltreatment, the child may be emotionally abused. [8]One or both parents may ridicule or belittle the child. [9]In this case, physical problems may be absent, but the child's self-esteem will be seriously undermined.

_____

*nutrients: substances the body needs for good health.
*thrive: grow or develop well.

Topic Sentence   _____

Irrelevant Detail   _____

2. [1]Do you need to memorize a list of items in a particular order? [2]If you do, you should take the *serial position effect* into account. [3]The serial position effect refers to the tendency of many people to make the most errors when trying to remember the middle of a list or series. [4]If, for example, you are introduced to a long line of people, you are most likely to forget the names of those in the middle of the line. [5]Many people refuse to believe that the ability to remember is a skill that can be improved with training. [6]Anytime you need to learn a long poem or speech, be sure that you take the serial position effect into account.

Topic Sentence   _____

Irrelevant Detail   _____

3. [1]Although the statistics vary about how many women there are in the technology industry, no one argues against the idea that men dominate the field while women are in short supply. [2]That current shortage of women in the tech industry might have surprised Ada Byron Lovelace (1815–1852), who is widely credited for being a prophet of the computer age. [3]The daughter of the poet George Gordon Byron (more commonly known as Lord Byron) and Anne Isabella Milbanke, Ada never met her famous father, who abandoned the family shortly after Ada was born. [4]While she was growing up, young Ada was tutored in mathematics, largely because her mother did not want her to turn into a Romantic‡ poet like her father. [5]Whip-smart in mathematics and eloquent to boot, teenage Ada met up with and much impressed a math professor from Cambridge named Charles Babbage, who was working on what he called an Analytical Engine. [6]When Babbage—credited now for coming up with the idea of a programmable computer—wanted a discussion of his work translated into English, he called upon Ada to do it. [7]Babbage knew that Ada understood the workings of the machine almost as well as he did. [8]And as it turns out, she was better than he at pointing out its potential. [9]The translation she did for Babbage is dotted with her own insights about what Babbage's computer-like machine might be

---

‡Romantic: With a capital R, the word refers to a school of poetry that was popular toward the end of the eighteenth century on into the nineteenth. It emphasized the expression of passionate emotion and focused on the feelings aroused by nature.

able to accomplish in the future. [10]She correctly thought, for instance, that it might be able to create music. [11]As one Babbage biographer has pointed out, Ada was the first person to suggest that a machine might be able to "manipulate symbols in accordance with rules" and that numbers could represent more than quantity, an insight that lies at the foundation of computer science. (Source of quotation: http://www .computerhistory.org/babbage/adalovelace/. Last accessed on November 2, 2014.)

Topic Sentence   _____

Irrelevant Detail   _____

4. [1]Because of the ease with which the English language can adopt new words, it has a large and colorful vocabulary. [2]Still, even English doesn't always have the perfect word for some common experiences; for those words, we have to look to other languages. [3]For instance, have you ever walked in the woods and felt wonderfully alone in the peace and quiet of the woods? [4]Even if you are a city dweller, you have probably had that experience at least once in your life. [5]What you didn't have was a word for it. [6]The Germans, however, do. [7]It's *Waldeinsamkeit.* [8]Compound words are more common in German than they are in English. [9]English also doesn't have a word for that mark left on a table by a cold glass. [10]The Italians, however, do. [11]It's *culaccino.* [12]The English language also has no precise word to describe a joke told so badly that one actually has to laugh at the botched attempt. [13]If you spoke Indonesian, however, you'd have the word *jayus* at your disposal.

Topic Sentence   _____

Irrelevant Detail   _____

5. [1]Most people run or scream in terror when they see a snake. [2]Yet if snakes are examined without prejudice, they prove to be fascinating and relatively harmless members of the reptile family. [3]Like other reptiles, they are cold-blooded, and their temperatures change with the environment. [4]Although most people think that snakes are slimy and wet, the opposite is true. [5]Their skins are cool and dry, even pleasant to the touch. [6]The Hopi Indians perform ritual dances with live rattlesnakes in their mouths. [7]Despite their reputation, most snakes do more good than harm by helping to control the rodent population.

Topic Sentence   _____

Irrelevant Detail   _____

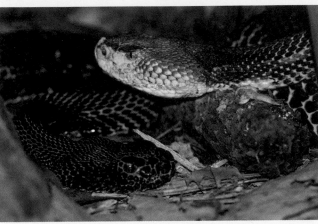

The snake on the right doesn't belong to the harmless category. It's a rattlesnake.

Major and Minor Supporting Details

To understand how a supporting detail can be labeled major or minor, consider the following paragraph. The major supporting details appear in **boldface**, the minor ones in *italics*.

> Psychologists have identified three basic styles of parenting. **Controlling parents think their children have few rights and many responsibilities.** *They tend to demand strict obedience to rigid standards of behavior and expect their children to obey their commands unquestioningly.* **Permissive parents, in contrast, require little responsible behavior from their children.** *Rules are not enforced, and the child usually gets his or her own way.* **Effective parents find a balance between their rights and their children's rights.** *They control their children's behavior without being harsh or rigid.*

In this paragraph, the topic sentence announces that psychologists have identified three different parenting styles. The natural response of most readers would be to say: "What are the three styles of parenting?" Notice how all the major details (printed in boldface) speak directly to that question.

Based on this illustration, we can say then that **major details** further define key words or phrases essential to understanding the main idea expressed in the topic sentence. Major details anticipate the questions readers might raise about the main idea and start to supply answers. Sometimes they supply answers that are complete and need no further support. However, sometimes major details need the help of minor details. **Minor details** are more specific sentences that follow major ones. They further explain, illustrate, or emphasize a term or point introduced by the major details.

▶ **EXERCISE 3**   **Diagramming Major and Minor Details**

DIRECTIONS   Read each paragraph. Then fill in the boxes with brief paraphrases of the major and minor details.

EXAMPLE   ¹It seems impossible that large prehistoric creatures are alive today. ²Yet huge creatures from the dinosaur age may still exist beneath the sea. ³After all, as fossil remains show, dinosaurs had relatives called plesiosaurs, who lived in the sea. ⁴They were huge and had long necks and snakelike heads. ⁵People who maintain that plesiosaurs still live point to recent accounts of strange sea creatures that fit the description of ancient sea monsters. ⁶According to reports, the modern-day sea creatures also have long necks and snakelike heads.

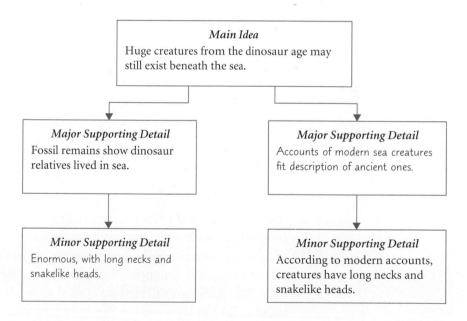

EXPLANATION   The topic sentence claims that huge creatures from the dinosaur age might still exist beneath the sea. Two major supporting details help make that statement more convincing. Each major detail is followed by a minor one that adds more information.

1. ¹To the ordinary observer, Earth appears to be a solid mass. ²Scientists, however, know that Earth is composed of several distinct layers. ³Called the *crust*, the layer closest to the surface consists of lightweight rock that extends for about twenty miles beneath Earth's surface. ⁴Just underneath the crust is a second layer, about two thousand miles thick, known as the *mantle*. ⁵Portions of the mantle are extremely hot. ⁶The third layer, or the *core* of Earth, is made up primarily of nickel and iron, and it too reaches extremely high temperatures. ⁷The temperatures are hot enough to melt both metals, but the fifty pounds of pressure borne by each square inch keeps them solid.

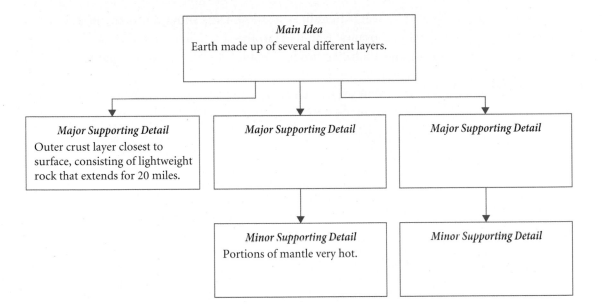

2. ¹Between 1959 and 1975, the American psychologist Harry Harlow conducted a series of experiments with rhesus monkeys. ²The goal of the experiments was to determine the effects of maternal deprivation and social isolation. ³Then and now, Harlow's experiments have been harshly criticized on ethical grounds because of the intense suffering they caused the monkeys under observation. ⁴In 1959, Harlow and fellow researcher Robert Zimmerman placed one group of infant monkeys in a cage with both a terrycloth figure designed for physical contact and a wire figure that dispensed

food. [5]A second group of monkey subjects only had contact with a wire food dispenser. [6]When the study was completed, the monkeys that had been given food and a chance to cuddle with the terrycloth figure were much better adjusted than those who had had food but no experience of physical contact. [7]In 1962, Harlow and his wife, Margaret, raised one group of monkeys with a cloth figure for comfort and another group in complete isolation. [8]At the end of the experiment, the monkeys raised in isolation would bite their arms and legs and attack others who approached them. [9]By the 1970s Harlow was engaging in experiments that called for infant monkeys to be housed in steel chambers that were appropriately nicknamed "the pits of despair." [10]Not surprisingly, the monkeys who spent time in the chambers were devastated by the experience.

Harry Harlow's monkey subjects craved affection as much as they craved food.

From Reader to Writer Before Harry Harlow's experiments took place, it was assumed that an infant's need for food bonded infants to their caretakers. Give the child enough food and it would be happy was the general opinion. Harlow's experiments, however, showed the importance of touch to an infant. Deprived of touch, the infant monkeys in Harlow's experiments grew up disturbed and violent. While Harlow's experiments helped us better understand what was essential to rearing a healthy human being, they did it at the cost of immense suffering to the infant monkeys who were his subjects. Write a few paragraphs explaining why you think Harlow is a hero, a villain, or something in between. (For more research on both Harlow's experiments and his life, try the reading here: http://www.boston.com/news/globe/ideas/articles/2004/03/21/monkey_love/?page=full, last accessed November 2, 2014.)

Evaluating the Contribution of Minor Details

From looking at the paragraph on styles of parenting, you might assume that minor details aren't important. Within the sample paragraph, the major details do the work of defining "the three basic styles of parenting." The minor details only repeat, with greater specificity, the point of the major details.

However, that's not always the case. Could you, for instance, react the same way to the minor details italicized in this next paragraph? They follow the major details. They are more specific than the major details, which they serve to explain. But are they unimportant?

Topic Sentence
[1]The human ear is a complicated structure that can be divided into three main parts. [2]The external part is the outer ear. [3]*It collects sound waves and directs them to the auditory canal, which ends at a membrane called the tympanum or eardrum.* [4]The middle part of the ear contains three small bones. [5]*These are called the hammer, anvil, and stirrup.* [6]*These three small bones channel the vibrations collected from the eardrum into the inner ear.* [7]The inner ear contains the actual hearing apparatus,* a small, shell-like organ filled with fluid and nerve endings. [8]*It is called the cochlea.* [9]*When the nerve endings receive vibrations from the fluid in the cochlea, they transmit them directly to the hearing portion of the brain.*

The human ear consists of three main parts: the outer ear, middle ear, and inner ear.

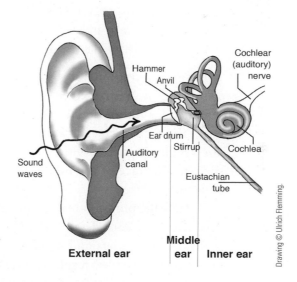

Figure 6-1 The Parts of the Human Ear

In this case, the topic sentence tells you that the human ear has three main parts. The first major detail identifies one of those parts as the "outer ear." But look closely at the minor detail modifying the first major one. The minor detail explains the function of the outer ear. Ignore that piece of information and all you know about the outer ear is what it's called. You don't know what it does.

*apparatus: a part or device that performs a specific function.

The same is true for the next new major detail in the sample paragraph (sentence 4), which introduces another part of the ear. Here again it's the two minor details that provide the real meat of the explanation.

When Minor Details Double Up, the Reader Needs to Think Twice

And what about this next paragraph? In this case, here again there are two minor details following one major one. Would you say that both of the minor details are irrelevant, or unnecessary, for your understanding of the underlined topic sentence?

Topic Sentence

[1]Vision is the slowest of the senses to develop in infants. [2]Infants have blurry vision at birth, but their visual world is not a complete blur. [3]They can see closer objects more clearly and can discern meaningful patterns. [4]For example, newborns show preferences for looking at facelike patterns over nonfacelike patterns. [5]They can recognize their own mother's face and even show a preference for looking at her face over other faces. (Nevid, *Psychology*, 3rd ed., p. 336, © Cengage Learning.)

In this case, the major detail further explains the topic sentence's claim that the "visual world is not a complete blur" for infants. Then sentence 4, a minor detail, gives us an example of a "meaningful pattern," the human face. That minor detail is followed by another minor detail, sentence 5, which makes the previous sentence even more specific. The face of the infant's mother is a particularly meaningful pattern.

Because the phrase "meaningful patterns" is so general, we definitely need the first minor detail to clarify the phrase, making that detail essential to our understanding of the paragraph's message. The second minor detail describes a specific face that is meaningful to infants. But while it's interesting to learn that babies can tell the difference between their mom's face and the faces of others, it's not a detail we need in order to understand the point of the paragraph.

The moral of both previous examples is this: Don't equate the label "minor" with a lack of importance. Minor details flesh out, or further develop, some part or point of the major detail. Sometimes they are critical to your understanding of a paragraph. Sometimes they are not.

WEB QUEST
Use the Web to write brief answers to these questions: What are cochlear implants, and why are they the source of controversy?

_____

_____

_____

SUMMING UP THE KEY POINTS

Major Details
- are less general than topic or introductory sentences.
- provide the examples, reasons, statistics, and studies that help make the main idea clear and convincing.
- anticipate readers' questions about the main idea.
- are essential to your understanding of the paragraph.

Minor Details
- are the most specific sentences in the paragraph.
- follow and further explain major details.
- must be evaluated because they may or may not be important enough to include in reading notes.

▶ **EXERCISE 4**   **Recognizing Major and Minor Details**

DIRECTIONS   Use the underlined topic sentence to determine if the sentences that follow are major or minor details. Then answer the accompanying questions.

EXAMPLE

Topic sentence provokes the question, "What were those attempts?"

[1]Over the last fifty years, Native Americans have made numerous attempts to gain more political power. [2]In late 1969, a group of Native Americans publicized their grievances by occupying Alcatraz, the abandoned prison in San Francisco Bay, for nineteen months. [3]In 1963, tribes

Sentences 2 and 3 introduce two of those attempts.

The remaining sentences add more specific information about the fight to gain political power.

in the Northwest waged a campaign to have their fishing rights recognized in parts of Washington State. ⁴These were eventually granted by the Supreme Court in 1968. ⁵In 1972, a group of Native Americans marched on Washington, D.C., to dramatize what they called a "trail of broken treaties" and present the government with a series of demands. ⁶In 1973, members of AIM, the American Indian Movement, took over Wounded Knee, South Dakota, for seventy-two days to protest the government's treatment of Native Americans. ⁷Since the early 1980s, several tribes have filed lawsuits to win back lands and mineral rights illegally taken from their ancestors. (Adapted from Thio, *Sociology*, 4th ed., p. 255.)

1. How many major details appear in this paragraph? ___5___

2. Which sentence or sentences provide major details? _2, 3, 5, 6, 7_

3. What question or questions do the major details answer about the topic sentence?

   How did Native Americans try to go about gaining more political power?

   What were the attempts that the author referred to in the topic sentence?

4. How many minor details appear in the paragraph? ___1___ Which sentence or sentences are minor details? ___4___

5. How essential is/are the minor detail(s)? Please explain your answer.

   In this case, the minor detail doesn't add information essential to understanding

   the main idea. It just tells the reader more about the success of one specific

   attempt to gain more political power.

EXPLANATION   Sentences 2, 3, 5, 6, and 7 are all major details that answer the obvious questions raised by the topic sentence. How have Native Americans gone about demanding more political power? What are some of those "attempts"? The exception is sentence 4, which further explains sentence 3. It's a minor detail that tells us how Native Americans triumphed in one particular court case. While it certainly adds information to the preceding sentence, it doesn't add much to your understanding of the topic sentence, so it's not an essential detail.

1. ¹Some basic distinctions can be made between *self-assertion* and *aggressive* behavior. ²Self-assertion involves standing up for your

rights by speaking out on your own behalf; it is a direct, honest expression of feelings and desires. ³It is not exclusively self-serving. ⁴In contrast to self-assertion, aggression involves hurting another person or achieving one's goals at the expense of another. ⁵Aggression does not take into account the feelings or rights of others. ⁶It is an attempt to get one's own way no matter what. (Adapted from Dennis Coon and John O. Mitterer. *Psychology: A Journey*, 5th ed., p. 587, © Cengage Learning.)

1. How many major details appear in this paragraph? _____

2. Which sentence or sentences provide major details? _____

3. What question or questions do the major details answer about the topic sentence?

   _____

   _____

4. How many minor details appear in the paragraph? _____

5. Which sentence or sentences provide minor details? _____

6. How essential is/are the minor details(s)? Please explain your answer.

   _____

   _____

   _____

2. ¹It's not exactly news that men and women tend to use speech in different ways. ²In conversation, men interrupt more than women and are far more likely to assert strong opinions without indicating that another point of view might exist, for instance, "Bank fees are a form of highway robbery." ³Women, however, are more likely to express opinions as questions, e.g., "I think bank fees are excessive, don't you?" ⁴The assumption has been that the differences in speech were a result of cultural training. ⁵But a book published in 2011, *Duels and Duets,* offers an alternative point of view; it suggests that the difference in speech patterns is a result of evolutionary* history rather than social inequality. ⁶According to the

_____

*evolutionary: related to gradual change or development over the course of time.

author, John L. Locke, a professor of linguistics[†] at Lehman College, women tend to be less assertive in conversation because, historically, they were the physically weaker sex. [7]As the weaker sex, they needed to create social or group bonds as a form of protection. [8]They had to find strength as part of a group because they could not rely on brawn and muscle. [9]But for men the evolutionary story was very different. [10]Men who publicly displayed their assertiveness,[*] in conversation and in combat, often gained in status, particularly if the man was physically strong enough to beat his rivals. [11]In the early stages of human development, men were encouraged to duel, or fight, even in conversation, while women, for safety's sake, were more given to duets, to pairing up for safety's sake. [12]If the author of *Duels and Duets* is correct, it appears that old habits die hard.

1. How many major details appear in this paragraph? _____

2. Which sentence or sentences provide major details? _____

3. What question or questions do the major details answer about the topic sentence?

   _____

   _____

4. How many minor details appear in the paragraph? _____ Which sentence or sentences provide minor details? _____

5. How essential is/are the minor detail(s)? Please explain your answer.

   _____

   _____

   _____

---

†linguistics: the study of language and its structure.
*assertiveness: boldness, having confidence in one's ideas or actions.

From Reader to Writer Using the paragraph on being self-assertive or aggressive as a model, write a paragraph or two explaining the differences between friends and acquaintances. But don't just explain the differences. Illustrate them with concrete examples of the kind of behavior that goes with each relationship.

✔ CHECK YOUR UNDERSTANDING

1. In the context of a paragraph, what's the purpose of major supporting details?

    _____

    _____

2. What do minor supporting details do?

    _____

    _____

3. Why do minor details need to be evaluated?

    _____

    _____

Category Words in Topic Sentences Signal Major Details

Especially in textbooks, topic sentences are likely to include broad category words. **Category words** sum up and generally refer to a variety of more specific activities, events, and behaviors. They usually appear as part of a larger phrase, for instance:

1. Child abuse can take several different *forms*.

2. Psychologists have identified three *styles* of parenting.

3. Even when identical twins are reared in different homes, they often show many *similarities* in taste and behavior.

Using Category Words to Keep Readers on Track

Topic sentences like the three shown above tell readers to be alert to each sentence introducing another member of the larger category or group. Based on the topic sentence, readers know immediately that every new *form*, *style*, or *similarity* is a major detail.

For an illustration, read the following paragraph. Note the circled phrase in the underlined topic sentence. That phrase tells you that each myth described will be a major detail. It also tells you that there are *three* major details in the paragraph. Guided by the topic sentence, skilled readers look for references, both explicit and implicit, to the word *myth* to sort out the three major details. (This paragraph, by the way, is another illustration of how important minor details can often be).

"One classic" is an elliptical phrase that expects the reader to supply the word *myth*.

"Another myth" signals another major detail.

The introduction of another long-held belief in sentence 7 suggests another myth and another major detail.

[1]Education is one of those much-discussed topics that seem to attract misinformation like a magnet attracts iron. [2]Thus, it's not surprising that there are at least (three common myths) about education that have almost no factual basis. [3]One classic is the belief that IQ scores don't change when in fact they can and do. [4]Especially among children, IQ shifts of five to ten points can occur over the course of a few months. [5]According to another myth of long standing, grouping students by ability improves their performance. [6]But, in fact, very little research supports this claim. [7]For at least two decades, many in education have also insisted that "discovery learning," in which students master scientific principles through problem solving rather than direct instruction, was the best way to teach science. [8]Yet a review of research indicates that direct instruction is often superior to discovery learning in the context of teaching science. (Source of information: Lillienfeld et al., *Fifty Common Myths*, p. 114.)

The sample paragraph illustrates how useful category words in topic sentences can be when it comes to identifying major and minor details. In the above example, each reference to a new myth is a major detail.

Similarly, if you were reading a paragraph where the topic sentence said something like "Three different kinds of behavior separate alcoholism from social drinking," you would know immediately that each sentence introducing one of those "three kinds of behavior" was a major detail.

Commonly Used Category Words ●	Behaviors	Groups	Stages
	Categories	Incidents	Standards
	Causes	Kinds	Steps
	Characteristics	Materials	Strategies
	Classes	Methods	Studies
	Components	Mores	Symptoms
	Consequences	Motives	Tactics
	Differences	Objectives	Talents
	Disparities	Offices	Techniques
	Distinctions	Pointers	Traditions
	Effects	Precautions	Traits
	Elements	Problems	Ways
	Examples	Reasons	Values
	Factors	Rules	Virtues
	Functions	Similarities	
	Goals	Skills	

> **EXERCISE 5**   **Using Category Words to Identify Major Details**

DIRECTIONS   Underline the topic sentence and circle the category word or phrase that guides your search for major details. Then label the sentences that follow as *M* (for major) or *m* (for minor).

1. Parents typically discipline children in one of three ways. *Power assertion* refers to physical punishment or a show of force, such as taking away toys or privileges. _____ Another alternative is for parents to use *withdrawal of love* or the withholding of affection. _____ They can, for instance, refuse to speak to the child, threaten to leave, or act as if the child were temporarily unlovable. _____ *Management techniques* combine praise, approval, rules, reasoning, and the like to encourage desirable behavior. _____ (Adapted from Coon, *Essentials of Psychology*, 9th ed., p. 101, © Cengage Learning.)

2. At one time, lotteries were illegal. But that time has clearly passed as more than forty states now allow and regulate lotteries. Several factors account for the birth of what some have called the lottery or "bettor government." Obviously, lotteries can bring in

meaningful sums of money—some \$23 billion in "profits" in 2008 alone. _____ That's a huge portion of state revenue. _____ Lotteries are also popular and entertaining. _____ What's more, they are voluntary. _____ No one can force you to participate in a lottery. _____ In addition, lotteries help relieve the pressure to increase taxes. _____ In some states, net lottery earnings have taken the place of a one-cent increase in the sales tax. _____ By taking control of lotteries, states offer a legal and fair alternative to illegal gambling operations, such as neighborhood numbers games. _____ (Adapted from Bowman and Kearney, *State and Local Government*, 8th ed., p. 364, © Cengage Learning.)

Outside the Topic Sentence, Category Words Can Turn into Transitions

If a broad category word appears in a topic sentence, you can usually expect to see that same word repeated or referred to within the paragraph. The author will use it, at least once, probably more, as a transition introducing a major detail.

For instance, in this next paragraph, the second sentence is the topic sentence. It tells us that honeybees can only survive in a community where they all have "a number of special functions." If you think that the phrase "a number of special functions" is a clue to the major details, you are correct. But note as well how new major details are integrated, or blended, into the paragraph by the repetition of or reference to the word *function*.

In sentence 3, *for example* is a reference to the *number of special functions.*

In sentence 5, the word *functions* is used in connection to worker bees to indicate a *new* function is being introduced.

In sentence 8, the word *function* is attached to another member of the colony, *drones*, as a way of indicating to readers that yet another function is being addressed.

[1]The honeybee is a highly social insect that can survive only when it is part of a community. [2]Within the honeybee community, the members have a *number of special functions* that help ensure survival. [3]The queen, for example, is the only sexually productive female; she gives birth to all of the drones, workers, and future queens. [4]Her capacity for laying eggs is enormous, and her daily output exceeds 1,500 eggs. [5]Although they lack the ability to mate or reproduce, worker bees also perform important functions. [6]They secrete wax, construct the honeycomb, gather food, turn nectar into honey, guard the hive against intruders, and regulate the hive's temperature. [7]If, for instance, the hive becomes too hot, worker bees cool the air by fanning their wings. [8]In contrast to worker bees, drones have only one function—to mate with the queen. [9]After the mating, which takes place in flight, a drone immediately dies; he has served his sole function. [10]He is no longer necessary to the community.

Like humans, honeybees don't thrive in isolation; they need to be part of a larger community.

© Ulrich Flemming.

▶ **EXERCISE 6** **Using Category Words in Paragraphs**

DIRECTIONS Use one of the category words listed below to fill in the blanks in the topic sentences. Then use the same word in its singular form to create a transition to the first major detail.

EXAMPLE Halloween is one of those holidays that has a lot of ___traditions___ associated with it. Perhaps the most famous ___tradition___ is trick or treating.

EXPLANATION Note how the category word in the topic sentence gets repeated in order to create a transition from the topic sentence to the first supporting detail, in this case "trick or treating."

advantages	traditions	symptoms
studies	techniques	objectives

1. Journalists need a number of good _____ to make their subjects speak freely during an interview. The most important _____ is the ability to draw people out and encourage them to talk freely.

2. Dengue fever has several horrifying _____. The most obvious _____ is a red rash that spreads over the entire body, causing it to swell.

3. The high school writing program has four _____. One _____ is to help students better understand what they believe to be true about the world.

4. There are several _____ to making the reading of novels, poetry, and plays a major part of the elementary and high school curricula. The most essential _____ is the ability they have to encourage empathy, or understanding of others.

5. Numerous _____ suggest that multitasking is a bad idea. In one _____, subjects who were heavy multitaskers made more mistakes completing a simple sorting task than did those who did not multitask or who engaged in it infrequently.

From Reader to Writer Start your paragraph with a topic sentence like this one, "All of my friends have several qualities in common," or maybe this one, "The person I marry has to have three key characteristics." Then use the category word you chose for your topic sentence as a transition to help your reader follow your description of the characteristics, attitudes, behaviors, etc., you expect to find in a friend, mate, teacher, or co-worker.

Addition Transitions Are Clues to Major Details

Topic sentences that include category words often appear in combination with addition transitions like *first*, *second*, *third*, *furthermore*, *moreover*, and *also*. (A more complete list appears on page 315.) However, even if addition transitions don't turn up in the company of category words, they still provide excellent clues to major details.

Addition transitions are the author's way of saying to readers, "I'm not introducing a completely different point here; I am adding to what I said before." When linked to category words, addition transitions are even more specific: They tell the reader, "Here's another major reason, illustration, advantage, or consequence to consider."

Look, for example, at the following passage and notice how the italicized transitions help readers sort out the subgroups included under the larger category word *reasons*, which appears in the topic sentence.

The transition *first of all* tells readers to be on the lookout for the first reason why children should not watch wrestling.

The transition *furthermore* announces the second reason.

The transition *in addition* tells readers that yet another reason is on its way.

[1]Even though the World Wrestling Federation, Inc. has changed its name to suggest it's nothing more than entertainment—It's now called World Wrestling Entertainment, Inc. (WWE)—there are a number of reasons why parents should not allow young, impressionable children to watch wrestling. [2]*First of all*, wrestling suggests to children that physical violence causes no real harm. [3]In a wrestling match, no one seems to get hurt and most of the wrestlers come back the following week. [4]*Furthermore*, wrestling suggests that people are valued according to the damage they can do since the superstars of wrestling are those men and women who most effectively hurt and humiliate their opponents. [5]This is not an especially good message to be giving children. [6]*In addition*, wrestling celebrates crude and loutish behavior. [7]Watching a wrestling match on television or on YouTube, it's hard to say whose behavior is more despicable.* [8]It's a toss-up between the wrestlers shouting at the top of their lungs that they are going to demolish their opponent and the scantily clad women who parade around exhibiting score cards and occasionally jump in the ring to join the fray.*

In this paragraph, the author says there are several reasons why young children should not be allowed to watch wrestling matches. The transitions then help the reader recognize each of the reasons presented.

Transitions That Signal Addition or Continuation ●		
After all	Furthermore
Also	In addition
And	Last
As a matter of fact	Lastly
As an illustration	Last of all
Finally	Moreover
First	Next
First and foremost	One point, example, kind, etc.
First of all	Second, Third, Fourth
For example	Similarly
For instance	Then
For one thing	Therefore
For this reason	Too

*despicable: unworthy of respect, disgraceful.
*fray: fight, intense activity; to wear down or unravel.

▶ **EXERCISE 7**   **Using Category Words**

DIRECTIONS   Read each paragraph. Circle the category word or phrase used in the underlined topic sentence. Circle as well the addition transitions. When you finish, answer the questions that follow.

EXAMPLE   ¹Human activities are disrupting and degrading many of the world's freshwater rivers, lakes, and wetlands. ²These activities affect freshwater systems in (four major ways.) (First,) dams and canals fragment up to 40 percent of the world's 237 rivers, thereby altering or destroying wildlife habitats, or living spaces, both on land and in the water. (Second,) flood control levees and dikes built along rivers disconnect the rivers from their flood plains, destroy habitats, and alter or reduce the functions of nearby wetlands. (Third,) cities and farms add pollutants and excess plant nutrients to streams, rivers, and lakes. ⁶And (fourth,) many inland wetlands have been drained or filled to grow crops or have been covered with concrete, asphalt, and buildings. (Adapted from Miller and Spoolman, *Sustaining the Earth*, 9th ed., p. 65, © Cengage Learning.)

1. What does the topic sentence signal you to look for as you read the rest of the passage?
     the four major ways human activities are affecting the world's freshwater systems

2. Which sentence introduces the first major detail? ___3___

3. How many major details are there? ___4___

4. How many minor details are there? ___0___

EXPLANATION   As it was meant to, the topic sentence sends the reader in search of the four major ways human activities affect our freshwater systems. Note, then, how the author introduces each of the four ways with an addition transition. No minor details follow the major details because the major details communicate their point all by themselves.

1. ¹One approach to minimizing the limitations of both computers and humans is to have them work together in ways that create a better outcome than either could achieve alone. ²In medical diagnosis, for example, the human's role is to establish the presence and nature of a patient's symptoms. ³The computer then combines this information in a completely unbiased way to identify the most likely diagnosis. ⁴Similarly, laboratory technologists who examine blood

samples for the causes of disease are assisted by computer programs that serve to reduce errors and memory lapses by (1) keeping track of findings from previous tests, (2) listing possible tests that remain to be tried, and (3) indicating either that certain tests have been left undone or that a new sequence of tests should be done. [5]This kind of human-machine teamwork can also help with the assessment of psychological problems. (Bernstein et al., *Psychology*, 8th ed., p. 300, © Cengage Learning.)

1. What does the topic sentence signal you to look for as you read the rest of the passage?

   _____

   _____

2. Which sentence introduces the first major detail? _____

3. How many major details are there? _____

4. How many minor details are there? _____

2. [1]Mixed martial arts (MMA) is a full-contact combat sport that, as the name suggests, combines a mix of martial arts, ranging from jujitsu to kickboxing and wrestling. [2]For a while, the sport was confined to grown men and women, but it has gotten a toehold among kids, who are training to learn the various moves, holds, and blows that may one day permit them to participate in the Ultimate Fighting Championship (UFC), which is wildly popular on cable television. [3]While many are horrified by the idea of children learning mixed martial arts, some parents argue that real benefits are derived from children training for this sport. [4]Supporters of MMA for children claim that the training teaches them discipline. [5]To participate, they have to follow regimented* routines that do not allow for laziness or a careless attitude toward instructions. [6]Supporters also argue that in the United States where childhood obesity* is steadily growing, the physical activity demanded by MMA is a blessing, rather than a curse. [7]Moreover, proponents insist that mixed martial arts will encourage children to work hard and compete to win, teaching them, at the same time, how to learn from defeat.

---

*regimented: strictly controlled and ordered.
*obesity: a condition in which the body has begun to store a large amount of excess fat.

1. What does the topic sentence signal you to look for as you read the rest of the passage?

   _____

2. Which sentence introduces the first major detail? _____

3. How many major details are there? _____

4. How many minor details are there? _____

From Reader to Writer If you have kids or plan on having kids, explain why you would or would not encourage them to participate in UFC events.

When Addition Transitions Are Used More Sparingly

Sometimes writers mark every new major detail with an addition transition. But the emphasis here is on the word *sometimes*. Despite the example shown on page 315, you can't assume that every major detail will have a transitional marker. Look, for example, at this next paragraph.

Topic Sentence

Sentence 2 introduces the first "way" Houdini exposed fakery.

The opening transition *moreover* tells readers another "way" is coming up.

In addition announces the third and final "way."

[1]Although the famed magician Harry Houdini could have benefited from his audience's belief in the world of spirits, he tried in a number of ways to expose the fakery behind supposed supernatural* happenings. [2]Throughout his career, Houdini carefully investigated and proved false hundreds of claims by people who said they could communicate with the spirit world. [3]*Moreover*, he kept a file of fake mediums† and he instructed that, after his death, the file be made public. [4]To ensure that his wishes were carried out, Houdini entrusted a key to the file to his friend and fellow magician Joseph Dunninger. [5]*In addition*, Houdini purposely eliminated the "magic" behind his tricks by explaining how they were performed. [6]This was his way of proving to people that miracles could actually be faked.

In the sample paragraph, the writer doesn't use a transition to introduce the first "way" Houdini tried to expose fakes. Based on the location of the topic sentence, the writer expects readers to infer that sentence 2 describes the first of the "ways" Houdini exposed the fakery behind supernatural events.

---

*supernatural: other worldly, magical.
†mediums: people who claim that they are in touch with the world of spirits.

Because it is further away from the topic sentence, sentence 3 opens with the addition transition *moreover*. The transition signals to readers that this sentence describes a new and different way that Houdini tried to outwit the fakes. Sentence 4 is a minor detail modifying sentence 3; it includes no addition transition. To do so would confuse the relationship between the sentences. In sentence 5, however, the author uses the transitional phrase *in addition* to highlight another "way" Houdini tried to expose fakery. Once again the transition serves to keep the reader in touch with the writer's train of thought.

A Note on Two Common Addition Transitions

Addition transitions like *for instance* or *for example* are common in all kinds of writing. But they are particularly common in textbooks. Writers use them to tell readers, "Here's an illustration of the general statement you just read."

Experienced readers respond based on their understanding of the material. If they think they already understand the point of the general sentence, they skim the example. If they find the general sentence confusing, they read the example slowly. They might even read it twice.

▶ **EXERCISE 8**   **Using Addition Transitions**

DIRECTIONS   Fill in the blanks in each paragraph with one of the addition transitions in the following list.

also	first	finally	moreover	second

1. Polls sponsored by the American Automobile Association and other highway safety organizations consistently suggest that many Americans are bad drivers who don't want to improve. Because most states do not require motorists to periodically refresh their skills, adult drivers have generally not taken a test on road rules, road signs, or driving skills since they first got their driver's license as teenagers. _____, the majority of drivers polled admit to speeding, while one-third say they frequently run yellow or even red lights. Many drivers _____ engage in distracting behaviors while behind the wheel. In a poll by Vlingo, a mobile application company, one in four adults said that they text while driving. As the age of the driver

decreased, the amount of texting increased. According to the pollsters at Vlingo, 66 percent of "the *least experienced* drivers, those sixteen to nineteen," admitted to texting while driving." (Source of the Vlingo study: Breitbart.com.)

2. People who engage in "extreme couponing" i.e., who make coupon clipping practically a full-time job in the name of saving money, need to put down the scissors and think twice about what they are doing. If you are into extreme couponing, consider _____ the basis for your shopping list. Is it based on what you like to eat or on what's good for your health? Or are you basing your shopping list on what bargain some fast food corporation has decided to of-fer for that week? If any of these patterns fit how you make up your shopping list, you need to remember that there's no guarantee good nutrition or enjoyable meals automatically come with a coupon at-tached. _____, coupons frequently accompany processed food, and processed food is likely to have a great many chemical ingredients. Given the number of chemicals in processed foods, you might want to think twice before you stock up on frozen pizza and french fries, even if you do have a coupon that lets you buy two packages and get one free. _____, cooking your own food from scratch is probably cheaper than using coupons. It takes less than a dollar and a half to buy a package of dried beans or lentils, and those beans and lentils can be turned into a soup, which will last you for two or three meals.

From Reader to Writer Forty-four states ban texting while driving. Write a paragraph (or more) explaining why that ban is effective or useless. Please make sure to give reasons for your opinion, or point of view.

 ## Concluding Sentences Versus Supporting Details

Most of the time, the last sentence in a paragraph does exactly what you would expect it to do. Directly, as a major detail, or indirectly, as a minor one, it supports the main idea. Sometimes, however, the last sentence of a paragraph does not play the role of supporting detail. Instead, it func-tions as a **concluding sentence** that tells you how a situation described in the paragraph was or should be resolved.

Take, for example, the following paragraph. The underlined topic sentence tells us that between 1692 and 1693, Salem, Massachusetts, was the scene of witchcraft trials. Except for the last one, all the remaining sentences in the paragraph tell us more about what happened in Salem during those trials.

> [1]From 1692 through 1693, Salem, Massachusetts, was the scene of a series of witchcraft trials. [2]The trials began when four young girls, Betty Parris, Abigail Williams, Elizabeth Hubbard, and Ann Putnam Jr., appeared to be suffering fits of madness during which they threw themselves on the floor screaming in terror or whimpered and hid under the bed. [3]During these bouts, the girls accused several men and women in the town of dealings with the devil. [4]The girls' accusations were believed and before the townspeople came to their senses, nineteen men and women had been hanged. [5]Many others were cruelly tortured, tormented, and imprisoned, until it became clear that the girls had been lying all along and there were no witches in Salem. [6]Following the events in Salem, witchcraft trials practically disappeared from the colonies.

In this illustration, sentences 2–5 further explain the main idea expressed in the opening sentence. They talk about the Salem trials, how they got started, and what went on as a result. The last sentence, however, moves away from the main idea of the paragraph. It tells us what happened in the colonies *after* the Salem experience. Writers frequently use the last sentence of a paragraph in this way, to say to readers, "OK this is how things stand now" or "This is where the subject or situation is headed."

Such concluding sentences are not unrelated to the main idea of the paragraph, even if they do not directly explain it. Concluding sentences like the one in the paragraph on witchcraft trials almost always help you understand more about the topic or issue under discussion.

READING TIP

Don't ignore concluding sentences. Evaluate them and decide how important they are to your understanding of the material and your purpose in learning it.

Concluding Sentences Look Ahead to the Next Paragraph

Concluding sentences help readers predict what's coming up next. For instance, based on the last sentence of the previous paragraph, readers might rightly expect the next paragraph to explain why witchcraft trials disappeared from the colonies. That expectation would be correct, as the following paragraph illustrates.

> [1]From the very beginning, many colonists had been appalled by the Salem trials but were too frightened to speak out against them. [2]After all, the girls could easily accuse them next. [3]However, when the wife of the governor of Massachusetts was also named as a witch, the trials had run their course. [4]Paris, Putnam, Hubbard, and Williams had gone too far with their wild accusations. [5]They had attacked a respected woman, whose husband was in a position of power. [6]As a result, people began speaking out against the Salem trials and their awful accomplishments. [7]Increase Mather, the influential president of Harvard, expressed the new anti-witch hunting mood of Salem and the rest of the colonies when he said, "It were better that ten suspected witches should escape than one innocent person should be condemned."

Evaluating the Final Sentences

Whenever you come to the end of a paragraph, make sure you are clear on the function of the last sentence. Is it a supporting detail that develops the main idea? If so, what does it add to your understanding of that main idea? If the last sentence is a concluding sentence, make sure you understand how it sums up an event or situation described in the paragraph. Use it as well to shape your expectations about the direction the author's thought will take in the next paragraph.

WEB QUEST
Use the Web to discover the meaning of "spectral evidence" and the role it played in the Salem witchcraft trials.

_____

_____

_____

SUMMING UP THE KEY POINTS

1. Be alert to category words appearing in topic sentences. When words like *rules*, *laws*, *differences*, and *varieties* appear, you can use them to identify major details. Each new *rule*, *law*, *difference*, or *variety* described will usually be a major detail.

2. To provide a transition for a major detail, writers frequently repeat the category word used in the topic sentence.

3. *Addition transitions* such as *moreover*, *similarly*, *first*, and *second* can also signal that a major detail is on its way.

4. *Concluding sentences* describe how a situation or event described in the paragraph turned out. That information is relevant to your understanding of the topic or issue addressed in the paragraph.

5. Concluding sentences also frequently point to the direction the next paragraph will take. Thus, they can help shape your expectations as you move from paragraph to paragraph in longer readings.

▶ **EXERCISE 9**   **Recognizing the Function of the Last Sentence**

DIRECTIONS   Read each paragraph and notice the underlined topic sentence. Circle the letter of the answer that best describes the function of the last detail in the paragraph.

EXAMPLE   ¹In 1856, Henry Bessemer developed a new method for manufacturing steel, one that consisted of three basic steps. ²First, a blast of cold air was forced through the mass of hot melting iron. ³The enormous heat created then burned out the impurities in the iron and left it ready for the final step. ⁴During the last step, carbon, manganese, and other substances were added in order to make the steel stronger. ⁵The introduction of the Bessemer process revolutionized the steel industry, making steel a profitable American export.

    a. The last sentence in the paragraph provides a supporting detail that develops the main idea.

    ⓑ The last sentence in the paragraph is a concluding sentence that explains how someone or something mentioned in the paragraph turned out or might develop over the course of time.

EXPLANATION   The last sentence does not describe one of the three basic steps in the Bessemer process. That eliminates answer *a*, making answer *b* the correct choice.

1. [1]In 1886, French chemist Louis Pasteur believed that he had found a vaccine to combat the dreaded disease called rabies. [2]Pasteur, however, was fearful of using the rabies vaccine on human beings and did not use it on humans until the decision to do so was forced on him. [3]On July 6, 1885, a young boy named Joseph Meister was brought to Pasteur for treatment. [4]The boy had been bitten on the arms and legs by a rabid dog. [5]Pasteur consulted with several physicians who assured him that the boy was going to die. [6]It was only then that Pasteur decided to use his rabies vaccine. [7]Meister lived to become gatekeeper of the Pasteur Institute and committed suicide fifty-five years later.

   a. The last sentence in the paragraph provides a supporting detail that develops the main idea.

   b. The last sentence in the paragraph is a concluding sentence that explains how someone or something turned out or might develop over the course of time.

2. [1]Can robot authors write books that people want to read? The answer to that question depends on whom you to talk to. [2]There are some who believe that robot authors—software programs that collect information about a topic and organize it into book form—are the wave of the future, while others consider such books to be of limited value at best. [3]The inventor and economist Philip Parker, for instance, sees a rosy future for computer-generated books. [4]More than a decade ago, Parker began using automatic text-generating software to "write" books, and he has written or published over 100,000 of them. [5]Parker claims that his books and others like them are the perfect solution for people who speak languages that are not widely shared, like Chichewa, the African language of Malawi. [6]Thanks to robot-authored books, the farmer who needs to understand the latest planting techniques can, indeed, find a book on the subject and written in his or her own language no less. [7]Talk to Chris Csikszentmihalyi, of the Massachusetts Institute of Technology, however, and you will hear a different story. [8]Csikszentmihalyi points out that disaster can occur if the software makes an error in, for instance, dispensing

medical advice. [9]As he puts it, "Would you really want to bet your life on text generated by a robot?" (Source of quotation: Pagan Kennedy, "I-Robot Book," *The New York Times Book Review*, October 16, 2011, p. 15.)

    a. The last sentence in the paragraph provides a supporting detail that develops the main idea.

    b. The last sentence in the paragraph is a concluding sentence that explains how someone or something turned out or might develop over the course of time.

3. [1]In 2005, Cyndy Bizon thought her husband, Joel, was dying. [2]Anguished at the thought of losing him, she watched her spouse being wheeled into the operating room. [3]Shortly after, she collapsed from a condition known as "broken heart syndrome," a physical response that mimics a heart attack without really being one. [4]Broken heart syndrome, like the attack that afflicted Cyndy Bizon, occurs when the body absorbs a huge shock, even one with positive associations like winning the lottery. [5]In most cases it strikes not men but women over the age of fifty-five. [6]Out of the 6,229 cases reported, only 671 involved men. [7]Using a government database that gathered information from 1,000 hospitals, Dr. Abhishek Deshmukh of the University of Arkansas has tried to pinpoint why women outnumber men as victims. [8]But as of yet, he has found no answer. [9]Theories abound. [10]It might be hormonal differences. [11]It might be that men are more used to handling stress and, as a result, their bodies have adapted to it better. [12]But so far, no one knows for sure what causes the syndrome. [13]The good news is that most people recover from an attack of broken heart syndrome with little or no signs of permanent damage. (Source of statistics: http://news.yahoo.com/women-more-likely-broken-heart-syndrome-184939504.html.)

    a. The last sentence in the paragraph provides a supporting detail that develops the main idea.

    b. The last sentence in the paragraph is a concluding sentence that explains how someone or something turned out or might develop over the course of time.

4. [1]In the nineteenth century, opium was brought into China by British merchants, who profited handsomely from the opium trade and fought hard to maintain their money-making export. [2]Thanks to

British merchants, use of the drug became so widespread in China that the Chinese government banned the importation of opium altogether. [3]Despite the ban, the British smuggled the drug in, and the attempt to eliminate its use was unsuccessful. [4]Confiscation of large quantities of opium by the Chinese government led to the Opium War of 1839, in which the Chinese battled the British for control of the opium trade. [5]The Chinese lost the war, and the British were able to force the Chinese government to legalize opium use. [6]Eventually China drove the British out, and the country became the main source of opium for the rest of the world. (Adapted from Waughfield, *Mental Health Concepts,* 5th ed., p. 354, © Cengage Learning.)

a. The last sentence in the paragraph provides a supporting detail that develops the main idea.

b. The last sentence in the paragraph provides a detail that explains how someone or something turned out or will develop over the course of time.

CHECK YOUR UNDERSTANDING

1. Why are category words in topic sentences important?

   ___Bc those words could_____

2. What are some examples of addition transitions?

   _____

3. Why do authors frequently repeat the category word used in a topic sentence?

   _____

   _____

4. The last sentence in a paragraph may not directly support the main idea, but if it doesn't, what two other functions might it fulfill?

   a. _____

   _____

   b. _____

   _____

DIGGING DEEPER Obedience—Would You Electrocute a Stranger? *Dennis Coon and John O. Mitterer*

Looking Ahead Harry Harlow's experiments with monkeys, which you learned about earlier, are among the most famous experiments in the twentieth century. The same can be said about the experiments conducted by Stanley Milgram, which were designed to discover the limits of obedience.

Getting Focused The title already indicates the topic is obedience. Therefore, you need to be looking for the author's point *about* obedience. However, in *Looking Ahead*, you also learned that Milgram conducted one of the most famous experiments of the twentieth century. That means you need to understand how the experiments were conducted and what conclusions were drawn from them.

1 If ordered to do so, would you shock a man with a heart condition, who is screaming and asking to be released? Certainly few people would obey. Or would they? Think about it, in Nazi Germany, obedient soldiers (who had once been average citizens like ourselves) helped slaughter more than 6 million people in concentration camps. Do such inhumane acts reflect deep character flaws? Are they acts of heartless psychopaths or crazed killers? Or are they simply the result of obedience to authority? These are questions that puzzled social psychologist Stanley Milgram (1965) when he began a controversial series of studies on obedience—a special type of conformity to the demands of an authority figure.

Milgram's Obedience Studies

2 Perhaps the best way to understand Milgram's experiments is to imagine yourself as a participant. Imagine answering a newspaper ad to take part in a "learning" experiment at Yale University. When you arrive, a coin is flipped and a second participant is designated the "learner." By chance you have become the "teacher."

3   You are told by those running the experiment that your task is to read a list of word parts. The learner's task is to memorize them. You are to punish him with an electric shock each time he makes a mistake. The learner is then taken to another room and you watch as he is seated in an "electric chair" apparatus. Next, electrodes are attached to his wrists. You are then escorted to your position in front of a "shock generator." On this device is a row of thirty switches marked from 15 to 450 volts. Corresponding labels range from "Slight Shock" to "Extreme Intensity Shock"

and finally "Danger: Severe Shock." Your instructions are to shock the learner each time he makes a mistake. You must begin with 15 volts and then move one switch (15 volts) higher for each additional mistake.

4   The experiment begins, and the learner soon makes his first error. You respond by flipping a switch. The learner makes more mistakes. You rapidly reach the 75-volt level. The learner moans after each shock. At 100 volts, he complains he has a heart condition. At 150 volts, he says he no longer wants to continue and demands to be released. At 300 volts, he screams and says he can no longer give answers.

5   At some point, you, in the role of teacher, begin to protest the experiment. "The man has a heart condition," you say, "I'm not going to kill him." The experimenter says, "Please continue." Another shock and another scream from the learner and you say, "You mean I've got to keep going up the scale? No sir, I'm not going to give him 450 volts!" The experimenter says, "The experiment requires you to continue." For a time, the learner refuses to answer any more questions and screams with each shock. Then he falls chillingly silent for the rest of the experiment.

Milgram's Results

6   Milgram had doubted that many people would obey the order to keep inflicting shocks on a seemingly tortured subject. He was not the only one. When he polled a group of psychiatrists before the experiment, they predicted that less than 1 percent of those tested would obey. What's astounding is that in Milgram's experiments, 65 percent of the subjects obeyed and went all the way to the 450-volt level; almost no one stopped short of 300 volts. The first substantial drop in obedience occurred at the 300-volt level. Whatever his expectations had been, Milgram had discovered that his subjects were obedient to the extreme and willing to inflict pain if an authority figure required them to do so.

7   As it turned out, though, the experiment was a fake. The "learner" was actually an actor who turned a tape recorder on and off in the shock room. No shocks were ever administered. However, the dilemma for the teacher was quite real. Participants protested, sweated, trembled, stuttered, bit their lips, and laughed nervously. Clearly, they were disturbed by what they were doing. Nonetheless, most obeyed the experimenter's orders. This was an outcome that shocked not just Milgram but also most of those working in the social sciences.

Milgram's Follow-Up

8   When Milgram's results were published, some suggested that the prestige of Yale University added to the participants' willingness to obey. Surely a Yale professor would not really allow anyone to be truly hurt during the experiment. To test this possibility, the study was re-run in a shabby office building in nearby Bridgeport, Connecticut. Under these conditions, fewer people obeyed. This time it was only 48 percent. Still, that was a large number, and even without the prestige of Yale influencing their behavior, participants in Milgram's experiment were far more obedient than anyone had expected.

9   Milgram was so disturbed by the willingness of people to knuckle under to authority and senselessly shock someone that, in later experiments, he tried to understand what circumstances might actually reduce obedience. What he found was that individuals whose concerns were backed up by others were more likely to refuse to increase the voltage when commanded to do so. Where obedience is concerned, there seems to be strength in numbers. Adapted from Coon and Mitterer. *Introduction to Psychology*, 12th ed., pp. 547–548, © Cengage Learning.

Sharpening Your Skills

DIRECTIONS   Answer the following questions by filling in the blanks or circling the letters of the correct response.

Previewing   1. What would be a good question to guide your reading of the section titled Milgram's Results?

_____

_____

Using Context Clues   2. In paragraph 2, how would you define the word *designated* in the following sentence: "When you arrive, a coin is flipped and a second participant is designated the 'learner'"?

_____

3. Which definition best fits the word *dilemma* used in this sentence: "However, the dilemma for the teacher was quite real"?

a. a wide range of possible choices

b. chance meeting

c. two choices with no positive outcome

d. chain of events

Following the Writer's Train of Thought

4. Which words are repeated and referred to so often in the reading that they must be essential to the main idea?

   a. Milgram, polls, Yale University, Bridgeport University

   b. Milgram, experiments, obedience, authority

   c. newspaper ad, polls, Milgram experiments, Nazis

5. This sentence appears at the beginning of paragraph 5: "I'm not going to kill him." Who is "him"?

   _____

6. The second sentence in paragraph 6 is

   a. a topic sentence.

   b. a major supporting detail.

   c. a transitional sentence.

7. This sentence appears near the end of paragraph 7: "Clearly, they were disturbed by what they were doing." In that sentence, the pronoun *they* refers to _____. The words *what they were doing* is another way of saying _____

   _____

8. Paragraph 7 includes the sentence "Nonetheless, most obeyed the experimenter's orders." What phrase does the author expect readers to mentally add between *most* and *obeyed*?" _____

   _____. When authors leave words out that they think the reader can supply, they are making use of

   a. transitions.

   b. introductory sentences.

   c. ellipsis.

   d. explanatory patterns.

Main Ideas and Explanatory Patterns

9. The main idea of the entire reading appears in

   a. the first sentence of paragraph 1.

   b. the last sentence of paragraph 1.

   c. the first sentence of paragraph 2.

   d. the first sentence of paragraph 3.

10. In paragraph 6, the topic sentence is

    a. the first sentence in the paragraph.

    b. the second sentence in the paragraph.

    c. in the middle of the paragraph.

    d. at the end of the paragraph.

Understanding the Function of Supporting Details

11. These two sentences appear in paragraph 7: "However, the dilemma for the teacher was quite real. Participants protested, sweated, trembled, stuttered, bit their lips, and laughed nervously." Which of the following statements correctly describes the relationship between the sentences?

    a. The first sentence is the topic sentence; the second sentence is a major detail.

    b. The first sentence is a major detail; the second sentence is a major detail.

    c. The first sentence is a major detail; the second sentence is a minor detail.

12. The last sentence in paragraph 7 is

    a. the topic sentence.

    b. a major supporting detail.

    c. a minor supporting detail.

    d. a concluding sentence.

13. Paragraph 5 opens with these two sentences: "At some point, you, in the role of teacher, begin to protest the experiment. 'The man has a heart condition,' you say, 'I'm not going to kill him.'" Which of the following statements correctly describes the relationship between the two sentences?

a. The first sentence is the topic sentence; the second sentence is a major detail.

b. The first sentence is a major detail; the second sentence is a major detail.

c. The first sentence is a major detail; the second sentence is a minor detail.

14. Why is Bridgeport, Connecticut, mentioned in the reading and how does that reference help support the main idea?

_____

_____

_____

15. In paragraph 9, which category word should guide your search for major details?

_____

From Reader to Writer Milgram summed up his experiments in an article for *Harper's* magazine. He titled the article "The Perils of Obedience." In the article, he said the following: "The essence of obedience is that a person comes to view himself as the instrument for carrying out another person's wishes, and he therefore no longer regards himself as responsible for his actions." Write a paragraph or two explaining when and why being obedient in the way Milgram described has had (or can have) disastrous consequences. Source of quotation: http://www.physics.utah.edu/~detar/phys4910/readings/ethics/PerilsofObedience.html. Last accessed November 6, 2014.)

▶ TEST 1   **Reviewing Key Concepts**

DIRECTIONS   Answer the following questions by filling in the blanks.

1. The form supporting details take _____

    _____ .

2. What are some of the different forms supporting details can take in order to support the main idea?

    _____

3. Explain the difference between major and minor details.

    _____

    _____

    _____

    _____

    _____

4. How should the reader treat minor details?

    _____

    _____

5. What kinds of words in topic sentences are clues to major details?

    _____

6. What are some examples of these words?

    _____

7. What kinds of transitions are clues to major details?

    _____

8. What are some examples of these transitions?

    _____

9. Concluding sentences fulfill two functions. What are those two functions?

   _____

   _____

   _____

10. When taking notes, are you free to just ignore the information in concluding sentences? _____ Please explain.

    _____

    _____

▶ TEST 2   **Recognizing Supporting Details**

DIRECTIONS   The first sentence in each group of sentences is the topic sentence. That topic sentence is followed by five supporting details. Circle the letters of the three sentences that help make the topic sentence clear and convincing.

Topic Sentence **1.** Over the years, salamanders—small, lizardlike creatures that walk on four legs—have been the focus of numerous legends.

Supporting Details

a. In England, a salamander is also the name of a portable stove.

b. The philosopher Aristotle claimed that salamanders could put out fires simply by walking through them.

c. The word *salamander* comes from the Greek word *salamandra*.

d. It was once believed that twining a salamander around a tree would kill the tree and poison its fruit.

e. According to legend, 4,000 soldiers died when they drank from a stream into which a salamander had fallen.

Topic Sentence **2.** The Walt Disney film *Pinocchio* is based on a novel by nineteenth-century Italian writer Carlo Collodi, but the novel was far more violent than the film.

Supporting Details

a. In both the novel and the film, Pinocchio is transformed into a donkey.

b. Disney's *Pinocchio* did not achieve the popularity of the fabulously successful *Snow White*.

c. In Collodi's novel, when Pinocchio is attacked by a cat, he bites off the cat's paw.

d. In the Italian version, Pinocchio kills a talking cricket when the insect tries to keep him from getting into trouble.

e. In the novel, when Pinocchio falls asleep by the fire, he wakes up with his wooden feet burned off.

Topic Sentence **3.** Until a cure was discovered in the nineteenth century, scurvy, a disease caused by a lack of vitamin C, plagued sailors on long sea voyages.

Supporting Details

a. In the late 1490s, the explorer Vasco da Gama lost more than half of his crew to scurvy.

b. In his autobiography, *Two Years Before the Mast*, nineteenth-century writer Richard Henry Dana described the sufferings of a fellow sailor who had contracted scurvy: "His legs swelled . . . his flesh lost its elasticity . . . and his gums swelled until he could not open his mouth."

c. Scurvy no longer plagues sailors who spend long periods of time at sea.

d. During the Napoleonic wars (1803–1814), French soldiers, who did not have daily doses of vitamin C, suffered from scurvy, but British soldiers, who drank daily doses of lime juice, escaped the disease.

e. British sailors became so associated with the drinking of lime juice that they were nicknamed "limeys."

Topic Sentence 4. For centuries, dogs have held a very special place in the hearts of humans.

Supporting Details

a. In the fifteenth and sixteenth centuries, no high-born lady was complete without her lap dog, and many fine ladies took their pets to church.

b. Unlike most dogs, border collies would rather work than play.

c. Rudyard Kipling (1865–1936), one of the most popular writers of his time, celebrated the British military but he also found time to write a poem in praise of dogs, titled "Four Feet."

d. The French Emperor Napoleon (1769–1821) claimed that his beloved Josephine preferred her dog Fortune to him.

e. Some people do not understand the bond that can develop between human beings and their pets.

▶ **TEST 3**　　　**Identifying Topic Sentences and Supporting Details**

DIRECTIONS　Circle the appropriate letter to identify the one sentence in each group that could function as the topic sentence.

1. a. The digestive system performs several important functions from which the body benefits.

    b. During digestion, food is broken down into smaller pieces.

    c. The digestive juices turn the food we eat into fat, carbohydrates, and protein, all of which are needed by the body.

    d. During the digestive process, nutrients are absorbed into the bloodstream.

    e. At the end of digestion, waste products are eliminated from the body.

2. a. The California Department of Fish and Game uses GIS to track and monitor endangered species of plants and animals.

    b. The fire department in Greenville, South Carolina, uses GIS to map the best routes to a fire.

    c. Chicago uses GIS for parking violations and meter repair.

    d. Police in Denver use GIS to track crime trends throughout the city.

    e. The technology known as geographic information systems (GIS) is transforming the policies and operations of state and local governments. (Adapted from Bowman and Kearney, *State and Local Government*, p. 238.)

3. a. According to Gordon Allport, mature adults are interested in others and consider the welfare of others as important as their own.

    b. Gordon Allport believed that mature adults are problem solvers, who have developed the necessary skills to complete current and future tasks.

    c. The psychologist Gordon Allport developed several criteria, or standards, for what he considered to be the "mature" personality.

    d. The ability to relate emotionally to other people was yet another of Gordon Allport's criteria.

    e. Self-insight was another character trait Gordon Allport associated with maturity.

4. a. People suffering from test anxiety worry they will perform poorly and be considered stupid as a result.
   b. Test anxiety is a very common problem with profound consequences.
   c. Test takers who suffer from test anxiety often know the right answers, but their minds go blank due to high anxiety.
   d. Some children who suffer from test anxiety refuse to go to school.
   e. Boys and girls seem to suffer equally from test anxiety.

5. a. With the passage of the North American Free Trade Agreement (NAFTA) in 1994, it became easier for U.S. companies to move their plants to locations where labor was much cheaper than in the United States.
   b. Rulings by the World Trade Organization made it easier for foreign products to be imported into the United States.
   c. American workers are no longer competing with one another; they are competing with workers around the world.
   d. In India and Russia, wages for computer programmers average less than 10 percent of the wages for programmers in the United States.
   e. During the recession of 2001–2003, more than 15 percent of the American jobs lost were outsourced to workers from other countries where the labor was cheap.

▶ **TEST 4**   **Distinguishing Between Major and Minor Details**

DIRECTIONS   Read each paragraph. Circle any addition transitions. Then fill in the boxes using the numbers of the sentences to identify the major and minor details.

1. ¹Biologically, chimpanzees and humans differ by little more than 1 percent of their DNA, which means that chimpanzees are actually more closely related to humans than they are to gorillas. ²The anatomy of a chimpanzee's brain and central nervous system is amazingly like that of humans. ³And like humans, chimpanzees can also create and use tools, make decisions, and cooperate in groups. ⁴Chimpanzees also demonstrate many human communication skills. ⁵They use sign languages and gestures to indicate what they want. ⁶They use nonverbal behaviors such as kissing, hugging, back patting, and fist shaking in the same ways humans do. ⁷Furthermore, chimpanzees feel and express human emotions such as happiness, sorrow, fear, and despair. ⁸These animals are like us in many of their behaviors, too. ⁹For example, mother chimpanzees care for their offspring during their long childhood, and chimps also divide into groups that go to war against one another.

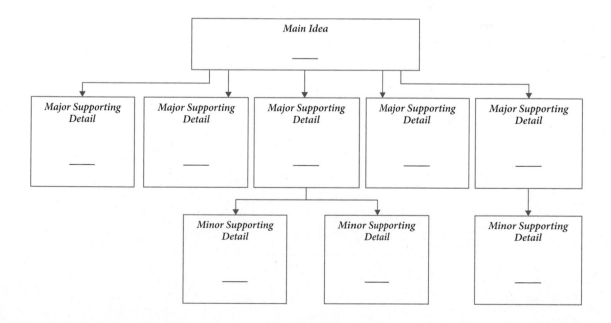

2. [1]Defined in general terms, monarchies are systems of government ruled, or appearing to be ruled, by one person, and four types of monarchies are still in existence throughout the world. [2]The first type includes monarchies in which the king (or queen) is both head of the government and head of state, and the monarch is directly involved in ruling the country. [3]This kind of monarchy, found mostly in the Middle East, includes Jordan, Saudi Arabia, and Morocco. [4]The second type of monarchy is one based on religious authority. [5]In Japan, Thailand, Nepal, and Bhutan, for example, monarchs are actually above the government, and they remain remote from politics and the public while observing formal rituals of conduct. [6]Monarchs in the third category, which includes democracies of Northern Europe and the Scandinavian states, have no political or religious role, serving instead as symbols of national unity. [7]The Netherlands, Denmark, and Luxembourg all have this type of monarch. [8]The fourth and final type of monarchy is the hybrid type illustrated by Britain, where the queen has some political authority, serves a religious role as head of the Anglican Church, and also functions as a symbol of her nation's identity.

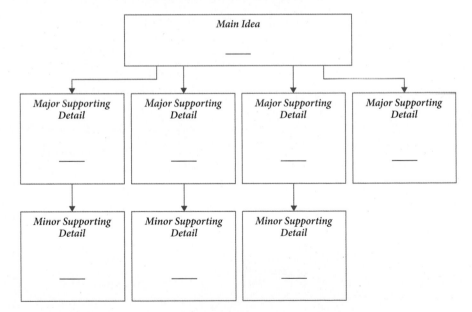

▶ **TEST 5**   **Using Category Words as Clues to Major Details**

> **DIRECTIONS**   Read each paragraph. Then underline the topic sentence and answer the questions that follow the reading.

1. [1]Many of us use recitation as a memory aid. [2]Having finished reading an essay, for instance, we mentally repeat the key points. [3]But even those of us who use recitation to remember don't realize that there are two different methods: active and passive. [4]When we use *active* recitation, we paraphrase the material, repeating key points in our own words. [5]When we use *passive* recitation, we simply repeat what we see before us in the text. [6]We don't even attempt to replace the author's words with our own. [7]Over the years, numerous studies have shown that active recitation, especially when combined with visualization, is a much better device for remembering than passive recitation.

   a. Based on the topic sentence, what category word or phrase will help you locate major details? _____

   b. Which sentence introduces the first major detail? _____

   c. How many major details are in the paragraph? _____

   d. How many minor ones are there? _____

   e. How would you label the last sentence? Is it a concluding sentence or a supporting detail? _____

2. [1]Most middle-class Americans generally maintain four principal zones of distance in their personal and professional relationships. [2]*Intimate distance* covers a space varying from direct physical contact with another person to a distance of six to eighteen inches. [3]This is the distance considered appropriate for close friends, romantic partners, and family members. [4]It's the one used for intimate situations. [5]*Personal distance*—eighteen inches to four feet—is the distance married couples use in public; it's also the distance used for conversation about things not considered especially private. [6]*Social or business distance* covers a four- to twelve-foot zone that is used for casual social exchanges and business negotiations. [7]Eye contact is almost always maintained at this distance, because the lack of it suggests that someone's attention is wandering. [8]*Public speaking distance*

can be a separation of only twelve feet, but usually it's not more than twenty-five. ⁹The goal of public speaking distance is to put a barrier between one's self and one's audience while making sure that listeners stay within the speaker's field of vision. (Source of information: www .linus-geisler.de/dp/dpo3_distance.html.)

a. Based on the topic sentence, what category word or phrase will help you locate major details? _____

b. Which sentence introduces the first major detail? _____

c. How many major details are in the paragraph? _____

d. How many minor ones are there? _____

e. How would you label the last sentence? Is it a concluding sentence or a supporting detail? _____

3. ¹Many people have superstitions, beliefs about good or bad things that will or will not happen in response to totally unrelated actions or events. ²But professional sports, fueled by the fear of failure in front of a crowd, seems to be an especially fertile ground for superstitious beliefs, and some of the most famous athletes have also been the most superstitious. ³Baseball Hall of Famer Wade Boggs wouldn't eat anything but chicken the night before a game, and before every turn at bat, he would write the Hebrew word *Chai*, meaning "life," into the dirt. ⁴If tennis player Goran Ivanisevic won a match, the next time he played, he would make sure to follow the exact same routine he had used on the winning day. ⁵He would wear the same clothes, eat the same meal at the same restaurant, and, if possible, talk to the same people. ⁶Tennis great Serena Williams says that closely following a specific routine contributes to her victories on the court. ⁷For that reason she always brings her shower sandals courtside and bounces the ball exactly five times before her first serve, but only twice before the second. ⁸Patrick Roy, perhaps the greatest goaltender in hockey history, believed he had a spiritual relationship with the goal posts, whom he called his friends. ⁹When a puck hit the posts, Roy always made it a point to say thank you to the goal posts he tended.

a. Based on the topic sentence, what category word or phrase will help you locate major details? _____

b. Which sentence introduces the first major detail? _____

c. How many major details are in the paragraph? _____

d. How many minor ones are there? _____

e. How would you label the last sentence? Is it a concluding sentence or a supporting detail? _____

4. [1]What everyday rules for behavior guide parents' efforts to socialize their children? [2]To answer that question, Heidi Gralinski and Claire Kopp (1993) observed and interviewed mothers with their children. [3]The research by Gralinski and Kopp suggests that maternal rules vary with the child's age. [4]They found that for fifteen-month-olds, mothers' rules and requests centered on ensuring the children's safety, respecting basic social niceties ("Don't bite"; "No kicking"), and learning to accept delays. [5]As children's ages and thinking abilities increased, the numbers and kinds of prohibitions and requests expanded. [6]The focus now was on family routines, self-care, and other concerns regarding the child's independence. [7]By the time children were three, new kinds of rules emerged: "Do not scream in a restaurant, run around naked in front of company, pretend to kill your sister, hang up the phone when someone is using it, fight with children in school, play with guns, or pick your nose." (Adapted from Seifert, Hofnung, and Hofnung, *Lifespan Development*, 2nd ed., p. 179, Boston: Houghton Mifflin.)

a. Based on the topic sentence, what category word or phrase will help you locate major details? _____

b. Which sentence introduces the first major detail? _____

c. How many major details are in the paragraph? _____

d. How many minor ones are there? _____

e. How would you label the last sentence? Is it a concluding sentence or a supporting detail? _____

▶ **TEST 6**   **Recognizing Supporting Details and Concluding Sentences**

DIRECTIONS   Read each paragraph. The topic sentence in each paragraph is underlined. Label each of the sentences that follow the topic sentence as a major (*M*) or minor (*m*) detail. If you think the paragraph ends with a concluding sentence, write a *c* in the final blank.

1. ¹<u>Although we associate penguins with the Antarctic, only two of approximately twenty species live on the continent of Antarctica.</u> ²These are the two largest, the emperor and the king penguins. _____ ³Both of them stand about four feet high. _____ ⁴Most other species are found on the islands in the Antarctic region, but a few breed as far north as Australia, New Zealand, South Africa, and South America. _____

2. ¹<u>Leadership and management are in some ways similar forms of influence, but in one very crucial way they are quite different.</u> ²Managers can direct the efforts of others because of their status or power within an organization. _____ ³Simply put, employees follow the directions of a manager largely because they know that not to do so would endanger their jobs. _____ ⁴Leaders, in contrast, don't have to rely on their position or rank; often it is the power of their personality that makes them an influence to be reckoned with. _____ ⁵At the Marriott Corporation, for example, employees often go beyond their normal duties largely because they respect and admire Bill Marriott. _____

3. ¹Surprising as it may seem to those of us who grew up with him, Santa Claus was not always pictured as a roly-poly figure with chubby cheeks, a big belly, and a long white beard. ²<u>The Santa Claus we know today was created in the mid-nineteenth century by the cartoonist Thomas Nast.</u> ³The European ancestor of our Santa Claus, Saint Nicholas, was always pictured as a tall, lean, and bearded bishop who bore no trace of extra fat. _____ ⁴However, during the years 1863 to 1885, Nast was commissioned by *Harper's Weekly* to do a series of Christmas drawings; during that twenty-two-year period, he created the pudgy figure so beloved by children today. _____ ⁵It was Nast who decided that Santa should wear

a fur-trimmed red suit and hat. _____ [6]Nast's cartoons also showed the world how Santa spent his entire year—making toys, checking on children's behavior, and reading their letters. _____ [7]Ultimately, however, Nast's fame rests not on his Santa Claus drawings but on his cartoons attacking political dishonesty and wrongdoing. _____

4. [1]The first American comic strip appeared at the end of the nineteenth century. [2]Comic books, however, arrived after the turn of the century, and it wasn't until the 1930s that comic books successfully became part of American culture. [3]The first comic book, published by Dell Publishing Company, was a huge failure, but the second one, also published by Dell, succeeded. _____ [4]Called "Famous Funnies," the comic book cost ten cents, and all thirty-five thousand copies quickly sold out. _____ [5]Not surprisingly, many more comic books followed, most of them featuring cartoon characters, such as Popeye and Flash Gordon, that had originally appeared in newspapers. _____ [6]The biggest comic book breakthrough, however, came in 1938 with the introduction of a red-caped, blue-suited figure called Superman. _____ [7]Appearing in the first issue of *Action Comics*, Superman was an immediate sensation. _____ [8]Today, that first issue of *Action Comics* can fetch its owner around $100,000. _____

7 Focusing on Supporting Details in Longer Readings

IN THIS CHAPTER, YOU WILL LEARN

- how to adapt what you know about supporting details in paragraphs to longer readings.

- how to recognize connections between paragraphs.

- how to use informal outlines for taking notes.

> "Beware of the person who can't be bothered by details."
>
> —WRITER AND PUBLISHER WILLIAM FEATHER

Chapter 7 shows you how experienced readers think their way through a longer, multi-paragraph reading. In particular, the chapter focuses on how supporting detail paragraphs clarify and support the main idea of an extended reading. Equally important, the chapter illustrates how writers help readers make connections between paragraphs.

By the end of Chapter 7, everything you know about supporting details in paragraphs and in longer readings will come together when you learn how to make an *informal outline* for note-taking. Informal outlines are a great way to sort out complicated information by reducing it to a bare bones blueprint of the main idea and the major and minor details.

Responding to Supporting Details in Longer Readings

Supporting details in paragraphs are single sentences. But in longer readings, one major detail might get an entire paragraph of explanation. It might even get two paragraphs.

But you can relax. That's not a major obstacle. When you are working with supporting details in longer readings, you don't have to do anything you haven't already done within the context of a paragraph. Once again, you need to (1) look for familiar patterns of general and specific sentences, (2) pay attention to words that are consistently repeated or referred to, and (3) check for any category words that might help you identify major details. With longer, multi-paragraph readings, you get a little more help from the author. That help comes in the form of major and minor headings, which provide clues to the author's topic and main idea.

Once you think you have a handle on the main idea of the entire reading, then you need to determine if there is a thesis statement† that sums up that main idea. If there is, you know you are on the right track, and you can start consciously figuring out what each supporting detail paragraph contributes to the main idea expressed in the thesis statement. Frequently, the opening sentence of a supporting detail paragraph is where the author is most likely to explain or suggest how the new paragraph connects to both the previous paragraph and to the main idea governing the entire reading.

As with paragraphs, supporting details in multi-paragraph readings can fulfill a variety of functions depending on the needs of the main idea. They can be examples, reasons, studies, statistics, exceptions, and definitions. The role they fill depends on the questions raised by the main idea expressed in the thesis statement.

READING TIP

If you can't find a thesis statement that matches the main idea you came up with *and* none of the paragraphs in the reading support the main idea you were considering, then you know you have to re-think your first guess about the overall or controlling main idea.

Thesis Statement Locations

The location of the thesis statement in a chapter section should affect your expectations about and search for major details. If you think the author starts right off with the thesis statement summing up the main idea of the reading, some of the major details might well appear in the opening paragraph. But if the thesis statement concludes the first paragraph, then you can expect the next paragraph to introduce the first major detail.

---

†At this point, depending on the chapters that you have covered, you might want to review the meaning of the term *thesis statement* introduced in Chapter 5.

When It Comes to Reading, There Are No Rigid Rules

Remember, though, there's no rule saying the author has to open or close the first paragraph of a chapter section with the thesis statement. These are just typical locations, particularly in textbooks, where authors use thesis statements just like they use topic sentences—to get their general point across as quickly as possible. Even in textbooks, though, thesis statements can move around, and the textbook templates, or explanatory patterns, you learned about in the previous chapter will not always apply.

Thesis Statements Can Turn Up in Unexpected Places

The following reading comes from a sociology text. In this instance, the opening paragraph does *not* introduce the thesis statement of the reading. The thesis statement is neither the first sentence nor the last. There is no opening question guiding you to the thesis statement and no reversal transition telling you, "Forget that introduction; here comes the real main idea."

The question now is what do you do since none of the previous explanatory patterns fit the reading? Well, you'll do what you did with paragraphs when they became more complicated. You'll look for patterns of general and specific sentences, along with repetition and reference of key words. In addition, you'll have the chapter heading to help guide your thoughts and make sure they match up with the author's.

What does the title suggest to you? What question does it raise?

All of the sentences in paragraph 1 are equally specific. What does that suggest to you?

What words or phrases are repeated in paragraphs 1 and 2?

Becoming Human

1 Several years ago a Seattle judge gave permanent custody of a six-year-old boy to the county welfare department. The judge asked that efforts be made to have the child taken away from his biological parents and adopted, despite protests from the child's father and mother. The judge based his decision on the fact that the child could not speak intelligibly, crawled rather than walked, and barked like a dog when people approached him. . . . Clearly, the little boy's tragic condition was the result of isolation and almost total neglect. From infancy he had spent most of his days and nights alone in a filthy one-room house. His father was in prison and his mother was rarely home, stopping by only now and then to feed him.

2 There have been countless cases like this, of children whose parents so neglected them and so isolated them from all human contact that when they were discovered, they acted more like wild animals than human beings. In fact, children like this are often called feral children (the word *feral*

How could stories of feral children help you understand how we become human?

means "untamed"), because some people mistakenly assume that such children were reared in the wild by an animal.

3   Human children cannot be raised by mother wolves, dogs, or other animals—such stories are fantasies. Unfortunately, cruel and unfit parents can raise their children like animals. Sometimes children thought to be feral are actually victims of mental retardation or severe mental illness, not neglect. But others, like the little boy in Seattle, are born with normal capacities, for they make rapid progress once they are rescued from isolation.

What general word in the first sentence of paragraph 4 suggests the writer might be zeroing in on the main idea?

4   Feral children demonstrate an important principle: Our biological heritage alone cannot make us into adequate human beings. Only through social relations—constant intimate interaction—can the rich cultural legacy that sets humans apart from other animals be transmitted to humans. An infant is born without culture. Reared in isolation, a human being will not even learn to talk or walk, let alone sing or read. . . .

5   The learning process by which infants are made into normal human beings possessed of culture and able to participate in social relations is called *socialization*. This process, which literally means to be "made social," begins at birth and continues until death. We never cease to be shaped by our interactions with others. (Adapted from Stark, *Sociology*, 10th ed., p. 148, © Cengage Learning.)

Edward Julius Detmold/Blue Lantern Studio/Fine Art/Corbis.

Rudyard Kipling's *The Jungle Book* features Mowgli, a boy raised by wolves and befriended by a panther named Bagheera.

In this case, the main idea doesn't appear until the fourth paragraph. That means the paragraphs that precede it fulfill a dual function. They act as an introduction to the controlling main idea—"We need interaction with others in order to learn human, as opposed to animal, behavior." But at the same time, they function as supporting details. They tell readers what happens when we don't have the "intimate interaction" with others referred to in paragraph 4. The examples of feral children are proof that we need others in our efforts to become human.

When the thesis statement turns up in the middle or the end of a reading, it is not unusual for the opening paragraphs to serve a dual function, as introduction and support.

From Reader to Writer   In fiction like Kipling's *The Jungle Book*, feral children may lead happy, even joyous lives. The reality for such children is usually much sadder. One of the most studied and most famous feral children was a little girl named Genie. After being rescued from isolation and abuse, Genie began to make progress in learning how to speak and behave like a normal human being.

Use the Web to discover the details of Genie's life and recreate it in your writing. Answer questions like the following: Where was Genie found? What happened to her after she was discovered? How did she end up? Is she still alive?

READING TIPS

1. If a chapter section does not fit an explanatory pattern you are familiar with, start thinking about the relationship between general and specific sentences, and be on the lookout for chains of repetition and reference.

2. Use the heading of a chapter section to guide your search for the main idea and the supporting details that explain it.

3. When you start to get answers to your questions about the heading, you are also zeroing in on the main idea of the entire reading.

Major and Minor Details Revisited

Sometimes writers can't fully explain a major supporting detail in one paragraph. They need a second paragraph for further clarification. That makes the second paragraph a minor detail.

As they do in single paragraphs, minor details in longer readings vary in their significance. If they simply repeat the same point for emphasis or provide an additional or obvious example, they can be skimmed and forgotten.

But here again *minor details need to be evaluated.* If a writer takes two paragraphs to develop the same point and the second paragraph is needed to fully explain the first, then the minor detail paragraph needs close attention. The information it contains probably also needs to appear in your notes.

READING TIP

To determine the relationship between major and minor details, *look carefully at the opening sentences of each paragraph.* The sentence openings are where writers usually link what came before to what's coming next. Sentence openings will usually give you the best clues to how paragraphs relate to one another.

SUMMING UP THE KEY POINTS

1. Understanding the function of supporting details in longer readings calls upon the same skills you used to understand them in paragraphs. Once you have a sense of the main idea, start looking for a thesis statement that confirms you are on the right track.

2. The relationship between general and specific sentences and the repetition and reference in the reading will help you determine both the main idea and the function of the supporting details.

3. The heading of a chapter section will also help you understand the function of the supporting details. The heading will raise questions and the supporting details will help answer those questions.

4. Major details in longer readings answer questions about the heading and the main idea. Minor details further clarify major ones and must be evaluated for importance with each new reading.

5. As they do in paragraphs, major and minor supporting details can fulfill any number of functions depending on the needs of the main idea. They can be examples, reasons, studies, statistics, definitions, exceptions, etc. Whatever form they take, they answer the questions readers might have about the main idea of the chapter section or reading.

▶ **EXERCISE 1**   **Recognizing Main Idea and Supporting Detail Paragraphs**

DIRECTIONS   When correctly assembled, the six paragraphs labeled a–f make up a complete, multi-paragraph reading about hiking a famous trail in the rain. One paragraph is pure introduction. One paragraph introduces the thesis statement. There are three major detail paragraphs and one minor one. On the blanks following the reading, use the paragraph letters to indicate how the paragraphs should be arranged in order to make sense to the reader.

The Half Dome peak in Yosemite National Park is a gorgeous sight, but some have died trying to reach it.

Jarno Gonzalez Zarraonandia/Shutterstock.com.

Half Dome in the Rain Turns Deadly

a. Yet many hikers don't fear the rain's effect on Half Dome. Thinking, as most people do, that tragedy won't strike them, they charge ahead, despite the posted signs and warnings of park officials that rainy weather and Half Dome's trail are a dangerous mix. In the fall of 2011, the problem of hiking Half Dome in bad weather came to a head because the rains were unusually heavy. Although the heavy rains were making the Half Dome trail treacherous, even deadly, some hikers kept on trying to beat the odds, with disastrous, even deadly results.

b. The Half Dome trail is the most demanding day hike in California's Yosemite National Park. Hikers with the strength and stamina to walk to the top of Half Dome go straight up a mountain of rock, climbing a total of 4,800 feet.[†] At the top, the view is glorious. It's certainly worth the effort. But if it's raining, the demanding day hike can turn deadly because the rock becomes slippery and treacherous.

c. Twenty-six-year-old Hayley LaFlamme did not have Castillo's luck with her the day she set out to climb Half Dome along with her sister and two friends. It had rained in the morning and rain and lightning were still threatening when the small group set out. Despite the slippery conditions, though, LaFlamme made it to the top of Half Dome. It was on the descent that tragedy struck. Making her way down the cable ladder that threads its way along Half Dome's trail, LaFlamme lost her grip and fell 600 feet to her death.

d. While Castillo may have lacked common sense, he didn't lack nerve. An experienced salsa dancer, he convinced himself that he was in good physical condition and could successfully make the trip back to safety. When the rain stopped, he started out on foot. But after a fall, he sat down and scooted the rest of the way down the mountain. It wasn't a particularly dignified trip. But he made it and lived to tell his story. In fact, he says he is going back to complete the hike under better weather conditions.

e. For Armando Castillo, hiking Half Dome in the rain proved dangerous and terrifying, but in the end he made it back alive. About three-quarters of the way up Half Dome, Castillo and some other hikers were confronted by a hailstorm. When the storm cleared, the other hikers

---

[†]Half Dome is more than 8,800 feet high, but hikers don't usually start at the very bottom.

turned back, unwilling to trust their luck. Castillo decided to trust his and kept going, feeling he had come too far to turn back. When a freezing thunderstorm hit, he was trapped at the 8,842 foot summit. He called 911 to get rescued, but rangers don't fly in weather that might kill them along with the stranded hikers. His only alternative was to find shelter under a rocky ledge and try to figure out how to make it back alive.

f. In addition to LaFlamme, at least twenty people have died attempting to scale or return from Half Dome. According to park officials, in most of those deaths rain was a factor, and there is a growing worry that if unseasonably heavy rains continue due to climate change, the number of tragic deaths might multiply as hikers continue to tempt fate. Park officials are currently mulling over alternatives for how to best prevent hikers from attempting Half Dome in the rain. But they are pessimistic since so many people in the past have assumed that warnings about rain on Half Dome being deadly didn't apply to them.

1. Introductory Paragraph: _____

2. Thesis Statement Paragraph: _____

3. Major Detail Paragraph: _____

4. Minor Detail Paragraph: _____

5. Major Detail Paragraph: _____

6. Major Detail Paragraph: _____

READING TIP Even more than in single paragraphs, category words like *circumstances*, *reasons*, and *consequences* at the beginning of a reading are a clue to the major details.

▶ **EXERCISE 2**   **Understanding the Function of Supporting Details**

DIRECTIONS   Read through each selection. Note the underlined thesis statement. Then answer the questions that follow.

EXAMPLE

Is Romance Essential to Marriage?

1   The majority of Americans and Europeans believe that couples should first fall in love and then get married. Yet in many other countries, including India and China, the reverse is much more common. First, an individual marries someone chosen by family members; *then* the couple finds love. Anthropologists say that the arranged marriage is actually common throughout history, with even colonial* Americans approaching matrimony in this way. Today, in fact, as many as 60 percent of the world's marriages are still arranged. There appear to be two main reasons why arranged marriages have never gone out of fashion.

2   First, in many cultures, marriage is viewed as the union of two families, rather than just two people. Because marriage is a valuable tool for creating alliances* that benefit both parties, the selection of a mate is considered too important to be left up to the young and inexperienced. Often with the help of professional matchmakers, parents search for someone who possesses the specific temperament, interests, and background that will suit both their child *and* their family.

3   Unlike Western relationships, which usually begin from chance encounters between two people who may or may not have much in common, the arranged marriage involves a focused search that ends by matching up two very compatible* people. Thus, children are raised with the expectation that their parents will help them find the best possible husband or wife so that the blending of the two families will be permanent.

4   The other reason why the tradition of arranged marriage remains strong is the belief that romantic love can hinder the establishment of a lasting partnership. Proponents* of arranged marriage believe that in a union based on romance, serious problems can arise when the excitement of courtship begins to fade and the partners' flaws and differences become more apparent. Because arranged marriages are not based on love to begin with, they are not usually dissolved, as many Western marriages are, once passion dies. Thus, while about half of romantic marriages end in divorce, only about 5 percent of arranged marriages fail.

---

*colonial: relating to the period of time in which America was a colony under British control.
*alliances: unions of two or more people who share a legal or informal connection or relationship, a union, or an association that benefits both sides.
*compatible: fitting together well, sharing a common background and interests.
*proponents: supporters.

5   Still, arranged marriages are not necessarily loveless. On the contrary, in societies that arrange marriages, couples often become loving life partners. Because the spouses were matched based on compatible characteristics, they usually possess the necessary foundation* for building mutual respect, affection, and even love. In Western marriages, passionate love is often damaged by the intrusion of everyday life. In arranged marriages, however, couples begin their courtship *after* the wedding as they blend gradually blossoming affection with the realities of day-to-day existence.

In India, arranged marriages are not at all unusual.

© Ulrich Flemming.

1. Based on the underlined thesis statement, what question or questions do you think the supporting detail paragraphs will answer for the reader?

    What are the two reasons why arranged marriages have remained popular?

2. Which of the supporting detail paragraphs answer that question?
    2 and 4

3. Are there any minor supporting detail paragraphs in this reading?
    ___yes___ If your answer was yes, which paragraphs introduce minor details? __3 and 5__

*foundation: basis; body or ground on which other parts rest.

EXPLANATION   "Two main reasons" is the key phrase in the thesis statement, which appears at the very end of the first paragraph, a typical location of main ideas in longer readings (see pages 254–56 in Chapter 5). Having used this phrase, the writer who wants to communicate with readers has to start the next paragraph with the first of the two reasons.

Paragraph 3 doesn't introduce another reason but describes the focused search for a partner, continuing the theme of the previous paragraph—that marriage is an alliance, or a union, between families. Paragraph 4 does introduce the second reason, as the opening transition signals it will.

1. No Diet Books on the Fiji Islands

1 On the Fiji Islands of the South Pacific, diet books would never be the big sellers they are in the United States. Although Fiji Islanders have definite ideas about how a person should look, they don't much care about being overweight. On the contrary, Fijians like sturdy muscles and a generally well-fed look in both men and women. To a large degree, the preference for plumpness among Fijians stems from their culture's emphasis on community rather than appearance.

2   Unlike Americans, who prize individualism, the Fijians care more about the good of the community than they do about themselves as individuals. For them, standing out in a crowd is never as important as showing a caring attitude toward friends. And what is the main vehicle for showing your friends you care? It's serving them food, of course. For the Fijians, offering food to friends and family shows you're concerned about their physical and emotional well-being. At dinnertime, Fijians routinely open their windows and doors so that the aroma of the meal will waft outside and attract passersby. Extra food is always prepared so that anyone attracted by the smell of dinner can stop by for a snack. It is, in fact, a social disgrace not to have enough food for drop-in guests.

3   Because they believe that sharing food encourages a sense of community, Fijians consider dieting socially unacceptable. Dieting prevents a person invited to dine with friends from accepting the invitation. In addition, what dieter would willingly prepare huge, tempting meals for friends and family? Suspicious of diets, parents watch their children carefully for signs that they might be losing weight. They do so not because they want their children to achieve and maintain a certain weight but because they want to make sure their children are fully participating in the community through the sharing of food.

4   As a result of the Fijians' attitude toward food, children in particular are spared the painful experience so common to Americans of all ages—the failed diet. Children aren't obsessed by their personal appearance, and they don't constantly compare themselves to those a bit trimmer or thinner. If anything, they pity others for failing to be appropriately plump. However, the Fijian emphasis on food and the celebration of body fat does have one drawback. Children who need to limit their intake of calories for reasons of health—say, a child with diabetes—can become anxious or depressed because they are unable to fully participate in the community's common feasting. (Source of information: Seifert, Hoffnung, and Hoffnung, *Lifespan Development*, pp. 264–65, © Cengage Learning.)

1. Based on the underlined thesis statement, what question or questions do you think the supporting details answer for the reader?

_____

_____

2. Which of the supporting detail paragraphs answer that question?

_____

3. Are there any minor supporting detail paragraphs in this reading? _____ If your answer was yes, which paragraphs introduce minor details? _____

2. Remembering Ebbinghaus

1   At the end of the nineteenth century, a German psychologist named Hermann Ebbinghaus became interested in the carefully controlled laboratory experiments being used to do scientific research. He decided to introduce similar methods into the study of human memory.

2   Using only himself as a subject, Ebbinghaus devoted six years of research to his experiments. In one of them, he memorized lists of nonsense syllables, put them aside for specified amounts of time, and then relearned them. By comparing the time taken to learn the lists with the time taken to relearn them, Ebbinghaus was able to reach several important conclusions about the role of memory in learning. After more than a century of research, these conclusions have been repeatedly confirmed.

Rates of Forgetting

3   As a result of his research, Ebbinghaus maintained that the rate of forgetting becomes progressively slower over time. A list of nonsense syllables that he had memorized and put aside for an hour required more than half the original study time to relearn. But a list that had been put aside for nine hours was not, as one would expect, totally forgotten. The rate of forgetting had slowed down, and only two-thirds of the original study time was required to relearn the nonsense syllables.

4   Since 1885, when Ebbinghaus first published his work, investigators have continued to study the rate of forgetting. They have used not only nonsense syllables but also passages of prose, lists of facts, and excerpts from poetry. Like Ebbinghaus, they have discovered that the rate of forgetting slows down over time. It is rapid at first. But it becomes slower as the amount of time between learning and relearning increases. This was the first of Ebbinghaus's conclusions to be confirmed.

Overlearning

5   Another of Ebbinghaus's conclusions confirmed by modern research is that overlearning during the initial learning period makes relearning at a later time easier. Based on his experiments, Ebbinghaus maintained that the more repetitions involved in the original learning experience, the fewer repetitions needed for relearning. Later investigators have come to a similar conclusion. However, they have also concluded that each repetition will not produce an equal return in time saved during the relearning period. After a point, the repetition of material already memorized does not produce a sufficient reward.

Distributed Learning

6   Research that followed Ebbinghaus's experiments by more than half a century also confirmed his belief that learning sessions devoted to memorizing are more effective if they are distributed over time. In 1940, an American psychologist, A. P. Bumstead, conducted a series of experiments to determine whether it was better to have several short learning sessions spaced out over a period of time or one long, unbroken learning session. Using only himself as a subject, Bumstead memorized several different poetry selections, spacing his learning sessions at intervals that varied from one hour to eight days. After finishing the experiment, Bumstead concluded that increasing the time between learning sessions actually decreased the amount of time needed to memorize the material.

1. Based on the underlined thesis statement, what question or questions do you think the supporting details answer for the reader?

   _____

   _____

2. Which of the supporting detail paragraphs answer that question or those questions? _____

3. Are there any minor supporting detail paragraphs in this reading? _____ If your answer was yes, which paragraphs introduce minor details? _____

WEB QUEST
One issue that Ebbinghaus did not research is context-specific or context-dependent remembering. What does that term mean and how might you apply it to learning?

_____

_____

_____

From Reader to Writer Write at least three or four paragraphs explaining why you think romance is (or is not) a necessary ingredient for marriage. Use a brief discussion of arranged marriages as an introduction to your main idea. Start your paper by saying that countries where arranged marriages are common have the right (or the wrong) idea.

✔ CHECK YOUR UNDERSTANDING

1. If the chapter section you are reading does not fit a common explanatory pattern, what should you do?

   _____

   _____

2. What should you do once you think you have a sense of the overall main idea of the reading?

_____

_____

3. What's the relationship between the heading of a chapter section and the supporting details?

_____

_____

4. What dictates the function of supporting details in longer readings?

_____

5. Do readers need to pay attention to minor supporting details in longer readings? Explain.

_____

_____

_____

From Reader to Writer Write a few paragraphs describing the different relationships people have to food. Make your thesis statement sum up the different connections to food that you've noticed among friends and family. (You can also focus on one friend or family member.) Then use concrete examples for supporting details. For instance, if your thesis statement refers to people who use food to calm anxiety, try to describe, as concretely as possible, someone you know who won't confront a problem without a Snickers in one hand and a bag of Moose Munch in the other.

The Value of Visuals Aids in Longer Readings

Up to this point, you've worked mostly with visual aids that illustrated or added to the information in relatively short readings. Visual aids become even more important, however, as the readings get longer, and there is more information to learn. That's because visual aids encourage **dual coding**.

The term *dual coding* was coined by Allan Paivio, a cognitive psychology professor who conducted a number of studies on long-term learning. Dual coding occurs when the learner processes the same information in two different ways. Paivio's studies showed that learning improved when learners absorbed new information by both text and image. Certainly, research[†] on the brain suggests Paivio may be right. As Chapter 1 points out, the more pathways in the brain that are activated at the same time, the more likely it is for long-term learning to take place.

For an example of how visual aids double your chances for remembering new information over the course of time, look at the following text, the topic of which is "hate crimes." When you finish the reading, look at the pie chart (Figure 7-1) as well. Notice how often the accompanying pie chart repeats, in visual terms, the same point made in the text, thereby helping the reader to dual code the information.

Hate Crimes Motivated by Bias

Readers would be correct to assume that the first paragraph is pure introduction. The sentences are all on the same level, and none of them cries out for further clarification. On their own, the statements are all too painfully clear.

1   In June 2011, 49-year-old James Craig Anderson, an African American auto plant worker, was robbed, beaten, and run over by a truck near a hotel in Jackson, Mississippi. Deryl Dedmon, the 18-year-old who drove the truck that ran over Anderson, was charged with murder. Dedmon and a group of other white teenagers were reportedly out looking for a black person to assault when they found Anderson. During the brutal attack, which was captured on hotel security video, the teenagers used racial slurs, making it clear that the teens' actions constituted a "hate crime."

2   A hate crime is an unlawful act of violence motivated by prejudice or bias against a particular group. Hate crimes are also known as "bias-motivated" crimes, which include intimidation (threats), destruction or damage to property, physical assault, and murder. Unfortunately, hate crimes have proven difficult to track.

[†]See, for example, *Research-Based Strategies to Ignite Student Learning* by neurologist Judy Willis.

3   In 2010, the Federal Bureau of Investigation reported a total of 6,604 hate crime incidents in the United States. However, FBI hate crime data undercount the number of hate crimes for several reasons. Unfortunately, not all U.S. jurisdictions report hate crimes. Also, it is often difficult to prove that crimes are motivated by hate or prejudice. Then, too, law enforcement agencies shy away from classifying crimes as hate crimes because it makes their community "look bad." In addition, out of fear of reprisals, victims are often reluctant to report hate crimes to the authorities.

4   Starting with the first time the FBI published hate crime data in 1992, most hate crimes have been based on racial bias. In 2009, a large percentage of racially based hate crimes were directed against blacks. As the Leadership Council on Civil Rights Education has pointed out, "From lynching, to burning crosses and churches, to murdering a man by chaining him to a truck and dragging him down a road for three miles, anti-black violence has been and still remains the prototypical* hate crime, intended not only to injure and kill individuals but also to terrorize an entire group of people.

5   However, religious bias is also a powerful motivation for hate crimes. Most hate crimes with a religious bias are directed against those of the Jewish faith. Ethnic bias is also a contributing factor, with the majority of hate crimes in this category being focused on Hispanic individuals. Hate crimes against Hispanics are usually motivated by a more general hatred of immigrants. Men and women perceived as not having a "normal" sexual orientation are also the focus of hate crimes, with gay and transgendered men and women subjected to attacks, despite the society's growing acceptance of sexual differences.

6   In a 1995 study, researchers Levin and McDevitt found that the motivations for hate crimes were of three distinct types. Thrill crimes are committed by offenders who are looking for excitement and attack victims for the "fun" of it. Defensive hate crimes involve offenders who view their attacks as necessary to protect their community, workplace, or college campuses from "outsiders," or to protect their racial and cultural purity from being "contaminated." Mission hate crimes are perpetrated by white supremacist group members or by those who, on their own, have dedicated themselves to a lifetime of bigotry. (Adapted from Linda A. Mooney et al., *Social Problems*, 8th ed., pp. 293–94, © Cengage Learning.)

---

*prototypical: illustrating the most common or typical qualities of a group or class, in this case of hate crimes.

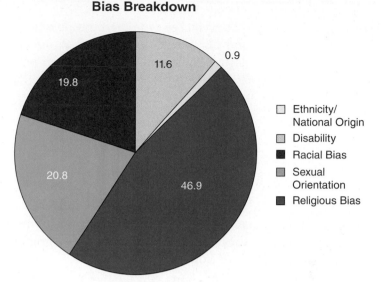

Figure 7-1 Categories of Hate Crimes

(Source of data: Federal Bureau of Investigation).

On Reading Pie Charts

Pie charts are likely to turn up whenever the author wants to show you the parts or categories that make up some larger whole. Usually, an author will supply a different visual aid if there are more than eight or nine categories involved. However, even when more subcategories are involved, authors sometimes stick with pie charts if one or two categories are huge and the remaining ones are very small. That's because the pie chart nicely highlights the differences in size. For the previous reading on hate crimes, a pie chart offers the perfect visual representation of the five bias categories.

In general, pie charts are an excellent way of showing differences in the size of subgroups comprising a larger whole. Since that was part of the message of this reading—that some categories of bias are much larger than others—the author selected a pie chart to reinforce that point.

Steps in Reading a Pie Chart ●

1. When you see a pie chart during a chapter preview, read the title and caption. Make it a point to understand what the pie chart is supposed to show readers, even before you read the excerpt it illustrates. The pie chart shown in Figure 7-1, for example, is clearly labeled to indicate that there are several different categories of hate crimes.

2. If the text is particularly difficult, it may help to look at the pie chart while you read, checking the chart when it is referred to in the passage. Like most visual aids, pie charts will usually be marked with a figure number that is referenced in the text. If the text does not seem too difficult, look at the pie chart when you finish reading so that your brain gets a chance to process the information visually as well as verbally. But whatever you do, don't skip over it.

3. Pay attention to the number and size of the individual pieces in the pie chart. Then make a mental note of the number or record it in your notes. Use it to review later on by asking yourself questions such as, "What are the five categories of bias?" If you can remember race, ethnicity, and religion but not the other two categories, then you know you have to take another look at the pie chart, because that's where all five categories are neatly summed up.

4. Be sure you understand what point the author wants to reinforce by including the pie chart. Is it the main idea or a supporting detail? The pie chart on hate crimes, for example, provides a visual summary of the supporting details.

5. If the author provides two pie charts, make sure you know what each one represents. Pay attention to similarities in the makeup of the segments. However, pay particular attention to differences. Writers usually include two pie charts side by side in order to provide information about two different groups in relation to two different topics. For instance, a writer might use two pie charts to highlight the differences between Democrats and Republicans when it comes to voting on educational spending and online voter registration.

▶ **EXERCISE 3**   **Learning with Pie Charts**

DIRECTIONS   Look at the title of the reading and the pie chart in order to predict what you think the reading will say. Then read the text and answer the questions that follow.

Partners in Pollution: China and the United States

1   Ever since the arrival of the Industrial Revolution in the nineteenth century, carbon dioxide (CO_2) emissions from the burning of fossil fuels—coal, gas, and oil—have been escalating at a dramatic and dangerous rate, increasing by 40 percent since the start of the Industrial Revolution. Despite general agreement among governments about the need to limit emissions of carbon dioxide into the air and water we need to survive, the emissions have been increasing, with the one exception being the year 2009, when the world was in a financial crisis. Since then, though, emissions from fossil fuels have grown by about 2.6 percent a year, despite the fact that limiting the amount of CO_2 emitted is crucial for our future and the future of our children. CO_2 is a heat-trapping gas that directly contributes to the warming of the air and oceans, which in turn has serious consequences for the health and safety of both humans and wildlife. Governments all around the world need to do more to limit carbon emissions.

2   Some governments, however, have more to do than others, a point that has been repeatedly made by officials from other governments, like those of India and Japan. While the amount of CO_2 these countries emit into the air is not small by any means, it is still dwarfed by the huge output of the United States and China. Together, the two countries account for more than half of all greenhouse gas emissions.[†] It's no surprise, then, that countries such as Mexico and Brazil have not taken kindly to suggestions from the United States about the need to control carbon output into the air.

3   There may, however, be some good news on the horizon for those who were furious at the big two's refusal to sign on or ratify[†] the 1997 Kyoto Protocol, with its international plan for fixed reductions in CO_2 emissions and other greenhouse gases. China and the United States have unveiled a secretly negotiated agreement to reduce the emission of greenhouse gases—prime among them CO_2—by significant amounts. Greenhouse gases trap heat in the atmosphere, thereby increasing temperatures that can severely damage the environment and harm the health and safety of Earth's inhabitants. Commenting on the agreement, UN climate chief Christiana Figueres, perhaps unintentionally, underscored how big a

---

[†]greenhouse gas emissions: carbon dioxide, methane, nitrous oxide, and fluorinated gases.
[†]The United States signed on but did not ratify, or formally agree to, the Kyoto Protocol. China refused when it became clear that the United States was not going to be a party to the Kyoto Protocol.

role China and the United States have played in endangering the global environment through their high levels of carbon emissions and other greenhouse gases when she said, "These two crucial countries have today announced important pathways towards a better and more secure future for humankind." (Source of quotation: http://www.theguardian.com/environment/2014/nov/12/china-and-us-make-carbon-pledge. Last accessed November 16, 2014.)

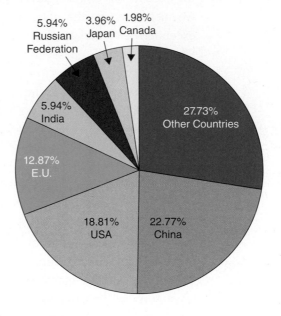

Figure 7-2   Global Emissions
When it comes to CO_2 emissions, China and the United States are more than a match for the rest of the world.

(Source of data: Environmental Protection Agency.)

1. Which of these statements best sums up the main idea of the reading?

   a. Other countries resent China and the United States for their role in polluting the environment.

   b. Following in the United States' footsteps, the Chinese government has finally decided to make reducing CO_2 emissions a priority.

   c. While all governments need to make the reduction of CO_2 emissions a priority, China and the United States share the greatest responsibility to do so.

   d. China and the United States have agreed to make huge cuts in greenhouse gas emissions.

2. What point made in the text is supported by the pie chart?

_____

_____

3. Which purpose does the pie chart fulfill?

   a. It restates the main idea in visual terms.

   b. It adds a supporting detail not mentioned in the reading.

   c. It repeats, in visual terms, the point of a supporting detail.

 # Outlining (Informally) Multi-Paragraph Readings

In some of your courses, you may find that taking notes in the margins of your text would be enough for you to understand and remember what you have read. But when the material is detailed and difficult, informal outlining is a great way to sort and record information.

With an informal outline, you know exactly what you need to remember and what you can safely forget. An informal outline is also a terrific tool for figuring out relationships between ideas. It forces you to determine which ideas are central to a reading and which are not.

Making an Informal Outline

As you know from Chapter 1, informal outlines have no fixed format. You can mix phrases with sentences and leave an _a_ without a _b_. The only test of an informal outline is how well it works for you. If your outline (1) records the main idea of the entire reading, (2) identifies and paraphrases the supporting details essential to understanding that main idea, and (3) shows the relationship between them, then it's perfect. Here, as another illustration, is a brief reading followed by an informal outline.

Each Species Plays a Unique Role in Its Ecosystem

The repetition of _niche_ in the opening paragraph makes that word a key candidate for being part of the main idea.

1 An important principle of ecology* is that each species has a distinct role to play in the ecosystems where it is found, which is called an _ecological niche_, or simply **niche** (pronounced "nitch"). A species niche includes everything that affects its survival and reproduction, such as how much water

_____

*ecology: branch of biology dealing with living things in nature and how they interact.

and sunlight it needs, how much space it requires, and the temperatures it can tolerate. A species niche should not be confused with its habitat, which is the place where it lives.

2   Scientists use niches to classify species broadly as *generalists* or *specialists*. Generalist species have broad niches. They can live in many different places, eat a variety of foods, and often tolerate a wide range of environmental conditions. Flies, cockroaches, mice, rats, white-tailed deer, raccoons, and humans are generalist species.

3   Specialist species, on the other hand, occupy narrow niches. For example, tiger salamanders are specialists because they can breed only in fishless ponds where their larvae will not be eaten. Another specialist is the red-cockaded woodpecker, which carves nest holes almost exclusively in longleaf pines that are at least 75 years old. China's highly endangered giant pandas are also specialists. They feed almost exclusively on various types of bamboo.

4   Is it better to be a generalist than a specialist? It depends. When environmental conditions are fairly constant, as in a tropical rain forest, specialists have an advantage because they have fewer competitors. But under rapidly changing environmental conditions, the generalist usually is better off than the specialist. (Miller and Spoolman, *Sustaining the Earth*, 9th ed., p. 69, © Cengage Learning.)

The author's explanation of how niches help scientists create two basic categories makes the opening sentence a possible thesis statement. The remainder of paragraph 2 along with paragraph 3 confirm that prediction.

Look now at the informal outline used to take notes on the reading:

Title:	Each Species Plays a Unique Role in Its Ecosystem
Main Idea:	Based on their ecological niche, scientists classify species as generalists or specialists.
Supporting Details:	1. Ecological niche refers to everything that sustains the species from drinking water to space and temperature.
	2. Generalists survive almost anywhere.
	Ex. flies, roaches, raccoons, and humans

> 3. Specialists need "special" conditions.
>
>   Ex. tiger salamanders thrive only in fishless ponds, red-cockaded woodpecker needs old pines, and pandas have to have bamboo.
>
> 4. If there are rapid changes in the environment, generalists fare better than specialists.

To a large degree, how you organize an informal outline is up to you. Still, there are some definite guidelines to follow if you want to take notes that are brief, complete, and well organized.

Guidelines for Informal Outlining ●	1. **Indent to show relationships.** Even with a quick glance, your outline should clearly identify the main idea of the entire reading. Always start off by writing the main idea close to the left-hand margin. Underneath and indented, list the supporting details used to explain it.
	2. **Condense and abbreviate.** Whenever you can, use phrases instead of sentences. Make up your own shorthand for common words and use it consistently. If a name appears several times, spell it out once, and then use initials. For example, if you are reading about President Lyndon Baines Johnson's[†] role in creating the Great Society, use the initials L.B.J. and G.S. to refer to the man and his most famous project.
	3. **Paraphrase the author's words.** If you just copy the author's words into your outline, you can't be sure you've understood them.
	4. **Leave plenty of space.** As you gather additional information from lectures or outside reading, you may want to add to your outline, so leave plenty of space both in the margins and between sentences.
	5. **Reorder the material if it helps you remember it.** There's no law saying you have to re-create the author's original order. If you think combining facts or ideas that appeared in separate paragraphs will help you remember them more easily, then, by all means, do it.

[†]Johnson, the thirty-sixth president (1963–1969), put together an ambitious plan to eliminate poverty in the United States. The plan was called the "Great Society."

▶ EXERCISE 4   Outlining Longer Readings

DIRECTIONS   Read and outline each selection. Make sure to paraphrase rather than copy sentences from the original. *Paraphrasing note*: If you have trouble paraphrasing a sentence, start by paraphrasing any words or phrases set off by commas. Often that will make it easier for you to find the language you need for the rest of the sentence.

EXAMPLE

Harriet Tubman and the Underground Railroad[†]

1   Even though the famed abolitionist[†] Harriet Tubman (1820?–1913) gave several interviews about her early life, the facts are hard to verify.[*] There are, for example, no exact records of her birth, although most history books cite 1820 as the year she was born. However, one item in Harriet Tubman's biography needs no verification: Because of her efforts, hundreds of slaves found their way to freedom.

2   According to Tubman's own account, she decided on her life's work when she was only thirteen years old. Badly beaten and wounded in the head by her owner, she prayed that guilt would make him repent and see the light. But when he came to visit her, intent only on seeing if she was well enough to sell, the girl realized that prayers were not enough. From that moment on, she knew that she had no choice but to escape to the North and wage a battle against slavery.

3   Although Tubman married in 1844, she did not forget her vow to fight. Quiet as she seemed to those around her, she was only biding her time until she could escape with her two brothers, and, in 1849, the three set out together. Although her brothers eventually gave up, Tubman did not. Hunger and exhaustion could not deter her. From her point of view, death was a better alternative than slavery. Spending long nights alone in the woods, Tubman traveled hundreds of miles until she arrived in Philadelphia, a free woman. The year was 1850, and Tubman was just thirty years old.

[†]Underground Railroad: The nineteenth-century organization dedicated to helping slaves gain their freedom.
[†]abolitionist: person who fought to eliminate slavery in the nineteenth century.
[*]verify: prove true or accurate.

4　　Before long, Tubman made contact with members of the Underground Railroad, an organization dedicated to helping slaves make an escape to freedom. Tubman made it a point to learn all the names of people and places that could guarantee safety for fleeing slaves. With her knowledge of the secret network, Tubman returned to the South for her sister and her sister's children. One year later, in 1851, she returned again for her brothers. That same year, she returned for her husband, only to find that he had a new family and was content to stay where he was.

5　　During the next ten years, Tubman traveled back and forth between the free and slave states, making about twenty secret journeys in all. Ultimately, she was personally responsible for the escape of more than 300 men, women, and children.

6　　Because some of the escapes were extraordinary and because she was subject to strange seizures, some people thought Harriet Tubman had magical powers. But those who traveled with her knew otherwise. To them, Tubman's success was not mysterious. It was the result of brains, daring, and ingenuity.* Magic had nothing to do with it.

7　　Tubman planned her rescues with enormous attention to detail and flatly refused to take any chances that might endanger her charges. If, for example, wanted notices were posted describing the number and appearance of her group, she would change the group's makeup. If the description said one man and two women, she would dress one of the women in men's clothes to outwit her pursuers. If any member of her party aroused her suspicions, she would refuse to take that person. It was this attention to minute detail that made her rescue attempts so successful and earned her the nickname "Moses."

8　　Yet another black American to escape slavery and become an influential abolitionist was Frederick Douglass, whose contributions are outlined in the section that follows.

Main Idea	Harriet Tubman enabled hundreds of slaves to gain freedom.
Supporting Details	1. After being badly beaten, she decided to escape slavery and take action against it.
	2. 1844; got married but did not forget her determination to fight.
	a. 1849; escaped.
	b. 1850; arrived in Philadelphia a free woman at the age of thirty.

*ingenuity: imagination, originality.

3. Made contact with the Underground Railroad to learn who could guarantee safety.

   a. Made twenty secret journeys.

   b. She was so successful, people thought she had magical powers.

4. Planned her rescues with great attention to detail.

   a. If wanted notices described her party, she would change the group's appearance.

   b. If she had doubts about a person, she wouldn't take that person.

   c. Earned the nickname "Moses."

EXPLANATION Because most of the reading deals with Tubman's efforts to free other enslaved people, the last sentence in paragraph 1 is the thesis statement. It effectively sums up the reading. Although there are eight paragraphs, only four of them contain major details that are essential to explaining the main idea. Note, too, the transitional sentence that ends the reading. This kind of transition could help you focus your reading of the next section, but it need not appear in your notes.

1. Parents as Victims

1 Most of us find it difficult to imagine children attacking their parents because it so profoundly violates our image of parent-child relations. Parents possess the authority and power in the family hierarchy.* Furthermore, there is greater social disapproval of a child striking a parent than of a parent striking a child; it is the parent who has the right to hit. Although we know fairly little about adolescent violence against parents, scattered studies indicate that it is almost as prevalent as spousal violence.

2 Most children who attack parents are between the ages of thirteen and twenty-four, but incidence* of abuse differs according to gender. Sons are slightly more likely to be abusive than daughters. The rate of severe male violence tends to increase with age, whereas that of females decreases. Boys apparently take advantage of their increasing size and the cultural expectation of male aggression. Girls, in contrast, may become less violent because society views female aggression

*hierarchy: order of importance or power, ranking.
*incidence: frequency of occurrence.

more negatively. Most researchers believe that mothers are the primary targets of violence and abuse because they may lack physical strength or social resources to defend themselves (Gelles and Cornell, 1985).

3   **Abuse of Elderly Parents**   Of all the forms of hidden family violence, only the abuse of elderly parents by their grown children (or in some cases, by their grandchildren) has received considerable public attention. Elder mistreatment may be an act of commission (abuse) or omission (neglect) (Wolf, 1995).

4   It is estimated that approximately 500,000 elderly people are physically abused annually. An additional 2 million are thought to be emotionally abused or neglected. Although mandatory reporting of suspected cases of elder abuse is the law in forty-two states and the District of Columbia, much abuse of the elderly goes unnoticed, unrecognized, and unreported (Wolf, 1995). . . . Although some research indicates that the abused elder may have been an abusing parent, more knowledge must be gained before we can draw firm conclusions about the causes of elder abuse. (Adapted from Strong, Devault, and Cohen, *The Marriage and Family Experience*, 11th ed., pp. 476–77, © Cengage Learning.)

Main Idea   _____

_____

Supporting Details   _____

_____

_____

_____

_____

_____

_____

_____

_____

_____

2. The Positive and Negative Effect of First Impressions

1   Labeling people according to our first impressions is an inevitable part of the perception process. These labels are a way of making interpretations. "She seems cheerful." "He seems sincere." "They sound awfully conceited."

2   The problem is that first impressions have a lasting effect and sometimes that works in our favor, sometimes not. If first impressions are accurate, they can be useful ways of deciding how to respond best to people in the future. Problems arise, however, when the labels we attach based on a first impression are inaccurate.

3   Maintaining an opinion formed on the basis of a first impression is most clearly illustrated in what sociologists call the **halo effect**, a term that describes the tendency to form an overall positive impression of a person on the basis of one positive characteristic. Most typically, the positive impression comes from physical attractiveness, which can lead people to attribute all sorts of other virtues to the good-looking person.

4   For example, employment interviewers tend to rate mediocre but attractive job applicants higher than their less attractive candidates. And once employers form a positive impression, they often ask questions that confirm the image of the applicant. An interviewer might, for instance, ask leading questions aimed at supporting her positive views, such as "What lessons did you learn from that setback?" The interviewer might also be inclined to interpret any answer given in a positive light, "Ah, taking time away from school to travel was a good idea, makes you a more well-rounded human being!"

5   The opposite of the halo effect is "the devil effect." When this effect is in play, the first impression formed is negative. From that point on, no positive information gets processed by the person holding the negative opinion. "So you were a straight-A student, don't you think school should be about more than grades?" (Adapted from Adler and Proctor, *Looking Out, Looking In*, 12th ed., p. 104, © Cengage Learning.)

Main Idea   _____

_____

Supporting Details

_____

_____

_____

_____

_____

_____

_____

_____

DIGGING DEEPER   **Is Risk-Taking in Our Genes?** *Paul Roberts*

Looking Ahead The reading about hiking the Half Dome in Yosemite National Park pointed out that people sometimes take risks that common sense tells them could cost them their lives. The more timid among us probably wonder how anyone could think the thrill of the risk was worth the loss. The following reading from *Psychology Today* suggests that how willing we are to take or avoid risks may actually be in our genes.

Getting Focused Use the question in the title to focus your reading. When you finish, you should be able to answer with more than a *yes* or *no*. You should also be able to generally explain how the author, journalist Paul Roberts, supports his claim.

1   In the land of seatbelts and safety helmets, the leisure pursuit of danger is a growth industry. Some experts say that courting uncertainty is the only way to protect the inner force America was founded on. Or to define the self. Whatever the reason, RISKY BUSINESS HAS NEVER BEEN MORE POPU-LAR. Mountain climbing is among the fastest growing sports. . . . Extreme skiing—in which skiers descend cliff-like runs by dropping from ledge to snow-covered ledge—is drawing wider interest. Sports like paragliding and cliff-parachuting are marching into the recreational mainstream while the adventurer-travel business, which often mixes activities like climbing or river rafting with wildlife safaris, has grown into a multimillion-dollar industry. "Forget the beach," declared *Newsweek* last year. "We're hot for mountain biking, river running, ice climbing, and bungee jumping."

2   Thirty-six-year-old Derek Hersey knew a thing or two about life on the edge. Where most rock climbers used ropes and other safety gear, the wiry, wise-cracking Brit usually climbed "free solo"—alone, using nothing but climbing shoes, finger chalk, and his wits. As one climbing buddy put it, Hersey went "for the adrenaline and risk," and on May 28, 1993, he got a dose of both. High on the face of Yosemite's Sentinel Rock, Hersey met with rain and, apparently, a slick rock. Friends who found the battered body reckon he fell several hundred feet. In the not-too-distant past, students of human behavior might have explained Hersey's fall as death-wish fulfillment. Under conventional personality theories, normal individuals do everything possible to avoid tension and risk.

3   In fact, as researchers are discovering, the psychology of risk involves far more than a simple "death wish." Studies now indicate that the

inclination to take high risks may be hardwired into the brain, intimately linked to arousal and pleasure mechanisms, and may offer such a thrill that it functions like an addiction for some. The tendency probably affects one in five people, mostly young males, and declines with age. It may ensure our survival, even spur our evolution as individuals and as a species. Risk-taking probably bestowed a crucial evolutionary advantage, inciting the fighting and foraging of the hunter-gatherer.

4　　In mapping out the mechanisms of risk, psychologists hope to do more than explain why people climb mountains. Risk-taking, which one researcher defines as "engaging in any activity with an uncertain outcome," arises in nearly all walks of life. Asking someone on a date, accepting a challenging work assignment, raising a sensitive issue with a spouse or a friend, confronting an abusive boss—all involve uncertain outcomes, and present some level of risk. Understanding the psychology of risk, understanding why some individuals will take chances and others won't, could have important consequences in everything from career counseling to programs for juvenile delinquents.

5　　Researchers don't yet know precisely how a risk-taking impulse arises from within or what role is played by environmental factors, from upbringing to the culture at large. And, while some level of risk-taking is clearly necessary for survival (try crossing a busy street without it), scientists are divided as to whether, in a modern society, a "high-risk gene" is still advantageous. Some scientists, like Frank Farley, Ph.D., a University

Risk-takers are not inclined to play it safe.

Vixit/Shutterstock.com.

of Wisconsin psychologist and past president of the American Psycho-logical Association, see a willingness to take big risks as essential for suc-cess. The same inner force that pushed Derek Hersey, Farley argues, may also explain why some dare to run for office, launch a corporate raid, or lead a civil-rights demonstration.

6   Yet research has also revealed the darker side of risk-taking. High-risk-takers are easily bored and may suffer low job satisfaction. Their crav-ing for stimulation can make them more likely to abuse drugs, gamble, commit crimes, and be promiscuous. As psychologist Salvadore Maddi, Ph.D., of the University of California-Davis warns, high-risk-takers may "have a hard time deriving meaning and purpose from everyday life."

7   Indeed, this peculiar form of dissatisfaction could help explain the explosion of high-risk sports in America and other postindustrial Western nations. In unstable cultures, such as those at war or suffer-ing poverty, people rarely seek out additional thrills. But in a rich and safety-obsessed country like America, land of guardrails, seat belts, and personal-injury lawsuits, everyday life may have become too safe, predictable, and boring for those programmed for risk-taking. ("Risk" by Paul Roberts from *Psychology Today*, November/December 1994. Reprinted with permis-sion from *Psychology Today* magazine. Copyright © 1986 Sussex Publishers, LLC.)

Sharpening Your Skills

DIRECTIONS   Answer the following questions by filling in the blanks or circling the letter of the correct response.

Following the Writer's Train of Thought

1. Based on the title, along with the repetition and reference in the first two paragraphs, what's the likely topic for this reading?

   a. Derek Hersey

   b. mountain climbing

   c. risk-taking

   d. extreme skiing

Main Ideas and Explanatory Patterns

2. Which paragraph introduces the thesis statement?

   a. paragraph 1

   b. paragraph 2

   c. paragraph 3

Understanding the Function of Supporting Details

3. Based on the overall main idea expressed in the thesis statement, how would you classify paragraph 4, as a major or a minor detail?

_____

Please explain the reasoning behind your answer.

_____

_____

4. How would you classify paragraph 5, as a major or minor detail?

_____

Please explain the reasoning behind your answer.

_____

_____

5. How would you classify paragraph 6, as a major or minor detail?

_____

Please explain the reasoning behind your answer.

_____

_____

6. Why does the author open paragraph 6 with the reversal transition "yet."

_____

_____

7. How would you classify paragraph 7, as a major or minor detail?

_____

Please explain the reasoning behind your answer.

_____

_____

_____

Paraphrasing

8. In your own words, what two views do researchers hold about the value of risk-taking?

_____

_____

_____

_____

9. According to the article, have researchers clearly identified the source of risk-taking? _____ Please paraphrase statements in the reading that support your answer. Write the paragraph number in which the statements appear after your paraphrase.

_____

_____

_____

_____

Following the Author's Train of Thought

10. In paragraph 7, the opening phrase, "this peculiar form of dissatisfaction," refers to what in the previous paragraph?

_____

From Reader to Writer

In 2015, the legendary climber and base jumper†, Dean Potter and his climbing partner and friend Graham Hunt, died when they attempted a wingsuit BASE jump from Taft Point in Yosemite Park. Wing suit BASE jumping, which is illegal in all state parks, involves a bat-like suit that keeps the jumper aloft for longer periods of time than BASE jumping from high altitudes without a wingsuit allows.

Upon hearing of Potter's death, the chief of staff of Yosemite National Park, Mike Gauthier, described Potter as one of the "great athletes that people idolize and look up to." Potter had lived in the Yosemite Valley for over twenty years and had challenged the limits

_____

†BASE jumper: someone who jumps from high altitudes off of a fixed structure like a bridge or mountain. It is considered the most extreme of extreme sports.

of what was possible for climbers the entire time. Thus, many shared Gauthier's opinion. But perhaps just as many did not. Instead, they criticized Potter harshly. Some called him a dare devil who left three children without a father. Others labeled him a self-indulgent thrill seeker, who thought the rules did not apply to him.

Use the Web to do some research on Potter and then write a paragraph or two expressing your point of view. Was he a pioneer and a hero or a man who "took major risks without care or thought to the concerns of the family and friends who loved him"? (Source of quotations: http://adventureblog.nationalgeographic.com/2015/05/17/pioneering-climber-dean-potter-died-in-base-jumping-accident/, last accessed May 21, 2015).

▶ **TEST 1**   **Reviewing Key Concepts**

DIRECTIONS   Answer the following questions by filling in the blanks.

1. Once you think you know the overall main idea of a reading, what two things do you need to do to see if you are on the right track?

   _____

   _____

   _____

   _____

2. If you think the first sentence or two of the opening paragraph is the thesis statement, where should you look for the first major supporting detail?

   _____

3. If you think the last sentence in the first paragraph of a chapter section introduces the thesis statement, where should you look for the first major supporting detail?

   _____

4. If the chapter section you are reading doesn't seem to fit any of the familiar explanatory patterns you know about, what should you do?

   _____

   _____

5. How would you define the term "dual-coding"?

   _____

   _____

6. What's the main difference between major and minor supporting details in paragraphs and in longer, multi-paragraph readings?

   _____

7. What's an essential similarity between minor details in paragraphs and minor details in longer, multi-paragraph readings?

   _____

   _____

8. In longer readings, where is the author most likely to tell you how the paragraph you are reading connects to the one that came before?

   _____

9. In both paragraphs and longer readings, what kinds of words offer solid clues to the major details?

   _____

10. Why is it important to indent when making an informal outline?

    _____

▶ **TEST 2**   **Recognizing Thesis Statements and Supporting Details in Longer Readings**

DIRECTIONS   After reading each selection, answer the questions by circling the appropriate letter and filling in the blanks.

1. The Debate over Legalizing Marijuana

1   Controversy exists over whether marijuana should be legalized for the limited use of pain relief and nausea control for seriously ill individuals, including cancer patients and those individuals suffering from AIDS. Many medical professionals have testified in state and federal hearings that they believe that marijuana is more effective and has fewer side effects than other forms of legal pain relief. Others dispute the findings. There has been a move in several states to pass medical marijuana laws that allow for limited use of small amounts of marijuana if it's medically prescribed.

Laws

2   The federal government's drug laws do not make an exception for the medical use of marijuana. California passed a law allowing medical uses of marijuana to be regulated but decriminalized. The Supreme Court held that the federal laws "trumped" California law. As of 2015, 23 states have passed some version of a medical, or a medical and recreational, marijuana law, allowing for some limited prescription of marijuana, but federal laws against any use still remain.

Policy

3   Federal drug officials under President George W. Bush made it clear that they would enforce the federal laws against doctors and medical co-ops that distribute marijuana. In a new development, after President Obama took office, the Justice Department has indicated that they will not pursue these types of cases in states that have laws allowing for the use of medically prescribed marijuana. This is a major change in policy for the Justice Department. (Adapted from Pollock, *Ethical Dilemmas and Decisions in Criminal Justice*, 7th ed., p. 15, © Cengage Learning.)

1.   Which of the following sentences is most likely to be the thesis statement of this reading?

 a.   "Controversy exists over whether marijuana should be legalized for the limited use of pain relief and nausea control for seriously ill individuals, including cancer patients and those individuals suffering from AIDS."

   b. "Many medical professionals have testified in state and federal hearings that they believe that marijuana is more effective and has fewer side effects than other forms of legal pain relief."

   c. "The federal government's drug laws do not make an exception for the medical use of marijuana."

2. In paragraph 2, the description of the California law and the Supreme Court decision is there to illustrate what word in the thesis statement? _____

3. In paragraph 3, the description of how the federal law against marijuana for medical purposes has been pursued by different administrations is present to illustrate what word in the thesis statement? _____

4. In this reading, what question about the main idea is answered by the supporting details?

_____

_____

2. Anorexia Nervosa: The Starvation Disease

1 When their children begin talking about dieting, most parents don't worry. In weight-conscious America, everyone wants to be a size smaller than they are. However, for some teenagers, dieting is no laughing matter. For them, dieting is not a momentary whim to be pursued and forgotten; instead, it is the symptom of a serious emotional disorder called *anorexia nervosa*, a disease that can have terrible, even fatal, consequences.

2   The disease usually strikes adolescent and preadolescent girls who have no reason to diet. They are not overweight, nor have they been told to diet by their doctors. They are not preparing to take part in specialized sports activities requiring a slender figure. These girls stop eating because, despite all evidence to the contrary, they believe they are fat. Determined to lose the imaginary excess poundage, they refuse to eat more than a few morsels of food per day. Usually, weight loss is rapid, sometimes over fifty pounds in a matter of months.[†]

[†]According to the South Carolina Department of Mental Health, one in two hundred American women suffers from anorexia, and around 90 percent of those suffering from eating disorders are female. All statistics for this reading come from this source.

3   Some teenagers who are obsessed with the need to diet seek treatment because they or, more typically, their parents realize that the diet is leading to starvation. Others do not seek treatment but simply begin eating normally again on their own. However, because the disease comes in waves, or bouts, a few victims manage to keep it a secret and so avoid both exposure and treatment.

4   Unfortunately, members of this group are in the most serious danger. Although they may be able to keep their secret into adulthood, the disease, if left untreated, almost always goes out of control, with tragic results. In fact, some victims—like gymnast Christy Henrich, pop singer Karen Carpenter, and models Ana Carolina Reston and Isabelle Caro—die from the physical effects of prolonged starvation. Mortality rates are high: Between 5 and 10 percent of all anorexics will die within ten years of the disease being diagnosed; 18 to 20 percent will die after twenty years. Current statistics indicate that only 30–40 percent of anorexics will fully recover.

5   To date, the actual cause of the starvation disease has not been determined. According to one theory, teenagers may be starving themselves in order to rebel against parental authority. Traditionally, the refusal to eat has been a young child's weapon against parental discipline. The parent may plead and even demand that the child eat, but, by refusing, the child demonstrates his or her power over the situation. Unconsciously, teenagers who diet to the point of starvation may be attempting to teach their parents the same lesson: Control is not in the hands of the parents.

6   According to another theory, anorexia may indicate a young girl's deep-rooted fear of growing up. From this perspective, starving the body can be viewed as a way of maintaining its childish contours and rejecting adult femininity. Yet another hypothesis views the disease as a form of self-punishment. The victims may have extraordinarily high standards of perfection and punish themselves for failing to meet their goals. A growing body of evidence links anorexia to depression. However, it's not completely clear yet which comes first, the depression or the eating disorder. The difficulty untangling cause from effect exists because being severely underweight can cause physiological changes in the brain that lead to depression.

1. Which of the following sentences is most likely to be the thesis statement of this reading?

   a. "When their children begin talking about dieting, most parents don't worry. In weight-conscious America, everyone wants to be a size smaller than they are."

   b. "However, for some teenagers, dieting is no laughing matter. For them, dieting is not a momentary whim to be pursued and forgotten; instead, it is the symptom of a serious emotional disorder called *anorexia nervosa*, a disease that can have terrible, even fatal, consequences."

   c. "The disease usually strikes adolescent and preadolescent girls who have no reason to diet. They are not overweight, nor have they been told to diet by their doctors."

2. In paragraph 2, the description of the girls' refusal to eat and resulting rapid weight loss is there to illustrate what word in the thesis statement? _____

3. Does paragraph 3 illustrate the same word in the thesis statement? _____ Please explain.

   _____

   _____

4. What do the opening words in paragraph 4 signal about its relationship to paragraph 3?

   _____

   _____

▶ **TEST 3**   **Recognizing Thesis Statements and Supporting Details in Longer Readings**

DIRECTIONS   After reading each selection, answer the questions by circling the appropriate letter and filling in the blanks.

1. Henry Ford's Model T

1   Long before he invented the car known as the Model T, Henry Ford made the American public a promise: "I will build a car for the great multitude." Ford kept his promise and forever changed the life of working Americans. Using an assembly-line method of production, which he refined for maximum efficiency, Henry Ford produced a car that ordinary working people could afford. The first Model T appeared in 1908. By the following year, close to 10,000 Model Ts were putt-putting their way across America's frequently bumpy roadways. Unlike in earlier years, the drivers were no longer wealthy businessmen but farmers and factory workers.

2   Light in weight, the Model T was still strong enough to be driven on rough country roads that had never known pavement. At a price of less than $900, even farmers could afford to save up and buy one. And buy them they did, using their cars for everything from carting eggs to making Sunday calls. As one farmer's wife delightedly wrote to Ford, "Your car has lifted us out of the mud."

3   To be sure, the Model T was not restricted to rural areas. As cities continued to spring up across the nation, more and more people began using cars to drive to and from work. When the weekend rolled around, what could be cheaper than piling the family into the Model T for an excursion? By the time production stopped in 1927, more than 15 million Model Ts had been sold, and the price had been reduced, making the cars even more affordable for the masses of people who wanted to buy them.

4   What made the Model T so cheap to produce for a mass audience—and ultimately such a gold mine—was the interchangeability of its parts. Every Model T was like the previous one. That meant the Model T could be mass produced on assembly lines, whereas other cars had to be put together one by one. But Ford didn't stop there. Always looking to cut production costs, he introduced the *moving* assembly line, making it easier and quicker for factories to turn out Model Ts, again at a cheaper price.

5   An astute businessman, Ford was also willing to pass on his savings to consumers because he knew full well that lowering the price of the Model T would increase its sales, which is exactly what happened. The decrease in price boosted sales and broadened the spectrum of ordinary working people who could afford to buy a car. By 1923, the price of a Model T, which had started out selling for $850, was at an all-time low of $290, a price not beyond the range of average working people. Thus, between 1908 and 1927, Ford sold a whopping 15.8 million Model Ts. He also established a production record that was not shattered until the arrival of the Volkswagen Beetle during World War II.

1. Which of the following sentences is most likely to be the thesis statement of this reading?

   a. "Using an assembly-line method of production, which he refined for maximum efficiency, Henry Ford produced a car that ordinary working people could afford."

   b. "The first Model T appeared in 1908. By the following year, close to 10,000 Model Ts were putt-putting their way across America's frequently bumpy roadways."

   c. "Light in weight, the Model T was still strong enough to be driven on rough country roads that had never known pavement. At a price of less than $900, even farmers could afford to save up and buy one."

2. Which of the following statements accurately describes the quote from the farmer's wife in paragraph 2?

   a. The quotation is a major detail in both the paragraph and in the reading as a whole.

   b. The quotation is a major detail in the paragraph but a minor detail in the reading as a whole.

   c. The quotation is a minor detail in both the paragraph and in the reading as a whole.

   Please explain the reasoning behind your answer.

   _____

   _____

3. Which sentence best expresses the main idea of paragraph 4?

   a. Henry Ford invented the assembly line.
   b. Henry Ford may have developed ways to cheapen the price of the Model T, but he also turned factory life into a workers' nightmare.
   c. The Model T's ability to be mass produced on an assembly line made the car both cheap and profitable.
   d. Henry Ford revolutionized factory production in America.

   In relation to the main idea of the entire reading, the main idea of paragraph 4 is a

   a. major detail.
   b. minor detail.

   Please explain the reasoning behind your answer.

   _____

   _____

4. Which sentence best expresses the main idea of paragraph 5?

   a. Ford boosted sales by passing his savings on to consumers in the form of lower prices.
   b. When it came to passing on his savings to consumers, Ford was an exception to the general rule of millionaire businessmen who never cut prices no matter how cheap the labor costs.
   c. Ford's production record was not challenged until the arrival of the Volkswagen Beetle.
   d. Like Ford's Model T, the Volkswagen Beetle was very much a "people's car."

   In relation to the main idea of the entire reading, the main idea of paragraph 5 is a

   a. major detail.
   b. minor detail.

Please explain the reasoning behind your answer.

_____

_____

2. Medical Remedies: Leeches, Maggots, and Dirt

1 If a patient became ill with a fever in the eighteenth century, a surgeon might prescribe leeches. Several of these glossy black worms would be placed on the patient's body, where they would puncture the skin and draw small amounts of blood. If the doctor thought that the patient should be drained of more blood than leeches could drink, he would next turn to bloodletting, which involved cutting a vein and allowing ounces or even whole pints of blood to flow from the body, often until the patient fainted.

2 During the Civil War, physicians sometimes treated a soldier's open wound by putting maggots, the wormlike larvae of flies, directly onto the patient's damaged flesh. If a patient complained of intestinal problems, the physician might order him to eat dirt.

3 Do you shudder when you think of such revolting remedies? Are you relieved that advances in medical knowledge have put a stop to these kinds of treatments? You may be surprised to know that scientists have discovered that many of these old cures work; in some cases, they are actually more effective than other, more modern techniques. As a result, a number of disgusting medical remedies are making a comeback in today's hospitals.

4 **Leeches to the Rescue**   For instance, doctors are once again using leeches for bloodletting. The crawly creatures are proving to be particularly useful after surgeries involving the reattachment of severed body parts. When areas swell with congested blood, leeches are applied to relieve the pressure by sucking up the blood. Leech saliva contains a natural anesthetic, so the bite is pain free. The saliva also contains substances that prevent bacteria from infecting the wound area and cause blood vessels to open wider. Therefore, the worms promote the circulation of blood necessary for healing. Leech saliva also contains a chemical that keeps blood from clotting. Thus, the creatures also have been used to unclog blood vessels during heart surgery.

5 **Maggots Make a Comeback**   Another creepy-crawly making a comeback in doctors' offices is the wormlike maggot. In the nineteenth and early twentieth centuries, battlefield physicians noticed that

maggot-infested wounds healed better than those injuries that were bug free. It turned out that maggots eat dead flesh and kill harmful bacteria that cause infection, which make them highly beneficial as healing agents. Today's laboratories grow the larvae and put them into special bandages that keep the creatures in a wound. Then they ship the bug-filled bandages to the more than 200 hospitals in the United States and Europe that have prescribed maggots for patients with bedsores, leg ulcers, stab wounds, or any other injury that won't heal. The practice is even referred to now as *biosurgery*.

6 **The Healing Power of Dirt**   One more disgusting treatment that actually works is *geophagy*, or dirt eating. For thousands of years, people suffering from intestinal disorders have eaten a little soil to settle their stomachs. As a matter of fact, geophagy has always been relatively common in central Africa and in parts of the southern United States. Scientific research has confirmed that some forms of clay and earth neutralize acid, which is why the antidiarrhea product Kaopectate when first manufactured contained a white clay called kaolin, and the laxative-antacid milk of magnesia contained the same ingredients as soil found around Magnesia in Greece. Dirt also contains phosphorus, potassium, copper, zinc, manganese, and iron—minerals that are essential to the body's functions—so doctors may even prescribe geophagy for patients suffering from deficiencies of these nutrients.

7   They may not have known *why* these therapies worked, but doctors of days gone by knew their remedies were effective. Today, of course, modern scientific research has revealed the reasons for the success of these treatments. The next time you're in one of our modern, sterile hospitals, don't be surprised if you see a few bugs and a little dirt.

1. Which of the following sentences is most likely to be the thesis statement of this reading?

   a. "During the Civil War, physicians sometimes treated a soldier's open wound by putting maggots, the wormlike larvae of flies, directly onto the patient's damaged flesh. If a patient complained of intestinal problems, the physician might order him to eat dirt."

   b. "You may be surprised to know that scientists have discovered that many of these old cures actually work; in some cases, they are actually more effective than other, more modern techniques. As a result, a number of disgusting medical remedies are making a comeback in today's hospitals."

    c. "Another creepy-crawly making a comeback in doctors' offices is the wormlike maggot."

2. Which sentence best expresses the main idea of paragraph 4?

    a. Leeches are particularly helpful to people undergoing surgery for the reattachment of body parts.

    b. Leeches may one day make surgery unnecessary.

    c. Leeches are again being used to draw off the build-up of blood.

    d. Leeches are now a required element of all microsurgeries.

In relation to the main idea of the entire reading, the main idea of paragraph 4 is a

    a. major detail.

    b. minor detail.

Please explain the reasoning behind your answer.

_____

_____

3. Which sentence best expresses the main idea of paragraph 5?

    a. Maggots are also experiencing a medical revival.

    b. Already in the nineteenth century physicians were using maggots to treat wounds.

    c. Maggots eat flesh and the bacteria it contains.

    d. Today, entire laboratories are devoted to the production of maggots.

In relation to the main idea of the entire reading, the main idea of paragraph 5 is a

    a. major detail.

    b. minor detail.

Please explain the reasoning behind your answer.

_____

_____

4. Which sentence best expresses the main idea of paragraph 6?

   a. Over-the-counter remedies like Kaopectate are actually not very safe.

   b. Geophagy is an age-old treatment for stomach problems.

   c. As it turns out, eating dirt actually has health benefits.

   d. Dirt-eating is common the world over.

In relation to the main idea of the entire reading, the main idea of paragraph 6 is a

   a. major detail.

   b. minor detail.

Please explain the reasoning behind your answer.

_____

_____

8 Focusing on Inferences in Paragraphs

IN THIS CHAPTER, YOU WILL LEARN

- about the different kinds of inferences essential to reading.

- how to tell the difference between logical inferences and illogical inferences.

- about the importance of linking pronouns and antecedents* in topic sentences.

- how to combine information from two or more sentences to create a main idea statement that sums up the paragraph.

- how to infer implied main ideas.

- when and how to add information and connections to supporting details.

> "An inference is a statement about the unknown made on the basis of the known."
>
> —S. I. HAYAKAWA, *LANGUAGE IN THOUGHT AND ACTION*

Words like *imply*, *infer*, and *inference* have been turning up regularly in the previous chapters. There's a reason for that. To some degree, all writers expect readers to infer, or create, some of the text they read. Experienced writers know they don't have the time, energy, or space to put every single word necessary to their message on the page or screen. Instead, they rely on readers to fill in gaps by adding the words, ideas, or relationships essential to completing their written message.

If you think about it for a moment, you will realize that this is no different from what we do in speech, where more is implied than what's actually said. After all, if the person bagging your groceries at the supermarket asks you, "Paper or plastic?" you know immediately that he or she is asking you, "Do you want a *paper* or a *plastic* bag?" Language almost always says more than the spoken or written words.

---

*antecedents: the nouns to which pronouns refer.

That's why drawing inferences is so essential to understanding what you hear and read.

How Inferences Work

As you move through this chapter, you will see that different kinds of inferences are required for different aspects, or parts, of a text. Sometimes readers have to infer connections between sentences. At other times, they have to supply background knowledge. Often, they have to come up with the general main idea suggested by the more specific supporting details.

At the same time, you'll also get a solid understanding of the difference between logical inferences that help readers get the author's message and illogical inferences that lead them astray. **Logical inferences** are evidence-based guesses that rely on the author's words, subject matter, and context to determine what the author has implied, or suggested, but not directly stated. **Illogical inferences** over-rely on the reader's personal experience and are not firmly grounded in the author's actual language. For the most part, they lack supporting evidence and don't fit the writer's context. Sometimes they even contradict the author's actual words or give too much emphasis to one sentence while ignoring others.

Evaluating Inferences

We'll talk more about logical and illogical inferences later on. But for now, you'll get a general understanding of the difference by looking at the drawing on page 399 and deciding which of the four captions that follow fits the details of the drawing.

1. "I wish I was as fabulous as my dog thinks I am."[†]

2. "Dogs define the word *loyalty*."

3. "Dream big! Dare the impossible!"

4. "Dogs are a source of unconditional love."

[†]This is actually a popular saying on bumper stickers.

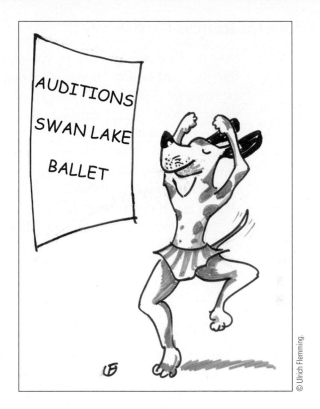

© Ulrich Flemming.

Most people who look at this drawing correctly pick number 3 as the caption. They arrive at the right caption by looking at the clues in the drawing and figuring out which caption fits or follows from the details shown. What are those clues and how do they add up? See the list below.

1. The dog is wearing a tutu; in the real world, dogs don't dress up as ballet dancers.

2. Dogs also don't dance; in particular, they don't do ballet, but this dog seems to be not only dancing but trying out for a part in the famous ballet *Swan Lake*.

3. The ability of a dog to stand *en pointe*† is a seemingly impossible feat. Yet the drawing shows a dog doing just that, or close to it, which fits the words "Dare the impossible."

4. The drawing makes the impossible—a dog auditioning for a part in the famous ballet *Swan Lake*—look possible.

---

†*En pointe* is a dance term meaning to be raised up on the tip of your toe.

When Inferences Go Astray

Now imagine that you had picked caption 2 on page 398, "Dogs define the word *loyalty*." If you are a dog lover, this caption might well express your point of view. Most people who know anything about dogs would probably feel the same way. But your personal feelings about dogs can't—and shouldn't—make up for the fact that nothing in the drawing suggests loyalty, either to humans or other dogs. After all, the only one in the drawing is the dancing dog, so there is no one for her to be loyal to. In short, caption number 2 would be an illogical inference because it doesn't match the clues provided.

That, in a nutshell, is the key to drawing logical inferences. The idea or conclusion you come up with has to fit the information explicitly given. If it doesn't, it's illogical and will probably lead you away from the author's meaning rather than toward it.

▶ EXERCISE 1   Matching Your Inferences to the Visual and Verbal Clues

DIRECTIONS   Look at the following cartoon. Read the clues provided in each frame. Then on the blanks that follow, explain the inference the reader is supposed to supply to make sense of the cartoon.

CALVIN AND HOBBES © 1995 Watterson. Dist. By UNIVERSAL UCLICK. Reprinted with permission. All rights reserved.

1. What does the first frame tell you about Calvin's state of mind?

_____

_____

2. Why does the second frame show Calvin smiling with an exclamation point over his head?

_____

_____

3. What does the third frame show Calvin doing, and how do his actions relate to the first frame?

_____

_____

4. Why does Calvin say he loves loopholes and what does the last frame have to do with the first?

_____

_____

_____

▶ **EXERCISE 2**   **Drawing Inferences from Quotations**

DIRECTIONS   The following statements or claims require inferences to make sense. Rewrite each one to make the meaning more explicit than implicit.

EXAMPLE   "My lyrics are pretty straightforward; I don't Shakespeare 'em up."—Singer Bruno Mars in an interview with *Rolling Stone*

What does Mars imply when he says, "I don't Shakespeare 'em up"?

The language of my lyrics is not elaborate or unfamiliar like Shakespeare's language.

It's easy to understand.

EXPLANATION   No matter how beautiful the language of Shakespeare might be, it's not easy to read. It takes some time to understand. Mars compares his language to Shakespeare's to say that the language of his songs is the exact opposite. In the song "Grenade," for instance, he sings about giving his love "all he had" only to have her toss it "in the trash." The lyric is clearly not open to multiple interpretations. Note that to make sense of what Mars says in the interview, it's the reader who has to *infer* the connection between the opening statement and the allusion, or reference, to Shakespeare.

1. "I do not weep at the world. I am too busy sharpening my oyster knife."—Zora Neale Hurston, author of *Their Eyes Were Watching God*

   What does Hurston imply about her attitude toward life's difficulties?

   _____

   _____

2. "If men were angels, no government would be necessary."—James Madison, Federalist Paper #51[†]

   What does Madison suggest about human character with this quote?

   _____

   _____

3. "It is the mind that makes the body."—Sojourner Truth, ex-slave and abolitionist

   What does Sojourner Truth imply about the relationship between mind and body?

   _____

   _____

4. "You don't forget the face of the person who was your last hope."—Suzanne Collins, *The Hunger Games*

   What does Katniss Everdeen in *The Hunger Games* mean when she makes this statement?

   _____

   _____

[†]James Madison, John Jay, and Alexander Hamilton wrote a series of articles in 1787–1788 that came to be known as "The Federalist Papers." The purpose of the papers was to convince New Yorkers that the country needed to be united under the laws laid out by the Constitution.

From Reader to Writer Write a sentence or two describing someone famous. But don't say who the person is. Instead, select details that will make your audience recognize the person without being named, for instance, "Married to the King of Rap, she's a star in her own right, a true Destiny's Child, whose talent propelled her to fame and fortune long before the queen met her king."

Connecting Topic Sentence Pronouns to Their Antecedents

Connecting pronouns to antecedents is one of the most basic inferences readers draw while reading. Consider, for instance, these two sentences below, excerpted from a history text:

> In the early nineteenth century, as reformers launched changes in many cities and considered ways to improve society, Robert M. La Follette pushed Wisconsin to the forefront of reform. A Republican, he entered politics soon after graduating from the University of Wisconsin. (Adapted from Berkin et al., *Making America*, 6th ed., p. 535, © Cengage Learning.)

You are so used to connecting pronouns like *he* and *she* to their antecedents, or the nouns to which they refer, you probably didn't even think about it when you connected the pronoun *he* to its antecedent, Robert La Follette. Still, it's you, the reader, who infers the connection. The author doesn't connect pronoun and antecedent for you.

Connecting Pronouns and Antecedents in Topic Sentences

Like any other sentence in a paragraph, topic sentences often need some help from readers. To communicate the message of a paragraph, topic sentences often need readers to connect pronouns to antecedents. Take, for instance, the underlined topic sentence in the following paragraph. The sentence doesn't state the topic. Instead, a pronoun stands in for the topic. Writers do this all the time, expecting readers to infer the topics represented by the pronouns.

[1]At one time, the right side of the brain was regarded as the minor hemisphere, or half. [2]We now know, however, that it has its own special set of talents and isn't "minor" at all. [3]The right hemisphere is superior at recognizing patterns, faces, and melodies. [4]It's also involved in detecting and expressing emotions. [5]The right brain is actually better than the left at visualization skills, such as arranging blocks to match a pattern, putting together a puzzle, or drawing pictures.

The first sentence in the sample paragraph is an introductory sentence. As introductory sentences so often do, this one tells you what people *used to think* about the right side of the brain, the topic under discussion. If you doubt that's the topic, notice how many times the phrase is repeated and referred to. Keep in mind, too, that *hemisphere* is a synonym for *side*. That means every sentence has something to say about this topic.

Based on that kind of opening, you'd be correct to expect the topic sentence to arrive soon. And, indeed, it does. It's also accompanied by another dead giveaway, the reversal transition, *however*.

But suppose you wanted to take notes on the topic sentence. How would you paraphrase it? (1) *It* isn't a minor hemisphere but has its own talents or (2) *The right brain* isn't the minor hemisphere; it has its own talents? If you wanted to understand your notes two or three weeks after you read the paragraph, you'd definitely opt for sentence 2. That means you'd make sure to infer the correct antecedent and include it in your paraphrase of the original.

READING TIP

Whenever a topic sentence uses a pronoun to refer to the topic, be sure to mentally connect the pronoun to its antecedent. Include the antecedent, rather than the pronoun, in your notes.

▶ **EXERCISE 3**   **Filling in the Gaps in Topic Sentences**

DIRECTIONS   Underline the partially complete topic sentence in each paragraph. Then in the blanks at the end of the paragraph, write a topic sentence that includes any necessary information missing from the original. *Note*: Sometimes the completed topic sentence will only need a noun. However, be prepared to add more information when necessary.

EXAMPLE   ¹Who was Will Rogers? ²He was the cowboy-philosopher who won America's heart in the 1920s. ³Born in Oklahoma, Rogers began his career onstage playing a rope-twirling cowboy-comedian and in 1915 joined the Ziegfeld Follies.† ⁴Soon his widely quoted wisecracks about the American political scene made him famous nationwide. ⁵The public loved the way he ridiculed politicians. ⁶"I am not a member of any organized party—I am a Democrat." ⁷By the time he died in a plane crash in 1935, Rogers had made more than twenty films, and quotes from his newspaper column had appeared on the front page of the *New York Times*.

Will Rogers was the cowboy-philosopher who won America's heart in the 1920s.

EXPLANATION   In this case the completed topic sentence required only the addition of Will Rogers's name.

1. ¹As a relatively young man, the actor Bela Lugosi became rich and famous. ²Taken by his 1931 performance as the blood-drinking Count Dracula, movie audiences willingly paid to see Lugosi's special brand of elegant evil. ³But all that changed as Bela Lugosi grew older. ⁴When he died, he had nothing left of the fame and fortune playing Dracula had brought him. ⁵Because Lugosi had become so closely identified with the figure of the count, producers were hesitant to cast him in other roles. ⁶In addition, his thick Hungarian accent, so effective in *Dracula*, was a handicap for other parts. ⁷As a result, Lugosi was reduced to making ridiculous, low-grade thrillers like *Bela Lugosi Meets a Brooklyn Gorilla* and *Mother Riley Meets the Vampire*. ⁸By the mid-1950s, Lugosi was all but forgotten by Hollywood and his fans. ⁹By 1956, he was dead, a victim of drugs and alcohol.

_____

_____

_____

†Ziegfeld Follies: Flo Ziegfeld was famous for his stage shows, which bore his name. Follies are stage shows with very elaborate costumes and special effects.

2. [1]Throughout the 1800s, explorers had dreamed of reaching the North Pole. [2]But it wasn't until 1909 that anyone claimed to have arrived at the North Pole. [3]Who did it first, though, is still the subject of argument. [4]Dr. Frederick Cook claimed that he had reached the Pole on April 21, 1908, spending two days there until drifting ice forced him to move westward. [5]The world press celebrated Cook's achievement until cables began arriving from Robert Peary, who insisted that he had been the first man to reach the Pole. [6]The controversy continued even after the two men had died. [7]In fact, some historians insist that both claims lacked the appropriate proof and therefore cannot be honored. [8]They propose instead that Richard Byrd was the first man to really arrive at the North Pole, flying over it in 1926. [9]Some Russian historians, for their part, dispute any such claims. [10]They insist that in 1937 the Russian scientist Otto Schmidt was the first person to ever set foot at the North Pole.

_____

_____

3. [1]When baseball was still ruled by the strict segregation, or separation, of players into white or black teams, Satchel Paige was the highest paid player in the Negro Leagues. [2]And without a doubt, he was worth every penny of his $40,000 salary; he was the most talented pitcher baseball has ever seen, now or then. [3]Batters who came up against him could expect to strike out. [4]In 1932, he pitched sixty-two straight scoreless innings. [5]To get a hit off him, you had to be at the top of your game, and not many were up to the challenge. [6]Joe DiMaggio, considered by many to be one of the greatest players of all time, said Paige was "the best I ever faced, and the fastest." [7]People came from all over to watch Paige play, and even all-stars were in awe of his legendary bag of pitches, each with its own Paige-bestowed nickname. [8]There was the bee ball, the trouble ball, the Long Tom, the two-hump blooper, and, perhaps the most famous of them all, the hesitation pitch.

_____

_____

4. [1]By most standards, the new sharing economy is a huge success, with Internet intermediaries matching suppliers to consumers needing anything from a ride across town to a room for the weekend. [2]Still, there are some problems to be solved before it can be called a complete success. [3]When it comes to the sharing of living spaces, some of those doing the sharing have discovered that their short-term guests don't always respect personal property. [4]When comedian Ari Teman lent his apartment via Airbnb, he came home to find, in his words, "things all over the floor, bottles of alcohol, wrappers. The furniture had been disassembled. . . . [5]As it turned out, Teman's apartment had been the scene of a sex orgy. [6]The company claims to vet all of its applicants for rentals, but as Teman's experience shows, the process is not foolproof. [7]While Airbnb offers a Host Guarantee reimbursement of one million dollars to owners, it doesn't always make up for the misery the experience causes and not everything that could get damaged is covered by the guarantee. (Pets, photos, and artwork, for example, are not.) [8]Although Airbnb paid Teman $25,000 in damages, the bill for repairs was higher than that, and Teman's understandably furious condo board threatened him with eviction. [9]Like Airbnb, ridesharing apps like Lyft, Uber, and Sidecar offer convenience for those in need of a quick ride. [10]But if an accident occurs, it's not at all clear whose insurance will take care of the damages and medical costs. [11]Lyft and Sidecar say the driver's personal insurance will handle at least some of the costs. [12]Insurance companies, however, do not agree, and some Lyft drivers have publicly complained that their insurance got cancelled when it was discovered that they drove for a ride share company. [13]According to one Lyft driver, he got this advice from his employer: "If you get into an accident, end your ride immediately and turn off your app, so you cannot be identified as a ride-service driver." (Source of information about Teman's disaster: http://www.today.com/news/sharing-economy-can-bring-convenience-cash-trouble-1D79562415; Source of quotation about insurance cancellation: http://goodnewsgreens .blogspot.com/2014_01_01_archive.html. Last accessed November 26, 2014.)

_____

_____

WEB QUEST
When forty-one-year-old Satchel Paige was signed to play in the American league, some complained that he was too old to play. How did Paige respond?

Piecing Together Main Idea Statements

Topic sentences, those single sentences that sum up a paragraph's main idea, are very popular in textbook writing. They're popular because they provide a quick and efficient way for writers to tell readers, "Here's my point."

Still, topic sentences are not the only way textbook authors communicate the main idea of a paragraph. While authors of business texts rely on them almost exclusively, the same is not true for authors of history and psychology texts. Authors in these disciplines certainly use topic sentences. But they also vary their introduction of the main idea by presenting parts of it in two or occasionally three different sentences. Then they leave it up to the reader to knit the parts together into a main idea statement.

This method of introducing the main idea is particularly popular with paragraphs that rely on a question-and-answer format, for example:

¹In 2008, the tanker *Sirius Star* was hijacked by pirates; carrying two million barrels of oil, it was the largest tanker ever taken at sea. ²Boarded in waters off the coast of Somalia, where the majority of pirate attacks occur, the seizure of the *Sirius Star* raised, yet again, the question haunting shipping companies, sailors, and maritime security organizations: How can ships at sea be kept safe from pirate attacks? ³Vahan Simidian, the chief executive officer of HPV Technologies, believes his company's magnetic acoustic device (MAD), which functions as both alarm and weapon, provides the answer. ⁴If the ship's captain is concerned about an approaching vessel, he can use MAD to produce a siren-like sound that tells pirates they have been sighted. ⁵If the pirates keep coming, MAD can be notched up to another level of piercing sound. ⁶At this point, the sound the

device produces is so loud it's painful to the ears and can disorient and confuse those who hear it. [7]As Mr. Simidian says, when asked if MAD can do serious harm, "Absolutely." (Source of information: Daniel Emery, "Technology Sets Sights on Piracy," BBC News.)

In this example, sentence 2 poses a question. Sentence 3 provides the answer. Left on its own, though, neither sentence provides a clear statement of the main idea. To arrive at that, you need to combine question and answer, taking a piece from each one: "Vahan Simidian thinks his company's magnetic acoustic device, which functions as both alarm and weapon, can keep ships safe from pirate attacks."

Paragraphs that rely on readers to weave together parts of different sentences don't have to focus on answering a question. Look, for example, at the following:

> [1]Unlike most minorities, Native Americans directly benefited from the New Deal.[†] [2]They had a strong supporter in Secretary of the Interior Harold Ickes and an even stronger one in the Commissioner of Indian Affairs, John Collier. [3]Both opposed existing Indian policies that since 1887 had sought to destroy the reservation system and eradicate* Indian cultures. [4]But it was Collier who really maintained the momentum for change. [5]At Collier's urging, Congress passed the Indian Reorganization Act in 1934. [6]The act returned land and community control to tribal organizations. [7]It provided Indian self-rule on the reservations and prevented individual ownership on tribal lands. [8]To improve the squalid* conditions found on most reservations and provide jobs, Collier organized an agency for Indians and ensured that other New Deal agencies played a part in improving Indian lands and providing jobs. [9]He also promoted Native-American culture. [10]Working with tribal leaders, Collier took measures to protect, preserve, and encourage Indian customs, languages, religions, and folkways. (Adapted from Berkin et al., *Making America*, 6th ed., p. 744.)

In this case, the main idea statement has to be pieced together from sentences 1 and 2: "Unlike most minorities, Native Americans directly benefited from the New Deal, largely *because* they had a strong supporter

---

[†]New Deal: When Franklin D. Roosevelt became president in 1932, he announced a program of economic reforms called the New Deal. The goal of the program was to kickstart the country out of a terrible economic depression.
*eradicate: eliminate, wipe out.
*squalid: poverty-stricken.

in Secretary of the Interior Harold Ickes and an even stronger one in the Commissioner of Indian Affairs, John Collier." In principle, this main idea statement was produced by precisely the same method as the previous example. To come up with a statement of the main idea, the reader had to combine the information from two different sentences.

However, to create an effective main idea statement summing up the above paragraph, readers had to do more than combine information from different sentences. They also had to infer the right connection or relationship between those sentences. That relationship is cause and effect—the idea that one thing is produced by, or the cause of, another— and, in this case, it is expressed by the word *because*. *Because* is a **conjunction**, or linking word, that says one event (the effect) was the result of another (the cause).

As you can see, the sample main idea statement makes explicit what the authors only implied—that Native Americans benefited from the New Deal *because* of effort put forth by Harold Ickes and the even greater efforts of John Collier.

Recognizing the Role of Bridging Inferences

The more conscious you become of the role inferences play in reading, the more you'll realize that writers constantly expect readers to infer connections between sentences. They expect them to make what reading researchers call **bridging inferences**. These are inferences that clarify relationships between sentences and paragraphs.

Although there are other relationships beyond cause and effect that you will have to infer when you read (more in Chapters 10 and 11), cause and effect is probably the most common. Writers of all kinds, from textbook authors to novelists, expect their readers to bridge the gap between sentences by inferring that one event led to or produced another. Keep that in mind while you complete the next exercise.

▶ **EXERCISE 4**   **Constructing Main Idea Statements**

DIRECTIONS   Combine different parts of sentences to create a main idea statement that sums up the paragraph in the same way a topic sentence would. *Note*: If you need to change the wording to make the sentences combine more smoothly, feel free to do so. Just don't alter the meanings of the sentences.

EXAMPLE   [1]For more than twenty years, Billy Tipton was a popular jazz musician, who played both the saxophone and the piano. [2]Tipton, however, had a secret. [3]He was a woman who had decided to live her life as a man. [4]Although Tipton has been dead for over two decades, it's still not clear what his motive was. [5]The general consensus is that Tipton was desperate to pursue a career in jazz and assumed that being a female would inhibit his chances. [6]Jazz was and is a largely male club. [7]How Tipton kept his secret for so long is unclear. [8]He married three times and adopted three sons, claiming that an old injury prevented him from having sexual relations. [9]With age, Tipton's health deteriorated. [10]But he refused medical care, probably fearing his secret would come out. [11]He died of a bleeding ulcer in 1989. [12]He could have survived the condition if he had sought care. [13]But getting medical attention meant he would have had to reveal his true sex. [14]That was apparently a secret he wanted to take to his grave.

Main Idea Statement   Billy Tipton was a popular jazz musician who kept a secret for years: He was a woman who had decided to live life as a man.

EXPLANATION   Sentence 1 introduces the topic Billy Tipton. It tells the reader who he was and what he did. Sentence 2 announces that Tipton had a secret without saying what it was. That piece of information is left for sentence 3. Since the remaining supporting details describe the lengths Tipton went to to keep his secret, we need to combine all three sentences to come up with the main idea statement those supporting details develop.

1.   [1]In 1871, the *New York Herald* sent Henry Morton Stanley to Africa in search of David Livingstone, the English missionary.* [2]Stanley faced sickness, unfriendly natives, and starvation to find the missionary and win himself a reputation as one of the bravest men in the world. [3]Since that time, history books have celebrated Stanley as a hero. [4]But Henry Morton Stanley had another side, one not so prominently* displayed in the history books. [5]His cruelty toward his men was legendary. [6]Like many men who have led a hard life, he considered the world a hard and brutal place. [7]His response to his vision of the world was to

*missionary: a person who goes to foreign countries to do religious or charitable work.
*prominently: obviously, openly, overtly.

eliminate all trace of humanity from his personality. [8]Underlings who didn't obey his orders were severely beaten. [9]Subordinates who challenged his authority were shot. [10]Ashley Jackson, a professor of military history, has written: "Stanley had one of the biggest kill rates of all the great African explorers in terms of the number of people who died during his journeys, and you can't gloss over the fact."

Main Idea Statement

_____

_____

2. [1]In the early nineteenth century, many runaway slaves sought refuge among Florida's Seminole Indians. [2]As a result, the U.S. government ordered the Seminoles to leave Florida, but they refused. [3]They were encouraged to rebel by their much-respected leader, Osceola. [4]Osceola's response to the order was to spear the announcement with a dagger and proclaim, "There, this is the only treaty I will make with the whites." [5]His words weren't empty boasting. [6]When government troops arrived to subdue the Seminole rebellion, they were killed. [7]The war between the Seminoles and the United States government had officially begun. [8]Even after Osceola was captured and died in prison, the war continued as Osceola's Seminole followers fought in his name. [9]In 1842, however, the tribe was finally defeated and force-marched to the state of Oklahoma.

Main Idea Statement

_____

_____

_____

3. [1]Writer Barbara Ehrenreich has always liked putting traditional wisdom to the test. [2]Thus, when President Bill Clinton pushed through legislation forcing people who had been living on welfare to go into the job market, she decided to test the administration's claim that anyone willing to work hard could become self-supporting. [3]Traveling around the country, Ehrenreich worked as a hotel maid, cleaning woman, fast food waitress, Walmart sales clerk, and nurse's aide. [4]It didn't take her long to realize just how empty that optimistic claim was when applied to unskilled labor. [5]As Ehrenreich put it in her book, *Nickel and Dimed*, no one ever told her "that you could work hard—harder than you ever thought possible—and still find

yourself sinking ever deeper into poverty and debt." [6]What the author also discovered was that, given the money she was earning, her diet had to be very limited. [7]She lived mostly on canned and fast foods. [8]Money for groceries was in short supply because the minimum wage she earned seldom added up to enough for a security deposit on a rental apartment. [9]As a result, she usually rented by the week and ended up paying high rents. [10]That left her with less money for food. [11]Throughout her travels, Ehrenreich often juggled two jobs to stay financially afloat and was painfully aware that her budget did not allow her to get sick.

Main Idea Statement

_____

_____

_____

Inferring the Main Idea from Start to Finish

Sometimes writers don't supply even parts of the topic sentences. Instead, they provide a series of specific statements designed to lead readers to the implied main idea of the paragraph. The statements can't be combined into a main idea statement. But they do add up to an **implied main idea**, an idea that is strongly suggested by the author without ever being directly stated. For an illustration, read the following paragraph:

T. E. Lawrence, nicknamed Lawrence of Arabia, dreamed of an independent Middle East that he did not live to see.

[1]As a young man, the British soldier and writer T. E. Lawrence took part in an archaeological* expedition in the Middle East. [2]The work fascinated him, as did the land, and he became possessed by a dream: The Arabs would one day overthrow Turkish rule and take control of their own country. [3]Lawrence sought to make his dream become reality during World War I when the British, at war with the Turks, seemed ready to help the Arabs revolt. [4]Seeing a chance for Arab independence, Lawrence arranged a meeting between British and Arab leaders. [5]Supplied with British arms and aided by Lawrence's military strategy, the Arabs rose up and captured several major Turkish strongholds, helping the British cause in the process. [6]By 1919, when the war ended, the Turks had been defeated. [7]Thrilled by what he saw as an

---

*archaeological: related to discovering the remains of lost civilizations.

Arab victory, Lawrence was now convinced that Arab self-rule would become a reality. [8]But when he was called to the Paris Peace Conference that formally ended the war, he was stunned to discover that the British had no intention of giving up their newly won control of the Middle East.

The author hasn't included a topic sentence in this paragraph. Instead, she leaves a trail of clues and expects readers to infer the implied main idea: "Although T. E. Lawrence believed helping the British during World War I would win independence for the Arab countries, the British betrayed him and replaced the Turks as the Arabs' new rulers." The basis for that inference is found in the following statements:

1. According to the author, Lawrence was "possessed" by the dream of Arab independence. The word *possessed* suggests Lawrence was passionately committed to the idea of Arab autonomy.

2. The author says Lawrence tried to turn "his dream" into a reality during World War I.

3. Believing the British were going to help the Arabs if they could beat the Turks, he arranged a meeting between the British and Arab leaders.

4. Guided in part by Lawrence's military strategy, the Arabs did help the British defeat the Turks.

5. Lawrence went to the Paris Peace Conference believing the British were going to reward the Arabs for their help.

6. The author uses the word *stunned* to describe the shock Lawrence felt about learning that the British were not giving up control of the Middle East.

7. Instead, they were taking over the countries the Turks had lost, thanks to the Arab revolts.

Given both the language and the content of the paragraph, it would be hard not to infer that Lawrence was betrayed by the British refusal to give the Arabs self-rule. The clues also suggest that the British led Lawrence to believe they were backing his attempts to gain Arab independence. Instead, as soon as the Arabs helped them beat the Turks, the British took control of the countries once ruled by the Turks.

When Should You Think About Inferring the Main Idea?

Any time you read a passage and can't find a general sentence that even partially sums up the main idea, look at all the specific statements supplied by the author and ask yourself what they suggest about the topic.

Look, for instance, at the following paragraph. The repetitions and references running through the paragraph suggest the topic is "fear of spiders." Look over all the specific details related to that topic. Then, at the end, write what you think is the implied main idea of the paragraph.

[1]Ms. B, a twenty-three-year-old woman, complained of a phobia, or fear, of spiders that she had had for as long as she could remember. [2]She had no history of any other psychiatric symptoms. [3]In treatment, when first approached with a closed glass jar containing spiders, she breathed heavily, wept, and rated her distress as extremely high. [4]Suddenly she began scratching the back of her hand, stating she felt as though spiders were crawling under her skin, although she knew this was not really the case. [5]The sensation lasted only a few seconds and did not recur. [6]Her total treatment consisted of four one-hour sessions distributed over the span of a month. [7]At completion, she had lost all fear of spiders and was able to let them crawl freely about her arms, legs, and face, as well as inside her clothing, with no distress. [8]She remained free of fear at a one-year follow-up exam and expressed disbelief that she had allowed such a "silly fear" to dominate her life for so long (Curtis, 1981, p. 1095). (Adapted from Sue et al., *Understanding Abnormal Behavior*, 8th ed., p. 136, © Cengage Learning.)

If your implied main idea goes something like, "Ms. B's treatment helped her overcome her fear of spiders," you drew a logical inference. It's logical because it is solidly based on the following details:

1. Ms. B arrived for treatment unable to even look at spiders without having a violent reaction.

2. She then had four one-hour treatments.

3. After the treatments, she did not have a violent reaction and was actually able to let spiders crawl on her body.

Mrs. B. is not alone. Fear of spiders is a common phobia.

© Ulrich Flemming.

Now, of course, you could claim that Ms. B's new response was a miracle. But that wouldn't be a logical inference. It wouldn't be based on or fit what's actually said in the paragraph, which explicitly describes the actions Ms. B took to combat her fear. The paragraph doesn't just say that Ms. B. suddenly and miraculously stopped being afraid of spiders. If it did, then calling her response a miracle would make more sense.

Making a Logical Inference

To be logical, reading inferences have to derive, or come from, what's actually said in the paragraph. You must be able to say: This is the implied main idea *because* of these words and statements. If you cannot point to anything in the paragraph that supports your version of the implied main idea, you and the author are no longer thinking along the same lines.

READING TIPS

1. Paragraphs that open with a question along with paragraphs that compare and contrast two topics often imply rather than state the main idea.

2. In paragraphs that imply the main idea, many of the sentences are likely to be equally specific.

SUMMING UP THE KEY POINTS

1. If the topic sentence uses a pronoun in place of the topic, make sure to mentally link the pronoun to the correct antecedent.

2. When two or three sentences in the paragraph almost but not quite sum up the main idea about the paragraph's topic, consider combining them into a main idea statement that would function just like a topic sentence.

3. If no general sentence seems to sum up a main idea about the topic, and you can't find any sentences that even come close, then you need to look at all the specific statements in the paragraph and consider what idea they suggest when taken together.

4. Inferring implied main ideas is a two-step process. First, you need to understand what each sentence contributes to your knowledge of the topic. Next, you need to ask yourself what all the sentences combine to suggest about the topic. The answer to that question is the implied main idea of the paragraph.

▶ **EXERCISE 5**   **Recognizing the Implied Main Idea**

DIRECTIONS   Each item in this exercise contains four sentences that combine to imply a main idea. Circle the letter of that implied main idea.

EXAMPLE

a. During the nineteenth century, factory owners hired young orphans, whom they could force to work fifteen hours a day.

b. Many factory owners preferred hiring women, who could move quickly among the machinery and were easily frightened by threats of dismissal.

c. Whenever possible, the employers increased their profits by reducing the workers' wages.

d. Workers who complained about the hours or poor working conditions were promptly fired; whenever possible, employers saw to it that rebellious workers were thrown into jail.

Implied Main Idea (a.) Nineteenth-century factory owners cruelly exploited the men, women, and children who worked for them.

b. In the nineteenth century, factory owners were quick to hire women because they were too timid to make any demands.

c. In the nineteenth century, children were expected to work rather than play.

EXPLANATION   The first four sentences give examples of the way nineteenth-century employers abused *all* their employees, not just women and children. Thus, *a* is the only implied main idea that follows from all the specific statements given. It's certainly the only sentence that could summarize the first four.

1. a. On October 15, 1917, the famed Dutch exotic dancer Mata Hari was brought before a French firing squad and executed as a spy.

   b. Although Mata Hari had agreed to spy for the Germans, there is no evidence that she ever gave them any information.

   c. Information about a new British tank, said to have been given to the Germans by Mata Hari, was actually provided by a British prisoner of war.

   d. The case against Mata Hari was based largely on telegrams supplied by the head of France's espionage agency, who had tampered with them before the trial.

Implied Main Idea

   a. Mata Hari was executed not because she was a spy but because she was hated by the head of France's espionage bureau.

   b. Mata Hari may not have been guilty of the crimes that earned her a death sentence.

   c. There is no evidence Mata Hari agreed to spy for the Germans.

2. a. Thanks to Henry Ford's invention of a cheap automobile—called the first "people's car"—farmers from small rural towns were able to sell their products to larger markets located some distance away.

   b. Ford's Model T was introduced in 1908 and priced at $850; by 1923 it cost only $290, and people from all walks of life had the chance to own a car.

    c. Ford's Model T was so famous, popular songs and jokes alluded to it.

    d. In the early part of the twentieth century, almost half the American population lived in the country, but Ford's Model T made access to city life much easier, and the rural population began to diminish.

Implied Main Idea
    a. The invention of the Model T had a profound effect on American life.

    b. Henry Ford was determined to make a car that even working people could afford.

    c. Henry Ford was a genius when it came to making money.

3. a. The month of January got its name from Janus, the Roman god of beginnings.

    b. Saturday was named after Saturn, the Roman god of agriculture.

    c. The sporting goods company Nike took its name from the Greek goddess of victory.

    d. The planet Neptune was named after the Roman god of the sea.

Implied Main Idea
    a. The gods and goddesses of Greek and Roman mythology had exotic and colorful names.

    b. The names of the ancient gods and goddesses live on in our language.

    c. Our calendar is a constant reminder of Greek mythology's long-lasting influence.

READING TIP The main idea you infer from the specific details should sum up the paragraph in the same way a topic sentence does.

▶ EXERCISE 6   **Inferring Main Ideas**

DIRECTIONS   Read each of the six supporting details. Then infer the main idea you think they suggest.

EXAMPLE

a. In Chinese weddings, red plays a central role, appearing in the invitations and decorations.

b. In Hindu wedding ceremonies, both the bride and groom smear themselves with the spice turmeric in preparation to be married.

c. Orange blossoms, or *azahares*, are the typical flower choice for Spanish weddings, because they symbolize happiness and fulfillment.

d. The bride and groom's sharing of the liquor saki is an important Japanese wedding tradition.

e. In Nigeria, many couples follow the Yoruba ritual called Tasting the Four Elements, in which the newlywed couple tastes food representing four different flavors representing different parts of a relationship: sweet, bitter, sour, and hot.

f. In Muslim weddings, the bride and groom, along with friends and family, celebrate with a feast, called Walima, which can last for two days.

Implied Main Idea   Wedding traditions vary according to the country or culture.

_____

EXPLANATION   Two key threads of meaning run through these groups of sentences: (1) wedding traditions and (2) wedding traditions from different cultures. Because each sentence introduces another tradition from a different culture, the inference "Wedding traditions vary according to the country or culture" is supported by the sentences supplied and could be used to summarize them. That makes it a logical answer, although there are other ways of expressing a similar point, for instance, "Different cultures embrace different wedding traditions."

1. a. Marjoe Gortner's parents put him on stage at the age of four, claiming that those plagued by illness could be healed by their young son's touch.

   b. Gortner continued to pretend to be a healer on into adulthood but eventually admitted in a documentary that he was a fraud.

   c. A middle-aged woman who attended a faith healing session conducted by the well-known faith healer Kathryn Kuhlman threw off her back brace as a result, claiming to no longer have cancer of the spine.

d. Shortly afterwards, the woman's backbone collapsed; four months later she was dead.

e. James Randi's *The Faith Healers* describes numerous acts of healing that were motivated more by the desire for money than by faith in a god.

f. In 1994, television repairman Larry Maxwell was sentenced to three months in jail for claiming he could channel god's power and cure an undercover state trooper of AIDS.

Implied Main Idea _____

_____

2. a. When Meaghan Ybos was raped at the age of sixteen by a man in a ski mask, she reported it to the police and evidence was gathered from her body; that evidence, called a rape kit, was never analyzed to uncover the suspect's DNA.

b. When Ms. Ybos's rape kit was analyzed, years later, the evidence it provided helped identify and convict a man who had gone on to rape a series of women.

c. Backlogs of rape kits have recently been rediscovered in police departments across the country and used to track down suspects identified in other rape attempts.

d. Prosecutor Tim McGinty has been quoted as saying, "The rape kits are a gold mine for law enforcement."

e. Sarah Tofte, director of policy at the Joyful Heart Foundation, an advocacy group for victims of sexual assault, says that hundreds of thousands of untested rape kits that could provide clues to serial rapists are lying on shelves in cities all over the United States.

f. In cities like Detroit and Cleveland, police and prosecutors have started analyzing rape kits that have been gathering dust for years and that analysis has led to the identification or conviction of numerous men who were traced via their DNA.

Implied Main Idea _____

_____

Questions for Evaluating Inferences ●	1. **Is your inference solidly based on statements in the paragraph?** If asked to defend the main idea you inferred, you should be able to point to specific words and sentences that support it.
	2. **Are you relying more on the author's words than on your own personal point of view?** Don't draw an inference based mainly on what you think or feel about the subject. When drawing inferences, it's the writer's mind you have to read, not your own.
	3. **Are you sure that none of the author's statements contradict your inference?** If any of the sentences in a passage contradict the idea you've inferred, you probably haven't hit upon the main idea the author intended.
	4. **Do the sentences in the paragraph connect to the main idea you inferred?** If you jot your inference in the margins, you should immediately see how the supporting details help develop it.

▶ EXERCISE 7   Recognizing Implied Main Ideas

DIRECTIONS   Read each paragraph. Then circle the letter of the implied main idea.

1. In the past, many men and women decided to become flight attendants because they were attracted to the glamorous, fun, jet-setting lifestyle that came with the job. Now, however, flight attendants are spending most of their workdays dealing with rude, disgruntled passengers who are frustrated by delays, crowded flights, and the disappearance of perks like free food. These cranky travelers often leave their manners in the airport terminal and bombard flight attendants with complaints. Flight attendants must also worry about the possibility of terrorism. Since the terrorist hijackings of four airliners on September 11, 2001, flight attendants have to carefully scrutinize passengers' behavior, check suspicious baggage, and take additional security measures. What's more, the crew must endure the stress and anxiety of working in an environment that is a terrorist target. Working in an industry that is struggling financially, flight attendants also now worry constantly about layoffs and wage or benefit cuts.

Implied Main Idea
    a. The airline industry is in a state of massive confusion.

    b. The job of flight attendant has lost much of its glamour.

    c. The September 11, 2001, terrorist attacks have significantly affected the airline industry.

2. Adolescent yearnings for independence often lead to some withdrawal from family members and to arguments with parents over issues of autonomy and decision making. Some distancing from parents may be healthy during adolescence, as young people form meaningful relationships outside the family and develop a sense of independence and social competence. As it turns out, and despite popular misconceptions to the contrary, most adolescents and their parents express love and respect for each other and agree on many of the principal issues in life. Though disagreements with parents are common, serious and prolonged conflict is neither normal nor helpful for adolescents. (Adapted from Nevid, *Psychology*, 3rd ed., p. 374, © Cengage Learning.)

Implied Main Idea
    a. While there is some benefit to adolescents withdrawing from their parents, a major break is neither typical nor beneficial.

    b. Adolescents need to learn how to live on their own, and it's healthy for them to pull away from their parents.

    c. Adolescents who withdraw from their parents are the exception; in general, adolescents feel affection and respect for their parents.

3. Already in 1967, a study done at Harvard Medical School showed that during meditation, people use 17 percent less oxygen, lower their heart rates by three beats per minute, and increase the type of brain waves that occur during the state of relaxation preceding sleep. Other studies of the brain have confirmed that meditation shifts activity from the right hemisphere of the prefrontal cortex[†] to the left hemisphere. As a result, the brain switches to a calmer, more content state. For this reason, meditation can eliminate the need for medication to treat anxiety, tension, and even pain. In fact, many individuals are managing the pain of chronic diseases or injuries not with painkillers but with meditation, which helps people learn to accept their

---

[†]prefrontal cortex: Part of the brain that is highly developed in humans, the prefrontal cortex plays a large role in regulating thought, emotion, and behavior.

discomfort rather than struggle against it. Other patients suffering from diseases like cancer are meditating to actually boost their immune systems. Studies show that people who meditate have higher levels of disease-fighting antibodies in their blood.

Implied Main Idea

a. Meditation offers some significant health benefits.

b. Meditation is growing in popularity.

c. Meditation can sharpen one's ability to think.

4. Was the 5,300-year-old, mummified body discovered in 1991 and now known as the "Iceman" killed, or did he freeze to death after being caught in a storm? One of the hikers who discovered the body in the Italian Alps said that before the Iceman was freed from a melting glacier, he had been clutching a knife in one hand. In 2001, an Italian radiologist discovered an arrowhead embedded in the shoulder of the Iceman; its position indicated that he had been hit from behind. Medical examiners have found a deep gash in one of the corpse's hands, in addition to a cut on his other hand and bruises on his body. Furthermore, DNA specialists have analyzed blood found on the arrows the Iceman was carrying. They have also found blood on the back of his cloak and his knife. They say that this blood came from four different people. The blood of two people was found on the same arrow in the Iceman's quiver, suggesting that this arrow had struck two different individuals and then been pulled free.

A well-preserved corpse, now known as the "Iceman," was found in the Italian Alps in 1991.

Sven Hoppe/dpa/Corbis Wire/Corbis.

Implied Main Idea

a. Scientists cannot decide if the Iceman froze to death or was murdered.

b. Evidence suggests that the Iceman was probably killed in a fight.

c. DNA testing has finally proven that the Iceman died after being shot in the back with an arrow.

5. Dogs trained by the military are remarkably effective at locating improvised explosive devices (IEDs). IEDs are composed of chemicals, not metals, making them especially hard to detect via electronic monitoring systems. Dogs, however, can sniff the explosives out and that talent has made them a common sight on the fields of war. In addition to bomb detection, dogs in the military are widely used to help treat soldiers with post-traumatic stress disorder, or PTSD, both at home and in the field of war. But their service comes with a price. Military veterinarians have noted that dogs who spend many months on the battlefield often start exhibiting behavior that is similar to some of their human companions. The sound of gunfire, for instance, can suddenly begin to elicit wild barking, even if in the past the dog seemed to tolerate it without anxiety. Other battle-weary dogs will start refusing to go into buildings or enter cars. Giving the dogs more time off from the job seems to help. The anti-anxiety drug Xanax also seems to help.

Implied Main Idea

a. Dogs trained in the military are a huge help to soldiers on the ground.

b. Dogs trained in the military usually end up completely broken by the horrors of war.

c. Some military dogs seem to be suffering their own version of PTSD.

✔ CHECK YOUR UNDERSTANDING

1. When writers put parts of the main idea into different sentences, what should readers do?

_____

2. When writers don't give readers even parts of topic sentences, how should readers respond?

_____

_____

 ## Reviewing Logical and Illogical Inferences

To see the difference between logical and illogical inferences, read the following passage about Joan of Arc. Then look carefully at the two possible implied main ideas or inferences that follow. One is a logical inference that follows from, or is based on, the paragraph. The other is an illogical inference. It reflects the reader's point of view more than the author's. Your job is to decide which is which.

> Joan of Arc, the national heroine and patron saint of France, was born in 1412 to a family of poor peasants. In 1425, at the age of thirteen, Joan claimed to hear voices that she believed belonged to the early Christian saints and martyrs.* Four years later, in 1429, those same voices told her to help the young king of France, Charles VII, fight the British, who were trying to take control of France in the Hundred Years War.† When the king believed her story and gave her troops to command, Joan put on a suit of armor and led her soldiers to victory. Yet when the British captured Joan in 1430 and tried her for heresy* and wearing masculine dress, Charles refused to help her, allowing her to be condemned to death. On May 30, 1431, Joan was burned at the stake, still swearing loyalty to the king of France.

Which of the following implied main ideas effectively sums up the previous paragraph?

Implied Main Idea 1 Even though Joan of Arc sacrificed her life to save his throne, the king of France failed to return her loyalty.

---

*martyrs: people willing to die for their faith or to save the lives of others.
†Hundred Years War (1337–1453): an episodic struggle on land that lasted a century and varied from times of peace to periods of intense violence.
*heresy: challenging church law.

Implied Main Idea 2   Although she died swearing her loyalty to the king of France, Joan of Arc must have hated him for his betrayal.

Did you decide that the first implied main idea was a more logical inference than the second? If you did, you are absolutely correct. The paragraph definitely implies that Joan sacrificed everything for a king who did not return her loyalty.

Statement 2, in contrast, is an illogical inference. It could easily lead the reader away from the writer's real point. There is simply no evidence in the paragraph to support the notion that Joan hated the king for his betrayal. On the contrary, the last sentence of the paragraph contradicts the idea that Joan hated the king.

SUMMING UP THE KEY POINTS

1. Logical inferences
   - follow from or are based on what's said in the paragraph.
   - do not favor the reader's experience or knowledge over the author's words.
   - are not contradicted by any statements appearing in the paragraph.
   - do not divert the reader from the author's intended meaning.
   - could function as the topic sentence.
2. Illogical inferences
   - give more weight to the reader's thoughts than they do the author's words.
   - are based on a few stray words or one or two sentences rather than most of the sentences in the paragraph.
   - are likely to be contradicted by one or more statements appearing in the paragraph.
   - couldn't effectively function as topic sentences.
   - are likely to lead readers away from the author's intended meaning.

▶ **EXERCISE 8**   **Identifying Implied Main Ideas That Follow from the Text**

DIRECTIONS   Read each paragraph. Then circle the letter of the implied main idea. *Note:* Be sure the answer you choose fits the description of a logical inference.

1. The drug called cocaine was formally identified in 1855. By the 1870s, surgeons used it as an anesthetic for minor surgery. In the 1880s, it was used to treat opium addiction, alcoholism, and depression. The drug came to the notice of the young Sigmund Freud when he read reports of how small doses could restore the spirits of soldiers exhausted by war. Freud was so enthusiastic about the beneficial uses to which cocaine could be put he prescribed it for a young colleague who was addicted to morphine. The drug, however, did not cure the addiction. Instead, the young man began hallucinating wildly. Believing that snakes were crawling under his skin, he committed suicide, leaving Freud devastated by what he had done.

Implied Main Idea

a. Sigmund Freud believed the reports of cocaine's beneficial effects and prescribed it for his patients.

b. Sigmund Freud never got over the mistake he made when he prescribed cocaine for a colleague who then killed himself.

c. Sigmund Freud was sadly mistaken in his early enthusiasm for cocaine.

d. Sigmund Freud's own drug addiction was the source of a tragic mistake concerning his young colleague.

2. Entrants in the "Little Miss of America" beauty pageant—girls between the ages of three and six—are not asked to pay a fee. Their indulgent* parents, however, willingly pay hundreds of dollars just to have their children's photographs included in the pageant catalog. They also must pay for the singing and dancing lessons that will allow their child to participate in the talent section of the contest. But perhaps even more costly than the lessons are the extensive* wardrobes of party dresses and costumes that the girls must have in order to participate in the contest and its related functions. Furthermore, traveling expenses for the children and the relatives who accompany them can easily run into thousands of dollars.

*indulgent: ready to spoil, overly fond.
*extensive: wide-ranging, large, covering a lot of territory.

Implied Main Idea

    a. It costs a lot of money to enter the Little Miss of America beauty contest.

    b. Little girls should not be encouraged to participate in beauty pageants.

    c. When parents enter their little girls into beauty pageants, they have no idea of the costs associated with being in the pageant.

    d. Parents who enter their children in beauty contests are doing their children great harm, whether or not they know it.

3. On January 30, 1889, young Crown Prince Rudolf of Austria was found shot to death in his hunting lodge on the outskirts of Vienna. Lying next to him was the body of his lover, seventeen-year-old Baroness Marie Vetsera. She, too, had been shot. In the years since that tragic event, some have claimed that Rudolf ended his life because he was depressed over a terminal* illness. According to this theory, when Marie found him, she decided to take her life. Others insist, however, that Rudolf was murdered by members of the court who feared his progressive* beliefs would become public policy when Rudolf reached the throne. According to another theory, Marie and Rudolf entered into a suicide pact when their parents forbade the couple to marry.

Implied Main Idea

    a. Although there are many theories about how Crown Prince Rudolf and Marie Vetsera died, the theory that they were murdered makes the most sense.

    b. No one really knows for sure how Crown Prince Rudolf and Marie Vetsera died.

    c. Love drove Crown Prince Rudolf of Austria to suicide.

    d. In despair at their inability to wed, Crown Prince Rudolf and Marie Vetsera decided to die together.

4. Can babies inside the womb hear what's going on outside of the mother's body? Although earlobes start to form in the eighth week of pregnancy, it takes three months for the ears to become fully functional. At that point, the baby can hear the mother's heartbeat or her growling stomach. Moms-to-be report that babies also respond to voices outside the womb, particularly the mother's. Although infants

---

*terminal: ending in death, having a limit or boundary.
*progressive: forward-thinking, open-to-change.

in the womb respond to voices in general, their heartbeat is more likely to slow at the sound of the mother's voice. This suggests that, to some degree, infants can not only hear but also distinguish between voices. Sonograms have also revealed that babies in the womb turn their heads in response to noises. They also jerk or kick at the sound of loud and unexpected noises like a car backfiring or a door slamming.

Implied Main Idea

a. There is evidence that babies do hear what's going on outside the womb.

b. Without question, babies remember everything they experience in the womb.

c. Babies inside the womb can hear the sounds of the mother's body very clearly but they hear sounds outside the womb just faintly.

d. Already in the womb, babies seem to have highly developed tastes for what they like to hear.

5. By the end of the nineteenth century, the United States was turning its attention to Hawai'i. In 1881, Secretary of State James Blaine declared the Hawaiian Islands "essentially part of the American system." By 1890, Americans owned about three-quarters of Hawai'i's wealth and subordinated its economy to that of the United States. Hawai'i's sugar exports, for example, entered the United States duty free. In Hawai'i's multiracial society, Chinese and Japanese nationals far outnumbered Americans, who represented just 2.1 percent of the population. To gain more influence over the workings of the government, prominent Americans on the islands organized secret clubs and military units to contest the rule of Hawai'i's government. As early as 1887, American interests on the island had gained enough influence to force the king to accept a constitution granting foreigners the right to vote. The new constitution also shifted power away from the monarchy and granted more decision making to the legislature, which was more open to foreign influence. By the turn of the century, many native Hawaiians (53% of the population) believed that *haole* (foreigners)—especially Americans—were stealing their country. (Adapted from Norton et al., *A People and a Nation*, 10th ed., Brief Edition, p. 556, © Cengage Learning.)

Implied Main Idea

a. When the American government turned its attention to Hawai'i at the end of the nineteenth century, it tried hard to help the islands' struggling economy and got only unjust criticism as its reward.

    b. Hawai'i's inhabitants unfairly criticized the role the United States was taking in the islands' affairs.

    c. Thanks to the actions of Secretary of State James Blaine, Hawai'i lost control of its native government.

    d. When the American government turned its attention to Hawai'i at the end of the nineteenth century, it did so to benefit its own interests.

From Reader to Writer Using paragraph 4 as a model, write a paragraph that opens with a question. Answer the question with a topic sentence and supporting details, or let a series of specific sentences imply or suggest your answer to the reader. Here are some questions to consider answering in your writing: Why are selfies so popular on social media? Why do so many girls post belfies on Instagram? What can be done to stop bullying in the schools? What makes a good teacher or friend?

▶ EXERCISE 9   Inferring the Implied Main Idea

DIRECTIONS   Read each paragraph. Then, in the blanks that follow, write the implied main idea of the paragraph.

EXAMPLE   Everyone knows that smoking cigarettes is bad for you. There's no dispute about that. But what about electronic cigarettes; are they bad for you? To be sure, marketing campaigns by the makers of e-cigarettes suggest they are a healthy alternative to smoking. This is probably one reason why many people, especially women, have started smoking, or, as those familiar with the practice call it, "vaping." The main advantage of vaping with e-cigarettes (or your own personal vaporizer) is the lack of tobacco and toxic chemicals, such as ammonia, arsenic, and tar, which are used to create real paper and tobacco cigarettes. The whole purpose of electronic cigarettes, however, is to supply nicotine to the user, and nicotine has its own nasty side effects. Even in small doses, it is addictive. It also constricts blood vessels and can cause high blood pressure that, in turn, limits the flow of blood to the heart. Nicotine has also been linked to poor sleep quality, diabetes, and cancer. Currently, electronic cigarettes are not regulated by the Food and Drug Administration (FDA), but an FDA study has found cancer causing substances in at least half of the samples analyzed. Of particular concern is the growing use of e-cigarettes among middle and high school kids, who are running the risk of nicotine addiction. (Source of FDA study information: http://www.cancer.org/cancer/cancercauses/tobaccocancer/questionsaboutsmokingtobaccoandhealth/questions-about-smoking-tobacco-and-health-e-cigarettes. Last accessed 5/16/2015).

Implied Main Idea   Even without tobacco in them, electronic cigarettes may be bad for you.

_____

EXPLANATION   The sample paragraph poses a question about the safety of electronic cigarettes. The author, however, provides no explicit answer. Instead, she focuses mainly on the drawbacks associated with e-cigarettes. Emphasizing only the drawbacks without saying anything positive about them in response to the question suggests that the author wants readers to think e-cigarettes are not a positive alternative to smoking.

1. Anyone who orders a milkshake in Rhode Island and expects a drink made with ice cream is in for a surprise. In Rhode Island, a "milkshake" contains no ice cream. It's made only of milk and flavored syrup. If you want ice cream in your drink, you'd better call it a "cabinet." The name comes from the wooden cabinet encasing the mixer that shakes up the milk. Similarly, anyone in search of a long sandwich made with layers of meat and cheese should ask for a "sub" or a "hero" in the North. But in the South, you had better request a "poor boy," or the waiter will be confused. If you want a soda in Boston, you should probably ask for a "tonic." However, if you are in Minneapolis, you'd better ask for a "pop," or else you're likely to get a glass of flavored seltzer water.

Implied Main Idea   _____

_____

2. Body modification, the altering of the body for non-medical reasons, may seem odd to those not given to the practice. But there are those who believe that consciously modifying, or changing, the body is a way of taking control of one's life and identity. To that end, no risk or expense is too much. Corneal tattooing, for instance, used to be done to improve the appearance of an eye that had some injury

or defect. But now it is more frequently done by a tattoo artist, who, upon request, can put a heart, a star, or a patch of blue in the corner of a person's eye. Can the procedure go wrong and end in blindness? It certainly can. But to the committed believer in body modification, the risk is worth it. For some young women, corset piercings have become a desirable body modification. To achieve the right look, the women have their back pierced in two vertical columns. That way a ribbon can be laced through eyelet closures tacked into the skin, giving the naked back the appearance of an old-fashioned corset. Time-consuming and painful, corset piercings are, for those who desire them, worth both the time and the pain. The same holds true for those who think branding is a desirable body modification. Body branding is the result of third-degree wounds inflicted by the heat of a white-hot iron applied directly on the skin to form symbols and shapes of assorted sizes. During the branding, there is no way to completely dull the pain. But for those who think brands are beautiful, the pain is no obstacle.

Implied Main Idea _____

_____

3. The Beatles' song "I Am the Walrus" was inspired by Lewis Carroll's classic work of children's literature, *Alice's Adventures in Wonderland*. The same book also gave rock group Jefferson Airplane the idea for its song "White Rabbit" and Steely Dan its idea for "The Mock Turtle's Song." Mary Shelley's horror novel, *Frankenstein*, inspired songs performed by the rock band Blue Oyster Cult and singer-songwriter Bob Dylan, who also got many of his ideas for lyrics from great works of literature like Samuel Taylor Coleridge's "The Rime of the Ancient Mariner," Dante's *The Inferno*, and the poetry of William Blake. Several of Led Zeppelin's songs are derived from J. R. R. Tolkien's *The Lord of the Rings*. The band Styx also performed a song based on that same fantasy classic. Rock group Pink Floyd's entire *Animals* album was inspired by George Orwell's classic, *Animal Farm*. Homer's *The Odyssey* has influenced songs by Steely Dan, Cream, and others. It's well known that Kate Bush's song "The Sensual World" was inspired by James Joyce's *Ulysses*, while Crash Test Dummies' "Afternoons & Coffeespoons" is a clear reference to T. S. Eliot's "The Love Song of J. Alfred Prufrock."

Implied Main Idea _____

_____

4. Quick, what comes to mind when you hear the phrase "war hero"? Is it the famous statue of soldiers planting the flag at Iwo Jima? Is it John Kerry, who earned a silver star and a bronze medal before going on to become a senator from Massachusetts? Or do you think of Pat Tillman, the courageous young man who gave up a promising career in football to die in the mountains of Afghanistan, while fighting for his country? What probably doesn't come right to mind are the more than six hundred female soldiers who dressed up as men so they could fight in the country's Civil War, even though they could have stayed safely at home and never dodged a bullet. Like those six hundred female soldiers, you also probably never even heard of Manuela Sáenz (1797–1856), who was a colonel in the rebel Peruvian army. Yet you are probably familiar with her famous lover, another soldier hero, Simón Bolivar (1783–1830). Similarly, World War II war hero Audie Murphy had a film made of his heroic actions during wartime. It was called _To Hell and Back_. Yet World War II's most decorated woman warrior, Nancy Wake, famous as a guerilla fighter who made it to the Germans' most wanted list, gets barely a mention in the history books.

Implied Main Idea _____

_____

5. When people behave in a way that is odd or dangerous, it's not unusual for someone to link his or her behavior to a full moon. Epilepsy patients, for example, have sometimes claimed that their seizures were triggered by the arrival of a full moon. Yet when Dr. Selim Benbadis, from the University of South Florida College of Medicine, investigated these claims, he found that, over the course of three years, most of the seizures his subjects experienced took place during the moon's last quarter rather than the first. According to the results of Dr. Benbadis's study, seizures actually declined during the full moon. Similarly wrong-headed is the belief that madness occurs when the moon is full. When two researchers—James Rotton of Florida International University and Ivan Kelly of the University of Saskatchewan—reviewed studies linking bouts of lunacy (*luna*

means "moon" in Italian) to the size of the moon, they found next to no connection between the two. About the only place that a full moon has a powerful effect on behavior is in the animal kingdom. During a full moon, for example, prey animals move about less. But there is nothing mysterious or supernatural about their behavior. They simply know that the light of the full moon makes it easier for predators to find them.

Implied Main Idea

_____

_____

✔ CHECK YOUR UNDERSTANDING

Explain the difference between logical and illogical inferences.

_____

_____

_____

_____

 ## Inferring Supporting Details

Main ideas are not the only text element readers need to infer. Inferences also play a big role in making supporting details meaningful. For an illustration, read the following example. As you do, consider what information you have to infer in order to fully understand what the supporting details contribute to the main idea.

Topic Sentence

Notice how the reader has to supply the meaning

[1]According to social exchange theory, the development and continuation of intimate relationships are associated with the rewards and costs involved. [2]Research has shown that dating couples who experience an increase in rewards as their relationship progresses are likely to stay

appropriate to the context. These are not financial rewards and costs.

The reader also has to figure out how the comparison level contributes to expectations.

together. [3]In contrast, dating couples who experience fewer reward increases are less likely to stay together. [4]Rewards and costs, however, do not arise on their own and in isolation. [5]People bring to their relationships certain expectations. [6]John Thibaut and Harold Kelley coined the term "comparison level" (CL) to refer to the expected outcome in relationships. [7]A person with a high CL expects his or her relationships to be rewarding. [8]Someone with a low CL does not. [9]Even a bad relationship can look pretty good to someone who has a low CL. (Adapted from Brehm, Kassin, and Fein, *Social Psychology*, 5th ed., p. 208, © Cengage Learning.)

Inferring the Meanings Appropriate to the Context

Note that the writers of the paragraph on social exchange theory do not specifically define the meanings of the two key words, *rewards* and *costs*, even though both words need to be understood in a particular way: as emotional rather than financial rewards and costs. If those two words aren't defined in this way, the social exchange theory wouldn't make much sense when applied to intimate relationships. Yet the writers don't supply those specific meanings. They just supply the context for the two words. It's up to readers to draw the right inferences.

Inferring Relationships and Adding Information

The need for reader-supplied supporting details, however, does not end with the definitions of these two words. Sentences 2 and 3 in the previous paragraph can only develop the topic sentence if readers draw a bridging inference. They have to infer a cause-and-effect relationship in which one event produces another. Dating couples who get an increased number of rewards stay together *because* they like the rewards. Similarly, couples who experience fewer rewards are less likely to stay together *because* there aren't enough rewards in the relationship.

Even sentence 4, which looks so simple, requires readers to infer two implied phrases shown here in brackets: "Rewards and costs [*within couple relationships*], however, do not arise on their own and in isolation [*from all other influences*]." In short, this entire paragraph only makes sense if the reader is willing to work with the author and supply the necessary content and connections.

READING TIP

Writers don't always identify relationships with specific transitions like *however* and *for example*. It's up to you, the reader, to keep asking yourself, What does the sentence I am currently reading have to do with the one that came before?

SUMMING UP THE KEY POINTS

1. The need to draw inferences in reading does not apply solely to main ideas. It also applies to supporting details, where readers sometimes need to supply part of the content.

2. In addition to information, readers may also need to infer the connections between sentences, figuring out for themselves why one sentence follows another.

▶ **EXERCISE 10**   **Drawing Inferences About Supporting Details**

DIRECTIONS   Read each paragraph and underline the topic sentence. Then circle the appropriate letter to identify the inference readers need to add to the supporting details.

EXAMPLE   ¹Knowledge about emotions is learned, at least in part, from parents. ²Children who display knowledge about emotions—who can label emotional expressions on faces, describe the feelings of another person in an emotional situation, and talk about the causes of emotions—typically have mothers willing to discuss and explain the power of emotions. ³In the context of learning about emotions, these mothers are good "coaches." ⁴However, when parents react negatively to children expressing emotion (e.g., "You're overreacting!"), children's understanding of emotions is poorer and, as a result, the children are less socially competent. ⁵Parents who engage in such negative behaviors are missing opportunities to explain to their children the key elements of emotional responses. ⁶The extreme case is represented by children who are physically abused or neglected by their parents. ⁷These children lack the ability to call up the emotional expressions appropriate to particular situations, such as going to the zoo and getting a balloon or losing a pet to disease. (Adapted from Bukatko and Daehler, *Child Development*, 5th ed., p. 393, © Cengage Learning.)

1. To make sentences 2 and 3 fit together in a meaningful way, which inference does the reader need to add to the supporting details?

   a. Mothers who criticize their children for not expressing how they feel create adults who are emotionally cold.

   b. Mothers open to talking about their own emotions provide role models that help their children deal with their own emotional life.

   c. Some mothers who are open to discussing emotions are likely to do so only when their children express negative emotions.

2. To make sentences 6 and 7 fit together in a meaningful way, which inference do readers need to add to the supporting details?

   a. Parents who discourage their children from showing emotion do so because they themselves don't know how to express their feelings.

   b. When parents discourage their children from showing emotion, they do so because they equate showing emotion with weakness.

   c. Neglectful or abusive parents probably spend very little time showing their children how to express what they feel.

EXPLANATION   Sentence 2 tells us that children who know how to handle their emotions typically have a mother willing to discuss her own emotions. But the authors don't tell us exactly how the mother's ability is handed on to her offspring. Instead, in sentence 3, the authors use the word *coaches* to imply that some mothers teach their children about emotions in the same way coaches teach kids about sports. However, it's up to readers to draw that inference, which is answer *b*.

Although the authors don't say it explicitly, it's very unlikely that abusive or neglectful parents would spend much time coaching their children in how to go about handling their emotions. This is the inference readers have to draw for the second question, making answer *c* correct.

1. ¹What would become one of the most dramatic events of the civil rights movement occurred in Mississippi in 1955. ²In September, Emmett Till, a fourteen-year-old black youth from Chicago, visited relatives near Greenwood, Mississippi. ³After buying some candy at a local store, Till supposedly said "Bye, baby" to the white female clerk. ⁴Three days later, after midnight, the girl's husband and brother dragged Till from his relatives' home, shot him through the head, brutally beat him, and dumped his body in the Tallahatchie River. ⁵After her son's death, Till's mother insisted on an open casket at the

funeral so that, in her words, "All the world can see what they did to my boy." [6]The image of Till's mutilated body, captured on television, seared itself into the consciousness of a generation of black leaders. [7]Yet despite overwhelming evidence of guilt, an all-white, all-male jury found the two white suspects innocent of kidnapping. (Adapted from Gillon and Matson, *The American Experiment*, 2nd ed., p. 1123, © Cengage Learning.)

1. To make sentences 3 and 4 fit together in a meaningful way, which inference do readers need to add to the supporting details?

   a. The husband and brother of the female clerk were outraged that a black man would speak in such a familiar way to a white woman.

   b. Emmett Till was dragged from his relatives' home by people who were ready to make trouble with the first person who crossed their path.

   c. The people who kidnapped Emmett Till were trying to avenge a similar crime that had been committed against another teenage boy who was white.

2. To make sentences 5–7 fit together in a meaningful way, which inference do readers need to add to the supporting details?

   a. Till's mother never really cared about her son, and she showed her feelings by leaving the casket of her son open for all to view.

   b. The mother's attempt to make others experience her grief succeeded with a generation of black leaders but seemed not to have affected the white jurors sitting in judgment on the men who kidnapped and killed Till.

   c. Till's mother was so distraught from grief, she could not think straight.

2. [1]The turning point of the 1960 presidential campaign came in a series of four televised debates between September 26 and October 24. [2]Facing off against Richard M. Nixon, John F. Kennedy used the debates—the first-ever televised debates between presidential contenders—to demolish the Republican charge that he was inexperienced and poorly informed. [3]And he succeeded far better than his opponent in communicating the qualities of boldness, imagination, and poise. [4]Kennedy appeared alert, aggressive, and cool. [5]Nixon, who perspired profusely, looked nervous and

uncomfortable. [6]Not surprisingly, radio listeners divided evenly on who won the debate. [7]However, the overwhelming majority of television viewers gave Kennedy a decisive edge. [8]The performance energized Kennedy's campaign, and the debates institutionalized television's role as a major force in American politics. (Adapted from Gillon and Matson, *The American Experiment*, 2nd ed., p. 1130, © Cengage Learning.)

1. To make sentences 1–5 fit together in a meaningful way, which inference do readers need to add to the supporting details?

    a. Kennedy was also perspiring, but he knew how to stand in front of the camera so that his perspiration did not show.

    b. Kennedy was just as uncomfortable as Nixon was on television, but he didn't show it while Nixon did.

    c. The contrasting image of a cool Kennedy and a sweating Nixon made the 1960 debate a major turning point in the campaign.

2. To make sentences 6 and 7 fit together in a meaningful way, which inference do readers need to add to the supporting details?

    a. Because the reception was not good, people who listened to the debate on radio couldn't hear what the candidates said with the same clarity as those watching it on television.

    b. Kennedy had spent a good deal of time being coached on how to debate, whereas Nixon had not.

    c. People who saw the debate on television were heavily influenced by the appearance and manner of the two men, whereas people listening on radio were not.

CHECK YOUR UNDERSTANDING

What two kinds of inferences do readers need to add to supporting details?

_____

_____

_____

DIGGING DEEPER Schooling Resistance

Looking Ahead The paragraph on page 409 explains how the lives of Native Americans benefited from Franklin Roosevelt's New Deal.[†] This reading, in contrast, focuses on the lives of Native Americans at a time when the U.S. government was mainly interested in destroying, rather than supporting, Native American culture.

Getting Focused The word *schooling* refers to education or training, and the title tells us the reading is about training resistance. So here's one question to focus your reading: How were Native Americans trained in resistance? But Looking Ahead offers another clue. It tells us that the U.S. government was intent on destroying Native American culture. Put the two pieces of information together, and you can use this question to focus your reading: How did the U.S. government's attempts to destroy Native American culture lead to resistance?

1 By 1876 gold had been discovered in the Black Hills of South Dakota and Montana, and it was Major General George Armstrong Custer's job to see to it that the Sioux Indians, to whom the land belonged by treaty, stopped attacking the gold miners who had been pouring into the region. Although skirmishes in the Black Hills had been growing steadily more dangerous since the Sioux and Cheyenne had begun working in tandem, Custer was confident of victory and didn't bother to wait for reinforcements. What Custer didn't know was that he had badly underestimated the size of the Indian camp. He was expecting a few hundred. But, in fact, almost triple that number responded to his attack. Within a matter of hours, what came to be known as the Battle of Little Bighorn was over, and the only thing left alive from Custer's entire regiment of 256 men was one horse. Even worse, every soldier had been stripped naked and, except for Custer, scalped.[†]

2   "Custer's Last Stand," as the debacle came to be called, unleashed an avalanche of public fury, which boded no good for the Native Americans living on the western Plains. For those sympathetic to the Indians, the fear was that the government, goaded by public demands

---

[†]New Deal: a series of social programs created by the U.S. government and designed to get the country out of an economic depression.
[†]Custer's scalp may have been spared because he wasn't in uniform. He was dressed in buckskin. Thus, the Indians may have mistaken him for a local scout.

for vengeance, might pursue a policy of total annihilation. However, the battle at Little Bighorn had a second consequence: It also re-energized social reformers, who had been arguing for decades that assimilating the Plains Indians through education was the best way to end the bloody and costly confrontations between Native Americans and the U.S. military. In the past, government officials had paid lip service to the idea. But now, with Custer's devastating defeat staring them in the face, they were ready to listen. More to the point, they were ready to act. In the wake of Custer's humiliating failure, the American government began moving away from the use of force to subdue the Plains Indians. The new federal goal was to educate Native Americans and thereby assimilate them into white culture. Unfortunately, that policy shift, despite a few economic incentives, proved devastating to the lives of those Indians living on the western Plains.

3   At the time the American government had its change of heart, one of their own, Army Captain Richard C. Pratt, was on hand to provide a ready-to-implement educational model. In the military, Pratt had worked with Indian scouts and thought highly of their abilities. He believed that Indians, with the appropriate training, could achieve the level of "civilization" attained by white people and abandon what he referred to as their "savagery." In 1879 Pratt had his chance to prove that the red man could become white when he convinced the Secretary of War to let him open the Carlisle Industrial Training School in Carlisle, Pennsylvania. Pratt even had a motto ready which summed up his educational objective: "Kill the Indian in him and save the man."

4   Thus, at the Carlisle Institute—attended by Native American students as young as three and as old as sixteen—native languages were banned along with all signs of Native American dress, custom, or worship. This was Pratt's way of, in his words, planting "treason to the tribe and loyalty to the nation at large." While some basic academics were part of the curriculum, the emphasis was on agricultural labor, with students being sent to local farmers and other businesses to learn a trade and collect a small wage.

5   Although those who attended Pratt's school have left behind testimony suggesting they did not share his conviction that the school was an overwhelming success, Pratt persuaded the administrators of Indian affairs in Washington that assimilation based on his military model of schooling would solve what was commonly referred to as "the Indian problem." As a result, the school at Carlisle became the standard for all the other government-sponsored Indian boarding schools that fanned

out throughout the nation as the idea of assimilation increasingly took hold. By the century's end, there would be over one hundred and fifty Indian boarding schools, with at least one quarter of them explicitly following the Carlisle model, and the rest introducing some variations on Pratt's training. In one thing, none of the schools deviated: Their common goal was to obliterate all traces of the children's Indian identity.

6   According to the Pratt pattern, the government's boarding schools were purposely set up far from the children's homes so there was no chance that they could be tainted by contact with their parents. Upon arrival at boarding school, students generally got new names like Thomas Jefferson Price or George Washington Brown. They then had their hair cut and were issued uniforms or hand-me-down European clothing. As part of their training, they attended Christian services, learned to speak and read English, and were taught basic vocational skills. Most importantly, they were forbidden to speak their own language or carry on any Native American traditions, such as the wearing of traditional medicine bundles, which were small bags containing objects gathered from the natural world. To do so was considered a dangerous symptom of "returning to the blanket" (i.e., showing an attachment to tribal customs or rituals).

7   Under the Pratt model, every attempt to "return to the blanket" had to be stamped out through rebuke, penalty, or punishment. It depended on the school which measure was taken. Some students who were caught speaking their native tongue got only a reprimand, while others reported having their hands strapped raw for speaking in their own language. In boarding schools with the harshest regimes, runaways were sometimes placed in solitary detention or forced to cut the grass with scissors. Boys who ran away might have their heads shaved and be made to stand in the schoolyard wearing a dress. Students of both sexes were forced to eat lye soap for uttering even a few words of a tribal language. As one female student recalled, "Mother Garrett [the boarding school matron] jerked me by the collar of my dress and dragged me into the bathroom. That lye soap was about that big and about that high. She said, 'Don't you ever speak Indian again, or I'm going to wash your mouth again. . . .' My tongue got blistered from that lye."

8   Despite the harsh treatment they received, for many students, the schools still offered a way out of what was otherwise a hopeless future with no way to eke out a living on or off the reservation. In fact, school records show that some Native American boarding schools were

swamped with applications made by parents eager to help their children find a place in what had become a white man's world.

9   What the school records say less about is what happened when parents, despite the financial advantages, didn't want their children to become assimilated. Some did not, but refusal was not an option. Parents who tried to keep their children out of boarding schools had them taken away by force. By 1931, nearly one-third of all children belonging to the western tribes were in boarding schools either on or off the reservations.

10   Yet despite the proliferation of Indian boarding schools in the West, what Captain Pratt and those who followed in his path seem not to have realized is that giving up all outward expressions of one's ethnic history does not mean the past is forgotten or less cherished. As former boarding school student Mitch Walking Elk explained it, "They put me in the boarding school and they cut off all my hair, gave me an education, but the Apache's still in there." Even more revealing is the story of Chehia Red Arrow, who freely acknowledges, in her memoirs, that her education at the Phoenix Indian School in Arizona prepared her "to bring in money from the white man's world." But acknowledging the value of what she had learned at the boarding school does not in any way mean that Chehia Red Arrow, or, as she was called at school, Anna Moore, had forgotten her true identity. Years later, after leaving the boarding school and raising her family, Chehia Red Arrow helped start a tribal newsletter. She was also a founder of the Pima Indian Museum; editor of a little book called *Pima Indian Legends*; and author of *A Pima Past*, her autobiography. When it was safe to do so, Anna Moore had returned to the blanket after all. (Sources of information and quotations in this reading appear in the manual.)

Sharpening Your Skills

DIRECTIONS   Answer the following questions by filling in the blanks or circling the letters of the correct response.

Using Context Clues

1. Based on the context clues, what do you think *in tandem* means in the following sentence: "Although skirmishes in the Black Hills had been growing steadily more dangerous since the Sioux and Cheyenne had begun working *in tandem*, Custer was confident of victory and didn't bother to wait for reinforcements"?

2. Based on the context clues, what do you think *debacle* means in the following sentence: "Custer's Last Stand," as the *debacle* came to be called, unleashed an avalanche of public fury, which boded no good for the Native Americans living on the western Plains"?

_____

3. Based on the context clues, what do you think *annihilation* means in the following sentence: "For those sympathetic to the Native Americans, the fear was that the government, goaded by public demands for vengeance, might pursue a policy of total *annihilation*"?

_____

4. Based on the context clues, what do you think *assimilate* means in the following sentence: "The new federal goal was to educate Native Americans and thereby *assimilate* them into white culture"?

_____

Recognizing Main Ideas and Explanatory Patterns

5. Which of the following explanatory patterns best describes this reading?

a. The reading starts off with the main idea that controls the entire reading.

b. After a brief introduction, the author introduces the overall main idea of the reading.

c. The main idea of the entire reading opens the second paragraph.

d. After a brief introduction, the main idea appears at the end of the second paragraph.

6. Which of the following is the reading's thesis statement?

a. "Custer's Last Stand," as the debacle came to be called, unleashed an avalanche of public fury, which boded no good for the Native Americans living on the western Plains. For those sympathetic to the Native Americans, the fear was that the government, goaded by public demands for vengeance, might pursue a policy of total annihilation."

    b. "By 1876 gold had been discovered in the Black Hills of South Dakota and Montana, and it was Major General George Armstrong Custer's job to see to it that the Sioux Indians, to whom the land belonged by treaty, stopped attacking the gold miners who had been pouring into the region. Although skirmishes in the Black Hills had been growing steadily more dangerous since the Sioux and Cheyenne had begun working in tandem, Custer was confident of victory and didn't bother to wait for reinforcements."

    c. "The new federal goal was to educate Native Americans and thereby assimilate them into white culture. Unfortunately, that policy shift, despite a few economic incentives, proved devastating to the lives of Indians living on the western Plains."

Paraphrasing   **7.** How would you express the thesis statement of the reading in your own words?

_____

_____

_____

8. According to paragraph 5, the schools created to educate the country's Native Americans never deviated on one point. In your own words, what was that point?

_____

_____

9. In your own words, what is the main idea of paragraph 7?

_____

_____

Understanding the Function of Supporting Details   **10.** Which of the statements following this excerpt from paragraph 7 best describes the relationship among the supporting details?

Students of both sexes were forced to eat lye soap for uttering even a few words of a tribal language. As one female student recalled, "Mother Garrett [the boarding school matron] jerked me by the collar of my dress and dragged me into the bathroom. That lye soap was about that big and about that high. . . ."

a. The excerpt contains one major detail followed by two support-ing minor details.

b. The excerpt contains two major details followed by one minor detail.

c. The excerpt contains one major detail followed by a minor de-tail and a new major detail.

d. The excerpt starts off with a minor detail followed by two major details.

Drawing Inferences

11. Which bridging inference does the reader need to supply to make sense of the two sentences in paragraph 8?

a. The records mentioned in sentence 2 are the writer's way of proving that treatment in the boarding schools was extremely harsh.

b. The records mentioned in sentence 2 illustrate how students who graduated from boarding schools found good jobs after they finished.

c. The reference to the records is the author's way of providing evi-dence for the claim that, despite harsh treatment, many students saw the school as a way of escaping a hopeless future.

12. Which bridging inference does the reader need to supply to make sense of the first two sentences in paragraph 10?

a. Mitch Walking Elk was someone whose ethnic identity was de-stroyed by his years in a federal boarding school.

b. Mitch Walking Elk was one of the few boarding school stu-dents whose sense of his heritage remained undamaged by the experience.

c. Mitch Walking Elk is an example of someone who did not aban-don his Native American identity despite all attempts to sup-press it.

d. Once he was out of a white-run boarding school, Mitch Walking Elk had a hard time getting accustomed to life among his own people.

13. In paragraph 10, the author says that the story of Chehia Red Arrow is "even more revealing." The author expects readers to infer

the rest of the comparison. What words are readers expected to infer?

_____

_____

14. What the comment by Mitch Walking Elk and the story of Chehia Red Arrow reveal is never explicitly explained. Can you infer what the author wants them to suggest?

_____

_____

15. Why do you think the author uses the verb *fanned out* in the following sentence? What does the word suggest? "As a result, the school at Carlisle became the standard for all the other government-sponsored Indian boarding schools that *fanned out* throughout the nation as the idea of assimilation increasingly took hold."

_____

_____

_____

From Reader to Writer   By the 1880s, Native Americans had little hope of reclaiming their lost lands and many were in despair. But something called the Ghost Dance gave them new hope. Use the Web to find out what the Ghost Dance is (if you don't already know). Then write about it. Start by explaining what it was and what it was supposed to accomplish. Then explain how, for most Native Americans,[†] the Ghost Dance came to an end with the death of the great Indian chief Sitting Bull. Sitting Bull was shot because the government mistakenly believed he was using the Ghost Dance to fuel rebellion.

_____

[†]Even today, there are some Native Americans who perform the Ghost Dance and believe in its power.

When you edit your writing, be conscious of how you connect your sentences to make it easy for the reader to understand your point. Are the inferences you need the reader to supply easy to come up with given the clues you provide? They should be. Put yourself in the reader's place and see if the inferences you expect readers to make are clearly implied by your words. Ask a friend to read what you have written and see if there are any places where he or she struggles to infer the right detail or connection.

·Use the Web to find the information you need. Here are two websites to get you started: http://www.legendsofamerica.com/na-ghostdance .html and http://www.history.com/this-day-in-history/sitting-bull-killed-by-indian-police

▶ **TEST 1**   **Reviewing Key Concepts**

DIRECTIONS   Answer the following questions by filling in the blanks or circling the letter of the correct response.

1. Readers who draw logical inferences base them heavily on _____
   _____.

2. Readers who draw illogical inferences are inclined to ignore ____
   _____ in favor of _____
   _____.

3. Readers need to avoid illogical inferences because they can have what effect?

   _____.

4. If the topic sentence identifies the topic through a pronoun, the reader needs to be clear about the pronoun's _____.

5. When parts of the main idea appear in different sentences, it's the reader's job to _____.

6. If you have to infer the main idea of a paragraph, the main idea you infer should _____.

7. Inferences about relationships between sentences are called _____
   _____.

8. When it comes to supporting details, reader-supplied inferences

   a. are not as important as they are for main ideas.
   b. are seldom necessary.
   c. are as central to supporting details as they are to main ideas.

▶ **TEST 2**   **Linking Pronouns to Antecedents in Topic Sentences**

DIRECTIONS   Underline the topic sentence. Then rewrite it in the blanks, making sure to replace the pronoun with its antecedent. *Note*: If you need to, add any other necessary information that is implied but not stated in the topic sentence.

1. [1]Because of research indicating that drinking coffee contributes to diseases ranging from cancer to heart attacks, coffee has long been a guilty pleasure for many. [2]New research, however, suggests that it may actually offer significant health benefits. [3]For instance, researchers at the National Institute of Diabetes and Digestive Diseases found that coffee significantly reduces the risk of chronic liver disease. [4]Turning old research on its head, two studies of American nurses have shown that the biggest coffee drinkers actually have a lower risk for developing high blood pressure. [5]Drinking too much sometimes causes the heart to race, but the effect is apparently harmless. [6]Similarly, coffee's connections to breast cancer, osteoporosis, and dehydration have been exposed as weak and unproven. [7]What coffee does do is improve athletic ability by triggering a release of adrenaline that strengthens muscle contractions while improving speed and endurance. [8]And coffee's benefits aren't just physical. [9]Caffeine, functioning as a mild antidepressant, also helps to chase away the blues.

_____

_____

_____

2. [1]Like the famed *Titanic*, the British cruise ship *Lusitania* was another "floating palace" that sank. [2]The target of a German torpedo, it plummeted into the depths of the ocean a little more than three years after the *Titanic*, on May 7, 1915, with similar tragic results. [3]The death toll for the *Lusitania* was a devastating 1,198 people (or 61 percent of those aboard). [4]Those victims, too, died from injuries, drowning, and cold exposure. [5]Images of the sinking ship still horrify to this day. [6]Because the ship sank in less water than the length of the ship, it ended up with the bow on the ocean floor and the stern facing the sky. [7]The tragedy also had significant international impact. [8]The ship

had been carrying over one hundred Americans, and the public outcry against the Germans was huge. [9]The United States government had, up to that point, been reluctant to enter World War I. [10]But the sinking of the *Lusitania* put an end to that reluctance.

---

3. [1]Wilbur and Orville Wright are usually credited with being the first to fly an airplane. [2]However, some people argue that New Zealand farmer Richard Pearse and aviation pioneer Gustave A. Whitehead were the first to do it. [3]Pearse designed his own engine-powered flying machine. [4]On March 31, 1903, his aircraft rose fifty yards into the air. [5]That was eight months before the first Wrights' flight. [6]But the only accounts of the flight are from eyewitnesses so Pearse has not generally been given credit for his achievement. [7]Whitehead built his first airplane with flapping wings in 1897 but failed to get it into the air. [8]He didn't give up, however. [9]He kept experimenting and flew his aircraft for the first time in Bridgeport, Connecticut, on August 14, 1901, more than two years before the Wrights' aircraft took flight. [10]Like Pearse, Whitehead's flight has been documented by witnesses, not photographs, and his accomplishment remains in dispute.

---

4. [1]In 2003, researchers at the Harvard University School of Public Health wanted to find out if it's healthier for men to express their anger or to keep angry feelings to themselves. [2]They conducted a study of 23,522 male health professionals, aged fifty to eighty-five, and concluded that it's healthier for men to express anger than to keep it under wraps. [3]Relying on questionnaires, researchers asked the subjects to identify how they behaved when they got angry. [4]The subjects were asked to choose among options such as "I argue with others" and "I do things like slam doors." [5]The study went on for two years and revealed that men who expressed their anger in moderate ways were half as likely to suffer from a non-fatal heart attack as men who almost never showed

their anger. [6]The study also showed that the risk of stroke decreased as the levels of anger expression increased.

_____

_____

_____

5. [1]Unpleasant as anxiety can be, it's not necessarily a serious problem. [2]It only becomes a serious problem when it gets out of control and prevents people from getting what they want out of life. [3]An example is a college student named Jian who became unbearably anxious when he took exams. [4]By the time Jian went to see a counselor, he had skipped several tests and was in danger of dropping out of school. [5]Like Jian, people with anxiety problems often can't find the will to do anything constructive about their emotional distress. [6]Instead of trying to handle anxiety alone, they would be better off seeking therapy. [7]In therapy, they would discover that they are not alone and that, in itself, would help. [8]In any given year, roughly 18 percent of the adult population suffers from an anxiety disorder. (Adapted from Dennis Coon and John O. Mitterer. *Psychology*, 5th ed., p. 508, © Cengage Learning.)

_____

_____

▶ **TEST 3**   **Constructing Main Idea Statements**

DIRECTIONS   Read each paragraph and look for sentences that sum up parts of what you think is the main idea. Combine those sentences and write the main idea statement on the blanks.

1. [1]The white-tailed deer was one of the first animals to be protected by legislation. [2]But as it turns out, they don't need protection. [3]The white-tailed deer has proven to be a highly adaptable creature. [4]They have actually flourished and their population has not diminished despite the loss of wooded areas. [5]In most cases, the wooded areas that have been demolished have been given over to suburban developments. [6]Fortunately for the deer, suburban landscaping has provided quite a bit of vegetation to munch on, and they haven't minded adding, say, holly bushes to their diet. [7]It's also true that suburbia is not welcoming to hunters. [8]Thus, the deer have generally been able to roam the suburban landscape without fear. [9]Suburbanites also like gardens and, once again, woodland deer have been happy to expand their diet to include garden-grown produce.

Main Idea
Statement   _____

_____

_____

2. [1]Melvin L. Kohn was for many years chief of the Laboratory of Socio-environmental Studies of the National Institute of Mental Health in Washington D.C. [2]In 1956, he conducted a study of the values guiding child-rearing practices among American parents. [3]The results revealed some notable class differences. [4]For example, working-class parents (manual laborers and blue-collar workers) placed greater stress on such values as obedience, neatness, and cleanliness than did middle-class parents. [5]Middle-class parents thought such values as curiosity, happiness, consideration for others, and especially self-control were more important. [6]Both groups gave equally high importance to honesty. (Adapted from Stark, *Sociology*, 10th ed., p. 163, © Cengage Learning.)

Main Idea
Statement   _____

_____

_____

3. [1]Bill collection agencies aren't known for caring much about the people behind the debts they collect. [2]Their position is if you can't pay your debts, we will harass you until you do. [3]But in a time when debts and unemployment are particularly high, the agencies are even going a step further. [4]They are employing—some say abusing—old state laws that are still on the books. [5]These ancient laws make failure to pay a debt a crime and some collection agencies are using them to put people with unpaid debts into jail. [6]Although around one-third of U.S. states have such laws, Illinois has been singled out as a state where the practice is particularly popular among collection agencies. [7]As a result, the state's attorney general, Lisa Madigan, is fighting to get state judges to throw debtor cases out of the courts. [8]Getting into a debt is not a crime according to the federal government, and debtor prisons have not been legal since the 1850s. [9]But if a person does not show up after a collection agency has filed a charge against him or her in the courts, judges have been known to find in favor of the agency.

Main Idea Statement

_____

_____

_____

4. [1]Following the 2011 nuclear crisis in Japan in the wake of a towering tsunami, long-suppressed fears about nuclear power resurfaced. [2]This was true at least in some countries around the world. [3]But it wasn't true for all. [4]In the wake of Japan's nuclear disaster, Switzerland froze plans to build any new nuclear plants. [5]The Germans did the same, while Austria's minister of the environment proposed a stress test for plants all across the European Union. [6]Public opposition to nuclear plants broke out in places as far apart as Turkey and South Africa. [7]The Spanish government, however, did not follow suit. [8]Nor did the governments of Russia, Poland, China, and Chile. [9]Their official stance is that no hasty decisions should be made on the basis of the Japanese experience. [10]The United States appears to be on the side of the Russians and the Chinese. [11]Government officials say, however, that safety lessons need to be learned from the Japanese experience.

Main Idea Statement

_____

_____

_____

▶ **TEST 4**   **Recognizing the Implied Main Idea**

DIRECTIONS   Read each paragraph. Then circle the letter of the implied main idea.

1. The word *natural* in advertisements clearly sells products. Juices and foods filled with "natural" goodness along with "natural" vitamins and herbs are big money makers. Consumers seem to believe that anything coming straight from nature has to be good for you. Yet if you're one of those consumers, you might want to reconsider your trust in Mother Nature. Aflatoxin, one of the most potent cancer-causing substances that exists, is a natural product of mold. Ricin, one of the deadliest poisons on Earth, comes from nature's own castor beans. Take just one bite of the naturally growing mushroom *Amanita phalloides*, and you won't be around long enough to discuss its bitter aftertaste. Next time you're thinking of buying an herbal supplement because it's "natural"—and therefore has to be good for you—just remember, bee stings and poison ivy are also "natural."

Implied Main Idea   a. Synthetic products are better for you than natural ones are.

   b. We shouldn't just assume that "natural" products are safe.

   c. The word *natural* is a big selling point for all kinds of products.

2. In 1995, gray wolves, listed as an endangered species, were reintroduced into Yellowstone National Park, where they had once roamed freely. To the surprise of biologists, the wolves multiplied faster than expected, so much so that their status is now listed as "threatened" rather than endangered. Perhaps because of the population spurt, the wolves have begun to stray outside the park's boundaries. In a few cases, they have ventured onto bordering ranch lands and killed domestic livestock. The U.S. Fish and Wildlife Service responded quickly by shooting or capturing the wolves believed to be preying on livestock. But some ranchers have taken the law into their own hands and shot the wolves themselves. The ranchers want the legal right to shoot any wolf that ventures onto their property.

Implied Main Idea   a. The reintroduction of gray wolves was a bad idea from the beginning.

   b. The reintroduction of gray wolves into Yellowstone National Park proves that endangered animals can be saved by human intervention.

c. The 1995 reintroduction of gray wolves into Yellowstone National Park has saved them from extinction; however, it has also caused some serious problems.

3. Currently, children in the United States receive more vaccinations than ever before. On average, they get approximately twenty-four inoculations for fourteen different diseases. As a result, potential killers such as polio and diphtheria are all but unknown in the United States. One would think that would be cause for gratitude among parents anxious to protect their children from illness. But some parents are not so thrilled. Instead, they worry about the possible adverse effects of so many vaccinations. Wary about the possibility that vaccines might do their children harm, a growing number of parents are limiting the number of vaccinations their children can receive, a practice known as "shot limiting." In some cases, they are refusing to let their children be vaccinated at all. According to a 2011 study reported in the journal *Pediatrics*, one in ten parents has decided to delay vaccinations, refused to grant permission for all the standard vaccinations, or refused to vaccinate altogether. Public health officials worry that parental reluctance concerning vaccinations will have dangerous consequences. Diseases once considered threats of the past, thanks to vaccinations, may make a comeback. In 2010 and 2012, for instance, outbreaks of whooping cough occurred for the first time in decades.

Implied Main Idea

a. Although vaccinating America's children has had obvious benefits, some parents still worry about possible adverse reactions and are limiting or refusing inoculations.

b. Parents who delay, limit, or refuse vaccinations for their children are doing them more harm than good.

c. Anxious about their children's health, some parents have launched a very public fight against unnecessary vaccinations.

4. It's common knowledge that bullying is a problem both in elementary and high school. When we think of bullying, we think of it as a kid-on-kid issue. Donald Brian Wood, however, might not agree. Wood is an algebra teacher who had a meltdown in front of his students after he could not get them to quiet down. When the students kept on goading him, Wood threw a chair out the window. One of Wood's students filmed the teacher's emotional collapse and put

it on YouTube. Wood was placed on administrative leave, since it was clear from the video that he had lost control of himself and his classroom. Kathy Klein, a 68-year-old bus monitor, did keep control of herself, limiting her reaction to the elementary school students taunting her by saying quietly, "If you can't say something nice, don't say it." But her mild reprimand didn't help. Surrounded by jeering students shouting insults, Klein, too, ended up on YouTube because someone on the bus filmed her humiliation. According to Elizabeth Englander, executive director of the Massachusetts Aggression Reduction Center, this kind of behavior among students occurs when students feel themselves part of a pack and individual responsibility evaporates. Englander argues that students need to learn "digital citizenship." Let's hope they learn it soon since according to a 2012[†] report, one in five teachers claims to have been the victim of what's come to be known as *cyberbaiting*, incidents in which students goad a teacher or an aide into breaking down, film the emotional collapse, and then post it on YouTube.

Implied Main Idea

a. Cyberbaiting may or may not be a real issue of concern, since so far there has been only one major attempt to verify its existence.

b. Cyberbaiting is a new term, coined to identify a troubling phenomenon in which students goad a teacher or an aide into a public meltdown so they can film it and post it on the Web.

c. Cyberbaiting is another indication that technology in the classroom is not having the beneficial effect many expected.

[†]The report was conducted by Symantec, the maker of anti-virus software.

> ## TEST 5   Recognizing the Implied Main Idea

DIRECTIONS   Read each paragraph. Then circle the letter of the implied main idea.

1. According to the rules of their order, Carmelite nuns begin their days at the crack of dawn. Rising at 5:00 a.m., they sing hymns and eat breakfast. Breakfast, like the rest of their meals, is simple. The nuns are not allowed to eat meat. In addition, they have taken a vow of poverty, so rich food is out of the question. Once breakfast is over, the Carmelites spend their days doing chores or saying prayers. Conversation of any sort is forbidden, as are visitors. If the nuns speak at all to outsiders, it is through an iron grill that symbolizes their separation from the world. As one might expect, radio, television, and computers are not usually found among the Carmelites.

Implied Main Idea

   a. In time, the rules of the Carmelite order are bound to become less strict.

   b. Most Carmelite nuns enter the order because they have been wounded by the world.

   c. The Carmelites will never change the strict rules of their order.

   d. The rules of the Carmelite order ensure that the nuns lead a life of solitude and simplicity.

2. History books have long insisted that the Spanish explorer Hernando Cortés defeated the Aztec Empire after Montezuma, the empire's too-trusting king, welcomed Cortés into Tenochtitlan (now Mexico City) and extended him his hospitality. Cortés returned the courtesy by throwing Montezuma into jail. Then, with the help of a few hundred men and the arrival of European diseases like typhus and smallpox, he turned the Aztec Empire into a Spanish colony. That, in any case, is the conventional version of events. But now researchers at an archaeological dig about 100 miles east of modern Mexico City have unearthed hundreds of skeletons, bones, and ancient objects that tell another story. The remains found are from a 1520 caravan of Spanish conquistadors, their families, and servants, all of whom were on their way to Tenochtitlan, probably to help put the finishing touches on Cortés's defeat of the Aztecs. According to Enrique Martinez, director of the dig, the newfound evidence strongly suggests that the travelers were set upon and captured by

Aztec warriors. The captors then apparently kept their victims in cages for an extended period of time, perhaps up to six months. During that time, Aztec priests made regular selections of those who were to be used as human sacrifices in religious rituals. Close examination also suggests that the caravan's captors engaged in cannibalism, eating the bodies of those who had been sacrificed. This seems to explain why Cortés named the town where it all happened "Tecuaque," which means "where people were eaten."

Implied Main Idea

a. Historians have underestimated the courage of Montezuma's warriors.

b. Enrique Martinez has found conclusive evidence that cannibalism was part of Aztec society.

c. A new archaeological discovery disputes the notion that the Aztecs let themselves be conquered without fighting back.

d. In at least one instance, Cortés's followers got exactly what they deserved for plundering the great Aztec Empire.

3. Spectacled cobras—six-foot-long brown snakes that can kill with a single bite—are everywhere in the country of Sri Lanka. It's not surprising, therefore, that thousands of people are bitten yearly. Many victims are children, and some of them die. What's surprising is that most Sri Lankans will not harm a cobra that happens to venture into a nearby woodpile or rice field. The majority of Sri Lankans are Buddhists. According to their religion, the spectacled cobra once gave shelter to Buddha by opening the hood at the back of its neck. To show that the cobra was under his protection, Buddha is said to have given the snake the spectacles-like red mark that appears on the back of its head.

Implied Main Idea

a. Given the number of people who die from snake bites, the people of Sri Lanka should stop worshipping cobras.

b. The people of Sri Lanka should do something about the threat of cobra bites to their children.

c. The people of Sri Lanka do not kill cobras because they believe the snakes are under the protection of Buddha.

d. Should the number of victims suffering from cobra bites continue to rise, the people of Sri Lanka are bound to change their attitudes toward cobras.

4. Listeria is a food-borne bacterium that has been found in hot dogs, deli meats, soft cheeses, undercooked meat, poultry, and seafood. On a yearly basis, listeria sickens about 2,500 Americans. One serious outbreak of listeria poisoning, in 1998, was traced to meat processed at a Sara Lee Corporation plant in Michigan. The company had to recall fifteen million pounds of hot dogs and luncheon meats. In 2002, seven people died after eating Wampler brand turkey tainted by listeria. In 2011, thirteen people died and seventy-two were sickened after eating cantaloupe contaminated by listeria. In the healthy, listeria is an unpleasant nuisance, causing flu-like symptoms that last several days. But if the elderly are stricken by listeria poisoning, they can die from it. If a pregnant woman ingests the bacterium, a miscarriage or a stillbirth often results, even if the mother herself experiences no symptoms.

Implied Main Idea

    a. Processed meats have long been the source of food poisoning.

    b. Given the high incidence of listeria poisoning, it is surprising that meatpacking plants are not required to test for it.

    c. Outbreaks of listeria poisoning are bound to increase.

    d. Depending on who is stricken, listeria poisoning can be an unpleasant nuisance or a deadly tragedy.

5. Those who claim that a U.S. president must be exceptionally smart to be elected to the office might want to consider the career of our twenty-ninth president, Warren G. Harding (1921–1923). Harding was considered none too bright by most of the people he worked with. An incurious man, he mainly liked to play poker and golf, drink, and chase women. Thought by many historians to be one of the worst presidents in history, Harding never really wanted the job. But his wife Florence wanted him to be president, and she pushed him hard. Prodded by Florence, Harding rose from one office to another. Elected to the U.S. Senate in 1914, he was absent for most of the important votes. What Harding had going for him were his looks. The man looked presidential. He also had a magnificent speaking voice, which served to disguise the fact that he had little or nothing to say. According to former Secretary of the Treasury William McAdoo, Harding had mastered the art of making flowery speeches that consisted of fancy "phrases moving over the landscape in search of an idea."

Implied Main Idea

a. Warren G. Harding was lucky to have a wife like Florence.

b. The career of Warren G. Harding suggests that not all presidents are exceptionally smart.

c. Historians have never treated Warren G. Harding fairly.

d. Warren G. Harding's magnificent speaking voice and gift with words were what got him the job as president.

▶ **TEST 6**   **Inferring the Implied Main Idea**

DIRECTIONS   Read each paragraph. Then write the implied main idea in the blanks that follow.

1. Some people claim that declawing a cat does no real harm, but for reasons of their own, they are denying the obvious. Cats remove old skin and dry hair by scratching themselves. A cat without claws can't groom itself properly. Cats also need their claws to jump. A cat's claws are like landing gear. They help cats maintain their balance. If deprived of claws, the animals find it hard to jump from place to place. Worst of all, if a declawed house cat escapes its home, it could quickly die of starvation. Grabbing for a mouse or bird would be an empty gesture, leaving the cat to starve. An even more horrible fate awaits the declawed cat who gets into a fight with another animal.

Implied Main Idea   _____

_____

2. On December 18, 1912, an amateur archaeologist named Charles Dawson and his friend, Arthur Smith Woodward, presented what they claimed were extraordinary findings to the Geological Society of London. Woodward and Dawson presented the skeleton of a creature alleged to be half-man and half-ape. The two men claimed they had discovered what was believed to be the missing link between humans and apes. With relatively little investigation, Piltdown man—as the skeleton came to be called—was accepted as genuine. As time went by, however, doubts began to surface, and researchers examined and reexamined the skeleton. In 1953, close analysis of the skeleton revealed that someone had created it by fusing together the bones of a human being and an orangutan.

Implied Main Idea   _____

_____

3. Why do so few women pursue careers in science and engineering?[†] A common answer has been that these are socially defined as male

---

[†]It should be noted here that the percentage of women in engineering and science has been steadily increasing.

occupations, and women are discouraged from entering them, either by negative attitudes or by actual discrimination. Even more popular is the idea that childhood socialization gives women negative feelings about these careers. Some even have proposed that biological differences are involved, that women excel at relational thinking, while men excel at linear thinking, which is better suited for doing science. Ironically, some feminists have, perhaps unwittingly, encouraged this biological view by claiming that women do think differently and that a feminist approach would lead to better science. (Adapted from Stark. *Sociology*, 10th ed., p. 169, © Cengage Learning.)

Implied Main Idea _____

_____

4. Vitamin A helps with vision, bone growth, and healthy skin. A deficiency in vitamin A can produce eye diseases. Dairy products, nuts, and yellow vegetables all contain vitamin A. Vitamin C helps fight colds and is essential to healthy teeth. Oranges, lemons, tomatoes, and strawberries all contain this important vitamin. Vitamin D, the sunshine vitamin, helps keep bones and teeth strong; a lack of this vitamin can contribute to arthritis. Fish and eggs are the best sources of vitamin D. The vitamin B complex—B_1, B_2, B_6, and B_{12}—is also extremely important. It keeps the skin healthy and develops muscle tone. Vitamin B may even help reduce stress and tension. Green, leafy vegetables, milk, and grains help supply this important group of vitamins.

Implied Main Idea _____

_____

▶ **TEST 7**   **Inferring the Implied Main Idea**

DIRECTIONS   Read each paragraph. Then write the implied main idea in the blanks that follow.

1. During the Civil War, the first war to be covered by newspaper journalists, some reporters considered it their duty to rally the troops. During the famous battle of Bull Run, for example, Edmund Clarence Stedman of the *New York World* would wave the regiment flag whenever he thought the troops he was covering were losing their will to fight. Junius Browne from the *New York Tribune* went a step further. If he thought a rebel sniper was in the surrounding area, he would pick up a gun and start firing. Aware that Union[†] leader Ulysses S. Grant liked to drink, Sylvanus Cadwallader of the *Chicago Times* did his part to win the war: He locked himself and Grant in the bathroom to keep the general from hitting the bottle. Even more than his colleagues, Samuel Wilkeson of the *New York Times* participated in the war he covered. After the bloody battle of Gettysburg, Wilkeson wrote his report standing beside the grave of his oldest son.

Implied Main Idea   _____

_____

2. In the stable and moist conditions of the tropical rain forests, plants and animals are more varied and diverse than anywhere else on Earth. The variety and diversity of the rain forest makes it a treasure trove for all kinds of riches, from exotic perfumes to cures for deadly diseases. Yet every year, a rain-forest region the size of Belgium is cut down to make way for agriculture. The cutting occurs despite the fact that the soil in the rain forest is not particularly suitable for either growing or grazing. The soil is sandy. Lacking nutrients from the trees, it quickly becomes too dry to be useful for farming or herding. Still, the cutting continues, although no one knows what miraculous cure for disease has been lost in the process.

Implied Main Idea   _____

_____

_____
[†]Union: loyal to the U.S. government during the Civil War.

3. Lasers, devices that produce an intense, focused beam of light, have been around since 1960, when Theodore H. Maiman put the first one together. At the time, however, no one quite knew what to do with the laser. In fact, in the 1960s and early 1970s, the laser was often described as a solution looking for a good problem. But today, no one makes that little joke any more. Laser technology is being used to correct vision problems. Many who undergo laser surgery no longer need glasses to see. Lasers are also now commonly used to remove cataracts and gallstones. Heart surgeons also use them to remove blood clots from coronary arteries. In addition to medical uses, lasers are important tools of the military. They are central to all kinds of weaponry, including the so-called "smart" bombs. Moreover, traveling at the speed of light, lasers can burn a hole in missiles or their warheads and thereby render them ineffective. They are also a central part of military warning and detecting systems. In addition, lasers have found their place in industry. They play a key role in machine-tool operations, communication systems, tunnel construction, and welding.

Implied Main Idea _____

_____

4. The first successful blood transfusion was performed in the seventeenth century, but the practice was outlawed because of the dangers it posed to the patient. The practice was revived in the nineteenth century, but it was accompanied by terrible risks, like blood clots and kidney failure. Austrian-born Karl Landsteiner (1868–1943), however, had a theory. He argued that the blood of humans had inborn differences and similarities. The key, from Landsteiner's perspective, was to understand both the differences and the similarities. Once they were understood, Landsteiner thought the risks of blood transfusion might be eliminated. To that end, he analyzed numerous blood samples. By 1901, he had classified blood donors into three different categories called A, B, and O (AB was added in 1902). Following that discovery, the transfusion of blood became a relatively safe procedure.

Implied Main Idea _____

_____

5. In 1789 the French Revolution exploded in France with far-reaching consequences. The revolution even reached across the ocean to the tiny island of Saint Dominique, which was under French control. A slave on the island named Toussaint Bréda heard and took to heart the revolution's passionate slogans about extending rights and independence to all men, not just those wearing royal cloth and not just those with white skin. When slave owners on Saint Dominique rebelled against the new revolutionary government's demand to end slavery on the island, France's revolutionaries backtracked, unwilling to live up to the promise of their early slogans. Bréda, however, had taken the promise of freedom for all seriously, and he wasn't backing down. Calling himself Toussaint L'Ouverture ("the one who finds an opening"), the now ex-slave successfully fought the French soldiers who came to support not the rights of man but the rights of slaveholders. The war to end slavery on the island continued for fourteen years with Toussaint L'Ouverture outwitting all those who came up against him. The situation looked so hopeless for the French that France's new leader, Napoleon Bonaparte, invited L'Ouverture to negotiate terms of peace with the promise of safe conduct. When L'Ouverture arrived for the meeting, Napoleon had him thrown in jail, where he died of cold, hunger, and neglect. His soldiers fought on despite his loss until 1803 when Napoleon granted the island its independence and it assumed the name it had always been called by its black inhabitants, Haiti, meaning "land of mountains."

Implied Main Idea   _____

_____

9

Understanding the Role of Inferences in Longer Readings

"Much of what we understand—whether when listening or reading—we understand indirectly, by inference."

—WRITER DAN KURLAND

"The common characteristic of inferences is that they are statements about matters which are not directly known, statements made on the basis of what has been observed."

—S.I. HAYAKAWA, *LANGUAGE IN THOUGHT AND ACTION*

You already know how to infer the main ideas of paragraphs. But as you might have guessed, implied main ideas aren't limited to paragraphs. They also turn up in longer, multi-paragraph readings. This chapter will give you some examples of readings unified by an implied, rather than a stated, main idea. It will also show you how to use the writer's clues to come up with your inferred version of a thesis statement.

Chapter 9 will also talk more about another kind of inference essential to reading longer selections. It will show you how readers supply the inferences that link paragraphs together in support of an overall meaning or main idea. And finally, it will look at a skill essential for just about every college course, summary writing.

Implied Main Ideas Can Sum Up Longer Readings

In longer readings, the controlling main idea is usually expressed in a thesis statement. Although the length of the reading plays a key role in the location of that thesis statement, somewhere within the first three or four paragraphs is the most likely location. This is particularly true of chapter sections within textbooks, because textbook writers are not concerned with creating a mood or heightening suspense. They want to make sure their readers absorb a lot of new information as quickly as possible. With that goal in mind, they are likely to introduce the thesis statement fairly quickly so readers don't miss it. Only occasionally does it appear at the very end.

That doesn't mean, however, that every chapter section will have a thesis statement. Writers of all kinds, and that includes writers of textbooks, do sometimes expect readers to infer the implied main idea that unifies an entire reading. Here's an example:

The Gorilla's Two Faces

Paragraphs 1 to 2 suggest the reading is only about Gorilla Monsoon being wrestling's first real bad guy.

1   Even many die-hard wrestling fans don't remember his name anymore, but in the mid-sixties, the wrestler Gorilla Monsoon was a major star. At 6 feet and 5 inches, Monsoon was a towering figure. He weighed more than four hundred pounds and fought some eight thousand bouts. When announcers said his name, their voices tended to quaver a little, for Gorilla was wrestling's first real "bad guy." He was the wrestler audiences loved to hate because he was tougher and meaner than anyone else around.

2   Wearing a body suit with one strap draped over a massive shoulder, Gorilla would enter the ring looking as if he could, in a hungry moment,

Bettmann/Corbis.

One of the stars of wrestling in the sixties and seventies, Gorilla Monsoon, a.k.a. Robert Marella, went on to become a play-by-play announcer for the World Wrestling Entertainment company.

chew and digest rusty nails. After toying with his opponent for a while, he usually liked to end the bout with the "airplane spin," the wrestling hold that made him famous. Knocking his opponent to the floor, he would wrap the man's feet around his enormous waist. Seemingly without effort, he would then lift and twirl his opponent round and round, keeping him at waist level for at least thirty seconds. To further embroider his image of pure evil, Gorilla would cackle with laughter the entire time. Staged or not, it was a terrifying display, and the audience couldn't get enough of it.

Notice now how the transition "out of the ring" sets the reader up for a change in perspective.

3   Out of the ring, however, Gorilla Monsoon was Robert Marella. Quiet and soft-spoken, Mr. Marella, as he liked to be called, was college educated. Prior to becoming a professional wrestler, he had thought about becoming an English teacher. But teaching wasn't particularly lucrative. Wrestling paid better, and so "Gorilla Monsoon" was born.

4   Despite his brutal appearance in the ring, Marella had a way with words. When asked why anyone would ever pay to see grown men throw one another around in a ring, he paraphrased St. Augustine:[†] "For those who believe in our sport, no explanation is necessary."

5   He was equally articulate* when interviewed, long past his heyday, about the current state of wrestling. Asked about the new and more profitable face of wrestling, he shrugged it off as little more than people from the pages of "comic books." From Marella's perspective, wrestling in the old days was a more serious sport, and wrestlers were treated with both respect and fear. As he put it, "People really thought I was the Devil." (Source of quotations: David Hadju, "When Wrestling Was Noir,"[†] *New York Times Magazine*, January 2, 2000, p. 43.)

Drawing the Logical Inference

The sample reading breaks into two sections. The first section, paragraphs 1 and 2, deals with the man in the ring. Here is where we learn about Gorilla Monsoon's public image. He was the wrestler everyone loved to hate. But in the second section of the reading—paragraphs 3–5—a new and different image emerges, along with Gorilla's real name, Robert Marella. We are told that, out of the ring, Marella was anything but the hulking bully he portrayed in it. He was soft-spoken, well-read, and an intellectual.

[†]St. Augustine (354–430): Catholic saint who, when questioned about his faith, responded, "For those who believe, no explanation is necessary."
*articulate: well-spoken, good with words.
[†]noir: a term usually applied to books or movies about characters who were dangerous and living outside the mainstream.

Yet if we look for a thesis statement that sums up both sides of Gorilla's personality, we won't find it. Almost all the sentences in the reading are equally specific. No general statement sums them up. Instead, readers are left to infer one like the following: "Sixties wrestler Gorilla Monsoon may have been a brute in the ring, but out of it, he was a smart, thoughtful man who took his profession seriously." As it should, that inference functions like a thesis statement. It sums up the main idea of the entire reading.

Like paragraphs with topic sentences, longer readings usually express the main idea in a thesis statement. But that's not always the case. If you read an article, an essay, or a chapter section and don't find any general statements that summarize the meaning of the more specific ones, you need to infer one.

READING TIPS

1. Readings that break apart in the middle with the author moving on to a point different from the one developed by the opening paragraphs are very likely to imply rather than state the main idea of the reading.

2. Writing that (1) compares and contrasts two topics, (2) talks about the difference between the past and present, and (3) opens with a question but doesn't follow with an immediate answer is very likely to imply rather than state the main idea of the reading.

From Reader to Writer Write two or three paragraphs that contrast how you think about a person, place, or event now as opposed to when you were a child. Start by explaining how you felt as a kid (e.g., "When I was little, I thought my dad was much too strict"). Make sure to give a specific example or two that illustrates what you mean, for instance, "We were in serious trouble if we came home even five minutes after curfew." When you finish the section on childhood, use a reversal or time transition to take your reader with you as you describe how your feelings have changed. "Now that I have kids of my own, I realize that my dad was trying. . . ." Again, be specific about how your thinking has changed. Overall, let the contrast between then and now tell your readers what they need to know. Don't provide a thesis statement to sum up the difference between you as a kid and you as an adult. Let your examples speak for themselves.

Checking Your Inference Against the Author's Words

As with paragraphs, you need to make sure that the main idea you infer fits the information provided by the author. Once you infer the main idea, go through each paragraph and check to see what it adds to your understanding of the main idea you inferred. If the individual paragraph main ideas and the overall main idea you inferred don't seem to have any relationship, you need to re-think your initial inference.

SUMMING UP THE KEY POINTS

1. Like individual paragraphs, longer multi-paragraph readings don't always state the main idea directly. Sometimes they leave out the thesis statement and provide enough clues for readers to infer the overall or controlling main idea of the reading.

2. Inferring the implied main idea of a reading is only part of the reader's job. The next step is to check the implied main idea against the author's actual words. There has to be a connection between them. If the supporting paragraphs don't match the main idea the reader has inferred, then there is something wrong with the reader's inference.

▶ **EXERCISE 1**   **Recognizing Implied Main Ideas**

DIRECTIONS   Read each selection. Then circle the letter of the statement implied by the reading.

1. The Future of Genetic Testing

1   In August 2000, a test-tube baby named Adam Nash was born in Denver, Colorado. After cutting Adam's umbilical cord, doctors collected some cells from that cord. A month later, they infused those same cells into the body of Adam's six-year-old sister, Molly. The procedure saved Molly's life.

2   Afflicted with a rare bone marrow disease called Fanconi anemia, Molly's only hope was a cell transplant from a sibling. Because both parents carried the Fanconi gene, which gave them a 25 percent chance of giving birth to a child carrying the same disease as Molly, doctors needed to select an embryo not affected by the disease-carrying gene. That selection process could only be carried out in an

in vitro†-produced pregnancy followed by sophisticated gene testing. Doctors would test embryo cells to discover which of them did not carry the diseased gene and then impregnate the mother with only those cells that tested normal.

3   In part at least, the Nash case† resembles a similar one from 1989, which involved sixteen-year-old Anissa Ayala, a young girl diagnosed with a lethal form of leukemia. In an effort to save her life, the girl's father, Abe Ayala, had his vasectomy reversed so that he and his wife, Mary, could have a third child who would be a bone marrow donor for Anissa. Although the Ayalas had a one-in-four chance of having a child with the right cells to be a donor, luck was on their side. Genetic testing showed that Anissa's newborn sister, Marissa, had inherited all the right genes, and she did, in fact, prove to be an ideal donor. Thanks to Marissa, Anissa got a new lease on life.

4   In situations like these where a child's suffering can be cured, genetic testing does indeed seem like a godsend. Certainly, this position is promoted by Charles Strom, director of the Illinois Masonic Medical Center, which was heavily involved in both cases. Thanks to genetic testing, lives can be saved and tragedy avoided. As long as the children born to be donors are loved, says Strom, that's all that matters; and in both cases, the children born to save their siblings are very much cherished.

5   Yet both cases have raised a central question: Are the increasing sophistication and use of genetic testing where reproduction is involved always a cause for jubilation?* If you ask Leon Kass, former chief of the President's Council on Bioethics,† the answer is no. Like other bioethicists before him, Mr. Kass takes issue with the idea of children coming into the world to be donors. He fears that eventually the children will feel exploited by their parents and angry at the siblings they helped save. Other bioethicists like Jeffrey Kahn, director of the University of Minnesota's Center for Bioethics, don't take issue with parents bringing a child into the world in order to be a donor. Instead, Kahn fears a future in which reproductive technology allows some parents—primarily those who can afford it—to choose their children's physical and mental makeup.

---

†in vitro: taking place in a test tube.
†As of 2014, both Adam and Molly Nash were doing fine. If you would like to know more about the two siblings, there is also a 2012 YouTube video of Molly Nash talking about her life and about Fanconia anemia.
*jubilation: joy, triumph, celebration.
†bioethics: the study of moral and ethical implications caused by new scientific discoveries. The Council on Bioethics was a group appointed by then president George W. Bush, and it met between 2002 and 2009.

6   Kahn, who is as pessimistic as Strom is hopeful, claims that having a child "is quickly becoming like buying a new car." Parents can choose the options they do or do not want. He believes that as genetic tests become more available to the public, there will be more and more parents attempting to create "designer babies," and parents will be asking for "embryos without a predisposition* to homosexuality or for kids who will grow to more than six feet tall." (Sources of information: Abigail Trafford, "Miracle Babies Draw Us into an Ethical Swamp," *Washington Post*, November 14, 2000, p. 28; Dan Vergano, "Embryo Genetic Screening Controversial—and Successful," *USA Today*, January 10, 2010, available on the Web.)

Implied Main Idea

a. The negative consequences of genetic testing far outweigh its positive uses.

b. Genetic testing should not be allowed to play a role in human reproduction.

c. Thanks to genetic testing, children like Molly Nash now have a chance to lead a normal life.

d. Genetic testing as the basis for human reproduction has become the center of an ethical controversy.

2. The Pros and Cons of Tort Reform

1   In Houston, a woman who scalded herself with hot coffee sued McDonald's and won $2.9 million (later reduced to a "mere" $480,000). In Maine, a woman golfer hit a shot that bounced off an obstacle and struck her in the face. She sued the country club and won $40,000. In Connecticut, a twelve-year-old Little League baseball player uncorked a wild throw that conked a woman in the stands. The woman promptly sued the player and the local government. In New York City, several prison inmates somehow shot themselves in the feet and then sued the city for negligence.

2   Such stories seem to be increasingly common, as 800,000 lawyers in the United States seek to justify their existence and citizens look for an easy dollar instead of for a sense of personal responsibility. The results are a reduction in the gross national product of an estimated $2.5 million per attorney, personal and corporate financial tragedies, and local governments that must hike taxes to cover legal fees and liability settlements.

---

*predisposition: leaning, inclination, or tendency toward a particular condition or behavior.

3   The biggest problem is that of *torts*, damage suits over product liability,* personal injury, medical malpractice, and related claims. Throughout the twentieth century, state courts gradually eliminated restrictions on tort liability and substituted legal doctrines favoring plaintiffs* over defendants. For example, nearly all states have a strict liability rule for product safety. This means that manufacturers of defective products (or even very hot coffee) may be held fully liable for damages caused by their product, regardless of whether the manufacturer was negligent.

4   Today, state legislatures are actively engaged in tort reform that shifts the advantage more toward defendants. Punitive damage awards have been capped in Alabama, New Jersey, Illinois, Texas, and other states. Laws protecting local governments and their employees from exorbitant* liability awards have been adopted in several states. There has been a surge of business interest in judicial* elections in California and other states, as judges known for generous tort decisions have come under electoral* attack and, in some cases, gone down to defeat.

5   Aligned against tort reform are powerful trial lawyers; litigation,* product liability, and personal injury suits are their bread and butter. Also against tort reform are certain consumer groups, who see unlimited tort liability as a fundamental right for injured citizens and a means to hold individuals and firms accountable for shoddy and dangerous practices and merchandise. These opponents of tort reform are fighting against insurance companies, manufacturers, and others in courtrooms and in state capitols. They have been aided in their battle by the supreme courts of several states (e.g., Indiana, Ohio, and Oregon), which have overturned tort reforms. (Adapted from Bowman and Kearney, *State and Local Government*, 7th ed., p. 268, © Cengage Learning.)

Implied Main Idea

    a. Tort reform has been a long time coming, but the public, fed up with lawsuits, has decided to take the plunge and reduce the rewards of litigation.

    b. While many states are actively engaged in tort reform, both lawyers and consumers fear that the reforms will go too far.

---

*liability: responsibility for a mistake or malfunction.
*plaintiffs: people who bring a suit to court in order to win damages.
*exorbitant: excessive, especially in the sense of price or demands.
*judicial: related to the courts and judges.
*electoral: related to voting in elections.
*litigation: legal proceeding in a courtroom, lawsuit to win damages.

c. Lawsuits over product liability are a menace to the economy and to citizens' sense of personal liability; they are fueled more by the lure of easy money than by any real harm done by a product.

d. Although state legislators are working hard to protect companies from lawsuits over product liability, consumers do not support their efforts.

From Reader to Writer Use the Web to define the term *savior sibling*. Then read three or four discussions of why some people support the birth of savior siblings while others are appalled, or outraged, by the idea. Consider where and how you agree or disagree with the two different points of view. Follow your definition of the term with reasons why you are for or against this practice. The two websites that follow offer two different perspectives or points of view. http://www.cbc-network .org/2011/03/savior-siblings-start-us-down-harrowing-ethical- path/ and http://www.rsrevision.com/GCSE/christian_perspectives/ genetics/saviour_siblings/for.htm.

READING TIP

Look to the beginning of paragraphs to infer the answers to two questions that should *always* be on a reader's mind: Why does this paragraph follow the previous one? What connects them to one another?

▶ EXERCISE 2   Inferring Implied Main Ideas

DIRECTIONS   Read each selection and infer the implied main idea. Then write your inference in the blank lines that follow.

EXAMPLE

Are You Sure You Want to Be a Leader?

1 The word *leader* has positive connotations for most people. Thus, most of us, if asked whether we would like to be in a position of leadership, will say yes. To be sure, being a leader has its satisfactions. Leadership brings with it power and prestige. Often it brings status, respect, and opportunities for professional advancement and financial gain. Yet those of us intent on pursuing leadership roles in our professional lives don't always take into

account the fact that leaders are usually expected to work longer hours than other employees are. Actually, people in organizational leadership positions typically spend about fifty-five hours per week working. During periods of peak demand, this figure can rise to eighty hours per week.

2   Being a leader is also a good way to discover the truth of Murphy's law: "If anything can go wrong, it will." A leader is constantly required to solve numerous problems involving both people and things. Because of those problems and the difficulties attendant* on solving them, many people find leadership positions enormously stressful. As a result, many managers experience burnout and abandon their positions.

3   In addition, people in managerial positions complain repeatedly that they are held responsible for things over which they have little control. As a leader, for example, you might be expected to work with an ill-performing team member, yet you might not have the power to fire him or her. You might also be called on to produce a high-quality service or product but not be given the staff or the funds to get the job done effectively.

4   In a sense, the higher you rise as a leader, the more lonely you are likely to be. After all, leadership limits the number of people in whom you can confide. It is awkward, not to mention unprofessional, to complain about one of your employees to another employee. Then, too, you need to be wary about voicing complaints against your superiors to the people who work for you. Such complaints are bad for morale. Even worse, they can threaten your job security. Not surprisingly, people in leadership positions complain that they miss being "one of the gang."

5   People at all levels of an organization, from the office assistant to the chairperson of the board, must be aware of political factors. Yet you can avoid politics more easily as an individual contributor than you can as a leader. As a leader you have to engage in political byplay from three directions: below, sideways, and upward. Political tactics such as forming alliances and coalitions are a necessary part of a leader's role. (Adapted from Dubrin, *Leadership*, 6th ed., pp. 16–17, © Cengage Learning.)

Implied Main Idea   Although being a leader has some very positive consequences, it also has some negative ones that need to be carefully considered.

EXPLANATION   The first paragraph opens by describing the positive consequences of being a leader. The remaining paragraphs describe the negative effects of assuming a leadership role. Yet if you look for a

*attendant: related to, connected to.

general statement that sums up both the positive and the negative consequences of leadership, you won't find it. What this means is that the reader has to draw an inference like the one shown above.

1. The Reality of Prison Life

1   Many Americans firmly believe that prison inmates spend their days lifting weights, watching television, or playing basketball while hardworking taxpayers pay for prisoners' food, clothing, shelter, education, and health care. However, in a minimum-security prison, the day typically begins with a wake-up call at 6:00 a.m. Prisoners then head for the community bathrooms. Because hundreds of men often share a bathroom, they usually wait in line to use the facilities. Inmates are also expected to make their beds and clean their cells.

2   Prisons are noisy. Arguments, fistfights, and robberies among convicts are common. Many prisons, even those in sweltering southern states, are not air-conditioned. In spite of regular cleaning, they often smell of urine and body odor because fresh air cannot enter the sealed buildings.

3   At many institutions, prisoners might attend psychological counseling or educational programs for part of the day, the goal of which is to provide personal improvement. But everyone who is able usually works between four and eight hours daily. At some of this country's penal institutions, inmates labor in prison factories where they are paid between $0.10 and $1.35 per hour. Others are assigned to food service, laundry, maintenance, or janitorial service. A typical workday lasts from 7:30 a.m. to 3:30 p.m., with a break for lunch. Yet the majority of prisoners earn less than $25 a month, out of which they must buy their snacks, sodas, aspirins, and toiletries.

4   At 4:00 p.m. every day, prisoners must be in their cells and on their feet while guards count heads and make sure everyone is present. From 4:30 p.m. until the evening meal and then again until about 9:30 p.m., prisoners read mail, watch one of three available television channels, exercise, play cards and board games, or receive visitors. After these visits, prisoners are strip-searched before going back to their cell blocks, where they can watch television, wait in long lines to use the telephone, or visit with other inmates until lights out at 11:30. (Source of information: http://people.howstuffworks.com/prison1.htm.)

Implied Main Idea

_____

_____

2. Is Local News Really News?

1   Do you consider yourself an informed citizen because you're in the habit of watching the local news? If you do, you might want to consider how you are defining the word *informed*. Think about it. While watching your local news, it's unlikely that you will see or hear many reports about significant events concerning politics, culture, business, and government. Instead, you're probably learning about violent crimes, major accidents, deadly disasters, and celebrity breakups.

2   In a half-hour local news broadcast, only about fifteen minutes are left once the time for commercials, weather, sports, traffic, and bantering by news anchors is subtracted. This is not much time to relate all of the news of the day. Therefore, each individual news story is, by necessity, quite short. In fact, studies have shown that 70 percent of all news stories are no more than a minute long. Forty-three percent are less than thirty seconds long. Only about 16 percent of stories are longer than two minutes; in the television news industry, any story more than a minute and a half long is billed as an "in-depth" report.

3   Typically, the television news anchors who introduce or read these stories are not experts in any of the fields—such as education, the environment, business, government, and health—that are covered. Most are hired not for their understanding of the news but for their ability to read a story well while conveying the appropriate emotion (anger, fear, sympathy, admiration, disgust, etc.). The reporters who gather the news are not experts either. They are hired primarily for their ability to communicate well on camera, as well as for their writing skill and general common sense.

4   Local news reporters are under tremendous pressure to produce a story. They usually get their assignments about mid-morning. That leaves them only a few hours to gather the facts and write the story so that it can be ready for a 5:00 or 6:00 p.m. broadcast. As a result, reporters have little time for research, making their sources rather thin: Only 25 percent of TV news stories have more than one source. Not surprisingly, news directors avoid assigning hundreds of important stories that would require some real research.

5   The truth is that television news broadcasts feature stories that readily lend themselves to videotape footage and pictures. For that reason, there's little coverage of events that are important but difficult to illustrate, such as political speeches, school board meetings, or city council sessions. One survey revealed that only about 7 percent of news stories cover economic issues. Another study of six thousand news stories showed that only 9 percent of them concerned poverty

or welfare. Instead, TV news focuses on events that are relatively trivial but also very visual, and it tends to sensationalize those events by making them look even more dramatic than they actually were.

6   In addition to avoiding non-visual news stories, TV newscasts seldom include negative stories about their advertisers or about police officers and firefighters. According to one survey, more than half of news directors interviewed said that they had been pressured by advertisers to either kill critical stories or promote favorable ones. The largest number of consumer complaints concern new car dealerships, but because car dealers buy a lot of commercial airtime, they are rarely subjected to a news station's scrutiny.

7   Neither will viewers see many critical stories about grocery and cloth-ing stores, shopping malls, banks, insurance and health care providers, soda manufacturers, or fast food restaurants, all of which buy a signifi-cant amount of commercial airtime. Police and firefighters are also rarely cast in a negative light on local TV news stations because reporters need the cooperation of law enforcement and public safety officials to get the crime stories that are their lifeblood. That's why viewers see few, if any, stories about issues like radar traps, brutality, and/or police or firefighter mistakes. (For source of statistics: Amy Mitchell, "The Big Picture," in the online archives of the *Columbia Journalism Review*, January/February 1999; see also Greg Byron, "TV News: What Local Stations Don't Want You to Know," http://jerz.setonhill.edu/EL227/2009/08/31/.)

Implied Main Idea   _____

_____

✔ CHECK YOUR UNDERSTANDING

1. What should you do if you are reading a chapter section and don't find a general sentence or two that sums up the point of the reading?

_____

2. If the author hasn't put the main idea of the reading into a thesis statement, how can you know that your inference is correct?

_____

3. Which three methods of organizing information are very likely to imply rather than state the main idea?

_____

 ## Drawing Inferences to Connect Paragraphs

Reader-supplied inferences are essential for figuring out implied main ideas as well as supporting details. But you also need them to understand why one paragraph follows another. For an illustration of how drawing inferences is essential to tracking the author's train of thought through an extended reading, paragraph by paragraph, look at this next selection. Notice how readers need to draw inferences to determine why one paragraph follows another. Note as well that paragraph openings are particularly rich in clues to help readers determine how each new paragraph connects with the one that came before.

Projective Tests

The reading starts out focused on the Rorschach test. The title should encourage readers to infer that the Rorschach is a projective test. It should also encourage the idea that there is more than one projective test under discussion.

Here, to connect the first and second paragraph, the reader has to infer that the TAT is another kind of projective test, even though the author doesn't say so explicitly. But this is the only inference that fits the title, which tells the reader that more than one test will be discussed.

1   In projective tests, subjects are asked to describe or make up a story about images that are open to different interpretations. The **Rorschach** (Roar-shock) **Inkblot Test** is among the oldest and most widely used projective tests. Developed in the 1920s, it consists of 10 standardized inkblots that vary in color, shading, form, and complexity. Each time test subjects are shown an inkblot, they have to describe what they see in it. Differences in interpretation of the inkblot's content—"I see blood dripping from a dagger" versus "I see flowers in bloom"—are used to identify personal conflicts and fantasies. Particularly important are the parts of the inkblot that are used to construct an image. The goal of the test is to detect emotional disturbances by observing how differences in personality shape one's perception, or view of the world.

2   Less abstract than the Rorschach test, the **Thematic Apperception Test (TAT)** consists of 20 drawings. The drawings show people in situations that are open to various interpretations. During testing, subjects are shown each sketch and asked to make up a story about the people in it. Later on, they look at the drawings again and elaborate on their original story or else create a new one. In studying the stories produced, a psychologist might count, for instance, the number of times the central figure in a TAT story

From the opening phrase, with its emphasis on projective tests in general, the reader should immediately infer here that the author is ready to discuss both tests, not just one or the other.

Note how the opening phrase encourages the reader to infer that the author is now going to talk about what makes projective tests useful rather than unreliable.

is angry about being overlooked or ignored. If the same theme comes up frequently, then that might provide a therapist with some insight into a patient's general attitude toward the world.

3   Although projective tests have been around a very long time and are quite well known, how reliable they really are is open to question. After those undergoing testing interpret the inkblots or drawings, the interpretations are analyzed and further interpreted by the test scorers. In a sense, the interpretation of a projective test can be a projective test for the scorer, who may also be influenced by personal experiences.

4   Yet despite these drawbacks, projective tests still have value. This is especially true when they are used as part of a test battery (collection of assessment devices and interviews). In the hands of a skilled clinician, projective tests can be a good way to detect major conflicts, to get clients to talk about upsetting topics, and to set goals for therapy.

Focusing on Paragraph Openings

"What goes on at the beginning strongly determines how readers will understand what follows."
—Writer and researcher Joseph Williams, from *Style: Ten Lessons in Clarity and Grace*

Writers often use the openings of paragraphs to tell readers the direction they are taking. Consequently, you need to pay especially close attention to the beginnings of paragraphs. This is where you will get your strongest sense of what connects the previous paragraph to the one you are about to read. As you move from paragraph to paragraph, keep asking yourself questions like these:

1. Why is this paragraph here?

2. What does this paragraph have to do with the one that came before?

3. What connection does the author want me to make between the previous paragraph and the one I am reading now?

Over time, you'll get a good sense of the different kinds of clues to connections writers leave in order to guide readers along the path of their thinking.

Common Paragraph Relationships
●

When one paragraph follows another, the new paragraph might do any of the following:

1. show how the personal experience previously described has wider or general significance.

2. offer a more specific illustration of what's just been said.

3. add to the example or examples previously introduced.

4. explain how the traditional thinking described in a previous paragraph has been changed, reversed, or modified.

5. describe what happened as a result of the events related in a previous paragraph.

6. provide evidence for a point previously introduced.

7. identify the cause of the situation described in the previous paragraph.

8. offer a solution to the problem just introduced.

9. give a reason for the claim just made.

10. outline a point of view that opposes the one just cited in the previous paragraph.

SUMMING UP THE KEY POINTS

1. Writers often use opening phrases in new paragraphs to tell readers the direction they are taking. Pay attention to those sentence openings. Let them help you follow the writer's train of thought.

2. Whenever possible, use the concluding sentences of paragraphs to determine the direction the next paragraph will take.

3. For each new paragraph, ask yourself, "Why is this paragraph here?" "What is the relationship of this paragraph to the one that came before?"

▶ **EXERCISE 3**   **Drawing Inferences Based on the Writer's Clues**

DIRECTIONS   Read each of the following selections. Then answer the questions about how the author's thought develops paragraph by paragraph.

1. **An Arctic Mystery**

1   When the Napoleonic Wars[†] ended in 1815, the British victors were faced with the problem of what to do with a navy no longer needed to wage war. It was easy enough to ignore the ordinary sailors coming home. They could be left to starve on the streets like most of Britain's poor. A much bigger problem was how to employ returning naval officers. Socially connected, the officers' extended unemployment would be considered an insult by their well-placed families, causing aristocratic support for the British government to decline. But then members of the British Admiralty got an idea, one that could solve the unemployment problem while bringing glory to England.

2   As Britain's war with Napoleon was ending, British Arctic exploration was just beginning. What better way to keep Britain's newly unemployed naval officers busy than to send them on a journey to explore the frigid regions around the North Pole? Thus, in 1818 Sir John Ross, an officer in the British Royal Navy, was sent by the British Admiralty to explore Baffin Bay, which he did successfully. Sir William Edward Parry, Ross's second in command, quickly followed on a voyage of his own in 1821 and again in 1827, becoming the first man to overwinter in the Arctic. However, it was the 1845 Arctic voyage of naval officer Sir John Franklin that truly caught the public's attention in both Europe and America. Already renowned as an Artic explorer, Franklin had made three Arctic voyages prior to 1845, and his last one had covered more of the Arctic than any of his previous expeditions. Yet it was the mysterious disappearance of Franklin and his two ships—*Erebus* and *Terror*—along with his entire 129-man crew that placed his name in the history books and inadvertently* stimulated greater exploration of the Arctic's frozen terrain.

3   In addition to keeping its high-born naval officers employed, the British Admiralty had sent Sir John sailing into the Arctic seas in the hopes of discovering the legendary Northwest Passage, a narrow channel connecting the Pacific and Atlantic Oceans. However, the Admiralty probably would have done better to assign Franklin's second in command, Francis Moira Crozier, to head the expedition. While Franklin had great experience with Arctic trekking,* Crozier was much more experienced. Franklin had not sailed through ice-packed waters

---

[†]Napoleonic Wars: wars fought between France and other European nations, among them England, during the French emperor Napoleon Bonaparte's reign.
*inadvertently: unintentionally, by chance.
*trekking: walking on rough terrain or land.

for almost two decades. In a personal letter, Crozier had openly acknowl-edged misgivings about Franklin's judgment. Yet he had no choice but to obey his commander, and that may have been his undoing.

4   But whatever Franklin's shortcomings were or were not—and Franklin's competence is the subject of argument to this day—the expedition he commanded was probably doomed from the start. Both the *Terror* and *Erebus* were heavily stocked with something new on the market—canned food. There was enough of it, in fact, to last five years if necessary. But as later analysis of several cans showed, many of them were not properly constructed, and the food in them quickly became loaded with infectious bacteria. In addition, lead used in the tin casing seems to have bled into the food and poisoned those who ate the cans' contents. It's also true that during the years of the expedition, 1845 to 1850,[†] Arctic winters were especially severe. As if that weren't enough, the huge, steel-tipped, icebreaker ships the British were extremely proud of producing needed deep water to sail efficiently; in the Arctic, deep water froze early, leaving the *Terror* and the *Erebus* stuck in ice.

5   Although no one knows what took the biggest toll— the weather, the ships, or the poisoned food—Franklin and his entire crew just seemed to vanish from the face of the Earth. After August of 1845, no one in England heard a word from the men aboard the *Erebus* and the *Terror*. But if the British Admiralty was ready to assume Franklin was dead and forget about him, his wife, Lady Jane Franklin, was not. Tirelessly, she badgered government officials to keep looking. Because Lady Jane had both money and influential friends, keep looking they did, while at the same time exploring more and more of the previ-ously unexplored Arctic regions. Even the Americans got into the act, sending out an expedition to find the missing ships and above all the missing leader of those ships.

6   It wasn't until 1854, after more than a dozen search expeditions had slogged their way through Arctic snow in search of Franklin, that the mystery came to be, at least partially, resolved. That was the year that Sir John Rae, a surveyor for the Hudson Bay Company, spoke with some local Inuit[†] after noticing that one of the group was wearing a scrap of what looked like a naval uniform. The Inuits said they had seen and spoken to a band of perhaps forty white men trudging through

[†]1850 was the last year that any members of the crew were seen, although they might have survived somewhat longer.
[†]*Inuit* is the term that has replaced *Eskimo*.

the ice and snow. Although the men were clearly suffering from starvation, the native Inuit could not help them because they themselves had so little food. When Rae, excited by the news, offered a reward for more information, the Inuit offered what they had found in the area where the men had first been seen: pieces of naval instruments, some silver plate, even one of Franklin's medals. They also told Rae that they had seen some of the men a second time. Only this time, they were dead. Perhaps even worse, there was evidence of cannibalism on the bodies left lying in the snow.

7   When Rae returned to England with the first shred of news about what had happened to Franklin and his men, Franklin's wife was outraged at the suggestion that men of England, particularly men such as her husband, would engage in cannibalism instead of starving to death. In an effort to prove she was right and Rae wrong, she funded yet another search expedition. This time the searchers found a note left by Crozier, Franklin's second in command. The note said that Franklin had died on June 11th, 1847. The note also said that nine officers and fifteen other men had died, but those who were left would start out on foot the next day, in the hopes of finding supplies or help to fend off starvation. Exactly what happened to those remaining men as they struggled to survive in an Arctic wilderness is unknown to the present day. There are rumors that some men simply gave up on being found and went to live with the Inuit, who took them in. Others suggest that they died during their search for help and their bodies were covered over by snow and ice and then devoured by animals when the cold eased up. The truth is no one knows what happened to Crozier and the gang of starving men who followed him once Franklin had died. (Sources of information: Pierre Berton. The Arctic Grail: The Quest for the Northwest Passage and the North Pole, 1818–1909. Lyons Press, 2000; http://www .thecanadianencyclopedia.ca/en/article/to-touch-the-hand-of-franklin-reaching-across-the-beaufort-sea-feature/ (last accessed March 21, 2015.)

1. Based on the first paragraph, what do you think is the topic of the entire reading?

_____

2. The last sentence of paragraph 1 was written to make readers ask what question?

_____

3. What does the last sentence of paragraph 2 suggest the reading will explain?

_____

_____

_____

4. By paragraph 3, how would you express the topic of the reading? Is your topic different or the same as the one you chose for question 1?

_____

_____

5. What does the opening of paragraph 4 suggest about its relationship to paragraph 3?

_____

6. In paragraph 5, what words in the opening sentence does the author use to help readers make a connection to paragraph 4?

_____

7. What words in paragraph 5 did the author use in order to encourage readers to make a connection to this statement in paragraph 2: "Yet it was the mysterious disappearance of Franklin and his two ships—*Erebus* and *Terror*—along with his entire 129-man crew that placed his name in the history books and inadvertently stimulated greater exploration of the Arctic's frozen terrain"?

_____

_____

8. Paragraph 6 introduces Sir John Rae. How is he connected to the title of the reading?

_____

_____

9. By paragraph 7, how would you answer the question: "What is the Arctic mystery described in the title?"

_____

_____

_____

10. Is the main idea of the reading implied or stated? _____

If you think it is stated, please write the thesis statement on the following lines. If you think it's implied, write the main idea you inferred on the following lines:

_____

_____

_____

_____

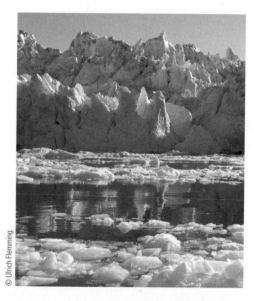

This is the kind of frozen landscape that surrounded Crozier and the ships he commanded.

2. When You're Haunted by a Past That Isn't Yours

1 The Data Protection Act of 1998 went into force in 2000. It was meant to ensure that companies or organizations that provided personal data, or information, about individuals got their facts right. As a result of the Data Protection Act, individuals could get access to their personal information and, if necessary, challenge its accuracy. The thinking was that if people could get access to background information and discover it was wrong, they might sue the data provider. Thus, fear of litigation would keep personal data providers on their toes and ensure that the information they gave out was accurate. That was the assumption anyway.

2   Dennis Teague might have his doubts that things worked out as planned. When Teague was rejected for a job at the Wisconsin State Fair, he pushed to find out why. He was astonished to learn that he had a long criminal record. Or at least that's what his background check showed. According to the Wisconsin Department of Justice, Teague had a lengthy criminal history.

3   As it turned out, though, the record wasn't Teague's. His second cousin had used his name when he was arrested. Although the fake name had eventually been discovered and the real culprit identified, Teague's name was still attached to a long list of crimes he didn't commit. Teague sued the Wisconsin Department of Justice claiming that the system used to perform background checks is flawed, generating information about the person being checked as well as about people who might have used the person's name as an alias.

4   Kathleen Ann Casey probably shares Dennis Teague's skepticism. Casey applied for a job as a pharmacy assistant. But she didn't get the job. Her background check had turned up a criminal past that showed Casey repeatedly being charged with forgery. Casey not only didn't get the job, she also ended up losing her apartment because she couldn't pay her rent. Yet Kathleen Ann Casey had never done anything illegal. The same could not be said, though, for Kathleen A. Casey, a much younger woman who lived in another town and didn't have her namesake's scruples about forging other people's names onto checks and credit card slips.

5   The arrival of computers and the Web was supposed to make doing background checks easier. After all, if someone wanted to do a background check, that person no longer needed to go to a courthouse and thumb through records. All he or she had to do was pay a fee to a company or an institution that had gathered the information electronically, often from public records available online. Unfortunately, many of the companies that now routinely collect and sell information so easily don't necessarily double-check for accuracy or even update their files regularly, as Gina Marie Haynes learned to her dismay.

6   Haynes refused to pay for a used car that broke down as soon as she drove off the lot. The used car company filed fraud charges, which were eventually dismissed. To her shock, Haynes discovered through a background check that companies collecting information from public records on the Web had noted the fraud charge but neglected to remove it from the records. She spent a year trying to get the fraud

accusation off the records of the many different companies and organizations that now freely sell her data, accurate or not, to anyone who asks for it. (Source of information about Dennis Teague: Bruce Vielmetti, "Wisconsin Sued Over Criminal Reports," www.thebackgroundinvestigator.com/current_issue/index .asp?id51479; about Kathleen Ann Casey and Gina Marie Haynes, http://finance.yahoo .com/news/ap-impact-criminal-past-isnt-182335059.html.)

1. What does the last sentence of paragraph 1 suggest about how the reading will develop?

   _____

2. Based on the first paragraph, what might be the main idea?

   _____

   _____

3. Does paragraph 2 continue the train of thought begun by the last sentence of paragraph 1? Please explain your answer.

   _____

   _____

4. In paragraph 3, how does Dennis Teague's story help explain the meaning of the title?

   _____

5. In paragraph 4, why has Kathleen Ann Casey been introduced by the author? What role does she play in developing the main idea?

   _____

   _____

6. What does the author imply about Kathleen A. Casey?

   _____

   _____

7. How does paragraph 5 help explain the title of the reading?

   _____

   _____

8. What does the last sentence in paragraph 5 suggest you are going to learn about Gina Marie Haynes?

   _____

   _____

9. Is the main idea of the reading implied or stated? _____

10. If you think the main idea is stated, please write the thesis statement on the following lines. If you think it's implied, write the main idea you inferred on the following lines.

    _____

    _____

    _____

CHECK YOUR UNDERSTANDING

1. Where are you most likely to find clues to the relationships between paragraphs?

   _____

2. Each time you start a new paragraph, what kinds of questions should you be asking?

   _____

 # Writing Summaries

"Summarizing is, then, like paraphrasing, a tool of understanding."
—David Rosenwasser and Jill Stephen, authors of *Writing Analytically*

At this point you are familiar with the way writers, particularly writers of textbooks, state or imply main ideas in both paragraphs and longer readings. That means you are ready to think about a skill that is absolutely central to college success—the ability to write summaries.

Except for mathematics, instructors in just about every discipline assign written summaries for homework. In preparation for these assignments, you need a clear understanding of what a summary is and how to go about writing one.

Summarizing: Paraphrasing with a Difference

A **summary** is a condensed version of a writer's original thoughts. However, it doesn't use the writer's original language except, perhaps, to introduce names or key terms. Unlike paraphrasing for a term paper where you try to reproduce in your own words most of the original text, *paraphrasing for a summary requires you to exclude some of the original.* A good summary should include the author's main idea and only those supporting details essential to understanding that main idea. Introductory sentences, extra examples, concluding sentences, and obvious or repetitive details can and should be left out.

Let's say, for instance, that you were summarizing the following paragraph. Which supporting details would you need to keep in your summary and which ones do you think you could leave out?

[1]To the inexperienced listener, *narcocorridos* are ballads that sound like pumped up polkas. [2]But unlike polkas with their harmless, often trivial, lyrics, *narcocorridos* are no laughing matter. [3]Those who write and sing the ballads are putting their lives on the line, and some have, literally, died for a song. [4]*Narcocorridos* tell the story of Mexican drug lords and the lengths they go to maintain control of drug trafficking to and from the United States. [5]Although a *narcocorrido* singer can make a fortune if he is commissioned by a gang who wants to be celebrated in song, the singer is then linked to that gang. [6]That link makes him an enemy of opposing gangs. [7]This is the likely reason why Sergio Vega, known as "El Shaka," was shot and killed. [8]It's also why Sergio Gómez was kidnapped right after a concert, tortured, and strangled. [9]Valentín Elizalde's *narcocorrido* "To My Enemies" put his name on a hit list, and Elizalde ended up being gunned down in front of witnesses right after performing at a concert in Texas. [10]The name of *narcocorrido* singer Gerardo Ortiz was almost added to that list when his car was attacked after a concert. [11]Two people in the vehicle were killed, but the singer escaped and went into hiding.

Read the paragraph through and you'll see that the author keeps coming back to the dangers associated with singing a *narcocorrido*. The general statement of that point is sentence 3, which, with the addition of the word *narcocorridos* from sentence 2, forms the main idea statement: "Those who write and sing narcocorridos are putting their lives on the line, and some have literally died for a song." Along with the summary's purpose, the main idea is what determines the selection of details that go into the final summary.

Start with the Main Idea

As you might suspect, a good place to start your summary is with a paraphrased statement of that main idea. So here's one possibility: "Narcocorrido singers pen lyrics that sometimes get them killed."

Consider Your Purpose and Audience

The next sentence you add to your summary depends on two things: (1) your purpose in writing and (2) your audience. If you are summarizing in order to take notes for a paper you are writing, then you'll want to make it clear why *narcocorrido* singers come under fire. You'll also want to add some names to your summary to illustrate your point. That means your summary would look like this:

Summary 1

Narcocorrido singers pen lyrics that sometimes get them killed because the lyrics angered a rival gang. Among those who have died because their songs glorified one gang and infuriated another are Sergio Vega, Sergio Gómez, and Valentín Elizalde.

But if you're writing a summary for an instructor's assignment, then you can't take for granted that your instructor knows what *narcocorrido* music is. Therefore, you'll need to paraphrase the definition and add that to the summary. You'll also need to provide the author and source of the original article. For instance,

Summary 2

As Ellis Ward points out in his *New York Times* article "Balladeers for the Drug Cartels," *narcocorrido* singers put their lives on the line when they sing, and more than one has died for a song. *Narcocorrido* ballads make drug lords sound like heroes, but in glorifying one drug kingpin, the singer infuriates a rival gang and makes enemies. Sergio Vega, Sergio Gómez, and Valentín Elizalde are among those *narcocorrido* singers whose songs led to their being killed by rival gangs.

Mimic the Author's Underlying Structure

Recognizing the author's underlying explanatory pattern or structure is a huge help when you write a summary. Once you recognize the structure, it's easier to decide what to leave in and what you can leave out. In the case of the paragraph introduced on page 493, the author introduces a general point and then illustrates it with specific examples. To summarize the paragraph, then, you just need to decide how many examples you need to include to make the main idea believable.

Narcocorrido singers celebrate the bravery and daring of drug cartels, and some have lost their lives for their songs.

Jose Miguel Gomez/Files/Reuters.

WEB QUEST
What war popularized the singing of corridos?

_____

While the word *corridos* is currently linked in the press to the drug wars, historically, what was the subject of the early corridos?

_____

_____

▶ **EXERCISE 4**   **Evaluating Summaries**

DIRECTIONS   Read each paragraph. Then circle the letter of the better summary. On the blank lines explain why one summary is better than the other when it comes to taking notes.

EXAMPLE

Original: Between 300,000 and 600,000 U.S. citizens a year survive a suicide attempt, and about 19,000 of those survivors are permanently disabled. Suicide is the eighth leading cause of death in the United States. Young people between the ages of fifteen and twenty-four constitute* the largest increase in suicides during the past thirty years. Men kill themselves at approximately four times the rate for women. The highest risk for many years has been Caucasian men over thirty-five, but the suicide rate among teenagers and young black males has been dramatically increasing since the middle of the twentieth century. Native Americans kill themselves at about one and one-half the times the national U.S. rate. Even though the elderly make up roughly 10 percent of the total population, 25 percent of all suicides occur in the over-sixty-five population, and suicide rates increase after age seventy.

(Adapted from James, *Crisis Intervention Strategies*, 6th ed., pp. 180–81, © Cengage Learning.)

Which of the following summaries used to take notes on the paragraph is better?

(a.) Suicide is a major problem in the United States. It is the eighth leading cause of death, with young people, men over thirty-five, African Americans, Native Americans, and the elderly being the populations hardest hit.

b. Between 300,000 and 600,000 U.S. citizens a year survive their attempt to commit suicide. But many who try do succeed, making suicide the eighth leading cause of death. More and more young people are killing themselves, although, for the most part, it is the elderly who are most likely to commit suicide.

Please explain the reasoning behind your choice.

Summary b doesn't infer any main idea from all of the statistics, even though, taken

together, the figures suggest a serious social problem. Summary b also leaves out

entirely some of the populations in which suicides are high.

*constitute: make up, comprise, consist of.

1. *Original*: To believe that only women who are partners in a conjugal* relationship are victims of violence is to be badly mistaken. Studies on courtship violence estimate that it occurs in anywhere from 22 to 67 percent of courtship relationships and cuts across college, high school, and nonschool dating populations. A conservative estimate is that violence occurs in approximately 25 percent of courtship relationships. As simplistic as the following may sound as a predictor of violence, one study found that the number of dating partners and dating frequency had the highest positive correlation* and that grade point average had the highest negative correlation.

   (Adapted from James, *Crisis Intervention Strategies*, 6th ed., p. 284, © Cengage Learning.)

   Which of the following summaries used to take notes on the paragraph is better?

   a. To think that only women who are partners in a conjugal relationship are victims of violence is to make a mistake. Studies on courtship violence in romantic relationships estimate that violence also occurs in courtship relationships, with different studies suggesting figures that range from 22 to 67 percent. At a conservative estimate, around one-quarter of all dating relationships include some degree of violence. As for predicting which relationships will tend to include violence and which ones will not, one study found a high correlation between violence in a relationship and numerous dating partners. The study also found that people with high grades had the least chance of being in a relationship that was violent.

   b. It's not only married women who can be the victims of violence. Violence can be part of courtship as well as marriage. Even with a conservative estimate, at least 25 percent of all romantic relationships are marred by violence.

   Please explain the reasoning behind your choice.

   _____

   _____

   _____

---

*conjugal: related to marriage.
*correlation: a mutual connection or relationship between two events, parts, or things that seem to influence one another.

2. *Original*: Marxists[†] and anarchists[*] have been trying to claim Emiliano Zapata (1879–1919) as one of their own ever since his assassination in 1919. But Zapata was never motivated by political ideology, or theory. He fought for economic justice. When the price of sugar went up and produced huge profits, Mexican *haciendeos*, or plantation owners, began forcing small farmers off their land in order to grow more sugarcane. Zapata tried first by peaceful, political means to convince the big landowners to give back the land they had taken illegally. When those attempts failed, he founded a guerilla movement known as the Zapatistas and focused on his now famous slogan *Tierra y Libertad* or Land and Liberty. Zapata was so successful at taking back land from the wealthy, Mexico's new political leader Venustiano Carranza, who was opposed to land reform and feared Zapata's influence and success, laid a trap for his opponent. On April 10, 1919, Zapata arrived for what he thought was a meeting with a colonel defecting from Carranza's forces and was shot to death by federal soldiers.

Emiliano Zapata was a horse trainer by profession but ended up becoming a heroic leader of the Mexican revolution.

Which of the following summaries used to take notes on the paragraph is better?

a. Emiliano Zapata (1879–1919) fought to bring justice to Mexico's small landowners. Using guerilla tactics, he and his supporters forced the large plantation owners to give up the land they had taken from small farmers. Under his leadership, the Zapatistas were so successful fighting for "Tierra y Libertad," or Land and Liberty, that Mexico's leader Venustiano Carranza, who was on the landowners' side, had Zapata killed.

b. Marxists and anarchists have always tried to claim Emiliano Zapata as a political supporter of their theories, but Zapata was his own man and that's what made him an enemy of Mexican leader Venustiano Carranza, who had Zapata assassinated.

[†]Marxists: people who believe in the economic theories of Karl Marx.
[*]anarchists: people who believe that government is a source of evil.

Please explain the reasoning behind your choice.

_____

_____

_____

WEB QUEST
Emiliano Zapata was a major figure in the Mexican revolution that took place between 1910 and 1920. Who was the other major revolutionary figure who fought in the North while Zapata did battle in the South?

 ## Summarizing Longer Readings

Summaries of longer readings should start off just like paragraph summaries do—with the main idea. But then you also have to determine (1) which main ideas from the supporting detail paragraphs you need to include and (2) how much additional description or explanation the supporting details need in order to be clear. Once again, both of those decisions depend on the purpose, overall main idea, and audience for your summary.

Say that you were writing a summary of the reading on pages 485–87 about the doomed Arctic journey of the two ships *Terror* and *Erebus*. But, because your purpose was to describe the fate of the expedition in preparation for writing a paper about changes in the Arctic due to global warming, your audience consisted of only you. In other words, you wanted to have the gist of the reading clear in your mind but knew it wasn't going to play a major role in your paper. It would merely be part of the introduction. In that context, the following summary would work just fine.

Summary 1

Even though John Franklin's expedition to the Arctic (1845–1850) ended with the disappearance of the ships and crew, the trip made

Franklin posthumously* famous and encouraged the exploration of the Arctic. When Franklin's ships *Terror* and *Erebus* froze in the ice and did not return, the public was fascinated and wanted to know what happened to Franklin and his men. In addition, his determined and influential wife Lady Jane Franklin kept the Navy looking for her husband and thereby furthered the exploration of the Arctic.

Here again, the summary of a longer reading starts off with the overall main idea. But the supporting details about what went wrong on the expedition are kept to a bare minimum.

If the Purpose Changes, So Can the Details

In the next example, the purpose of the summary has changed. The summary is included to help make a larger point—that the British are willing to celebrate as heroes those who fail at what they set out to do. Notice how the change in purpose changes the details included in the summary.

Summary 2

As many admirers and critics have pointed out, the British are just as likely to celebrate those who fail as those who succeed.[†] Take, for instance, the last voyage of Sir John Franklin, who set out in 1845 to find the Northwest Passage but ended up with his ships, *Terror* and *Erebus*, stranded in ice and his men reduced to cannibalism. Franklin may not have been suited for the job to begin with since he had not sailed through ice in over twenty years. But even had he been well-prepared, he faced several obstacles that all but guaranteed his failure. The winters of his journey were especially cold, his ships were too large to stay out of freezing water, and his food supply was tainted. Yet, despite his failure to achieve his goal, Franklin achieved great posthumous fame, and efforts to locate both him and the men under his command furthered Arctic exploration.

If the purpose were changed again, say to fulfill an assignment asking you to summarize the gist or essential elements of the reading, there would be yet another shift in the details included. Then the summary would

---

*posthumously: after death.
[†]For a discussion of Britain's fondness of heroic failures, see this website: www.screenon line.org.uk/tours/heroes/tour5.html.

touch on all the supporting main ideas in the reading: (1) Franklin's lack of expertise, (2) the obstacles the expedition faced, (3) the horror Franklin's crew underwent after his death, (4) Rae's gruesome discoveries, and (5) the Arctic exploration that came out of the many searches instigated by his wife.

Pointers for Summary Writing
●

1. Summaries are *paraphrased* and *abbreviated* versions of original text. Thus, your summary should never be as long as the original article, essay, or chapter section. Summaries, however, don't have a fixed length. How long or short they are depends on the audience, main idea, and the purpose of the summary.

2. In a summary, the language and length of the original changes; the message or point does not.

3. The number of major or minor details you include in a summary will vary with the purpose, main idea, and audience.

4. If the reading you are summarizing implies but doesn't state the main idea, your summary should express the implied main idea directly in a thesis statement.

5. If you are writing a summary for someone other than yourself, always assume that person hasn't read the original. Then decide what major and minor details are essential to making the main idea of the reading clear to the reader.

6. While a summary should not change the meaning of the original, it can change the order in which ideas are presented.

7. When you are considering what can be eliminated, look closely at illustrations or examples. Often one example will do for a summary and you can eliminate the rest. Quotations, for the most part, can usually be left out of the summary. Quotations almost always provide emphasis, and in a summary you don't need to say things in different ways. Once is enough.

8. Unlike examples, reasons for a particular idea or action should not be cut although they can be trimmed down. Reasons are there to prove a point in the original text and should always make their way into a summary.

9. Authors sometimes use repetition for emphasis. But repetition has no place in a summary. Eliminate any sentences that serve that purpose.

10. If you are summarizing an article for an assignment, make sure to include the author and source of the article somewhere in the opening lines.

11. While you may use a date or a bit of background from the original introduction, most introductory material should not find its way into your summary.

12. Leave your personal opinion out of the summary unless, of course, you are instructed to include it.

SUMMING UP THE KEY POINTS

1. Summaries are abbreviated versions of longer texts. Never let the summary match the original in length.

2. Unlike a paraphrase for a term paper, a summary requires you to eliminate some of the original material.

3. A good summary should include the author's main idea and only those supporting details essential to understanding the main idea.

4. A good summary should exclude introductory sentences, extra examples, concluding sentences, and obvious or repetitive details.

5. The form and content of a summary varies with the purpose and audience.

▶ EXERCISE 5   Writing Summaries

DIRECTIONS   Summarize the following readings. Include the title of the article at the beginning of your summary.

EXAMPLE

The Role of Culture in Listening and Learning

1 Culture influences listening as well as learning. While, for example, Americans and Europeans tend to think mostly about imparting information to others when they speak, people from other cultures, particularly those in Asia, place a heavier emphasis on listening. They concern themselves as much with the receiving of messages as they do with the giving

of them. The Japanese, for example, who consider listening central to polite behavior, spend less time talking and more time listening than Europeans and Americans do.

2   Cultural differences are also obvious when it comes to learning something new that requires time to process and remember. In numerous polls, American students mention the difficulty they have maintaining long-term concentration. Asian and Indian students do not experience the same level of difficulty with maintaining concentration. One explanation for this may be that Buddhism, a religion prominent in Asian countries, teaches the importance of *mindfulness*, or focusing completely on the thought or task at hand. In countries like India, Nepal, and Japan, training in the ability to maintain concentration and attention starts in childhood. Europeans and Americans are far less likely to receive such training and, not surprisingly, report greater difficulties staying focused for extended periods of time.

3   In order to describe cultural differences in listening and learning, communication researchers, influenced by the work of anthropologist Edward T. Hall, often speak of low- and high-context cultures. In low-context cultures, such as the United States and Canada, communicators frequently expect to give and receive a great deal of information. Generally speaking, they tend to believe that most messages of significance come through words. High-context cultures such as Japan and Saudi Arabia tend to place much more emphasis on elements of a message that go beyond words, for instance, setting, social position, relationship, and gesture. Members of high-context cultures are also more likely to pay attention to other components of their message besides words, believing that they play a big role in how words are understood. (Source of information: Berko et al., *Communicating*, 9th ed., p. 94, © Cengage Learning.)

Summary   In "The Role of Culture in Listening and Learning," the author says our culture influences how we both listen and learn. For example, while Europeans and Americans tend to think that offering information is the most important part of communication, people from Asian cultures are more likely to emphasize listening. The Japanese, for instance, don't talk as much as Americans and Europeans do. And while maintaining concentration is a struggle for many Americans, staying focused is far less difficult for members of Asian countries, particularly those where Buddhism encourages the practice of "mindfulness."

Those who study culture and communication often use two descriptive terms invented by anthropologist Edward T. Hall, labeling cultures as high- or low-context. People from high-context cultures expect the listener to be aware of more than words, taking into account factors like gesture, location, relationship, and status. People in low-context cultures focus mainly on the language of a message and are less likely to take other factors into account.

EXPLANATION   As it should, the summary includes the main idea of the original reading and only enough of the examples to clarify the main point. Because high- and low-context cultures are defined, the summary repeats those definitions in different words. The decision to leave the definitions out of the summary would depend on the reader's background knowledge. Those familiar with the terms might not include them.

1. Children in Alcoholic Families

1   Children raised in homes where open communication is practiced and consistency of lifestyle is the norm* usually have the ability to adopt a wide variety of roles. Children growing up in alcoholic homes seldom learn the combination of roles that mold healthy personalities. They become locked into roles based on their perception of what they need to do to survive and bring some stability into their chaotic lives. The following roles of children in alcoholic families have been identified.

2   **The Scapegoat**   The scapegoat is the typical troubled child in the alcoholic family. This acting-out child is the one who comes to the attention of school administrators, police, and social services. These children have extremely poor self-images and attempt to enhance themselves by rebellious, attention-seeking behavior. Scapegoat children use unacceptable forms of behavior to say, "Care about me," or "I can't cope."

3   **The Hero**   The oldest child is most likely to be a very sophisticated child or family hero. This is the little adult who takes care of the alcoholic, the spouse, and the other children. In attempting to care for the family, the responsible child enables the alcoholic by giving her or him more time to drink. Not only are such children highly responsible to the family, they are also highly responsible in their academic and extracurricular activities.

---

*norm: standard or typical pattern, the usual way things happen.

4 **The Lost Child**   This is usually the middle or younger child. The lost child follows directions, handles whatever has to be handled, and adjusts to the circumstances, however horrible they may be. The lost child outwardly appears to be more flexible, spontaneous, and somewhat more selfish than others in the home. These children don't feel, question, get upset, or act in any way to draw attention to themselves. They enable the alcoholic by not being a "bother."

5 **The Family Mascot**   The family mascot is usually the youngest child, who placates and comforts everybody in the family and makes them feel better. This child thinks that by making family members feel better, he or she can divert attention from the problem, and it will go away. The mascot may also assume a role of sympathetic counselor to the rest of the family. The mascot abets the alcoholic by distracting the family from the constant conflict alcoholism causes in a family setting.

(James, *Crisis Intervention Strategies*, 6th ed., p. 318, © Cengage Learning.)

Summary
_____
_____
_____
_____
_____
_____
_____
_____
_____
_____
_____
_____
_____

2. Getting Real

1 While young girls comparing themselves to supermodels has always been a problem, the models of previous generations, like Cindy Crawford and Naomi Campbell, were at least wearing a size six. Many of today's models wear size zero. To get and maintain that size, they starve themselves. As a result, they often suffer from depression and eating

disorders. But that physical and mental misery is not what young girls see when they flip through the pages of a fashion magazine. What they see are the super-thin, heavily photoshopped, and often surgically enhanced women they think they are supposed to become when they grow up. For a very few young readers of fashion magazines, this is not a problem. Just naturally, they look a lot like the long-legged, very thin but still bosomy young girls on those magazine pages. But most young readers do not share in that supposed physical perfection, and they suffer from a negative body image as a result. The more the fashion industry glorifies excessive thinness, the more likely it is that young girls will end up deeply dissatisfied with their bodies.

2   That situation is not going to get better without a profound change in attitude by both those who create fashion images and those who consume them. For starters, we need more dress designers interested in creating clothes that look good on women of all sizes, not just on those who wear a size zero or, tops, a size two. That's why it's a good thing that the adorable and definitely not a size two actress Melissa McCarthy started her own plus-size clothing line. McCarthy learned the hard way that designers don't want to create clothes for women her size. After being nominated for an Oscar, she asked several top designers to create a dress for her and was turned down by every one of them.

3   Models themselves could also do a lot for young readers if they would refuse to perpetuate the notion of super-thin, female perfection. Certainly Australian model Meaghan Kausman took a positive step in this direction when she outed the swimsuit company that photoshopped her body to make her size-eight figure appear to be a size four. Kausman was so outraged by the pounds-thinner image of herself that ended up on the company's catalogue pages, she posted the original photo on Instagram, right alongside the one that had been altered. The daughter of a body image expert whose organization supports young people with eating disorders, Kausman has a clear understanding of why her body was altered as well as why she wasn't about to let it happen without a fight: "I was really taken aback that they could take the creative license to alter it because of what they thought would fit into their cultural ideal of what beautiful was."

4   Social media offers another avenue of change, and those on Facebook, Twitter, and Instagram should make it a point of publicly celebrating women like tennis player Serena Williams and television star Lena Dunham, who simply refuse to conform to the wafer-thin ideal promoted by the fashion industry. And more teenagers should follow in the footsteps of young Julia Bluhm, who posted a petition on Change.Org titled "Seventeen Magazine: Give Girls Images of Real Girls!"

5   Bluhm's petition garnered 84,000 signatures, and *Seventeen* responded by saying it would no longer photoshop or digitally alter their models in any way. *Seventeen*'s editorial board also promised to feature a more diverse range of beauty in its pages. That's a huge victory for both the signers of the petition and their future heirs. As one mother who signed the petition wrote, "I have a 7-year-old daughter who told me she was fat yesterday. She is not fat. We have to save our daughters." (Source of data: http://thinkprogress.org/health/2014/08/28/3476691/model-swimwear-photoshop/; https://www.change.org/p/seventeen-magazine-give-girls-images-of-real-girls.)

Summary

_____

_____

_____

_____

_____

_____

_____

_____

_____

_____

_____

_____

From Reader to Writer The reading titled "Getting Real" said that girls are faced with unrealistic images of female beauty that cause many young girls to feel bad about how they look. What about young boys? Are they faced with an impossible ideal of what it means to be an attractive male?

Write a few paragraphs explaining why you think boys are (or are not) under pressure to conform to an impossibly high standard of what it means to be an attractive man. In editing your writing, check the paragraph openings to make sure the reader can easily follow your train of thought from paragraph to paragraph.

✔ CHECK YOUR UNDERSTANDING

1. How does writing a summary differ from paraphrasing for a term paper?

   _____

   _____

2. A summary should never _____ .

3. A summary should always include _____

   and only those _____ .

4. What should a good summary exclude?

   _____

5. The form and content of a summary varies according to _____ and

   _____ .

DIGGING DEEPER   Winning Legal Rights for Animals

Looking Ahead The reading on tort reform (pages 475–76) suggested that there might be too many lawyers at work in the United States. This reading suggests that their number might well increase due to a growing number of cases involving the legal rights of animals.

Getting Focused Read to get a more specific sense of what the author means with the phrase "legal rights for animals."

1 A little more than two decades ago, something called "animal law" started gaining public notice. There were several pet custody and wrongful death cases mentioned in the press that immediately became fodder for late-night comedians. Except for those involved, almost everyone seemed to think that talking about the legal rights of animals was a huge joke. In addition to the comic monologues, there were numerous cartoons showing a dog or cat sitting in the witness chair of a courtroom with paw raised in preparation for taking an oath. These were often accompanied by editorials with titles like "It Really Is a Kangaroo Court."[†]

No Joke Anymore

2 But make no mistake; these days, no one is laughing. Animal law, once unheard of both in and out of law school, is now being taught at more than a dozen law schools. Among them are some of the most prestigious: Georgetown, Harvard, and the University of California at Los Angeles. According to Stephen Wise, a Boston lawyer who teaches animal law at Harvard, the number of animal law classes is "sky-rocketing." Wise himself, the former president of the Animal Legal Defense Fund, wrote one of the first books on animal law, *Rattling the Cage: Toward Legal Rights for Animals* (2001). But numerous others have followed his lead and explored the position of animals in the legal system in books like *Animal Law: Cases and Materials* (2009), *An Introduction to Animals and the Law* (2010), and *A Worldview of Animal Law* (2011) and journals like *The Global Journal of Animal Law*.

3   Widespread interest in animal law was ignited in 1999 when an appellate court of appeals in New York reversed a trial court decision and awarded custody of Lovey, a ten-year-old cat, on the basis of the

---

[†]kangaroo court: a court that's dishonest or illegal.

cat's "best interests." This was in direct contrast to what had been the basis for awarding pet ownership: the animal would go to whoever came up with the bill of sale or certificate of adoption. Simply put, the animal was a piece of property. The New York decision, however, challenged the long-held assumption that, like jewelry or furniture, animals are property, devoid of interests or rights.

4   In 2000, Tennessee became the first state in the nation to approve emotional-distress damages for a pet's loss, and according to Michigan State's Animal Legal & Historical Center, other states followed Tennessee's lead. Attorneys specializing in animal law are intent on making the legal system recognize and respond to the human suffering caused by the loss of a beloved pet.

5   The noticeable toughening of anticruelty laws is further evidence that animal law is being taken seriously. In 1994, all but six states considered cruelty to animals a misdemeanor and punished it with small fines or short jail sentences. By 2014, "aggravated cruelty" to animals had been elevated from a misdemeanor to a felony in all fifty states. If someone intentionally kills or causes serious physical injury to a pet or other animal, that person can end up spending time in prison. Such tough sentencing is a far cry from the days when hurting or killing an animal was punished with a fifty-dollar fine. It is also a further indication of the justice system's changing attitude toward animals.

6   The much-publicized 2007 case of Atlanta Falcon quarterback Michael Vick is a perfect illustration of how much the law has revised its stance on cruelty to animals. Indicted by a grand jury in July 2007, Vick was sentenced to twenty-three months in prison. Although many people thought the sentence too short given the deadly abuse Vick and his co-conspirators had meted out to the dogs they had used as fighters or, even worse, as bait, there was a time when imprisonment would not have been part of the penalty. After all, Vick's dog fighting ring had harmed only animals, not people, and it was once generally assumed that laws were designed to protect only the latter, not the former.

7   In a country of devoted pet owners, though, that assumption has been re-examined and found wanting. Witness the fact that there now exist a variety of textbooks devoted to animal law. There are also websites focusing on the same subject and many of the sites link to a "Bibliography of Animal Law Resources." There are also student chapters of the Animal Legal Defense Fund across the country, and law schools routinely host discussions and debates dedicated to the subject of animal law. Although some of the groups involved in monitoring and changing the laws

governing relationships between humans and animals sport amusing names like "Pawtropolis" and "Kitty Crusaders," their intent is serious—to make the general public aware that animals can no longer be neglected, hurt, or, in the worst cases, killed with impunity. If the toughening stance *vis-à-vis* animal cruelty wasn't evidence enough, the number of lawyers registered with the Animal Legal Defense Fund continues to rise, and no one thinks that number has anywhere to go but up.

Sharpening Your Skills

DIRECTIONS   Answer the questions by circling the letter of the correct response or by writing out the answer.

Using Context Clues

1. Based on the context in which the words *misdemeanor* and *felony* appear in paragraph 5—"By 2014, 'aggravated cruelty' to animals had been elevated from a misdemeanor to a felony in all fifty states"—which makes more sense to you?

   a. A misdemeanor is the more serious crime.

   b. A felony is the more serious crime.

2. Based on the context in which *vis-à-vis* is used in paragraph 7, "If the toughening stance *vis-à-vis* animal cruelty wasn't evidence enough, the number of lawyers registered with the Animal Legal Defense Fund continues to rise, and no one thinks that number has anywhere to go but up," which definition makes the most sense?

   a. in contrast to

   b. in relation to

   c. up against

   d. as a way out of

Main Ideas and Explanatory Patterns

3. Which statement best expresses the main idea of the entire reading?

   a. Animal law is better known than it once was, but it is still not being taken seriously by legal scholars.

   b. The penalties for the abuse of animals need to be harsher.

   c. If animal law gains serious recognition, all experiments involving animals will result in lawsuits.

   d. Animal law is no longer the subject of jokes; it is taken seriously by both the legal system and the general public.

4. The main idea

    a. opens the reading.

    b. appears at the end of the first paragraph.

    c. appears at the end of the second paragraph.

    d. is implied.

Following the Writer's Train of Thought

5. What does the pronoun *this* refer to in sentence 2 of paragraph 3?

    a. a court in New York

    b. Lovey's custody being awarded on the basis of her "best interests"

    c. August 1999

    d. conflict over a cat in a divorce case

6. What does the phrase "simply put" (paragraph 3) signal about the sentence that follows?

    a. The author is going to reverse the previous point.

    b. The author is going to introduce a new point.

    c. The author is going to restate the previous point.

Paraphrasing

7. Which sentence best paraphrases the topic sentence of paragraph 3?

    a. The 1999 appellate court decision awarded Lovey to the person who had the cat's best interests at heart.

    b. The 1999 appellate court decision undermined the notion that pets are property.

    c. In the past, pets involved in divorce cases were treated as property.

    d. Thanks to the 1999 appellate court decision involving Lovey the cat, animals involved in divorce cases will never again be treated like property.

8. Which statement best paraphrases the topic sentence of paragraph 5?

    a. Although a few states have made cruelty to animals a felony, the majority have not followed suit.

    b. Anyone who purposely injures an animal deserves to serve time in prison.

    c. The growing tendency to make animal cruelty a serious crime is another indication that animals are winning legal rights.

    d. There was a time when people who purposely injured animals would be punished with nothing more than a small fine.

Following the Writer's Train of Thought

9. Here's the last sentence in paragraph 5: "It is also a further indication of the justice system's changing attitude toward animals." What's the connection between this sentence and the description of the Michael Vick case that follows in paragraph 6?

_____

_____

10. In paragraph 7, the phrase "that assumption" refers to what idea summed up at the end of paragraph 6?

_____

From Reader to Writer   Use the Web to read up on why Michael Vick went to jail. Then write a few paragraphs explaining why you think his punishment did or did not fit the crime. It's up to you if you write an introduction, but do make sure that you take a stand one way or another and give reasons for your position.

    In writing your final draft, be conscious of how many inferences you are expecting the reader to draw to understand why sentences and paragraphs follow one another. Ask yourself if there are any places where you might be better off making the connections more explicit? While readers are expected to draw inferences to make meaning, too many can overburden readers, making their attention wander out of frustration.

▶ **TEST 1** **Reviewing Key Concepts**

DIRECTIONS Answer the following questions by filling in the blanks.

1. After you infer the main idea of a longer reading, what should you do?

   _____

   _____

2. If the supporting paragraphs don't match the main idea the reader has inferred, what should the reader do?

   _____

   _____

3. What three kinds of texts are likely to imply rather than state the controlling main idea?

   _____

   _____

   _____

4. Where are you most likely to find clues to the relationships between paragraphs?

   _____

   _____

5. Each time you start a new paragraph, what kinds of questions should you be asking?

   _____

   _____

6. A summary is _____.

7. Unlike a paraphrase for a term paper, a summary requires you

   to _____.

8. A good summary should include _____

   and _____ .

   It should exclude _____

   _____ .

9. What three key elements affect the contents of a summary?

   _____

10. A summary should never be as long as _____ .

▶ **TEST 2** **Recognizing the Implied Main Idea**

DIRECTIONS Answer the following questions by circling the letter of the correct response.

1. Victimless Crime

1 Prostitution, pornography, illegal drug use, music and movie pirating, and ignoring car seatbelt and motor cycle helmet laws are all examples of victimless crimes. Victimless crimes are voluntary acts that violate the law but are perceived by some to present little or no threat to individuals or society. Up to 50 percent of all arrests in urban areas are estimated to be on charges of victimless crimes.

2 Some people argue that such crimes should be wiped off the books because those who engage in these activities participate willingly. Thus, a strong case can be made for legalizing, regulating, and taxing prostitution and recreational drugs. People will pursue these activities anyway, the argument goes, so why criminalize a large portion of the population unnecessarily. Instead, why not get a little piece of the action for the public purse? State regulation of gambling helps diminish the role of organized crime in gambling. Similarly, regulation of prostitution could help prevent the spread of sexually transmitted disease by requiring regular medical checkups for prostitutes.

3 In states where criminal behavior includes victimless crimes, there are extra burdens on the criminal justice system. Prosecutors and law enforcement authorities find much of their time consumed by relatively minor and non-threatening activities when they could be concentrating on more serious crimes. The courts must also spend a great deal of time processing these cases. The legalization of victimless crimes would immediately shorten the dockets† of prosecutors, police, and judges. For example, a growing number of states and localities have decriminalized possession of small amounts of marijuana. Even more have legalized the use of marijuana for medical purposes.

4 Opponents of decriminalizing victimless crimes say that "victimless" is the wrong word to describe actions that fall under this category. For example, with the selling of sex, prostitutes and their clients can become infected with the virus that causes AIDs and other communicable diseases. It is not uncommon for prostitutes to commit other types of crime and endure serious emotional and physical costs. Opponents

———————

†dockets: a calendar or list of cases to be heard in a courtroom.

also insist that legalization of drugs such as methamphetamines, heroin, or crack cocaine might lead to a significant rise in addiction and require higher taxes for treatment and health care. And if legalization were selective (say, only marijuana, cocaine, and ecstasy were made available legally), then new, more powerful designer drugs would likely debut on the market. (Adapted from Bowman and Kearney, *State and Local Government*, 8th ed., p. 450, © Cengage Learning.)

Which sentence best expresses the implied main idea of the reading?

a. Victimless crimes do no one any harm, and the activities that fall under this category should be made legal.

b. There is strong disagreement about whether or not victimless crimes should be legalized.

c. The idea that victimless crimes should be wiped off the books because no one suffers from them is misguided.

d. Making victimless crimes legal activities will have a host of unexpected and extremely negative consequences.

2. America Cools Off

1   In 1902, mechanical engineer Willis Carrier needed to solve a problem for one of his employer's clients, a printing company that was having trouble with its paper, which expanded and contracted in the heat and humidity. As Carrier pondered the problem, he figured out the relationship between temperature, humidity, and dew point. Then he went ahead and invented the air conditioner, which cooled the printing plant for the first time on July 17, 1902, solving the paper problem. Carrier's system was the first one that chilled, cleaned, and dried the air, resulting in an indoor climate that could remain a comfortable 72 degrees even on the hottest of summer days.

2   But the printing industry was not the only one that benefited from the invention of air conditioning. This new control over interior climates resulted in increased efficiency and productivity for a variety of industries, including textiles, cigars, chocolate, pasta, and celluloid film, among many others. As a result, air conditioning was in common use in commercial buildings by the 1940s. The technology also had a significant economic impact on the retail and entertainment industries. Department stores, movie theaters, sports arenas, and shopping malls have grown and prospered thanks in part to their ability to entice customers into their comfortably cool buildings. Air conditioning

allowed businesses—such as movie theaters—that were once forced to close during the sweltering summer months to stay open year-round. And air conditioning itself has grown to a huge $32-billion-a-year industry.

3   The technological impact of air conditioning, too, has been profound. It not only opened up many new areas of medical and scientific research, but it made space travel possible as well. Without air conditioning, astronauts could never have explored the moon.

4   Air conditioning affected where Americans lived. It opened up the steamy South and the desert Southwest for settlement. As a result, migration from southern states reversed in the 1960s, and cities such as Phoenix, Houston, Las Vegas, and Miami grew in size. Without air conditioning, these booming cities would probably still be small towns.

5   All over the country, air conditioning caused significant changes in architecture. Thanks to climate control, skyscraper windows could be sealed, allowing buildings to rise higher and higher. Residential architecture was transformed, too. Windows that were once placed in order to provide cross-ventilation were rearranged and reduced in size, the overhanging eaves and large porches that once helped cool a house were eliminated, and two-story Victorian homes with high ceilings were replaced by suburban, single-story ranch homes.

6   These architectural changes went on to produce profound social changes. People who once sought relief from the heat out on their front porches, where neighbors could interact regularly with one another, began staying inside their cooler, air-conditioned houses. As the streets emptied, social interaction outside the home diminished. America became a much more private place.

Which sentence best expresses the main idea of the entire reading?

a. The invention of air conditioning caused a number of dramatic changes in the way Americans lived and worked.

b. Willis Carrier was a technological genius, who single-handedly figured out how to protect paper from the effects of heat and humidity, thereby saving the printing industry from bankruptcy.

c. Thanks to Willis Carrier, the printing industry was saved from complete financial ruin.

d. The invention of air conditioning gave birth to the great American symbol—the skyscraper.

▶ **TEST 3**   Inferring the Implied Main Idea

DIRECTIONS   Write the implied main idea on the blank lines.

1. The Jury Deliberation Process

1   During a courtroom trial, the jury listens as both the defense and the prosecution present their witnesses and their evidence. Both sides finish presenting their cases by making closing arguments to the jury. Then, the judge sends the jury to the jury room to deliberate, i.e., decide on a verdict of "guilty" or "not guilty."

2   The first stage in making that decision is a relaxed period of *orientation*. The jury members select a group leader (the foreperson), set an agenda, and discuss the judge's instructions. Next, jurors begin to explore what they have heard in the courtroom. They talk about the evidence the lawyers have presented and raise questions. This initial discussion ends with a vote, and each jury member reveals his or her opinion about the verdict.

3   If the necessary consensus, or agreement, is not reached, the jury shifts into a period of *open conflict*. During this phase, the discussion becomes more argumentative. The two opposing groups go over the evidence and try to construct stories to explain it. If some members disagree, the majority group tries to convince those in disagreement by presenting information to support its argument. The majority group may also try to pressure the minority group to conform to the majority's opinion.

4   When a consensus is finally reached, the group enters a *reconciliation* phase. During this period, group members smooth over the conflicts between them. They express their satisfaction with their decision. On some juries, however, the majority is not able to persuade the holdouts to change their minds. In that case, the jury is "hung." A hung jury causes a mistrial, and the case must be retried with a new jury. (Source of information: Brehm, Kassin, and Fein, *Social Psychology*, 5th ed., p. 460, © Cengage Learning.)

Implied Main Idea   _____

_____

2. Texting and Driving

1   We all know that drinking and driving don't mix. Usually the people who do mix the two have already drunk too much to realize that they are doing something dangerous and stupid. But when it comes to texting, even people who are completely sober seem to think that texting

while driving is not a real problem. In any case, it's not as dangerous as drinking and driving. Or is it?

2   As it turns out, some skeptics at *Car and Driver* magazine did some research in order to find out which is a bigger threat: drinking while driving or texting while driving. They rigged a car so a red light would go off when the driver had to brake suddenly. Then they tested driver reactions under four different conditions: (1) unimpaired, (2) legally drunk at .08, (3) reading an email, and (4) texting. Texting while driving produced the slowest reaction time, while emailing came in second.

3   If that doesn't make you think about turning off your cell phone while you drive, consider the tragic chain of events set off when a 19-year-old Missouri driver was texting his friend about a visit to the country fair. The teenager was driving around fifty-five miles per hour and looking at his cell phone. Thus, he didn't notice that the pickup truck in front of him had slowed down for a construction site. By the time he slammed on his brakes, it was too late. The boy crashed into the truck at 55 mph. Then two buses coming up behind the crumpled vehicles couldn't stop fast enough to avoid the crash site. The result was a pileup that left two people dead and many others injured.

4   The incident in Missouri is not an isolated one. The University of North Texas Health Science Center looked at traffic data from the Fatality Accident Reporting System and came to an alarming conclusion: Between 2001 and 2007, texting while driving was responsible for 16,141 deaths. Because cell phone use and texting has only increased since that study was done, it's doubtful that this number has declined. A 2011 study by the National Highway Traffic Safety Administration places the number of drivers likely to be holding a cell phone to their ears at any given moment at 660,000. This means that there are over half a million drivers on the road who, at some point, are looking at the screens on their cell phone, not at the road, all the while assuming that they aren't doing something incredibly dangerous. Like the person who drinks four beers and picks up his or her car keys to get on the road, those who are texting and driving need to consider the potentially lethal consequences of their actions. (Source of statistics and accident description: http://techcrunch.com/2010/09/24/study-texting-while-driving-r; Jim Suhr and Jim Slater, "Texting While Driving Ban Isn't Academic for Missouri Students," *Huffington Post*, December 17, 2011.)

Implied Main Idea _____

_____

▶ **TEST 4**   **Inferring Connections Between Sentences and Paragraphs**

DIRECTIONS   Read the selection through once. Then re-read it and answer the questions following each selection.

1. The Birth of Vaccines

1   **Immunization** refers to the processes designed to induce immunity, or protection, from disease. In active immunization, a vaccine that contains an antigen (a substance that triggers an immune response from the body) is given by mouth or by injection. The first immunization elicits a primary immune response, just as an infection would. A second immunization, or booster, elicits a secondary immune response and increases immunity to disease. In passive immunization, a person receives antibodies purified from the blood of another individual. The treatment offers immediate benefit for someone who has been exposed to a potentially deadly agent or disease such as tetanus or rabies.

2   The first vaccine was the result of desperate attempts to survive smallpox epidemics that repeatedly occurred all over the world. Smallpox is a severe disease that kills up to one-third of the people it infects. Before 1880, no one knew what caused infectious diseases or how to protect anyone from getting them. But there were clues. In the case of smallpox, survivors seldom contracted the disease a second time. They were immune, or protected from infection.

3   The idea of acquiring immunity to smallpox was so appealing that people had been risking their lives on it for two thousand years. For example, many people poked into their skin bits of scabs or threads soaked in pus. Some survived the crude practices and became immune to smallpox, but many others did not.

4   By the late 1700s, it was known that dairymaids did not get smallpox if they had already recovered from cowpox, a mild disease that affects cattle as well as humans. To better understand the mysterious connection, Edward Jenner, an English physician, injected liquid from a cowpox sore into the arm of a healthy boy. Six weeks later, Jenner injected the boy with liquid from a smallpox sore. The boy did not get smallpox. Thus, Jenner's experiment showed directly that the agent of smallpox confers, or gives, immunity to smallpox.

5   Jenner named his procedure "vaccination" after the Latin word for cowpox (*vaccinia*). The use of Jenner's vaccine spread quickly through Europe, then to the rest of the world. The last known case of naturally

occurring smallpox was in 1977, in Somalia. The vaccine had eradi-cated the disease. (Adapted from Starr et al., *Biology: The Unity and Diversity of Life,* 12th ed., p. 674, © Cengage Learning.)

1. What does the topic of paragraph 1, immunization, have to do with the "vaccines" introduced in the title?

   _____

2. What do the opening words of paragraph 2—"The first vac-cine was the result of"— suggest about how the author's train of thought will continue?

   a. The author will continue to discuss immunization and the benefits of each type.
   b. The author will describe some of the diseases that can be controlled through the use of vaccines.
   c. The author will tell readers how vaccines came to be discovered.

3. In paragraph 3, why do the authors tell readers what people had been doing for two thousand years? What does this contribute to the main idea of the reading?

   _____

   _____

   _____

4. What connection does the writer expect readers to make between the title of the reading and paragraph 4?

   _____

5. If the main idea of the reading is expressed in a thesis statement, write the thesis statement here:

   _____

   _____

If you had to infer the main idea, write your inference here:

_____

_____

_____

_____

2. China's Adoption Problem

1   For at least a decade, couples desperate to adopt a child and tired of the paperwork and long waits required in the United States have turned to China. As a consequence of the government's population control policy, Chinese orphanages had a ready supply of healthy little girls available for adoption. China's one-child-per-family policy had re- sulted in many parents abandoning their first child if it was a girl rather than a boy. The hope was that the second child, or if need be, the third, would be a boy child because a boy could contribute more money to the household and take care of the parents in their old age.

2   Once the consequences of China's one-child-per-family policy became public knowledge in the United States, China became a haven for parents who wanted to adopt. According to the State Department, between 1999 and 2010, American parents adopted 64,043 Chinese children. Most of the children adopted were girls.

3   For the adoptive parents, there was an added bonus to adopting from a Chinese orphanage. They could adopt with a clear conscience. Unlike other countries, such as Ecuador, Vietnam, and Romania, there were no rumors about Chinese babies being stolen from their parents and sold on the black market.

4   New reports coming out of China since 2009, however, have altered that initially positive picture. At least one orphanage in the province of Hunan has been publicly accused of selling children for the explicit purpose of adoption by foreign parents. There are rumors of other orphanages doing the same. Since orphanages that arrange inter- national adoptions get hefty fees of around $5,000 or more from the couples seeking to adopt, it's clear that international adoptions are a profitable venture.

5   But the profitability of arranging adoptions is not what's come into question currently. What's being discussed in China and in the inter- national press is the question of how the orphanages got the children

in the first place. There was a time when the standard of living was so poor and the attitude toward girls so negative that orphanages had a steady supply of girl babies to put up for adoption. However, as living standards rose and families began practicing selective abortion,[†] fewer children became available for adoption. That's when stories about government officials searching homes for a second child began to surface. If one were found, the parents would be forced to give it up for adoption. Even twins were separated, with population control officials insisting that there were no exceptions to the one-child-per-family rule. The confiscated children would then be sent to an orphanage that specialized in arranging international adoptions.

6   Some U.S. parents with Chinese adoptive children have been devastated by the news of China's underground adoption policies. One mother interviewed by the *New York Times* said she was "haunted" by the idea that her child might have been taken away from her birth mother by threats or force. Other parents insist that their children could not have been forcibly removed from their families. They argue that their adoption agency would never have allowed such a thing to happen.

7   This position infuriates Karen Moline, a New York writer and board member of the group "Parents for Ethical Adoption Reform." She insists that the amount of money that changes hands in an international adoption and the difficulty accounting for that money (many of the payments are made in cash) makes the situation ripe for corruption.

8   Moline's belief that China's adoption process has been tainted by greed has some backing from a mother who reports bringing home two adopted girls from two different Chinese provinces. One of the daughters, from an orphanage in Guangxi province, was adopted with eleven other children, who came to the states at the same time. When the parents of the children discussed their experiences, they discovered that the twelve adopted children from Guangxi province had, almost word for word, recounted the exact same stories about their lives in the orphanage. As the mother of the two newly adopted girls explained, it was "all too specific to be believable." (Source of information: John Leland, "For Adoptive Parents, Questions Without Answers," *New York Times*, Sunday September 18, 2011, pp. C-1 and C-6.)

[†]selective abortion: When the parents find out the sex of the child, if it's a girl, the wife will get an abortion.

1. How does the reading define the word *problem* in the title?

    _____

    _____

2. What is the relationship between paragraphs 1 and 2?
    a. then and now
    b. comparison and contrast
    c. cause and effect

3. What key category word at the beginning of paragraph 2 helps readers grasp the relationship between the two paragraphs?

    _____

4. In paragraph 7, what position does the opening phrase of the paragraph refer to?

    _____

    _____

    _____

5. If the main idea of the reading is expressed in a thesis statement, write the thesis statement here:

    _____

    _____

    If you had to infer the main idea, write your inference here:

    _____

    _____

    _____

    _____

▶ **TEST 5** **Writing a Summary**

DIRECTIONS Read the following selection. Then write a summary that is six to twelve sentences long. Consider the purpose of the summary to be notes for your own use. Thus, you don't need to include the source of information.

Celebrating Singlehood

1   A quick question: Do you know what the third week of September is? Not Labor Day, that's weeks earlier. Give up? According to a report by the U.S. Census Bureau, the third week of September is "Unmarried and Single Americans Week," a week in which we are supposed to acknowledge the contributions single people make to society.

2   First started as "National Singles Week" in 1982 in Ohio by the Buckeye Singles Council and taken over by the American Association for Single People in 2001, the weeklong "celebration" was renamed in recognition that many unmarried people are in relationships or are widowed and don't see themselves as "single."

3   Although the week dedicated to singles has been around for more than a quarter century, and is recognized by mayors, city councils, and governors in some thirty-three states, it has yet to be legitimized and incorporated into mainstream American culture, as indicated by both the absence of greeting cards for the occasion and the number of people (including millions of unmarried people) unaware that the weeklong recognition of singlehood exists.

4   Yet even a casual inspection of demographics[†] in this country illustrates the increasing phenomenon of singlehood. The trend, which has taken root and grown substantially since 1960, includes divorced, widowed, and never married individuals. Each year more adult Americans are single.

5   According to the U.S. Census Bureau, the percentage of unmarried Americans varies by race and ethnicity. Among non-Hispanic whites, 20.6 percent have never married. Among African Americans, that figure is 39.4 percent. Among Hispanics, 28 percent have never tied the knot. In the Asian population, 28.5 percent have never married. Altogether the population of singles is quite large.

[†]demographics: statistical data, or information, describing the various groups in a larger population of people.

6   The varieties of unmarried lifestyles in the United States are too numerous to fit under one "umbrella" and too complex to be understood with any one category. They include: never married, divorced, young, old single parents, gay men, lesbians, widows, widowers, and so on. In research on the unmarried, however, those generally regarded as "single" are young or middle aged, heterosexual, not living with someone, and working rather than attending school or college. Although there are numerous single lesbians and gay men, they have not traditionally been included as singles in such research. (Adapted from Strong, Devault, and Cohen, *The Marriage and Family Experience*, 10th ed., p. 303, © Cengage Learning.)

Summary _____

_____

_____

_____

_____

_____

_____

_____

_____

_____

10 Learning from Organizational Patterns in Paragraphs

IN THIS CHAPTER, YOU WILL LEARN

- how to identify six organizational patterns commonly used to highlight or emphasize relationships between general and specific sentences.

- about common clues to those six patterns.

- how to determine the primary pattern of organization.

- how to make your notes reflect the patterns.

"The human brain really looks for structure in the world. We are set up to find patterns."

—PROFESSOR OF PSYCHOLOGY SCOTT HUETTEL

"What we call chaos is just patterns we haven't recognized."

—NOVELIST CHUCK PALAHNIUK

Chapter 10 continues the discussion of explanatory patterns begun in the previous chapters. But the focus here is on explanatory patterns that convey a specific type of content and, therefore, rely on a particular type of organization. The organizational patterns covered in this chapter are the following: *definition, time order, simple listing, comparison and contrast, cause and effect*, and *classification*.

The ability to recognize these six organizational patterns will help you (1) identify key points, (2) grasp relationships between ideas, (3) decide how best to take notes, and (4) provide a mental framework for remembering individual details.

It's the Thought That Counts

The organizational patterns introduced in the following pages (see the table on page 530) describe the ways writers, particularly writers of textbooks, organize information in order to communicate their thoughts. Organizational patterns are the verbal frameworks that writers frequently turn to when they want to do any of the following:

Type of Thinking	Organizational Pattern
1. Give readers the meaning or meanings associated with a word or term.	Definition
2. (1) Trace a fixed sequence of steps that produce an outcome or a product. (2) Help readers follow a chain of events that happened in real time and are central to understanding a significant period in history or the achievements of a person's career.	Time Order: Process Time Order: Sequence of Dates and Events
3. Describe the characteristics associated with a typical event or experience.	Simple Listing
4. Show readers how two people, events, or experiences do or do not resemble one another.	Comparison and Contrast
5. Help readers see how one event made another event happen.	Cause and Effect
6. Describe the various smaller groups that comprise, or make up, some larger group or whole.	Classification

The organizational patterns described individually in this chapter occur frequently in your textbooks and will serve you well as you attempt to understand your assignments. The characteristics of these patterns, though, are not fixed in stone. You can't assume that every time an author wants to compare and contrast two people or events, he or she will always use the typical transitions associated with the comparison and contrast pattern, such as *in contrast* and *similarly*. By the same token, a writer may describe a cause-and-effect relationship implicitly without ever saying directly that one event *caused* or was the *result* of another.

Thus, your job as a reader is to be alert to the thought relationships that connect the writer's ideas. As you read, keep asking yourself, what's the author trying to do here? Is he showing me how this event caused the one described in the next sentence? Is she telling me that despite some superficial similarities, two events normally linked together are really quite different?

In other words, it's the relationships between the ideas that should be your focus. Knowing the *characteristics associated with the patterns will help you spot those relationships*. These relationships are central to the way we think about the world, whether in school or out.

 ## Pattern 1: Definition

Although the definition pattern of development appears in all kinds of texts, this pattern in its purest form is found in business, sociology, science, and government texts.[†] When writing about these subjects, authors make a point of using whole paragraphs to define specialized vocabulary central to the discussion of their subject matter.

It's rare, however, for the definition pattern to govern an entire paragraph in a history text. Often, where history is concerned, definitions of key terms are included as part of larger explanations, and the most authors do is highlight the term they want you to remember. Sometimes they don't even do that, and you'll only recognize a key term by the amount of attention the author pays to its explanation.

Particularly in business and psychology texts, the **definition pattern** starts off with a general topic sentence identifying and defining the key word or term under discussion. That definition is followed by more specific sentences, which might do any of the following: (1) add to the definition by offering specific examples; (2) provide information about history, location, context, or usage; (3) explain how the term differs from a similar word or phrase; and (4) further define the key term by introducing its antonym, or term opposite in meaning.

In the illustration that follows, the definition for *puberty* starts out quite general but quickly becomes more specific.

[†]The definition pattern is also common in science and health texts, but, in these contexts, it's usually combined with the cause and effect pattern, as you will see in Chapter 11.

The topic sentence highlights and generally defines the key term *puberty*.

Supporting details zero in on the physical changes referred to in the topic sentence.

Puberty *denotes two general types of physical changes that mark the transition from childhood to young adulthood.* The first set of changes that define puberty concern physical appearance. These usually include a dramatic increase in height and weight, as well as changes in the body's fat and muscle content. The second defining change concerns sexual maturation, including change in the reproductive organs and the appearance of secondary sexual characteristics, such as facial and body hair and the growth of breasts. (Adapted from Kail/Cavanaugh, *Human Development*, 5th ed., p. 294, © Cengage Learning.)

Typically for this pattern, the topic sentence provides the broadest definition of the word *puberty*, and the reader learns that it refers to "two general types of physical changes." The supporting details then further define the two types of physical changes. Note that the authors have also used boldface to highlight the term they are defining and put the definition itself into italic.

Pattern Variations

Although much of the time, the definition pattern follows the sequence described above, you will encounter variations, particularly when you are reading sociology texts. Within sociology texts, it's just as likely for the author to start off with a specific description of how the term being defined came into being or is applied. Then, somewhere in the middle of the paragraph, the author will introduce and formally define the term central to the paragraph, for instance:

The paragraph starts off discussing early views of female crime.

The first part of the paragraph is then summed up in the phrase "This perspective."

An early view of female crime focused on the supposed dynamics* of sexual relationships. Female criminals were viewed as either sexually controlling or sexually naïve. They either manipulated men for profit or were manipulated by men. Thus, the female's criminality was often masked because criminal justice authorities were reluctant to take action against a woman. This perspective is known as the ***chivalry hypothesis***, which holds that much female criminality is hidden because of the culture's generally protective and forgiving attitude toward women. In other words, police are less likely to arrest, juries are less likely to convict, and judges are less likely to put female offenders into prison. (Adapted from Siegel, *Criminology*, 10th ed., p. 54, © Cengage Learning.)

*dynamics: psychological interaction in relationships.

Despite the variation in structure, the key element of this paragraph is the definition of the term *chivalry hypothesis*. That definition should be the focus of both your attention and your notes.

Typical Topic Sentences

When topic sentences like the following open a paragraph, it's extremely likely that the supporting details will all be devoted to further explaining the term mentioned in the topic sentence.

1. Nineteenth-century America was guided by the concept of **Manifest Destiny**, the belief that the United States was on a mission from God to occupy North America from coast to coast.

2. The *greenhouse effect* is the name for what happens when excessive carbon dioxide and other gases build up in Earth's atmosphere.

3. A *flashbulb memory* is an especially vivid image that seems to be frozen in memory at the time of a personal tragedy, an accident, or other emotionally significant events. (Adapted from Coon and Mitterer, *Introduction to Psychology*, 12th ed., p. 271, © Cengage Learning.)

4. A *database* is a collection of information arranged for easy access and retrieval. (Pride, Hughes, and Kapoor, *Business*, 10th ed., p. 354, © Cengage Learning.)

Taking Notes on Definition Patterns

Notes on the definition pattern should include three elements:

1. the term being defined

2. a complete definition

3. any other more specific details that might help clarify the definition— e.g., examples, contrasting words, origins

To illustrate, here are notes on the definition paragraph from page 532:

Main Idea The term *puberty* refers to two major changes that mark the transition from being a child to being considered an adult.

Supporting Details 1. Bodily changes like increases in height and weight.

2. Arrival of sexual maturity with changes in reproductive organs and secondary sexual characteristics like breasts and facial hair.

When authors include background material about how a word came into being, or they define a key term by telling you what it is *not*, this information is not always essential. Read it through carefully. Then decide if you need it to understand and apply the definition.

NOTE-TAKING TIP

When taking notes in the margins of your textbook, it's a good idea to make the word or words being defined stand out by circling, boxing, underlining, or highlighting them. This way, during review, you'll be sure to study important key terms.

If you are a fan of diagramming, you'll be happy to learn that definition passages readily lend themselves to mapping, for instance:

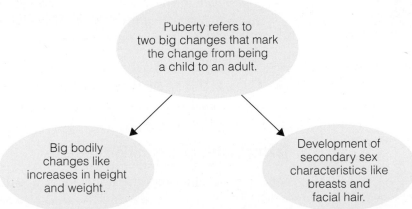

Puberty refers to two big changes that mark the change from being a child to an adult.

Big bodily changes like increases in height and weight.

Development of secondary sex characteristics like breasts and facial hair.

SUMMING UP THE KEY POINTS

1. Organizational patterns are standard ways of exploring specific types of content.

2. Recognizing standard organizational patterns can tell you what you should pay attention to as you read. But since all the elements of the pattern are not always on the page, it's your job to look for the thought relationships underlying the authors' words. *It's the thought that counts and the pattern follows.*

3. In business, psychology, and science texts, paragraphs relying on the definition pattern frequently open with a topic sentence that

defines a key term. That term is typically highlighted in some way, through boldface, italic, colored ink, or marginal notation.

4. In sociology texts, authors sometimes build up to the definition that is central to the paragraph rather than starting out with it. In history texts, key terms are usually presented as part of a larger explanation and may or may not be highlighted in bold or italic.

5. Topic sentences in the definition pattern often use phrases such as "refers to," "is the name for," "is said to be," and "is defined as."

6. Notes on the definition pattern should include (1) the term defined, (2) a clearly stated definition, and (3) examples or explanations of origins that clarify the word's meaning.

▶ EXERCISE 1   Understanding Definition Patterns

DIRECTIONS   Read and take notes on each paragraph, making sure to paraphrase and abbreviate in your notes.

The word *psychodrama* in bold is the first major clue to the definition pattern. The phrase "refers to" is an additional clue.

The rest of the paragraph explains the word's origin.

EXAMPLE   The psychiatric term **psychodrama** refers to a particular kind of group therapy created and developed by therapist Jacob Moreno in the early 1950s. In a psychodrama, individuals act out disturbing incidents from their lives, often playing multiple roles. The purpose of a psychodrama is to help patients better understand the troubling situations that may have contributed to their psychological problems. Moreno believed that the insights gained during a psychodrama could then be transferred to real life. For example, a teenager jealous of and in conflict with a twin might better understand both his own feelings and the feelings of his brother by acting out one of their quarrels.

Main Idea   In the 1950s, Jacob Moreno developed a special kind of group therapy called psychodrama.

Supporting Details   1. During psychodrama, individuals act out disturbing real-life situations.

2. Objective is to better understand situations that may contribute to psychological disturbance.

3. Moreno thought insights gained during a psychodrama could be applied to real life.

   a. A teenager in conflict with his twin might gain understanding by acting out a typical quarrel.

EXPLANATION   Here, the key term is *psychodrama* and our notes define it. They also include some essential background about the word—the name of Jacob Moreno and the approximate time when the term came into being. Note, too, that an example clarifying the key term has been included.

1. A **self-concept** is a person's perception, or view, of his or her personality and character traits. It consists of all your ideas and feelings about how you define yourself. To discover your self-concept, you might ask yourself, "What kind of person am I? Am I compassionate?* Selfish? Stubborn?" Self-concepts are built out of daily experiences and our reactions to those experiences. For example, let's say that you consistently do well in sports but find it hard to be part of a team. You might then begin to describe your self-concept in the following terms: "I'm a good athlete, but I'm not much of a team player." Self-concepts, however, can—and sometimes should—be revised, particularly if they are overly negative.

Main Idea

_____

_____

Supporting Details

_____

_____

_____

_____

_____

_____

_____

2. In neighborhoods where people know one another and feel mutual trust, children are less likely to become involved with deviant peers. They are also less likely to engage in problem behaviors. In these neighborhoods, kids are able to use their wits to avoid violent confrontations and to feel safe in their own neighborhood. They have what's known as **street efficacy**, the ability to navigate their world without

---

*compassionate: caring of others.

resorting to violence. In contrast, kids who don't live in such neighbor-hoods lose confidence in their ability to avoid violence. As research by sociologist Patrick Sharkey has shown, kids with a high level of street efficacy are less likely to resort to violence or to associate with delin-quent peers. (Adapted from Siegel, *Criminology*, 10th ed., pp. 189–90, © Cengage Learning.)

Main Idea

_____

_____

Supporting Details

_____

_____

_____

_____

_____

_____

✔ CHECK YOUR UNDERSTANDING

1. How do paragraphs based on the definition pattern generally begin in a business text?

_____

2. What variation might you expect in a sociology text?

_____

_____

3. What variation can you expect in a history text?

_____

_____

4. Topic sentences signaling the definition pattern often include what phrases?

_____

5. Notes on the definition pattern should include what?

_____

_____

Pattern 2: Time Order

Writers use the time-order pattern when they want to describe the steps in a process that produces an outcome or a product. They also use it when they want to chart someone's career, explain what made a span of time noteworthy, or describe a sequence of events that led up to a larger, more significant event.

Time Order: Process

Writers use the **process pattern** to tell their readers how something works, happens, or develops in real time. Because explaining how a product, process, being, or event develops over the course of time is crucial to writing about both science and business, these are the two contexts in which you will see this pattern most often. For an illustration, look at the following paragraph, where the author describes the three stages of growth in identical twins.

Identical twins can be hard to tell apart.

The word *stages* in the underlined topic sentence signals that the process pattern is coming up.

The supporting details describe each stage.

There are three basic stages involved in the development of identical twins. Their growth begins when the father's sperm pierces the egg of the mother. The fertilized egg then splits and divides into equal halves, each half receiving exactly the same number of chromosomes* and genes.* The halves of the egg then develop into two babies who are of the same sex and who are identical in all hereditary traits, such as hair and eye color.

Because the author wants to tell readers how identical twins develop in the womb, she uses a process pattern of development. Typically for this pattern, the topic sentence tells us there are three specific stages. The supporting details then describe each of the stages.

Transitional Signals

An author who wants readers to understand the steps or stages in a process is likely to use time-order transitions like the following.

Time-Order Transitions ●			
After	In	Over time	
At the onset	In the beginning	Right after	
At this point	In the early stages	Shortly after	
Before	In the end	Soon	
By	Last	Then	
During	Later	Today	
Eventually	Meanwhile	When	
Finally	Next	Within hours (or days)	
First, second, third	Now		
Following	Once		

Typical Topic Sentences

Any time a topic sentence uses words and phrases like *process*, *sequence of steps*, or *series of stages*, you are probably dealing with a paragraph that employs the process pattern of explanation. Note, however, that this

---

*chromosomes: bodies within a cell that consist of hundreds of clear, jellylike particles strung together like beads. They carry the genes.
*genes: the elements responsible for hereditary characteristics, such as hair and eye color.

pattern does not always employ a topic sentence that includes one of these words or phrases.

1. The process of photosynthesis is essential to plant life.

2. Storing information in long-term memory involves several distinct steps.

3. The barn owl follows an intricate courting ritual.

4. Learning gender roles begins immediately after birth. (Coon and Mitterer, *Introduction to Psychology*, 12th ed., p. 366.)

You should also know that authors sometimes just describe the steps or stages and let them imply a main idea such as "Elizabeth Kübler Ross's model of the grief process includes five stages."

Telltale Visual Aids

Flow charts use circles, boxes, and arrows to individualize and highlight the steps in a process. They are a dead giveaway to the process pattern. If you see a paragraph or chapter section accompanied by a flow chart like the one shown below, which outlines the general steps a consumer goes through to make a big purchase, then it's almost a given that the process pattern organizes the selection.

Taking Notes on Process Patterns

Notes on paragraphs describing a process should include the following:

1. the larger process being described

2. the specific steps in the process

3. the order in which they are presented

4. any specialized vocabulary used to describe the steps or stages

Notes based on an outline format would look something like this:

Main Idea There are three stages in the development of identical twins.

Supporting Details 1. Father's sperm pierces mother's egg.

2. Fertilized egg splits and divides into equal halves; each half receives same number of chromosomes and genes.

3. Halves of eggs develop into two babies of same sex, identical in all hereditary traits, such as hair and eye color.

However, some readers prefer setting off the steps or stages in a process with a flow chart. If the author doesn't include one in the text, you might consider making a flow chart to take notes. The result would look something like this:

Three stages in development of identical twins.

| Father's sperm pierces mother's egg. | → | Egg splits and divides into halves; each half has same number of chromosomes. | → | Halves of egg develop into twin babies identical in all hereditary traits. |

NOTE-TAKING TIP

When you are taking notes on the process pattern, don't get so caught up in describing the individual steps and fail to identify the overall process. By the same token, make sure to note anything the author says about the importance or complexity of the larger process being described.

SUMMING UP THE KEY POINTS

1. The process pattern explains how something works, functions, or develops by outlining the crucial steps according to the order in which they happen in real time. The process pattern is particularly common in science and business texts.

2. In the process pattern, time-order transitions that introduce each new step in the larger sequence are especially important. The presence of words and phrases such as "in the first step," "then," "next," and "finally" all signal an underlying process pattern.

3. Flow charts frequently accompany the process pattern. Writers use them to make the individual steps clear to readers.

4. Notes on the process pattern need to clearly identify the overall process being described. They should also list and describe, *in the correct order*, the individual steps that make up the larger whole.

5. When specialized vocabulary is included in the pattern, it should appear in your notes.

6. Flow charts are a good note-taking strategy for recording information organized by the process pattern.

▶ **EXERCISE 2** **Understanding Process Patterns**

DIRECTIONS Read and take notes on each paragraph. Circle the time-order transitions.

Notice how transitional phrases help mark off the steps or stages in the courtship ritual.

EXAMPLE In spring, the stickleback, a small fish found in both fresh and salt water, goes through a strange courtship ritual. (With the coming of the spring months,) the male stickleback begins to look for a place where he can build his nest. (Once he has found it,) he grows aggressive and fights off all invaders. (After finishing the nest,) he searches for a female. (When he finds one,) he leads her to the nest, and she enters it. The male (then) hits the tail of the female, forcing her to deposit her eggs. (Once she lays the eggs,) the female swims off, and the male enters the nest.

Main Idea   In spring, the stickleback goes through an odd courtship ritual.

Supporting Details

1. Male stickleback looks for place to build nest.

2. Finding one, he grows aggressive.

3. After finishing nest, he looks for female.

4. Leads her to nest, which she enters.

5. Male hits female's tail, forcing her to deposit eggs.

6. Once eggs are laid, she swims off and male enters nest.

EXPLANATION   Because the notes contain the main idea and all the steps described in the paragraph, we have everything of importance.

1. The first act of a newly hatched queen bee is to seek a mate. Three to five days after hatching, she attempts her first flight, flying far from the hive to avoid inbreeding. When she is far enough, the queen produces a scent that attracts drones from distant hives. Once a drone arrives, mating takes place at an altitude of about fifty feet. Following the mating, the queen flies home to lay her eggs. A queen who does not mate by the time she is two weeks old will never mate and will remain barren.

Main Idea

_____

_____

Supporting Details

_____

_____

_____

_____

_____

2. The psychological disorder known as paranoia develops in four basic stages. At the illness's onset, victims begin to distrust the motives of others. The paranoid are constantly alert for ulterior, or secret, motives in the actions of others. If suspicion marks the first stage, self-protection is central to the second. At this point, any personal failure is seen as the fault of others, and victims no longer take responsibility for their actions. In the third stage, paranoia sufferers become hostile; they are openly angry at their supposed ill treatment at the hands of other people. This period of anger usually leads to a moment of paranoid illumination.* In this final stage, everything falls into place, and the truly paranoid wholeheartedly believe that a plot or conspiracy is being directed against them. Seeing enemies everywhere,

_____

*illumination: understanding.

they are now convinced that someone, often a whole group, is trying to do them bodily harm and perhaps even kill them.

Main Idea

_____

_____

Supporting Details

_____

_____

_____

_____

_____

_____

Time Order: Sequence of Dates and Events

Textbook authors in all fields—except perhaps in mathematics—frequently use a **sequence of dates and events** to (1) describe what made a particular span of time eventful or memorable; (2) chart the career of an important figure; or (3) explain how some theory, invention, or activity came to be part of culture or history. Here, for example, is a time-order paragraph tracing a sequence of dates and events according to the order in which they occurred. The purpose or goal of the reading is to help readers see how the Internet developed over time and became part of daily life.

Notice how many sentences start with dates.

Putting dates at the beginning of sentences is purely intentional on the author's part. The dates make it easier for the reader to follow the sequence of events.

What we now call the Internet began in 1969 when the U.S. Defense Department linked up computers at four universities to create ARPANET (Advanced Research Projects Agency Network). By 1972, thirty-seven universities were connected over ARPANET. In 1983, ARPANET inter-linked with other computer networks to create the Internet. Between 1983 and 1990, the Internet was used mainly to transmit messages known as electronic mail, or e-mail, among researchers. In 1991, a group of European physicists devised a system for transmitting a wide range of materials, including graphics and photographs, over the Internet. By 1994, households all over the world were logging on to the Internet's

World Wide Web. By 2014, global Internet usage was a staggering 3,068,563,168 and climbing by the second. (Adapted from Janda et al., *The Challenge of Democracy*, 5th ed., p. 181, © Cengage Learning; statistic from www .internetworldstats.com/stats.htm.)

The main idea of this paragraph is implied. Taken together the dates, and the events attached to them, suggest a thought like the following: "Although the Internet did not start out as a technological tool for ordinary people, in a little over thirty years it became an essential way to communicate for people around the world."

Notice how the dates and events in the paragraph all contribute to this implied main idea. The first dates mark events that show how the early Internet was really very specialized in its goals. Then, as researchers expanded the Internet's capabilities, the dates indicate when it started to become important to ordinary people.

Transitional Signals

The previous sample paragraph includes some typical time-order transitions that appear when a paragraph is organized to present a sequence of dates and events. They are the authors' way of saying, "We've finished describing the previous event; get ready for the next one." Here are more transitions likely to appear in a paragraph tracing a sequence of dates and events.

Transitions Commonly Used to Organize Dates and Events ●	After that
	At that time or point
	Before
	Between _____ and _____
	By the end of the year
	By the year _____
	During _____
	During that time, period
	Finally
	From _____ to _____
	In January (etc.) _____
	In the days (weeks, months, years, century) following

In the spring (summer, fall, winter) of _____

In the following year

In the next year

In the years since

In the year _____

On the day (afternoon, evening) of _____

Until

When

While

Years later

Typical Topic Sentences

The sequence of dates and events organizational pattern often has a main idea that is implied rather than stated. However, when a topic sentence is included, it's likely to make some reference to a period of time, as do all of the topic sentences listed below.

1. The years leading up to the Great Depression were filled with a sense of optimism that disappeared almost overnight.

2. Between 1939 and 1944, most of Europe descended into a nightmare world of terror, violence, and death.

3. In their youth, the inventors of the airplane, Wilbur and Orville Wright, seemed destined for failure.

4. Between 1872 and 1889, soldiers, railroad workers, and trophy hunters almost managed to complete the wholesale destruction of the American bison.

Taking Notes on Dates and Events Patterns

When you take notes on paragraphs devoted to dates and events, include the following information:

1. the main idea

2. the dates and events used to develop the main idea

3. any other supporting details that lack dates but still seem essential to developing the main idea

Here, to illustrate, are notes on the paragraph about the Internet.

Main Idea   Although the Internet started out as a tool for researchers, it only took three decades

to enter regular households.

Supporting Details   1. 1969: The first step toward developing the Internet came when the Defense

Department linked computers at four universities to form ARPANET (Advanced

Research Projects Agency Network).

2. 1972: Thirty-seven universities were connected over ARPANET.

3. 1983–1990: ARPANET interlinks with other computers to create Internet, used

primarily for e-mail among researchers.

4. 1991: European physicists created a standardized system for encoding and

transmitting graphics.

5. Early 90s: Ordinary citizens start exploring the Net.

6. By 2014, billions of people making use of the Internet.

NOTE-TAKING TIP

The supporting details in the sample notes all start off with the dates mentioned in the paragraph. This is a good format to use when taking notes on dates and events.

READING TIPS

1. Readings accompanied by timelines are likely to include paragraphs tracing a sequence of dates and events.
2. Although paragraphs can rely on the dates and events pattern, it's in longer multi-paragraph readings that this pattern really makes its presence felt. This is particularly true of history texts.

SUMMING UP THE KEY POINTS

1. In the sequence of dates and events pattern, the *order* of events as they happened in real time plays an essential role.

2. Paragraphs using this pattern often describe how a series of separate events made some time period special or significant. The pattern is also used to chart the career of famous people or explain how some institution, activity, or invention became part of the culture.

3. Transitional phrases like "in 1999," "before 2001," and "after the election of 2008" are clues to this pattern. So, too, are topic sentences that emphasize a particular span of time; for instance, "*During the 1950s,* America underwent some startling changes in lifestyle."

4. Notes on this pattern should include the dates and events used to explain the main idea, along with any other undated details that seem relevant to the main idea.

▶ **EXERCISE 3**   **Understanding Dates and Events Patterns**

DIRECTIONS   Read and take notes on each paragraph. Circle the time-order transitions.

This is a case where the underlined topic sentence needs an antecedent to be complete. Note too how the topic sentence refers to a span of time.

The supporting details following the topic sentence open with dates to give a precise meaning to the phrase "every few years."

EXAMPLE   In the mid-nineteenth century, after the California mines played out, prospectors looking to strike it rich fanned out over the mountains and deserts of the West. For more than a generation, they discovered new deposits almost annually and very rich ones every few years. (In 1859,) there were two great strikes. A find in the Pike's Peak area of Colorado led to a frantic rush. (About the same time,) gold miners in northern Nevada discovered that the "blue mud" stalling their machinery contained one of the richest silver ores ever discovered. (In 1862,) Tombstone, Arizona, was founded on the site of a gold mine. (In 1864,) Helena, Montana, rose atop another. (In 1876,) rich deposits were discovered in the Black Hills of South Dakota. Whites were forbidden by a treaty with the Sioux from entering the Black Hills, but they went anyway and, as usual, the government defended them. (Conlin, *The American Past*, 9th ed., p. 511, © Cengage Learning.)

Main Idea When miners went West in search of gold and silver, they found rich deposits every

few years.

Supporting Details 1. In 1859, two big strikes, one in Colorado and another in Nevada.

2. 1862, city of Tombstone, Arizona, marks the site of a gold mine.

3. 1864, city of Helena, Montana, marks another gold mine.

4. 1876, gold discovered in the Black Hills — Treaty with the Sioux forbid prospecting

in the Black Hills, but prospectors moved in anyway and the government backed them.

EXPLANATION　　Because the author wants to give specific examples of his claim that "every few years" prospectors found rich veins of gold and silver, he uses the sequence of dates and events pattern. Those dates and events are then repeated in the notes.

1. Born in 1912, future German rocket scientist Wernher von Braun demonstrated his interests early on. As a boy, he tried to make his wagon fly by attaching rockets to its sides. By 1932, von Braun had already earned an engineering degree and was heading a newly created rocket program in Kummersdorf, Germany. By 1934, von Braun had received a doctorate in physics and his work was being funded by the new German leader, Adolf Hitler, who was enthusiastic about the potential of rocket science. It was only four years later that von Braun's team had developed the deadly V-2 missile, which could carry explosives almost two hundred miles. The V-2, in fact, was instrumental in Germany's deadly bombing raids on London. However, by 1945, the Nazi regime was collapsing. Von Braun, always careful to advance his own interests, decided to get on the winning side and surrendered to American troops. Initially skeptical of von Braun's motives, the Americans quickly realized how valuable he was to their own rocket program and decided to overlook his past. The Cold War was heating up, and von Braun was a gold mine of information. By 1960, von Braun was the head of NASA's George C. Marshall Flight Center. He was jubilant when his agency landed a man on the moon in 1969, and the country celebrated with him. In 1975, he was awarded the National Medal of Science. Wernher von Braun's story is worth remembering the next time anyone tells you with great certainty that "what goes around, comes around."

Main Idea

_____

_____

Supporting Details

_____

_____

_____

_____

_____

_____

_____

_____

_____

_____

_____

Josephine Baker

2. Given the amount of sunbathing that goes on, despite the associated hazards,* it's probably hard to believe that having a tan was once considered unattractive. In fact, it's only recently that being tan became desirable. Throughout the nineteenth century, tanned skin suggested that a person was poor and forced to work out-of-doors. Being tan was a sign of low social status. But by the early twentieth century, the more therapeutic properties of sunlight began to be recognized. In 1903, for instance, Niels Finsen got the Nobel Prize for Finsen Light Therapy, which used the vitamin D in sunlight to treat the once crippling disease called rickets.† Exposing one's body to sunlight, called heliotherapy, also became popular around the turn of the century. By 1915, sunbathing was becoming fashionable with the leisure class. But it took the famous French fashion designer Coco Chanel and the American singer and dancer Josephine Baker to make being tan a fashion trend. In 1923, Chanel accidentally got tan while sailing. When she returned to Paris a luscious

---

*hazards: dangers.
†rickets: a disorder brought on by a lack of vitamin D that can weaken the bones and cause crippling of the body.

golden brown, the designer was admired by everyone who saw her, and the tanning trend got its start. Ironically, the fad was cemented into place by the naturally brown, African American Baker, who was well known in the United States as a gorgeous chorus girl with comic gifts. But Baker, like many other African American entertainers, did not like being treated as a second-class citizen in her own country, and in 1925 she went to Paris, where her color was celebrated as much as her dancing. Thanks to Chanel and Baker, the idea that sun-browned skin was glamorous took hold across two continents and became associated with being both attractive and healthy.

Main Idea
_____

_____

Supporting Details
_____

_____

_____

_____

_____

_____

_____

From Reader to Writer Here is a list of people who accomplished great things. Look them up on the Web.[†] Then write a one- or two-paragraph biography that (1) identifies their contribution or accomplishment and (2) traces the key events that led up to those moments. For a model, look at the paragraph on Louis Zamperini on page 601. The Zamperini paragraph begins with his birth date and identifies key events of his

_____

[†]It's your choice, but I'd suggest looking at sites other than Wikipedia. Wikipedia tends to include so much information, it's hard to sort through all of it. And in its attempts to be completely objective, the language of the site is so colorless, it's not a model you want to imitate in your own writing.

youth. However, don't think you automatically need to include the date of birth. Feel free to start with a later date that triggered the actions of your subject, for instance, "When the twin towers went down in 2001, American football player Pat Tillman[†] knew immediately that he had to take action against his country's enemies."

1. Jack Andraka
2. Taryn Davis
3. Karen Silkwood
4. Paul Ridley
5. Sylvia Rivera
6. Sonia Sotomayor
7. Claudette Colvin
8. Charles R. Drew
9. Audie Murphy
10. Stella Ameyo Abadevoh

CHECK YOUR UNDERSTANDING

1. In the sequence of dates and events pattern, how does the author organize the events covered in the reading?

   _____

2. Paragraphs organized in a sequence of dates and events pattern are likely to fulfill what three purposes?

   _____

   _____

   _____

3. Give three examples of transitions likely to be used in this pattern of organization.

   _____

4. What should notes on this organizational pattern include?

   _____

   _____

[†]Pat Tillman left a promising career as a pro football player and enlisted in the U.S. Army in 2002. In 2004, his family was notified of his death in Afghanistan.

Pattern 3: Simple Listing

In time-order explanations of events, the dates and events or the steps in a process have to be presented according to how they occur (or occurred) in real time. The same is not true, however, for the **simple listing pattern**. With this pattern, the order of the details can vary with the writer. That's because the content does not rely on any specific order. Look, for example, at the following paragraph:

Introductory Sentence

Topic sentence doesn't suggest that individual differences need to be presented in any special order.

Supporting details don't use any transitions suggesting that the order of events plays a big role.

If you ask several American citizens who the country's greatest presidents were, don't expect complete agreement. For each person, greatness in a president depends on an individual's sense of what presidents should accomplish for the country. Those who believe it's the government's job to create social equality are likely to name Abraham Lincoln, Franklin Delano Roosevelt, maybe even Lyndon Johnson, all of whom proudly announced their determination to use the power of government for the creation of social justice. For those convinced, though, that the best president is one who governs least, Ronald Reagan is likely to be named the greatest president of all time. It was Reagan who repeatedly proclaimed that each individual was responsible for his or her own destiny. The government could not and would not step in to help those who had failed to adequately advance on society's economic ladder. For those who argue, however, that the Constitution is what makes the country both strong and special, the greatest presidents will be men like Thomas Jefferson, James Madison, and John Adams,[†] all of whom helped frame the Constitution that guides our lives to this very day.

According to the above paragraph, Americans decide who is the best president based on their personal ideas of how government should function. The writer then expands on that general point by giving examples. Those examples, however, do not have to be presented in any particular order. In fact, after adding some transitional links, the details could reappear with a totally different order:

If you ask several American citizens who the country's greatest presidents were, don't expect complete agreement. For each person, greatness in a president depends on the individual's sense of what

---

[†]Adams's contribution was somewhat indirect. He wrote the Massachusetts Constitution, which became a model for the U.S. Constitution.

presidents should accomplish for the country. Those who believe that what makes our country great is its Constitution would be likely to choose presidents like Thomas Jefferson, John Adams, and James Madison, men who played central roles in framing the Constitution. However, for those convinced that the best president is the one who governs least, Ronald Reagan is likely to be named the greatest president of them all. It was Reagan who repeatedly proclaimed that each individual was responsible for his or her own destiny. The government could not and would not step in to help those who had failed to adequately advance on society's economic ladder. But for those citizens passionately convinced that it's the government's job to help create social equality, the greatest presidents would be men like Abraham Lincoln, Franklin Delano Roosevelt, maybe even Lyndon Johnson, all of whom proudly announced their determination to use the power of government for the creation of social justice.

As this paragraph shows, the simple listing pattern does not rely on the order of events or steps to make a point.

Typical Topic Sentences

Topic sentences that signal the listing pattern often contain some general category word that needs to be illustrated to be meaningful—for example, "African honeybees have a number of *characteristics* that make them especially dangerous." But again, category words are *typical* in these sentences. That doesn't mean, they are always present. Neither of the sample paragraphs on how we choose our favorite president includes a category word.

The following are all topic sentences that suggest a listing pattern.

1. Emotions are strong motivators of behavior. (Jeffrey S. Nevid, *Psychology*, 4th ed., p. 286, © Cengage Learning.)

2. More than ever before, there is a wide range of digital games expressly created for educational purposes.

3. Abused children tend to exhibit similar behavior patterns.

4. Diseases of the bronchi and lungs are usually severe and can be life threatening. (Adapted from Neighbors and Tannenhill-Jones, *Human Disease*, 2nd ed., p. 159, © Cengage Learning.)

READING TIP In the listing pattern, the topic sentence is most likely to appear at the beginning or end of the paragraph.

Transitional Signals

Transitions like *for instance* and *for example* are likely to appear in the listing pattern. So, too, are transitions such as *first*, *second*, *third*, *next*, and *finally*.

Taking Notes on the Simple Listing Pattern

Notes on the simple listing pattern should include the following:

1. the main idea

2. any supporting details necessary to itemize and explain the plural word or phrase included in the topic sentence—for example, *ways*, *digital games*, *patterns*, and *diseases*.

Because order does not play a significant role in this pattern, you might consider using a Mind Map to take notes. A Mind Map is a particular kind of diagram that lacks the variety of diagrams as a whole. With a Mind Map, the main idea always appears in a larger center box or oval while the supporting details appear on branches stemming from the main idea to indicate their subordinate status. The details may or may not be surrounded by circles or boxes. A Mind Map gives you a bird's eye view of the relationships between ideas.

SUMMING UP THE KEY POINTS

1. In the simple listing pattern, the order of the supporting details can vary dramatically, depending on how the writer chooses to arrange the details.

2. Because the order of information is not a significant factor in this pattern, your notes can present the details in any way that makes them easy to remember.

3. Topic sentences in this pattern will appear at the very beginning or at the very end.

4. Topic sentences in the simple listing pattern are also likely to include some general category word that needs more specific examples to be meaningful, for instance, *characteristics*, *indications*, and *strategies*.

5. Typical transitions are *for instance* and *for example*, along with transitions like *first*, *second*, and *third*. These transitions help readers identify the individual items being listed.

▶ **EXERCISE 4**   **Understanding Simple Listing**

DIRECTIONS   Read each passage. Then take notes using the space provided to create an outline or a Mind Map.

The phrase "signs and symptoms" in the topic sentence suggests the simple listing pattern.

Supporting details requiring no particular order confirm the simple listing pattern.

EXAMPLE   There are many common signs and symptoms of respiratory disease. One typical symptom is difficulty breathing in a prone position. This symptom is especially significant if breathing becomes easier when the person sits or stands up straight. Coughing is another common symptom, and it's caused by irritation of the airways or a buildup of fluid in the lung tissue. Coughing up blood is called *hemoptysis* and can be a sign of serious respiratory disease. Nasal discharge is another symptom of respiratory problems and is present in both inflammation and allergic respiratory reactions. Most frequently, nasal discharge is a symptom of the common cold, but it can also be a symptom of other more serious respiratory disorders. Surprisingly, hiccups, at least if they are persistent, can be a sign of respiratory disease. A barrel-chested appearance and enlarged fingertips can also be signs that a respiratory disease is present.

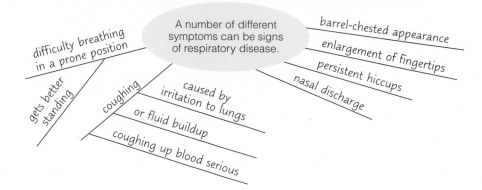

EXPLANATION As is typical of this pattern, the topic sentence appears at the beginning and includes a phrase, "signs and symptoms," that needs to be narrowed if it is to convey any information to the reader. The symptoms are then listed in a way the writer finds effective. However, another writer might just as easily choose to start with the most severe symptoms followed by those that are less severe because the material requires no fixed order of presentation.

1. Offering an apology would seem to be a simple act. All you have to do is say, "I'm sorry." Right? Well, not exactly. For some people apologizing is easy. They just admit they made a mistake. But for others, it's more difficult. The different ways people view making an apology may be the reason there are, at the very least, three different kinds. For example, there's the "I'm sorry you feel that way" apology. This is an irritating apology to those on the receiving end. It suggests that the person apologizing didn't do anything wrong and is only sorry that the person who was hurt is such a super-sensitive creature, thin-skinned enough to interpret harmless actions in the wrong way. A more satisfying apology for the person being apologized to goes something like this, "I'm sorry. That was a mistake on my part. I won't do it again." But this is one of the toughest apologies to make and many people just can't bring the words across their lips. Easier, perhaps because it suggests an exchange principle that levels the playing ground and eliminates guilt, is an apology like this one. "I'm sorry that what I did hurt you. How can I make it up to you?"

2. There are three learning strategies students should use to make sure they understand and remember new information. One strategy is *rehearsal*, or repetition, of what's just been read or heard. Thus, students who repeat the main idea of a paragraph right after they finish reading it are more likely to understand and remember the paragraph's point. *Synthesizing** is another key learning strategy. For instance, students reading a chapter that compares the press's role during the first and second Gulf War will have a better understanding of the material if they can link the chapter sections with a synthesis statement. A synthesis statement makes connections between different chapter sections (or even different readings), for example: "During the first Gulf War, the government and the military, worried about a possibly adversarial* press, imposed blanket censorship. But in the second, they used embedding† to keep the press informed and cooperative." The third strategy, *elaboration*, requires the learner to relate new information to prior knowledge by, for instance, comparing the author's point of view to another writer who disagrees or shares the same opinion, for example: Biographer "Robert Caro despises Lyndon Johnson as a man while

---

*synthesizing: the combining of separate thoughts to create a new idea.
*adversarial: challenging, ready to criticize.
†embedding: journalists were assigned to military units engaged in armed conflicts.

admiring his domestic policy as president; Robert Dallek is a sympathetic critic on both counts."

CHECK YOUR UNDERSTANDING

1. How does the simple listing pattern differ from the time-order pattern?

_____

_____

_____

2. In the simple listing pattern, where is the topic sentence most likely to occur?

_____

_____

3. What kind of word is likely to appear in a topic sentence that introduces the simple listing pattern?

_____

_____

4. What are some transitions that are likely to accompany this pattern?

_____

_____

From Reader to Writer Pick a topic like friendship, marriage, pets, studying, debt, and so on, and write a paragraph that organizes the details in the simple listing pattern. The paragraph should open or close with a topic sentence like "There are three things you should never do if you want to make a good impression the first day on a new job." The supporting details should then further explain each of those things to be avoided.

 ## Pattern 4: Comparison and Contrast

Paragraphs based on **comparison and contrast** describe the similarities and/or differences between two people, events, animals, or objects. Take, for example, the following paragraph:

Emphasis on differences in the introductory sentence and topic sentence suggest comparison and contrast.

Supporting details emphasize differences between the two topics discussed, Japanese and American management.

Much attention, perhaps too much, has been paid to the differences between Japanese and American workers. *But* perhaps we should examine more carefully the differences between Japanese and American management at the highest levels of decision making. In Japan, the heads of companies are discouraged from earning more than sixteen times the salary of their highest-paid workers. In America, *in contrast*, the company's chief officer can be expected to earn as much as 300 to 500 times more than the highest-salaried worker. In Japan, if someone in top management makes a serious blunder, he is in disgrace and will publicly acknowledge it. *However*, if the same thing happens in America, the company may suffer bankruptcy. But the person who erred is unlikely to publicly take responsibility. On the contrary, past experience suggests he or she, although statistically it's usually he, will often depart from the company with a hefty financial package.

While the introductory sentence suggests a paragraph that will focus on the differences between Japanese and American workers, the transition *but* reverses the opening train of thought and paves the way for the topic sentence—"But perhaps we should examine more carefully the differences between Japanese and American management at the highest levels of decision making." That topic sentence makes it clear that the paragraph will concentrate on differences between Japanese and American management rather than workers. The major supporting details then describe the specific differences.

In some cases, however, paragraphs do both: They compare *and* contrast two topics. Here's an example:

The topic sentence suggests the paragraph discusses similarities and differences between two kinds of bees.

Italicized verbs and comparative adjectives also signal the comparison and contrast pattern.

The African or so-called killer bees have entered the United States, and their arrival has, for good reason, aroused intense fear. *While in some ways* African honeybees *resemble* harmless American honeybees, they are different in a significant and extremely dangerous way. *When it comes to similarities*, the African honeybee's venom is *no more poisonous* than the American honeybee's. It's *also* true that the African bee is *not much more aggressive* than the honeybee. What *distinguishes* the African honeybee from the American honeybee is its determined defense of territory. If African honeybees are disturbed in their nest, they mount a furious attack and pursue intruders for miles. American honeybees, *in contrast*, quickly get bored and give up the chase.

In this paragraph, the topic sentence moves away from the focus of the introductory sentence, which talks about African killer bees. The topic sentence tells readers to expect a discussion of the similarities and differences between African *and* American honeybees: "While in some ways the African honeybees resemble harmless American honeybees, they are different in a significant and dangerous way." The supporting details fulfill the promise of that sentence, specifically identifying two similarities and one dangerous difference.

Transitional Signals

Notice the italicized transitions in the sample paragraphs. They are typical of transitions that signal the comparison and contrast pattern, as are the transitions that follow.

Transitions That Signal Similarity ●			
Along the same lines	In like fashion (manner)	Just as	
Also	In much the same way (manner)	Just like	
By the same token	In terms of similarities	Like	
Comparatively	In the same vein	Likewise	
In comparison		Similarly	

Transitions That Signal Difference ●	Actually	In reality	Opposing that position
	Although	Instead	Rather
	And yet	Ironically	Still
	But	Just the opposite	Though
	Conversely	Nevertheless	Unfortunately
	Despite that fact	Nonetheless	Unlike
	Even though	On the contrary	Whereas
	However	On the one hand	While
	In contrast	On the other hand	Yet
	In opposition		

Typical Topic Sentences

Transitions like those listed above are clues to the comparison and contrast pattern. So, too, are topic sentences like the following:

1. In contrast to African Americans, Mexican Americans were not forced into segregated military units during World War II.

2. Researcher Susan Harter found that some children view achievement tasks as a means of satisfying personal needs (**intrinsic motivation**), whereas others strive to do well primarily to earn external rewards such as grades, prizes, or social approval (**extrinsic motivation**). (Adapted from Shaffer, *Social and Personality Development*, 6th ed., p. 210, © Cengage Learning.)

3. Prior to the Spanish-American War of 1888, the media engaged in intense propaganda designed to promote a war with Spain, but, in contrast, members of the media were oddly restrained at the beginning of World War II, despite the threat of Germany and its allies.

4. One of the oldest controversies among education theorists is the nature versus nurture issue. (Adapted from Shaffer, *Social and Personality Development*, 6th ed., p. 210, © Cengage Learning.)

Topic sentences that identify two topics and refer to a similarity and/or difference between the two are almost sure to be indicators of the comparison and contrast pattern. However, it's also true that authors frequently identify the similarities and differences between two topics and let the details imply the overall point.

Taking Notes on Comparison and Contrast Patterns

Notes on a paragraph using a comparison and contrast pattern should clearly identify three essential elements:

1. the two topics being compared and/or contrasted

2. the similarities and/or differences between the two

3. the main idea they explain or support

Here, to illustrate, are notes on the paragraph on page 561.

Main Idea Although there are some similarities between American honeybees and African honeybees, there is an important and dangerous difference.

Supporting Details

1. African bees' venom no more poisonous than honeybees'.

2. The two bees about equally aggressive.

3. What makes African bees different and dangerous is determined defense of territory.

   a. Attack in a group and pursue for miles.

   b. Honeybees quickly give up the chase.

When taking notes on the comparison and contrast pattern, consider as well making a diagram that highlights similarities and differences:

Despite some similarities between American honeybees and African bees, there is a dangerous difference.

Similarities
1. venom about the same
2. equally aggressive

Differences
1. African bees will attack and pursue for miles
2. honeybees quickly give up

Linking Pattern to Purpose

In Chapter 12, we will talk at some length about persuasion in writing. But at this point, you need to know a key detail about the comparison and contrast pattern of organization. Within textbooks, readings with this pattern are likely to have a primarily informative purpose. But outside of textbooks, writers frequently compare and contrast to persuade. They try, that is, to prove, or at least make convincing, a point that others might disagree with. When the writer's intent is to persuade, the similarities and differences cited are usually present in order to make a value judgment convincing and encourage readers to share it.

Topic sentences like these two, for instance, suggest a persuasive purpose and practically demand a discussion of similarities and differences. "The remake of the movie classic *King Kong* was far inferior to the original" or "When it comes to court battles over child custody, dads are doing a good deal worse than moms."

READING TIP

Don't get so caught up identifying similarities and differences that you forget about the point they illustrate. Make sure you always know what main idea is developed by the author's description of differences and similarities.

SUMMING UP THE KEY POINTS

1. Paragraphs based on the comparison and contrast pattern of organization always present the reader with two different topics. Based on the needs of the main idea, the supporting details then highlight similarities and differences between the two. Some paragraphs using this pattern describe both similarities and differences.

2. Transitions such as *likewise, similarly, but,* and *however* are clues to this pattern. However, the real clues are the presence of the two topics and the references to similarities and/or differences.

3. Topic sentences that explain how two things, people, ideas, or events do or do not resemble one another are also a clue to this pattern. It's also true that in the comparison and contrast pattern, the main idea is frequently implied rather than stated. In this case, the author lets the similarities and differences speak for themselves.

4. Notes on the comparison and contrast pattern need to include the two topics being compared and/or contrasted. They also need to include the central similarities and differences between the two, along with the implied or stated main idea that the details develop.

5. Crucial to notes on the comparison and contrast pattern is the presence of the main idea. Sometimes readers get caught up in the similarities and differences and forget to indicate why they are present in the paragraph.

6. In textbooks, writers compare and contrast in order to communicate information about two topics. In editorials and essays, however, writers usually compare and contrast in order to convey a point of view they want you to share.

▶ EXERCISE 5   Understanding Comparison and Contrast Patterns

DIRECTIONS   Read each paragraph. Then circle the appropriate letter to indicate whether the author has (1) compared two topics, (2) contrasted two topics, or (3) compared *and* contrasted two topics. Circle all comparison and contrast transitions, and use the blank lines to take notes on the paragraph. *Paraphrasing note*: Don't worry if you can't find new language to refer to the topics. That may not be possible. Focus more on finding different words to discuss similarities or differences.

When immigrants arrived on Ellis Island in the late nineteenth century, all they had were the clothes on their back and any bundles they were able to carry.

Note how the main idea is implied based on the contrasts identified in the supporting details.

The transitions *but* and *instead* emphasize the focus on contrast.

EXAMPLE   Between 1890 and 1910, millions of people from southern and eastern Europe left their homes in search of the American dream. The new immigrants hoped to find a comfortable place where they could settle and live out their lives. (But) the cities to which they came were not prepared for the influx of immigrants, and many immigrant families ended up in ugly apartments that were poorly supplied with light, heat, and water. The new arrivals had dreamed of finding work that could make them independent, even rich. (Instead,) they found that jobs were scarce. Immigrants often had to take jobs for which they were unsuited, and the work left them exhausted and depressed. Moreover, many found that they were treated as outsiders, and their accents were subject to insults or ridicule.

In this paragraph, the author

a. compares two topics.
(b.) contrasts two topics.
c. compares and contrasts two topics.

Main Idea   Immigrants who came in search of the American dream between 1890 and 1910 were

terribly disappointed.

Supporting Details   1. Instead of comfortable place to live, had to settle for cold, ugly, and poorly lit

apartments.

2. Instead of suitable jobs, found unemployment or hard, tedious work.

3. Instead of warm welcome, ridiculed as outsiders with odd customs and funny way

of speaking.

EXPLANATION   The paragraph contrasts what immigrants hoped to find in their new country with what they actually found. Each difference reinforces the implied main idea: "Immigrants who came in search of the American dream between 1890 and 1910 were terribly disappointed."

1. Mary Shelley's *Frankenstein* (1818) and Bram Stoker's *Dracula* (1897) are the grandparents of the modern day horror story. Both novels are over a century old, yet they are still read and enjoyed today. Much of their staying power comes from the monsters who inhabit them. Similar in their ability to compel fear and allegedly based on real historical figures,[†] they also differ in several important respects. Shelley's nameless monster, constructed out of stolen body parts, suggests that scientific knowledge, used without ethical guidance or moral conscience, can wreak havoc* on the world. Stoker's *Dracula*, in contrast, is a reminder that there are things in the world that science can neither explain nor control. Stoker's Dracula, for all his paleness and red eyes, is a sexy presence, a fact that movies based on the novel have emphasized. Women, in particular, are drawn to him and readily fall under his spell. The monster in *Frankenstein* is so far from sexy that a blind man is the only one who doesn't scream at the sight of him. If anything, it's the monster's repulsiveness that separates him from Stoker's Count Dracula. Smart and articulate, Shelley's monster would like to be part of society but is an outcast because of his gruesome appearance. Count Dracula, on the other hand, has no desire to be part of a community except when he is in need of new blood. The count doesn't long to be normal in the way Shelley's desperate monster does.

In this paragraph, the author

a. compares two topics.

b. contrasts two topics.

c. compares and contrasts two topics.

Main Idea

_____

_____

Supporting Details

_____

_____

_____

_____

_____

_____

[†]Stoker is believed to have based Count Dracula on a nobleman called Vlad the Impaler, who had a taste for spilling and drinking the blood of his victims. Shelley is said to have visited Castle Frankenstein, where a man named Johann Konrad Dippel was believed to have carried out experiments that involved stitching together human bodies.
*havoc: confusion, chaos.

_____

_____

_____

2. To some degree, all societies are altered by time. But for Nigerian society, the changes between life in early-nineteenth-century Nigeria and now are especially striking. Most notable is the shift in economic and political power, which was originally in the hands of local leaders who governed Nigeria's twenty-three individual states. Currently, power is concentrated in the hands of a small group of business and military leaders. While local leaders in the early nineteenth century often waged war in pursuit of expanding the territory they controlled, modern tribal leaders exert influence through behind-the-scenes political wheeling and dealing rather than military conquest. Although the power and influence of local leaders has been dramatically curtailed by the arrival of democratic traditions, one thing has not altered. Community leaders are still regarded as the custodians of past tradition and as the final word on questions about what it means to be a Nigerian in moral or ethical terms. Another area where dramatic change has occurred is in the conduct of courtship. In the past, there was no such thing as dating. If a couple was seen together in public, they were expected to marry. City couples, at least, are now free to date without expectations of marriage. In the countryside, however, courtship rules are somewhat stricter, and dating as we know it is not encouraged.

In this paragraph, the author

a. compares two topics.

b. contrasts two topics.

c. compares and contrasts two topics.

Main Idea _____

_____

Supporting Details _____

_____

_____

_____

_____

_____

_____

From Reader to Writer You just read a paragraph that compared Mary Shelley's monster in *Frankenstein* to Count Dracula in Bram Stoker's *Dracula*. Write a paragraph in which you compare and contrast two heroes, villains, or monsters from a movie or comic series. Contrast, for instance, Freddy Krueger from the *Nightmare on Elm Street* series with the creepy Michael Myers of the *Halloween* series. Are they more similar than different? Or are they strikingly different in the way they embody evil? Remember the similarities and differences have to add up to some larger point such as "While some movie monsters are meant to inspire sympathy because of their isolation, Freddy and Michael embody pure evil."

CHECK YOUR UNDERSTANDING

1. What are the essential characteristics of the comparison and contrast pattern?

_____

_____

2. Name four transitions that are typical of this pattern.

_____

3. What kind of topic sentence is likely to appear in this pattern?

_____

_____

4. What should notes on this pattern include?

_____

_____

5. What mistake do readers sometimes make when taking notes on this pattern?

_____

_____

 ## Pattern 5: Cause and Effect

"Life is a perpetual instruction in cause and effect."
— American writer and philosopher Ralph Waldo Emerson

Whatever type of reading you do, you are bound to run across passages that explain how one event—the **cause**—leads to or produces another event—the **effect**. Look, for example, at the following paragraph:

Fear has a profound effect on the human body. When you become frightened, you breathe more deeply, thereby sending your muscles more oxygen and energy. *Consequently*, your heart beats faster, making your blood circulate more quickly and thereby rushing oxygen to all parts of your body. *In response* to fear, your stomach and intestines stop contracting and all digestive activity ceases. Your saliva also stops flowing, causing your mouth to become dry. Fear also causes the body's blood vessels to shrink, making your face lose its natural color.

For her portrayal of a woman in the grip of all-consuming fear in the movie classic *Psycho*, actress Janet Leigh was nominated for an Oscar.

Bettmann/Corbis.

In the above paragraph, the topic sentence identifies the cause and effect relationship under discussion: Fear has a profound effect on the human body. Introduced by italicized cause and effect transitions, the supporting details then describe the effects more specifically.

Cycles of Causes and Effects

Note that some details describe *cycles of causes and effects* in which one effect turns into the cause of another. Fear, for example, causes your blood vessels to shrink, which, in turn, produces another effect—your face loses color. If diagrammed, the relationships among these statements would look like this:

Transitional Signals

As the italicized transitions in the paragraph above suggest, transitions are often clues to the cause and effect pattern. Should you see any of the following in a paragraph, there's a good chance that the cause and effect pattern is at work.

Cause and Effect Transitions ●	As a result	For this reason	In the aftermath of
	As a side effect	Hence	Thanks to
	Consequently	In consequence	Therefore
	Due to	In response to	Thus

Cause and Effect Verbs

In addition to the above transitions, watch for the following verbs. They, too, are clues to the cause and effect pattern. Like the transitions, they can also help you sort out the individual causes and effects mentioned in a paragraph.

Verbs Linking Cause and Effect ●	Affect	End	Result
	Begin	Foster	Revolutionize
	Bring about	Generate	Set in motion
	Cause	Halt	Set off
	Change	Increase	Spur
	Contribute	Induce	Start
	Create	Introduce	Stimulate
	Decrease	Lead to	Stop
	Encourage	Produce	Trigger

Typical Topic Sentences

Topic sentences like those listed below all suggest a cause and effect pattern.

1. Self-esteem that does not seem to be based on anything can lead to later difficulties. (From Kaplan, *Adolescence*, 1st ed., © 2004 Cengage Learning.)

2. Brutally determined in their efforts to create an Islamic state in the Middle East, the terrorist group known as ISIS has carried out numerous, bloody attacks on innocent civilians.

3. The fabulous success of Daddy Yankee's album *Barrio Fino* brought the music known as Reggaeton international interest and acclaim.

4. A principal factor in bulimia is the pressure many young women feel to achieve an unrealistic standard of thinness. (Nevid, *Psychology: Concepts and Applications*, 4th ed., p. 302, © Cengage Learning.)

If you encounter a topic sentence that says one event led to or caused another, you are undoubtedly dealing with a cause and effect pattern.

Taking Notes on Cause and Effect Patterns

As you might expect, cycles of causes and effects such as the one already illustrated should be included in your notes along with the following:

1. the general cause and effect relationship described by the topic sentence

2. the specific causes and/or effects mentioned in the paragraph

Using Diagrams

Especially if the cause and effect relationship described in your reading relates to a physical process, consider taking notes using a diagram like the one shown below:

Diagrams take a while to get right. That's because it takes time to match the visual image to the verbal statement. But diagrams are worth the extra effort creating what cognitive psychologists call "desirable difficulty." In other words, if you have to work at learning something, you will probably understand it better than if you didn't have to struggle. However, if you don't want to spend the extra time to create a diagram, an outline will also get the job done:

Main Idea   Fear has a powerful effect on the human body.

Supporting Details   1. Breathe more deeply, sending muscles more oxygen and energy.

2. Heart beats faster, making blood circulate more rapidly.

    a. Blood rushes oxygen to all parts of body.

3. Stomach and intestines stop contractions so that all digestion ceases.

4. Saliva stops flowing and mouth gets dry.

5. Blood vessels shrink.

    a. Causes face to lose color.

From Reader to Writer The writer Dorothy Thompson said, "Only when we are no longer afraid do we begin to live." Use that quotation to begin your writing. Then explain what she meant by paraphrasing the quotation, for instance, "What Thompson suggests is that fear stops us from doing what we want. Freed of it, we begin to discover what we want to make of our lives."

Next, give one or two concrete examples of how getting rid of fear can help someone begin to live. Use people you know as examples or make up some examples that illustrate the point of the quote. Here's an example: "Take, for instance, the student who would like to participate in class discussions but is afraid he is not clever enough to do so. If he is brave enough to voice his opinion, he will likely discover that he actually gets a lot of support and praise for his originality and will start viewing himself with greater confidence. In a very real way, confidence breeds action."

SUMMING UP THE KEY POINTS

1. Paragraphs organized to show cause and effect always explain how one event produced or created another or other events.

2. Although they do not always appear, transitions such as *thus, therefore, consequently*, and *as a result* suggest that the cause and effect pattern is present. So, too, does the presence of verbs such as *triggers, causes*, and *stimulates*.

3. Topic sentences in the cause and effect pattern are likely to explain how some event or series of events led to specific effects or had powerful consequences—for example, "The study indicates that letting small children watch television throughout the day increases their risk of having concentration problems later on in school."

4. Topic sentences in this pattern may also describe the causes leading up to some larger event or experience—for example, "The topography of the land and the failure to heed the warnings of scientists led to a catastrophe that left thousands dead."

5. When a paragraph describes a cycle of causes and effects, it shows how one effect can become the cause of yet another effect, producing what amounts to a chain of cause and effect relationships.

6. Notes on this pattern should include the overall cause and effect relationship outlined in the topic sentence, along with any specific causes and effects identified in the paragraph.

▶ **EXERCISE 6**   **Understanding Cause and Effect Patterns**

DIRECTIONS   Read each paragraph. Circle any cause and effect transitions or verbs that appear in the paragraphs. Then take notes on each pattern. *Paraphrasing Note*: Come up with substitute language for, first, the cause, and then the effect. This strategy works well for this pattern *unless* the cause or the effect is a proper name or specialized term. When that's the case, use the proper name and concentrate on the other half of the cause and effect relationship.

The first two sentences need to be combined to create a main idea statement, which describes one of the most important causes of the American Revolutionary War.

The supporting details focus on the cause.

The concluding sentence restates the cause and effect relationship.

EXAMPLE   No one would deny that several events (led to) America's Revolutionary War. But one of the most important was the introduction of the Coercive* or Intolerable Acts, which were designed to punish Americans for the Boston Tea Party,† The Port of Boston was closed until the tea that had been destroyed was paid for. In addition, any English officials accused of committing murder in the course of suppressing a riot or enforcing the law could no longer be tried in the colony where the incident had taken place. Moreover, Massachusetts officials would no longer be locally elected; instead, they had to be appointed by the king. Perhaps most offensive to the Americans was the new Quartering Act. It specified that British troops could be housed in all inns or homes even without the owners' permission. (As a result) of the Coercive Acts, many Americans who had been undecided about rebellion became committed to the idea of throwing off British rule.

Main Idea   The Coercive Acts played a key role in America's decision to rebel against the British.

Supporting Details   1. Coercive, or Intolerable, Acts introduced after Americans dumped British tea into the ocean.

2. The Port of Boston was closed until tea was paid for.

3. English officials who committed murder while putting down a riot or enforcing laws couldn't be tried where murder had occurred.

4. Massachusetts officials had to be appointed by king rather than locally elected.

5. Most infuriating was Quartering Act, which put British soldiers into inns and homes of the colonists without asking their permission.

---

*coercive: forcing someone to do something against his or her will.
†Boston Tea Party: In 1773, Bostonians angry over British taxes on tea hurled 342 chests of English tea into the ocean.

EXPLANATION   This paragraph tells readers that Americans fought the Revolutionary War (the effect), in part at least, because of the hated Coercive Acts (the cause). The major details describe the acts so that readers understand the source of the hatred.

1. In his book *The Bounty of the Sea*, Jacques Cousteau, the underwater explorer, writer, and filmmaker, painted a terrifying portrait of what will happen if, in his words, we let the ocean "sicken and die" from pollution. From Cousteau's point of view, the death of the ocean, or extinction of sea life, will have terrifying consequences for all of humanity. Without sea life, the ocean would become a rotting grave. Billions of decaying bodies would create a stench* that would make its way into coastal regions. Consequently, people would have to abandon their homes to escape the smell. In addition, the death-filled seas would no longer be able to maintain a balance between the gases that make life possible. The carbon dioxide in the atmosphere would increase, trapping the heat that normally radiates outward from Earth into space. As a result, temperatures at sea level would dramatically increase. Yet another consequence would be visible on the ocean's surface. The surface would be covered with a thick film of decayed matter. Thus, the ocean would no longer give water to the skies through evaporation. Rain would be a rarity. Drought would range* over the land, and multitudes would starve.

Main Idea
_____

_____

Supporting Details
_____

_____

_____

_____

_____

_____

---

*stench: smell, stink.
*range: move about, travel.

_____

_____

2. Seasonal Affective Disorder (SAD) is a depressive condition that occurs during the winter months. According to one theory, SAD is related to an increase in the hormone melatonin. This hormone is released by the pineal gland during dark hours and is suppressed by light. In winter when the light decreases, increased amounts of melatonin in the body can cause drowsiness and fatigue. Further evidence for this theory is the fact that SAD occurs more commonly among those living in regions with shorter daylight hours. Medications to reduce melatonin in the body have been of some benefit in treating SAD.

(Neighbors & Tannehill-Jones, *Human Diseases* 2nd ed., p. 436, © Cengage Learning.)

Main Idea

_____

_____

Supporting Details

_____

_____

_____

_____

_____

_____

_____

_____

 ## Pattern 6: Classification

"In the last few years, we've learned that the formation and maintenance of categories have their roots in known biological processes in the brain."
—Behavioral scientist Daniel Levitin

In the classification pattern, the order of the supporting details is, once again, not important. However, there is a critical difference between simple listing and classification. Paragraphs relying on the classification pattern always make the same point: They tell the reader how some larger group can be divided into smaller subgroups, or classes, each with its own defining set of characteristics. For example, in the following paragraph, the authors classify voting methods in the House of Representatives.

The topic sentence covers all of the ways that voting can take place in the House of Representatives.

The supporting details then further describe those ways, giving each one a name and a brief description.

Members of the House of Representatives may vote in four different ways. The most common method is the *voice vote*. Members in favor of a bill say "yea," while those opposed say "nay." The Speaker of the House then judges, largely by volume, which side has the most voice votes and announces the result. If any member feels that the Speaker is mistaken, the Speaker can be forced to call for a *division* or *standing vote* in which the members stand to be counted for or against. A third method is the *yea or nay vote*. If one-fifth of the members present demand, all the members of the House present must be recorded as saying *yea* or *nay* to the measure being proposed. The *recorded vote* is taken when at least twenty-five members of the House request it, and the results are tallied electronically. (Source of Information: Shick and Pfister, *American Government: Continuity and Change*, p. 29.)

Typically for the classification pattern, the authors open by telling their readers two things: (1) the larger group to be subdivided, voting in the House of Representatives, and (2) the number of categories produced by classification, four. They then proceed to describe each category in more specific detail.

Typical Topic Sentences

Topic sentences like those listed here practically guarantee that a classification pattern organizes the paragraph.

1. Psychologists have identified four key determinants of attraction.
   (Adapted from Nevid, *Psychology: Concepts and Applications*, 4th ed., p. 528, © Cengage Learning.)

2. Researchers of human behavior insist that everyone, no matter what we claim or want to believe, lies, and the lies we tell fall into eight different categories, from little white lies to criminal deception.

3. According to the Köppen Climate Classification System, Mexico has seven main climate regions.

4. The Indian caste system once assigned human beings to four different groups, with Brahmins at the top of the heap and the untouchables at the bottom.

Frequently Used Words in Classification Topic Sentences ●	Categories Classes Components Elements Factors Features Fields	Groups Kinds · Parts Problems Ranks Types

Telltale Tables

Tables like the following frequently signal the presence of the classification pattern. Keep in mind, though, that you can also use tables to review (just cover the right-hand side and see what you can remember about each classification category).

Table 10.1: The Four Basic Components of a Strategy

Scope	• Identifies the markets or industries in which firm will compete
Resource Deployment	• Indicates how company will allocate or use resources
Competitive Advantage	• Specifies what advantages a firm has relative to competitors
Synergy	• Reflects extent to which businesses inside the firm can draw upon one another

Source of information: Van Fleet and Peterson, *Contemporary Management*, 2nd ed., pp. 73–74, © Cengage Learning.

Taking Notes on the Classification Pattern

To be complete, notes on the classification pattern require the following information:

1. the name of the larger group being broken down into subgroups

2. the names of the categories if they are supplied

3. a brief description of each category

Making Classification Charts

Consider making a classification chart to give your brain a visual image that mirrors the verbal pattern.

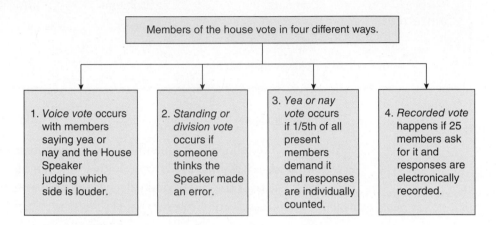

If names of categories do appear in the classification paragraph, put those names first in your notes. This note-taking format highlights the individual categories. Keep in mind, though, that the subgroups in this pattern are not always named.

 SUMMING UP THE KEY POINTS

1. Like simple listing, the classification pattern does not require that supporting details be presented in a particular order. However, the classification pattern, unlike simple listing, always makes the same point: It explains how some larger group can be broken down into smaller subgroups. Then the supporting details describe each subgroup in detail.

2. The topic sentence of the classification pattern usually names the number of subgroups that make up the larger whole—for example, "Currently, there are *three different kinds* of medication that deal with anxiety."

3. Categories in the classification pattern are not always identified by name. However, if they are identified by name, the names should be included in your notes. Include as well the characteristics that describe each subgroup.

▶ **EXERCISE 7**   **Recognizing and Understanding Classification Patterns**

DIRECTIONS   Read and take notes on each paragraph. *Paraphrasing Note*: If the categories have names, those should not change. Concentrate on paraphrasing the descriptive details used to differentiate between or among the categories.

The words *classified* and *categories* in the topic sentence give the pattern away.

The supporting details then describe each subgroup of the larger category.

EXAMPLE   Psychological problems are generally classified into two categories: externalizing disorders and internalizing disorders. The **externalizing disorders** are characterized by aggression turned outward, such as striking out at other people or the environment. People suffering from these kinds of disorders exhibit behaviors such as lying, stealing, disobedience, and delinquency. Other common symptoms of externalizing disorders include fighting, cruelty to animals, property destruction, temper tantrums, hostility toward authority figures, and violating the rights of others. The **internalizing disorders** are directed inward. These affect the individual rather than other people or the environment. These disorders are characterized by anxiety, depression, worrying, withdrawal, phobias, and panic attacks. (Source of information: Kaplan, *Adolescence*, 1st ed., pp. 463–64, © Cengage Learning.)

Main Idea Psychological problems are generally divided into two groups: externalizing disorders and internalizing disorders.

Supporting Details 1. Externalizing disorders are directed toward others or the environment.
   a. Include not telling the truth, theft, refusing to obey rules, and delinquency.
   b. Also include violence, fighting, animal cruelty, property damage, temper blowups, hostility, and ignoring the rights of others.
2. Internalizing disorders are directed inward, toward self.
   a. Include worry, depression, self-isolation, irrational fears, and panic attacks.

EXPLANATION   The notes contain the essential elements of the classification pattern. The larger group is divided into two smaller categories, and the names and characteristics of each group are listed.

Arteries carry blood away from the heart; veins carry it back.

1. In the human body, blood circulates through elastic, tube-like canals called *blood vessels.* Consisting of three different types, blood vessels are well adapted to their functions. The vessels called *arteries* carry blood away from the heart to all parts of the body. The largest artery in the human body is the *aorta.* Arterial blood appears bright red because it is filled with oxygen. In contrast, blood in the *veins,* another type of blood vessel, appears purplish because it is no longer carrying a supply of oxygen. Veins, which carry blood back to the heart, contain small valves that prevent the blood from flowing backward. This is important in the lower parts of the body where the blood has to move against the pull of gravity. The third type of blood vessel is the *capillary.* Capillaries are tiny vessels connecting arteries and veins. Capillary walls are extremely thin. They have to be thin so that digested food can pass through them to the cells of the body.

Main Idea

_____

_____

Supporting Details

_____

_____

_____

_____

_____

_____

_____

_____

_____

_____

2. Researcher John Lee has identified what he calls six different styles of love. The **erotic lover** focuses on the physical aspects of being in love. He or she is not especially jealous or possessive, and although emotions are intense, this lover is not likely to undergo much self-sacrifice in an effort to obtain love. The **ludic lover** sees love as a

game played for fun. This individual avoids deep relationships and may juggle a number of partners at the same time. Just the right degree of emotionality is maintained so that personal commitment never becomes too demanding. The **storgic lover** sees love as a slow, steady climb toward commitment. Neither intense emotions nor sexual encounters are central to the relationship. Instead of seeking the ups and downs of a passionate relationship, the storgic lover approaches love as a relationship mostly based on shared activities and interests. The **manic lover** is the opposite of the storgic lover. The manic lover is obsessed with his or her partner. Jealous and possessive, he or she is filled with anxiety that something will ruin the relationship. The **pragmatic lover** knows what he or she wants and "shops" to find a partner with the desired interests and goals. The relationship that ensues is not a highly passionate or intense one; rather, it is one that fits into a well-defined pattern. The **agapic lover** is patient, kind, altruistic, and compassionate. Love is given without any conditions and may involve self-sacrifice. Lee found no examples of pure agapic love in his research but did find some aspects of agape in a number of relationships. (Adapted from Kaplan, *Adolesence*, pp. 348–49, © Cengage Learning.)

Main Idea

_____

_____

Supporting Details

_____

_____

_____

_____

_____

_____

_____

_____

_____

_____

_____

_____

_____

_____

✔ CHECK YOUR UNDERSTANDING

1. What's the major difference between the simple listing pattern and the classification pattern?

   _____

   _____

   _____

2. What does the topic sentence in the classification pattern usually do?

   _____

3. When taking notes on the classification pattern, what should you include in your notes?

   _____

From Reader to Writer As a quick look at YouTube will tell you, animal videos are one of the biggest draws on the Web. But not all animal videos have the same purpose. Type the phrase "animal videos" (or another phrase you think more appropriate) into a search box and scan at least two screens worth of titles. Read the captions as well. And if you can do it without frittering the entire day away, watch some of the videos. Then write a paper that classifies them into the different categories your research has uncovered. You can decide if you want to give each category a name or not. However, you do need to describe each category's purpose and give a typical example of each one.

Identifying the Primary Pattern

Until now, you've been working with one organizational pattern at a time. But in the next exercise, you'll be asked to select one particular pattern among several possibilities. That means it's time to introduce the notion of the primary pattern.

When writers rely on a particular organizational pattern, that doesn't mean every sentence will reflect the **primary pattern**, or overall pattern. There may be a sentence or two that doesn't. Consider, for instance, sentences 6 and 8 in the following paragraph:

Sentences 1, 2, and 3 make up a main idea statement that describes a change or shift in the country's reliance on outsourcing.

The supporting details provide the causes behind the shift. Note how the phrases "one reason" and "another cause" suggest the cause and effect pattern.

[1]Mention the word *outsourcing* to most American workers and you are not likely to put a smile on their face. [2]The practice of sending jobs out of the country in order to increase corporate profits by using cheap labor has left many workers in the United States scrambling to earn a living. [3]But that situation might be changing as more and more companies once again think about turning out made-in-America products. [4]One reason for the shift in thinking is the rising cost of labor among big suppliers. [5]In some sections of China, for instance, the price of labor has gone up by 15 percent. [6]Another cause for the shift from outsourcing to *insourcing*—the newly coined term that perfectly describes the corporate world's change of heart—is the rising price of shipping costs around the world. [7]As shipping costs rise, profits decrease and directly undermine one of the main reasons for outsourcing in the first place. [8]Companies considering producing their wares in the United States also know that American workers are, with the exception of workers in Ireland and Norway, among the world's most productive. (Source of productivity statistic: http://www.csoonline.com/article/221017/is-insourcing-the-new-outsourcing.)

If you trace the repetition and reference in the paragraph, you'll see that practically every sentence tries to help explain *why* more companies are thinking about producing goods at home rather than out of the country. That makes the primary pattern of organization cause and effect, even though sentence 6 introduces a definition and sentence 8 makes a comparison. It would be a mistake to say that the primary pattern of this paragraph is either definition or comparison and contrast. One or two sentences do not a pattern make.

There will be times when patterns balance each other out so equally we can talk about mixed paragraph patterns. We'll discuss those in the next chapter. But much of the time, and certainly within this chapter, you'll be working mainly with primary, rather than mixed, patterns.

▶ **EXERCISE 8** **Recognizing Primary Patterns of Organization**

DIRECTIONS Read each paragraph. Then circle the appropriate letter to identify the primary pattern of organization.

1. A **generic product**, sometimes called a **generic brand**, is a product with no brand name at all. Its plain package carries only the name of the product—applesauce, peanut butter, potato chips, or whatever—in black type. Generic products, available in supermarkets since 1977, usually are made by the major producers that manufacture name brands. They appeal mainly to consumers who are willing to sacrifice consistency in size or quality for a lower price. However, generic products are not necessarily lower in quality. Even though generic brands may have accounted for as much as 10 percent of all grocery sales several years ago, they currently represent less than 1 percent. (Pride, Hughes and Kapoor, *Business* 10th ed., p. 403, © Cengage Learning.)

   a. definition

   b. comparison and contrast

   c. cause and effect

   d. classification

2. Child psychologists are inclined to label aggressive behavior as *overt* or *relational*. *Overt aggression* harms others through actual physical damage or the threat of physical harm. Children who engage in overt aggression are likely to push, hit, or kick a peer. At the very least, those who are overtly aggressive will make explicit threats to do some kind of physical harm in the future. Unlike overt aggression, relational aggression is more psychological than physical, and it revolves around threats to or criticism of peer relations. Children who use relational aggression don't physically hurt their victims. Instead,

they may taunt a peer by saying that he or she is unlikable and has no friends. At one time, parents and educators focused on strategies to avoid overt aggression among children, because this kind of aggression seemed the more harmful of the two. But research has shown that children also suffer from being the target of relational aggression. Although there are other kinds of aggression among children, these two forms tend to be the most common.

a. time order: process

b. simple listing

c. cause and effect

d. comparison and contrast

3. The painting known as the *Mona Lisa* has fascinated art lovers for centuries. But it wasn't until the twentieth century that one man fell so in love with the *Mona Lisa* that he decided to steal her from the Louvre.† In 1909, Italian-born Vincenzo Peruggia was employed by the Louvre to do some painting; it was at this point that Peruggia first got a look at the masterpiece that was to get him into so much trouble. On August 21, 1911, Peruggia returned to the Louvre as a visitor and headed straight for the *Mona Lisa.* Twenty minutes later, he left the museum with the painting tucked inside his jacket. For more than two years, investigators hunted unsuccessfully for the painting. Then, on November 29, 1913, a wealthy Italian art dealer received a letter saying the *Mona Lisa* would be returned for a price. On December 10, 1913, the art dealer arranged to meet with the painting's new owner. After Peruggia produced the painting, police took him into custody. At his trial in 1914, Peruggia explained that he had stolen the *Mona Lisa* because he couldn't forget her smile. The unsympathetic judge sentenced the would-be art collector to three years in jail.

a. time order: dates and events

b. comparison and contrast

c. cause and effect

d. simple listing

4. Certain attitudes toward life help make us successful. However, if those same attitudes are strictly maintained and never deviate, or

---

†Louvre: a famous museum in Paris, France.

change, they often prove to be an obstacle to happiness. The behavior of a problem-solver, someone who immediately tries to find solutions to difficult situations, perfectly illustrates how a positive attitude can turn negative. There simply are problems and questions in life with no solutions or answers. Why is it, for example, that some perfectly wonderful people die young while some evil ones survive and thrive? Unfortunately, people who insist on coming up with the right solution for every difficulty are inclined to get frustrated with such situations and they search for answers that can't be found. Relying relentlessly on logic is another attitude that can become harmful when pushed to extremes. There are situations in life where sympathy and empathy are more crucial than logic. But the person who has made reliance on logic a religion never figures that out. Yet another attitude that can have a down side is fear of failure. If we try hard to succeed because we fear failure, that's a good thing. But if we are overly terrified of failing, we are unlikely to engage in the original thinking creativity requires.

a. comparison and contrast

b. simple listing

c. classification

d. time order: process

5. The human brain has two hemispheres—the right and the left. Although the hemispheres cooperate for many functions, research suggests that they control highly different activities. Thanks to the left side of our brain, we are able to master and manipulate language, using it to communicate our thoughts. The left side of our brain helps us make sense by giving order and logic to our utterances.* The right hemisphere is less crucial to language production and appears to be more concerned with the creation of images. Research suggests that the right brain dominates during infancy. Babies make sense of the world by visualizing, rather than naming, and visualization is controlled by the right side of the brain.

a. time order: dates and events

b. comparison and contrast

c. cause and effect

d. simple listing

---

*utterances: verbal statements.

6. Can't tell the difference between emoji and emoticons? Don't let Carnegie Mellon Professor Scott Fahlman hear you say that. Fahlman, widely credited with creating the first emoticons in 1982 on the school's online message board, has no use for emoji, the standardized icons that originated in Japan in the nineties, extending beyond faces to display everything from smiles and frowns to weather conditions. For Fahlman, emoticons, text characters that the user thinks up to express emotions, are more creative than the predefined emoji images, which are limited in number and require no imagination on the user's part. Right now emoticons and emoji seem to be equally popular, but anecdotal evidence* suggests that emoji may be taking the lead. NBA player Mike Scott had his arm tattooed with emoji. Beyoncé marketed some emoji-themed tee shirts, and Katy Perry made a video of her hit song "Roar" with the lyrics translated into, you guessed it, emoji.

a. time order: process

b. comparison and contrast

c. cause and effect

d. classification

7. An attacker has put you in a wristlock to force you to submit. He has grabbed your wrist, pressing hard on the bones and nerves to cause you pain. If you try to pull away, you cause yourself more pain, and you could actually break your own wrist in an attempt to escape. However, if you remember a simple self-defense technique, you can free yourself. First, fight your instinct to tighten the muscles in your hands and arms. Doing so will actually cause you more pain because the tension will exert more pressure. If you are in pain, you cannot strike out to free yourself from your opponent. Second, let your hand and wrist relax and go limp. This will lessen the pain you're experiencing long enough for you to punch, kick, or bite your attacker as a way of forcing him to let you go. Relaxing your hand may also surprise him, causing him to loosen his grip for a moment. Third, the thumb is the weakest link in a person's grip, so rotate your

---

*anecdotal evidence: evidence collected from personal accounts rather than scientific studies.

arm and pull your hand toward your attacker's thumb for the best chance of breaking free.

a. definition
b. time order: process
c. comparison and contrast
d. classification

8. There are four common types of vegetarians, each of whom follows a different set of rules. Lacto-ovo vegetarians don't eat meat, but they do eat eggs and dairy products. Lacto vegetarians consume dairy products but won't touch eggs, whereas ovo vegetarians eat eggs but avoid dairy products. For members of the fourth category, vegans, eggs and dairy products are completely off the menu. So, too, are all animal by-products. Some vegans won't even touch honey. The restriction on animal by-products can extend to other aspects of life: Some vegans refuse to wear leather, silk, or wool.

a. comparison and contrast
b. classification
c. cause and effect
d. time order: process

9. The comic book superhero Superman first appeared on magazine racks in 1938. Wonder Woman arrived just three years later in 1941. But ever since her arrival, there's been an ongoing debate among fans arguing about which superhero could defeat the other in combat. Use the Web to follow discussion threads on the topic, and you'll find that the tone can become quite heated. Superman's supporters insist that, in terms of raw power and brute strength, Wonder Woman is no match for her brawny male counterpart. Unimpressed, Wonder Woman's fans point out that their hero has always shown herself capable of outfoxing her opponents with smart tactics, imaginative weapon use, and savvy strategy. Up against such smarts, they insist, Superman, despite his muscle, would not stand a chance. Unfortunately, fans of the two comic book characters may never get to see the two heroes duke it out and find out who wins. The confrontation probably won't take place because DC Comics has launched a new series titled Superman/Wonder Woman, and, clearly, romance, not war, is in the air. Issue #1 is titled "Power Couple." Issue #13 is called

"Battlefield of Love." Issue #4 shows the two in a passionate clinch. However, there will be 52 issues in the series, and if love doesn't conquer all, fans may still get to see a showdown between the two superheroes in the final installment of the series.

a. comparison and contrast

b. classification

c. cause and effect

d. time order: process

10. In the world of corporate America, there seems to be no penalty for incompetence, and there are numerous examples of high-priced executives who did a poor job yet received big rewards. When Pacific Gas and Electric filed for bankruptcy, it paid all of its top executives big bonuses as rewards for their splendid work. Coca-Cola's CEO, after supervising the loss of $4 billion, was given a check for $18 million. American Telephone and Telegraph fired CEO John Walther after nine months because he "lacked intellectual leadership." After giving Walther his walking papers, AT&T wrote him a final check for $26 million. Under the management of Jill Barron, a toy manufacturer, Mattel, lost $2.5 billion. She joined the line at the unemployment office with $40 million in pay and bonuses in her purse. (Adapted from Conlin, *The American Past*, 9th ed., p. 846, © Cengage Learning.)

a. comparison and contrast

b. classification

c. simple listing

d. time order: process

DIGGING DEEPER **What Causes the Thrill of Passion?** *Saul Kassin, Steven Fein, and Hazel Rose Markus*

Looking Ahead Is it possible that what we like to call "passion" is actually based on a confusion between cause and effect? The theory of *excitation transfer* described in this reading from a sociology text suggests that this is a very real possibility.

Getting Focused Preview the reading and you will see only one term in boldface: *excitation transfer theory*. It's pretty clear, then, that you need to know the meaning of that term. You also have to figure out what it might have to do with the thrill of passion, which is introduced in the title and the opening preview.

1 Passionate love is an intense emotional, heart-thumping state of absorption in another person. From ecstatic highs to agonizing lows, it is the bittersweet stuff of love poems, romance novels, pop music, and soap operas. But what is passionate love, and where does it come from? Researchers Ellen Berscheid and Elaine Walster have argued that passionate love is an emotion that can be analyzed like any other emotional response humans display or feel. Drawing on a two-factor theory of emotion developed by Stanley Shachter and Jerome Singer, Berscheid and Walster believe that passionate love is fueled by two ingredients: (1) a heightened sense of physical arousal and (2) the (sometimes mistaken) belief that the arousal was triggered by romantic desire.

2 According to this two-factor theory, the symptoms of arousal—pounding heart, sweaty palms, churning stomach, weak knees—are not always a response to a potential love interest. They can also occur when we misinterpret, or misunderstand, the cause of that physiological upheaval. In other words, they can occur when we confuse the effect of one stimulus with the effect of another.

3 According to **excitation transfer theory**, bodily arousal triggered by one stimulus can be misattributed to a second stimulus that benefitted from but did not necessarily cause the strong physiological reaction. For example, the energy springing from dancing can intensify a person's feelings for his or her partner, thereby fanning the flames of passion. The combined arousal effects of both the person and the dance then seem to be caused *only* by the second stimulus—the presence of the person. This may well be why intense sexual attraction and passion may not always make the best basis for a relationship. The passion felt may, in fact, be based on a confused sense of cause and effect.

4   Donald Dutton and Arthur Aron first tested this controversial hypothesis in a study that took place on two bridges above British Columbia's Capilano River. One was a narrow and wobbly suspension bridge (450 feet long and 5 feet wide with a low handrail) that sways 250 feet above rocky rapids—a nightmare for anyone the slightest bit afraid of heights. The other bridge, in contrast, was wide, sturdy, and only 10 feet above the ground. Whenever an unaccompanied young man walked across one of these bridges, he was met by an attractive young woman, who introduced herself as a research assistant, and then asked him to fill out a brief questionnaire. She also gave him her phone number in case he wanted more information about the project.

5   According to excitation transfer theory, it would be likely that the young men shaken by the experience of crossing the flimsy suspension bridge would be more likely to call the researcher than those men whose crossing had been less fear-inducing. As it turned out, that prediction proved correct. The men who crossed the scary bridge made the call more often than the men who crossed the sturdier, less anxiety-producing bridge. In a similar study called "Love at First Fright," researchers Cindy Meston and Penny Frohlich took their subjects to an amusement park. They discovered that men and women in the study rated photographs of potential partners as decidedly more or less attractive depending on whether or not they had looked at the photographs before or after taking a scary ride. Those who hadn't gone on an anxiety-inducing ride were far less likely to give high ratings to the photos, while those who had gave higher attractiveness ratings. Perhaps terror can fan the hot flames of romance.

6   And then again, maybe not. Perhaps it's just a relief to be with someone when we are in distress. In an attempt to rule out the possibility that relief rather than desire is what fuels attraction, Gregory White and his colleagues tried to create physiological arousal without the presence of distress. To do this, they had male participants run in place for either two minutes or fifteen seconds. Then both groups watched a videotape of a woman they expected to meet. One woman was made up to look attractive, the other to look unattractive. What the researchers found was that the men who ran for a longer period of time had a stronger reaction to both women. Men who ran longer were highly attracted to the woman made up to look pretty while men who had run a shorter period of time were less intensely attracted to the same woman. Similarly, the longer-running men had a strong, negative reaction to the woman made up to look unattractive. In contrast, the men who had run for only

a short period of time had a less intense negative response. This study suggested that the physiological arousal caused by physical activity—even without distress—intensifies emotional reactions, both positive and negative.

7   The research described above suggests that passion is not simply guided by our hearts. Instead, our passion might well be at the mercy of shaky bridges, roller coasters, tall buildings, and anything else that causes our hearts to race. This is an intriguing hypothesis. Certainly, it is consistent with the common observation that people are more likely to fall in love when they feel overwhelmed and anxious. But can we say for sure that passion is the result of misattributing the effect of one stimulus to another? Not really.

8   Based on the review of thirty-three experiments, Craig Foster and a team of researchers confirmed that *excitation transfer* does exist. But it's hardly the whole answer to what causes us to have a physiological response to passion so intense, we almost feel physically ill from the experience. The thrill we feel about a new and exciting, possibly dangerous, experience does sometimes get transferred to the people we meet during or right after the experience is over. Yet passion also occurs in the midst of exciting events when the person experiencing them knows full well that the excitement is playing into the feeling of sexual attraction. For the person experiencing passion, the original source just doesn't matter all that much. Researchers have also found, however, that wild, heart-thumping passion occurs when people have not undergone some wildly exciting experience prior to meeting someone new. All of which is to say, passion, the kind that makes your knees week, your stomach turn over, and your heart beat so fast you can barely breathe, cannot be so easily explained after all. (Adapted from Saul Kassin et al., *Social Psychology*, 8th ed., pp. 370–71, © Cengage Learning.)

Sharpening Your Skills

DIRECTIONS   Answer the following questions by filling in the blanks and circling the letter of the correct response.

Using Context Clues   1. Based on how the word *hypothesis* is used in paragraph 4, which definition for hypothesis would you choose and why?

   a. proven theory

   b. as of yet unproven theory

   c. theory proven to be false

Please explain. _____

_____

_____

2. Based on the context of paragraph 4, how would you define *controversial* in the following sentence: "Donald Dutton and Arthur Aron first tested this *controversial* hypothesis in a study that took place on two bridges above British Columbia's Capilano River"?

   a. subject to strong disagreement

   b. backed by sound evidence

   c. based on common sense

   d. widely shared by the population

3. Based on the context of paragraph 4, how would you define *suspension* in the following sentence: "One was a narrow and wobbly suspension bridge (450 feet long and 5 feet wide with a low handrail) that sways 250 feet above rocky rapids—a nightmare for anyone the slightest bit afraid of heights"?

   a. made of concrete

   b. well-built

   c. hanging

   d. poorly built

Main Ideas and Explanatory Patterns

4. Which statement best expresses the main idea of the reading?

   a. Passionate arousal has more to do with our exercise routine than it does with the person we are drawn to. We are most likely to experience passion as a result of engaging in some strenuous or dangerous physical activity that causes an intense physical response. That response encourages us to confuse fear with passion.

   b. While there is some evidence supporting the "theory of excitation transfer"—the idea that physical sensations produced by both fear and exercise may contribute to feelings of intense physical passion—passion is much too complicated to be explained by one cause.

   c. Passionate love is a heart-pounding experience that usually doesn't last very long, mainly because it's based on an exercise-high that we all too often misinterpret as love.

d. According to the theory of "excitation transfer," the experience of fear heightens our senses in general and makes us more prone to feeling intense passion for someone we barely know.

5. Which explanatory pattern best fits this reading?

a. The thesis statement opens the first paragraph.
b. The thesis statement ends the first paragraph.
c. The thesis statement is introduced by a reversal transition.
d. The main idea is implied.

Recognizing Organizational Patterns

6. What organizational pattern helps tie the details in this reading together?

_____

7. What two patterns of organization do you see at work in paragraph 5?

_____

Which one is primary? _____

Paraphrasing

8. In your own words, what is excitation transfer theory when used within the context of passionate love?

_____

_____

Understanding and Evaluating the Function of Supporting Details

9. According to the reading, what does dancing have to do with excitation transfer?

_____

_____

10. What is the authors' evidence for the following statement? "Perhaps terror can fan the hot flames of romance."

_____

_____

_____

Following the Author's Train of Thought

11. In paragraph 2, the phrase " that physiological upheaval" refers to what specific words previously introduced in the same paragraph?

_____

_____

12. What message do the words in opening paragraph 5 send to the reader?

_____

_____

13. What do the words *to do this* in the fourth sentence of paragraph 6 refer to?

_____

14. In paragraph 8, what does *it's* refer to in the second sentence?

_____

Drawing Inferences

15. Does this reading support the claim made by Ellen Berscheid and Elaine Walster?

___ Please explain. _____

_____

_____

From Reader to Writer For love to last, what do you think is the key ingredient, passion or friendship? Explain what ingredient or ingredients you consider essential. Since, to some degree, you will be using a cause and effect pattern of organization, look over the list of cause and effect transitions to see if there are places in your writing where a transition would increase the clarity.

▶ **TEST 1** **Reviewing Key Concepts**

DIRECTIONS Answer the following questions by filling in the blanks.

1. Paragraphs relying on the definition pattern frequently open _____

   _____.

2. In the time-order pattern of organization, the goal is to explain steps or events according to _____.

3. _____ are a good alternative to informal outlines when it comes to taking notes on the process pattern of development.

4. When a writer uses the simple listing pattern of organization, the topic sentence is likely to include a _____ word.

5. Paragraphs organized by the comparison and contrast pattern absolutely must have _____.

6. When readers take notes on the comparison and contrast pattern, they should not get so caught up in listing the _____ ____ that they forget about _____.

7. Paragraphs organized around _____ always explain how one or more events _____ another event or set of events.

8. Transitions such as _____ are likely to appear in the cause and effect pattern as are the verbs

   _____.

9. Some paragraphs explain how one effect becomes a cause of another and that cause, in turn, produces a new effect. This is called a

   _____ .

10. Paragraphs that use the classification pattern usually open with a

    _____

    _____ .

▶ **TEST 2**   **Recognizing Primary Patterns**

> **DIRECTIONS**   Identify the primary pattern of organization by circling the letter of the correct response.

1. The meaning of silence can vary with one's culture. Americans, for example, often view silence as negative. At business meetings, participants frequently force themselves to speak. They fear that being silent will make them appear as if they have nothing to say. On a personal level, silence is often interpreted as a sign that things are not going well. In a group, for example, members frequently mistrust the person who remains silent. It's assumed that he or she is bored or disinterested in the group's activities. In Japan, however, silence is viewed in an altogether different light. Silence, in a personal or a professional context, is often seen as positive. People who are silent at meetings are thought to reflect more deeply on the issues under discussion. During personal conversations, remaining silent so that the other person has a chance to speak is considered the height of politeness and courtesy. The Japanese, in general, prefer silence to speech.

    a. definition

    b. time order: process

    c. comparison and contrast

2. As a result of the tsunami disaster that struck Japan in 2011, hundreds of thousands of men, women, and children were left homeless. In response to the tragedy, many people began suffering from the signs and symptoms of severe depression. While efforts are being made to reunite families and rebuild lost housing, all of these efforts to return to normal will take time. In this period of intense sorrow and heartache, though, one small, quick fix has emerged in the shape of a fluffy, robot seal called Paro. Paro is programmed to respond to human touch and is being used to combat depression among those who have lost everything but their lives. The seal robots are housed in community shelters, where people can come to pet and play with them. In response to being stroked, the seals emit gurgling sounds of pleasure and wiggle their flippers. Although it remains to be seen how many people can actually be helped by the robot pets, there are some signs that the seals are doing some good.

One woman reported that she and her friends liked visiting the seals because they had lost their pets in the tsunami-caused flooding. Those who had lost their pets didn't want to get new ones until they knew where they would eventually be living. The robot seals helped fill the gap left by the animals' loss.

a. time order: process

b. cause and effect

c. comparison and contrast

3. During the Middle Ages (600–1500) in Europe, most ordinary people could not read. They had to rely on village gossip and on tales relayed by bands of storytellers. During this period, four main types of storytellers developed, each specializing in particular themes and characters. In northern Europe, *bards* recited poems about heavenly gods and earthly heroes. The poem *Beowulf*, for example, was probably first recited by an English bard. In France and Spain, *minstrels* related the great deeds performed by King Charlemagne's knights in stories like the *Song of Roland*. In France and Italy, *troubadours* spun tales of courtly romance that placed women on a pedestal with men under their command. In Germany, poet-musicians called *minnesingers* performed stories of passion and romance.

a. comparison and contrast

b. time order: dates and events

c. classification

4. Born to immigrant parents in 1917, it wasn't immediately clear that Louis Zamperini would become a war hero whose story would be the subject of both biography and film. Always in trouble as a kid, Zamperini was the neighborhood bad boy. Disgusted by his antics, neighbors predicted he'd end up in jail. Louis's older brother Pete, however, encouraged the fifteen-year-old Louis to learn discipline and self-control by becoming a runner. To everyone's surprise, including Zamperini's, the teenager was a natural, who ran in the 1936 Olympics at the age of nineteen. Although Zamperini didn't win any races, he finished with the fastest 5,000-meter time for an American and was looking to the 1940 Olympic games to prove he could medal. But that hope was dashed after the Japanese bombed Pearl Harbor in 1941, and the games were cancelled. Zamp, as his friends

called him, was headed not for the Olympic Games but for the military, where he became a bomber pilot. In 1943, on a search and rescue mission, Zamperini's plane crashed into the Pacific Ocean, and he and two survivors ended up drifting on a life raft for over six weeks, living off rain water and the few raw fish they could catch. Finally, Zamperini and the remaining survivor—the other man had died—were "rescued" by the Japanese, who put Zamperini into a series of interrogation camps, each one more brutal than the last. Amazingly, the Japanese knew about the young man's performance at the Olympics and wanted to use him to make radio broadcasts casting the Japanese in a favorable light. When Zamperini refused, they tortured him even more brutally than the other prisoners. But he could not be broken, and he survived until the war's end in 1945. Although Zamperini published his autobiography, *Devil at My Heels*, it was Laura Hillenbrand's biography *Unbroken* that made Zamperini a hugely admired public figure and the focus of Angelina Jolie's film by the same name.

a. definition

b. time order: dates and events

c. simple listing

5. In Northern India, a wasp known as *Rogas indiscretus* kills the gypsy moths that harm trees in the foothills of the Himalayas.[†] Scientists say the wasp's methods are simple yet quite efficient. The female wasp stings a gypsy moth caterpillar and deposits an egg inside it. After hatching, the wormlike baby wasp eats the moth's insides. The infant wasp then spins a cocoon inside the moth's dead body; the cocoon is protected by the mummified husk, or shell. Within a few weeks, the infant wasp grows into an adult—which, if female, is ready to lay at least two hundred eggs in other gypsy moth caterpillars. (Source of information: *U.S. News & World Report*, April 7, 1997, pp. 70–71.)

a. time order: process

b. comparison and contrast

c. classification

[†]Himalayas: mountains in south central Asia.

▶ **TEST 3**   **Recognizing Primary Patterns**

DIRECTIONS   Identify the primary pattern of organization by circling the letter of the correct response.

1. If you are thinking about leaving your job either by choice or at the request of your employer, here are some things you should and should *not* do when you leave. Don't tell off either your co-workers or your superiors, even if you feel that you have been badly treated. You never know when you might meet them again in a professional setting. Unless you have been fired for some truly horrible offense in which you have been caught red-handed, do ask for a reference. In looking for your next job, you will have to indicate where you have worked before, and even if it's bad, you want to know what your previous employer will say if asked for a recommendation. Plus, many employers who might have written a bad evaluation if they thought you weren't going to see it might well write a more neutral one if they know you are going to be reading what they've written. If a replacement has already been hired, don't tell him or her anything bad about the company. Your problems may have been a matter of personal chemistry, and your replacement might not share your difficulties. By the same token, when you interview for a new job, don't criticize your previous employer. Your criticism may be justified, but your potential new employer doesn't know you and is likely to assume you are a complainer or a troublemaker.

   a. definition

   b. time order: process

   c. simple listing

   d. comparison and contrast

2. The body's response to fresh wounds is remarkably quick and efficient. The first stage in the body's response occurs when the blood begins to clot. Next, tiny bodies in the bloodstream called **platelets** rush to the wound site and disintegrate, or dissolve. Fibrous proteins begin to form, and the blood that has already escaped hardens into a scab. Once the bleeding stops, the body releases chemicals called **pyrogens**. These chemicals cause the area surrounding the wound to grow warm. In turn, blood vessels grow wider, allowing nutrients, oxygen, and white blood cells to feed the wounded area and start the formation of new tissue.

    a. definition

    b. time order: process

    c. simple listing

    d. comparison and contrast

3. Few events are more bizarre or unbelievable than sudden death said to be caused by "voodoo" or "magic." Nevertheless, death caused by voodoo does, indeed, seem to occur. In his influential and still cited article on the subject,[†] the researcher Walter Cannon believed he had found an answer to why some people really did sicken and die when exposed to what others would consider harmless voodoo charms like bones, dead animals, and stuffed dolls. Cannon, a well-known medical researcher, argued that there was a physiological basis for death by voodoo. He claimed that the victims, who had to be believers in voodoo magic, were literally scared to death. Their bodies, that is, were overwhelmed by the physical changes that took place in response to intense fear. Cannon argued that profound fear and its effects on the body are what caused believers in voodoo to die if they considered themselves cursed.

    a. cause and effect

    b. time order: dates and events

    c. simple listing

    d. comparison and contrast

4. **Genetic screening** is the widespread routine testing for alleles[†] associated with genetic disorders. Genetic screening provides information on reproductive risks and helps families that are already affected by a genetic disorder. If a genetic disorder is detected early enough, treatments can sometimes minimize the effects of the disease. Hospitals routinely screen newborns for genetic diseases. Besides helping individuals, genetic screening can help us estimate the prevalence and distribution of harmful alleles in populations. (Starr, Taggert, Evers, & Starr, *Biology: The Unity and Diversity of Life*, 12th ed., p. 199, © Cengage Learning.)

    a. definition

    b. time order: process

    c. simple listing

    d. comparison and contrast

[†]Cannon's article originally appeared in the *American Journal of Public Health*, and it was titled "Voodoo Death."

[†]alleles: a pair of genes that occupies a specific position on a chromosome.

5. Private–prison businesses have been turning profits in America since the early 1600s, when English entrepreneurs began shipping convicts to the Virginia settlements and selling them as servants. Following the Civil War (1861–65), when manpower was in short supply, prison labor powered manufacturing in the North. By the mid-to late 1800s, convict labor leasing was encouraged by policy in over a dozen states. San Quentin, which was built in 1852 from rock and clay by convicts living on a nearby prison ship, was initially operated as a for-profit business. Although state and federal agencies took control of prisons starting in the 1920s, state-run prisons were not always typical for the United States. With the arrival of the drug wars in the late twentieth century, for-profit prisons made a comeback as stiff, new sentencing policies caused prison overcrowding. Faced with the need to expand the prison system, many lawmakers turned to the private prison industry. Today, 10 percent of the country's prisons are again run for profit, and in some states that figure goes as high as 44 percent. (Adapted from: Michael Ames. "Captive Market." *Harper's*, February, 2015, p. 39.)

   a. definition

   b. time order process

   c. time order: dates and events

   d. cause and effect

▶ **TEST 4**   **Recognizing Primary Patterns**

DIRECTIONS   Identify the primary pattern of organization by circling the letter of the correct response.

1. Though the U.S. president, unlike a prime minister, cannot command an automatic majority in the legislature, he does have some impressive powers. Simply by virtue of the office, the president is the official commander-in-chief of the armed forces. He can also grant reprieves and pardons for federal offenses, call Congress into special sessions, receive visiting dignitaries, and commission officers of the armed forces. Along with the Senate, the president has the power to make treaties with foreign countries, appoint judges to the Supreme Court, and place other high officials, like the Secretary of State, in office. The president also has the right to veto legislation and the power to ensure that legislation, once passed, is properly enforced. (Adapted from Wilson and DiIulio, *American Government*, 11th ed., p. 373, © Cengage Learning.)

   a. time order: process
   b. simple listing
   c. comparison and contrast
   d. cause and effect
   e. classification

2. If you are not a snake lover, you probably won't understand the lengths some people go to in order to procure an exotic snake. But snake lovers do exist. Just type the phrase "people who love snakes" into a search engine, and you will be amazed at how many sites come up. People who love and want to own exotic snakes will pay huge amounts of money to get their hands on, say, a gold-colored tree boa, a deadly black mamba, or a rare Boelen's python. And therein, of course, is the source of a lot of misery for snakes who get ripped out of their native habitats and stored in places snakes were never meant to be, like inside suitcases, handbags, briefcases, even strapped to the human body. Although there are some fairly stiff restrictions against trading in exotic reptiles, greed consistently overcomes fear of the law, and snake traders run risks most people would never dream of. They will, for instance, anesthetize deadly reptiles and put them inside their clothing, all the while praying that the snakes don't wake up earlier than expected. Often, snake traders get caught or

bitten. But then the traders knew what they were in for. The snakes didn't. Yet as Jennie Erin Smith writes in *Stolen World: A Tale of Reptiles, Smugglers, and Skullduggery,* far too many snakes never make it to their would-be owners. They die in transit, sometimes frozen in a plane's baggage compartment or infected with disease. Most typically, they die through suffocation, after being stuffed into a too tight container by an inexperienced snake trader who forgot that snakes need air to survive.

a. definition

b. time order: process

c. comparison and contrast

d. cause and effect

e. classification

3. Firms with an eye on the market often sponsor contests and sweepstakes to introduce new goods and services and to attract additional customers. Contests require entrants to complete a task such as solving a puzzle or answering questions in a trivia quiz, and they may also require proof of purchase. Sweepstakes, on the other hand, choose winners by chance, so no product purchase is necessary. Sweepstakes are more popular with consumers than contests because they do not take as much effort for consumers to enter. Marketers like them, too, because they are inexpensive to run and the number of winners is predetermined. With some contests, the sponsors cannot predict the number of people who will correctly complete the puzzles or gather the right number of symbols from scratched off cards. (Boone and Kurtz, *Contemporary Marketing,* 15th ed., p. 591, © Cengage Learning.)

a. definition

b. time order: dates and events

c. comparison and contrast

d. cause and effect

e. classification

4. Spanish poet Federico García Lorca was born near the city of Granada, Spain, in 1898. His creative genius showed itself early on. As a teenager, he was already writing poems and reciting them in neighborhood cafes. Although Lorca started out studying

philosophy and law, by 1919, he had abandoned both in favor of writing poetry and plays. His first play, *The Butterfly's Evil Spell*, was staged in 1920. It closed in one night, but that did not discourage its creator. A year later, Lorca published a book of poems and seven years later, another volume called *The Gypsy Ballads*. This one made the thirty-year-old Lorca famous, earning him the nickname the "Gypsy Poet." Annoyed by what he saw as the public's attempt to pigeonhole his work, Lorca moved to New York to study English at Columbia University. He returned to Spain in 1931, and by 1933 he had another play staged, *Blood Wedding,* the story of a woman who runs off with her lover on her wedding night. This play was a success, and Lorca followed it with *Yerma,* the tale of a woman who murders her husband because he cannot give her a child. It was at this point that the poet caught the eye of the conservative political party that seized power in Spain in 1936. The group's leader, Francisco Franco, disapproved of plays that did not celebrate family values. Even worse in Franco's eyes, Lorca had made it clear that his sympathies lay with working people, not the wealthy industrialists who supported Franco. On the morning of August 19, 1936, Franco had Lorca shot and buried in an unmarked grave. The poet's writings were burned in Granada's central square.

a. time order: dates and events

b. simple listing

c. comparison and contrast

d. cause and effect

e. classification

11 Combining Patterns in Paragraphs and Longer Readings

IN THIS CHAPTER, YOU WILL LEARN

- why writers sometimes combine organizational patterns in paragraphs and longer readings.
- how skillful readers respond to combined patterns in paragraphs and extended readings.
- how to decide which patterns are central to the main idea and which ones are not.
- how to take complete notes on mixed patterns.

> "The brain tries to make sense of information by reducing it to familiar patterns."
>
> —FROM THE TALKING PAGE LITERACY ORGANIZATION

Until now, you've worked with paragraphs based *primarily* on one organizational pattern. Some main ideas, however, rely equally on more than one pattern of organization. This is particularly true for longer readings, where authors frequently combine two, three, sometimes even four patterns in order to explain a complex idea.

Thus, it's important for you to learn how to (1) identify the different organizational patterns used in a longer reading, and (2) figure out which pattern or patterns are essential to developing the controlling main idea. Then you can use the underlying structure of the patterns to decide what's important and figure out how to best store the new information in your long-term memory.

Combining Patterns in Paragraphs

When the main idea calls for it, writers combine patterns rather than just relying on one. You can see that in the following paragraph, where two organizational patterns are necessary to develop the underlined topic sentence. The question for you is, Which two? Read the paragraph and answer the questions in the margin.

What pattern is
suggested by the
topic sentence?

¹Increased spells of warm weather and decreased use of pesticides have <u>resulted</u> in a plague of fire ants. ²Indeed, pleasant weather and an absence of pesticides have *encouraged* whole armies of ants to make their homes in farmers' fields, where they can leisurely munch on potato and okra crops. ³Should a tractor overturn one of their nests, the furious ants swarm over the machine and attack the driver. ⁴Using their jaws to hold the victim's skin, they thrust their stingers into the flesh, maintaining the same position for up to twenty-five seconds. ⁵The sting *produces* a sharp burning sensation and frequently *causes* painful infections that can last weeks and even months. ⁶Some victims who were especially allergic to the ants' poison have not survived a fire-ant attack.

What pattern
does the author
need to describe
the ant's attack?

Trace the repetition and reference that weave their way through this paragraph and you'll see that the author wants to talk about fire-ant attacks. That's the topic. Every sentence addresses this subject.

What does the author want to say about that topic? She wants to tell readers that due to pesticides being used less, fire-ant attacks are on the rise. That's the main idea, and it's based on a cause and effect relationship that looks like this:

| Decreased use of pesticides | → | Increase in fire-ant attacks |

But now look what happens in sentence 3. At this point, the writer wants to tell readers what the fire-ant attack feels like. To that end, the writer explains step by step what happens when fire ants get aggressive. Thus, we can rightly say that the paragraph is organized according to two different patterns, cause and effect *and* process. The two patterns are just about equal in importance because the author wants to communicate two kinds of information: (1) why the attacks are on the rise and (2) what an attack feels like.

Taking Notes on Mixed Pattern Paragraphs

Because the paragraph on fire ants describes a cause and effect relationship and outlines the steps in a process, you should first identify the key elements in each pattern. Then decide if all of those elements are essential to the main idea.

Since the cause and effect relationship is what structures the main idea of the paragraph, we definitely have to (1) identify and link both cause and effect in our notes and (2) provide any details about specific causes and effects. We should also include, as the author does, the steps or stages of an attack, because the author's purpose in describing the steps is to say to readers, "Here's why this main idea is worth talking about in the first place; fire-ant attacks can be scary, painful, even deadly."

But where the steps are concerned, there's some leeway in terms of what we can put in or leave out. Because the writer wants readers to understand how intense and awful the attack is, we don't necessarily have to include in our notes the fact that the ants eat potatoes and okra. We can also abbreviate or even eliminate any details that don't directly fulfill the author's purpose of telling readers why fire ants can be dangerous.

Notes on the fire-ant paragraph, then, would look something like this:

Main Idea More warm weather and decreased use of pesticides have produced a big increase in fire ants.

Supporting Details
1. Armies of ants have moved into farmers' fields.

2. If tractor overturns nest, ants swarm the machine and attack driver.

3. The ants thrust stingers into flesh, holding the same position for up to twenty-five seconds.

4. Sting produces painful burning sensation and can cause infections.

5. Some people with allergies have died following fire-ant attacks.

Not All Patterns Are Equal

In the paragraph on fire ants, both organizational paragraphs were equally essential to explaining the main idea. However, when taking notes on a paragraph with two or more organizational patterns, don't assume all the patterns included are always equal in importance. Instead, decide which pattern or patterns are most important based on two questions: (1) Which pattern or patterns are central to explaining the main idea? (2) Which pattern or patterns organize the most sentences? The answers to those two questions will tell you which patterns are essential to developing the main idea. Then some or all of the *key elements* of those patterns should appear in your notes.

Pattern Details Aren't All Equal Either. The phrase "key elements" in the previous sentence is italicized for a reason. Even after you decide what patterns are central to a reading, that doesn't mean every detail covered by the organizational pattern is significant.

For instance, in the reading on page 610, it is hardly necessary to mention that armies of fire ants were moving into farmers' fields *in order to eat potatoes and okra.* Thus, that detail from the process pattern did not make its way into the sample notes. As with so much else in learning, be selective about how you make use of organizational patterns. Decide which aspects of each pattern you need to include and which aspects you don't.

This is definitely the time to decide how central to the whole discussion the minor details in the paragraph might be. A minor detail might be absolutely essential, and then again it might add little except emphasis or human interest. It's up to you to decide what function it serves.

SUMMING UP THE KEY POINTS

1. The pattern or patterns of organization used in a paragraph are dictated by the main idea they develop. Some thoughts lend themselves perfectly to one pattern of organization, e.g., "Panda bears were once thought to be relatives of raccoons, but the differences between the two creatures eventually made it clear that they were not related."

2. Other ideas, however, clearly require more than one organizational pattern in order to be fully explained: "According to researchers Raymond Cattell and John Horn, there are two types of intelligence, fluid and crystallized, and each one follows a unique developmental course." In this case, the topic sentence demands two patterns of organization, comparison and contrast *and* process. In response, the reader would look for the details included in both patterns.

3. Because an author combines patterns in a paragraph, it doesn't mean that all the patterns present are equally important. Only those essential to developing the main idea are really significant. The elements of the patterns that develop the main idea are the ones that should go into your notes.

4. Even if a paragraph or reading does include two or more patterns, don't assume that every detail associated with the pattern is essential and needs to be recorded. Be selective and focus only on those pattern elements that enhance your understanding of the main idea.

▶ **EXERCISE 1**   **Recognizing Mixed Patterns**

DIRECTIONS   Read each paragraph and write the main idea in the blanks that follow. Then circle the appropriate letter or letters to identify the organizational pattern or patterns used to explain the main idea.

Note the boldface and italic signaling the presence of a definition.

There's an implicit cause and effect relationship developing in sentence 2.

The category word *efforts* suggests simple listing.

EXAMPLE   ¹One type of drinking that is particularly troublesome among young adults, especially college students, is **binge drinking**, *defined for men as consuming five or more drinks—and for women as consuming four or more drinks—within two hours*. ²Binge drinking has been identified as a major health problem in the United States since the 1990s and is the focus of several efforts to reduce the number of college students who binge. ³These efforts include establishing low tolerance levels for the antisocial behaviors associated with binge drinking. ⁴They also include working with athletes, fraternities, and sororities, changing the expectations of incoming freshmen, and increasing the number of activities that don't include the presence of alcoholic beverages. ⁵These efforts come at a time when national and international attention is directed at the problem of binge drinking. (Adapted from Kail and Cavanaugh, *Human Development*, 5th ed., pp. 365–66, © Cengage Learning.)

In your own words, what's the main idea of this paragraph?

Many different efforts are being made to control binge drinking among college students.

What pattern or patterns are needed to develop the main idea?

     (a.) definition

     b. time order

     (c.) simple listing

     d. comparison and contrast

     (e.) cause and effect

     f. classification

If you were taking notes on this paragraph, would you include information from the last sentence? ___No___ Please explain your reasoning. The main idea of the reading is that binge drinking is a problem among college students. My notes need to define the problem and explain what's being done to combat it. That information is central to the main idea. The last sentence doesn't do anything to clarify that point or resolve some situation described in the paragraph.

EXPLANATION Two main chains of repetition and reference run through the passage. They refer to "binge drinking among students" and "efforts to prevent it." Thus, the main idea has to include, connect, or make reference to these two phrases. As you can see, the paraphrased main idea statement does precisely that.

The organizational patterns necessary to explain that main idea are (1) definition for the reader who might ask "What exactly is binge drinking?" and (2) cause and effect to clarify the potential health problems produced by binge drinking. The category word *efforts* brings into play the simple listing pattern because the reader needs to know what those efforts are.

1. In a **longitudinal study**, *the same individuals are observed or tested repeatedly at different points in their lives.* As the name implies, the longitudinal approach studies changes over *long* periods of time and is the most direct way to watch development occur. More important, it is the only way to answer certain questions about the stability or instability of behavior: Do characteristics such as aggression, dependency, or mistrust observed in infancy or early childhood persist into adulthood? Does a regular exercise program begun in middle age have benefits in later life? Does people's satisfaction with their lives remain the same or change across adulthood? Such questions can only be explored by longitudinal testing, in other words, by testing people at one point in their development and retesting them again over the course of time.

   (Adapted from Kail and Cavanaugh, *Human Development*, 5th ed., p. 28, © Cengage Learning.)

In your own words, what's the main idea of this paragraph?

_____

_____

_____

What pattern or patterns are needed to develop this main idea?

a. definition

b. time order

c. simple listing

d. comparison and contrast

e. cause and effect

f. classification

If you were taking notes on this paragraph, would you record all three questions mentioned in the text? _____ Please explain your reasoning. _____

_____

_____

2. In a classic study begun in 1939, H. M. Skeels and H. B. Dye conducted research in an orphanage on infants whose intellectual development at nineteen months was judged so poor that they were considered unfit for adoption. These infants were transferred to an institution for the mentally handicapped, where Skeels and Dye arranged for each child to be put under the personal care of an adolescent girl who herself had limited intellectual ability. However, for the purpose of the study, the girls had been instructed at length in how to "mother" the children by giving them attention, affection, and mental stimulation. Meanwhile, a control group stayed at the orphanage and received medical care but little personal attention. Twenty-seven years later, Skeels did a follow-up study of these same subjects. Most of the orphans who had been raised by the older, developmentally challenged young women had graduated from high school and one-third had gone to college. Nearly all of them were self-supporting and rated as normal. However, most of those who had been in the control group and remained in the orphanage had not progressed beyond the third grade. They had either remained in institutions or were not self-supporting. (Adapted from Stark, *Sociology*, 10th ed., p. 168, © Cengage Learning.)

In your own words, what's the main idea of this paragraph?

_____

_____

_____

What pattern or patterns are needed to develop this main idea?

a. definition

b. time order

c. simple listing

d. comparison and contrast

e. cause and effect

f. classification

If you were taking notes on this paragraph, would you record information about the follow-up study twenty-seven years later? _____

Please explain your reasoning. _____

_____

_____

3. Who are the Democrats and the Republicans? These parties tend to attract different groups of supporters. Democrats maintain their greatest strength among African Americans and Hispanics, Catholics and Jews, women, and individuals between the ages of eighteen and twenty-nine and those over age fifty. White southerners were once a critical part of the Democratic coalition, but a majority of them have voted for the Republicans over the past three decades. Democrats, though, still maintain a foothold in the South through the support of African Americans. Republicans are scattered across the country. They tend to be white, Protestant, and middle to upper class, and their views are comparatively conservative. (Adapted from Gittelson, Dudley, and Dubnick, *American Government*, 10th ed., p. 161, © Cengage Learning.)

In your own words, what's the main idea of this paragraph?

_____

What pattern or patterns are needed to develop this main idea?

a. definition

b. time order

c. simple listing

d. comparison and contrast

e. cause and effect

f. classification

If you were taking notes on this paragraph, would you record the information in these two sentences? "White southerners were once a critical part of the Democratic coalition, but a majority of them have voted for the Republicans over the past three decades. Democrats, though, still maintain a foothold in the South through the support of African Americans." _____ Please explain your reasoning.

_____

_____

4. Although the most beautiful actress of her day, Elizabeth Taylor, played Cleopatra on film, the Egyptian queen was not especially beautiful. Images of her show a woman who was not unattractive, but not movie star gorgeous either. Yet she managed to mesmerize two of the most powerful men of her time. In 48 BCE when Julius Caesar, famed Roman general and statesman, arrived in Egypt, his mission was to make the Egyptians pay their debts to Rome. Caesar, however, quickly got distracted. Married at the time, he began an affair with the twenty-two-year-old Cleopatra, who bore his child in 47 BCE. But when Caesar was assassinated in 44 BCE, Cleopatra lost both her lover and her protector. That loss set the stage for the arrival of the Roman general Mark Antony in 43 BCE, who also came to Egypt on political matters but quickly turned his attentions elsewhere. Like Caesar, Antony became Cleopatra's lover, and for twelve years they ruled Egypt together. But when the Romans and Egyptians went to war, Mark Antony made the mistake of taking Cleopatra's military advice. Antony wanted to fight on land. Cleopatra insisted on the sea. The result was the disastrous Battle of Actium (31 BCE), which destroyed the Egyptian fleet. Humiliated by the crushing defeat, Antony and Cleopatra vowed to take their lives. Cleopatra, however, only pretended to kill herself while Antony actually did. It was only when Egypt's Roman conqueror, Octavian, swore he would take Cleopatra back to Rome in chains that Cleopatra took her life on August 12, 30 BCE.[†]

In your own words, what's the main idea of this paragraph?

_____

_____

_____

[†]The date of Cleopatra's death varies from source to source by as much as two weeks. The date given here turns up most frequently in various reference works on the Web.

What pattern or patterns are needed to develop this main idea?

a. definition

b. time order

c. simple listing

d. comparison and contrast

e. cause and effect

f. classification

If you were taking notes on this paragraph, would you include the information about the Battle of Actium? _____ Please explain your reasoning. _____

_____

 WEB QUEST
To this day, historians debate the reason behind Antony's mysterious behavior in the Battle of Actium. What did Antony do that, to this day, scholars puzzle over?

_____

_____

CHECK YOUR UNDERSTANDING

1. What decides the pattern (or patterns) of organization a writer uses?

_____

2. Should you assume that every pattern present in a paragraph is equally important? Please explain your answer.

_____

_____

_____

3. Once you identify an organizational pattern that's central to the main idea, should you assume that every element of that pattern is essential for your notes? Please explain your answer.

_____

_____

 ## From Pure to Mixed Patterns in Longer Readings

Longer, multi-paragraph readings do occasionally rely on a single pattern of organization. Look, for example, at the following selection, which relies almost exclusively on the comparison and contrast pattern of development. As you read, note the italicized transitions that are clues to that pattern.

Mating Strategies Differ Between the Sexes

This first paragraph focuses on similarities, but it's an introduction to the thesis statement below.

From this point on, differences dominate the reading in order to support the underlined topic sentence of the paragraph, which is also the thesis statement of the reading.

1   In selecting a mate, both men and women seek out those who are attractive, kind, honest, and good-natured. In addition to wanting the same basic qualities in a potential mate, both sexes avoid certain characteristics such as insensitivity, bad manners, loudness or shrillness, and the tendency to brag about sexual conquests.

2   _Despite these similarities,_ though, males and females differ in the emphasis they place on physical appearance and social status, at least for long-term relationships. Men are more concerned with appearance and women are more concerned with status. _How do we explain those differences?_ Women's preference for status over attractiveness depends on several factors, such as whether the relationship is short or long term (looks are more important in the short term) and whether the woman perceives herself as attractive. Women who consider themselves very attractive appear to want it all—status and good looks (Buss and Shackelford, 2008).

3   In one study, men and women reported kindness and intelligence as necessary in their selection of mates. _But_ their views of status and attractiveness differed. For the average woman seeking a long-term mate, status was a necessity. Good looks were a luxury. _In contrast_, men viewed physical attractiveness as a necessity rather than a luxury in mate selections—looks matter most when men are searching for mates (Le, Bailey, Kenrick, and Linsenmeier, 2002).

4   In another study, a researcher [Buss] asked ninety-two married couples which characteristics they valued most in their spouses. Women generally preferred men who were . . . good earners, ambitious, career oriented, from a good family, and fairly tall. Men tended to value good looks, cooking skills, and sexual faithfulness. Across some thirty-seven cultures studied, females valued a good financial prospect more than did men (Buss, 1989). In addition, women in all thirty-seven cultures tended to marry older men, who often are more settled and financially stable. (Adapted from Michael Gazzaniga, Todd Heatherton, and Diane Halpern, *Psychological Science*. New York: W. W. Norton and Company, 2010, p. 400.)

As long as the vocabulary and subject matter are familiar, readings like this one are fairly easy to interpret because the comparison and contrast pattern is so obvious. You know almost immediately that you have to understand the similarities and differences and link them to an overall point, which in this case appears in paragraph 2: When it comes to long-term relationships, men and women differ in how they view the importance of physical appearance and social status.

From Reader to Writer Write three to four paragraphs explaining what you think are some basic differences between male and female behavior at the start of a romantic relationship. Or, if you prefer, point out how similar the sexes are when it comes to romance.

When Patterns Combine in Longer Readings

In general, textbook readings are more likely to combine organizational patterns rather than relying solely on one. In this next example, three different patterns intermingle. Thus, the reader has to figure out (1) what each one contributes to an explanation of the main idea and (2) which ones are most critical to understanding the material.

Read the following selection. After you finish each paragraph, answer the questions posed in the margins. When you complete the reading, write the main idea and the organizational patterns that develop it on the blank lines that follow:

The presence of dashes after a term in boldface suggests what pattern?

What Role Do Instincts Play in Human Behavior?

1   Birds build nests, and salmon return upstream to their birthplaces to spawn. They do not acquire these behaviors through experience or by attending nest-building or spawning schools. These are **instinctive behaviors**—fixed,

How does the author answer the question that opens paragraph 2?

Why does the author mention specific dates in the last sentence of paragraph 2 and the first sentence of paragraph 3?

What's the big difference between paragraph 2 and paragraph 4?

inborn patterns of response that are specific to members of a particular species. **Instinct theory** holds that behavior is motivated by instincts, or inborn patterns of activity that do not have to be taught.

2   Does instinct theory explain the motives for human behavior? One man who thought so was William James, the father of American psychology. In his 1890 *The Principles of Psychology*, James listed thirty-seven instincts that he believed could explain most of human behavior. In 1908, in his very influential textbook, *An Introduction to Social Psychology*, the psychologist William McDougall added to James's list. From that point on, the list kept growing and growing until, by the 1920s, it had ballooned to ten thousand instincts covering a wide range of human behavior.

3   By the 1930s, however, the instinct theory was beginning to fall out of favor. One reason for its decline was that the lists of instincts had simply grown too long to be useful. Another was that explaining behavior on the basis of instincts didn't explain all that much. Saying a person is lazy because of a laziness instinct or stingy because of a stinginess instinct doesn't really explain the person's behavior. It merely attaches a label to it.

4   Psychologists today recognize that human behavior is much more variable and flexible than would be the case if it were determined by instinct. Moreover, instinct theory fails to account for the important roles of culture and learning in determining human behavior. Though instincts account for some behavior in other animals, most psychologists reject the view that instincts motivate complex human behavior. They argue instead that human behavior is the result of the interplay between heredity and the social and cultural environment. (Adapted from Nevid, *Psychology*, 4th ed., pp. 288–89. © Cengage Learning.)

What's the main idea?

_____

_____

_____

What organizational patterns explain that main idea?

_____

Evaluating the Organizational Patterns

The first thing to notice here is the role the sequence of dates and events pattern plays in the reading. Each reference to a year or time period is connected to a key point about the topic, which could be expressed as "psychologists' belief in instincts" or "theories of behavior," or even "psychologists' changing theories of behavior."

What main idea *about* that topic did the author want to convey? There's no thesis statement to point to in the reading. But an implied main idea does emerge based on the opening question and how the reading begins and ends. That main idea can be expressed as something like this: "Although at one time, psychologists were convinced that instinct determined behavior, that attitude changed dramatically over time. Today they believe that heredity and environment are the twin sources of behavior."

Implicit in that main idea is the need for the time order, sequence of dates and events pattern. That pattern is always a good guess when the author uses dates to contrast how something was viewed in the past versus how it's viewed "today." After all, a writer can't show readers how ideas changed over time without bringing the sequence of dates and events pattern into the reading. For those readers who might not be completely sure how to define instinct, the definition pattern is also essential to the mix.

But guiding the reading overall is the cause and effect pattern of organization. Some aspects of that pattern have to be present in notes because the author begins by explaining what psychologists used to think motivated behavior, and it ends with a more up-to-date view of why we do what we do. At the same time, paragraph 3 explicitly outlines a specific cause and effect relationship: There were two reasons why instinct theory fell out of favor. Diagrammed, the relationship would look like this:

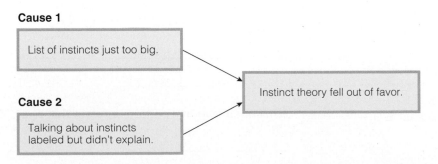

Cause 1

List of instincts just too big.

Cause 2

Talking about instincts labeled but didn't explain.

Instinct theory fell out of favor.

Taking Notes on Combined Patterns

While definition and sequence of dates play key roles in the instinct theory reading, it's the cause and effect pattern that requires the most attention. And it's cause and effect that dominates the selection of details for complete notes, which in outline form would look like this:

Main Idea   The idea that instincts determine behavior was very popular in the late nineteenth and early twentieth century, but psychologists now believe that biology and environment are the sources of human behavior.

Supporting Details

1. William James (*The Principles of Psychology*) and William McDougall (*An Introduction to Social Psychology*) were among those who believed that instincts were what motivated behavior.

    —By the 1920s, over 10,000 different instincts had been identified.

2. By the 1930s, the theory fell out of favor for two reasons:

    a. too many instincts

    b. didn't explain behavior, just called it an instinct, e.g., lazy people had the lazy instinct

3. Today's psychologists believe that our environment and our genetic inheritance are what influence behavior.

READING TIP

As soon as you see that a reading has numerous references to dates and periods of time, make sure you understand what events or shifts in thought occurred during the times identified.

SUMMING UP THE KEY POINTS

1. Multi-paragraph readings can and do rely on one organizational pattern. However, like paragraphs they often need more than one pattern to communicate their overall main idea to readers. That's because the content of the main idea frequently calls for different organizational patterns.

2. In response to readings that combine elements of different patterns, readers need to consider the main idea and ask this key

question: Which pattern elements are essential to explaining the overall main idea and which ones are not?

3. The basic rule of note-taking is simple: The main idea is always essential to your notes. But you can pick and choose the number of pattern details you include based on what they add to your understanding of the main idea.

▶ EXERCISE 2   Identifying Patterns in Longer Readings

DIRECTIONS   Answer the following questions by filling in the blank lines and circling the letters of the correct response. *Paraphrasing Note*: If you are struggling to paraphrase a thesis statement or an implied main idea, ask questions about the stated or implied main idea, for instance: What action was taken? Who or what was the source of the action? What were the consequences? Use your answers to those questions to put the main idea into words of your own.

EXAMPLE

Scott Joplin: The King of Ragtime

1   Born in 1868 in Texarkana on the Texas-Arkansas border, musician and composer Scott Joplin began his career playing piano in the saloons of St. Louis, Missouri, at the age of seventeen. During the next ten years, he perfected the jazz style that came to be known as ragtime. Then, from 1896 to 1900, Joplin studied at George R. Smith College in Sedalia, Missouri, so that he could write down the music he played so naturally.

2   In 1899, Joplin published his first piece of music, "Maple Leaf Rag." Less than a year later, ragtime—a unique American blend of African and European musical forms—took the country by storm. Suddenly, everyone wanted to hear "Maple Leaf Rag," and Scott Joplin became the first composer in the world to sell more than one million copies of a single tune.

3   But the King of Ragtime didn't want to devote his life to writing popular music. A serious artist, he resented white America's tendency to dismiss his music as trivial* because it grew out of African-American culture. To prove the value and beauty of ragtime, Joplin decided to compose an opera that would have ragtime rhythms at its core. By creating an opera, Joplin was

---

*trivial: insignificant, not serious.

demanding direct comparison with the greatest European composers and trying to prove to Americans that his music should be taken seriously. In the end, Joplin's opera would get him the acclaim* he dreamed of. Unfortunately, it would be too late for him to care.

4 The opera, titled *Treemonisha*, is the story of a poor black girl, Treemonisha,† who grows up to battle ignorant superstition and become a leader in her community. The opera combines new forms of ragtime, created specifically to accompany different kinds of dance including ballet. It also includes black work songs and soaring gospel music. When Joplin published it at his own expense in 1911—no one else was willing to take the job on—he called it "an entirely new form of operatic art." Yet despite Joplin's intense efforts to make the opera a success, the timing was wrong. The composer had invested all his money, energy, and hope in a work that displayed a strong social conscience at exactly the moment when the paying public was clamoring for more frivolous* entertainment. Even worse for the play's prospects, the ragtime beat, which was threaded throughout the opera's music, was declining in popularity.

5 The one performance in New York City in 1915 was a disaster, with members of the audience leaving in mid-performance. Joplin had financed the production himself. It left him both bankrupt and humiliated. Two years later he was dead.

6 Had he lived to see it, Joplin would have been overjoyed to read the review of *Treemonisha* that appeared in the *New York Times* when the opera was staged again fifty-seven years later in 1972. The *Times* music reviewer, Harold Schonberg, called the opera "harmonically enchanting"* and said "it refuses to leave the mind." According to Schonberg, the audience at the performance "went out of its mind." *Treemonisha* was then successfully staged in Houston, Seattle, Washington, and New York City. Ironically,* the modern audiences wildly applauded the very same opera that, for Scott Joplin, had symbolized nothing but financial ruin and critical failure. (Source of quotation: From Argyle, *Scott Joplin and the Age of Ragtime*, p. 146.)

---

*acclaim: enthusiastic and public praise.

†The girl's name combines her mother's name with the fact that the girl liked to play under a supposedly sacred tree.

*frivolous: unserious, light.

*enchanting: delightful, engaging.

*ironically: contradicting what one might expect to be the case.

1. In your own words, what's the main idea of this reading?

   In an attempt to make Americans take ragtime seriously, Scott Joplin wrote and
   produced an opera, but it failed miserably and it was only after his death that it
   got the admiration and praise he dreamed of.

2. What organizational patterns help develop that main idea?

   a. definition
   b. time order: sequence of dates
   c. time order: process
   d. simple listing
   e. comparison and contrast
   f. cause and effect
   g. classification

EXPLANATION In this reading, the author makes the main idea convincing by explaining (1) how Scott Joplin tried to have his music taken seriously over the course of his career and (2) how his dream came true. To fulfill those goals, she uses two patterns: the sequence of dates pattern to trace the composer's career, and a cause and effect pattern to explain how the opera *Treemonisha* eventually made his dream a reality. Only it was too late for him to know it.

1. Ridding the Brain of Demons

1   Early societies did not pity the victims of mental illness. Abnormal behaviors, from simple headaches to convulsions,* were believed to be caused by evil spirits that lived in the victim's body. According to this system of belief—called *demonology*—mental illness could only be cured by driving out the demons living in the victim's body. If the patient died in the process, that was just an unfortunate side effect of treatment. And treatment was essential.

2   That the victims of mental illness suffered more from the treatment than the malady is reflected in the evidence suggesting that Stone Age cave dwellers treated mental illness by a surgical method called *trephining*. During this procedure, part of the skull was chipped away to make an opening. Once the skull was opened, the evil spirits could

---

*convulsions: uncontrolled fits in which the muscles contract wildly.

escape. It was believed that when the evil spirit left, the person would return to his or her normal state. Surprisingly, several trephined skulls that healed over have been found. This indicates that some patients survived what had to be an extremely crude surgery. (Adapted from Sue et al., *Understanding Abnormal Behavior*, 5th ed., p.16, © Cengage Learning.)

1. In your own words, what's the main idea of this reading?

_____

_____

2. What organizational patterns help develop that main idea?

    a. definition

    b. time order: sequence of dates and events

    c. time order: process

    d. simple listing

    e. comparison and contrast

    f. cause and effect

    g. classification

2. Capital Punishment

1 What sets capital punishment apart from all other punishments is its quality of irrevocability.* This type of punishment leaves no way to correct a mistake. For this reason, some believe that no mortal should have the power to inflict capital punishment because there is no way to guarantee that mistakes won't be made. The growing number of innocent men and women who came perilously close to being executed indicates that we have an imperfect system.

2   Public support for capital punishment has swung up and down. Public opinion polls reveal that public support for the death penalty declined gradually through the 1960s, reaching a low of 44 percent in 1966, but has increased over the past 30 years. In the late 1990s, 75 to 80 percent supported the death penalty. Public support seems to be declining in more recent years. In a poll in 2008, only 63 percent of Americans supported capital punishment.

---

*irrevocability: incapable of being changed or altered.

3   Research indicates that certain groups are more likely to favor the use of capital punishment; for instance, support is higher by 20 to 25 percentage points among whites as compared to blacks. Membership in fundamentalist Protestant churches predicts higher support for the death penalty as well. Political conservatism* also predicts higher support. Interestingly, church activity negatively predicts support (the more active one is in one's church, the less likely one is to support the death penalty).

4   *Retentionists* (who believe that we should continue to utilize capital punishment) argue that capital punishment is just because it deters, or inhibits, others from committing murder and it definitely deters the individual who is executed. This is a utilitarian† argument. They also argue that capital punishment is just because murder deserves an equal punishment. They also say that the Bible dictates an "eye for an eye." This is, of course, a Judeo-Christian religious justification for capital punishment.

5   *Abolitionists* argue that capital punishment has never been shown to be effective in deterring others from committing murder, and, therefore, the evil of capital punishment far outweighs any potential benefits for society because there is no proof that it actually deters. Abolitionists also point to the religious command to "turn the other cheek," as an argument against any Christian justification for capital punishment. (Pollock, *Ethical Dilemmas and Decisions in Criminal Justice*, 5th ed., p. 332, © Cengage Learning.)

1. In your own words, what's the main idea of this reading?

_____

_____

2. What organizational patterns help develop that main idea?

   a.   definition

   b.   time order: sequence of dates and events

---

*conservatism: a political or social philosophy that emphasizes maintaining existing traditions and promoting individual responsibility over help from the government or other members of society.

†utilitarian: having a useful function that benefits the greatest number of people. Derived from the work of philosophers John Stuart Mill and Jeremy Bentham, who called their philosophy "utilitarianism."

c. time order: process

d. simple listing

e. comparison and contrast

f. cause and effect

g. classification

3. The Donner Party Goes West

1 Some time during 1845, brothers Jacob and George Donner caught the emigration fever and decided to head west to California. They sold their land, houses, farm equipment, and most of their belongings. They also talked their friend James Reed into moving his family west with theirs. Together they bought oxen, cattle, bagged and barreled food, and heavy Murphy wagons.

2 Their plan was daring but not unusual. Already thousands of Americans had left behind land, jobs, and culture to move west. But from the start, the Donner party, as the group came to be called, met with more than its share of disappointments, failures, and, in the end, deadly disasters.

3 The disappointments started already upon arrival at Independence, Missouri, in 1846 when members of Donner and Reed's group learned that most of the twelve hundred wagons going west had already departed. They took heart, though, after catching up with fifty other California-bound wagons. Still, being surrounded by other migrants* during the days and weeks that followed didn't help as much as those traveling west under Donner and Reed's leadership had thought it would. Instead, fear and anxiety mounted as the homesteaders trekked across the inhospitable land that seemed unfit for cultivation.* Dust storms, thunderstorms, muddy roads, stubborn mules, and bad water further strained tempers.

4 Desperate to speed up the pace, Donner and Reed began talking about a "shortcut" around the southern edge of a settlement in Salt Lake City. A couple of California trappers who overheard them warned about the dangers of taking a large number of wagons, animals, and people through the shorter route, saying that it had never been

---

*migrants: people on the move from one place to another.
*cultivation: farming, soil preparation.

attempted by wagon trains. But knowing that they had to reach the far side of the mountains before snow began to fall, the tired travelers decided to take the risk.

5   By September 30 the Donner party was facing the Sierra Nevada Mountain range, and the weather was worsening. Seasoned "mountain men" had predicted a late snowfall for the winter of 1847. But they were wrong. The exhausted travelers were hit with a blizzard already in November. Not sure what to do, the group split in two with one group waiting out the storm while another, headed by Donner and Reed, moved on.

6   As hunger gnawed, the fifteen members who had followed Donner and Reed managed to catch a scrawny coyote, an owl, and a squirrel. Then they ate their dogs, oxen, and horses. After nine days and nights in the cold, two men and two children had died. Their corpses became food for the starving survivors. Four more of the party died over the next twenty-three days, and their bodies, too, were used as food.

7   Back at the second encampment, thirty-seven of those who had hoped to wait out the storm perished in the grueling struggle for life. When the blizzard broke in February of 1847, seven of the Donner-Reed group made it to safety. Then they organized a rescue party to bring back more of the stranded survivors.

8   At the start, the Donner party had included eighty-one[†] people. In the end, there were forty-five survivors. George Donner, the man whose idea it was to move west, was not among them. He had already died on March 17, 1847. His wife died a little more than a day later. George's brother, Jacob, and his wife, Elizabeth, met the same fate. The third leader of the party, James Reed, survived and made it to California, where he built up a fortune in real estate and ended up becoming the sheriff of San Jose. (Source of information: Gillon and Matson, *The American Experiment*, 2nd ed., pp. 494–95; www.donnerpartydiary .com/survivor.htm.)

[†]This number varies from account to account, largely because, in the beginning at least, the Donner party gained and lost members as people decided to join up or leave.

1. In your own words, what's the main idea of this reading?

   _____

   _____

   _____

2. What organizational patterns help develop that main idea?

   a. definition

   b. time order: sequence of dates and events

   c. time order: process

   d. simple listing

   e. comparison and contrast

   f. cause and effect

   g. classification

4. Personality and Body Type

1 In the 1940s, some researchers tried to revive a much-debated theory of human behavior called *constitutional typology*. According to this theory, body type determines personality. Although critics point to the theory's lack of scientific evidence, constitutional typology still has some believers who argue that human beings fall into three basic categories of physique, or body type, with each one producing a particular set of character traits.

2 According to constitutional typologists, *endomorphs* tend to be round and soft, with protruding abdomens. They love gracious living and good food. They have gentle, relaxed temperaments and prefer to keep life uncomplicated. Said to embody the cliché about fat people being friendly, endomorphs like to be surrounded by their friends and are not comfortable being alone for any length of time.

3 The exact opposite of the endomorph, the *ectomorph* is described as all skin and bones, with a flat belly and long legs. Much less social than the fun-loving endomorph, the ectomorph prefers intellectual pursuits, especially if they can be carried on in relative isolation from people. Less good-natured than the endomorph, ectomorphs are nervous and high strung. Given to quick reactions and high-intensity relationships, they suffer from the aftermath of tension and have difficulty relaxing and falling asleep.

Even today, there are those who claim that body type can predict personality.

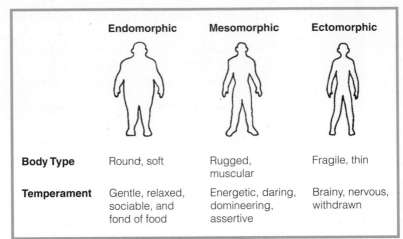

	Endomorphic	**Mesomorphic**	**Ectomorphic**
Body Type	Round, soft	Rugged, muscular	Fragile, thin
Temperament	Gentle, relaxed, sociable, and fond of food	Energetic, daring, domineering, assertive	Brainy, nervous, withdrawn

4   The *mesomorph* is neither fat nor thin but broad and muscular, with a strong, rugged physique. People in this category are said to love physical activity—the more daring and fast paced, the better. They also enjoy games of risk or chance. Domineering by nature, mesomorphs like to be around people but prefer to be in situations they can control.

1. In your own words, what's the main idea of this reading?

_____

_____

_____

2. What organizational patterns help develop that main idea?

a. definition

b. time order: process

c. time order: sequence of dates and events

d. simple listing

e. comparison and contrast

f. cause and effect

g. classification

From Reader to Writer The Donner party is not the only expedition that seemed to have been doomed from the start. On June 17, 1527, Captain Pánfilo de Narváez led five Spanish ships with 600 men on board on a journey to reach the New World. But in 1528, a hurricane struck the ships, triggering a chain of disasters that left only four men alive when the journey finally ended. Use the Web to find out more about this ill-fated expedition and write about it, making sure to correctly describe the chain of events as well as the causes of its disastrous end.

✔ CHECK YOUR UNDERSTANDING

1. Why do writers sometimes combine organizational patterns?

    _____

2. Do multi-paragraph readings always combine organizational patterns? _____
    Please explain.

    _____

    _____

3. When it comes to taking notes, what should readers do in response to readings that combine more than one pattern?

    _____

    _____

Evaluating the Patterns

Whether you are dealing with one paragraph or several, the principle remains the same: When more than one organizational pattern is present, focus on the pattern or patterns most central to explaining the main idea. For instance, to get the most out of the following reading, start by determining the main idea. Next, figure out which organizational patterns support that idea. Then decide if the patterns are equally important or if one is more central to explaining the main idea.

Barbie

1   Barbie, the all-American doll, is—like many Americans—an immigrant. Although introduced in 1959 by the American toy company Mattel, Barbie's origins lie in Germany where she was called Lilli. The German Lilli doll was a novelty toy for adult men (as evidenced by her proportions, equivalent to 39-21-31 in human terms). She was based on a character that cartoonist Reinhard Beuthin drew for the German tabloid[†] newspaper *Das Bild* in 1952. Lilli was so popular that she became a regular feature, later made three dimensional as Bild Lilli, an eleven-and-a-half-inch-tall blonde doll with the figure Barbie would make famous.

2   Lilli came to America with Ruth Handler, one of the founders and co-directors of the Mattel toy company. While vacationing in Europe, she got a glimpse of Barbie in a store window. Handler bought three of the dolls and gave one to her daughter Barbara, after whom Lilli would be re-named. Mattel bought the rights to Lilli and unveiled her as Barbie in March 1959. Despite mothers' hesitations about buying a doll that looked like Barbie, within the first year of the doll's debut Mattel had sold 351,000 Barbies at $3 each (or about $17 in 2000 dollars). By 1997, over one billion Barbies had been sold.

3   Within the United States, Barbie has been controversial—at least among adults. Some have worried that Barbie's wildly unrealistic figure fosters girls' dissatisfaction with their own body—a serious problem in a culture plagued by eating disorders. Others claim that, despite Barbie's 1980s "Girls Can Do Anything" makeover, Barbie represents an empty-headed version of femininity, focused on little more than fashion and appearance. Many have also noted that blonde, blue-eyed Barbie failed to represent the diversity of America's people.

4   In 2012, a U.S. Congressional Committee cited studies showing that half of all Barbies are made by exploited young women in Mainland China, who earn very little for their work because Chinese factories receive only 35 cents per doll to cover their costs, including labor. Saudi Arabia banned Barbie in 2003, arguing that her skimpy outfits and the values she

---

†tabloid: Technically, the word describes a newspaper of a particular size—11 × 17 inches, with shorter articles and more pictures. Many tabloids peddle scandals, so the word has taken on negative connotations. However, there are some respectable tabloids that report hard news.

Perhaps because of their sex toy origins, Barbie dolls have always had a highly sexualized image.

Aly Song/Reuters.

represents are not suitable for a Muslim nation. Still, the eleven-and-a-half-inch doll remains popular worldwide, selling in more than 150 countries. Today, the average American girl has ten Barbies—and the typical German girl owns five. For better or worse, Barbie continues to link the United States and the rest of the world. (Norton et al., *A People and a Nation*, Brief 9th ed., p. 777, © Cengage Learning.)

If you look for a thesis statement that sums up the details included in this reading, you won't find it. The main idea of this reading is implied.

Inferring the Main Idea

Look closely at the reading about Barbie, and you'll see it breaks into two parts. Up until paragraph 3, the reading is concerned with Barbie's history. It follows then that the first part of the reading relies heavily on the sequence of dates pattern.

By paragraph 3, though, the authors move away from Barbie's history to discuss how she causes the "controversy" mentioned in the topic sentence of the third paragraph. At this point, the underlying pattern becomes cause and effect with the authors identifying some of Barbie's alleged negative effects.

Put the two ideas together—(1) Barbie started in Germany and immigrated to the United States and (2) once she arrived in the U.S.

she was both popular and controversial—and you will come up with an implied main idea that might be worded something like this: "Barbie got her start in Germany, but made her debut in the United States in 1959, proving to be extraordinarily successful. She has, however, also proved controversial."

In this case, there is nothing to suggest that the authors want readers to consider one pattern more important than the other. The title does not lean in one direction or the other. Nor does the accompanying picture. In addition, each pattern governs two paragraphs, so there's no difference in coverage.

The only other factor that might influence how you handle the elements of each pattern in your notes is outside the context of the reading. If, for instance, your instructor had already emphasized the cultural consequences of Barbie's popularity with young girls, then the cause and effect pattern underlying the reading might well be the emphasis in your notes. For that matter, if you yourself are interested in Barbie's European past, then you might decide for your own purposes to take more detailed notes on her history.

Sifting and Sorting Pattern Elements

The sample notes that follow assume that both patterns are of equal significance for the main idea. They don't, however, assume that every element of each pattern needs to be recorded:

Main Idea Barbie got her start in Germany, but made her debut in the United States in 1959, proving to be extraordinarily successful. She has, however, also proved controversial.

Supporting Details

1. Barbie started out as German Lilli.

2. Based on a 1952 cartoon by Reinhard Beuthin.

3. Mattel executive Ruth Handler brought Lilli to America and Mattel bought the rights to Lilli, unveiling her as Barbie in 1959.

   a. Within a year Mattel sold thousands of Barbies.

   b. By 1997, a billion Barbies had been sold.

4. Barbie provoked controversy.

   a. Some people think her figure encourages girls to have a very unrealistic body image.

    b. Others think she encourages the notion of empty-headed femininity.

    c. She doesn't represent America's diversity.

    d. 2012 Congressional committee compiles studies showing Barbies are made by exploited young women in Mainland China.

    e. Saudi Arabia banned Barbie because her skimpy clothes didn't represent Muslim values.

As they should, the notes record the key dates and the events that accompanied them. But as with the notes on the fire ants on page 610, some details have been left out. The fact that Lilli became a regular figure in *Das Bild* doesn't add anything important to the main idea, so it doesn't appear. Nor does it seem crucial to record that Ruth Handler was on vacation when she spotted Barbie.

From Reader to Writer   Toys are often a controversial topic. Dolls of all kinds have been criticized for any number of reasons, from not reflecting racial diversity to encouraging girls to focus more on appearance than achievement. Toys that mimic the weapons of military combat have also aroused controversy. It's even been suggested that toy guns be banned from toy stores because they encourage the idea that gun ownership is harmless. Write a paragraph explaining why you think so many people are concerned about the toys children play with. Try to mention specific toys as illustrations. To get some ideas, use search terms like "bad (good) toys for kids." Then write a paragraph explaining why you think this concern is necessary or unnecessary.

▶ EXERCISE 3   Identifying Main Ideas and Evaluating Pattern Elements

DIRECTIONS   Identify the main idea of each reading along with the pattern or patterns used to develop it. Then evaluate the significance of those patterns to decide if they are equal in importance or one is more important than the other.

EXAMPLE

The Dual Nature of Curare

1 *Curare* is a blackish, powder-like substance made from the roots and bark of a woody vine that grows in South America. Although many people know

that curare is a deadly poison, they do not know that it can save life as well as take it. Once known only as the "flying death," curare has become one of medicine's most trusted weapons in the fight against disease.

2   Rumors of curare's deadly powers began to circulate as early as the sixteenth century, when explorers came back from journeys to the Amazon. Upon their return, they described Indian hunters who could bring down prey with a single blow from a dart gun. According to eyewitness accounts, hunters boiled the roots and bark of a woody vine into a heavy syrup. Then they dipped darts into the thick liquid. Expert hunters, capable of finding a target more than a hundred yards away, would blow the darts through hollow reeds, killing their prey almost instantly. Birds died in less than five seconds, and human beings in less than five minutes.

3   Because the jungles were all but unreachable to everyone but the Indians, no one really understood how curare worked until the mid-nineteenth century, when experimenters began to uncover its secrets. It was found that curare, if swallowed, is fairly harmless. But if it penetrates the skin, curare is lethal. Because it relaxes all the muscles in the body—including those that control breathing—the victim quickly suffocates and dies.

4   Once researchers knew how curare worked, they were in a better position to figure out how it might be used to more beneficial ends. However, researchers were reluctant to experiment with curare imported from South America. Its strength varied, and one could never be sure how strong a dosage to use.

5   During World War II, Daniel Bovet, an Italian pharmacologist, developed the first synthetic, or artificial, form of curare, and the stage was set to discover curare's benefits to humans. In 1942, Dr. Harold Griffith successfully used it as an anesthetic during surgery. From that time on, a synthetic form of curare was used in many operations because it relaxed the patient's muscles and made the surgeon's work easier. Eventually, it was also used to treat rabies and tetanus, diseases that produce severe muscle cramps.

1.   What is the main idea of the entire reading?

a. Curare is an incredibly dangerous poison that can kill in seconds.

(b.) A deadly poison, curare can also save lives.

c. Curare has a long and ancient history.

d. The jungle kept curare a secret for centuries.

2. Which pattern or patterns does the author use to develop that main idea?

(a.) definition

(b.) time order: sequence of dates and events

(c.) time order: process

d. simple listing

e. comparison and contrast

(f.) cause and effect

g. classification

3. If more than one pattern organizes the reading, identify the most important.

cause and effect; definition; sequence of dates and events

Please explain.

Without definition and the cause and effect pattern, the writer couldn't tell readers what curare is or how it kills and cures. Without the sequence of dates and events, the writer couldn't explain how scientists unraveled the poison's secrets with the passage of time.

EXPLANATION   Everything in the reading, including the title, points to answer *b* as the overall main idea: Curare has a double nature: It can kill *and* it can heal. To explain that main idea, the author needs the definition pattern to tell readers what curare is. The cause and effect organizational pattern is central to explaining curare's dual nature as killer and healer. The sequence of dates and events pattern plays a key role in organizing the description of how curare's other, more beneficial, uses came to light. Process, probably the least important pattern, helps explain how hunters turned curare into a poison so that they could dip their arrows into it.

1. Schizophrenia, the Mind in Two

1   The term *schizophrenia* was coined in 1911 by the Swiss psychiatrist Eugen Bleuler. Literally, the word means "split mind." Bleuler thought the term effectively expressed one of the disease's central symptoms—a split between the patient's internal world and the external world of social reality.

2   Since Bleuler's time, researchers still have not figured out what causes this mysterious and devastating disease. However, they have been able to identify and name three distinct types.

3   *Disorganized schizophrenia* expresses itself through bizarre and childlike behavior. Victims pay little attention to personal grooming. Sometimes they remain unwashed for days. Behaving like children, they are prone to making faces and spouting nonsense.

4   Those suffering from a second form of the disease, called *catatonic schizophrenia*, can remain immobile for hours. Mentally withdrawing from their environment, patients adopt rigid postures and fall silent for days, even months. Sometimes, without reason, sufferers will suddenly grow violent and attack anyone who comes near.

5   In *paranoid schizophrenia*, the most marked symptom is the presence of delusions or fantasies that bear no relation to reality. Patients suffering from this form fear that a person or group is trying to harm them. They often think they are surrounded by enemies and may, in response, become violent.

6   As research continues, it's becoming more and more likely that schizophrenia is not a single disease but a family of diseases that may arise from a variety of causes. By learning more about each type of schizophrenia, researchers hope to find more effective treatments.

1. What is the main idea of the entire reading?

   a. The term *schizophrenia* means "split mind," and was coined by Eugen Bleuler.

   b. Schizophrenia may well be a family of diseases.

   c. Although no one knows the cause of schizophrenia, researchers have identified three distinct types.

   d. Paranoid schizophrenia is perhaps the worst and most debilitating form of the disease.

2. Which pattern or patterns does the author use to develop that main idea?

   a. definition

   b. time order: sequence of dates and events

   c. time order: process

   d. simple listing

   e. comparison and contrast

    f.   cause and effect

    g.   classification

3. If more than one pattern organizes the reading, identify the most important.

_____

Please explain.

_____

_____

_____

_____

2. The Johari Window

1   The Johari Window, named after its inventors, Joseph Luft and Harry Ingham, is a useful model for describing the complex process of human interaction. The window, or box, is divided into four panes, or areas, with each area labeled to indicate the kind of information that can be revealed or concealed when we communicate or interact with others: (1) open, (2) blind, (3) hidden, and (4) unknown. Because each person's window reflects his or her psychological makeup, the size of each pane varies with the individual.

2   The **shared area** of the Johari Window represents your "public" or "awareness" area. This section symbolizes the information about yourself that both you and others recognize. It includes the information that you are willing to admit or make public. For example, you and everyone you know may be aware that you are a competitive person who doesn't like losing an argument or that your temper is easy to trigger when the subject is politics.

3   The **blind area** in the Johari Window represents the information about yourself that others may know, or think they know, but that you are not aware of. For instance, you may think that you have a tendency to be shy and a bit withdrawn, whereas others may see you as open, relaxed, and friendly. Over time, information in the blind area can shift to the open area if other people are willing to mention their view of your behavior.

4   The **hidden area** in the Johari Window shows information that you know but that others do not. This area reflects the private thoughts and feelings you prefer to keep to yourself. For example, you may not want people to know that you are terrified of public speaking despite the fact that you do it frequently. Unlike the open and blind areas, the hidden area may not change over time. In other words, you may always choose to keep certain things about your life a secret.

5   The **unknown area** of the Johari Window is made up of things unknown both to you and to others. This area is reserved for those feelings, talents, and motives that are below the surface of awareness and have never been acknowledged or displayed. For example, you may have a talent for verbal expression, but if you are shy and avoid speaking a lot, you may never know that you have the ability. To offer another example, you may know that you get angry when talking to authority figures but have no idea that your anger stems from an unhappy relationship with your older brother. Obviously, if you don't recognize the cause and effect relationship between your childhood and your adult behavior, no one else is likely to either.

The Johari Window is used primarily with groups on the assumption that self-disclosure and feedback improve communication among group members.

	Known to self	Unknown to self
Known to others	Shared	Blind
Not known to others	Hidden	Unknown

1. What is the main idea of the entire reading?

   a.   The Johari Window is the creation of Joseph Luft.

   b.   The Johari Window consists of four separate panes, or sections.

c. The Johari Window offers an effective way to describe inter-actions with others.

d. The size of the panes in the Johari Window varies with the individual.

2. Which pattern or patterns does the author use to develop that main idea?

a. definition

b. time order: sequence of dates and events

c. time order: process

d. simple listing

e. comparison and contrast

f. cause and effect

g. classification

3. If more than one pattern organizes the reading, identify the most important.

_____

Please explain.

_____

_____

_____

_____

DIGGING DEEPER

Can Whales Be Saved? *Tyler Miller*
Scott Spoolman

Looking Ahead Over-harvesting practically brought some species of whales to extinction. But regulation helped the whales make a comeback. That does not mean, however, that they aren't still under threat.

Getting Focused Both the title and the preview of the reading tell you that whales are in danger. Read to understand the nature of the threat and to see if you can answer the question posed in the title.

1 Whales are fairly easy to kill because of their size and their need to come to the surface to breathe. Mass slaughter became efficient with the use of radar and airplanes to locate the whales. Fast ships, harpoon guns, and inflation lances that pump dead whales full of air and make them float also aided in the harvesting of the huge creatures.

2 Whale harvesting, mostly in international waters, has followed a classic pattern with whalers killing an estimated 1.5 million whales between 1925 and 1975. Such over-harvesting reduced the population of eight of the eleven major species to commercial extinction (i.e., whales were so hard to find it no longer paid to hunt and kill them). It also drove some commercially prized species such as the giant blue whale to the brink of biological extinction. (Despite the whales being classified as endangered, which gives them some protection, biologists are not sure that the species can recover.)

3 In 1946, the International Convention for the Regulation of Whaling established the International Whaling Commission (IWC). Its mission was to regulate the whaling industry by setting annual quotas to prevent over-harvesting and commercial extinction.

4 This did not work well for two reasons. First, IWC quotas often were based on inadequate data or ignored by whaling countries. Second, without any powers of enforcement, the IWC was not able to stop the decline of most commercially hunted whale species.

5 In 1970, the United States stopped all commercial whaling and banned all imports of whale products. Under pressure from conservationists, the U.S. government, and the governments of many non-whaling countries, the IWC has imposed a moratorium on commercial whaling since 1986. It worked. The estimated number of whales killed commercially worldwide dropped from 41,480 in 1970 to about 1,300 in 2005.

6   Despite the ban, Japan, Norway, and Iceland kill about 1,300 whales of certain species each year for scientific purposes. Critics see these whale hunts as poorly disguised commercial whaling because the whale meat is sold to restaurants with each whale worth up to $30,000 whole-sale. In 2005, Japan more than doubled its whaling catch, allegedly for scientific purposes, from 440 minke whales to 850 minke whales and 10 fin whales, and began harvesting humpback whales in 2006.

7   Japan, Norway, Iceland, Russia, and a growing number of small tropical island countries—which Japan brought into the IWC to support its position—hope to overthrow the IWC ban on commercial whaling and reverse the international ban on buying and selling whale products. They argue that commercial whaling should be allowed because it has been a traditional part of the economics and culture of their countries. They also contend that the ban is based on emotion, not on updated scientific estimates of whale populations.

8   The moratorium on commercial whaling has led to a sharp rebound in the estimated populations of sperm, pilot, and minke whales. Proponents of whaling, therefore, see no scientific reason for not resuming controlled and sustainable hunting of these and other whale species with populations of at least 1 million. They argue that proposed hunting levels are too low to deplete stocks again.

9   Most conservationists disagree. Some argue that whales are peaceful, intelligent, sensitive, and highly social mammals that pose no threat to humans. Therefore, they should be protected for ethical reasons. Others question IWC estimates of the allegedly "recovered" whale species, noting the inaccuracy of past estimates of whale populations. Also, many conservationists fear that opening the door to any commercial whaling may eventually lead to widespread harvest of most whale species by weakening current international disapproval along with legal sanctions[†] against commercial whaling.

10   Proponents of resuming whaling say that people in other countries have no right to tell Japanese, Norwegians, and people in other whaling countries not to eat whales, just because some people like whales. This would be the same as people in India who consider cows sacred telling Americans and Europeans that they should not be allowed to eat beef.

(Adapted from Miller and Spoolman, *Living in the Environment*, 15th ed., pp. 257–58, © Cengage Learning.)

[†]sanctions: penalties for doing something that is unapproved or illegal.

Sharpening Your Skills

DIRECTIONS Answer the questions by filling in the blanks or circling the letters of the correct response.

Recognizing Patterns of Organization

1. The cause and effect pattern organizes the explanation in paragraph 1. The cause described is _____ . The effect is _____ .

2. What pattern organizes the explanation in paragraph 2?

   a. simple listing
   b. cause and effect
   c. comparison and contrast
   d. time order: process

Following the Author's Train of Thought

3. In paragraph 4, what does the opening pronoun "this" refer to?

   _____

4. What key category word appears in paragraph 4?

   _____

5. In addition to the category word, what other clues to the major supporting details do the authors provide?

   _____

Recognizing Patterns of Organization

6. What organizational patterns tie paragraphs 3, 4, and 5 together?

   _____

7. What is the primary pattern organizing the entire reading?

   _____

Identifying Main Ideas

8. Which of the following statements best sums up the main idea of the entire reading?

   a. The moratorium on whaling was not as successful as some would like to think. Many critics of whaling argue that the figures showing whale populations rebounding have been faked in order to roll back the ban on whaling.

   b. Efforts to save whales from biological extinction have been persistently undermined by Japanese whalers, who are determined to maintain a tradition that goes back hundreds of years.

   c. A moratorium on whale hunting saved many species of whales from extinction, but the increase in the whale populations has re-ignited the old controversy between supporters and critics of whaling.

   d. The most convincing argument for maintaining the moratorium on commercial whaling comes from those who make their living taking tourists whale watching. They argue correctly that whales are worth more alive than dead because whale watching is a $1 billion-a-year business.

Paraphrasing

9. In your own words, what was the mission of the IWC?

   _____

   _____

10. Paragraph 9 identifies the reasons why opponents of commercial whaling oppose the practice. In your own words, what are the reasons they offer for maintaining the moratorium?

    _____

    _____

    _____

    _____

    _____

11. Is it true that telling people in other countries to stop whaling is just like telling Americans they should stop eating beef?

_____

12. What does this line graph suggest about the effect of the moratorium on the whale population?

Figure 11-1 The effects of the 1986 moratorium on the whale population.

Source of data: http://whalingecosystems.weebly.com/effects-of-the-moratorium.html

_____

13. Does the author of the article believe the Japanese are whaling purely for research purposes?

_____

_____

14. Does the line graph that follows support or challenge the author's point of view?

_____

_____

_____

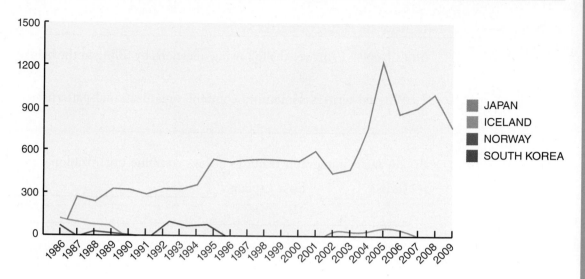

Figure 11-2 Tracking the growth of scientific whaling.

Source of data: http://whalingecosystems.weebly.com/effects-of-the-moratorium.html

15. The authors' purpose in this reading is to

   a. outline for readers the controversy surrounding the killing of whales.

   b. convince readers that the moratorium on killing whales must remain in place.

   c. show readers that those who want to lift the moratorium on killing whales have legitimate reasons for doing so.

From Reader to Writer Conservationists worry that if whaling continues, some species of whale might become extinct. That's one reason why the International Whaling Commission has banned whaling. Iceland, Norway, and Japan, however, continue to hunt for whales. Using the article you just read, plus some of your own Web research, write a paper explaining in more detail how these three countries get around the ban.

Once you describe how the three countries manage to ignore the ban, use the Web to discover what organization or organizations are fighting to protect the whales. What methods do they use? Are they successful? Are they considered legal? These are all questions that the second part of your paper should answer.

▶ **TEST 1**   **Reviewing Key Concepts**

DIRECTIONS   Answer the following questions by filling in the blanks.

1. Why do writers sometimes combine organizational patterns? ___

   _____

2. Do multi-paragraph readings always combine organizational patterns? _____ Please explain. _____

   _____

   _____

3. When a writer combines different organizational patterns, should
   the reader assume the patterns are all equally important? _____
   Please explain. _____

   _____

4. When readings combine different organizational patterns, how does
   the reader decide which elements of the patterns to include as notes?

   _____

   _____

   _____

5. What elements of a reading are always essential to your notes?

   _____

   _____

▶ **TEST 2**   **Identifying Main Ideas and Patterns of Organization**

DIRECTIONS   Read each selection. Write the main idea in the blanks that follow. Then circle the appropriate letters to identify the patterns organizing the reading.

1. Adopting New Products

1   Acceptance of new products—especially new-to-the-world products—usually doesn't happen overnight. In fact, acceptance of new products can actually take a very long time. People are sometimes cautious or even skeptical about new products. Those customers who do adopt new products usually go through an adoption process that has five stages.

2   The first stage is simple awareness, when the would-be consumer becomes conscious of the product's existence. Next, is the interest stage, when the individual seeks information about the product's price and comparative value. During the evaluation stage, potential buyers consider whether the product satisfies specific criteria, or standards, that are crucial to meeting their personal needs. In the trial stage, the people considering purchase find a way to experience the product without buying it. The individual may take advantage of free samples, purchase a small quantity, or borrow the product from someone else. In the final adoption stage, the decision is made to adopt the product because it appears to fulfill some specific need or needs.

3   Then, too, when an organization introduces a new product, people do not begin buying it all at the same time. Nor do they move through the process at the same speed. Some enter the adoption process quickly. Others wait. For most products, there is also a group of non-adopters who never even begin the adoption process. Because not everyone reacts to new products in the same way, people in marketing spend a good deal of time trying to understand what makes consumers buy or reject a new product.

4   Depending on the length of time it takes potential buyers to adopt a new product, marketers classify buyers into one of five major adopter categories: *innovators*, *early adopters*, *early majority*, *late majority*, and *laggards*. *Innovators* are the first to adopt a new product. They enjoy trying new products, tend to be adventurous, and like to be one of the first to own a new product. *Early adopters* choose new products carefully and are viewed as "the people to ask" by those in the other categories. People in the *early majority* adopt a new product just prior

to the average person. They are deliberate and cautious in trying new products. Individuals in the *late majority* are quite skeptical of new products but eventually adopt them because of economic necessity or social pressure. *Laggards*, the last to adopt a new product, are oriented toward the past. They are suspicious of new products. When they finally decide to adopt one, it may be in the process of being replaced by a newer product that the innovators and early adopters already possess. (Adapted from Pride and Ferrell, *Marketing*, 15th ed., p. 296, © Cengage Learning.)

1. What is the stated or implied main idea of the entire reading?

   _____

   _____

   _____

2. Which patterns does the author use to develop that main idea?

   a. definition
   b. time order
   c. simple listing
   d. comparison and contrast
   e. cause and effect
   f. classification

2. The Rise of Public Relations

1   You may think today's cash rebate programs from car manufacturers are relatively new. But in 1914, Henry Ford announced that if he sold 300,000 Model Ts that year, each customer would receive a rebate. When the company reached its goal, Ford returned $50 to each buyer. This was good business. It was also good public relations. *Public relations* involves creating an understanding for, or goodwill toward, a company, a person, or a product. Ford did precisely that with his fifty-dollar rebate.

2   There are three ways to encourage people to do what you want them to do: power, patronage, and persuasion. *Power* can be ruling by law or might. But it can also mean ruling by peer pressure—someone does something because his or her friends do. *Patronage* is a polite

term for bribery—paying someone to do what you want. The third method, persuasion, is the approach of public relations. *Persuasion* is the act of using argument or reasoning to induce someone to do something.

3   One of the first political leaders to realize the importance of public relations was Augustus Caesar, who in the first century commissioned statues of himself to be erected throughout the Roman Empire. The purpose of the statues was to enhance his image. Since then, many political leaders have ordered heroic images of themselves printed on coins and stamps.

4   The current public relations approach in the United States, however, can be traced not to the Romans but to journalists writing at the beginning of the twentieth century. Journalists were an important reason for the eventual emergence of public relations as a profession.

5   Before 1900, many businesspeople believed they could work alongside the press, or even ignore it. In general, stories that appeared in newspapers simply promoted companies that bought advertising. But after the Industrial Revolution[†] arrived in the United States at the end of the eighteenth century, and a new breed of industrialists began exploiting workers in pursuit of profits, the press's attitude toward industry began to change.

6   In response to what they saw as a great injustice, journalists like Lincoln Steffens (1866–1933) and Ida Tarbell (1857–1944) wrote stories that exposed corruption, with Tarbell taking on the oil industry and Steffens going after men who were manipulating the stock market. Thanks to the activities of these journalists, known as "muckrakers," the heads of big companies knew they could no longer just ignore the press. They had to get the press and the public on their side. Thus, 1900 saw the appearance of the first publicity firm. It was called The Publicity Bureau, and it was based in Boston. The Publicity Bureau signaled that public relations had become a formal profession that wasn't going to disappear any time soon. (Adapted from Biagi, *Media/Impact*, 10th ed., p. 236, © Cengage Learning.)

[†]Industrial Revolution: The Industrial Revolution began in England in the mid-eighteenth century, arriving later in the United States. Processes and products once done by hand were now being completed at high speed by machines.

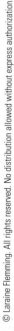

1. What is the stated or implied main idea of the entire reading?

    _____

    _____

    _____

2. Which patterns does the author use to develop that main idea?

    a. definition
    b. time order
    c. simple listing
    d. comparison and contrast
    e. cause and effect
    f. classification

▶ **TEST 3** Identifying Main Ideas and Patterns of Organization

DIRECTIONS Read each selection. Write the main idea in the blanks that follow. Then circle the appropriate letters to identify the patterns organizing the reading.

1. Outlawing Love

1 In 1947, India gained its independence from Britain. Shortly afterward, the country descended into a bloody civil war between Muslims and Hindus. As a result of the war, over 500,000 people died. A temporary peace only came about when what had once been a single country was divided, on August 14th and 15th, into the northern Islamic Republic of Pakistan and the southern Republic of India. At least four wars have occurred since the partition, and mistrust between the two countries remains strong to the present day.

2 The distrust shared by Muslims and Hindus is mirrored currently in what some conservative Hindus have labeled the "love jihad," a term meant to indicate that young Muslim men romance Hindu women as a way of converting them to Islam. These conservative groups have even claimed that Muslim men get paid to pretend to be in love with Hindu girls. There seems to be little or no evidence for such claims. This is certainly true in the case of Kaleem Sheikh, who has been imprisoned due to charges that he tried to forcefully abduct a young Hindu girl named only as *S* in court papers.

3 The girl, however, has come forward to say that the charges were made up by her Hindu parents, furious over her romance with a Muslim youth. According to the girl's account, the parents tormented her until she lodged a complaint against the young man, whom she insists she loves. Fearful that her parents might kill her for soiling their honor,[†] the girl made the charge but then recanted after the court guaranteed her safety. She also says that the young man insisted that she continue to practice Hinduism if that was her desire.

4 Concerns about Muslims launching a love jihad, however, are not limited to a few conservative parents living in rural areas. Many of those insisting that Muslim men have launched a love jihad possess a great deal of political clout. Some even belong to India's politically influential Bharatiya Janata Party. This is not as surprising as it might

---

[†]Honor killings, or murders carried out by family members who believe a female relative has behaved immorally, are on the rise in India.

seem since in heavily Hindu populations, the politician who claims to be protecting the purity of Hindu women can win votes.

5   Although a number of prominent Bollywood[†] male stars are Muslims while their equally famous Bollywood wives are Hindu, the subject of interfaith marriages has been a touchy issue in India for a very long time. But it's only recently that some have tried to turn such marriages into a crime, calling them an attack on the Hindu faith. The political speeches criticizing the Muslims' supposed love jihad have also triggered public assaults on Hindu-Muslim couples, something that never would have occurred two or three decades ago when attitudes toward interfaith romances and marriages were more tolerant.

(Sources of information: http://www.aljazeera.com/indepth/features/2014/10/jihad-war-romance-india-20141014923212607.html. Last accessed January 11, 2015; http://www.nytimes.com/2014/11/02/opinion/sunday/its-not-jihad-its-just-love.html?_r=0. Last accessed January 11, 2015.)

1. What's the stated or implied main idea of the entire reading?

_____

_____

_____

2. Which patterns does the author use to develop that main idea?

a. definition

b. time order

c. simple listing

d. comparison and contrast

e. cause and effect

f. classification

2. Grading Concussions[†]

1   *Concussions,* or head injuries that lead to a temporary loss of brain function, are fairly common. Often, however, the symptoms of a concussion may go unrecognized because symptoms vary widely and

---

[†]Bollywood: the Indian version of Hollywood.
[†]Some medical experts further sub-divide Grade 3 concussions to create five separate grades rather than three.

often come on hours after a person has been injured. The symptoms are also quite various and two people suffering from a concussion may not show the same reactions. Among the many symptoms are pallor, or paleness, slurred speech, nausea, vomiting, blurred vision, ringing in the ears, memory loss, and dizziness.

2   Loss of consciousness, however, is the most dangerous symptom of a concussion. Losing consciousness, for even a few seconds, means that the concussion is labeled Grade 3. Grade 3 concussions are considered "severe" and require treatment by a physician. When treating a patient suffering from a Grade 3 concussion, doctors use a series of questions to determine memory loss or profound mental confusion. They also test the patient's coordination and physical reflexes to determine if there is any damage to the central nervous system. If the questions and tests seem to suggest a serious brain injury, the doctor will order x-rays such as a CAT scan or MRI.

3   Some experts insist that loss of consciousness is also a symptom of a Grade 2 "moderate" concussion. However, most medical experts do not consider loss of consciousness, even for a very brief period of time, to be typical of Grade 2 concussions. The typical symptoms of a moderate concussion—memory loss, mental confusion, and severe headaches—can linger for as long as twenty-four hours, sometimes continuing for several days. Grade 2 concussions require at least twenty-four hours of observation in order to see if symptoms worsen.

4   The most widely accepted symptoms of Grade 1 or "mild" concussions are confusion, headache, and occasionally brief memory loss. Grade 1 concussions are not characterized by any loss of consciousness. They are usually the result of minor automobile accidents, sports involving bodily contact, and falls or other mishaps at work. When a concussion is mild, the symptoms usually disappear fairly quickly. However, they can linger in weaker form for days after the injury occurs. Grade 1 concussions, however, do not necessarily require treatment or observation. In fact, athletes who get Grade 1 concussions while playing contact sports are allowed to return to play after twenty minutes. Nevertheless, repeated Grade 1 concussions have become cause for concern. No matter how mild, repeated concussions have been linked to dementia* later on in life. (Sources of information: http://www.medic8.com/ healthguide/articles/mildheadinjury.html and http://www.injuryinformation.com/ injuries/concussions.php)

---

*dementia: persistent mental confusion and impaired reasoning.

1. What's the stated or implied main idea of the reading?

   _____

   _____

2. Which patterns does the author use to develop that main idea?

   a. definition

   b. time order

   c. simple listing

   d. comparison and contrast

   e. cause and effect

   f. classification

12 Responding to Persuasive Writing

IN THIS CHAPTER, YOU WILL LEARN

- how to tell the difference between informative and persuasive writing.

- how informative and persuasive writing sometimes overlap.

- how fact and opinion are central to identifying purpose.

- about the role of tone in informative and persuasive writing.

- how to evaluate arguments in persuasive writing.

"Almost everything worth writing about is worth arguing over."

—LEGENDARY TEACHER OF WRITING
MINA P. SHAUGHNESSY

"Without evidence, an argument is a windy, flimsy statement of one person's opinion."

—PROFESSORS ALISON PEASE AND LIVIA KATZ[†]

In previous chapters, we've concentrated mainly on how to determine the author's message or meaning. But before you leave the pages of this book, we need to look more closely at the characteristics that accompany persuasive writing. In addition to purpose, persuasive writing differs from informative writing in a number of ways, and you should know when your textbooks have, with or without the author's conscious intention, combined informative and persuasive purposes. Otherwise, you might unthinkingly absorb what are *opinions*, or personal points of view, as if they were proven facts that no one is likely to ever question.

What you'll learn from this chapter about persuasive writing will serve you well when reading textbooks. But it's also important for other kinds

---

[†]You can find the context for this quotation along with a brief but very good discussion of evidence here: www.jjay.cuny.edu/departments/english/Using_Evidence_to_Strengthen_Your_Arguments.pdf.

of reading from blogs to tweets to newspaper editorials, all of which have at their core an opinion that the writer wants readers to share.

By itself, though, an opinion is not an *argument*. To be considered an argument, an opinion needs evidence. Without evidence, statements of opinion are, as the opening quote suggests, not especially worthy of attention. That's certainly something to keep in mind when you are the writer. But it is equally important when you are the reader and are being bombarded by opinions from any number of sources. You need to be able to evaluate the evidence for those opinions and decide which ones you might consider sharing and which ones just don't have enough solid support for you to take them seriously without further proof. This chapter will give you the tools to make that evaluation.

 ## Recognizing the Primary Purpose

Like organizational patterns, purposes can mix together in one piece of writing. But one pattern is almost always **primary**, or more central to the author's intention than the other. In textbooks, the author's primary purpose is generally informative. However, passages of persuasion can make their way into textbooks without the authors even realizing they have revealed their personal point of view.

When that happens, you need to notice how and where informative writing has veered toward persuasion. If you do, you can be more conscious about deciding whether you actually agree with what's being said or need to know more before you do. What you don't want to do is absorb someone else's point of view without considering it first, and that can happen when you are not clear on how persuasive and informative writing can intermingle.

How does the reader know when the two purposes have begun to merge? In textbook writing, the balance of verifiable fact and non-verifiable opinion is a key indicator of whether or not the writer has maintained a strictly informative purpose. So let's start there.

 ## Facts and Opinions Are Clues to Purpose

The heavier the text is on facts, the more likely it is that the purpose of the writing is strictly informative. As you might expect, the more opinions that are present, the greater the chance that the author has taken on a persuasive purpose. However, in order to decide in which direction the author is leaning, you need to be absolutely certain about the difference between fact and opinion.

Facts

Facts are agreed upon pieces of information that can be verified or checked by turning to reference works, original documents, and knowledgeable experts. Look up, for instance, the dates of the American Civil War anywhere in the world, and they will be the same: 1861 to 1865. Similarly, you can check the date Nancy Pelosi was first elected speaker of the U.S. House of Representatives anywhere in the world. It will always be January 4, 2007, whether you look the date up today or ten years from now.

In addition to being verifiable, facts are usually expressed in language that is more denotative than connotative. In other words, the language packs little or no emotional punch. Take, for instance, the following sentence:

> Chunking—the grouping of bits of information into meaningful and manageable clusters—aids the retention* and retrieval of information.
>
> (Matsumoto, *People: Psychology from a Cultural Perspective*, p. 55, © Cengage Learning.)

Could you check if there are studies showing that chunking really does help people recall different bits of information? Yes, you could. That's what makes the statement a fact. Reinforcing the factual nature of the statement is the author's denotative language. Nothing in the sentence encourages the reader to feel anything about the situation described. The author conveys no judgment about the content. Nor does he encourage readers to see the information on chunking in a positive or a negative light.

To see the difference, compare the previous statement to this one:

> Probably the most effective aid to remembering is chunking—the grouping of bits of information into meaningful and manageable clusters—no other memory technique can match it.

With language like *effective* and *no other memory technique can match it*, we are getting into the area of opinions, or personal value judgments. After all, some people think visualizing is the key to

---

*retention: keeping something in one's memory.

remembering. Because there could be a difference of opinion about the best technique for remembering, the thoughtful reader would expect this statement to be followed by some proof that chunking really is the best strategy for remembering new information. Lacking any proof, the reader might well hold off before deciding that chunking is, indeed, the best technique.

> **Facts**
>
> 1. can be verified for accuracy through online and print reference works, personal interviews, original documents, and news sources.
>
> 2. rely on denotative language that doesn't express a point of view toward the topic under discussion.
>
> 3. are not shaped or affected by a writer's personality, background, or training and, therefore, do not vary from person to person or place to place.
>
> 4. frequently use numbers, statistics, dates, and measurements.
>
> 5. name and describe but do not evaluate.

Opinions

In contrast to facts, **statements of opinion** cannot be verified. Opinions are shaped by a person's background, personality, and training. They cannot be proven true or false. There is no way, for example, to prove to cat lovers that dogs make better pets. Nor can you convince a city lover that country life is really superior. Which pet a person favors or where best to live one's life are matters of opinion.

While opinions can't be verified, that doesn't mean they can't be evaluated. On the contrary, people speak all the time about *sound, valid,* or *informed* opinions. These are the terms used to refer to opinions based on solid evidence and logical reasoning. *Unsound, invalid,* or *uninformed* opinions lack evidence and rely on reasons not relevant, or related, to the opinion stated. While everyone has the right to an opinion, not every opinion is worthy of your attention or respect. Those lacking any supporting evidence definitely fall into this category.

In contrast to facts, opinions are likely to be laced with highly connotative language that carries with it some association or feeling. Look, for instance, at this statement drawn from a history textbook:

A ruthless land grab, the Cherokee removal exposed the *prejudiced and greedy* side of Jacksonian democracy. (Divine et al., *America Past and Present*, vol. 1, p. 285, © Cengage Learning.)

The two italicized phrases in this sentence have strong negative associations, which reveal that this statement—despite coming from a textbook—is more opinion than fact. There's nothing wrong with that. It happens all the time in textbooks because textbook authors are human. They have their personal likes and dislikes just like you do. And despite their best intentions to convey information to readers without making value judgments, their ideas or beliefs about their subject matter will occasionally emerge in a text.

That's only a problem if you don't pay attention and fail to notice that you are absorbing an opinion along with a statement of fact.

Opinions

1. cannot be verified for accuracy.

2. can only be labeled *valid* or *invalid*, *sound* or *unsound*, *informed* or *uninformed*, depending on the amount and type of support offered.

3. rely on connotative language that conveys a judgment or feeling.

4. are affected by a writer's personality, background, and training.

5. frequently express comparisons using words such as *more*, *better*, *most*, and *least*.

6. often make value judgments suggesting that some action or event has a positive or negative effect.

7. are likely to be introduced by verbs and adverbs that suggest doubt or possibility, such as *appears*, *seems*, *apparently*, *probably*, *potentially*, and *possibly*.

▶ EXERCISE 1   Labeling Facts and Opinions

DIRECTIONS   Label each statement *F* (for fact) or *O* (for opinion).

EXAMPLE   The part of the brain known as the amygdala helps in the storing of memories and plays a role in aggression and fear.   F

EXPLANATION   Thanks to fairly new brain scanning technology, we can call this statement a fact because its claim can be verified.

1. Harvard student Mark Zuckerberg first launched a version of Facebook in 2003. _____

2. If money is, indeed, the mother's milk of politics, efforts to make the money go away are not likely to work. (Wilson and DiIulio, *American Government*, p. 246, © Cengage Learning.) _____

3. Social scientists have coined the term *halo effect* to describe the tendency to form an overall positive impression of a person on the basis of one positive characteristic. (Adler and Proctor, *Looking Out/Looking In*, 12th ed., p. 104, © Cengage Learning.) _____

4. Bruno Mars's real name is Peter Gene Hernandez, and he was born in Hawaii. _____

5. In the general election for president, money does not make much difference, because both major-party candidates have the same amount, contributed by the federal government. (Wilson and DiIulio, *American Government*, p. 246, © Cengage Learning.) _____

6. The 1973 U.S. Supreme Court case *Miller v. California* resulted in a method for testing obscenity. _____

7. Beyoncé first became famous as a member of the girl group Destiny's Child. _____

8. Campaign contributions should not be considered a form of free speech. _____

9. The movie *The Imitation Game* does a terrible job recreating the life of the brilliant computer scientist Alan Turing. _____

10. One study (Begler, 2010) revealed that women are more likely than men to regard expressions of love as genuine statements rather than attribute them to some other cause. (Adler and Proctor, *Looking Out/ Looking In*, 12th ed., p. 104, © Cengage Learning.) _____

 # Combining Opinions with Facts

Up to this point, you have worked with statements that were either fact or opinion. But the truth is writers don't always keep fact and opinion neatly separated. Often, without realizing it, writers intent on informing their readers include a word or phrase that expresses their personal point of view.

For an illustration, read the following sentence in search of words that evaluate Sigmund Freud's discussion of dreams:

Sigmund Freud's revolutionary text *The Interpretation of Dreams* was published in 1900 and its impact is still relevant today. (Rubin et al., *Psychology: Being Human,* 3rd ed., Boston: Houghton Mifflin, p. 52.)

Did you decide that the words *revolutionary* and *relevant* expressed an evaluation? If you did, good for you. Those are precisely the words that push an otherwise factual statement into the realm of opinion. The statement is, to be sure, *primarily* factual. But it definitely puts a personal opinion into the mix. In this context, *revolutionary* carries with it positive associations that suggest Freud's theories were original and groundbreaking enough to survive until the present day.

Now consider this sentence:

Sigmund Freud's *The Interpretation of Dreams* was published in 1900, and the theories of dreaming it introduced are still used by some therapists despite the fact that Freud's theories have not been supported by scientific research on dreams and sleep.

Well now, there's another way to look at Freud's theories, which is not to say that this less positive view is the correct one. All it shows is that evaluations of Freud's book vary from person to person, making both of the above statements of opinion.

What the second sentence does suggest, though, is this: Before you assume *The Interpretation of Dreams* was so groundbreaking that its influence remains powerful over a century later, you might want to know a bit more about the current research on dreaming.

READING TIPS

1. An author's word choice counts a great deal when it comes to separating fact and opinion. A single word or phrase can inject a personal opinion into a statement that, at first glance at least, seems like hard fact.

2. Be wary of an author (or speaker) who starts a statement with the phrase, "It's a well-known fact. . . ." Often the claim made in the statement isn't well known. Much of the time, it isn't even a fact.

SUMMING UP THE KEY POINTS

1. Like organizational patterns, the author's purpose does not always neatly fall into one category or the other. Sometimes a piece of writing is both informative and persuasive and the reader has to determine which purpose is *primary*, or major.

2. Even when the purpose of writing is primarily informative, as it usually is in textbooks, the reader should be on the lookout for passages where the author has slipped into persuasion.

3. Statements of fact offer descriptions of topics or issues. They do not evaluate them.

4. Factual statements can be verified, or checked, against outside sources. They don't vary from place to place or person to person.

5. Factual statements employ a cool, neutral tone, using words that do not call up strong emotional associations.

6. Unlike facts, opinions can't be verified. They can't be proven right or wrong, true or false. That doesn't mean, however, that opinions can't be evaluated. They can.

7. Opinions backed by sound evidence and reasoning are termed *sound, informed,* or *valid.* Those that aren't backed by relevant evidence are labeled *unsound, uninformed,* or *invalid.*

8. Without realizing it, writers sometimes add a word or phrase with positive or negative associations. That word or phrase then mixes an opinion in with facts.

▶ **EXERCISE 2**   **Recognizing When Fact and Opinion Blend**

DIRECTIONS   Label each statement *F* (for fact), *O* (for opinion), or *M* (for a mix of both).

EXAMPLE   Men and women view and experience aging differently. As men approach their fifties, they fear the loss of their sexual capacity but not their attractiveness; for women, the reverse is true. (Bryan Strong et al., *The Marriage and Family Experience*, 11th ed., p. 196, © Cengage Learning.)

——— O ———

EXPLANATION   Although the information here is presented as if it were factual, it's impossible to verify how *all* men or *all* women experience aging.

1. In 1963, in a decision that was typical of the Supreme Court ruled by Chief Justice Earl Warren, the Court prohibited the Lord's Prayer and Bible reading in schools.

   ———

2. University students have a positive view of marriage therapy. (Knox and Schacht, *Choices in Relationships*, 10th ed., p. 479, © Cengage Learning.)

   ———

3. The heart is a hollow, muscular organ with four chambers that serve as two pumps. It is about the size of a clenched fist. (Hales, *An Invitation to Health*, 7th ed., p. 277, © Cengage Learning.)

   ———

4. Responding to increasing Republican accusations—including those from the House Un-American Activities Committee (HUAC)—that his administration let Communists into the government, Truman moved to beef up the existing loyalty program. . . . But Truman's loyalty program intensified rather than calmed fears about an "enemy within." (Adapted from Berkin et al., *Making America*, 5th ed., p. 803, © Cengage Learning.)

   ———

5. Government regulation and public awareness are external forces that have increased the social responsibility of business. (Pride, Hughes, and Kapoor, *Business*, 10th ed., p. 51, © Cengage Learning.)

_____

6. Cross-cultural studies . . . consistently indicate that some societies and subcultures are more violent and aggressive than others. (Shaffer, *Social and Personality Development*, 6th ed., p. 308, © Cengage Learning.)

_____

7. [Following the Mexican-American War], Mexico was dismembered like a carcass of beef. One-third of Mexican territory—an area larger than France and Spain combined—was detached because the Polk administration wanted it and the United States was strong enough to take it. (Conlin, *The American Past*, 9th ed., p. 393, © Cengage Learning.)

_____

8. On February 2, 1848, Trist [the American representative] signed the Treaty of Guadalupe Hidalgo, granting the United States all the territory between the Nueces River and the Rio Grande and between there and the Pacific. In exchange, Trist agreed that the United States would pay Mexico $15 million and any war reparations* owed to Americans. (Berkin et al., *Making America*, 6th ed., p. 325, © Cengage Learning.)

_____

9. Our friends who have children influence us to do likewise. (Knox and Schacht, *Choices in Relationships*, 10th ed., p. 311, © Cengage Learning.)

_____

10. These two great popular heroes of the revolution [Pancho Villa and Emiliano Zapata] could not have been more different in temperament. Zapata was reserved and cautious but determined, steadfast, and fair in carrying out his promises, while the more physically

_____

*reparations: payments to help make up for a wrong that's been done.

dominant and temperamental Villa embodied a frontier code of fearlessness, honor, violence, and vengeance in pursuing his objectives. (Adapted from Meyer et al., *The Course of American History*, Oxford University Press, 9th ed., 2010, p. 400.)

_____

✔ **CHECK YOUR UNDERSTANDING**

1. Is it true or false that all writing can be divided into two kinds, informative or persuasive? _____ Please explain. _____
_____

2. The key difference between a fact and an opinion is that statements of fact can be
_____ .

3. The language of facts is _____ rather than _____ .

4. Unlike facts, opinions can't be _____ . That doesn't mean, however, that opinions can't be _____ . They can be labeled _____
_____ .

5. Is it true or false that all statements can be labeled as fact or opinion? _____
Please explain. _____
_____

6. If the statement is a fact, put an *F* in the blank. Put an *O* in the blank if it's an opinion.
   a. China is home to the world's largest Web population. _____
   b. The Chinese government has been remarkably unsuccessful in its efforts to control what its citizens view on the Web. _____

Recognizing When Persuasion Is Primary

We started this chapter by talking about the way informative writing in textbooks can cross over into persuasion. But, like informative writing, persuasion can be a writer's sole purpose in writing. The question is, How do you know when persuasion *is* the author's primary purpose? In general, persuasion is the author's main purpose when he or she offers an opinion and strongly suggests that you share it. But there are other clues as well.

The Title Often Takes Sides

Writers determined to persuade often introduce an abbreviated version of their opinion in titles like "Say No to Higher Taxes" or "Stop Factory Farming." Thus, if you are trying to determine if the author's purpose is persuasive, start with the title. Does it simply identify the issue as it does here: "The Arrival of America's Railroads"? Or does the title itself take a stand: "Corporate Greed Equals Corporate Corruption"?

▶ **EXERCISE 3**   **Connecting Title with Purpose**

DIRECTIONS   Look at each title. Then write an *I* or a *P* in the blank to indicate if the title suggests an informative or a persuasive purpose.

1. A Controversial Supreme Court Decision Makes Headlines _____

2. Corporations Don't Have Civil Rights _____

3. Are Bullies Getting Younger and Younger? _____

4. Viagra Is No Medical Necessity _____

5. Education in Denmark _____

6. Standardized Testing Deserves a Failing Grade _____

7. New Standards for New York Teachers _____

8. The Status of Greenland's Glaciers _____

9. Daring Mother Nature to Strike Back _____

10. Skinny Scarecrows Aren't Sexy _____

The Author Takes a Stand

In purely informative writing, authors supply readers with information while keeping their **personal perspective**, or point of view, out of the discussion. However, when writing becomes primarily persuasive, the writer's point of view becomes central to the discussion. It becomes the controlling main idea.

Writers motivated by a persuasive purpose see an issue in a certain light. Convinced of their correctness, they believe it is important for readers to share their point of view, or at least to seriously consider sharing it. It's no surprise, then, that writing with a persuasive purpose includes thesis statements like these, which express a definite point of view in language that is more connotative than denotative.

1. Instead of being treated as heroes, whistle-blowers are unfairly made the subject of criminal investigations that are purposely designed to intimidate others from speaking out in the future.

2. Beauty contests for children may serve the vanity of the parents, but they are enormously stressful for the anxious children put on display.

3. At the heart of factory farming is the belief that the suffering of animals just does not count. What counts is profit.

Persuasive writing puts forth an opinion, an idea, a belief, or an attitude that some readers might disagree with. It does not put forth ideas that no one disputes. This sentence would not be the thesis statement for a persuasive piece of writing: "Thomas Jefferson was the third president of the United States." This one, however, might well turn up as the focus of a persuasive article or essay: "Publicly Thomas Jefferson seemed to stand against the extension of slavery, but his behind-the-scenes position was a good deal more complicated."

Statements that other people might not agree with or share are at the heart of persuasive writing. That's what makes recognizing persuasive writing so important. As a reader, you don't want to share a point of view without even realizing that you have accepted as fact an idea that is really only someone else's opinion.

▶ **EXERCISE 4**   **Distinguishing Between Informative and Persuasive Thesis Statements**

DIRECTIONS   Each of the following statements could provide the basis for either informative or persuasive writing. In the blank that follows each one, write *I* to indicate that the thesis appears to be primarily informative or *P* to indicate the opposite.

1. New reproductive technology has made it increasingly possible for parents over fifty to have children. _____

2. While reproductive technology has made it increasingly possible for parents over fifty to have children, the question those parents need to be asking is, Should parents in their sixties really be raising teenagers? _____

3. Recent studies show that more than half of U.S. employers block social media access because they fear social media can too easily distract their employees from work. _____

4. Companies that are blocking their employees from social media sites are damaging employee morale and decreasing, rather than encouraging, productivity. _____

5. The Obama administration passed health care legislation that strikes at the heart of individual freedom and responsibility. _____

6. If nothing else, the Obama administration's health care plan has eliminated a long-standing obstacle to health care in America— the ability of insurance companies to deny coverage for preexisting conditions. _____

7. In the spring of 2011, thousands of protestors in Egypt's Tahrir Square gave new and courageous meaning to the title of an old song, "Walk Like an Egyptian." _____

8. In the spring of 2011, Cairo's Tahrir Square was the scene of angry protests against the Egyptian dictator Hosni Mubarak, who, as a result, was forced to abdicate his role as Egypt's leader. _____

9. For decades, Pakistani husbands who threw acid into the faces of the wives they wanted to replace received minimal punishment, but the legal system in Pakistan has begun to take action and men found guilty now get fourteen years to life in prison. _____

10. Filmmaker Sharmeen Obaid-Chinoy's documentary about acid attacks on women in Pakistan, called *Saving Face*, is a tribute to the activists and victims who have courageously spoken out against this barbaric practice. _____

From Reader to Writer Use the phrase "children's beauty contests" to search the Web for different points of view, or perspectives on the subject. The French, for instance, want to ban them. The British generally don't think there's anything wrong with them. Then write two statements you think you could develop in writing, one with an informative purpose, the other persuasive.

The Supporting Details Provide the Evidence

Authors looking to persuade their readers know that they have to give them more than the title and point of view. Persuasion requires an **argument**. Arguments of any merit don't just state an opinion and repeat it. Instead, they supply evidence, selected to make readers say, "I see your point" or, even better, "Based on that evidence, I'm inclined to agree with you."

Evidence in an argument can take different forms. It can take the form of reasons, examples, studies, events, personal experiences, statistics, etc. Like all supporting details, evidence in an argument depends on the opinion, i.e., the thesis statement being put forth for readers' acceptance.

Here, for instance, the author argues that a writer who wrote a fake memoir* called *The Education of Little Tree* did so to cover up his violent racist past. Note how the evidence focuses on events from the subject's life. For the author of the argument, the subject's violent and racist past is evidence. It illustrates why Carter needed to disguise his past when the country began to change and blatant* racism was no longer tolerated.

---

*memoir: life story.
*blatant: obvious, overt, out in the open.

Asa Carter's Secret Past

The title offers a clue to the author's intention.

1 Although Asa Earl Carter originally claimed that his book *The Education of Little Tree* was autobiographical, there is very little evidence to prove his claim of Native American heritage, and the book is now generally accepted as fiction rather than the autobiography Carter suggested it was. Unlike the main character of his book, Carter was not orphaned at five years of age, and his Cherokee grandparents didn't raise him because he didn't have any Cherokee grandparents. Many of Carter's descriptions of Cherokee life have been widely disputed by those who are really Cherokee by birth. For the most part, the story of Carter's Indian past appears to have been invented to cover up the period of his life he wanted to keep hidden from the world—his years as a violent racist.

Here's the point of the author's argument: Carter tried to reinvent himself as a Native American orphan to cover up his history as a "violent racist."

Paragraph 2 presents evidence of Carter's violent racism.

2 Born in Anniston, Alabama, in 1925, Carter started his career as a radio announcer. He specialized in attacking Jews, blacks, Yankees, and any of what he termed the "lesser breeds." He was especially hard on those who dared challenge the superiority of the white race. When he wasn't assaulting minorities over the radio waves, Carter was managing the Anniston chapter of the Ku Klux Klan, which he himself had founded. Under Carter's leadership, the Anniston Klan had several vile* accomplishments: They threw stones at black students trying to integrate the University of Alabama campus, savagely beat the civil rights activist Reverend Fred Shuttlesworth, and castrated a mentally handicapped black handyman.

Notice the author's use of sarcasm in the phrases "vile accomplishments" and "credentials as a racist and a bigot."

3 Given Carter's credentials as a racist and a bigot, he was the natural choice of the 1962 gubernatorial candidate George Wallace, who thought he needed to show a more racist profile to make it into the governor's office. Anxious to escape the more liberal image of his mentor, Big Jim Folsom, Wallace tapped Carter as his speechwriter. After Wallace was elected, he again turned to Carter, who penned for Wallace his infamous inaugural slogan, "segregation now, segregation tomorrow, segregation forever."

The reference to Carter changing his name is important in light of the author's thesis that Carter was covering up his past.

4 The times were changing, though, and, after a while, even Carter figured out that spewing racist hatred was not the foundation for a successful career. After running, unsuccessfully, against his old friend Wallace for not being racist enough, Carter moved to Texas and started writing under the pseudonym Forrest Carter. His first novel, *The Rebel Outlaw: Josey Wales*, became a movie starring Clint Eastwood, but Carter really hit pay dirt when he penned his fake memoir, *The Education of Little Tree*. Although there were those suspicious of the book's authenticity

---

*vile: disgusting.

from the beginning, most accepted Carter's claims about his Cherokee past as fact, and the book eventually became a huge best seller.

5   Ironically, *The Education of Little Tree* was celebrated as a symbol of the country's growing acceptance of a multicultural history in which minorities played a key role. Unfortunately, Carter wasn't alive to be publicly shamed—if such a man could be shamed—when his literary sleight of hand was exposed in 1991 by a distant relative and Wallace biographer who described Carter's life as a Klansman in the pages of the *New York Times*. Asa Carter had died in 1979, while still being acclaimed for Forrest Carter's contribution to a growing body of literature written by people of color, precisely the people of color Carter had once insulted for being the "lesser breeds," who should know their place or suffer the consequences.[†]

> The author uses both first names to emphasize that Carter tried to keep the two parts of his life separate.

Typically for writing with an overtly persuasive purpose, it's not hard to determine the author's position or point. Carter wrote *The Education of Little Tree* to cover his tracks. He knew the times had changed and figured it would be a wise move to get on the winning side. Most of the evidence provided for the author's claim has to do with proving that Carter was a violent racist, and on that score the author does well.

> Asa Carter was a Ku Klux Klan member who, when it became profitable, transformed himself into a champion of Native American rights.

Jim McDonald/Documentary/Corbis.

[†] The information for this reading comes from Dan T. Carter's *The Politics of Rage*, a biography of George Wallace. Carter is also the "distant relative," who wrote the *New York Times* article "The Transformation of a Klansman" exposing Forrest Carter's true identity.

What's less grounded in hard fact is Carter's reason for writing *The Education of Little Tree*. Yes, he did write it at a time when the country was changing. Carter's brand of blind and vicious racism was coming under attack. Thus, he may well have wanted to hide the person he had been before moving to Texas.

But then again, he might also have simply been an opportunist. Realizing that works about minorities were being celebrated, he might have thought to himself, I can make some money by pretending to be a part-Cherokee writer who tells the story of his life. The claim about Carter's motives is simply harder to prove, and, for that reason, this part of the author's argument is less well substantiated, or backed up, than the claim about his past as a violent racist. That part of the author's argument is solid.

Choosing a Tone

"We often refuse to accept an idea merely because the tone of voice in which it has been expressed is unsympathetic to us."
—Philosopher Friedrich Nietzsche

In addition to offering an opinion and providing evidence, the reading on Asa/Forrest Carter reveals its persuasive purpose through the author's tone. **Tone** in writing resembles tone of voice in speaking. It's the feeling or attitude evoked, or called up, by the author's words. Tone in writing is, as the writer and blogger Mort Castle so perfectly expressed it, "the writer's voice in the reader's mind."

Unlike informative writing, which usually mutes the author's tone, writing designed to persuade uses tone as a way of encouraging readers' agreement. In the reading on Carter, the tone—a mixture of sarcasm and contempt—encourages readers to feel equally appalled and disgusted by Carter's behavior.

But tone varies with the opinion proposed and the audience addressed. (See the box on page 678 for a range of tones.) Writers with a persuasive purpose might use a friendly and highly personal tone to make readers feel sympathetic to the idea, attitude, situation, or action they propose. Or, they might employ a furious tone to make readers share their anger and demand some change.

In the following excerpt, the author has learned from intimate experience that organ donation can be a complicated and extraordinarily difficult affair. This is an opinion she wants her readers to share. Notice how she creates an earnest yet informal tone that encourages readers to take her situation seriously. The casualness of her tone is important, because she doesn't want to lapse into self-pity. That might make her readers less responsive to her situation:

Despite the seriousness of the situation, the author's use of the word *beans* helps keep the tone light.

The statement "I am an odd duck" diminishes the distance between reader and writer and affirms the author's refusal to be miserable.

Whaddya Have to Do to Get a Kidney Around Here?

It was almost a year ago that I found out my kidneys were slowly but ineluctably* failing. I'd been diagnosed with kidney disease a few years earlier, but the beans had been stable at 50 percent. Then a consult at Mass General concluded with the news that it could be as early as a year before I would need what was euphemistically* called "renal replacement therapy." Doctors are often discreet* in the way they describe things, but the message was clear. I would face three choices: death, dialysis, or transplant.

   I am an odd duck, but I was energized by what was now to be a great adventure. I was going to have the opportunity to face my own mortality. At sixty-five, I had a wonderful life, a public voice, and made a modest contribution to a better world. . . . I loved my life and would enjoy more if it were available, but death was OK. I would take it as the last wonderful journey. I'd also do what needed to be done to continue to live a long and fruitful life, free of infirmity.* That meant finding a person who would donate his or her spare kidney to me before mine failed. It was not, the doctors said, too soon to begin the search. (Frances Kissling, *Whaddya Have to Do to Get a Kidney Around Here?* Salon.com Archive, www.salon.com/2009/03/27/my_kidney/. March 27, 2009. Used by permission of the author.)

Right from the title, the author uses tone to say to readers, "If you are looking for a sob story, don't look here." The person she presents to her readers through her choice of tone is serious about her condition. However, she is neither miserable nor despairing. One way or another, she will manage the situation and face whatever happens. This is the message her tone conveys.

The Power of Tone

Tone may just be the most powerful device in the persuasive writer's toolbox. It's the voice readers "hear" on the page. If they like the voice, they are all the more ready to listen to what the author says.

   Because tone can be so inviting and encourage an emotional response that leaves logic behind, it pays to be aware of its effect on you. That means knowing how an author is using language, imagery, and detail to create it.

----

*ineluctably: inescapably.
*euphemistically: expressed positively despite having negative connotations.
*discreet: careful, tactful, careful about what's said or revealed.
*infirmity: weakness, illness.

Some Words to Describe Tone ●		
Admiring	Disapproving	Passionate
Amazed	Disbelieving	Patriotic
Angry	Disgusted	Proud
Anxious	Doubtful	Puzzled
Appalled	Enthusiastic	Regretful
Arrogant	Friendly	Respectful
Assertive*	Horrified	Rude
Breezy	Insulting	Sarcastic
Cautious	Ironic*	Shocked
Comical	Mistrustful	Skeptical
Confident	Neutral	Solemn
Contemptuous	Nostalgic (longing for a past time)	Sympathetic
Critical		Worried
Cynical	Objective	
Determined	Outraged	

Irony can also refer to something that is the opposite of what one might expect. In this case, the photo contradicts the words.

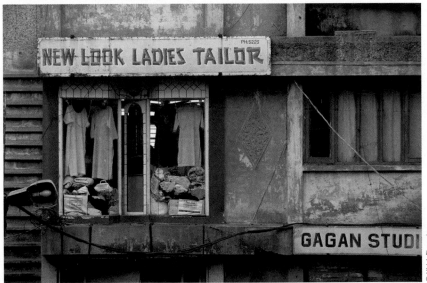

*assertive: said or done with great confidence and a sense that one is right.
*When the tone is ironic, the writer says the opposite of what is intended in such a way that the underlying meaning becomes more important than what the words actually say, "Of course Kim Kardashian is news! How could the world *not* want to know about a young woman who has never, in her entire life, accomplished anything of substance?"

▶ **EXERCISE 5**   **Hearing the Author's Tone**

DIRECTIONS   Read each excerpt. Then circle the appropriate letter to identify the author's tone.

1. After all the extravagant hype, it appears that Google Glass, the wearable technology that looks like ugly glasses your grandmother might have bought because they were on sale at fifty percent off, have failed in the marketplace. Now there's a surprise. Who wouldn't buy a product that made the owner an awkward standout in just about any situation imaginable? And then there was that $1,500 price tag. Clearly the glasses were a steal. After all, they encouraged others to get angry and pop you one in the head after they realized your glasses were being used to film them without their consent. And wearing them was bound to encourage intimacy in friendships, since no one speaking to someone wearing Google Glass could be sure the person wasn't watching YouTube instead of following the conversation. It's impossible to fathom* why such a terrific gadget didn't take off in the marketplace.

   a. neutral

   b. ironic

   c. amused

   d. fascinated

2. **Where Have All the Tools Gone?**

   The disappearance of tools from our common education is the first step toward a wider ignorance of the world of artifacts† we inhabit. And, in fact, an engineering culture has developed in recent years in which the object is to "hide the works," rendering many of the devices we depend on every day unintelligible to direct inspection. . . . A decline in tool use would seem to betoken a shift in our relationship to our own stuff: more passive and more dependent. And, indeed, there are fewer occasions for the kind of spiritedness that is called forth when we take things in hand for ourselves, whether to fix them or to make them. What ordinary people once made, they buy; and what they once fixed for

---

*fathom: figure out, understand.
†artifacts: objects made by human beings that are of historical interest.

themselves, they replace entirely or hire an expert to repair, whose expert fix often involves replacing an entire system because some minute component has failed. (Mathew B. Crawford, *Shop Class as Soulcraft*, Penguin Books, 2010, p. 1.)

The author's tone is

a. neutral.

b. warning.

c. curious.

d. discouraged.

3. **Joe Hill Was No Hero**

Americans seem always to have lusted for rags-to-riches heroes. Failing to find them, we are too often inclined to invent them. This certainly seems to be the case when it comes to the man born Joel Hägglund who later came to be known as Joe Hill.[†] A poet and song-writer, Hill first came to public attention when he wrote a series of songs that were adopted by the early American labor movement. His name, however, did not become notorious until he was arrested for armed robbery and murder. According to the legend, Hill never committed the murder; he was executed in an attempt to destroy the labor movement. Although it is true that Hill was tried and convicted on circumstantial evidence, it is equally true that his story contained numerous distortions and loopholes. At his best, he was a man unfairly tried and convicted; at his worst, he was a criminal who boldly proclaimed himself innocent. But in neither case was he a legendary hero, and the ridiculous tendency to call him heroic is a misguided attempt to make a hero out of a man totally unworthy of the name.

The author's tone is

a. neutral.

b. ironic.

c. mystified.

d. disgusted.

[†]Two of Hill's most famous songs were "The Preacher and the Slave" and "Casey Jones—the Union Scab." Hill's life was also the subject of a song titled "Joe Hill," which singer Joan Baez made widely known at a famous concert in Woodstock, New York.

4. **Sympathy for the Candidate**

If you dislike campaign oratory* put yourself in the candidate's shoes for a moment. Every word you say will be scrutinized, especially for slips of the tongue. Interest group leaders and party activists will react sharply to any phrase that departs from their preferred policies. Your opponent stands ready to pounce on any error of fact or judgment. You must give countless speeches every day. The rational reaction to this state of affairs is to avoid controversy, stick to prepared texts and tested phrases, and shun anything that sounds original (and hence untested). . . . Voters may *say* that they admire a blunt, outspoken person, but in a tough political campaign, they would probably find such bluntness a little unnerving. (Wilson and DiIulio, *American Government*, 10th ed., p. 243, © Cengage Learning.)

The author's tone is

a. neutral.

b. ironic.

c. puzzled.

d. sympathetic.

From Reader to Writer Colorado businessman James Beach was kicked off a flight for using a knee defender, a device that stops the passenger in front of the device user from reclining. When Beach used his, the woman in front of him was not happy. Look up the incident involving Mr. Beach on the Web. Write two accounts of it. Make the purpose of one purely and clearly informative, telling the reader simply what happened when. Keep your tone neutral.

Make the second description persuasive. Argue in favor of the person using the knee defender or the person unable to recline. Use a tone designed to make readers sympathetic to your side of the dispute.

---

*oratory: speech making.

In Persuasive Writing, Both Sides Rarely Get Equal Time

Writers whose intention is primarily to inform will present both sides of an argument just about equally so that readers can draw their own conclusion, for example:

Drug Use and Pregnancy

1 Court cases with policy implications for whether a woman can or should be arrested if she exposes a fetus to illegal drugs are continuing to be debated at the highest judicial levels, including the Supreme Court in the United States. Is this an effective way to reduce the likelihood of drug use and any of its accompanying risks for the fetus? That depends on your point of view.

What Are the Opposing Arguments?

2 Some say a concerned society should impose criminal or other charges on a pregnant woman who uses a drug that may be dangerous to the fetus. A number of jurisdictions in the United States and provinces in Canada have implemented laws permitting a newborn to be removed from a parent on the grounds of child abuse or neglect because of drug exposure during pregnancy. In some cases, the woman has been ordered to be confined to a drug-treatment facility during pregnancy. After all, anyone found to provide such illegal substances to a child would certainly expect to face criminal or other charges. Are the circumstances that much different in the case of a pregnant woman and her fetus?

3   Others believe the situation is vastly different and further claim that criminal charges, imprisonment, or mandatory treatment are counter-productive (Beckett, 1995; Farr, 1995). Legislation specifically targeted to pregnant drug users might actually drive prospective mothers, out of fear of being prosecuted, away from the care and treatment needed for both themselves and their fetuses. Moreover, the tendency to rely on criminal procedures could limit the resources available for the implementation of innovative, well-funded public health efforts for treating addiction and its consequences for the fetus (Chavkin, 2001). (Adapted from Bukatko and Daehler, *Child Development*, 5th ed., pp. 123–24, © Cengage Learning.)

To see the difference between pure informative and pure persuasive writing, compare this reading to the one about Asa Carter. The reading on Carter never even suggests that a different point of view exists. Yet it's sometimes argued that Carter wrote *The Education of Little Tree* to atone, or make up, for his despicable past,[†] after realizing late in life how wrong he had been.

In the author's mind, this point of view isn't even worthy of your consideration. Thus, you, the reader, don't hear about it. For a writer with persuasive intentions, that's not unusual. And even when a writer with a persuasive purpose mentions an opposing point of view, it's usually to tell readers precisely how that opposing point of view is in error.

Ten Signs of Informative Writing ●	**1.** Opens with a neutral title that does not judge or evaluate: "Latino Rock Pioneers of the 50s"; "World War II Propaganda."
	2. Describes a subject, an event, or an issue without offering a personal opinion, or making a value judgment: "In 2005, surgeons successfully performed a face transplant for the first time in medical history."
	3. Relies mainly on denotative language, which makes the author sound personally uninvolved: "On the first day of the riots, one hundred people died."
	4. Leans heavily on factual evidence that can be verified, or checked, in other sources: "In May of 1968, approximately nine million workers went on strike in France."
	5. Describes the opinions of others without revealing if the author agrees or disagrees: "In a recent *New York Times* editorial, William Baude argued that states might 'use custody laws to curtail the movements of pregnant women.'"
	6. Avoids using the first-person singular (*I*) or plural (*we*): "It has been argued by some" as opposed to "I would argue here."
	7. Often gives both sides of an issue: "Judge William Rehnquist, who died in 2005 at the age of eighty, was considered by many to be an arch-conservative who helped divide the country. Others saw him as a consensus builder."
	8. Expresses only value judgments that are attributed to others: "Some hold the opinion that both Republicans and Democrats failed to adequately help victims of Hurricane Katrina. Critics cite failures among Democrats at the local level and Republicans at the federal level."

[†]Interestingly enough, Carter's former friend and boss Governor George Wallace did try to atone for his racist past, apologizing publicly and privately for his past behavior.

9. Emphasizes the role of research that illustrates or supports the main idea: "The leading medical researcher at Harvard Medical School disputes the notion that eight glasses of water a day are essential for good health. His claim is supported by a number of studies done on athletes."

10. Commonly appears in reference works, textbooks, manuals, newspapers, and institutional reports.

Ten Signs of Persuasive Writing
●

1. Opens with a title that suggests a point of view: "Voting Matters" or "Turkey Haunted by the Nightmare of Armenia."[†]

2. Expresses a personal opinion about a subject, an event, or an issue: "From my perspective, the best thing about the Winter Olympics is that they are over."

3. Frequently uses language that reveals strong feelings: "How many stories about desperate, terrified, and homeless people do we need to hear before we seriously commit to providing more low-income housing in our cities, instead of turning our urban neighborhoods over to those wealthy enough to live there?"

4. Mentions an opposing point of view mainly to contradict it: "The notion that alcoholics can learn to drink moderately is wishful thinking."

5. Uses more facts that favor the writer's point of view. For instance, a writer who does not want readers to support the use of animals in research might include statistics about the number of mice killed in pursuit of a cancer treatment, while leaving out any statistic about the number of people living longer now that the drug is available.

6. Gives reasons why the author's opinion should be held by others: "There are several reasons why both censorship and propaganda are absolutely necessary during wartime."

7. Often uses the first-person pronoun (*I*) or addresses the audience: "I know that you too must cringe when politicians claim to speak for all Americans."

[†]Although many of his fellow citizens disagree with Turkish writer Orhan Pamuk, others share his point of view. Pamuk insists his country carried out genocide, or planned mass slaughter, against the Armenians in 1915.

8. Refers to the audience as if agreement had already been established between the writer and the audience: "We all know that elections are not won by merit; they are won by money."

9. Uses rhetorical questions that neither expect nor want an answer: "Except to undermine parental authority, what other reason could there be for telling a small child to question authority?"

10. Commonly appears in essays, editorials, biographies, and books written to make readers aware of an issue or revise a long-held opinion.

READING TIP

Any time an author gives both sides of an issue an equal amount of space, pointing out the pluses and minuses of each position, you are dealing with writing meant to primarily inform rather than persuade.

▶ **EXERCISE 6**   Recognizing Main Idea, Purpose, and Tone

DIRECTIONS   Read each of the following selections. Then, in the blank lines that follow, identify the author's main idea, purpose, and tone. *Note:* Feel free to suggest that informative and persuasive writing have blended together equally if you think that is the case.

EXAMPLE

Fingerprints on Trial

The title doesn't really make a judgment. It gives us the topic but not the purpose. However, the opening sentence has a definite "That was then this is now" feel to it.

The tone is fairly neutral, but the thesis statement comes close to taking a stand: Where

1   Fingerprints have long been considered an essential part of crime solving. If a trained expert said in a courtroom that fingerprints found at the scene of a crime matched those of the accused, the expert's testimony usually decided the case. The defendant was found guilty, case closed. But fingerprint evidence may no longer be considered unassailable proof of guilt. While fingerprints might not lie, the experts who analyze them can and do make mistakes. Sometimes poorly trained, they are not always subject to regular

fingerprints are concerned, mistakes have been made, making the tone somewhere between neutral and critical.

The use of the term *sacred cows*—ideas held sacred more out of tradition than for merit—suggests the author's point of view that fingerprint evidence might be another sacred cow.

The last paragraph is really the clincher. There are definitely two sides to this issue, but the author presents only the side that questions the value of fingerprint evidence.

This sentence moves the tone from neutral to critical.

review by outside experts. Consequently, the use of fingerprint evidence is currently on trial, and the jury is still out as to whether fingerprint analysis makes for reliable evidence.

2   Fingerprint evidence was first admitted into a U.S. courtroom in 1902 and went unchallenged for so long, in part, because no one really knew what standards should be applied to what was considered scientific evidence. However, all that changed with a 1993 case called *Daubert v. Merrell Dow Pharmaceuticals*. The case involved a child whose mother had taken a drug made by Merrell Dow Pharmaceuticals. The child suffered from serious birth defects, and lawyers representing the child's family argued that the drug had caused the defects. The pharmaceutical company insisted that there was no valid proof that the drug was at fault and raised the issue of what constituted scientific proof. The judge ruled in favor of the pharmaceutical company and laid down a set of standards for what could qualify as proof. Chief among them was the criterion that an evidence-gathering technique with a high error rate could no longer be accepted as solid evidence.

3   As a consequence of the *Daubert* ruling, judges were now required to take a more active role evaluating and deciding the "quality of evidence." It was at this point that the sacred cows of forensic* science came under attack. Handwriting evidence was no longer considered scientific, use of lie detector results as evidence was severely limited, and even ballistic tests claiming to match bullets to specific guns came into question.

4   Suddenly, questions were being asked that had rarely been posed in pre-1993 courtrooms: Has fingerprint identification been adequately tested? What's the error rate? What are the standards and controls for evaluating fingerprint experts? People like lawyer Robert Epstein, who has repeatedly challenged the validity of fingerprint evidence, would say that none of these questions has been adequately answered. And even when they have been answered, the result does not bode well for the survival of fingerprint analysis. Epstein is not alone in his opinion. Professor David Faigman of the University of California, Hastings College of Law, predicts "that . . . some judge somewhere in the country will write an opinion excluding fingerprinting. It's inevitable. The research is just too thin to let it in." (Source of statistics: Malcolm Ritter, "Fingerprint Evidence Faces Hurdles," April 7, 2001, www.scafo.org/Library/PDF/FP%20Evidence%20 Faces%Hurdlespdt.)

---

*forensic: related to courts of law and criminal investigations.

Given standards of proof introduced by the courts, some people say that fingerprints might not be a reliable source of evidence.

What is the main idea or point of the reading?

Fingerprint evidence is being attacked as not scientific enough to decide guilt or innocence.

The author's purpose is persuasive .

The tone is neutral but leaning toward critical .

EXPLANATION   In this case, the author argues that fingerprint evidence may not measure up to current standards of proof. Although the author uses a mostly neutral tone, the lack of a balance between those who still believe in fingerprint evidence and those who don't makes the purpose persuasive. In addition, phrases like "sacred cows" and "the result does not bode well" suggest a critical tone.

1. Congratulations, Dad! Are You Nuts, Mom?

1   Usually when a woman announces she is ready to give birth, most people, be they friends, relatives, or complete strangers, clap for joy. Impending motherhood is a miracle, after all, worthy of celebration. But that's hardly the response that British mother-to-be Elizabeth Adeney received when it was discovered in May 2009 that she was about to give birth.

2   Elizabeth Adeney, you see, was sixty-six years old and pregnant thanks to modern fertility treatments, which allow women long past childbearing age to bear children. As it was with sixty-six-year-old Adriana Iliescu, a Romanian woman who gave birth to a child in 2006, the public's view of Elizabeth Adeney was hotly critical. Her decision evoked numerous public attacks.

3   Among the nicer reactions was one from a blogger who said that much could be forgiven if Adeney, like some other older moms, had had a younger partner. Then the partner could presumably care for the child if anything happened to Adeney. But Adeney was divorced with no partner. She also didn't have brothers and sisters to step in if something happened to her.

4   Few took the position of one writer, who insisted that the whole affair was no one's business except the mother's. That mind-your-own-business take on the subject was, in fact, very much in line with what Adeney herself had said: that her pregnancy was no one's business except her own. As newspapers, blogs, and tweets around the world

confirmed, very few agreed. Adeney's situation was fodder for the tabloids, and everyone seemed ready and willing to take potshots at Adeney's decision to become an elderly mom.

5   Far fewer people asked the question posed by journalist Gail Parker of the *Belfast Telegraph*, who wondered in print why old moms, but not old dads, are the subject of scorn and abuse. As Parker wrote, "If Adeney had been a 66-year-old man, it would have been cigars all around and to hell with the actuary tables."[†] And she's right; no one batted an eyelash when Warren Beatty became a dad at fifty-five, Bruce Willis at fifty-seven, and even the stodgiest art critics can't restrain a smile at the mention of artist Pablo Picasso's fathering a child at sixty-eight.

6   Although there are probably legitimate reasons for thinking that having a child after the age of fifty is not the best idea in the world, it's clear that those reasons aren't applied equally. We seem to think old dads are a triumph over nature's limitations whereas old moms should have their heads examined. (Sources of quotations: www.anorak.co.uk/media/210798.html; www.belfasttelegraph.co.uk/opinion/columnists/gail-walker/why-are-the-old-mums-so-disliked-but-not-old-dads-14306592.html.)

What is the main idea or point of the reading?

_____

_____

_____

The author's purpose is _____ .

The tone is _____ .

2. The Long Road to Informed Consent

1   During the 1947 Nuremberg Trials following World War II, it was revealed that physicians in concentration camps had performed horrific medical research experiments on prisoners in the camps. That doctors, whose historic mission it was to heal, subjected their patients

---

[†]actuary tables: tables indicating the average length of life given specific circumstances.

to painful and often deadly experiments—doctors would force feed patients poison to determine what dosage would kill them—shocked the world and resulted in the Nuremberg Code, which set up guidelines for experiments that involved human beings:

> The voluntary consent of the human subject is absolutely essential. This means that the person involved should have legal capacity to give consent; should be so situated as to be able to exercise free power of choice, without the intervention of any element of force, fraud, deceit, duress, over-reaching, or other ulterior form of constraint or coercion; and should have sufficient knowledge and comprehension of the elements of the subject matter involved as to enable him to make an understanding and enlightened decision.[†]

2   The need for such a code became even more apparent in 1972 when the public learned of the Tuskegee Syphilis Project, carried on by the U.S. Public Health Service. During the course of the experiment, which lasted forty years, researchers had allowed syphilis to progress unchecked through the bodies of hundreds of black male sharecroppers, none of whom were told the real cause of their symptoms. The subjects of the experiment were also steered away from seeking outside treatment so that the disease's effects, among them blindness, madness, and death, could be carefully tracked. Even after it was discovered that penicillin could cure syphilis, the subjects of the experiment were kept ignorant of the cure.

3   When Peter Buxton, one of the physicians involved in the research, told a reporter what was happening in Tuskegee, the research was halted in response to the cries of public outrage. In 1997, in acknowledgment of the wrong that had been done, President Clinton publicly apologized for the government's actions. The victims of the experiment were also awarded ten million dollars as a result of a class action suit.

4   Immediately following Buxton's disclosure of the Tuskegee experiment's goals, the National Commission for the Protection of Human Subjects of Biomedical and Behavioral Research was established. Its expressed goal was to introduce legislation that would further ensure a patient's right to be informed about the details of

---

[†]The complete Nuremberg Code can be found on the National Institutes of Health (NIH) website.

any research in which he or she participated. Although the Public Health Service has admitted that mistakes were made in the Tuskegee research, no one has ever publicly acknowledged the similarities between the doctors tried at Nuremberg and the doctors working in Tuskegee.

What is the main idea or point of the reading?

_____

_____

_____

The author's purpose is primarily _____

_____.

The tone is _____.

3. Educational Innovation in the States

1   In the time since *A Nation at Risk*[†] called national attention to the acute need for educational reform, the states have responded on a large scale. Hundreds of task forces have thoroughly studied school problems and issued recommendations for resolving them. Many of these recommendations have been enacted into law as innovative programs to improve the quality of public education. The federal legislation No Child Left Behind (NCLB) incorporated many principles and innovations first adopted in the states.

2   State financial support for schools has risen dramatically—by more than 50 percent higher over a recent eight-year period. A broad and powerful coalition of state and local elected officials, professional educators, community organizers, parents, and business interests has been important in the reform drive. Improvement in education is a nonpartisan issue; Democrats, Republicans, and Independents agree that the economic future of the United States depends on the quality of schooling.

[†]*A Nation at Risk*: The name refers to a 1983 report written by members of an educational task force, who claimed that the U.S. educational system was under threat due to declining test scores and a high teacher dropout rate.

3   The states have been busily innovating in the four critical areas of standards, students, teachers, and the education bureaucracy. Every state has recorded remarkable program achievements in at least one of these categories, and in some instances, prodded by NCLB, a majority have implemented reforms in all four. But incremental* reforms have not been bold enough to reverse the strong tide of mediocrity in many troubled settings, opening up a growing demand for more far reaching restructuring of public education. (Ann O. M. Bowman and Richard C. Kearney, *State and Local Government*, 8th ed., p. 429, © Cengage Learning.)

What is the main idea or point of the reading?

_____

_____

The author's purpose is _____.

The tone is _____.

WEB QUEST
Who was Eunice Rivers, and what was her role in the Tuskegee Syphilis Project? How is she viewed as a result of that role?

_____

_____

_____

_____

_____

---

*incremental: changes or additions that come in small pieces.

Sound Arguments Need Sound Reasoning

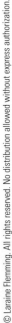

"At the end of reasons comes persuasion."
—Philosopher Ludwig Wittgenstein

To be persuasive, writers need to put forth a sound argument. They need to (1) clearly identify the opinion or point of view they would like you to share or consider and (2) provide evidence for their position. You have already seen several examples of authors who do precisely that, but looking at one more won't hurt, for example:

Facebook Doesn't Belong on the Mountaintop

The title announces the author's point of view.

1   In December of 2011, legendary rock climber Tommy Caldwell spent sixteen days trying to reach the summit of El Capitan, the huge mountain of granite that towers over Yosemite National Park. Caldwell didn't complete his free climb up the daunting face of El Capitan. The icy weather and the difficulty level of the climb forced him to give up his solitary quest to make it to the top. But then perhaps *solitary* isn't exactly the right word, because even after his wife left, ten days into the climb, Caldwell wasn't really alone. He had four thousand friends from all over the world along with him. They cheered him on as Caldwell chronicled his climb via his Facebook page.

At this point, the author is providing background through an introductory paragraph.

The author acknowledges that bringing Facebook up the mountain is an individual choice.

2   Charging his cell phone through portable solar panels, Caldwell did what many climbers do these days. He allowed people to follow him in real time as they received a running commentary from the man doing the climbing. The fans loved it, so did Caldwell's sponsors, and certainly Caldwell is perfectly within his right to bring his "friends" with him as he risks life and limb. Yet for those who see the sport of mountain climbing as a test of the climber's individual self-sufficiency, courage, and determination, there's something a little depressing about the arrival of social media on the once lonely mountaintop. It sets the stage for the climber to start thinking about the perfect Kodak moment, instead of the next crevice* to grab.

Note how the reversal transition *yet* moves away from seeming acceptance to introduce the opinion that matches the title.

3   This certainly seems to be the worry Katie Ives, the editor of *Alpinist* magazine, has expressed in saying that the "representation of the experience" might become the important part of the climber's experience. Therefore, something crucial about the feeling of the adventure would get lost. This sentiment has also been echoed by David Roberts, a writer and climber, who says that social media could introduce a "fatal self-consciousness." Caldwell himself has said that chronicling the experience on his Facebook page changed the experience: "It felt like there were a lot of people watching our progress like a football game."

The author uses quotations from experts on the subject as support for the point of view expressed. The first expert supplies one reason why social media should not be on the mountaintop: It takes away from the experience.

---

*crevice: crack in a rock that climbers use to pull themselves up a mountain.

The experts refer to the danger of being too conscious that others are watching.

4   But isn't that precisely the problem with bringing Facebook up the mountain? If you are conscious people are watching, you start playing to the crowd, and that can be a fatal mistake. Zack Smith, a world-class climber, put it best when he said, "Climbing mountains is a dangerous pursuit. When you mix in the potential desire to impress people, that's a very dangerous thing." (Source of quotations: Alex Lowther, "On Ledge and On Line: A Solitary Sport Turns Social," *New York Times*, December 9, 2011, p. 1.)

This example illustrates the core elements of an argument: (1) it offers an explicit statement of the author's perspective (although the perspective can also be implied), and (2) it provides relevant support for that perspective. The argument about mountain climbing and social media also includes a third common element, *recognition of an opposing point of view*. But as is typical for persuasion, that opposing point of view is quickly contradicted.

From Reader to Writer   Do some research on Eunice Rivers and her role in the Tuskegee Experiment. Write a paragraph or two that evaluates her actions. Was she duped by the people she worked with? Was she just desperate for a job and willing to do anything to stay employed? Or was she just plain evil? Whatever position you take, be sure to supply evidence for your opinion.

Recognizing Shaky Support

Supporting evidence for a writer's point of view can vary enormously. It can take the form of facts, examples, expert opinion, statistics, reasons, studies, and so on. However, there are times when writers let their **bias**, or personal prejudice in favor of or against an idea or person, get in the way of their ability to think carefully and logically. At times like these, the support for their opinions may get off track, and they may provide evidence that only appears convincing at first glance.

Here are some common errors writers sometimes make when they provide support for an opinion. If you see any one of them in a piece of writing, think twice before making the writer's point of view your own, at least until you know more about the topic.

Hasty Generalizations

One example or, for that matter, a few examples are never enough to prove a broad generalization about huge numbers of people. Yet, writers who want to persuade are sometimes guilty of offering readers precisely this kind of **hasty generalization**. Here's an example:

Generalization

Specific Study

Generalization

> Without a doubt, the 1.5 to 2 million American children who are being homeschooled are learning more and learning it faster than children who are attending public or private schools. According to a study conducted in 2004 by the Home School Advocates organization, which examined the progress of 102 homeschooled children in fifty families, students who are taught at home by their parents consistently score in the eightieth percentile or above on standardized achievement tests. This same study also revealed that 75 percent of these 102 home-schooled children are enrolled in one or more grades higher than their public- and private-school counterparts of the same age. Clearly, a homeschool education is far superior to that of an education in any institutional setting.

Don't be fooled by the presence of one study supporting the idea that children who are homeschooled do better than children who are not. One small study seldom proves anything. In this case, readers are being asked to accept a generalization about more than a million children based on a single study of 102 kids.

Where broad generalizations are concerned, writers need to give readers lots of examples. *The broader the generalization the more examples required.*

Irrelevant Evidence

When you analyze a piece of persuasive writing, always be on the look-out for **irrelevant**, or **unrelated**, **evidence**. Authors in the grip of excessive bias will sometimes supply you with a fact or reason that fills up space but has no particular bearing on the subject at hand. Look, for example, at the following paragraph, where the writer argues that John F. Kennedy does not deserve his high ranking on surveys of best presidents. Can you find a piece of irrelevant evidence?

When surveyed for its opinion about America's best presidents, the public consistently and mistakenly ranks John F. Kennedy either first or second. In reality, Kennedy was not a particularly effective president. No doubt, much of his appeal rests upon his image. He was seen as a dynamic leader reigning over a new "Camelot."[†] Kennedy's quick wit, excellent speaking skills, and good looks helped make him the media's darling, and his charm and charisma played well on television. Yet while the press portrayed him as a devoted family man, Kennedy actually was a womanizer who had a number of extramarital affairs, including one with a nineteen-year-old White House intern. He suffered from chronic health problems and took many drugs, including painkillers, to relieve colitis, back pain, and Addison's disease. His precarious physical state made him ill-suited to the nation's highest office, yet he irresponsibly duped the American people into believing that he was capable and fit. In truth, Kennedy was living on borrowed time; had he lived to be reelected to a second term, his failings eventually would have been exposed, and his house of cards would have come tumbling down.

The author of this passage argues that John F. Kennedy was not a particularly good president. To support that opinion, she offers two reasons: Kennedy was a womanizer, and he had serious health problems that he kept hidden.

John F. Kennedy may well have been a womanizer. However, unless the author can explain how that interfered with Kennedy's performance of his duties as president, the author has not supplied you with evidence relevant to her claim. To make Kennedy's immoral behavior matter in this context, the author would have to describe how Kennedy's affairs with women kept him from the business of the presidency.

More relevant to the author's point are Kennedy's hidden health problems and the medications he was forced to take. Painkillers are notorious for clouding a person's ability to think clearly, so they *may* have interfered with Kennedy's performance. But this potential piece of supporting evidence needs to be connected or related to the opening opinion to be convincing. The author needs to cite, for example, some instance in which President Kennedy's presidential decisions were affected by the drugs he took for his health problems. Just telling you Kennedy had health problems isn't enough.

[†]Camelot: according to legend, King Arthur's royal court. Now it's an allusion used to suggest a longed-for time when the world was a better place.

Circular Reasoning

It's easy to determine the opinion expressed in the following paragraph: The U.S. government should regulate night-shift hours. What's not as clear is why the author takes this position. Much of the paragraph simply repeats the opening opinion. That's why it's an example of **circular reasoning**: The opinion and the reason for holding it are one and the same.

Before a disaster occurs, the government of the United States should regulate the number of hours a worker can put in on a night shift. It is a disgrace that this has not been done already. The United States is one of only six industrialized countries that do not regulate night-shift hours. This lack of regulation is a dangerous and costly oversight that will one day prove disastrous.

But imagine now that the author had recognized his failure to provide an argument and revised the above paragraph to make it more persuasive.

In this example, the author follows the opening opinion with evidence— studies showing that loss of sleep is dangerous.

Before a disaster occurs, the government of the United States should regulate the number of hours a worker can put in on a night shift. According to studies completed by the National Commission on Sleep Disorders in 2012, the loss of sleep, whether voluntary or involuntary, is a dangerous and, sometimes, deadly threat. In studies of sleep disorders, the commission has repeatedly concluded that literally millions of accidents are caused every year by people trying to function normally on too little sleep. Earlier studies have come up with similar results. A study by the Congressional Office of Technology, completed in 1991, pointed to the importance that changes in the sleep cycle play in human errors within the workplace. Likewise, a 2007 study by Harvard's Medical School suggested that people are more likely to make errors in judgment if they have not slept seven to eight hours within the last twenty-four hours. They are also more likely to become more emotionally unstable.

The author interprets the studies to make it clear that they are evidence for the opening opinion.

These studies strongly suggest that limits be placed on disturbances of the human sleep cycle. Although the government cannot determine how many hours employees sleep, it can and should place limits on the number of hours they spend on night shifts.

In this paragraph, the author now anticipates and answers the question she rightly assumes readers might pose: "Why should I take this opinion seriously?" To argue that opinion and make it persuasive, the author identifies several studies that describe the possible dangers that can result from lack of sleep. Although thoughtful readers might not immediately embrace the author's opinion as their own, they would certainly seriously consider it, given the support provided.

Offering False Alternatives

Authors who have let bias interfere with logic often insist that there are only two possible alternatives or answers to a problem or question when, in fact, there are several. Here's an example:

Opening claim says product placement is a must.

The other alternative is not good and can't be considered, making product placement a necessity.

Moviemakers intent on creating a realistic atmosphere are forced to engage in *product placement*—the use of brand names in exchange for a fee. Were an actor in a scene to open a can simply labeled tuna, the audience's attention would be distracted by the label, and the effect of the scene would be destroyed. People are used to seeing brand names such as Chicken of the Sea and Bumble Bee. Filmmakers who want realism in their films aren't doing anything wrong when they engage in product placement.

According to this author's reasoning, either moviemakers must accept fees for using brand names or they will be forced to use general name labels that distract the audience. Left out of this reading are two other alternatives: (1) arrange the scene so that audiences don't see labels or (2) invent brand names and labels that resemble the real ones. Faced with the above either-or thinking, critical readers would start looking for other alternatives. As soon as the writer tells you there are only two choices, you can usually count on discovering that others actually do exist.

Making Careless Comparisons

Be wary of authors who use comparisons not to illustrate a point but to prove it. Often the differences between the two things compared are more crucial than the similarities. Here, for example, the author compares producers who get paid for product placement with athletes who get paid to wear their sponsor's clothing:

Filmmakers who accept fees for using brand names in their films are just like athletes who are paid to wear brand names in public.

Although that reasoning might sound convincing at first, the differences between the two practices may, in fact, be more important than the similarities. Certainly that is what the writer of the following passage believes:

> Product placement and celebrity endorsements are not the same at all. Highly publicized celebrity contracts have made the public fully aware that athletes are paid large sums of money to sport a sponsor's clothing or footwear. In contrast, the average moviegoer is not as knowledgeable about the fees paid to filmmakers using brand names. Thus, the effects of product placement in films work on a far more subconscious level. Audience members have no idea they are seeing paid advertising.

As the author of this passage points out, there are some crucial differences between athletes who wear brand-name clothing and filmmakers who use brand names in their movies. Those differences considerably weaken the first author's argument for product placement.

SUMMING UP THE KEY POINTS

1. To be taken seriously, opinions need to be backed by relevant reasons and evidence. They need to be part of a solid argument that offers readers a basis for sharing the opinion put forth in the reading.

2. Particularly when they are convinced that they are right beyond all doubt, writers can get careless and offer readers shaky evidence that doesn't provide adequate support for their opinion or claim.

3. Hasty generalizations cover large numbers of people, experiences, and ideas, while offering only one or two examples as proof—for instance, "Getting a college degree is worthless. My aunt dropped out of high school, and she owns her own company."

4. Irrelevant evidence is related in some way to the topic at hand but has nothing to do with backing up the opinion being put forth—for instance, "Despite swindling numerous people out of their pensions, the broker should not pay for his crimes with a prison term. After all, he founded several organizations that take care of abandoned animals."

5. Circular arguments restate the opinion being proposed in different language, and the restatement is supposed to function as evidence—for example, "Ten years from now, there will no longer be print books; everything will be digitalized. It's bound to happen because books composed of paper are going to disappear and e-books are going to take their place."

6. Writers using false alternatives insist that a problem with several solutions actually has only two—for example, "The only choice we have where swine flu is concerned is to either slaughter every single pig in countries where the disease emerges or face the death of millions around the world."

7. Careless comparisons use the similarities between two groups, experiences, or ideas to prove a point. Although comparisons are a useful step in an analysis, they are often shaky as evidence because the differences usually outweigh the similarities. For example, "Why is there always so much talk about the corruption of politics through campaign contributions? Campaign donations are just like speech. They are another form of self-expression."

▶ EXERCISE 7   Recognizing Shaky Arguments

DIRECTIONS   The following passages all present arguments in favor of an opinion. But each one reveals flawed logic. Circle the appropriate letter to identify the error.

EXAMPLE   In far too many American cities, homelessness has become a major problem. In some cities, whole families live on the street. In a country this rich, homelessness is a national disgrace. In response to this social problem, Americans must dig more deeply into their pockets to support the work of local charities, or the number of homeless people will continue to grow.

   a. irrelevant evidence

   (b.) false alternatives

   c. careless comparison

   d. hasty generalization

   e. circular reasoning

EXPLANATION   The author insists that we have only two choices about how to treat the homeless: give to local charities or allow the problem of homelessness to increase. It doesn't take a sociologist to realize that there are other alternatives as well.

1. Stephen King is an underrated artist who is every bit as gifted as Shakespeare. Evidence of King's greatness can be found by examining the similarities in the work of both authors. Shakespeare often wrote about love and relationships. An excellent example of this is his play *Romeo and Juliet.* Stephen King also writes about relationships. *The Stand* and *It* both focus on the importance of love and the power of friendship. Both authors examine issues of morality and are interested in the power of evil.

    a. irrelevant evidence
    b. false alternatives
    c. careless comparison
    d. hasty generalization
    e. circular reasoning

2. The works of Ernest Hemingway should no longer be part of the high school curriculum. His novels and short stories are too dated and of little interest to a modern generation. Although Hemingway is still beloved by high school English teachers, he writes about a world that is obsolete and to which people, particularly young people, can no longer respond. Everyone now knows about the destructive power of war and the impossibility of fulfilling the rigid masculine role. Hemingway doesn't tell young people anything they need to know anymore, although he might have done so when his first novel was published in 1926. But that was a long time ago.

    a. irrelevant evidence
    b. false alternatives
    c. careless comparison
    d. hasty generalization
    e. circular reasoning

3. Sociologists have long claimed that a lack of daily or weekly contact with a parent has few negative effects on the children of

divorce; however, new research shows that a lack of regular contact with one of the parents is actually destructive. In one study, fifty college freshmen with divorced parents completed a questionnaire about their experiences and feelings. A number of the students who were geographically separated from one of their parents following a divorce admitted to having a more difficult time adjusting. In comparison to those whose parents continued to live near each other after divorcing, this group also claimed to feel more hostility.

a. irrelevant evidence
b. false alternatives
c. hasty generalization
d. careless comparison
e. circular reasoning

4. Elementary school teachers often keep classroom pets such as gerbils, hamsters, guinea pigs, and reptiles. The teachers claim that these animals help young children learn about both responsibility and biology. However, animals in the classroom should be outlawed for ethical and health reasons. According to People for the Ethical Treatment of Animals and the American Society for the Prevention of Cruelty to Animals, keeping animals in cages for education or enjoyment teaches youngsters that cruelty to animals is acceptable if it serves human interests. Therefore, either we put a stop to keeping animals in the classroom or we destroy young peoples' compassion for the other creatures of our world.

a. irrelevant evidence
b. false alternatives
c. hasty generalization
d. careless comparison
e. circular reasoning

5. The growing movement toward using social media in the classroom is a misguided one at best. Students have enough trouble concentrating while they are in school; they don't need the lure of Facebook or Twitter to further distract them. Teachers enthusiastic about using social media in the classroom should look at studies from the PEW

Internet and American Life Project. When people use Facebook, they spend their time looking at friends' photographs, searching for former friends and classmates, and liking or not liking the posts they read. There is no way to connect these frivolous activities to learning in school.

a. irrelevant evidence

b. false alternatives

c. hasty generalization

d. careless comparison

e. circular reasoning

 # Turning the Tables: From Reader to Writer

Now that you know what experienced readers should look for when they read to determine purpose, you also know a lot about what goes into a well-written, persuasive essay. You know you should provide a clear statement of the main idea, include relevant evidence, connect general thoughts to specific details, keep your readers on track by referring to what came before, avoid excessive bias, and choose a tone likely to win readers over to your side.

At this point, you also know the things you should not do, such as include irrelevant information as evidence; fail to show readers how one idea leads to another; try to browbeat your readers into agreeing with you, and never quite nail down the idea you want your readers to share or act on. Knowing all this, you are ready to change roles and write a persuasive essay about any one of the topics listed below.

Taking a Stand

Each of the topics listed is at the center of a controversy, so you will need to read up on the one you choose, decide where you stand, and then figure out how you might get others to share your point of view.

1. letting teachers bring guns to schools to protect themselves and their students

2. legislation banning pit bulls

3. wearing fur clothing

4. declawing cats or letting cats roam free out of doors

5. police using military equipment

6. giving parents personal exemptions from vaccinating their children against infectious disease

7. beauty pageants for kids

8. using alternative medical treatments—herbs, acupuncture, special diets, etc.—in place of traditional medicine

9. flying with knee extenders or similar devices to protect your space during flight

10. using animals in medical experiments

11. admitting transgender students into women's colleges

12. playing high school football and risking repeated concussions

Diagramming Your Thoughts Instead of the Writer's

Up to this point, you have used diagramming to record the thoughts of other writers. But diagramming is a very useful device for getting your own thoughts down on paper and figuring out (1) what you want to say and (2) how you, initially at least, want to order the information.

Once you have an idea of where you stand on an issue, consider making a map, or diagram, of the argument you have in mind. Write the opinion at the top of the page and ask yourself, "What would I say to convince my audience that this is the right perspective to take?"

Each time you write down a reason or example you think might work, consider the questions these points might raise in the minds of your readers. Put the questions into your diagram as well and see if you can provide a rough answer. Give the questions a different shape so that, at a glance, you can see the difference between your reasoning and the questions about that reasoning you need to respond to.

Here, for instance, is an early diagram of the persuasive essay for the *Reader to Writer Assignment* on p. 673. Notice how the diagram tries to identify not just the opinion and the reasons for holding it, but also the questions those reasons might evoke in the minds of readers:

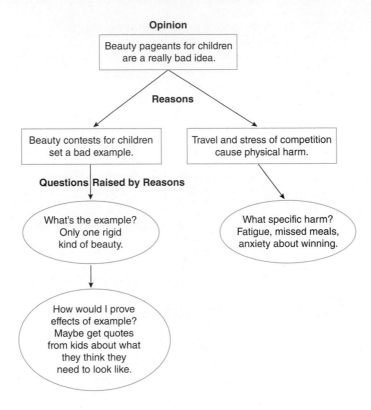

Diagram, Draft, Revise, and Diagram Again

When you are reading a really good persuasive piece of writing, it's easy to think that the writer just started writing and out came a perfectly written persuasive essay or article like, for instance, Paula McLain's essay on pages 762–64. But that is almost never the case. Writing, any kind of writing but particularly writing to persuade, requires a significant amount of drafting and revision (or re-seeing).

Once you write a first draft based on your initial diagram, make a second diagram to see if you might, in fact, have a new idea to add or an idea you think you might eliminate. Here, to illustrate, is a second diagram of the essay on children's beauty contests. Notice how the supporting details have been expanded.

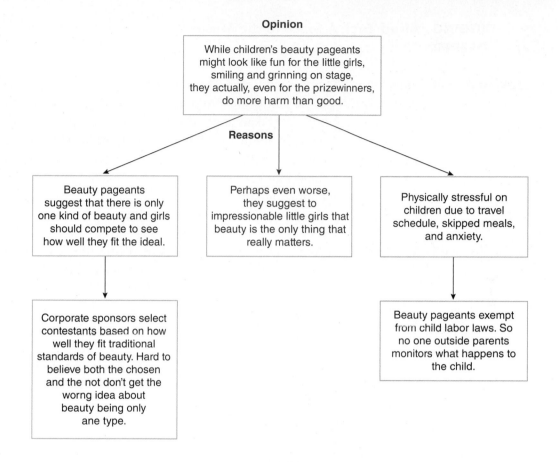

Opinion

While children's beauty pageants might look like fun for the little girls, smiling and grinning on stage, they actually, even for the prizewinners, do more harm than good.

Reasons

Beauty pageants suggest that there is only one kind of beauty and girls should compete to see how well they fit the ideal.

Perhaps even worse, they suggest to impressionable little girls that beauty is the only thing that really matters.

Physically stressful on children due to travel schedule, skipped meals, and anxiety.

Corporate sponsors select contestants based on how well they fit traditional standards of beauty. Hard to believe both the chosen and the not don't get the worng idea about beauty being only ane type.

Beauty pageants exempt from child labor laws. So no one outside parents monitors what happens to the child.

▶ **EXERCISE 8**   **Writing a Persuasive Essay**

DIRECTIONS   Pick and research your topic, either from the list on pp. 702–3 or one of your own choice. You may have to read up on several different topics before you find the one that truly interests you. Turn in a diagram indicating the opinion you want to communicate along with the evidence you intend to use to support your point of view. Remember to make your diagram reflect the questions you think readers might raise.

DIGGING DEEPER   Blind Tom: A Slave to the Music

Looking Ahead   Today Tom Wiggins would probably be called an *autistic savant.* The term refers to people who suffer from autism; but who, nevertheless, have some extraordinary talent or gift that earns them recognition.

Wiggins's gift was the ability to make music and mimic whatever he heard, not just sounds but entire speeches and songs. Performing all across the nation and internationally, "Blind Tom," as Wiggins came to be called, earned a fortune. But since Tom was a slave, he never saw a penny of the fortune he made for the family who owned him.

Getting Focused   As you read, think about why the author would title this reading "A Slave to the Music." Underline information from the reading that helps to explain that title. Ask yourself, "How is the word *slave* used? Is it meant literally or figuratively? Or is it, in fact, used both literally and figuratively?"

BLIND TOM.
vright 1880, by John G. Bethune.

Library of Congress Prints and Photographs Division [LC-USZ62-84287].

Notice who once owned the copyright to the photo.

1   Born blind and a slave, Thomas Green Wiggins (1849–1908), already, at birth, had two strikes against him. But those obstacles didn't stop him from going on to have a spectacular career as a musician and performer.

Capable, from an early age, of mimicking any tune and practically any sound he heard, Tom was something of a prodigy at the piano. He only had to hear a melody once and could play it. By the age of five, he was already composing music.

2   Given that Tom was encouraged to play the piano by his owner, lawyer James Bethune, his story might, at a glance, seem to be one of history's kinder narratives about life as a slave. Yet, while Tom was not physically brutalized like most slaves were, his life is a sad tale of greedy deceptions carried out by people determined to benefit from both Tom's extraordinary gifts and his inability to fully understand the world around him. When his life is viewed from the vantage point of today's medical knowledge, Thomas Green Wiggins seems to have suffered from autism, a disease characterized by extreme difficulty using language as a means of communication. Tom "spoke" through playing music and mimicking sounds, not through words. But music wasn't enough to save him from the rapacious intentions of the Bethune family who, one way or another, figured out how to own him for his entire life and profited handsomely from their possession of another human being.

3   James Bethune discovered Tom's talent when the four-year-old boy, who accompanied his mother to work in Bethune's house, began playing the piano music he had heard Bethune's children playing. Tom just had to listen to the youngsters play. After one hearing, he automatically knew how to find the right notes on the keyboard. Impressed by the boy's talent, Bethune decided to profit from it. Tom was only eight when Bethune hired a hall and had the boy play before a packed audience. It was clear from the ticket sales and the audience's reaction that Tom was going to be a huge draw.

4   When Tom was nine, Bethune hired him out to a show promoter named Perry Oliver for a number of years. Oliver billed Tom as the troubled savage whose spirit could be calmed by music. Before his performance on the piano, Tom would sit as he often did rocking back and forth with a blank open-mouth stare. Occasionally he would mimic some word or sound he heard from the audience. But the moment he sat at the piano, he was transformed. He played with mastery, grace, and confidence and seemed possessed by another spirit altogether. As one journalist wrote, "This poor blind boy is cursed with but little of human nature; he seems to be an unconscious agent acting as he is acted on, and his mind a vacant receptacle where Nature stores her jewels to recall them at her pleasure." The fact that the "poor blind boy," because of his autism, "was cursed" with "little of human nature" was fine with Oliver

and Bethune. They billed the boy as a "halfwit," whose artistry came from some supernatural source of energy, which flowed through him when he sat at the piano.

5   Bethune made around $20,000 on his venture with Tom's manager. For his part, Oliver pocketed $50,000. Tom got nothing except room and board, although he was on a grueling four-shows-per-day schedule and was separated from his family. He may have wanted to complain, but his speech was so bizarre, it's doubtful anyone would have understood what he wanted to say. And since he was a slave, it's even more doubtful that anyone would have cared.

6   Tom's popularity grew to such a degree that he was asked to perform all over the country. But Bethune knew that war with the North was imminent. Thus, he kept the boy's appearances close to home. When the Civil War broke out in 1861, Bethune had Tom perform for Confederate troops, with whom Tom was extremely popular. He even composed a southern war song called "The Battle of Manassas."[†]

7   In 1864, Bethune knew that the war would be over soon. He also knew that the Union was going to win and what that victory meant for his ownership of Tom. Calling on his legal background, Bethune talked Tom's mother and father into signing a contract that gave Bethune the right to manage Tom until he was twenty-one years of age. The boy would receive food and shelter and $20.00 a month. The parents would receive $500 a year along with meals and shelter in Bethune's residence. As it turned out, Bethune would sometimes receive upwards of $50,000 a year, thanks to the efforts of his contracted slave.

8   When the war ended in 1865, Tom was legally a free man. But since he had never been aware that he was a slave, freedom meant little or nothing to him. In any case, Bethune's contract was legally binding. Tom could not work for anyone else, least of all himself. Every penny he earned went to Bethune.

9   With the war finally over, Bethune thought it safe to bring Tom to tour in the North, where, once again, his performances drew huge, appreciative crowds. But Tom's entry into Indiana brought with it conflict when Tabbs Gross, a black entertainment promoter, claimed that Bethune had sold Tom to him for $20,000 in gold and then reneged on the deal without returning the gold. There must have been some-thing to the accusation because Bethune quickly fled Indiana with

---

[†]The Battle of Manassas: This battle, also known as the Battle of Bull Run, was the first major battle of the Civil War. The Union was badly beaten by the Confederacy.

Tom in tow. Gross and his lawyer followed and took him to court. Not surprisingly, the judge found in favor of the white Bethune, claiming that Tom was highly emotional and could be harmed if taken from the people who were "treating him so kindly."

10   For the next five years, Tom performed all over the United States and Europe. He even caught the attention of America's most famous novelist Mark Twain, who was fascinated by Tom's talents and wrote about his splendid gifts, suggesting to friends that they plan on seeing a performance. At the end of five years, though, when Tom was twenty-one, Bethune had to come up with another scheme to keep Tom under his control. Once again, he turned to the courts. This time, he claimed Tom was insane and asked to be made the young man's legal guardian. Given Tom's odd behavior, the constant rocking back and forth typical of autism, the strange speech, the mimicry of odd sounds, it was not hard to make the court decide in the lawyer's favor. Tom was given over to Bethune, this time, seemingly at least, for life.

11   Although Tom liked being at Bethune's country estate in Virginia, where he had a fine piano and the sounds of nature to inspire him, his guardian kept him on the road for most of the year, traveling from town to town, often from country to country. After a while, though, Bethune Sr. was too old for all the traveling, and his son John took over the tours. The constant touring continued even after Bethune Jr. married Eliza Stutzbach, the owner of a boarding house.

12   But then in 1884, while rushing to catch a train, John Bethune was killed and ownership of Tom reverted to his father. Eliza, now divorced from John Bethune but outraged at losing out on Tom's earnings, had apparently learned a thing or two from her husband and his father. She, too, turned to the courts. Dragging Tom's aged mother Charity back from her home in Georgia, she petitioned for Charity to take over the raising of her son with Eliza herself as second guardian should Tom's mother be unable to handle his care. When the court decided that Tom should, in fact, be in the custody of his mother, Eliza barely waited for the ink on the documents to dry before sending Charity back to Georgia. Tom was, again, in the control of a member of the Bethune family. By 1887, the year when Tom's "guardianship" went to Eliza, Tom Wiggins had been in the family's service for a total of thirty-eight years.

13   Although Tom had initially seemed distraught at being separated from the world he knew with Bethune Sr. and his son, one month later, he was on stage again. The only difference was that now he was a source of income for Eliza, who presented him, ironically, as the "last

slave set free by order of the Supreme Court of the United States." Although his glory days were past and the crowds were dwindling, as was the income Eliza collected, Tom continued to perform constantly until 1905 when a stroke took him away from the stage forever. He died of a second stroke at Eliza's house in Hoboken, New Jersey. The location of his burial is a subject of dispute. Records suggest that Eliza had him buried in Brooklyn. But a neighbor of the daughter of Tom's former owner, Fanny Bethune, claims that Fanny decided Tom should be buried in the family plot in Georgia. As a result, two memorial plaques to Blind Tom now exist, one in Brooklyn and one in Georgia. (Sources of information: http://www.blackpast.org/perspectives/confounded-enigma-blind-tom-wiggins and http://www.twainquotes.com/archangels.html.)

Sharpening Your Skills

DIRECTIONS   Answer the questions by filling in the blanks or circling the letter of the correct response.

Using Context Clues

1. Based on the context, write out the definition you think best fits the word *prodigy* from the following sentence: "Capable, from an early age, of mimicking any tune and almost any sound he heard, Tom was something of a *prodigy* at the piano."

The word *prodigy* means _____.

Identifying Purpose

2. Which is correct?

   a. The reading was written primarily to inform.

   b. The reading was written primarily to persuade.

Recognizing the Controlling Main Idea

3. Which of the following statements best sums up the main idea of the entire reading?

   a. Born blind and a slave, Thomas Green Wiggins (1849–1908) already, at birth, had two strikes against him. But those twin obstacles didn't stop him from going on to have a spectacular career as a musician and performer.

   b. Given that Tom was encouraged to play the piano by his owner, lawyer James Bethune, his story might, at a glance, seem to be one of history's kinder narratives about life as a slave. Yet, while Tom was not physically brutalized like most slaves were, his life is a sad tale of greedy deceptions carried out by people determined to benefit from both Tom's extraordinary gifts and his inability to understand the world around him.

c. When his life is viewed from the vantage point of today's medical knowledge, Thomas Green Wiggins seems to have suffered from autism, a disease characterized by extreme difficulty using language to communicate. Tom "spoke" through playing music and mimicking sounds, not through words, and it was his unique form of "speech" that brought him fame.

Drawing Inferences

4. In paragraph 9, the author writes, "Not surprisingly, the judge found in favor of the white Bethune, claiming that Tom was highly emotional and could be harmed if taken from the people who were 'treating him so kindly.'" Why is this judgment not surprising?

_____

_____

5. Before Tom's condition was better understood, many African Americans considered Tom to be a traitor to his race. What do you think was the basis for this criticism?

_____

_____

Following the Author's Train of Thought

6. In paragraph 2, what synonym for *story* does the author use to refer to what was said previously?

_____

7. The writer relies heavily on what kind of transitional devices to help readers follow her train of thought?

a. cause and effect

b. comparison

c. time order

d. contrast

8. In paragraph 12, the reader has to draw what inference in order to connect these two sentences: "Eliza, now divorced from John Bethune but outraged at losing out on Tom's earnings, had apparently learned a thing or two from her husband and his father. She, too, turned to the courts."

_____

_____

Recognizing Patterns of Organization

9. Which of the following is the primary pattern organizing this reading?

a. comparison and contrast

b. simple listing

c. time order

d. cause and effect

Considering Tone

10. What word best describes the tone of this reading?

a. neutral

b. disapproving

c. understanding

d. worried

From Reader to Writer *Autism Speaks* is a highly influential organization that claims, as the name suggests, to speak for those with autism. But the organization is a controversial one, with both strong supporters and even stronger critics. Research the group on the Web and decide how effectively you think the organization serves the interests of those who live with autism. Make your evaluation of the organization the core of your argument as you explain why the criticism is or is not well founded.

▶ TEST 1   **Reviewing Key Concepts**

DIRECTIONS   Answer the following questions by filling in the blanks.

1. How is determining the author's purpose similar to identifying organizational patterns?

    _____

    _____

2. The key difference between a fact and an opinion is that statements of fact can be _____ while statements of opinion cannot be _____.

3. While facts rely on _____ language, opinions are likely to employ _____ language.

4. Unlike facts, opinions can't be _____, but they can be _____. They can be labeled _____ _____.

5. How can a writer blend an opinion into a largely factual statement?

    _____

    _____

6. When an author's purpose is to persuade, you should expect the author to give you an _____.

7. Tone in writing is the _____ _____.

8. If an author provides facts or reasons unrelated to the point of an argument, then he or she is using _____. But if the author restates the point of an argument as evidence why readers should share his or her point of view, then the reasoning is

    _____.

9. If the author tells you that children in elementary school are not learning to read and offers as evidence the example of his neighbor's child who, at the age of eight, still can't read, then you are dealing with a _____.

10. If the author insists that there are only two ways to handle the situation described in a persuasive reading, then the chances are good that you are being presented with _____.
But if the author tells you that the government's handling of finances is no different from how ordinary people have to balance their budgets, then you are being confronted with a _____, because the government can print its own money. We can't.

▶ **TEST 2**   **Identifying Fact, Opinion, or Both**

DIRECTIONS   Label each sentence *F* for fact, *O* for opinion, or *M* for a mix of both.

1. Alan Mathison Turing (1912–1954) was an English mathematician whose brilliant career was senselessly destroyed when it was discovered that he was a homosexual.

    _____

2. A carcinogen is any agent that increases the chances of a cell becoming cancerous.

    _____

3. During World War I, Chile remained neutral.

    _____

4. People who post selfies on social media sites suffer from low self-esteem.

    _____

5. Although most people don't realize it, eyewitnesses to crimes are extremely unreliable.

    _____

6. Reality television shows appeal to people who have no lives of their own.

    _____

7. A new species of land mammal has been discovered in the forests of Vietnam.

    _____

8. The 2014 movie *American Sniper*, about military marksman Chris Kyle, aroused a huge controversy, with some people calling Kyle a hero and others labeling him a psychopath.

   _____

9. When it comes to Hip-Hop, Iggy Azaelea is no match for Nicki Minaj.

   _____

10. The Japanese mushrooms called *maitake* sometimes grow as big as footballs.

   _____

▶ **TEST 3**   **Identifying Tone**

DIRECTIONS   Circle the appropriate letter to identify the tone of each passage.

1. In August 2006, the *New York Times* published an article titled "Tale of the Tapeworm (Squeamish Readers Stop Here)." Readers who didn't take the warning seriously made a huge mistake. What the article reported on was the story of a woman who had, in the course of making gefilte fish,[†] ingested a tapeworm, and here's where the squeamish should have stopped reading. When the tapeworm was removed from the woman's body, it turned out to be three feet long. The source of numerous and vague symptoms like fatigue and indigestion, the worm had been happily living in the woman's stomach for who knows how long. Disgusting as the idea may be, tapeworms can, in fact, do just that: take up residence in your body without your knowing it. Unless the body gets irritated by its guest and produces some symptoms, the tapeworm can make use of it for as long as twenty years. As if that thought weren't gross enough, tapeworms can, if undetected, grow as long as thirty feet. Consider that the next time you think about eating sushi.

   The tone is

   a. humorous.
   b. horrified.
   c. neutral.
   d. lighthearted.

2. Chimpanzees, who share nearly 99 percent of our DNA, are almost human, but you would never know it from the way we treat them. As photographer Michael Nichols has shown in his disturbing book *Brutal Kinship*, we use and abuse them at will for medical research, for entertainment, or simply out of personal greed. Determined to remain blind to their suffering, we refuse to grasp how like us they are. Chimpanzees nurture their young and mourn their dead. They have distinct personalities and can express a variety of emotions, from love to rage. Yet for all their similarities, we appear to think

---

[†]Gefilte fish: A Jewish delicacy made with ground fish.

little of their pain and suffering if our interests are served. Leafing through the pages of Nichols's book, which is filled with images of chimps in cages or lying vacant-eyed with tubes dangling from their arms, it's practically impossible to understand how we can torture and maim creatures who look and behave so much like ourselves.

The tone is

a. disgusted.

b. confident.

c. ironic.

d. neutral.

3. I'm on the couch because the dog on the blanket gets worried at night. During the day she sleeps the catnappy sleep of the elderly, but when it gets dark her eyes open and she is agitated.[†] I'm next to her. We are in this together, the dying game, and I read for hours in the evening with one foot on her back, getting up only to open a new can of beer or take blankets to the basement. At some point I stretch out on the vinyl couch and close my eyes, one hand hanging down, touching her side. By morning the dog arm has become a nerveless club that doesn't come around until noon. My friends think I am nuts. (Jo Ann Beard, "The Fourth State of Matter," *The Best American Essays 1997*, ed. Ian Frazier and Robert Atwan. Boston: Houghton Miffin, 1997, p. 12.)

The tone is

a. angry.

b. grieving.

c. irritated.

d. neutral.

4. I'm afraid I have noticed an alarming development at our house. The dog is trying to talk. He is not at all interested in remaining The Creature in the Household Who Barks, which, I have explained to him again and again, is the only role for which he is suited. Oh, I've done all the right things to raise his self-esteem about this: I've assured him that forever and ever he will be the only one in the house who is permitted to bark, and that, in fact, is why we hired him as

---

†agitated: nervous.

the family dog in the first place, so he would bark and maybe protect us. I even told him that we *respect* him for his bark. You know what he says to this? "*Oowwww. . . .*" (Sandi Shelton, *You Might as Well Laugh*, St. Martin's Press, p. 74. © 1999.)

The tone is

a. surprised.

b. neutral.

c. comic.

d. angry.

5. For years, critics have argued about the ancient Greek play *Oedipus Rex*. Some have claimed that Oedipus knows nothing of his guilt until the end of the play, when it is revealed that he murdered his own father. Others have insisted that Oedipus is aware all along of his guilt. According to this point of view, Oedipus, the brilliant solver of riddles, could not possibly have ignored the mounting evidence that he was the king's murderer. Just how or why this debate has raged for so many years remains a mystery. The correct interpretation is so obvious. Oedipus knows from the beginning that he is guilty. He just pretends to be ignorant of the truth. For example, when a servant tells the story of the king's murder, he uses the word *bandits*. But when Oedipus repeats this story, he uses the singular form *bandit*. Sophocles provides clues like this throughout the play. Thus, it's hard to understand why anyone would think that Oedipus does not know the truth about his crime.

The tone is

a. lighthearted.

b. confident.

c. neutral.

d. outraged.

▶ **TEST 4**   **Getting to the Point**

DIRECTIONS   Read each selection and identify the point of view the writer wants readers to share. Then circle the appropriate letter to identify the author's tone.

1. **Do These Parents Talk to Their Kids?**

1   According to a report of the National Campaign to Prevent Teen Pregnancy, 20 percent of adolescents have had sex before their fifteenth birthday. The report also revealed that only a third of these adolescents' parents know their children are sexually active. Such alarming statistics should cause us to wonder why parents aren't communicating more with their children.

2   Communication between parents and children is important, and far too many parents seem to be falling down on the job. How can two-thirds of them not know what their own children are doing? And why aren't they talking to their kids and making them understand the risks of becoming sexually active? Are these parents that oblivious to the temptations bombarding modern young people? Or are the parents simply too lazy or self-absorbed to concern themselves with how their own kids are spending their free time?

3   Whatever the reason for parents' apathy and ignorance, it's the kids who will ultimately pay the price. One in seven sexually active fourteen-year-old girls gets pregnant. And sexually experienced adolescents are far more likely than virgins to smoke, drink alcohol, and use drugs. Thanks to parents who won't get their heads out of the sand and watch their own kids, America's young people are growing up much too fast.

The author would like readers to agree that _____

_____ .

The tone of the passage is

a. irate.

b. solemn.

c. ironic.

d. cautious.

2. The Genius of Camille Claudel

1   Camille Claudel (1864–1943) was an extraordinarily talented French sculptor, who initially was remembered largely for being the model, assistant, and mistress of the legendary artist Auguste Rodin, creator of the famous sculpture *The Kiss.* Camille Claudel, however, was a gifted sculptor in her own right. She created gorgeous marble and bronze sculptures such as *The Waltz*, *Wave*, and *The Age of Maturity,* which left even Rodin in awe of her talent.

2   These masterpieces have won Claudel posthumous, critical acclaim from many of today's art critics and historians. Yet, sadly, it took almost three-quarters of a century for her to get the recognition she fully deserved. For many years after her death, the genius she showed as a young artist was largely forgotten by all but a few art historians.

3   Some of those historians have argued that Claudel's talent was unfairly eclipsed by that of her teacher and lover. The respected and popular Rodin occupied a prominent place in French culture, and even though Claudel established her own reputation, she never quite managed to emerge from his shadow, especially during a time when being an artist was still considered a masculine calling.

4   After Claudel, pregnant with Rodin's child, lost their baby, she suffered serious bouts of depression. Her behavior became increasingly unstable and she was plagued by persecution fantasies. In despair because Rodin would not leave his wife, Claudel left Rodin in 1898 to strike out on her own, but her mental condition only worsened.

5   Tragically, Claudel's family, embarrassed by her free-wheeling lifestyle as an artist, used Claudel's depressed state to have her institutionalized in 1913 after her father died. However, her mother and brother refused all medical advice about providing Claudel with effective treatment, preferring to keep her locked away in order to protect the family name. While living on her own, Claudel had become notorious for insisting that she wanted to create her sculptures from nude models. That male artists used nude models was understood. But for a female artist of the time, it was a shocking demand. Her mother and brother seem not to have forgiven Claudel for her "wild" behavior, and it was their preference that she be hospitalized for the rest of her life, which she was.

6   Claudel spent thirty years in an institution, forbidden to have any visitors except members of her family. During that time, she destroyed most of what she had accomplished during her years of confinement.

However, close to one hundred pieces of her work have survived. They are the basis of the acclaim she began to receive in the 1980s when feminist art historians began writing about her work and a film was made of her tragic but artistically productive and creative life.

The author would like readers to agree that _____

_____.

The tone of the passage is

a. critical.

b. cool.

c. sarcastic.

d. admiring.

▶ **TEST 5**   **Identifying the Author's Point, Purpose, and Tone**

DIRECTIONS   Read each selection and answer the questions that follow.

1. Guns in the Schools

1   In August 2008, the school board in rural Harrold, Texas, became the first in the United States to permit teachers and administrators to carry concealed weapons into a school. After receiving forty hours of weapons training and a permit to carry a concealed handgun, a teacher would be "certified" to take his or her weapon into the classroom, lunchroom, or bathroom.

2   Why? To prevent a Columbine High School (thirteen dead, twenty-three wounded in 1999) or a Virginia Tech (thirty-two dead, numerous wounded in 2007) type massacre by gunmen. According to the school board's logic, a teacher could pull out a Glock 9 mm and waste a potential assassin before he unloaded his own weapon, thereby saving innocent lives. Even the public knowledge that old Mr. Crotch, the English teacher, or Ms. Slink, the attractive music teacher, might be carrying a pistol would probably be sufficient to deter an armed attack.

3   The reactions ranged from shock on the part of the teacher organizations and many teachers, administrators, and parents to enthusiastic endorsement by Texas governor Rick Perry, who supported similar statewide legislation proposed in the legislature. The National Rifle Association was ecstatic, as were gun rights supporters across the United States.

4   School violence is a problem in some schools, though students are much more likely to suffer harm at home or otherwise away from school. But school shootings capture the public attention and evoke feelings of horror and fear for one's own children. School kids— particularly boys—have always fought but what is different today is the easy availability of firearms and the willingness to use them to settle a dispute. But if we cannot keep guns out of schools, is arming teachers and staff the best alternative—fighting fire with fire?

5   Thirty-seven states currently ban guns from school. Only two states permit them. Utah allows concealed weapons on college campuses and South Carolina permits a student, teacher, administrator, or any other school employee or visitor to carry concealed weapons in his or her vehicle on school grounds. However, Michigan, Ohio, Alabama, Virginia, and several other states were considering permitting guns

on school property in 2009. Federal law prohibits taking a gun within 1,000 feet of a school under the Gun-Free School Zones Act of 1996.

6   Are concealed weapons in schools a good idea? Perhaps at first blush the concept has appeal, but like most everything else in the public policy world, the devil is in the details.

- Do teachers and administrators want the tremendous responsibility of carrying a weapon and possibly using it against an armed or threatening student?

- At what point in a potentially violent conflict should a teacher actually deploy and use his or her gun? When a credible threat is communicated? A knife pulled? A shot fired?

- Will teachers be asked to purchase and maintain their own pistol, or would the school board or state purchase and maintain it instead? Who pays?

- Who will be responsible for ensuring that weapon-carrying teachers maintain their permits and receive regular weapons training?

- What happens when a teacher's firearm accidentally discharges and injures someone?

- And most important: are there other, better policy options for handling violence in the schools? (Adapted from Ann O. M. Bowman and Richard C. Kearney, *State and Local Government*, 8th ed., © Cengage Learning.)

What is the authors' point? _____

_____.

What is the author's purpose? _____

How would you describe the author's tone? _____

_____

2. Columbus Revisited

1   When Columbus set sail in 1492, King Ferdinand and Queen Isabella of Spain wanted him to spread Christianity while fulfilling his promise of finding a route to Asia. Columbus, as it turned out, did neither, and it's a wonder why we have given him a national holiday.

2   When Columbus first sighted land, he thought he was somewhere in the East Indies, but he was actually stepping on shore of what is now Barbados. Claiming everything in sight as the property of Spain,

Columbus demanded that the native population pay tribute, preferably in gold. If they refused outright or seemed to be making insufficient efforts to pay, their hands were chopped off per order of Columbus.

3   In 1493, as the governor of Hispaniola, now Haiti and the Dominican Republic, Columbus gifted the New World population with imported European diseases, malnutrition, overwork, and painful punishment for any failure to follow his orders. Eventually, Columbus's rule and its aftermath took a terrible toll, reducing the population to a mere 22,000 people.

4   With time even the Spanish missionaries, sent to help Columbus spread God's word, were alarmed by his behavior. One missionary reported that Columbus was guilty of "robbing and destroying the land." The missionary was appalled because Columbus thought nothing of cutting down a whole forest in order to have enough wood for heat and building construction. By 1500, even his Spanish sponsors knew their man was a failure. Stripped of his authority, Columbus was returned to Spain in chains at the command of the new governor.

5   In the light of his failures, we have to wonder about those people who claim that Columbus's voyage began a new era of exploration and that his great achievement is worthy of a federal holiday.

What is the author's point? _____

_____

What is the author's purpose? _____

How would you describe the author's tone? _____

_____

▶ **TEST 6**   **Locating Errors in Logic**

DIRECTIONS   Read each selection and then circle the appropriate letter or letters to identify the error in logic.

1. Fast food restaurants such as McDonald's, Burger King, and Taco Bell should be required to display warning notices about the fat content of the foods they sell. Animal studies have suggested that eating fatty foods seems to provoke addictive behavior. For example, rats fed a diet high in sugar exhibit signs of anxiety when the sugar is removed. Other research suggests that high-fat foods may stimulate the brain's pleasure centers, producing an effect similar to that of drugs such as nicotine and heroin. As a result, consumers have the right to be informed that eating fast food is just like getting hooked on drugs. The government requires cigarette manufacturers to print warning labels on every pack to inform consumers that smoking is an addictive habit that causes cancer and death. It stands to reason, then, that every fast food wrapper and carton should be similarly labeled to make it clear that their addictive contents will lead to obesity and death.

   a. irrelevant evidence
   b. careless comparison
   c. false alternatives
   d. hasty generalization
   e. circular reasoning

2. Kids today are being assigned far too much homework, so schools should require teachers to limit their after-school assignments to a maximum of one hour's worth of work. When children are forced to spend school nights doing hours of homework, they quickly learn to dislike both school and learning. Kids burn out quickly if their free time is filled up with assignments and projects. Children need their evenings free to play and relax. Plus, now more than ever, children should be spending quality time with their families in the evenings. If kids are always doing homework instead of bonding with family members, how can they possibly grow up with any sense of family values? Either we limit homework now, or kids will grow up believing

that academic achievement is more important than cultivating family relationships.

a. irrelevant evidence

b. careless comparison

c. false alternatives

d. hasty generalization

e. circular reasoning

3. George Balanchine, the Russian-born choreographer and dance teacher, founded the School of American Ballet in 1934. Best known as the prime mover at the New York City Ballet from 1948 to 1983, Balanchine has been called one of the finest creators of ballets the world has ever known. But if we examine his career without the blinders of hero worship, it's obvious that Balanchine possessed neither enormous talent nor great artistic vision. Out of the studio, Balanchine ignored dancers he had trained for years, pretending not to recognize members of his troupe when he bumped into them in restaurants or stores. Even Balanchine's fellow choreographers had to endure rude treatment: He was so self-centered he could scarcely remember their names.

a. irrelevant evidence

b. careless comparison

c. false alternatives

d. hasty generalization

e. circular reasoning

4. According to an American Management Association report, 78 percent of U.S. firms monitor their employees' communications in some way, and 47 percent read their workers' e-mail messages. Companies may argue that they monitor their workers only to guard company secrets or to protect themselves from potential lawsuits over harassment and other violations. But the fact remains that employers are spying on Americans whose privacy is protected by the U.S. Constitution. Yet employers record telephone conversations and videotape employees with surveillance cameras. Employees should be outraged by their employers' attempts to monitor their every move. They should speak out against attempts to infringe

upon their privacy. What's more, companies themselves should realize that stooping to snoop on their workers sends a bad message about how little trust or respect they have for their employees.

a. irrelevant evidence

b. careless comparison

c. false alternatives

d. hasty generalization

e. circular reasoning

5. Today's zookeepers claim to have learned the lessons of the past and are creating habitats for animals that take into account the animals' needs. Unfortunately, though, no matter how many plants, trees, rocks, and waterfalls are added to create more naturalistic settings, the creatures confined in zoo exhibits are still suffering from mistreatment. They may not be cruelly locked up in cramped cages as in the past, but they are still neglected and even beaten. When an elephant handler at the Oregon Zoo inflicted 176 gashes and cuts upon one of the beasts in his care, the truth became clear. The pretty, naturalistic settings of modern zoos do nothing more than camouflage the animal abuse occurring in these lovely locations.

a. irrelevant evidence

b. careless comparison

c. false alternatives

d. hasty generalization

e. circular reasoning

Putting It All Together

The extended readings that follow give you a chance to review everything you have learned in Chapters 1–12. There are three sets of questions for each reading. *Getting the Gist* focuses on the kinds of questions that you might take on a standardized test in order to show that you have a general grasp of the material covered. The questions in *Taking a Closer Look* concentrate on both the content of the reading as well as the textual clues to meaning that writers have purposely left to help keep their readers on the right track. *Reading with a Critical Eye* tests your ability to evaluate what you have read and includes questions about word choice, fact and opinion, purpose, argument, and tone.

© Ulrich Flemming from *Found Art Around the World.*

▶ **READING 1**   Communication and Identity

Ronald B. Adler and Russell F. Proctor

Looking Ahead   This selection comes from a communications textbook titled *Looking Out/Looking In*. Each chapter of the book targets a particular aspect of how we present ourselves to the world in both one-on-one and group situations. Keep that larger context in mind as you read.

Word Watch   Some of the more difficult words in the reading are defined below. The number in parentheses indicates the paragraph in which the word appears. An asterisk marks its first appearance in the reading. Preview the definitions before you begin reading and watch for the words while you read.

> **fundamental (5):** essential, basic
>
> **hypothetical (6):** in theory rather than practice, imagined but not yet real
>
> **genetic (9):** related to the genes that we inherit from our parents
>
> **extroversion (9):** a tendency to turn outward toward others, the inclination to be sociable
>
> **spectrum (10):** range
>
> **appraisals (13):** evaluations
>
> **metaphor (14):** implied comparison of two seemingly different things that actually share a similarity

Getting Focused   The title is a strong clue to the content of the reading. By the time you finish it, make sure you can explain how self-concept influences communication.

TEXTBOOK TIP   Textbooks that explain how people think and behave—for instance, psychology, sociology, and communications texts—are very likely to introduce key theories by identifying the person or group who first publicly described or named the theory. When a name is introduced outside of parentheses or a footnote, check to see if a theory or term is associated with it. Record the name of the person along with the theory or definition in your notes.

Introduction: Defining Who You Are

1 Who are you? Take a moment now to answer this question and let the following list guide your answer. Try to include all the characteristics that describe you:

Your moods or feelings (for example, happy, angry, excited)
Your appearance (for example, attractive, short)
Your social traits (for example, friendly, shy)
Talents you have or do not have (for example, musical, nonathletic)
Your intellectual capacity (for example, school smart, street smart)
Your strong beliefs (for example, religious, environmental)
Your social roles (for example, parent, girlfriend)

2   Now take a look at what you've written. How did you define yourself? As a student? A man or woman? By your age? Your religion? Your occupation? There are many ways of identifying yourself. List as many ways as you can. You'll probably see that the words you've chosen represent a profile of what you view as your most important characteristics. In other words, if you were required to describe the "real you," this list ought to be a good summary.

Communication and the Self-Concept

3 What you've done in developing this list is to give a partial description of your **self-concept**: the relatively stable set of perceptions you hold of yourself. If a special mirror existed that reflected not only your physical features but also other aspects of yourself—emotional states, talents, likes, dislikes, values, roles, and so on—the reflection you'd see would be your self-concept. . . .

4   Of course, not every item on your self-concept list is equally important. For example, the most significant part of one person's self-concept might consist of social roles, and for another person it might be physical appearance, health, friendships, accomplishments, or skills.

5   Whatever aspect of your self-concept you consider fundamental,* the concept of self is perhaps our most basic possession. Knowing who we are is essential because without a self-concept, it would be impossible to relate to the world.

6   **Self-esteem** is the part of the self-concept that involves evaluations of self-worth. A hypothetical* communicator's self-concept might include being quiet, argumentative, or serious. His or her self-esteem would be

---

**Sidebar notes:**

Note how both the title and the questionnaire suggest the authors are writing about a topic like self-concept or personal identity.

The heading connects self-concept to communication, so be on the lookout for paragraphs that link the two.

Note the definition of *self-concept*, which is in boldface. It's a good idea to paraphrase key terms that aren't too technical.

What distinction is the author making in paragraph 6 between what and what?

determined by how he or she felt about these qualities: "I am glad that I am quiet," or "I am embarrassed about being so quiet," for example.

At the beginning of paragraph 7 the authors make a key connection between what two topics?

7   Figure 1 shows the relationship between self-esteem and communication behavior. People who feel good about themselves have positive expectations about how they will communicate. These expectations increase the chance that communication will be successful, and successes contribute to positive self-evaluations that reinforce self-esteem. Of course, the same principle can work in a negative way with communicators who have low self-esteem.

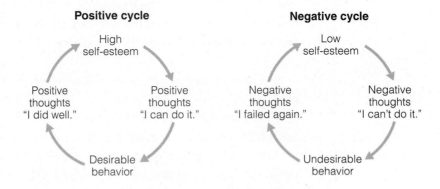

Figure 1   The Relationship Between Self-Esteem and Communication Behavior

Biological and Social Roots of the Self

8   How did you become the kind of communicator you are? Were you born that way? Are you a product of your environment? As you'll now see, the correct answer to the last two of these questions is "yes."

What is the relationship between the content of this heading and the previous chapter section?

9   **Biology and the Self**   Take another look at the "Who Am I?" list you developed at the beginning of the chapter. You will almost certainly find some terms that describe your personality—characteristic ways that you think and behave across a variety of situations. Your personality tends to be stable throughout your life. Often it grows more pronounced over time. Research suggests that personality is, to a large degree, part of our genetic* makeup. For example, people who were judged shy as children will show a distinctive reaction in their brains as adults when they encounter new situations. In fact, biology accounts for as much as half of some communication-related personality traits, including extroversion,* shyness, assertiveness, verbal aggression, and overall willingness to communicate. In other words, to some degree, we come "programmed" to communicate in certain ways. . . .

Note how the authors are using the phrase "genetic makeup" as a synonym for biology.

What in paragraph 9 would cause readers to worry in paragraph 10 that they are "stuck with a personality"?

10   But before you become distressed about being stuck with a personality that makes communication difficult, keep two important points in mind. First realize that these traits are a matter of degree, not an either-or matter. It's an over-simplification to think of yourself as shy *or* sociable, argumentative *or* agreeable, self-controlled *or* spontaneous. It's more accurate to realize that almost everyone's personality fits at some point on a spectrum* for each trait. You may be somewhat shy, a little argumentative, or moderately self-controlled.

The transition "second" signals continuation of the thought from the previous paragraph. The author is still saying "don't be distressed."

11   Second, while you may have a disposition toward traits like shyness or aggressiveness, you can do a great deal to control how you actually communicate. Even shy people can learn to reach out to others. And those with aggressive tendencies can learn to communicate in more sociable ways.

12   Finally, realize that although your personality may shape the way you communicate to a degree, your self-concept determines how you feel about the way you relate to others. Consider how different self-concepts can lead to very different ways of thinking about your method of communication:

Quiet	"I'm a coward for not speaking up."
	"I enjoy listening more than talking."
Argumentative	"I'm pushy, and that's obnoxious."
	"I stand up for my beliefs."
Self-controlled	"I'm too cautious."
	"I think carefully before I say or do things."

As you will soon see, our self-concept and self-esteem are shaped to a great extent by both the messages we receive from others and the way we think about ourselves.

Note how the heading serves to move the reader away from biological/genetic explanations.

13 **Socialization and the Self-Concept**   How important are others in shaping our self-concept? Imagine growing up on a deserted island, with no one to talk to or share activities. How would you know how smart you are—or aren't? How would you gauge your attractiveness? How would you decide if you're short or tall, kind or mean, skinny or fat? Even if you could view your reflection in a mirror, you still wouldn't know how to evaluate your appearance without appraisals* from others or people with whom to compare yourself. In fact, the messages we receive from the people in our lives play the most important role in shaping how we regard ourselves.

Remember the opening textbook tip. Paragraph 14 gives you a chance to apply it.

14   As early as 1912, sociologist Charles Cooley used the metaphor* of a mirror to identify the process of **reflected appraisal**: the fact that each of us develops a self-concept that reflects the way we believe others see us. In other words, we are likely to feel less valuable, lovable, and capable to the degree that others have communicated ego-busting signals; and we will probably feel good about ourselves to the degree that others affirm our value. The principle of reflected appraisal will become clear when you realize that the self-concept you described in the list at the beginning of this chapter is a product of the positive and negative messages you have received throughout your life.

Look what you have broken now! How can you be so clumsy!?

© Ulrich Flemming.

Notice how paragraph 15 opens with an introduction that identifies the function of the paragraph.

15   To illustrate this point further, let's start at the beginning. Children aren't born with any sense of identity. They learn to judge themselves only through the way others treat them. As children learn to speak and understand language, verbal messages contribute to a developing self-concept. Each day a child is bombarded with scores of messages about him- or herself. Some of these are positive: "You're so cute!" "I love you." "What a big girl." Other messages are negative: "What's the matter with you? Can't you do anything right?" "You're a bad boy." "Leave me alone. You're driving me crazy!" Evaluations like these are the mirror by which we know ourselves; and because children are trusting souls who have no other way of viewing themselves, they accept at face value both the positive and negative evaluations of the apparently all-knowing and all-powerful adults around them.

In paragraph 16, what does the phrase "this same principle" refer to?

16   This same principle in the formation of the self-concept continues in later life, especially when messages come from what sociologists term *significant others*—people whose opinions we especially value. Family

members are the most obvious type of significant others. Friends, teachers, and acquaintances, though, can also be significant others. To see the importance of significant others, ask yourself how you arrived at your opinion of yourself as a student, as a person attractive to others, as a competent worker, and you'll see that these self-evaluations were probably influenced by the way others regarded you. (Adapted from Adler and Proctor, *Looking Out/Looking In*, 12th ed., pp. 41–48. 12th ed., © 2006 Cengage Learning.)

Close Up on Visual Aids
●

In visual aids, the arrows are always important. The arrows in Figure 1 on page 732 help send a message to readers. Moving in a circle and pointing in the same direction, the arrows suggest which of the following?

a. High self-esteem leads to good behavior while low self-esteem leads to bad behavior.

b. Low self-esteem can produce negative thoughts and behavior that further contribute to low self-esteem.

c. Both positive and negative self-esteem affect how well we communicate and how well we communicate further raises or lowers our self-esteem.

Monitoring Your Comprehension
Review the marginal annotations and answer any questions posed. If you can't answer a question, mark the sentence or passage referred to and re-read it before turning to the comprehension and critical reading questions.

GETTING THE GIST   These questions are the kind you might encounter on a standardized reading test.

DIRECTIONS   Identify the general gist, or point, of the authors' words by circling the appropriate letter.

1. According to the authors, what's the relationship between our self-concept and communication?

   a. Until we develop a positive self-concept, it's unlikely that we would be good communicators.

   b. How we view ourselves has a strong influence on how well or how effectively we communicate.

    c. Communicating with others is a way of figuring out how they see us.

    d. The ability to communicate only develops after we have a sense of self.

2. According to the authors, your self-concept is

    a. largely a product of genetic inheritance.

    b. developed by your interaction with those who are close to you.

    c. a product of both genetic inheritance and interaction with others.

    d. the result of parental training.

3. What's the difference between *self-concept* and *self-esteem*?

    a. Self-concept refers to our conscience whereas self-esteem refers to our personality.

    b. Self-concept is the self we see reflected in the eyes of others whereas self-esteem refers to our positive sense of self.

    c. Self-concept refers to the internal image we have of who we are; self-esteem refers to the value we place on ourselves.

4. Which statement best paraphrases the term *reflected appraisal* in paragraph 14?

    a. How much success we have in life affects how we see ourselves.

    b. Our appraisal of ourselves influences the way we see others.

    c. We develop our sense of self by seeing ourselves reflected in the eyes of others.

5. The cartoon with the chicken and the chick that broke the egg appears in the section titled "Socialization and the Self-Concept" to illustrate which of these three statements?

    a. "Even if you could view your reflection in a mirror, you still wouldn't know how to evaluate your appearance without appraisals from others or people with whom to compare yourself."

    b. "Children are trusting souls who have no other way of viewing themselves; they accept at face value both the positive and negative evaluations of the apparently all-knowing and all-powerful adults around them."

    c. "As early as 1912, sociologist Charles Cooley used the metaphor of a mirror to identify the process of **reflected appraisal**."

TAKING A CLOSER LOOK This set of questions focuses on your understanding of the text, both its content and the language used to convey that content.

DIRECTIONS Answer the following questions on the blank lines provided or by circling the letter of the best response.

Paraphrasing

1. How would you paraphrase the author's definition of self-concept in paragraph 3?

_____

_____

Following the Author's Train of Thought

2. The title of the first chapter section is "Communication and the Self-Concept." In which paragraph do the authors connect communication with self-concept?

_____

Recognizing the Main Idea

3. In your own words, what is the connection between self-concept and communication?

_____

_____

Recognizing Patterns of Organization

4. What pattern of organization does the main idea of the reading suggest?

_____

Following the Author's Train of Thought

5. In paragraph 9, the authors use what word as a synonym for the word *self* introduced in the heading "Biology and the Self"?

_____

Understanding Figurative Language

6. Where's the metaphor in this sentence that appears at the end of paragraph 9, and what two things does it compare? "In other words, to some degree, we come 'programmed' to communicate in certain ways."

_____

_____

What is the point of the metaphor? What is it supposed to tell you about the communication?

_____

_____

Identifying and Evaluating Supporting Details

7. What category word in paragraph 10 helped you identify the major supporting details?

_____

8. Is the information in paragraph 11 essential or nonessential? _____ Please explain the basis for your answer.

_____

_____

Recognizing Sentence Functions

9. Which function does the concluding sentence in paragraph 12 fulfill?
   a. It provides a major supporting detail that supports the main idea of the paragraph.
   b. It explains how some person or event mentioned in the paragraph changed over time.
   c. It provides a transition to specific examples illustrating the main idea.

Following the Author's Train of Thought

10. At the beginning of paragraph 13, the authors pose this question: "How important are others in shaping our self-concept?" Where in the paragraph does that question get answered?

_____

Paraphrasing

11. In your own words, how do the authors answer the opening question in paragraph 13?

_____

Understanding Transitions

12. Paragraph 15 opens with a transitional phrase that tells *readers*

    a. the authors are making a new and different point.

    b. the authors are continuing the same thought but adding an example.

    c. the authors are going to slightly revise what's just been said.

Following the Author's Train of Thought

13. In paragraph 15, the following statements—some positive, some negative—all illustrate what previous phrase in the paragraph? "You're so cute!" "I love you." "What a big girl." "What's the matter with you? Can't you do anything right?" "You're a bad boy."

_____

14. Paragraph 16 opens with the phrase "This same principle." To what principle are the authors referring?

_____

Recognizing Patterns of Organization

15. What would you say is the primary organizational pattern in this reading?

_____

READING WITH A CRITICAL EYE The goal here is not to be critical in the negative sense, but rather to understand how fact, opinion, argument, and tone reinforce the authors' apparent purpose.

DIRECTIONS Answer the questions on the blank lines provided or by circling the letter of the correct response.

Fact and Opinion

1. How would you label this statement from paragraph 9? "In fact, biology accounts for as much as half of some communication-related personality traits. . . ."

    a. It's a fact.

    b. It's an opinion.

    c. It's a mix of both.

Analyzing Arguments

2. In paragraph 13, the image of the deserted island is used to make what point?

_____

_____

3. In paragraph 16, the authors say this: "To see the importance of significant others, ask yourself how you arrived at your opinion of yourself as a student, as a person attractive to others, as a competent worker, and you'll see that these self-evaluations were probably influenced by the way others regarded you." What's the point of the argument?

_____

_____

What's the evidence for that point?

_____

_____

4. How would you evaluate the evidence? Do you consider it solid or shaky? _____

Please explain. _____

_____

Identifying Purpose

5. How would you label the authors' purpose?
   a. purely informative
   b. purely persuasive
   c. primarily informative with some persuasion included
   d. primarily persuasive with some informative writing included

From Reader to Writer Describe the person who you believe contributed most significantly to your self-concept. Make sure to explain how that person shaped your sense of self and why he or she was so critical to your personal development.

▶ READING 2   Social Influence: Follow the Leader

Dennis Coon and John O. Mitterer

Looking Ahead You already know from the previous reading that the way others view us affects our sense of ourselves. But did you realize that just the mere presence of other people can affect how you or I behave? If you did not consider that possible, think again because the following reading suggests that we are profoundly affected by being in the presence of others.

Word Watch Some of the more difficult words in the reading are defined below. The number in parentheses indicates the paragraph in which the word appears. An asterisk marks its first appearance in the reading. Preview the definitions before you begin reading and watch for the words while you read.

> **facilitation (4):** the act of making things easier
>
> **uniformity (8):** the state of being mentally or physically in agreement
>
> **susceptible (12):** likely to be influenced or harmed by something outside the self

Getting Focused This reading is from a psychology textbook that makes heavy use of italicized opening questions as a way to guide the reader's attention. Each time you start a section that opens with a question, read for the answer. Then paraphrase it in the margins of the text.

TEXTBOOK TIP Textbooks that make heavy use of questions to guide the reader's attention often expect readers to infer the answer even though the answer is usually the main idea of the paragraph. Remember, too, when you infer the answer to a question posed at the beginning of a textbook section, that answer might govern not just the paragraph but the entire reading.

© Laraine Flemming. All rights reserved. No distribution allowed without express authorization.

The number of specific details used to explain how the presence of others affects behavior suggests that the second sentence is the main idea of the paragraph. The key question is this: Do you think that is also the main idea of the entire reading?

Now that you have finished the paragraph, how would you answer the opening question?

When it comes to distributing your attention, what does the last sentence tell you to do?

When you see examples like this one about the biker, make sure you know what larger general point the example illustrates.

This is a reading with lots of boldface terms. Be sure you link the definitions to the terms.

Note that the answer to

1   No topic lies nearer the heart of social psychology than social influence (changes in behavior induced by the actions of others). When people interact, they almost always affect one another's behavior. For example, in a sidewalk experiment, various numbers of people stood on a busy New York City street. On cue, they all looked at a sixth-floor window across the street. A camera recorded how many passersby also stopped to stare. The larger the influencing group, the more people were swayed to join in staring at the window.

2   *Are there different kinds of social influence?* Social influence ranges from mild to strong. The gentlest form of social influence is *mere presence* (changing behavior just because other people are nearby). We *conform* when we spontaneously change our behavior to bring it into agreement with others. Compliance is a more directed form of social influence. We *comply* when we change our behavior in response to another person who has little or no social power or authority. Obedience is an even stronger form of social influence. We *obey* when we change our behavior in direct response to the demands of authority. The strongest form of social influence is *coercion* (changing behavior because we are forced to or suffer unpleasant consequences).

Mere Presence

3   Mere presence refers to the tendency for people to change their behavior just because of the presence of other people. Let's explore some of the ways mere presence can induce us to modify our behavior.

4   Imagine that you are out riding your bike when another rider pulls up beside you. Will you pick up your pace? Slow down? Completely ignore the other rider? The very first investigation of social psychology by Norman Triplett in 1898 examined precisely this question. According to Triplett's results, which have remained unchallenged, you are more likely to speed up. This is an example of **social facilitation**,* the tendency to perform better in the presence of others.

5   *Does mere presence always improve performance*? No, if you are confident in your abilities, your behavior will most likely be facilitated in the presence of others. If you are not, then your performance is more likely to be impaired. Another classic study focused on college students shooting pool at a student union. Good players who were confident (sharks) normally made 71 percent of their shots. Their accuracy improved to 80 percent when they were watched by others. Less confident, average players (marks) who normally made 36 percent of their shots dropped to 25 percent accuracy when someone was watching them.

the opening question is not a simple *yes* or *no*. The answer changes with the context. That's not unusual. When you are reading to answer a question, make sure you understand the entire answer, not just part of it.

In addition to noting the definition of a boldface term, consider paraphrasing the definition in the margins.

A new heading signals the introduction of a new idea. Be on the lookout for what the author says about conformity.

Whenever you read a play-by-play account of an event or events, ask yourself what the event or events are meant to illustrate or prove.

If an experiment or study gets a heading all of its own, you can bet that it is really important to the reading and should therefore get extra attention. Paraphrase it in the margins or summarize its conclusions in your notes.

6   **Social loafing** is another consequence of having other people nearby. People tend to work less hard (loaf) when they are part of a group than they do when they are solely responsible for their work. In one study, people playing tug-of-war while blindfolded pulled harder if they thought they were competing alone. When they thought others were on their team, they made less of an effort.

Conformity

7   When Harry met Sally, they fell in love and were not shy about expressing themselves around campus. Some students in Harry's classes advised him to be a bit more discreet. Increasingly, Sally noticed other students staring at her and Harry when they were, well, expressing their love. Although they never made a conscious decision to conform, in another week their public intimate moments were a thing of the past. Perhaps the most basic of all group norms is, as Harry and Sally discovered, "Thou shalt conform." Like it or not, life is filled with instances of conformity.

8   Daily behavior is probably most influenced by group pressure for conformity. We all conform to a degree. In fact, some uniformity* is a necessity. Imagine being totally unable to anticipate the actions of others. In stores, schools, and homes, this would be frustrating and disturbing. On the highways, it would be lethal.

The Asch Experiment

9   *How strong are group pressures for conformity?* One of the first experiments on conformity was staged by Solomon Asch (1907–1996). To fully appreciate it, imagine yourself as a subject. Assume that you are seated at a table with six other students. Your task is actually quite simple. On each trial, you are shown three lines. Your job is to select the line that matches the length of a fourth "standard" line.

10   As the testing begins, each person announces an answer for the first card showing a line. (See Figure 2.) When your turn comes, you agree with the others. "This isn't hard at all," you say to yourself. For several more trials, your answers agree with those of the group. Then comes a shock. All six people announce that line 1 matches the standard, and you were about to say line 3 matches. Suddenly you feel alone and upset. You nervously look at the lines again. The room falls silent. Everyone seems to be staring at you. The experimenter awaits your answer.

11   In this study, the other "students" were all actors who gave the wrong answer on about a third of the trials to create group pressure. Real students conformed to the group on about one third of the critical trials. Of those

tested, 75 percent yielded at least once. People who were tested alone erred in less than 1 percent of their judgments. Clearly, those who yielded to group pressures were denying what their eyes told them.

Figure 2 These are examples of the lines students compared in the Asch experiment.

12   *Are some people more susceptible* to group pressures than others?* People with high needs for structure or certainty are more likely to conform. So are people who are anxious, low in self-confidence, or concerned with the approval of others. People who live in cultures that emphasize group coop-eration (such as many Asian cultures) are also likely to conform.

Group Factors in Conformity

13   *How do groups enforce norms?* In most groups, we have been rewarded with acceptance and approval for conformity and threatened with rejection or ridicule for nonconformity. These reactions are called *group sanctions*. Negative sanctions range from laughter, staring, or social disapproval to complete rejection or formal exclusion. If you've ever felt the sudden chill of disapproval by others, you will understand the power of group sanctions.

This would be a good place to circle the term and underline the definition of "group sanctions."

Here again, make sure you understand more of the answer than just a simple "yes."

14   *Wouldn't the effectiveness of group sanctions depend on the importance of the group?* Yes. The more important group membership is to a person, the more he or she will be influenced by other group members. The risk of being rejected can be a threat to our sense of personal identity. That's why the Asch experiments are impressive. Because these were only temporary groups, sanctions were informal, and rejection had no lasting importance. Just the same, the power of the group was evident.

Does this paragraph really discuss more than one factor affecting conformity?

15   *What other factors besides the importance of the group affect the degree of conformity?* In the sidewalk experiment described earlier, we noted that large groups had more influence. In Asch's face-to-face groups, the size of the majority also made a difference, but a surprisingly small one. In other studies, the number of people who conformed increased dramatically as the majority grew from two to three people. However, a majority of three produced about as much yielding as a majority of eight. The next time you want to talk someone into (or out of) something, take two friends along and see what a difference they make. (Sometimes it helps if the two are large and mean-looking.)

16   Even more important than the size of the majority is its unanimity (total agreement). Having at least one person in your corner can greatly reduce pressures to conform. When Asch gave subjects an ally (who also opposed the majority by giving the correct answer), conformity was lessened. Perhaps this accounts for the rich diversity of human attitudes, beliefs opinions, and lifestyles. If you can find at least one other person who sees things as you do (no matter how weird), you can be relatively secure in your opposition to other viewpoints. Incidentally, the Internet now makes it much easier to find that other like-minded person. (Dennis Coon and John O. Mitterer, *Psychology: A Journey*, 4th ed. © Cengage Learning.)

Monitoring Your Comprehension There are several headings in the reading. If you can look at each heading and paraphrase the point made in that section, your comprehension is good. Anytime the heading doesn't evoke any memory of what the author said about it, mark the section for a second reading.

GETTING THE GIST   These questions are the kind you might encounter on a standardized reading test.

DIRECTIONS   Identify the general gist, or point, of the author's words by circling the appropriate letter.

1. Which statement best expresses the overall main idea of the reading?
    a. Working in groups is likely to interfere with personal creativity.
    b. Solomon Asch's study of conformity is decades old, but remains highly influential among students of social psychology.
    c. Although many people tend to think conformity is a bad thing, there are numerous instances in daily life where conforming to what others do is morally correct.
    d. Studies in social psychology suggest that our behavior is influenced by the presence of others, particularly when we are part of a larger group.

2. According to the authors, people tend to loaf, or work less hard,
    a. when they feel under pressure.
    b. when they are part of a group.
    c. when they have experienced failure in the past.
    d. when they are with others who are not motivated to achieve.

3. Which statement best defines *compliance*?
    a. We comply when we imitate those we admire.
    b. We comply when we obey the commands of those higher in authority than we are.
    c. We comply when we go along with the requests of someone who has little real power over us.
    d. When we comply, we are coerced into doing so by those who have power over our lives.

4. According to the authors,
    a. confident people perform even better when they are being observed.
    b. those who are unsure of themselves are likely to improve their performance when being observed.
    c. people who are confident are unaffected by the presence of others.
    d. people who are really talented avoid working in the presence of a group.

5. The Asch experiment suggests that

   a. people in a group tend to break into small, constantly warring sub-groups.

   b. people in a group are always going to fight over control of the group.

   c. in a group, people are likely to change what they think in order to fit in with the other members.

   d. being in a group encourages the individual members to think with greater originality than they would on their own.

TAKING A CLOSER LOOK This set of questions focuses on your understanding of the text, both its content and the language used to convey that content.

DIRECTIONS Answer the following questions on the blank lines provided or by circling the letter of the best response.

Recognizing Thesis Statements

1. Which of the following is the thesis statement summing up the main idea?

   a. No topic lies nearer the heart of social psychology than social influence (changes in behavior induced by the actions of others). When people interact, they almost always affect one another's behavior.

   b. Social influence ranges from mild to strong. The gentlest form of social influence is *mere presence* (changing behavior just because other people are nearby).

   c. Obedience is an even stronger form of social influence. We *obey* when we change our behavior in direct response to the demands of authority. The strongest form of social influence is *coercion* (changing behavior because we are forced to).

   d. Even more important than the size of the majority is its unanimity (total agreement). Having at least one person in your corner can greatly reduce pressures to conform.

Recognizing Patterns of Organization

2. Overall, what is the primary pattern of the reading?

_____

3. Paragraph 2 combines which patterns of organization?

_____

4. Paragraph 10 opens with a _____ transition that is linked to what organizational pattern?

_____

Following the Authors' Train of Thought

5. Paragraph 3 ends with a sentence that
   a. introduces the main idea.
   b. provides a major supporting detail.
   c. offers a minor supporting detail.
   d. makes a transition.

6. In the last sentence of paragraph 8, what does the pronoun *it* refer to?

_____

7. Which statement best describes the relationship between paragraphs 7 and 8?
   a. Paragraph 8 repeats the main idea introduced in paragraph 7.
   b. Paragraph 7 illustrates the main idea introduced in paragraph 8.
   c. Paragraphs 7 and 8 are major details illustrating the main idea introduced in paragraph 6.

8. In the second sentence of paragraph 9, what does the pronoun *it* refer to?

_____

9. In paragraph 10, the sentence "Then comes a shock" is a
   a. topic sentence.
   b. major supporting detail.
   c. minor supporting detail.
   d. transition.

10. Why do the authors open the reading with a description of people standing on a sidewalk and looking at a sixth-floor window?

   _____

   _____

Paraphrasing 11. Which statement is the best paraphrase for these two sentences? "The more important group membership is to a person, the more he or she will be influenced by other group members. The risk of being rejected can be a threat to our sense of personal identity"

   a. Because being in a group threatens a person's sense of identity, those who have low self-esteem are likely to avoid groups that include more than three people.

   b. Group influence increases according to how much the members fear being excluded from the group.

   c. Rejection from a group is so painful for some that their lives are never the same once they are excluded from a group they considered important to their identity.

12. In your own words, how do the authors answer the question they pose: "Does mere presence always improve performance?"

   _____

   _____

   _____

Drawing Inferences 13. The authors open the section titled "The Asch Experiment" with a question: "How strong are group pressures for conformity?" But they expect readers to infer the answer. What answer do they want you to infer and why?

   _____

   _____

   _____

Understanding Supporting Details

14. In paragraph 8, the authors say this: "Daily behavior is probably most influenced by group pressure for conformity." Then they offer some examples meant to convince readers that conformity is essential to daily behavior. What other examples can you think of that would fit the authors' point?

_____

_____

15. Why do the authors bring up the Asch experiment? How does it support the main idea of the reading?

_____

_____

READING WITH A CRITICAL EYE   The goal here is not to be critical in the negative sense, but rather to understand how word choice, fact, opinion, argument, and tone reinforce the author's apparent purpose.

DIRECTIONS   Answer the questions on the blank lines provided or by circling the letter of the correct response.

Fact and Opinion

1. What are you dealing with in each of these statements, fact (F), opinion (O), or a mix of both (B)?

a. One of the first experiments on conformity was staged by Solomon Asch (1907–1996) _____

b. People with high needs for structure or certainty are more likely to conform. _____

c. Another classic study focused on college students shooting pool at a student union. Good players who were confident (sharks) normally made 71 percent of their shots. Their accuracy improved to 80 percent when they were being watched by others. _____

2. Reading 2 is from a textbook, but not all textbook authors assume the same tone. How would you describe the tone these two authors use to approach their audience?

a. informal and friendly

b. learned and informed

c. completely impersonal

3. What language in the reading encouraged you to choose that tone?

_____

_____

_____

Evaluating Arguments

4. What might a critical thinker say about the authors' suggestion that the pressure on group members to conform to the ideas held by a group is very strong (paragraphs 9–12)?

_____

_____

_____

_____

5. What evidence do the authors offer for the following claim? "Daily behavior is probably most influenced by group pressure for conformity."

_____

_____

From Reader to Writer Open your paper by briefly summarizing the experiment conducted by Solomon Asch. Then use a transitional sentence like the following to move the reader to the second part of your paper. If you agree with the results of Asch's experiment, your transitional sentence would be something like this: "Solomon Asch's experiment highlights a common tendency in human nature, a tendency I can attest to from personal experience." If you think the results of Asch's experiments do not fit your experience, use a transitional sentence like this one: "The tendency to conform to the ideas of the group may have been strong in 1956, but I'm not so sure that is true today."

Make the second part of your paper focus on one or two experiences that do or do not fit the conclusions social psychologists have drawn from Asch's experiment.

WEB QUEST
Use the Web to identify one or more criticisms that have been leveled at Asch's results.

_____

_____

_____

▶ **READING 3**   Failing Those in Our Care

Rita Soronen

Looking Ahead   Do you remember reading about the children from the orphan trains? They were among the first children in the United States to be put into foster care. Unfortunately, the system of foster care, formally founded[†] by Charles Loring Brace, the same man who started the orphan trains running, has a lot of problems, not the least of which is the issue the author focuses on—what happens to young people who turn eighteen and are officially "aged out" of the system.

Word Watch   Some of the more difficult words in the reading are defined below. The number in parentheses indicates the paragraph in which the word appears. An asterisk marks its first appearance in the reading. Preview the definitions before you begin reading and watch for the words while you read.

> **emancipated (1):** freed, given liberty
>
> **egregiously (3):** to a horrible degree, terribly
>
> **intact (3):** complete, not damaged, whole
>
> **conservative (6):** In a political context, preferring tradi-tion over change; in the context of making an estimate, guessing purposely low
>
> **trailblazer (7):** someone who does new things before anyone else, a pioneer
>
> **innate (8):** inborn, natural, not taught or acquired

Getting Focused   The title with its emphasis on failure tells you how to direct your attention. By the time you finish the reading, you should be able to explain how the foster care system is failing those who enter it.

[†]Foster care existed prior to Brace's time, but there wasn't much care in it. Nor was there any attempt to formalize the fostering process. The children were viewed largely as cheap help, and there was no supervision of the people supposedly caring for them. Brace is the first one who publicly thought of foster care as a way to help the children rather than the fostering adults. Whether his ideas worked or not is another matter.

Based on the opening paragraph, do you think the author believes foster care in the United States is what it should be?

1   In 2012 in the United States, 23,439 children in foster care turned 18 and were "emancipated"* or "aged out." In simple terms, most of them were put out into the world on their own without housing, financial assistance, or emotional support. Take Adrian, now 27. After being placed into foster care at 6 because of his mother's drug and alcohol abuse, he stayed in care, moving from home to home, until he was 18 and too old for the system. He found the strength to try to put himself through college, using the county van his caseworker helped secure to move there.

2   His roommate got to go home on school breaks and had a mother who called to check in on him. Adrian had no one to call when he struggled at school—nowhere to call home, no one to send a gift, no one to see how he was doing. He worked nearly 60 hours a week just to pay for college, and when eventually his grades slipped, he was kicked out. He struggled with the ups and downs of depression. As Adrian said of children in foster care: "We are not equipped to go through this world alone."

Authors don't supply facts and figures for no reason. Why are these numbers and statistics here?

3   In 2012, U.S. authorities received more than 3.3 million reports of abuse, representing about 6 million children, or 8% of the child population. From those reports, after investigation and intervention, about 400,000 children were placed in foster care, and of those, nearly 60,000 were permanently taken away from their families of origin. These are children who were neglected or abused by parents—physically or sexually or both—so egregiously* that a judge permanently severed the parents' rights to claim the children as their own. Terminating, or legally ending, the right of a parent to raise a child is not something a judge decides lightly. In fact, parents receive every legal, social, and system opportunity to keep their families intact*—too often putting the child at risk of emotional or physical harm.

4   Because we know that children thrive in families—not institutions or transient, temporary, care—we made a promise to those children. We promised the day they were permanently separated from their families that we would find them new ones. A place to call home, to be loved, supported, and cherished, as every child should. We failed 23,439 children last year, and legally emancipated them from care. This world is not an easy place for children to grow and thrive on their own. Too often it is not even a safe place.

5   Make no mistake, many dedicated and skilled adults step forward to try to care for these children, as their social workers, counselors, or temporary foster parents. Some even stay connected once a child leaves care. And some states have worked hard to extend foster care to 21, but resources for older youth are limited and difficult to access. A Health and Human Services report found that the federal Foster Care Independence

What does the last sentence of this paragraph lead you to expect from the paragraph that follows?

Was the expectation fulfilled by the paragraph?

When the author introduces a specific example, always ask yourself, What point does this example illustrate or suggest?

program meant to help foster children make the transition to adulthood is inconsistent from state to state and provides too little for these troubled young people. And it simply is not a substitute for a family. Considering the trauma these children have endured at a young age, the moves from foster family to foster family and the abandonment they feel, it's no wonder they are at a higher risk for a grim future.

6   Conservative* studies find one in five will become homeless after 18; at 24, only half will be employed; less than 3% will have earned a college degree; 71% of women will be pregnant by 21; and one in four will have experienced post-traumatic stress disorder at twice the rate of United States war veterans. And too often, many are at risk of moving back into government systems—from juvenile centers to prison.

7   Renee, now 25, was young when her mother became addicted to drugs and could no longer care for her and her brother. They were placed in foster care, moved around within the system, and eventually aged out. She had nowhere to go after foster care. Now on her own as a young adult, she's facing obstacles that could have been avoided. Renee told me that, "For children who have never been on their own before, they're really in a bad situation once those first few months of support stops. If I can't pay a bill, who's going to help me pay it? I had to be a trailblazer,* that's all I knew. It was a survival tactic. I still feel like I don't have any guidance. Everything for me is trial and error, and I hate that." And for Dante, it was really very simple: "I just wanted a family and a home," he said. After nearly 12 years, he left foster care with neither.

8   There is a cycle of violence and helplessness innate* in the lives of the hundreds of thousands of children in the U.S. foster care system. And yet millions of Americans are unaware that thousands of children remain in this cycle, and those charged with their protection fail to commit to better solutions for educational and vocational support, employment, life skills training, and secure homes.

9   It is our duty as a nation to end this cycle. We made promises to these 101,000 children in foster care waiting to be adopted that we would find them safe, supportive homes. We must take the lead and work harder to do that. If children have been permanently separated from their families and freed for adoption, it's unacceptable that they end up without one. April is National Child Abuse Prevention Month and is followed in May by National Foster Care Month. Take these opportunities to call your U.S. representative or senator, speak with your state representatives, or write a letter to your governor to urge them to focus on the foster care system to make the health, safety, and welfare of children in their states an uncompromised

priority. We can make the life of each and every American child a cause for celebration and joy. We must demand justice and safety at every level for children, not only because it is their basic human right but because those who grow and learn in just environments and with the protection of families ultimately create humane and thriving societies as adults. (Used by permission of the author © Rita Soronen.)

Monitoring Your Comprehension The reading is threaded through with factual information. Can you explain why the author has included those facts and what they are meant to prove? Can you explain what the author hopes to accomplish with her writing? If you can answer these two questions, you have understood the reading.

GETTING THE GIST These questions are the kind you might encounter on a standardized reading test.

DIRECTIONS Identify the general gist, or point, of the author's words by circling the appropriate letter.

1. Which statement best expresses the overall main idea of the reading?
    a. Foster children who leave the foster care system without any kind of job training are likely to have problems adjusting to making it through the world completely on their own.
    b. We need to take action to ensure that children who enter the foster care system don't end up fending for themselves but instead find a safe and supportive home as well as some kind of safety net for their exit from the foster care system.
    c. The foster care system in the United States needs to be completely overhauled because it is failing every child who gets caught up in it.
    d. Currently, those children who enter the foster care system have next to no chance of having a successful life. Once they leave the foster care system, it's a given that they will end up homeless, unemployed, and, if they are really unlucky, on their way to prison.

2. According to the author, foster care throughout the United States is
    a. exactly the same in every state.
    b. difficult to evaluate.
    c. inconsistent from state to state.
    d. non-existent in some states.

3. According to the author, the studies of what happens to foster care children who age out of the system suggest

   a. that those who really want to can still achieve their dreams.

   b. that they end up suffering from severe addictions.

   c. that many will become homeless and unemployed.

   d. only one in five will get a college degree.

4. The author claims that

   a. no adults in the foster care system are interested in what happens to the children they supervise.

   b. many adults in the foster care system do everything possible to find foster children a home, but they have limited resources.

   c. many adults do their best for the children in the foster care system, but they cannot overcome the children's early wounding.

   d. adults in the foster care system are too burdened by pointless paperwork to search for homes to replace the ones they were removed from.

5. Which of the following best paraphrases the final sentence?

   a. We need to take better care of foster children because how a society handles its most helpless members is a symbol of how morally successful a society is as a whole.

   b. We need to take better care of our foster children because if we do not, their only alternative is a life of crime.

   c. We need to take better care of our foster children; since they have suffered so much already, we need to help them realize that life is not one long cycle of pain and violence.

   d. We need to insist that foster children get the same chances as other children because that is their basic right as human beings and because taking care of foster children encourages the society as a whole to thrive.

TAKING A CLOSER LOOK This set of questions focuses on your understanding of the text, both its content and the language used to convey that content.

DIRECTIONS Answer the following questions on the blank lines provided or by circling the letter of the best response.

Recognizing Thesis Statements

1. Which of the following correctly identifies the location of the thesis statement?

   a. The first two sentences of the first paragraph sum up the main idea of the entire reading.

   b. The last two sentences of the first paragraph sum up the point of the entire reading.

   c. The last three sentences of the second paragraph sum up the point of the entire reading.

   d. The first four sentences of the last paragraph sum up the point of the entire reading.

Understanding Supporting Details

2. Paragraph 3 introduces a number of facts and figures. What are they meant to suggest to the reader?

   _____

   _____

3. Adrian and Renee serve to illustrate what main idea?

   _____

   _____

Following the Author's Train of Thought

4. In the second sentence of paragraph 1, what does the pronoun *them* refer to?

   _____

5. The last sentence in paragraph 5 leads readers to expect that the author will focus on what topic?

   _____

   _____

Drawing Inferences

6. Why does the author contrast the life of Adrian, introduced in paragraph 2, with the life of his roommate at school? How does that contribute to her overall point?

_____

_____

7. What inference does the author expect readers to make in order to understand how the second part of this sentence relates to the first? "In fact, parents receive every legal, social, and system opportunity to keep their families intact—too often putting the child at risk of emotional or physical harm."

   a. Judges don't care very much about the decisions they make concerning children in foster care.

   b. Judges who try to keep families together don't have enough information about the families they are trying to maintain; therefore, they are prone to error.

   c. In an effort to keep families together, judges sometimes put children back into the dangerous family situations that got them into court in the first place.

8. In paragraph 4, what inference do readers need to draw to understand the author's message?

_____

_____

9. In paragraph 5, what main idea does the author expect you to infer?

_____

_____

_____

Making Connections

10. Which statement accurately describes the relationship between paragraphs 5 and 6?

    a. Paragraph 5 introduces a general point that is made more specific by paragraph 6.

    b. Paragraph 6 changes the direction of the author's thinking and introduces a new main idea.

    c. Paragraphs 5 and 6 both further develop a main idea introduced in paragraph 4.

READING WITH A CRITICAL EYE The goal here is not to be critical in the negative sense, but rather to understand how word choice, fact, opinion, argument, and tone reinforce the author's apparent purpose.

DIRECTIONS Answer the questions on the blank lines provided or by circling the letter of the correct response.

Identifying Purpose

1. How would you label the author's purpose?

    a. informative

    b. persuasive

What made you choose that purpose?

_____

_____

_____

_____

Fact and Opinion

2. Which one of these statements is a fact (F) and which one is an opinion (O)?

    a. In 2012, U.S. authorities received more than 3.3 million reports of abuse, representing about 6 million children, or 8% of the child population. _____

    b. In fact, parents receive every legal, social, and system opportunity to keep their families intact—too often putting the child at risk of emotional or physical harm. _____

Tone 3. When the author used the italicized words in the following passage, what response did she want to create in the reader? Please explain your answer.

"In 2012 in the United States, 23,439 children in foster care turned 18 and were 'emancipated' or 'aged out.' In simple terms, most of them *were put out into the world on their own without housing, financial assistance, or emotional support*"?

_____

4. Paragraph 5 opens with the transition "Make no mistake." What does that transition suggest about how the author wants readers to view the idea coming up next?

_____

5. Overall, what kind of tone comes through in the reading?
   a. sympathetic and determined
   b. formal and neutral
   c. furious but hopeful
   d. angry and disgusted

   What elements of the reading helped you make your choice?

_____

_____

_____

_____

_____

From Reader to Writer   Look up the name Mary Ellen Wilson. As a little girl, Mary Ellen had a profound effect on the American foster care system. In your writing, explain who she was and how her life and the people who helped her profoundly changed the lives of many young children.

▶ **READING 4** Hand-Me-Downs

Paula McLain

Looking Ahead Once a foster child, Paula McLain went on to become a best-selling author. In other words, she defied the odds, as they are described in the previous reading. Clearly, though, she has not forgotten what it's like to grow up as a foster child.

Word Watch Some of the more difficult words in the reading are defined below. The number in parentheses indicates the paragraph in which the word appears. An asterisk marks its first appearance in the reading. Preview the definitions before you begin reading and watch for the words while you read.

> **adhering (1):** sticking
>
> **stipulated (2):** stated explicitly
>
> **wards* (2):** those who are under the formal control or protection of others
>
> **lascivious (3):** indecent, expressing sexual desire in a sleazy way
>
> **innovative (6):** new and different

Getting Focused The preview says that McLain has not forgotten what it's like to grow up in foster care. Read for the specific details, both people and events, that defined the experience for the author.

What two things does the author's simile compare?

1 When I was 20, I worked in a nursing home. One day I overheard a conversation between Minnie, one of the veteran nursing assistants, and a woman named Amelia, who called her patients her babies. I was microwaving chicken-noodle soup, trying not to listen to Minnie sell the idea of foster-parenting to Amelia as if it were a piece of questionable real estate. "It's not bad at all," Minnie said, "and you can't beat the money." If they took in one more foster kid, they'd be able to swing buying a hot tub. My soup had gone volcanic, salty broth bubbling over the sides, adhering* to the bowl like a chicken-colored membrane. There was nothing to do but chuck the whole thing or dump it over Minnie's head to watch the noodles burn worm tracks down her face. That was the other way to go.

What inference does the author expect you to make to get from paragraph 1 to 2?

2 I was 4 when my parents left—separately, a few months apart—and my sisters—the eldest, Teresa, and the youngest, Penny, and I—were made wards* of the Fresno County Court. It was 1970. Because the court

order stipulated* that my sisters and I stay together, our social worker, Mrs. O'Rourk, had trouble placing us. We were an instant difficult family. Just add water. Like Sea Monkeys. Going to a group facility hung over our heads, and Mrs. O'Rourk used this to gain sympathy. It worked on our third set of foster parents, a young couple plagued by infertility and the nicest people we'd ever known.

Why does the author mention Sea Monkeys? How do they develop the sentence that came before?

How does the sentence beginning "But sympathy could not. . . ." affect the previous train of thought?

3   Our first night they told us we could call them Mom and Dad if we wanted, but only if we were comfortable. The next day, they took us to each pick out a bicycle. Rows and rows stood on their kickstands like shiny dominos. I thought, if this is the only good thing that happens, it will be enough. But sympathy could not have possibly prepared Samantha and Tom for us. We couldn't stop wetting the bed—even though we were 7, 8, and 10 by then—or the crying jags that came out of nowhere. And then there were the nightmares featuring shadows that looked a lot like our previous foster father, Mr. Clay, who, though he was old enough to be our grandfather, wasn't grandfatherly at all. He was creepy and lascivious.*

4   I remember sitting on the edge of my bed with my new mom, Samantha, who had led me in there after finding me behind the couch, touching myself. "It's not wrong, masturbation," she said. "It's just . . . people keep it to themselves." I knew she just wanted a normal kid; if not a baby, then at least a girl who had become sexualized in appropriate ways at appropriate times. Her face seemed to be wrestling with itself, eyebrows in a tight V, her top teeth after the same bit of skin, over and over. I had never heard the word *masturbation* before, but I told her I wouldn't do it anymore. I could see she didn't know what to do with us. You're doing fine, I wanted to say, better than anyone else ever has.

Why does the author include this description of Samantha's face?

5   One night, seven months into our stay, Samantha and Tom sat us down for a family talk. "The Mod Squad" was on TV, and I couldn't stop watching as Tom told us very slowly that his office was transferring him to San Francisco. We were wards of the court. We'd have to stay and find new parents.

6   Enter Erika and Bub. In their bedroom there was a space between the water bed and dresser just big enough for a girl to sidle into. Penny hid there when she called our old number to talk to Samantha. It happened several times. Finally Samantha had to phone Erika: someone needed to explain to Penny why she couldn't call anymore. We all had to move on; it was for the best. Samantha and Tom hadn't been transferred after all. Maybe the job fell through, or maybe there hadn't been one.

7   I was in the system for 14 years, with my sisters the whole time. This saved my life, I'm sure of it, and yet I remember wondering then whether we kept getting passed along because there were three of us. Recently,

this question arose, stingingly, once more when I heard of a pilot program in Massachusetts, where a handful of families are earning at least $20,000 a year to care for sibling groups. The pilot program, called Sib-Links, is a costly and innovative* response to a crisis in the foster-care system: the number of children needing care—more than half a million—has doubled since 1985, while the number of foster families has diminished slightly. It's too early to tell whether the new program will increase the number of foster parents or boost the level of care, but I fear the financial incentive will draw families driven less by good intentions than by hard need.

8   That day in the nursing home, as I stormed down the wheelchair-lined corridors, I couldn't help wondering if some of our foster parents took us in just for the checks. Maybe, but would that be any more painful than what happened with Samantha and Tom? I thought someone finally wanted us enough to keep us, no matter how tough it got. I was wrong.

("Hand-Me-Downs" by Paula McLain, as appeared in the *New York Times*, September 29, 2002. Used by permission of the author, Barer Literary, LLC.)

Monitoring Your Comprehension

The reading opens with the author thinking about throwing hot soup in her co-worker's face. If you can answer the questions—(1) What is the source of her rage? and (2) Why did she take the discussion so personally?—you have understood the reading.

GETTING THE GIST   These questions are the kind you might encounter on a standardized reading test.

DIRECTIONS   Identify the general gist, or point, of the author's words by circling the appropriate letter.

1. Which statement best sums up the main idea of this reading?

    a. Growing up in foster care prepared the author for life's hard knocks.

    b. Growing up in foster care helped the author forge deep bonds with her siblings.

    c. Growing up in foster care left the author with deep emotional wounds that could still bleed when she was reminded of the experience.

    d. Growing up in foster care has made the author wonder if everyone who is nice to her now is just pretending because she has both fame and fortune, making her life worth something in the eyes of others.

2. According to the author, Sib-Links is
   a. a very ineffective way to deal with foster care.
   b. a new and pricey way of dealing with foster care.
   c. bound to fail.
   d. a program with a long history of success.

3. The author suggests that Samantha and Tom gave them back to the state because
   a. the husband and wife were cruel people at heart.
   b. they just didn't know how to handle kids with such enormous problems.
   c. Tom had to take an important job out of state and they badly needed the money.
   d. the author misbehaved.

4. The author is worried that the Sib-Links program
   a. won't solve the problem of children in foster care who can find no home to go to.
   b. will be too costly to last.
   c. will encourage people to become foster parents in order to collect the money.
   d. will be one of the first programs to go if there are spending cuts.

5. Which statement best describes the relationship of this reading to the previous one by Rita Soronen?
   a. Like Rita Soronen, Paula McLain is concerned about what happens to teenagers who get too old to be enrolled in foster care.
   b. Unlike Rita Soronen, Paula McLain doesn't think the public can do much to change the foster care system.
   c. While Rita Soronen looks at the foster care system as an outsider who wants to improve it, Paula McLain recounts her own personal experience from inside the foster care system.
   d. Rita Soronen and Paula McLain don't agree when it comes to how to go about solving the problems that plague the foster care system.

TAKING A CLOSER LOOK   This set of questions focuses on your understanding of the text, both its content and the language used to convey that content.

DIRECTIONS   Answer the following questions on the blank lines provided or by circling the letter of the best response.

Recognizing Main Ideas

1. The main idea of this reading is
   a. expressed in a thesis statement.
   b. implied.

   What is the main idea of this reading?

   _____

   _____

   _____

Drawing Inferences

2. What does the author's description of her alternatives in paragraph 1 suggest about her reaction to Minnie's discussion of foster care?

   _____

3. In paragraph 3, what does the author suggest about Mr. Clay, one of her previous foster fathers?

   _____

   _____

   Please explain your answer.

   _____

   _____

   _____

   _____

4. What does the author suggest in paragraph 4, when she says "I knew she just wanted a normal kid; if not a baby, then at least a girl who had become sexualized in appropriate ways at appropriate times."

_____

_____

5. How does that sentence in paragraph 4 reinforce what was suggested in paragraph 3?

_____

_____

_____

6. What does the author's description of Samantha's face in paragraph 4 suggest about Samantha's reaction to the author's behavior?

_____

Recognizing Transitions

7. What kind of transition opens paragraph 5?

_____

Following the Author's Train of Thought

8. In paragraph 7, what does the pronoun _this_ in the second sentence refer to?

_____

_____

9. In paragraph 7, the third sentence opens with the phrase "Recently, this question arose." To which question is the author referring?

_____

_____

_____

10. By the last paragraph, the author tries to decide which of two alternatives is worse. What are the two alternatives?

_____

_____

_____

What does she decide?

_____

_____

_____

READING WITH A CRITICAL EYE   The goal here is not to be critical in the negative sense, but rather to understand how word choice, fact, opinion, argument, and tone reinforce the author's apparent purpose.

DIRECTIONS   Answer the questions on the blank lines provided or by circling the letter of the correct response.

Understanding Figurative Language

1. The author uses the following simile in paragraph 1. What does she want to suggest with this comparison?
"I was microwaving chicken-noodle soup, trying not to listen to Minnie sell the idea of foster-parenting to Amelia as if it were a piece of questionable real estate."

_____

_____

_____

2. In paragraph 2, the author uses another simile, comparing her family to Sea Monkeys. Sea Monkeys were, for a while, a popular product in aquariums. Just add water and salt, and they came to life (for a little while at least). What is the author's comparison of her difficult family to Sea Monkeys meant to tell readers about her family's behavior?

_____

_____

Tone **3.** Which word best describes the author's tone?

    a. hopeful about the future

    b. cool and neutral

    c. sarcastic and angry

    d. bitter and sad

4. Why does the author describe how her sister hid in a little space in order to hide and call Samantha? Why include such a specific descriptive detail?

_____

_____

_____

5. In paragraph 1, the author says her soup had gone *volcanic*. Why do you think she chose that particular word?

_____

_____

From Reader to Writer Paula McLain does not fit the pattern described in the previous reading. She left foster care, worked at a variety of jobs, got herself through school, earned a Master of Fine Arts in poetry, and went on to write a best-selling novel called *The Paris Wife*. Write a few paragraphs explaining what you think it takes for people to overcome a childhood that suggests the world is a place of danger and disappointment. What characteristics do you think such people have? What role do friends play? What about just plain luck?

Use McLain's life as she describes it in the reading to introduce your ideas about what kind of people seem capable of overcoming a painful childhood. Of course you can also use someone else's biography to pave the way for your thoughts about people who survive and thrive despite childhood trauma. Maybe you have read *The Autobiography of Malcolm X* or about Temple Grandin, a woman who didn't let severe autism defeat her dreams of achievement.

Brief descriptions of their lives would also provide a good introduction to your ideas on what makes for a survivor. And the person in your introduction doesn't have to be famous. You can also use a relative or friend if you know someone who has created a relatively successful life despite a terrible start. The main point of your writing is to tell readers what you think makes a successful survivor.

▶ **READING 5**   The Altruistic Personality

Sharon S. Brehm, Saul M. Kassin, and Steven Fein

Looking Ahead   In this reading from a sociology textbook, the authors try to understand what makes some people willing to put the interests of others before their own.

Word Watch   Some of the more difficult words in the reading are defined below. The number in parentheses indicates the paragraph in which the word appears. An asterisk marks its first appearance in the reading. Preview the definitions before you begin reading and watch for the words while you read.

---

altruistic (2): exhibiting unselfish concern for the welfare of others

genetically (2): related to biological inheritance

empathy (5): understanding of another person's situation or feelings

fraternal twins (5): developed from two separate eggs (identical twins develop from one egg)

heritable (5): capable of being passed by birth from one generation to the next

variables (9): characteristics, events, or things that can change with time or context

pro-social (10): caring about the welfare of others

collectivist (11): valuing the group's well-being over all else

individualist (11): valuing the individual person's well-being over all else

extroversion (11): interest in other people, interest in the world outside one's own mind

---

Getting Focused   The title, "The Altruistic Personality," tells you the topic. But that's just the subject matter. Read to discover what the authors have to say about the altruistic personality. Does it exist? If so, what character traits does it seem to consist of? And what does the research say about the origins of an altruistic personality? Is it inherited or shaped by environment? These are the kinds of questions you should be able to answer once you finish reading.

TEXTBOOK TIP

As much as or even more than psychology texts, sociology text-books use research to back up their descriptions of how people function in society. In addition to understanding the details of each study mentioned (e.g., who conducted the study, what they were looking for, and what methods were used), make sure you know *why* the study is present in the text. That means knowing what main idea is explained or supported by the studies. Studies are in a text to prove or illustrate a point. Make sure you know what that point is.

Based on the title, preview, and quotation, what do you think this reading will explore?

"The purpose of human life is to serve and to show compassion and the will to help others."

—Albert Schweitzer[†]

1   When we think about extreme acts of helping, or of failing to help, or when we think about long-term, well-planned acts of helping such as volunteer-ing at a clinic or shelter or serving as a Big Brother or Big Sister, we tend to wonder about the nature of the people involved.

2   Researchers have even tried to identify an *altruistic* personality*, one that distinguishes people who help from those who don't. Some research has focused on whether certain people tend to be more helpful across situ-ations than others. Other research has asked whether and to what extent unselfishness and a willingness to give to others might be genetically* based. Several studies have sought to identify what general personality characteristics and traits comprise the altruistic personality.

Are Some People More Helpful Than Others?

As soon as the heading poses a question, start looking for the answer.

3   When Daniel Santos's friends and co-workers learned of his heroics in jumping 150 feet off the Tappan Zee Bridge to save a stranger, they were not surprised. "That's just how he is," said a fellow volunteer firefighter. "If he sees something, he's going to go and try to help out that person." A receptionist at the company where he worked as a mechanic added, "He will help anyone at any place and any time." His sister noted that he leaped into the water even though he's not a strong swimmer. "He has a good heart," she said (Fitz-Gibbon & Siemaszko, 1996, p. 7).

4   Are there people who are generally helpful across all situations? Are there others who are generally unhelpful? Although the specific situa-tion clearly can overwhelm individual differences in influencing helping

---

[†]Albert Schweitzer (1875–1965) was a doctor and philosopher, who devoted himself to medical missionary work.

behaviors, researchers have provided some evidence for individual differences in helping tendencies. These tendencies seem to endure in a variety of settings. People who are more helpful than others in one situation are likely to be more helpful in other situations as well. In addition, a long-term study by Nancy Eisenberg and others (1999) suggests that this individual difference may be relatively stable over time. Specifically, they found that the degree to which preschool children exhibited spontaneous helping behavior predicted how helpful they would be in later childhood and early adulthood.

Remember, if you see a reference to a study, make sure you know both what it proves and what it contributes to the overall main idea.

5   According to J. Philippe Rushton and his colleagues (1984), this individual difference in helpfulness is, in part, genetically based. Studies of twins offer some support for Rushton's argument. Genetically identical twins are more similar to each other in their helpful behavioral tendencies and their helping-related emotions and reactions, such as empathy,* than are fraternal twins* who share only a portion of their genetic make-up. These findings suggest that there may be a heritable* component to helpfulness.

What Is the Altruistic Personality?

6   Even if we identify some people who help others a lot and other people who don't, we have not addressed the question of what distinguishes people who help from those who don't—other than their helpfulness, of course. What are the various components of the altruistic personality? Can we predict who is likely to be altruistic by looking at people's overall personalities?

7   Consider some examples of people who have acted very altruistically. Do they seem to have very similar personality traits and characteristics? Think, for example, about Oskar Schindler[†] and how he cheated in business and in his marriage. Could anyone have predicted his altruistic actions from his overall personality? It is doubtful.

What do all the people described in paragraphs 7 and 8 have in common?

8   What about more contemporary models of altruism? In 1997, Ted Turner, founder of numerous cable stations and owner of professional sports teams, pledged a personal donation of one billion dollars to the United Nations. Not to be outdone, by July 2000 Microsoft Chairman Bill Gates had pledged 22 billion dollars to charity. Actor Paul Newman donated all of the millions of dollars in profits that were generated by his brands of salad dressing, spaghetti sauce, popcorn, and the like to charities, such as his camp for children living with a fatal disease. And until her

---

[†]Oskar Schindler (1908–1974): a German businessman famous for helping Jews to escape from Nazi Germany and the subject of the hit film *Schindler's List.*

death in 1997, Mother Teresa devoted her life to the poor in India. These four well-known figures seem quite different from each other in overall personality—except for their concern with helping others.

9   The quest to discover the altruistic personality has not been an easy one. Much of the research conducted over the years has failed to find consistent, reliable personality characteristics that predict helping behavior across situations. Situational variables* have predicted people's helping behaviors much better than personality variables.

10   Some researchers have changed the nature of the quest, however, focusing on personality variables that predict helping in some specific situations rather than across all situations; and their studies have been more successful in identifying traits that predict such behavior (Carlo et al., 1991; Penner et al., 1995). George Knight and his colleagues (1994) have suggested that an interacting group of personality traits influences pro-social* behavior and responses differ depending on the situation. For example, in dangerous emergencies, people who are high in self-confidence and independence are more likely to help than other people, but they are no more likely to help in response to a request to donate money to a charity.

11   Personality variables, or traits, that have been associated with greater helpfulness in some contexts include the following: empathy toward others; a tendency to attribute the causes of events to individual control rather than external circumstances; a collectivist* rather than an individualist* orientation; and extroversion,* openness to experience, and agreeableness (Bierhof et al., 1991; Kosek, 1995; Moorman & Blakely, 1995). And whether or not people have the traits associated with pro-social behavior, if they can be convinced or motivated to believe that they are altruistic, their behavior may follow. For example, labeling someone as a helpful person seems to increase that individual's helpful behavior.

The transition "in sum" is a sign to slow down; here's where a key point will be explicitly stated.

12   In sum, research provides some insight into the traits and characteristics that may be associated with helpful behavioral tendencies. However, more research is needed before a conclusion can be reached about the make-up of the altruistic personality. The research thus far does point to two qualities that seem essential for such a personality: empathy and advanced moral reasoning. (Adapted from Sharon S. Brehm, Saul Kassin, and Steven Fein, *Social Psychology*, 5th ed., © 2002 Cengage Learning.)

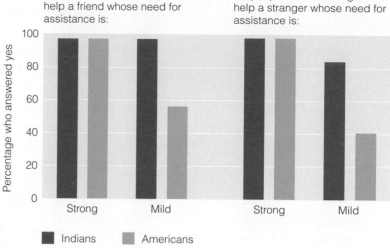

Figure 3 The Sense of Social Responsibility in India Compared to the United States

These results compare the proportion of children and adults in India with the proportion of children and adults in the United States who said that people have an obligation to help others, both friends and strangers. (Source of data: J. G. Miller et al., 1990.)

Close Up on Visual Aids

●

Bar graphs like the one shown in Figure 3 help readers make comparisons. They are a visual method of indicating degrees of difference between two groups. Longer bars indicate that one group has more of what's being measured while the group represented by the shorter bar has less. The caption following the figure number will usually tell you what is being measured.

1. In the case of the bar graph accompanying the reading on altruism, what two groups are being compared?

_____

2. What's being measured?

_____

3. The first set of bars on the left labeled "Strong" tells readers that

Indians and Americans _____

_____ .

4. The second set on the left labeled "Mild" indicates that _____

_____

_____.

5. On the right side of the graph, the bars labeled "Strong" empha-

size _____

_____ The bars labeled "Mild" show that _____

_____

_____.

Monitoring Your Comprehension Review the marginal annotations and answer any questions posed. If you can't answer a question, mark the sentence or paragraph referred to and re-read it before turning to the comprehension and critical reading questions.

GETTING THE GIST These questions are the kind you might encounter on a standardized reading test.

DIRECTIONS Identify the general gist, or point, of the authors' words by circling the appropriate letter.

1. Which statement best expresses the main idea of the entire reading?
   a. Research has proven that altruistic behavior has no genetic basis.
   b. Research on the altruistic personality suggests that certain personal characteristics and situations do seem to predispose, or encourage, an individual to help others.
   c. So far, researchers have been unable to construct any reliable studies for identifying the characteristics that make up an altruistic personality. However, one characteristic in particular, self-confidence, does seem to be mentioned as significant in several different studies.
   d. People who readily help others all have very similar personalities: They are affectionate by nature and enjoy extending a helping hand even if it means discomfort or danger for themselves.

2. According to the reading, researchers have discovered that
   a. we are all equally capable of altruism, but we don't all get the same chance to express it.
   b. we would all grow up to be hopelessly self-centered and self-absorbed if adults didn't model altruistic behavior for us.
   c. people differ in their capacity for altruism.
   d. women are more naturally altruistic than men.

3. Why do the authors mention Oskar Schindler, Ted Turner, Bill Gates, Paul Newman, and Mother Teresa?
   a. They illustrate the idea that donating large sums of money is a common behavior of people with altruistic personalities.
   b. They are all examples of people who were altruistic from childhood on.
   c. They illustrate the idea that people who behave in altruistic ways can have very different personalities.
   d. They support the authors' point that extremely altruistic people always become famous.

4. According to the reading, research on altruism
   a. has given us a clear picture of the altruistic personality.
   b. has indicated that true altruism does not exist.
   c. has been difficult to carry out for an extended period of time.
   d. hasn't come up with any definite conclusions about what makes a person altruistic.

5. According to the reading, which two characteristics seem likely to be essential to altruistic behavior?
   a. an affectionate nature and a high degree of self-confidence
   b. an outgoing personality and an enthusiastic attitude
   c. a capacity for empathy and advanced moral reasoning
   d. rigidity of character and a tendency to be outspoken

TAKING A CLOSER LOOK This set of questions focuses on your understanding of the text, both its content and the language used to convey that content.

DIRECTIONS Answer the following questions on the blank lines provided or by circling the letter of the best response.

Identifying Supporting Details

1. In general, the researchers described in this reading haven't come to many clear conclusions about the nature of altruism, but they haven't come up completely empty either. In your own words, name the three things we now know about altruism as a result of the research described.

   1. _____

   2. _____

   3. _____

   _____

Monitoring Your Comprehension

2. Having read this selection, how would you answer if someone asked you, "Are some people more inclined than others to be altruistic?" _____ What paragraph or paragraphs in the reading would support your answer? _____

3. Paragraph 4 opens with two questions. Where do the answers to these questions appear? _____

Recognizing Main Ideas

4. The work of J. Philippe Rushton supports what main idea about altruism?

   _____

Recognizing Patterns of Organization

5. The heading for paragraph 6, "What Is the Altruistic Personality?" suggests which pattern of organization?
   a. definition
   b. simple listing
   c. classification
   d. comparison and contrast

Constructing the Main Idea Statement

6. Which sentence in paragraph 8 could play the role of the topic sentence, as long as the reader added the names of the people discussed in the paragraph?

_____

Paraphrasing

7. Which statement is the best paraphrase of this sentence from paragraph 9? "Situational variables have predicted people's helping behaviors much better than personality variables."

   a. People are always ready to reach out to others when a situation is life threatening, but they are much less inclined to do so when financial help is needed.

   b. Researchers are more comfortable describing some specific situations that encourage altruism than they are defining the personality traits linked to altruistic behavior.

   c. Researchers have been able to determine the personality traits related to altruistic behavior, but they don't know what situations call forth expressions of altruism.

Drawing Inferences

8. To see to it that the opening sentence of paragraph 10 makes sense in terms of the rest of the reading, what word or words does the reader need to add after the word *quest*?

_____

Following the Author's Train of Thought

9. In paragraphs 10 and 11, what phrase do the authors start using to refer to altruistic actions?

_____

Transitions and Paraphrasing

10. By the end of the reading, the authors describe a shift in what researchers on altruism are looking for. What sentence opening announces that shift?

_____

Describe the shift in your own words.

_____

_____

_____

READING WITH A CRITICAL EYE   The goal here is not to be critical in the negative sense, but rather to understand how fact, opinion, argument, and tone reinforce the authors' apparent purpose.

DIRECTIONS   Answer the questions on the blank lines provided or by circling the letter of the best response.

Fact and Opinion   1. Label the following statements from the reading as *F* for fact, *O* for opinion, or *M* for mix of both.

a. "Researchers have even tried to identify an altruistic personality."

_____

b. "The quest to discover the altruistic personality has not been an easy one." _____

c. "George Knight and his colleagues have suggested that an interacting group of personality traits influences pro-social behavior."

_____

d. "Research provides some insight into the traits and characteristics that may be associated with helpful behavioral tendencies."

_____

Recognizing the Authors' Point of View   2. In paragraph 5, how do the authors indicate that they think researcher J. Philippe Rushton may be on the right track concerning the origins of altruism?

_____

_____

3. In paragraph 10, the authors discuss the research of George Knight. Do they also think that he is on the right track with his research? ____ Please explain.

_____

_____

Identifying Purpose   4. What is the authors' primary purpose?

a. The authors want to describe current research suggesting that altruism may be inborn.

b. The authors want to describe researchers' efforts to discover the nature and origin of altruism.

c. The authors want to encourage their readers to be more altruistic.

d. The authors want to convince readers that altruism has a genetic basis.

Tone 5. How would you describe the authors' tone?

a. confident

b. casual

c. skeptical

d. neutral

From Reader to Writer Martin Luther King Jr. said, "Every man must decide if he will walk in the light of creative altruism or in the darkness of destructive selfishness." Write two or three paragraphs in which you explain why King called altruism "creative" and "selfishness" destructive. In your final paragraph, explain why you think King was right or wrong in labeling altruism creative and selfishness destructive.

WEB QUEST

Who coined the word *altruism*? _____ . How was the word initially defined? _____

_____ . Around a century after the word *altruism* first came into being, a novelist and would-be philosopher named Ayn Rand took a stand on altruism. What was her position? _____

_____ .

▶ **READING 6**   Memory, Perception, and Eyewitness Testimony

Douglas A. Bernstein, Louis A. Penner, Alison Clarke-Stewart,
and Edward J. Roy

Looking Ahead   Reading 7 will talk about crime from the criminal's point of view. This one discusses it from the point of view of the eyewitness. In many criminal cases, defendants are convicted based on what eyewitnesses say they saw. However, in this selection from a psychology textbook, the authors point out the dangers of trusting eyewitness testimony.

Word Watch   Some of the more difficult words in the reading are defined below. The number in parentheses indicates the paragraph in which the word appears. An asterisk marks its first appearance in the reading. Preview the definitions before you begin reading and watch for the words while you read.

> **constructive memory (1):** the theory that memories can be transformed when the mind adds later experiences to the original remembrance
>
> **DNA evidence (1):** proof based on the body's DNA molecules, which are like a blueprint for everything in an individual's body; this means that, except in the case of identical twins, DNA evidence is unique to the person from whom it was derived
>
> **perceive (2):** recognize; absorb into consciousness
>
> **stimulus (2):** something that causes a response
>
> **assumption (4):** belief that is considered to be true and therefore does not require proof
>
> **prosecution (5):** related to the lawyers who make a case against a defendant during legal proceedings
>
> **inherent (8):** inborn; naturally a part of
>
> **amplified (8):** made more powerful
>
> **miscarriages (11):** failures
>
> **arrays (12):** arrangements

Getting Focused   In this selection, the authors are inclined to follow general statements with specific examples. Try paraphrasing the general statements in the margins. Then use arrows to point out the examples. To take your understanding a step deeper, write your own examples in the margins across from the authors' examples.

TEXTBOOK TIP Psychology texts usually include broad general statements about human behavior and thinking. But they seldom generalize without offering specific incidents, examples, or studies that support the general point. Each time you see a general statement about how people are likely to behave or think, make sure you can match the general statement with the proof of its accuracy.

As you read, notice the way references to mistakes have become a constant theme.

Here you have a typical textbook template in which the last sentence of the first paragraph tells readers what the chapter section will do.

1   There are few situations in which accurate retrieval of memories is more important—and constructive memory* is more dangerous—than when an eyewitness testifies in court about a crime. Eyewitnesses provide the most compelling evidence in many trials, but they can sometimes be mistaken. In 1984, for example, a North Carolina college student, Jennifer Thompson, confidently identified Ronald Cotton as the man who had raped her at knifepoint. Mainly on the basis of Thompson's testimony, Cotton was convicted of rape and sentenced to life in prison. After eleven years behind bars, DNA evidence* revealed that he was innocent (and it identified another man as the rapist). The eyewitness victim's certainty had convinced a jury, but her memory had been faulty (O'Neill, 2000). Let's consider the accuracy of eyewitness memory and how it can be distorted.

2   Like the rest of us, eyewitnesses can remember only what they perceive,* and they can perceive only what they attend to. Perception is influenced by a combination of the stimulus* features we find "out there" in the world and what we already know, expect, or want.

After you finish paragraphs 3 and 4, see if you can paraphrase two of the "limits" mentioned here.

3   Witnesses are asked to report exactly what they saw or heard; but no matter how hard they try to be accurate, there are limits to how faithful their reports can be. For one thing, during the time that information is encoded and stored in long-term memory, certain details can be lost. Further, the appearance of new information, including information contained in questions posed by police or lawyers, can alter a witness's memory (Belli & Loftus, 1996). In one study, when witnesses were asked, "How fast were the cars going when they *smashed into* each other?" they were likely to recall a higher speed than when they were asked, "How fast were the cars going when they *hit* each other?" (Loftus & Palmer, 1974). See Figure 4.

Note the category word *ways*. Make sure you can itemize them by the end of the paragraph.

4   There is also evidence that an object mentioned during questioning about an incident is often mistakenly remembered as having been there during the incident. So if a lawyer says that a screwdriver was lying on the ground (when it was not), witnesses often recall with great certainty having seen it. This *misinformation effect* can occur in several ways. In some cases, hearing new information can make it harder to retrieve the original

Question	Verb	Estimated mph
About how fast were the cars going when they _____ each other?	smashed into	40.8
	hit	34.0
	contacted	30.8

Original information — **External information** (About how fast were the cars going when they SMASHED INTO each other?) — **The "memory"**

Figure 4   The Impact of Questioning on Eyewitness Memory

After seeing a filmed traffic accident, people were asked, "About how fast were the cars going when they (smashed into, hit, or contacted) each other?" As shown here, the witnesses' responses were influenced by the verb used in the question; "smashed" was associated with the highest average speed estimates. A week later, people who heard the "smashed" question remembered the accident as being more violent than did people in the other two groups (Loftus & Palmer, 1974).

(From G. R. Loftus and E. F. Loftus, *Human Memory: The Processing of Information*. Copyright 1976. Reprinted with permission of Lawrence Erlbaum Associates, Inc.)

memory. In others, the new information may be integrated into the old memory, making it impossible to distinguish the new information from what was originally seen (Loftus, 1992). In still others, an eyewitness report might be influenced by the person's assumption* that if a lawyer or police officer says an object was there or that something happened, it must be true.

How can the way a witness testifies make a difference?

5   A jury's belief in a witness's testimony often depends as much (or even more) on *how* the witness presents evidence as on the content or relevance of that evidence (Leippe, Manion, & Romanczyk, 1992). Many jurors are impressed, for example, by witnesses who give lots of details about what they saw or heard. Extremely detailed testimony from prosecution* witnesses is especially likely to lead to guilty verdicts, even when the details reported are irrelevant (Bell & Loftus, 1989). When a witness gives highly detailed testimony, such as the exact time of the crime or the color of the criminal's shoes, jurors apparently assume that the witness paid especially close attention or has a particularly accurate memory.

What does "at first glance" suggest about what follows?

6   At first glance, these assumptions seem reasonable. However, the ability to divide attention is limited. As a result, witnesses might be able to focus attention on the crime and the criminal, or on the surrounding details, but probably not on both—particularly if they were emotionally aroused and the crime happened quickly. So witnesses who accurately remember unimportant details of a crime scene may not accurately recall more important ones, such as the criminal's facial features (Backman & Nilsson, 1991).

How can you tell from the first sentence that the authors are continuing the same train of thought?

7   Juries also tend to believe witnesses who are confident. Unfortunately, witnesses' confidence in their testimony often exceeds its accuracy (Shaw, 1996). Repeated exposure to misinformation and the repeated recall of misinformation can increase a witness's confidence in testimony, whether or not it is accurate. In other words, as in the Jennifer Thompson case, even witnesses who are confident about their testimony are not always correct.

8   The weaknesses inherent* in eyewitness memory can be amplified* by the use of police lineups and certain other criminal identification procedures (Wells & Olson, 2003). In one study, for example, participants watched a videotaped crime and then tried to identify the criminal from a set of photographs (Wells & Bradfield, 1999). None of the photos showed the person who had committed the crime, but some participants nevertheless identified one of them as the criminal they saw on tape.

What new element has been introduced that adds to the possibility of error?

9   When these mistaken participants were led to believe that they had correctly identified the criminal, they became even more confident in the accuracy of their false identification. These incorrect, but confident, witnesses became more likely than other participants to claim that it had been easy for them to identify the criminal from the photos because they had had a good view of him and had paid careful attention to him.

Remember Ronald Cotton from the opening of the reading? Why is he referred to now?

10   Since 1973, at least 115 people, including Ronald Cotton, have been released from U.S. prisons in twenty-five states after DNA tests or other evidence revealed that they had been falsely convicted—mostly on the basis of faulty eyewitness testimony (Death Penalty Information Center, 2004; Scheck, Neufeld, & Dwyer, 2000; Wells, Malpass, et al., 2000). DNA evidence freed Charles Fain, who had been convicted of murder and spent almost eighteen years on death row in Idaho (Bonner, 2001). Maryland officials approved $900,000 in compensation for Bernard Webster, who served 20 years in prison for rape before DNA revealed that he was innocent (Associated Press, 2003).

11   Frank Lee Smith, too, would have been set free after the sole eyewitness at his murder trial retracted her testimony, but he had already died of

cancer while awaiting execution in a Florida prison. Research on memory and perception helps explain how these miscarriages* of justice can occur, and it is also guiding efforts to prevent such errors in the future.

12   The U.S. Department of Justice has acknowledged the potential for errors in eyewitness evidence, as well as the dangers of asking witnesses to identify suspects from lineups and photo arrays.* The result was *Eyewitness Evidence: A Guide for Law Enforcement* (U.S. Department of Justice, 1999), the first-ever guide for police and prosecutors who work with eyewitnesses. The guide warns these officials that asking leading questions about what witnesses saw can distort their memories. It also suggests that witnesses should examine photos of possible suspects one at a time and points out that false identifications are less likely if witnesses viewing suspects in a lineup are told that the real criminal might not be included.

(From Douglas A. Bernstein et al., *Psychology*, 7th ed., © 2006 Cengage Learning.)

Monitoring Your Comprehension   Review the marginal annotations and answer any questions posed. If you can't answer the questions, mark the sentence or paragraph referred to and re-read it before turning to the comprehension and critical reading questions.

> **GETTING THE GIST**   These questions are the kind you might encounter on a standardized reading test.

> **DIRECTIONS**   Identify the general gist, or point, of the authors' words by circling the appropriate letter.

1. Which statement best expresses the main idea of the entire reading?
    a. The wording of questions can distort the memories of crime victims and eyewitnesses.
    b. Because eyewitnesses can and do make mistakes, innocent people have been wrongly convicted of crimes.
    c. People's memories are, in general, not very reliable, but eyewitnesses are particularly inclined to distort reality.
    d. Many innocent people have been convicted of crimes they did not commit; fortunately, DNA evidence has been used to exonerate them and set them free.

2. What do the authors say about police procedures used to identify wrongdoers?

a. Some of the techniques police use are helpful whereas others are not.

b. Having crime victims look at photographs is an ineffective criminal identification technique.

c. Procedures that police use to help eyewitnesses identify criminals can encourage distorted memories of events.

d. Eyewitnesses are intimidated by police authority and tend to say what the police want them to say.

3. Why do the authors mention victim Jennifer Thompson and/or accused rapist Ronald Cotton three times throughout the reading?

a. They illustrate the authors' point that the wording of questions often distorts eyewitnesses' memories.

b. Their example supports the idea that, in spite of its flaws, eyewitness testimony is usually accurate.

c. They illustrate the idea that bystander-eyewitnesses tend to recall details more accurately than victim eyewitnesses do.

d. Their story supports the idea that an individual can be falsely convicted on the basis of eyewitness testimony.

4. According to the authors, jury members often make the mistake of believing eyewitnesses who

a. speak clearly and slowly.

b. are confident and remember lots of details.

c. correct themselves during their testimony in order to make sure that what they say is accurate.

d. admit that they were scared during the commission of the crime.

5. According to the authors, the government

a. shares their point of view about the inaccuracy of eyewitness testimony.

b. doesn't believe that eyewitness testimony is prone to so much error.

c. recognizes the potential for error in eyewitness testimony.

d. has no interest in improving the accuracy of eyewitness testimony.

TAKING A CLOSER LOOK This set of questions focuses on your understanding of the text, both its content and the language used to convey that content.

DIRECTIONS Answer the following questions on the blank lines provided or by circling the letter of the best response.

Recognizing Thesis Statements

1. The thesis statement of the reading appears in
   a. paragraph 1.
   b. paragraph 2.
   c. paragraph 3.

   The thesis statement appears
   a. at the beginning of the paragraph.
   b. right after a reversal transition.
   c. at the end.
   d. at the beginning and the end.

Paraphrasing

2. In paragraph 2, the authors say perception is influenced by two factors. In your own words what are those two factors?

   1. _____

   2. _____

Recognizing Topic Sentences

3. The topic sentence in paragraph 3 is
   a. the first sentence.
   b. the second sentence.
   c. in the middle of the paragraph.
   d. the last sentence of the paragraph.

4. In your own words, what does that topic sentence of paragraph 3 tell readers?

   _____

   _____

Recognizing Transitions

5. What two transitions introduce support for the main idea of paragraph 3?

_____

Making Connections

6. Does paragraph 4 continue to develop the main idea from paragraph 3 or does it introduce a new point?

_____

Understanding Supporting Details

7. Why is a screwdriver mentioned in paragraph 4?

_____

_____

_____

Paraphrasing

8. Which of the following statements accurately paraphrases the *misinformation effect* introduced in paragraph 4?

a. Human memory is limited in the amount of detail it can store and some details of an experience are bound to get forgotten.

b. Information people hear or see after an event has occurred often gets added to the memory of the event.

c. When people are told by an authority figure that something is true, they are inclined to believe it.

Understanding Supporting Details

9. What category word in paragraph 4 directs readers to the major supporting details? _____

Following the Author's Train of Thought

10. Paragraph 6 opens with the statement, "At first glance, these assumptions seem reasonable." What does the phrase "these assumptions" refer to?

_____

_____

Making Connections

11. What should that opening phrase in paragraph 6 suggest to readers?

_____

Recognizing Topic Sentences

12. In paragraph 8, the topic sentence is
    a. the first sentence.
    b. the second sentence.
    c. the concluding sentence.
    d. the opening and closing sentences.

Understanding Supporting Details

13. Why are Ronald Cotton, Charles Fain, Bernard Webster, and Frank Lee Smith mentioned in paragraphs 10 and 11?

    _____

    _____

Recognizing Patterns of Organization

14. What is the primary organizational pattern in this reading?

    _____

Understanding Supporting Details

15. The reference to *Eyewitness Evidence: A Guide for Law Enforcement* appears in paragraph 12 to back up what point?

    _____

    _____

Close Up on Visual Aids
●

Look closely at Figure 4. Like the figure on page 732, this one makes use of arrows, and the direction of the arrows is important. In your own words, what do the arrows indicate about the relationship between *Question*, *Verb*, and *Estimated mph*?

_____

_____

Box by box, explain what the boxes labeled *Original information*, *External information*, and *The "memory"* illustrate for the reader.

1. "Original information" shows _____.

2. "External information" shows _____.

3. "The memory" indicates _____

    _____.

READING WITH A CRITICAL EYE   The goal here is not to be critical in the negative sense, but rather to understand how fact, opinion, argument, and tone reinforce the authors' apparent purpose.

DIRECTIONS   Answer the questions on the blank lines provided or by circling the letter of the correct response.

Fact and Opinion   **1.** The following statement in paragraph 5 is an opinion: "A jury's belief in a witness's testimony often depends as much (or even more) on *how* the witness presents evidence as on the content or relevance of that evidence." How would you describe this opinion?

    a. informed

    b. uninformed

Please explain.

_____

_____

Recognizing Tone   **2.** How would you describe the authors' tone?

    a. infuriated

    b. puzzled

    c. argumentative

    d. confident

Identifying Purpose   **3.** Can you cite passages in the text where the authors suggest an opposing point of view about eyewitness testimony? _____ What does that suggest to you?

_____

_____

4. What do you think is the authors' primary purpose?

    a. The authors want to tell readers about the various ways eyewitness testimony can occasionally be inaccurate.

    b. The authors want to convince readers that eyewitness testimony cannot be completely trusted.

Recognizing Bias 5. How would you describe the authors' attitude toward eyewitness testimony?

    a. The authors know that eyewitnesses can make mistakes, but they still have faith in eyewitness testimony as evidence.

    b. The authors think that eyewitness testimony is too flawed to be completely trusted as evidence.

    c. It's impossible to determine what the authors think.

From Reader to Writer Write two or three paragraphs summarizing the reasons why, according to the authors, eyewitness testimony can't be trusted.

▶ READING 7   Is Neutralization Necessary?

Larry J. Siegel

Looking Ahead This selection comes from a criminology textbook. But it too deals with the issue of how self-concept and self-esteem affect behavior.

Word Watch Some of the more difficult words in the reading are defined below. The number in parentheses indicates the paragraph in which the word appears. An asterisk marks its first appearance in the reading. Preview the definitions before you begin reading and watch for the words while you read.

> **subterranean (2):** underground
>
> **justifications (4):** explanations as to why behavior is appropriate or right
>
> **novice (4):** new, inexperienced
>
> **inconclusive (5):** not leading to a definite conclusion or eliminating doubt
>
> **norms (6):** rules or standards for social behavior
>
> **data (7):** information
>
> **gleaned (7):** gathered, figured out, gradually understood
>
> **provocation (8):** cause or reason for action
>
> **whim (9):** quickly changing mood or desire
>
> **opportunism (9):** readiness to take advantage of others without regard for the consequences
>
> **universally (10):** done or felt by all people in a group, appearing in all cultures

Getting Focused Make sure you determine what the term *neutralization* in the context of criminology means. Also, since the title questions how necessary it is, there must be some opposition, challenge, or contradiction described in the reading. Be on the lookout for some person or group who doesn't think neutralization is important.

TEXTBOOK TIP Criminology, like communications, sociology, and psychology, focuses on theories of behavior. Only within the context of criminology, the focus is on criminal behavior, rather than the everyday behavior of ordinary life.

Look for the names of the people who came up with theories about why people engage in criminal behavior. Make sure you understand the theory or theories they have proposed and be on the lookout as well for criticism or challenges to the explanations offered. Textbooks likely to offer theoretical explanations are just as likely to offer opposition to or criticisms of those explanations.

1   *Neutralization Theory* is identified with the writings of David Matza and his associate Gresham Sykes. They view the process of becoming a criminal as a learning experience in which potential delinquents and criminals master techniques that enable them to counterbalance or *neutralize* conventional, or traditional, values and drift back and forth between illegitimate and conventional behavior.

2   One reason this is possible is the subterranean* value structure of American society. **Subterranean values** are morally tinged influences that have become entrenched in the culture but are publicly condemned. They exist side by side with conventional values and while condemned in public may be admired or practiced in private. Examples include viewing pornographic films, drinking alcohol to excess, and gambling on sporting events.

Typically for academic writing, the pronoun this *is the link to the previous paragraph.*

3   Matza argues that even the most committed criminals and delinquents are not involved in criminality all the time. They also attend schools, family functions, and religious services. Their behavior can be conceived as falling along a continuum between total freedom and total restraint. This process, which he calls **drift**, refers to the movement from one extreme of behavior to another, resulting in behavior that is sometimes unconventional, free, or deviant, and at other times constrained and sober. Learning techniques of neutralization enable a person to temporarily "drift away" from conventional behavior and get involved in more subterranean values and behaviors, including crime and drug abuse.

What does drift *have to do with* neutralization?

4   Sykes and Matza suggest that people develop a distinct set of justifications* for their law-violating behavior. These techniques of neutralization include the following patterns:

1. *Deny responsibility.* Offenders sometimes claim their unlawful acts were simply not their fault. Criminal acts resulted from forces beyond their control or were accidents.

2. *Deny injury.* Criminals neutralize illegal behavior by denying the wrongfulness of the act. For example, stealing is viewed as borrowing. Vandalism is considered mischief that has gotten out of hand.

Never ignore a list, especially one with an italicized term after each number. This is practically an announcement for an essay question,

"Describe the techniques of neutralization."

3. *Deny the victim.* Criminals sometimes neutralize wrongdoing by maintaining that the victim of crime "had it coming." Vandalism may be directed against a disliked teacher or neighbor; or homosexuals may be beaten up by a gang because their behavior is considered offensive.
4. *Condemn condemners.* An offender views the world as a corrupt place with a dog-eat-dog code. Because police and judges are on the take, teachers show favoritism, and parents take out their frustrations on their kids, it is ironic and unfair for these authorities to condemn his or her misconduct.
5. *Appeal to higher loyalties.* Novice* criminals often argue that they are caught in the dilemma of being loyal to their own peer group while at the same time attempting to abide by the rules of the larger society.

In sum, the theory of neutralization suggests that people who engage in deviant behavior neutralize that behavior with slogans like "I didn't mean to do it." "They had it coming to them." "Everyone is picking on me."

Testing Neutralization Theory

The heading says the author's explanation is changing direction.

5 Attempts have been made to verify the assumptions of neutralization theory. But the results have been inconclusive.* So far the evidence is mixed. Some studies show that law violators approve of criminal behavior. Still others find evidence that even though they may be active participants themselves, criminals voice disapproval of illegal behavior.

Sometimes Being Bad Is Good

6 In their neutralization theory, Sykes and Matza claim that neutralizations provide offenders with a means of preserving a noncriminal self-concept even as they engage in crime and deviance. Sykes and Matza's vision assumes that most criminals believe in conventional norms* and values and must use neutralizations in order to shield themselves from the shame attached to criminal activity.

How does Topalli challenge the theory of neutralization?

7 Recent research by criminologist Volkan Topalli finds that Sykes and Matza may have ignored the influential street culture that exists in highly disadvantaged neighborhoods. Using data* gleaned* from 191 in-depth interviews with active criminals in St. Louis, Missouri, Topalli finds that street criminals living in disorganized, gang-ridden neighborhoods "disrespect authority, lionize honor and violence, and place individual needs above those of all others." Rather than having to neutralize conventional values in order to engage in deviant ones, these offenders do not experience guilt that requires neutralization. They are "guilt free." There is no need for them to "drift" into criminality, Topalli finds, because their

allegiance to nonconventional values and lack of guilt perpetually leave them in a state of openness to crime.

8   Rather than being contrite, or ashamed, the offenders Topalli interviewed took great pride in their criminal activities and abilities. Bacca, a street robber who attacked a long-time neighbor without provocation,* exemplified such sentiments:

> Actually I felt proud of myself just for robbing him, just for doing what I did. I felt proud of myself. I didn't feel like I did anything wrong. I didn't feel like I lost a friend cause the friends I do have . . . are lost. They're dead. I feel like I don't have anything to lose. I wanted to do just what I wanted to do.

9   Topalli refers to streetwise offenders such as Bacca as "hardcores," who experience no guilt for their actions and operate with little or no regard for the law. They have little contact with agents of formal social control or conventional norms because their crimes are not directed toward conventional society—they rob drug dealers. Most hardcores maintain no permanent home, staying in various residences as their whim* dictates. Their lifestyles are almost entirely dominated by the street ethics of violence, self-sufficiency, and opportunism.* Obsessed with a constant need for cash, drugs, and alcohol in order to "keep the party going," on the one hand, and limited by self-defeating and reckless spending habits on the other, they often engage in violent crime to bankroll their street life activities. They do not have to neutralize conventional values because they have none.

What change in attitude toward neutralization is the author outlining here?

10   Rather than neutralizing conventional values, hardcore criminals often have to neutralize deviant values. They are expected to be "bad" and have to explain good behavior. Even if they themselves are the victims of crime, they can never help police or even talk to them, a practice defined as snitching and universally* despised and discouraged. Smokedog, a carjacker and drug dealer, described the anticipated guilt of colluding with the police in this way, "You know I ain't never told on nobody and I ain't never gonna tell on nobody 'cause I would feel funny in the world if I told on somebody. You know, I would have regrets about what I did."

11   Street criminals are expected to seek vengeance if they are the target of theft or violence. If they don't, their self-image is damaged and they look weak and ineffective. If they decide against vengeance, they must neutralize their decision by convincing themselves that they are being merciful, respecting direct appeals by their target's family and friends. T-dog, a young drug dealer and car thief, told Topalli how he neutralized the decision not to seek revenge by allowing his uncle to "calm him down."

The older man, a robber and drug dealer himself, intervened before T-dog could leave his house armed with two 9 mm automatics. "That's basically what he told me. 'Calm down.' He took both my guns and gave me a little .22 to carry when I'm out to put me back on my feet. Gave me an ounce of crack and a pound of weed. That's what made me let it go." In other words, offenders claimed the target was just not worth the effort, reserving their vengeance for those who were worthy opponents. (Excerpted from Larry Siegel, *Criminology*, 10th ed., pp. 222–25. © 2010 Cengage Learning.)

Monitoring Your Comprehension   Review the marginal annotations and answer any questions posed. If you can't answer a question, mark the sentence or passage referred to and re-read it before turning to the comprehension and critical reading questions.

GETTING THE GIST   These questions are the kind you might encounter on a standardized reading test.

DIRECTIONS   Identify the general gist, or point, of the author's words by circling the appropriate letter.

1. Which statement best expresses the overall main idea of this reading?
   a. The neutralization patterns described by Sykes and Matza seem to be backed by solid evidence.
   b. Some recent research challenges the basis of neutralization theory suggesting that criminals are genetically programmed to commit crimes and are, therefore, not subject to the pangs of conscience.
   c. There are many different theories about the origins of criminal behavior.
   d. While Sykes and Matza suggest that criminals have to somehow neutralize, or justify, their illegal behavior, criminologist Volkan Topalli argues that criminals gain status from deviant behavior and don't have to neutralize it.

2. Which statement best paraphrases the views of criminologist Volkan Topalli?
   a. Criminals never quite overcome their fear of being outside of society and cut off from the life led by law-abiding citizens.
   b. Criminals are not born. They are created by lives that offer no hope for a better future and therefore make criminal behavior, with its immediate rewards, seem more appealing.

c. Criminals aren't ashamed of their behavior because they are following their own subculture's rules and don't need to neutralize society's rules or their behavior in order to commit a crime.

d. Criminals are genetically programmed to carry out illegal activities and thus remain untouched by the rules of society and have no need to neutralize deviant behavior.

3. Which definition of *hardcores* fits the definition in the text?

a. *Hardcores* are people who are addicted to pornography.

b. *Hardcores* are people who have no heart and no sympathy for others.

c. *Hardcores* are people who commit crimes and feel no guilt about their behavior.

d. *Hardcores* commit violent crimes without any hesitation.

4. Criminal culture, as defined in this reading, places a high emphasis on

a. loyalty.

b. courage.

c. vengeance.

d. secrecy.

5. Which statement best sums up Volkan Topalli's response to the theory of Sykes and Matza?

a. Neutralization theory doesn't take into account the genetic basis for criminal behavior.

b. Neutralization theory is just that, a theory without a strong basis in research.

c. Neutralization theory does not recognize the important role street culture plays in a criminal's value system.

d. Neutralization theory made more sense before the rise of an urban culture that left people feeling more disconnected from one another.

TAKING A CLOSER LOOK   This set of questions focuses on your understanding of the text, both its content and the language used to convey that content.

DIRECTIONS   Answer the following questions on the blank lines provided or by circling the letter of the best response.

**Recognizing
Patterns of
Organization**

1. What organizational pattern is central to the first paragraph?

_____

Paraphrasing

2. According to Sykes and Matza, what do criminals need to do?

_____

_____

**Following the
Author's Train
of Thought**

3. In the second paragraph, what does the opening pronoun *this* refer to?

_____

_____

Paraphrasing

4. In your own words, what is *drift*?

_____

5. What connection do Sykes and Matza make between drift and neutralization techniques?

_____

_____

6. According to the authors, what is Topalli's view of drift?

_____

**Following the
Author's Train
of Thought**

7. In the following pair of sentences, the phrase "these techniques of neutralization" refers to what phrase in the first sentence? "Sykes and Matza suggest that people develop a distinct set of justifications for their law-violating behavior. These techniques of neutralization include the following patterns."

_____

Seeing Transitions   8. In what paragraph do the authors begin to describe a challenge to the neutralization theory developed by Sykes and Matza?

_____

Monitoring Your Comprehension   9. Based on your understanding of paragraph 7, how would you fill in the blanks left in this statement?

According to Topalli, _____ don't have to

_____ their traditional _____

because they don't have them in the first place.

10. What evidence has Topalli offered in support of his claim?

_____

11. In paragraph 8, the story about Bacca is used to support what main idea?

_____

Following the Author's Train of Thought   12. Throughout paragraph 9, what do the pronouns _they_ and _their_ refer to?

_____

Understanding Supporting Details   13. Smokedog is introduced in paragraph 10 in order to illustrate what main idea?

_____

_____

14. In paragraph 11, why is the story of T-dog introduced? What point does it support?

_____

_____

_____

_____

Recognizing Patterns of Organization

15. Overall, what are the primary patterns of organization in this reading?

    a. classification, process, and definition

    b. definition and simple listing

    c. comparison and contrast, simple listing, and classification

    d. comparison and contrast, definition, and cause and effect

READING WITH A CRITICAL EYE The goal here is not to be critical in the negative sense, but rather to understand how fact, opinion, argument, and tone reinforce the authors' apparent purpose.

DIRECTIONS Answer the questions on the blank lines provided or by circling the letters of the correct response.

Analyzing Arguments

1. The reading presents two opposing points of view. Briefly describe each one.

   Sykes and Matza: _____

   _____

   Topalli: _____

   _____

2. What evidence do the authors offer for each side of the debate?

   Sykes and Matza: _____

   _____

   _____

   Topalli: _____

   _____

   _____

3. Based on the evidence, which argument to do you find more convincing?

_____

_____

_____

Purpose 4. How would you label the author's purpose?

    a. purely informative

    b. purely persuasive

    c. primarily informative with some persuasion included

    d. primarily persuasive with some informative writing included

Bias 5. Which statement best describes the author's attitude toward the issue discussed in the reading?

    a. The author supports the neutralization theory of Sykes and Matza.

    b. The author favors Topalli's explanation.

    c. It's impossible to determine the author's personal bias.

From Reader to Writer Write a brief paper that opens with a summary of the theory put forth by Sykes and Matza. Then use a reversal transition word, phrase, or sentence to point out how Topalli disagrees. In the last paragraph, explain your own position. Tell your readers which theory seems to make more sense and why.

Index

abstract versus concrete, 26
addition transitions, 314–15
"Altruistic Personality, The," 371
annotations. *See* marginal notes
antecedents in topic sentences, 397, 403–4
approximate definitions, 78
arguments
  diagrams for, 703–4
  evidence in, 673–74
  shaky support in, 693–98
  sound reasoning for, 692–93
  See also persuasive writing
automatic word recognition, 75–76

background knowledge
  comprehension and, 47
  role of in reading assignments, 17
  Web searches for, 48–50,
bar graphs, 6–7
bias
  defined, 50
  in arguments, 693–98
  in photos, 55
  on websites, 50
"Blind Tom: A Slave to the Music," 706–10
bridging inferences, 410

"Can Physical Aggression Be Learned?" 271–72
"Can Whales Be Saved?" 644–45
careless comparisons, 697–98
category words, 309–11
cause and effect patterns, 570–74
  defined, 570
  inference and, 410
  note-taking for, 572–73
  topic sentences for, 572
  transitions for, 571
  verbs signaling, 572
chapter headings. *See* headings
circular reasoning, 696–97

classification patterns, 577–80
  common words used in, 579
  defined, 577–78
  note-taking for, 579–80
  topic sentences for, 578
  visual aids for, 579, 580
"Combatting Infectious Diseases," 233–35
"Communication and Identity," 730–35
comparison and contrast patterns, 560–65
  defined, 560
  implied main ideas in, 562
  note-taking for, 563
  topic sentences for, 562
  transitional signals in, 561–62
  writing purpose and, 563–64
concentration
  questions for, 10–15
  varying assignments for, 18
concept maps, 29–30
concluding sentences, 320–22
conjunctions, 410
connotations, 101–2
  and opinions, 661
  changing with context, 101–2
  versus denotation, 101
context
  defined, 75
  impact on connotation, 101–2
  meaning and, 90
context clues, 77–82, 94–95
  approximate definitions and, 78
  contrast clues, 79
  example clues, 78–79
  general knowledge clues, 81
  for multiple meanings, 90
  restatement clues, 79–81
  with word analysis, 94–96
contrast clues, 79
contrast transitions, 79

definition patterns, 531–34
  defined, 531
  note-taking for, 533
  pattern variations for, 532–33
  topic sentences for, 533
definitions
  approximate, 78
  automatic, 76
  denotative, 101
  for specialized vocabulary, 80–81
  limitations of using dictionary for, 77–78
  Web-based, 105
  See also word meanings
denotations, of words, 101
details. *See* supporting details
diagrams
  for note-taking, 25–26, 534, 541, 555, 563, 571, 573, 580
  for recall and review, 25–26
dictionaries, 105–7
  and writing, 106
  basics elements of, 106–7
  figurative meanings in, 110
  multiple meanings in, 108
  print for writing, 105–6
  special context labels in, 108
  Web-based, 105
Digging Deeper readings
  "Blind Tom: A Slave to the Music," 706–10
  "Can Physical Aggression Be Learned?" 271–72
  "Can Whales Be Saved?" 644–45
  "Combatting Infectious Diseases," 233–35
  "Is Risk-Taking in Our Genes?" 378–80
  "Long Term Memory: Preserving the Past," 64–66
  "Obedience—Would You Electrocute a Stranger?" 327–29
  "Schooling Resistance," 441–44